PRESENCE
THROUGH
ABSENCE

"Harai Golomb is one of that exquisite breed, a Stradivarius among scholars. He knows how to unpack all the details, and weave them into a complex tapestry which reveals the full richness of whatever work of literature he chooses for his subject. His thorough, profound and innovative work on Chekhov is a model for teachers and students of how to read and extract the literariness of a text and how to construct a single author's poetics. This book is exemplary in its content and structure alike; it is the reward of many years of study, and an inimitable contribution to our understanding of Chekhov, and through him — of the very nature of literary and dramatic art."

BENJAMIN HARSHAV, Professor Emeritus of Comparative and Slavic Literatures, Yale University; Professor Emeritus of Poetics and Comparative Literature, Tel Aviv University; Founding Editor, *Poetics Today*; Founding Director, Porter Institute for Poetics and Semiotics, Tel Aviv University; Fellow of the American Academy of Arts and Sciences; Author, *Explorations in Poetics*

"A unique and extraordinary accomplishment. Professor Golomb's comprehensive and deep exploration of Chekhov's drama, his detailed and subtle discussions and analyses of almost every aspect of Chekhov's great plays — poetics, structure, genre, semantics, concept and creation of character, ends and beginnings, music and musicality, esthetic and philosophical dimensions, etc., and all this put in a comparative and historical context — not only will raise the study of Chekhov drama and theater to qualitatively new levels of scholarly and critical inquiry, but will powerfully impact upon the production, directing, and acting of Chekhov plays. Professor Golomb's masterful study of Chekhov drama and theater will be in the pocket of everyone interested in Chekhov and theater."

ROBERT LOUIS JACKSON, B.E. Bensinger Professor (Emeritus), Slavic Languages and Literatures, Yale University

"The publication of Harai Golomb's revelatory book is a celebration for the world of Chekhov studies. This book is bound to revolutionize the entire field: [...] A NEW POETICS of the major plays, it is as definitive as such a study can be. [...] The principles of Presence through Absence and Unrealized Potentials — the author's discovery — capture the brain, heart and soul of Chekhov's dramatic art and the uniqueness of its complexities. [...] Because of its innovative discoveries, analytical rigor, impeccable structure, depth and thoroughness, this book is a must for scholars, students, actors, directors, and the general Chekhov-loving public alike. Its path-breaking theoretical insights complement its meticulous textual analyses. All these qualities, together with its reader-friendly rhetoric, make it a masterpiece of its kind."

VLADIMIR B. KATAEV, Professor; Chair, the Department of the History of Russian Literature, Lomonosov State University, Moscow; Chairman, the Chekhov Commission of the Russian Academy of Sciences; Author, *If We Could Only Know — An Interpretation of Chekhov*

"Harai Golomb's welcome study on Chekhov's Poetics emerges from a lifetime's companionship with Chekhov and his plays. He succeeds in providing a valuable and insightful key to the essence of Chekhov's dramatic skills. He confronts questions others may have balked at asking; he questions received views, explains and demonstrates. To support his arguments, he offers close and subtle textual analyses. [...]

Golomb takes great pain to unpick the qualities and complexities of Chekhov's textual brilliance. Drawing on a lifetime of work in the creative arts, Golomb draws our attention to alluring new areas, for example indicating the value of comparing the plays and music. Judging, *inter alia*, from the extensive analysis of Russian name pronunciation, a wide readership is envisaged from drama and culture students and scholars to theatre goers and practitioners. All in all, Golomb has accomplished an adventurous study and a worthy addition to Chekhov scholarship."

CYNTHIA MARSH, Emeritus Professor of Russian Drama and Literature,
University of Nottingham. Author, *Maxim Gorky: Russian Dramatist*,
and many articles on Chekhov's theatre

"I was delighted to hear of the forthcoming book on Chekhov by Harai Golomb. After decades of seminal contributions to Chekhov studies in the form of articles, lectures, and appearances at international symposia, Professor Golomb has acquired a reputation as one of the most thoughtful and original Chekhov scholars in the world. He not only has an encyclopedic command of the entire Chekhov corpus and the surrounding scholarly literature, but he brings to Chekhov studies a vast erudition and sophistication in literary theory, in other literatures, and also in music. This book will undoubtedly be recognized as a major contribution, not only to Chekhov studies, including both drama and short stories, but to literary studies generally. I am honored to endorse it with the greatest enthusiasm."

HUGH MCLEAN, Professor Emeritus of Russian Literature,
University of California, Berkeley

"[...] Haraï Golomb does not provide definite and easy answers, but his book — a lifetime achievement — is true to both famous categories of Blaise Pascal: *esprit de finesse* and *esprit de géométrie*. His analyses of different moments in Chekhov's plays and short stories are always fine, subtle and illuminating. They offer an invaluable, precise and geometrical overview of the dramaturgy, style and theatricality. So the book is not only about one great playwright; it also deals with the way we can view theatre and its theory today.

Little by little, we begin to see and measure Chekhov's world and our own universe, with the precision of a labyrinth's surveyor. Golomb's book is a work of art in itself: we enjoy it at every turn. It confirms and deepens our love for Anton Pavlovitch. Thanks to both of them we keep going. There will never be an ending."

PATRICE PAVIS, Professor of Theatre Studies, University of Kent, Canterbury, UK;
Editor, French edition of Chekhov's Major plays; Author, *Dictionary of Theatre*;
Analyzing Performance; *Contemporary Mise en Scène: Staging Theatre Today*

"[...] Harai Golomb has undertaken here nothing short of a poetics of Chekhov's oeuvre as a whole. Moreover, arguing that Chekhovian meaning is produced precisely in the interactions between and among individual parts, he convincingly makes the case that nothing short of this will do. Indeed, even knowing Golomb's remarkable essays, I was unprepared for the extraordinary achievement of this book.

Golomb is the first to give an adequate account of the *isomorphism* of thematic and compositional workings that distinguishes Chekhov's dramatic project. This is more than illuminating; it is important. Golomb's understanding of "poetics" as work, activity, performance, establishes beyond dispute the dynamic complexity of Chekhov's artistic system and the signifying potential of each communicative or interpretive move. A similar affinity for function and morphology gives rise to some of Golomb's most innovative formulations Moreover, paying particular attention to Chekhov's choices — to what *isn't* there as much as what is — Golomb does greater justice to the justice Chekhov himself does to the complexity of the human condition, defined as it is by potentials, realized and unrealized alike. His analysis points the way toward an essential recognition of the interplay of textual and extra-textual elements, the mutual entailment of art and life, the interdependency of part and whole.

Rarely have I encountered such scrupulous explication, firmly rooting rhetorically powerful suggestion in concrete and substantive demonstration. Golomb's argument is distinguished by its logical rigor and its inspired use of textual material. It is also remarkable for its methodological self-awareness. Golomb keeps his cards on the table, acknowledging his own interests and interrogating his own procedures, raising more than once the thorny question of admissible (and inadmissible) evidence; the result is genuine probing and authentic inquiry.

What impresses me the most is Golomb's sense of both nuance and power when he examines relationships of all kinds — not only those between characters or between text and potential performances or between the work of art and its perceivers or even the vexed one between art and life — and his recognition of how complex and elusive all such relationships are, how dizzying the interpenetration of their respective parts, and how, in their borrowings and belongings, the components of each relationship effectively produce one another. No one reads Chekhov's dramas better.

As a scholarly contribution, the book will be invaluable to both those who study Chekhov and those who come to Chekhov via theater studies. But given its structural clarity, it will also be accessible — and no doubt extremely suggestive — for students at all levels and for directors, actors, and playwrights as well."

CATHY POPKIN, Jesse and George Siegel Professor in the Humanities and Professor of Russian, Columbia University. Author, *The Pragmatics of Insignificance: Chekhov, Zoshchenko, Gogol*; Editor, Norton Critical Edition of Anton Chekhov's Selected Stories

A NEW POETICS OF Chekhov's Plays

PRESENCE THROUGH ABSENCE

HARAI GOLOMB

sussex
ACADEMIC
PRESS
Brighton • Chicago • Toronto

2 4 6 8 10 9 7 5 3 1

First published in 2014 by
SUSSEX ACADEMIC PRESS
PO Box 139
Eastbourne BN24 9BP

and in the United States of America by
SUSSEX ACADEMIC PRESS
Independent Publishers Group
814 N. Franklin Street, Chicago, IL 60610

and in Canada by
SUSSEX ACADEMIC PRESS (CANADA)
8000 Bathurst Street, Unit 1, PO Box 30010, Vaughan, Ontario L4J 0C6

British Library Cataloguing in Publication Data
A CIP catalogue record for this book is available from the British Library.

Library of Congress Cataloging-in-Publication Data
Golomb, Harai.
A new poetics of Chekhov's plays : presence through absence / Harai Golomb.
pages   cm
Includes bibliographical references and index.
ISBN 978-1-903900-47-5 (h/b : alk. paper)
ISBN 978-1-84519-624-0 (pbk : alk. paper)
 1. Chekhov, Anton Pavlovich, 1860–1904—Dramatic works. I. Title.
PG3458.Z9D7347 2014
891.72'3—dc23

2013035787

Typeset & designed by Sussex Academic Press, Brighton/Eastbourne (UK) and Toronto (Canada).
Printed by TJ International, Padstow, Cornwall, UK.
This book is printed on acid-free paper.

Contents

PART II
VIEWING
CHEKHOV'S DRAMATIC TEXT AND WORLD

PART III
OVERVIEWING
A COMPREHENSIVE LOOK

Foreword
Donald Rayfield

About ten years ago I was rash enough to give a paper 'What is there left to say about Chekhov?' and annoy my colleagues by saying that, apart from biographical and textual questions, Chekhov criticism had reached an impasse and that perhaps we should have a moratorium for a decade until a new approach had been devised. Certainly, there was a problem in that the relatively small corpus of Chekhov's work — only four major plays, and only one stageable play and two unstageable ones in addition; narrative fiction of major literary importance that fits easily into one volume — was overwhelmed by the intensity and redundancy of many critical approaches, constantly rehashing the same interpretations and controversies, and over-obsessed with ideology and biographical reference points.

My point at that time is now completely invalidated by Harai Golomb's book. Those who have heard him speak (the ideal mode to appreciate the vigour of his performative approach) and read his papers will not doubt that they are about to feel a blast of fresh air in their faces. The fact that Golomb approaches Chekhov not as a Russianist or Slavist or comparativist, but from a background of musicology, drama and literary theory, aroused in the past suspicions among the supercilious and the conservative, but has been a source of inspiration for the open-minded. This is an approach to Chekhov that is equally valid in the original as in translation. True, it is oriented almost exclusively towards the four major plays (the prose fiction is little more than a prop, despite penetrating discussions of a couple of stories), but it opens up a diversity of interpretation and an insight into the mechanics of the Chekhov play which operate as a corrective to all the theoretical or practical work on Chekhov drama hitherto. Much of Golomb's approach is playful, or to use a more fashionable term, ludic. For instance, he imagines how different the play becomes if you chop off the final 30 seconds, 60 seconds, 90 seconds; he looks at apparent minutiae — choice of titles, for instance — which determine our reception of the work. You then realise that every word in Chekhov's drama is a butterfly which only has to flap its wings to cause a storm that affects the whole world. This is the best critical work on Chekhov I have read since Chudakov, and the broadest ever.

This is a book that highlights the structural genius in Chekhov's art, while constituting a feat in the structural organisation of its own text. It gives audience, reader, actor and director all they need, from how to pronounce Russian words, to the keys for unlocking the information and emotional treasures of the plays.

All of Golomb is food for thought; some of his ideas will generate controversy; a few may even be refuted, but this book certainly breaks through the sludge that has formed over the last century in the Chekhov pool and challenges professional *chekhovedy* to come out of their theoretical hermitages and get a life.

Preface
About and Around the Book

The Indefinite Article as Key to Ambitious Humility

My entire work on Chekhov has been inspired by one sentence I heard from the late Prof. Ronald Hingley.

I had the privilege of meeting him about thirty-five years ago, in Oxford. Even then he was an illustrious Chekhov scholar and biographer of world renown, the personification of the one-man-show called *THE OXFORD CHEKHOV* (nine volumes published for several years from 1964): this impressive collection of stories and plays was selected, edited, translated and introduced by him alone. I, on the contrary, was a young novice to the field; academically, an unknown and inexperienced nobody.

The reason for the meeting was my desire to share with him my initial views on Chekhov's poetics, which had started to crystallise. The key-terms that I hesitantly began to develop, designed to capture principles in Chekhov's poetics — *presence through absence* and *unrealised potentials* — were known in this capacity to no one but me and my students; I eagerly wished for an authoritative 'sounding board' that would tell me whether I was on the right track. Prof. Hingley's readiness to meet me realised these wishes.

It was during that talk that Prof. Hingley said that unforgettable sentence. After giving his undivided attention to my main theses, he looked at me with sympathetic and piercing eyes, and said (I am quoting from memory, but with certainty): "What you have here is **a** key to Chekhov"; he stressed the indefinite article with the maximum weight that that monosyllable can support, and after a short pause continued: "and this is the best one can do, because there can never be **the** key to Chekhov". Thus — in one brief, mostly monosyllabic, English sentence — Hingley managed to inspire the fusion of humility and ambition, which I experience as characteristic of my Chekhov project. It is *ambitious*, even audacious, in its attempt to face a formidable challenge: to capture in academic–analytical language the very gist of one of the pinnacles of world art — Chekhov's major plays — characterised by incomparable combination of structural complexity, emotional intensity, human sensitivity, verbal subtlety, and unspeakable wisdom. In other words, this means to schematise, and perhaps inevitably to simplify, an *oeuvre* justly renowned for its schematicism-repellent qualities. Yet it is also *humble*, precisely because of the awe-inspiring artistic greatness of the object of study, the intrinsic impossibility of ever finding **the key** to the artistic soul of Chekhov, just as his Túsenbach (*Three Sisters*, Act 4) will never find the lost key to the precious piano, which his beloved Irína compares to her soul. Similarly, Chekhov himself, repeatedly in his writing, shows with intrinsically non-religious fervour how adamant and uncompromising he is in pursuit of **a truth**, while resenting the very idea that there is, anywhere, a just claim for **the truth**.[1] Hingley's indefinite article, then, is the ever-fixéd star and the guiding compass of this work, circumscribing its intrinsic limitations and inspiring its quest to transcend them, while aspiring to grasp the essence of Chekhov's complexity and to guard against its oversimplification.

To conclude this point, let me point out that the title–subtitle complex, too, reflects the definite importance of the indefinite article in the way the Book, so to speak, defines itself. In the phrase *A New Poetics* the term *New Poetics* reflects an **ambition**: both to say something *new*, different from preceding works on the subject (while acknowledging their contribution to the present study), and to offer a *poetics* — a comprehensive artistic system of a corpus of an author's texts — rather than merely a study of single aspects, single works, etc. The indefinite article within the same phrase, however, reflects this work's **humility**: its modest goal is to offer *A New Poetics*, realising full well that *The Poetics* is forever unattainable. Let me also stress that the Book's explicit aim is to offer a poetics of Chekhov's **four major plays** (*The Seagull, Uncle Vánia, Three Sisters,* and *The Cherry Orchard*).

Characterising Chekhov

Chekhov's uniqueness is inimitable and unparalleled. Characterising this uniqueness is a major challenge of this Book. If it were possible to give several titles to the same book, I would opt for *Characterising Chekhov* as an alternative title, using both the adjectival and the gerundial senses of *characterising*: this is first and foremost an attempt characterise Chekhov as a 'characteriser' of his characters. Other aspects of his poetics are largely derivatives of this quality. In Chekhov, more than in many other masters, plot-events and narrative sequences are characteristically by-products of characters, their interactions, interrelationships and *reciprocal characterisations*, as demonstrated in the Book, rather than the other way around. Even *dramatic action*, though crucially central to Chekhov's plays (as to most plays, as such), is predominantly character-bound in his case. Generally speaking, this Book treats Chekhov's plays as literary potentials for theatrical realisation; it is deeply rooted in literary studies, but actively interacts with the study of drama and theatre.

One of the major facets of Chekhov's unique poetics is its particular brand of *inexhaustible complexity*, which makes his texts repositories of potential discoveries; potentially, not only every work, but often single sentences and phrases, even words, are interconnected with endless networks of meanings and analogies. Roughly, everything is connected with everything else, and these connections are

---

[1] This argument, as such, cannot be attributed to Chekhov's own thinking, which was moulded by a language that has no articles; however, beyond its surface formulation in English, the underlying meanings can be worded, though differently, in any language.

typically more meaningful than the elements connected by them if viewed in isolation. This particular brand of complexity makes it exceptionally difficult to write
about Chekhov's texts methodically, though this is precisely the main mission of
this Book. The challenge involved reminds me of what Winifred Nowottny (1965,
p. 19) said about the analysis of poetic language:

> The good analytical critic is not one who strips the layers off the onion one after
> another until there is nothing left inside; poetic language has the quality, para-
> doxical in non-poetic language, that when one layer of it is stripped off, the onion
> looks bigger and better than it did before — or, to speak more rationally, the
> process of examining its structure in critical terms sharpens the enquirer's appre-
> ciation of the power residing in the poetic configuration of words.

With some adjustment of the wording, this can be applied to "poetic language"
in a much wider sense, to include all complex works of verbal art in general. The
language (in a broader, figurative sense of this term) of Chekhov's artistic system
indeed has this quality, which it shares with all great art — a subject analysed in
the Book proper in greater detail. At this point I am stressing its impact on the Book
itself and the challenges that I faced in trying to shape its structure. The problematic interface between the linear, successive structure of academic discourse and
argumentation, on the one hand, and the complex density of Chekhov's artistic
structures, on the other hand, results in unavoidable repetitiveness within the
former.

This happens at least on two levels: (1) The same texts often come up for
analysis time and again, every time within a different context, under a different
heading, occupying a different position in a hierarchy of thematic superordination
and subordination, etc. (2) Identical or similar points in the argument are presented
more than once, each time differently configured, mainly, once again, in terms of
hierarchies of subordination and relationships of predication, to use a linguistic
metaphor. Indeed, some paradoxicality is inherent in the Chekhov phenomenon
itself; by some magic it seems to be one of its unifying forces, as will be argued in
the following pages. Even more so, paradoxicality characterises the mission of this
Book; thus, a study explicity dedicated to a single great master's art is occasionally 'compelled' to engage in theoretical preambles and implications (seen in
particular in Sections whose numbers include 0).

Technicalities

Translations Quotations from Chekhov's texts are translated by me, unless
otherwise stated. I have consulted several existing translations, but did not adhere
to any one of them in particular; rather, I 'concocted' my own versions based on
them.

Technical style In these as well as in other matters, total rigour and consistency seem to be genuinely unattainable. Some inconsistencies are simply errors
that attest to human imperfection and always escape the notice of authors, editors
and proofreaders alike; others are the result of borderline cases between various

categories and matters that can be differently interpreted. Thus, for instance, "p." or "pp." are supposed to be added to page-numbers only in cases of doubt; this, of course, is open to local interpretation, resulting in inconsistencies. The same applies to other matters of technical style, determined according to basic guide-lines applied sometimes flexibly and, once again, inconsistently. In most cases I am aware of these shortcomings and found no way around them; others may have escaped my notice in the first place.

Italics are used, according to academic conventions, for names of books and journals and for non-English words normally perceived as such (*inter alia*). In addition, *italics* are used in this Book for words and phrases that **function in context** as *professional terms* or *dictionary/lexicon entries*, whether they are indeed quoted from dictionaries and lexicons or not. It is the way a term functions within a given local context that determines whether it is italicised or not; assessing this kind of functioning is, again, a matter of personal decision, not always guided by clear principles. Terms deemed more familiar are usually italicised only when initially presented, others are italicised throughout the entire Book.

Bold is used for **semantic emphasis,** to stress a word or phrase for contextual importance and saliency; this emphasis is attributable to me as author, whether within my discourse or within a quotation, unless otherwise stated.

"Double quotation marks" are used, according to convention, for names of arti-cles within journals, stories and poems within books of similar works, etc. In addition, they are used in this Book for short quotations (when not indented in a separate paragraph), and whenever a word (or phrase) functions as a quote from a source. Thus, for instance, the term "philosophising" is given in double-quotes throughout the Book because Chekhov's personages themselves use the term in their fictional discourse, so that its use by me is quoted from them.

'Single quotation marks' are used, according to convention, for quotes within quotes; additionally, they are used here to convey irony, doubt, reservation, etc.; in this sense they complement **bold** emphasis, both being graphic representations of oral intonation. The combination of single quotation marks with italics is used in special cases of '*hypothetical statements*', e.g., when my authorial voice 'quotes' the inner thoughts of a personage, never verbalised in Chekhov's text, or what someone **would have said** in a given situation if s/he had been pressed to say something, or if s/he had been informed of something unknown, etc.

Superimpositions — e.g., of ***bold and italics*** — are the result of simultaneous presence of the qualities reflected in both types of fonts, e.g., **semantic emphasis** as well as *terminological function*.

A rather more rigorous distinction is attempted between three types of hori-zontal lines: (a) the *short hyphen* (-), always without spaces around it, (b) the *mid-sized dash* (–), also without spaces around it, and (c) the *long dash* (—), always preceded and usually followed by a space. (a) is used, conventionally, for compounds (e.g., *non-verbal*) and also to indicate (where deemed necessary) *grammatically-subordinated* hierarchies; (b) is used mainly for *coordinative–paratactical* pairs, often adjectives (e.g., *spatial–visual arts*, *unique–specific* character traits, etc.), but also nouns (e.g., *mind–brain*), adverbs (e.g., *socially–culturally*), etc., usually maintaining appositional relationship between them;

(c) is used for the separation of parenthetical clauses, statements etc., often instead of parentheses. This type of parenthetical statement, then — i.e., a syntactically-autonomous statement that maintains an *appositional–coordinative* relation to the statement preceding it — is enclosed between two long dashes, each separated from the words on both its sides by spaces.

Slash (/) is used to indicate *alternatives*, either–or relationships and complemetary views. Thus, *internal/external* would denote **either** *internal* **or** *external*, whereas *internal–external* would denote *internal* **as well as** *external*.

Capitalisation of certain words indicates internal cross-references to the book itself, to Chapters, Notes, Epigraphs, etc., within it. Thus, Book (in capitals) refers to this book; Chapter refers to chapters within this book; etc. A different use of capitalisation applies to the word "Act": when capitalised, it means an Act in a play, e.g., *Three Sisters*, Act 3; in all other senses, the word "act" is not capitalised, whether as noun or verb.

Three dots enclosed within square brackets [...] indicate deletions or omissions of a specific text within a quotation; however, three dots **without** brackets are originally supplied (Chekhov occasionally employs this punctuation mark as do other authors). In my authorial text this punctuation mark is also employed, though rarely, to encourage the reader to think further, as a hint that there is more to a statement than explicitly verbalised in its wording.

Diametrically opposed to books like Styan 1971 and Magarshack 1972, which analyse the texts of Chekhov's plays scene by scene in *close reading*, or even Gilman 1995 and many other books, which offer readings of his dramatic *oeuvre* play by play, the structure of this Book treats all four major plays, and occasionally some stories, on a par and simultaneously. The Chapter headings refer to theoretical and analytical categories, including major themes (e.g., *beginnings*, *endings*, *characterisation*, *communication*, etc.) across Chekhov's *oeuvre*, moving freely from play to play under such a thematic umbrella. In this crucial sense, the present Book connects to the late A. P. Chudakóv's *Chekhov's Poetics* (1983 [1973]) and deeply indebted to it, differences between the two approaches notwithstanding.

The analytical journey across Chekhov's major plays begins with discussing his beginning techniques and ends with discussing his ending techniques. This rhetorical and structural strategy is also faced with the formidable challenge of catering to the needs of readers who would like to read the book as an integral work, from start to end, and those who would like to concentrate on one Chapter, or just few, skipping or ignoring the rest. I believe that academic books are not novels, and need not be read cover to cover. I tried my best, then, to make each Chapter partly autonomous; this, in itself, required me to repeat some materials in different Chapters.

Terms and Terminological Problems

The use of certain terms in the Book requires explaining. Thus:

Addressee(s)/audience(s)/perceiver(s)/reader(s)/recipient(s)/spectator(s) — all these terms refer to the person(s) receiving or perceiving a message (in this context the message is a text by Chekhov). Differences as well as similarities between these terms are self-explanatory, especially between *readers* (recipients of written texts) and *spectators* (recipients of staged messages in theatre plays). In this Book all these terms are used, sometimes interchangeably, and sometimes selectively, stressing a certain nuance. Not all of them are strictly distinguished from the others.

Personage/character: these two terms are synonymous in the context of *drama*; therefore, they are often used interchangeably in the Book as well. However, the former (*personage*) is basically preferred, because the latter (*character*) has additional meanings (as in *character-trait, graphic character*, etc.). I find this term incomparably preferable to Pfister's (or rather to his translator, John Halliday's) choice of the term *Figure*, explicitly designed to solve the same problem (see Pfister 1988, 160–195). However, elsewhere in the Book the more generally accepted *character* is sometimes used, when stylistically preferable (e.g., in conjunction with *Characterisation* in Chapter 5) and when there is no risk of confusing between different senses of the word. In certain contexts the term *protagonist* is used, usually to denote a major personage, or 'hero', especially in *tragedy*.

Réplique: this French term denotes a *dramatic speech*, i.e., the consecutive text spoken by one personage until interrupted by another, or by silence. This basic building-block of texts of plays has no technical term in English, as it does in French (*réplique*), in German (*Replik*), in Russian (*реплика*), and probably in quite a few other languages. In this Book the French term is used, italicised.

Transliteration and other aspects of the use of Russian names and words throughout the Book are explained in the *Guide* at the end of the Book.

Gender references and other preferences In some cases, for clarity and flow of rhythm, masculine terms (e.g., he, his) are used to denote both genders; however, in most cases *s/he, his/her*, etc., are preferred. Such context-bound inconsistencies are admittedly debatable, reflecting local stylistic preferences.

The bibliographical list The title *Works Consulted* for the bibliographical list at the end of the Book was chosen advisedly. It is indeed neither a comprehensive bibliography of the field nor a list of references that are actually mentioned in the Book; rather, it is a personal list of the works that I have consulted throughout the years. Not all of them are actually quoted, and some of them could not be credited for specific inputs; omissions from this list are accidental and regretted. However they have all been, literally, consulted at some point. In untranslated Russian works, authors' names are given in the Book's transliteration; names of translated Russian authors are given as published in English, with the Book's transliteration in brackets. In certain cases it was almost impossible to apply rules of technical style consistently, and individual decisions had to be taken.

Appendixes All general/unspecified references to [*the*] Appendix refer to the Book's Appendix, pp. 332–350. References to the other Appendixes (to Chapter 5, pp. 128–133, and to Chapter 9, pp. 247–248) are referred to specifically by the relevant Chapter number.

Final Note Chekhov is a 19th-century Russian author, but the context in which this Book places him is largely beyond time and place; thus, he is considered here as a link in the chain of the most significant playwrights of all time (the Greeks, Shakespeare, Ibsen etc.), rather than as a link in the historical chain of Russian literature and drama. However, the Book is offered as complementary addition, rather than alternative, to other studies, which stress local and temporal aspects. Moreover, the existence and irreplaceable significance of those Slavistic studies is an integral part of the overall scholarly scene that makes the contribution of this study possible.

There is no abstract, general 'check-list' of features and categories supposed to apply to all authors, prompting the reader to "tick where applicable", as it were, whenever the chosen author (i.e., Chekhov in this case) conforms to that list. Rather, the concept of *a single author's poetics* is actioned in this Book *inductively*: *micro* textual analyses of scenes, hierarchies, and other elements in Chekhov's plays give rise to *macro* generalisations about his artistic system and its major features, not the other way around. This is how certain terms and categories — *Communication, Characterisation, Restraint*, etc. — have become so central in this Book's own thematic structure, and certain distinctions (e.g., between *art* and *reality*, variously worded) repeatedly discussed. Indeed, Chekhov's world slightly reverses Prospero's famous words in Shakespeare's *The Tempest* (IV, i, 156–157), saying, as it were, "Dreams are such stuff as we are made on". A hypothetical book attempting the characterisation of another author's poetics would most probably focus on different concepts in its study of that author; it could devote central chapters to other concepts — e.g., *ideology, plot and narrative structure, conflict*, etc., — and no chapter to *Communication* (here, Chapter 6) or *Restraint* (Chapter 7).

Chekhov's *World* and the Book's *Conceptual Structure* define each other.

Tel Aviv, October 2013

Acknowledgements

In all academic books known to me the author's acknowledgements begin with apologies, mainly with reference to those who for one reason or another were not mentioned. This is no exception. The sheer length of a list of names of all the people who have genuinely earned my thanks for their indispensable role in making this book possible is prohibitive. Unfair omission of some essential names is unavoidable and sincerely regretted.

Academic indebtedness to people whose written work has inspired and guided mine, or even stimulated it through disagreement and controversy, perhaps need not be acknowledged here, as it is amply (though, inescapably, not adequately) reflected in the Book itself, and recorded in the bibliographical list (*Works Consulted*). Insights gained through oral communication have often been just as crucial for my work, though giving them due credit is, unfortunately, much trickier; one is unable not only to acknowledge explicitly, but even to simply remember, everything one has internalised from relevant written and oral sources.

That said, I would like to single out the specifically relevant impact that the following three teachers and senior colleagues of mine had on the content of this Book: the late Poet–Professor Lea Goldberg (1911–1970), whose home-seminar on Chekhov's plays (Jerusalem, 1966) fatefully sparked off my enthusiasm for these masterpieces; Prof. Benjamin Harshav (now at Yale, formerly in Jerusalem and Tel Aviv Universities), who introduced me into the world of literary theory and text analysis; and the late Prof. Dalia Cohen (1926–2013), my mentor in music theory and analysis, who inspired my interart studies in this Book and everything else I have done in the study of music.

Out of the international communities of Chekhov, Russian, Literature, and Theatre Studies I gratefully acknowledge the collegial support of Professors Joe Andrew (Keele), Geoffrey Borny (Canberra), Erella Brown (Syracuse), Tat'iána Búzina (Moscow), Aleksándr Chepuróv (St. Petersburg), Douglas Clayton (Ottawa), Michael Finke (Urbana–Champaign), Boris Gasparov (Columbia), Robert Louis Jackson (Yale), Vladimir Kataev (Moscow), Cynthia Marsh (Nottingham), Hugh McLean (Berkeley), Margaríta Odésskaïa (Moscow), Michael O'Toole (Perth, Australia), Patrice Pavis (Paris and Kent), Manfred Pfister (Berlin), Cathy Popkin (Columbia), Roland Posner (Berlin), Donald Rayfield (Queen Mary, London), John Reid (Bristol), Herta Schmid (Berlin), Savely Senderovich (Cornell), Maria Shevtsova (Goldsmith, London), Andréï Stepánov (St. Petersburg), Darko Suvin (McGill), John Tulloch (London and Sydney), Maya Volchkévich (Moscow), and Seth Wolitz (Austin, Texas). These eminent scholars are 'shortlisted' here to represent a much longer list. I also sadly record the names of the late Professors Aleksándr Chudakóv and Èmma

Artém'ïevna Pólotskaïa from Moscow, who contributed to my Chekhov project through years of fruitful dialogue.

Special thanks to Dr. Valerie Lucas (Regent's College London) for years of involvement with my work, adding a perspective of international theatre research.

My peer-colleagues in Israeli universities who have helped and inspired my work throughout the years are indeed too many to enumerate here. The names of Ahuva Belkin, Ziva Ben-Porat, Menachem Brinker, Ariel Hirschfeld, Motti Lerner, Olga Levitan, Orly Lubin, Vladimir Paperny, Shlomit Rimmon-Kenan, Shimon Sandbank, Ziva Shamir, Uzi Shavit, Smadar Shiffman, Reuven Tsur and Tamar Yacobi are hardly recorded elsewhere in the Book, but all of them have generously supported my academic projects for many years.

As Deans of the Faculty of Arts and Heads of the Theatre Department at Tel Aviv University Professors Gad Kaynar, Nurit Kenaan-Kedar, Shimon Levy, Hannah Naveh, Freddie Rokem, Eli Rozik and Nurit Yaari have contributed in diverse ways to my professional life in recent years, and I am ever so grateful to every one of them.

It is an old rabbinical dictum that one learns from one's pupils more than from one's teachers and peer-colleagues. In this spirit I would like to thank my students throughout the years who have inspired my work on Chekhov through their presence in the classroom and, in their absence, in hours of solitary work at home, in libraries, while reading, writing and thinking. Specifically, it gives me great pleasure and satisfaction to list an admittedly too small number of senior post-graduate students, past and present — Ira Avneri, Meir Ben Simon, Dr. Yotam Benshalom, Rakefet Binyamin, Tali Hecht, Dr. Zmira Heizner, Karin Heskia, Moshe Perlstein, Daphna Silberg, and Dr. Omry Smith — whose direct and indirect inputs have been particularly invaluable, in certain cases even indispensable.

Words fail me to express my gratitude to my wife, Dr. Abigail Golomb. Living with this project under the same roof for decades is a consummation not to be wished, devoutly or otherwise; least of all for loved ones. My supporting, understanding and critical partner through the pleasures and ordeals of this work, offering sound and wise advice on matters large and small in and around the Book's production, it is mainly thanks to her that this Book reached the publisher before the Prózorov Sisters ever got to Moscow . . . My son, Dr. Uri Golomb, has been a sounding board in matters of substance and a helping hand in matters of academic–technical skill, sharing thoughts, doubts and discoveries.

Last but not least, my publisher and editor, Anthony Grahame, and his wife–partner, Anita Grahame, have been enormously helpful and supportive and unbelievably patient with this project. My gratitude to them is boundless.

HARAI GOLOMB
Tel Aviv, October 2013

Cover and Plate Section Illustrations

All cover images are taken from the production of *The Cherry Orchard*, the Khan Theatre, Jerusalem, Israel, 2010, directed by Michael Gurevitch; images © the Khan Theatre, reproduced by permission. Photographer: Gadi Dagon.

THE ACTORS (respective roles in parentheses on first identification):
Front cover image, from right to left: Leora Rivlin (Ranévskaïa), Erez Shafrir (Gáïev, lying down), Liron Baraness (Yásha), Yossi Eini (Lopákhin).
Back cover, right, alone: Erez Shafrir.
Back cover, left, images from top to bottom: (1) Nili Rogel (Duniásha, sitting); Shimrit Lustig (Ánia, lying down); (2), *right to left*: Yossi Eini, Avi Pnini (Firs), Erez Shafrir, Leora Rivlin, Arie Tcherner (Semeónov-Píshchik); (3) *right to left*: Florence Bloch (Charlótta), Liron Baraness, Orit Gal (Vária), Shimrit Lustig, Nili Rogel, Arie Tcherner; (4) *right to left*: Nili Rogel, Erez Shafrir, Leora Rivlin, Yossi Eini; (5) Avi Pnini.

The colour plate section (after page 254)
The Seagull (an adaptation of Chekhov's play) was premiered at Tmuna Theatre, Tel Aviv, in Autumn 2013. Adapted and directed by Ira Avneri. Translator (into Hebrew) and Literary Consultant: Prof. Harai Golomb. Stage and costume design: Dina Konson. Light design and projections: Yaron Abulafia. Sound design: Ehud Weisbord.

THE ACTORS (respective roles in parentheses):
Benny Eldar (Konstantín); Shiri Golan (Arkádina); Dudu Niv (Trigórin); Avi Oria (Sórin); Gaia Shalita Katz (Nína); Michal Weinberg (Másha); Yoram Yosephsberg (Dr. Dorn).

Photo credits: 1, 3, 4, 5, 6, 7 and 10 – Gadi Dagon; 2, 8 and 9 – Yaron Abulafia. Pictures reproduced with the kind permission of the photographers. Special thanks to Dina Konson (the Production's Stage and Costume Designer) and Ira Avneri (its Director and Adaptor) for their generous help in obtaining and processing these photographs.

In loving memory of my mother
Ada Golomb née Shertok (1897–1970)

Адочка

Who inspired my love for the beauty and depth
of the Russian Classics

Three Reasons Why the World needs Chekhov today

FIRST,
Chekhov listens. He was an extraordinarily receptive writer
and human being.

His listening was what Spinoza meant in his motto:
"Not to laugh, not to weep, but to understand."

SECOND,
Chekhov respects his readers. He does not try to liberate them, as did
Tolstoy and Dostoevsky, but left his readers free to liberate themselves.

THIRD,
Chekhov was endowed with a supreme sense of measure and restraint.

That is at the core of his art.

We need Chekhov and his art as we need water and life.

ROBERT LOUIS JACKSON
(Badenweiler, 2004)

PART

I

PREVIEWING

BASIC PRINCIPLES
OF CHEKHOV'S POETICS

CHAPTER

1

Basic Principles of Chekhovian Thematics *(What?)*

OPENING THE BOOK'S OUTER CIRCLE[1]

1.1 *Presence through Absence/Unrealised Potential*: Formulating a Chekhovian Universal

Major controversies in Chekhov criticism and scholarship in the past used to focus on such concepts as *optimism* vs. *pessimism* in his attitude to mankind as a whole, as indicated by his compassion *vs.* coldness/callousness towards his fictional personages. Such *thematic* discussions are complemented by other, seemingly unrelated, *compositional* ones, examining structural aspects of his plays (though these have hardly aroused comparable controversy). In this latter context I am referring to the artistic 'logic', or aesthetic motivation, governing such features as *exits and entrances* of personages, or the ordering and structuring of the thematic material (i.e., **what** and **who** is chosen to appear in a given play or scene, **why** and **when/where on page and stage**). It is my claim that these seemingly unrelated features are often governed by the same highly characteristic principle, which I shall formulate by the use of two pairs of interrelated concepts: *unrealised potentials* and *presence through absence.*

True, these thematic and compositional principles can be found in the work of other masters throughout the ages; yet, their dominance — centrality, totality and consistency — in Chekhov's work and world are quite unique and specific to him, amounting to a kind of *differentia specifica Chekhoviana*, a defining distinctive feature of the Chekhov phenomenon.

In fact, the terms *unrealised potential* and *presence through absence* are two mutually-complementary ways of presenting virtually the same complex, double-faced phenomenon. The former, stressing its 'negative'[2] aspect, is better applied to 'what-elements' in the text (i.e., *themes*); they are entities and phenomena that make up human life, such as love and marriage, work and responsibility, art and beauty, education and learning, etc. The latter, stressing its 'positive' aspect, is properly applicable also to 'who-elements' as well, i.e., to *characters/personages*, notably including offstage ones, whose absence is either total (e.g., General Prózorov in *Three Sisters* or the drowned seven-years-old Grísha in *The Cherry Orchard*), or partial, being significantly absent from a specific scene (e.g., Másha being absent from the ending of Act 3 of *Three Sisters*). Thus, these two terms will be treated almost interchangeably.

In short: Chekhov views the human world and condition as a network of *potentials* craving for *realisation*, which they hardly ever attain. I would go so far as to say that this way of looking at the human world gradually becomes almost obsessive, or at least all-pervasive, in his mind. Time and again he creates relationships between *potentials* and *(non)-realisation* almost everywhere in his works: externally, between and among personages, and internally, within many of them; in the portrayal of themes of great magnitude (major arenas and components of human life, as suggested above); in structuring chains of events, ideas, values, etc.; in treatment of *time* and *space/place*; and — last but not least — in the way his written texts are shaped, and, in the plays, also in the way they themselves serve as *potentials* for *realisation* on the theatre stage. In other words, this major hallmark of Chekhov's is typical of the way he 'passively' perceives the 'real' world as well as of the way he 'actively' creates his own, fictional 'worlds'.

1.2 Thematic Structuration in *Three Sisters: Trichotomies*

1.2.1 An Example: Education and Learning

The constant use of *unrealised potentials* often takes the form of contrasts organised in *trichotomies* (rather than *dichotomies*). This aspect is both structural and thematic, or in short, it is a feature of ***thematic structuration***. Thus, for instance, Andréï Prózorov says in Act 1 "Father, may he rest in peace, **oppressed** us with education" and in Act 4 he says "[…] irresistible sordid influence **oppresses** the children". Thus, a pattern (missed in most English translations) is created consisting of two types, or rather manifestations, of *oppressing*: (1) related to (the transmission of) *learning and education*; (2) related to (the effects of) *sordid/vulgar influence*.[3] There is, of course, a world of difference between these two applications of *oppression*; indeed, the emasculating effects of General Prózorov's "**oppressive** education", as manifest in the personalities of all his four distinctly individuated children, is sharply contrasted with the dehumanising effects of "irresistibly **oppressive** sordidness/vulgarity", personalised in the character of Natásha and her implied influence on her children. However, we do see their common feature, namely "*oppression*", further delimited by another common feature, the context of transmitting values from one generation to the next, whereas we do not see in the play an instance of the third member of the emerging *trichotomy*: learning and education transmitted **without** oppression. This positive option is an ***unrealised potential***, a ***present absence***, which we have to evoke in our minds, to complete the tripartite thematic structure. We, as audience, then, bring this positive constituent of the trichotomy into our perception of *Three Sisters*, though it is absent from the play's world of fictional reality. The positive, virtually ideal alternative — oppression-free education — is indeed so integral a part of the upbringing and culture of human beings in most societies, that we simply cannot help activating it in our minds when reading or watching the play, supplying a perspective, which is most obviously missing from the actual play as written. In constructing his text, then, Chekhov counts on this automatic response of the audience. He is playing with us a hide-and-seek game of *presences* and *absences*, as it were.

1.2.2 Other Themes

Education and learning is just one example out of quite a few themes organised in *trichotomies*. *Love and marriage* is another. Consider, for instance, three explicit pronouncements on the subject. In Act 1 Ól'ga says: "[...] it seems to me, that if I were married and sat home all day, it would be better... I **would have loved** my husband"; not long after that, in the same Act, Vershínin says: "If it were possible to begin life all over again, I would not get married... no, no!" [Note that at this very moment enters Kulýgin!] And in Act 2 Andréï says: "to get married is unnecessary; unnecessary, because it is boring", to which Chebutýkin replies: "well, it may be so, but loneliness... loneliness is a terrible matter, my friend". Once again, as with learning and education, we have a *Chomsky-like deep structure* of trichotomy. As before, we have (at least) two 'negative' representations of marriage: the lonely, unhappy and unmarried people (Ól'ga, Chebutýkin) lament their loneliness and **long for marriage** (of course in different ways), while the just-as-unhappy-and-lonely married people (Vershínin, Andréï) lament their loneliness and **negate marriage**. The contrast with Kulýgin is obvious, and adds to the subtlety of the overall picture. The 'positive' component — happy, fulfilled marriage based on love, understanding and communication — is conspicuously absent from the world of the play, but, again, it is activated in our minds, as contrasting background. The same applies to art, science, work, communication, and other themes that constitute major elements in life, whose relative dominance varies from play to play. In most of these cases, and in many others, the 'positive' component of the trichotomy is both *absent* from the play and *present* in it. Absent, because it is simply not there; present, because it is constantly generated in our minds, as active background that throws the 'negative' components into bold relief by contrast. The entire trichotomy has to be viewed *dynamically*, i.e., with its components reinforcing, weakening, and even cancelling out each other, **along the time axis of the play's unfolding**. Only such a view can claim to be an approximation of Chekhov's overall position towards a theme or a phenomenon, as can be inferred at a given point within a given text.

This is a crucial point: almost nowhere in Chekhov can we draw a conclusion from a single detail, however significant or powerful it may be; only interactions between isolated details, or between constituent elements of larger wholes, create the structured networks which carry Chekhovian meanings; and **meanings thus structured and generated are invariably and inevitably highly complex**.

1.3 Building a (Textual) Character: Doing, Talking, Wishing

Let us turn now from *theme* to *personage*. Here, of course, one can speak of a personage's unrealised emotional or intellectual potential, i.e., in the *non-realisation of potential fulfilment* in love, happiness, work, education, etc. This may seem as just another way of looking at the themes themselves (distinct from personages) as *unrealised potentials*. However, there is an additional angle, specific to personages.

Let us look at Chekhov's 1889 story "A Dreary Tale".[4] The story's first-person narrator, Professor Emeritus Nikolái Stepánovich (no surname given; see *A Guide*), says that in the past he used to judge people (himself and others) by their deeds and actions; however, experience taught him that these are contingent on circumstances, so now he judges people by their wishes. He concludes with the dictum: «Скажи мне чего хочешь, и я скажу кто ты» ["**Tell me what you want, and I will tell you who you are**"]. Indeed, when it comes to Chekhov one should exercise extreme caution in ascribing personages' views to the author. My colleague Nilly Mirsky, an eminent Israeli Chekhov translator and critic, goes so far as to claim that, as a rule, "the very fact that a Chekhovian character expresses an opinion, is reason enough to dissociate Chekhov from it".[5] According to her, then, one of Chekhov's techniques to dissociate himself from an idea is to let one of his personages express it. However, in this particular instance there is reason to believe that Chekhov is in basic accord with this personage's view that people should be judged by their wishes. Well, not quite: maybe Chekhov would have said that in order to understand people one has to look at their wishes **as well as** their actions. Anyway, **Tell me what you want <u>and what you do, and how the two relate to each other</u>, and I shall tell you who you are**[6] is much more clumsy and less elegant than the original aphoristic statement Chekhov attributes to his personage, but it corresponds much better to the author's world and poetics. Yet when formulating the dictum as he does Chekhov is making a point by typically activating and challenging his readers' expected conventional views, as if **no matter what you say, want, or dream about, only what you do matters**; or, as the elegant aphorism has it, "actions speak louder than words", and certainly louder than the kind of "airy nothing" dreams are made on. Chekhov's readers are thus encouraged to integrate the two views in their minds and produce a balanced mixture of them. Indeed one of Chekhov's major contributions to characterisation in drama and literature is the creation of fictional worlds in which what people say — and, more typically, what they think, want, and yearn for rather than say — is demonstrably as important as what they do, at least for determining **who they are.**

Chekhov's uniqueness in this context, then, lies undoubtedly in the extra stress that he lays on wishes as a distinctive feature of the personalities of his personages. In *The Seagull* Sórin suggests to Kóstia [=Konstantín] to write a play entitled «человек который хотел» (he suggests this title in Russian and in French; the English would be *The Man Who Wanted*), and goes on to enumerate things that he wanted to achieve in life and failed to: he wanted to get married, and remained single; wanted to become a "man of letters", and didn't; etc. etc. Now indeed it is clear to any spectator or reader of *The Seagull* that Sórin was a clerk in a public office. Like his colleagues in the office, he never became a writer or man of letters; yet, unlike them, he **wanted** to become one.[7] For Chekhov, then, what differentiates Sórin from Trigórin and Konstantín, who did become writers (with or without wanting it), is not greater than what differentiates Sórin from his colleagues in the office, who never dreamt of a literary calling.

Chekhov's plots, and his special brand of *dramatic conflict*, then, are often made of *wishes*, even *delusions*, rather than deeds and actions. And, by definition, wishes and yearnings, as such, are *unrealised potentials* and *present absences*. In Chekhov they are usually not merely unrealised, but **unrealisable.** Consequently, the *trichotomic principle* works here, too, possibly in a more complex manner: the unfulfilled wishes of *personage A* interact with those of *personages B*, and/or *C*, *D* etc.; for each of them the wishes are tangible mental reality, and this 'unreal reality', in turn, is primary evidence for the fact that the realisation of the wish is a non-reality, simply because it does not happen.

The main purpose of this discussion, though, is to show that the actual importance of *unrealisable wishes* in human life is, in itself, very real. Thus, for instance, in *Three Sisters*, the **reality** of faraway Moscow as a real city, and of the **real, painfully-near here-and-now** of the provincial township, are both rejected by the Prózorovs (in sharply varying degrees, ignored at this stage) as almost unreal within their mental reality; in contrast, however, their dream-world of past and future in the **painfully-faraway there-and-then** Moscow is almost the only reality they can mentally accommodate. This contrast sets the Prózorovs apart from other personages in the play. More significantly, it sets them apart from the reality-norms expected to characterise most potential audiences, and from the norms we would like to attribute to ourselves. Whether we are right or wrong in this self-characterisation — this is a question that Chekhov wants us to ask ourselves. A complex network of character-building is at work here, including the characterisation of the *implied* or *potential perceiver/addressee* (*reader/spectator*) as the target audience that the text presupposes.[8] It is typical of Chekhov's artistic system, that contrasts between the real and the imaginary within it do not take the shape of *symmetrical reversals* and neat contradictions, but *asymmetrical changes* and suggested *re-orderings of hierarchies*.

Most of the aforesaid applies to the construction of personages' wishes and delusions in fictional texts in general, rather than specifically in Chekhov's plays. What is specifically Chekhovian, once again, is the relative **dominance** of wishes, much **at the expense of** deeds and actions. Various aspects of this crucial matter are elaborated throughout the Book, especially in Chapters 4, 5 and 6.

To conclude: Chekhov's *human world* — just as his *thematics* and "*Realm of Ideas*" (Chudakóv's 1973 [1983] original term is «сфера идей») — usually rests on **merely-potential 'positive' *presence*s, made powerful and significant through their very *absence***. Now since it is usually natural to regard active action as 'positive' and passive inaction as 'negative', the *structural isomorphism* — usually *trichotomic* — between the ways Chekhov presents actions/inactions and good/bad components in life is even more striking. It does not follow from this structural isomorphism that in Chekhov's world action is **always** positive and inaction is **always** negative. As will be demonstrated below time and again, his world-view is much more complex: it usually challenges or undermines conventional views, but not necessarily negates or contradicts them.

1.4 Building a Text: Compositional Implications of the Principle of *Unrealised Potential/Presence through Absence*

Last but not least, the totality of the principle of *Presence through Absence* is apparent also within the domain of *textual composition*, in its relation to *thematics*. It is not at all logically inescapable that an artistic system characterised by *unrealised potentials* and *presence through absence* in the construction of *personages* and *themes* should also be characterised by the same principles in the construction of the text on the page. On the contrary: one can easily imagine a fictional text, which — though full of humanly unfulfilled personages, and/or *unrealised potentials* in love, work, education etc. — does not lead its readers through a maze of frustrated expectations. Likewise, one can imagine a text, which constantly frustrates its readers' expectations, and yet its personages are not necessarily portrayed as unfulfilled people. However, in Chekhov there is a remarkable *isomorphism* between these various levels and dimensions of his text and world, to match the isomorphism on a different plane, just suggested above. It is largely because of this isomorphism that one can speak of a totality of perception of the world in Chekhov, or even of obsessive search for the same *potential–non-realisation* pattern everywhere.

Though this principle of text construction is quite universal in Chekhov's late plays,[9] I shall confine myself to examples from *Three Sisters*, where it seems to be applied with iron clad consistency. In this play, almost invariably, the text frustrates **specific** expectations, i.e., potentials created or suggested at given moments by a textual unit, or a *dramatic speech (réplique)*.[10] Usually, in such cases Chekhov produces a textual continuation that takes an unexpected turn or twist; yet this twist is typically not diametrically opposed to the expected, but rather surprisingly 'goes sideways', as it were. This, too, is analogous to the technique of *asymmetrical reversals* just pointed out.

Let us look at the chosen examples from *Three Sisters*. In Act 2 Vershínin confesses his love for Másha, using banal compliments about what a wonderful woman she is, concluding with «Здесь темно, но я вижу блеск ваших глаз» ["It is dark here, but I see the sparkle in your eyes"], to which Másha replies, after moving to another chair, «Здесь светлей...» ["it's brighter here..."]. Then Vershínin, ignoring this surprising response, goes on with his banal love confession, to which Másha again replies unexpectedly: "When you talk like this I somehow laugh, though I'm scared... don't repeat that, please... [*in a low voice*] anyway, go on talking, it's all the same to me [...] people are coming, please talk about something else..." For our purposes suffice it to say that, as a reply to Vershínin's statements, one can reasonably expect a statement of *yes* or *no*, however worded. Even *maybe* or *not now* would do as a potential answer to the point. Vershínin's confession includes *a potential to be realised* in a number of direct ways as described. Másha's response leaves Vershínin's confession 'hanging in the air', as it were, without realising these potentials, but without negating them either.

To be sure, this *non-realisation* functions, *inter alia*, on the planes of events, plot construction, developing love relationships, etc.; but its main function and effect can be sensed on the *textual plane*, relating to any reader's or spectator's "what's-next?"-question. In the Chekhov's major plays there is a definite tendency, almost a consistent rule, which can be formulated, somewhat clumsily, as follows: **if the next textual element is expected to have a quality of banal sentimentality, or an explicit expression of bare or intense emotion, in most cases this expectation will not be fulfilled, thus remaining an *unrealised potential*.** There are several mechanisms that Chekhov uses to achieve this goal; the effect, though, is quite the same: it is the principle of *unrealised potential*, transferred from the planes of *characterisation*, *themes* and *events* into the plane of *textual composition*.

Finally, in this introductory Chapter it is important to stress that this Book is written from the standpoint of a reader of the play's text, the agenda of this Book and the arena in which it carries out its mission are focused on the *dramatic text* of Chekhov's plays, as handed down to us on paper by their author; in other words, the Book is focused on the dynamic interface between Chekhov's written text and the possible realisations of its spoken words and unspoken *stage directions* on stage. The Book, then, explores *potential→realisation* interactions not only in Chekhov's human–fictional worlds (shared by plays and stories), not only in the linear progression of his texts, but also in the plays' status as such — not shared by stories — as *literary–textual potentials* (*on page*) *for theatrical realisation* (*on stage*). The Book, then, does not include analyses of plays and productions, and even cursory references to actual performances are few and far between; rather, it treats the texts of Chekhov's plays both as fixed literary texts and as restless potentials for theatrical *realisations*. Indeed, a written verbal text of a play as such may be rich and complex literarily (as is the case in Chekhov, Shakespeare and other masters); but even in such cases, such a written text is also, and arguably mainly, a prompter that incessantly propels the staged action. It seems, then, that Chekhov — obsessed as he was with *potential→realisation* interactions — could not be satisfied with writing stories only, which cannot enact such interactions in its transmission from author to reader; only in the interactive interface between a written play and its staged production can the actual transmission from author to audience, literally, add an isomorphic dimension to the intricate *potential→(non)realisation* relationships in the play's *fictional world*. These matters will be elaborated in greater detail and depth throughout the Book.

1.5 *Negation vs. Annulment*: **Conservation of Artistic Mass**

In studying Chekhov's principles of *unrealised potentials* and *presence through absence* another important point has to be borne in mind. In exact and natural sciences, when something is stated and then annulled or negated, the result is nil. It is of little consequence, for instance, whether we detract 3 from 3 or 5 from 5:

in both cases the result is zero. In the arts, when something is presented and brought to mind and then negated, it is not annulled by its negation: it makes a lot of difference **what** had been suggested before it was ruled out, and how this process of 'suggesting' and 'ruling out' was executed. The negated entity stays on in our minds, as an *unrealised potential* and/or *present absence*. In all that we have seen — on any plane of Chekhov's artistic system — the potential is there, albeit unrealised. Moreover, in Chekhov it is often the unsaid, unspoken, undone, expected-in-vain — in other words, the clearly-defined-and-delimited — that is more powerfully *present* than anything that the eye can see and the ear can hear on the stage. This general principle — unlike the more specific one involving sentimentality and emotional outbursts — is not as absolutely consistent; even in Chekhov there are counter-examples of words and actions that do speak loud and clear. However, in these examples Chekhov is less unique, less different from other masters. His treatment of *presence **through** absence*, of *unrealised potentials*, is exceptionally powerful, and characteristic of his art.

Indeed, Chekhov's potentials on all planes gain potency **because** of being unrealised. They are forever held back, almost exploding with potential energy, which they are doomed never to release. The clouds over the terrain of his world keep gathering, ever greyer, ever denser, yet rains rarely fall, and storms hardly ever break out. It is erroneous to describe this quality as *understatement*; rather, it is comparable to violently boiling water in a pressure cooker covered with a hermetically sealed lid, hardly emitting any vapour. From the perspective of an outside observer it may look similar to a cold pot; yet, just try to remove the lid lightly, for a split second, and you'll be alarmed by the difference. And, indeed, Chekhov gives us hints, though sometimes hardly noticeable, to the existence of the controlled explosives. As Másha says, pointing at her chest, «Вот тут у меня кипит» ["here inside it is boiling"].

Historically speaking, Chekhov's position *vis-à-vis* his predecessors and successors in the history of European drama can also be viewed in terms of the principle of *unrealised potential*. By and large, roughly speaking, in classical drama the tendency is to present a fictional world of *realised potentials*, whereas in "*absurd*" drama the tendency is towards the *absence of potentials* in the first place. Thus, Chekhov's poetics is unique in **equally** stressing the existence of potentials and their non-realisation, making personages, themes, textual units, etc., powerfully present through their loaded absence.

Chekhov's special view of mankind also integrates into this system. To be human, for Chekhov, is (*inter alia,* of course) to have a great potential, and/or to have great yearnings, beliefs, even illusions and delusions, which are never annulled by their *unrealisability*. Such a view cannot be characterised as 'optimistic', as long as according to it humans are doomed never to realise the potentials of their lives; but it cannot qualify as plainly 'pessimistic' either, because of the strength of its underlying belief in the existence of a defiant, undying, indestructible *human potential*. To deny Chekhov's belief in the potential is falsely reductive; to deny his awareness of its unrealisability is equally shallow. In Chekhov's world, then, humans are destined to be caught between unquenchable potentials and their inescapable unrealisability.

Indeed, the inherent complexity of this view of mankind renders the entire argument about Chekhov's 'optimism *vs.* pessimism' shallow to the point of meaninglessness. The very idea that his irreducibly complex poetics can be subsumed under such simplistic labels is pathetically inadequate, being an attempt to force his evasive subtleties into dogmatic straitjacket. It is appropriate here to quote the late A.P. Chudakóv's (1983 [1973], p. 204) dictum: "The single dogmatic feature in Chekhov is his condemnation of dogmatism" [in the original: «Догматично у Чехова только одно — осуждение догматичности»]. I would suggest replacing *condemnation* with *abhorrence*, *negation*, or even simply *absence*, since *condemnation* has something dogmatic about it (which, indeed, appears to be Chudakóv's intention), whereas Chekhov creates a system that abhors dogmatism altogether and generates texts that are immune from it, rather than engaging in actively condemning it. Chekhov the man may well have consciously condemned dogmatism; his artistic system, however, has built-in immune system that rejects dogmatism to a quasi-dogmatic extent (if *dogmatic* is taken as merely an intensification of *consistent*). Most important for characterising Chekhov's **art**, then, is to state that it is non-dogmatic in its very essence, that he takes care to shun schematicism in the thematic and structural composition of his texts, rather than to ascribe to him, through his texts, judgemental censure or moral indignation towards dogmatic ideologies.

1.6 Paradoxes of the *(Un)Realisability* of Chekhov's Art

After the death of any great creative artist who leaves a significant legacy for posterity, it is futile to try to determine the nature of such a legacy in precise or absolute terms. Chekhov, of course, with his outstanding subtlety and complexity, is no exception; yet here is a proposed contribution to a general view of his specific brand of afterlife through looking at his art as a whole in the light of elements that make it up.

Thus, it can be said that while Chekhov's personages and themes were structured as *unfulfilled promises* and *unrealised potentials*, the author himself is one of the most fulfilled creative artists in human history; that, as a writer plays and stories, he realised his enormous potentials as fully as humanly possible. Indeed, this can be said of any creative artist of genuine greatness; yet, in Chekhov such a saying has a specific significance in the light of the ostensible paradoxical contradiction between his insistence on the universality and inescapability of the unrealisable human potential, on the one hand, and the specificity of the highly realised potential of his own genius, on the other. This, incidentally, is just one of a large number of ostensible and real contradictions that surround the Chekhov phenomenon. The Chekhov phenomenon itself, then, is one of the subversive shining exceptions to the total validity of a rule, which he dedicated his entire life as an artist to establish and substantiate.

And of course, last but not least, in Chekhov — as in any other great creative artist — the endless potential of greatness is ever-present, ever-active, in centuries to come. Such a potential is always realisable, yet never fully so; *greatness* in art is synonymous with *inexhaustibility*. Indeed, as long as there are theatres and theatre-goers, even in 200, 300, 1000 years — "the precise period is not the issue", says Vershínin — generations of new Vershínins will go on stage saying "in 200–300 [...] 1000 years [...] a new, happy life will dawn": like the horizon, ever keeping its distance from us, this promise of "new happy life" is never fulfilled, getting farther and farther away from those, who pursue it relentlessly while knowing full well that it is an *unrealisable potential*.

In a similar way, though in a totally different context, the horizon of 'saying the final definitive word' about any great art keeps getting away from us, precisely because of its *greatness*, alias its *inexhaustibility*. In this sense, then, we keep realising Chekhov's ever-replenishing, ever-regenerating potentials. So far we have been doing it for over a century; yet the journey will continue as long as there are human beings committed to the love and study of great art. Chekhov's is the eternal paradoxical saga of an art **about** **unrealised potentials**, which partly and significantly undermines its own premise through its sheer greatness. Pursuing its study and understanding is an unstoppable, everlasting human project.

Notes

1   The current Chapter (1) and the last one (11) 'frame' the Book, constituting its opening and closing statements. Both of them view the Chekhov phenomenon from outer perspectives, whereas the main body of the Book (Chapters 3–9) provides 'inner' perspectives for viewing the same materials.

2   The terms '*positive*' and '*negative*' as used here have nothing to do with moral *right* and *wrong*; they refer to the emphasis on *presence* as opposed to the emphasis on **non-realisation**.

3   Chekhov uses here the Russian word/term пошлость, whose near-untranslatability was discussed at length in Vladímir Nabókov's study of Gógol': see Nabokov 1944, 63–74.

4   The story's original Russian title [«Скучная история»] has been translated into English several times, with various titles ("A Dull Story", "A Boring Story", "A Tedious Story", "A Dismal Story", "A Tedious Business", and there are probably others). It is remarkable that almost all translators stick to the noun "story" in their translations while differing in their rendition of the adjective. To me, it is the translation of the noun that requires rethinking and revision. Thus, "A Dreary Story" is the title chosen by Ronald Hingley for his *The Oxford Chekhov*, Vol. 5 (London: Oxford University Press, 1970), pp. 31–83. The quoted sentence appears on p. 80 of this English version. It is my contention that *story* is wrong as an English equivalent for *история* as used by Chekhov in his title for the story; it would create a self-referential mechanism, wrongly attributing to Chekhov a view that his story itself is "boring"/"dull"/"dismal"/"dreary" etc. — a sense that is not suggested in the Russian original: in titling this story Chekhov avoids the regular Russian terms denoting a formal *narrative genre* (e.g., *рассказ*, *повесть*), that could create such a confusion. My own suggestion here, *Tale*, is motivated by two considerations: (a) it does not refer to a formal *genre* of prose fiction; (b) for the English reader, it may invoke a Shakespearean association — "It is a tale told by an idiot, full of sound and fury, signifying nothing" (*Macbeth*, V, v, 26–28). This association, though undoubtedly never intended by Chekhov, supplies a thematic and poetic resonance, whose tone is appropriate to the content and emotional world of this story.

5   This aphoristic dictum is included in "Unattainable Moscow", an article published in

Hebrew in the literary supplement of the Israeli daily *Yediot Achronot* (August 19, 1977). While I take exception to the totality implied in the wording of this generalisation, I do subscribe to the basic principle it expounds, and will return to it in other parts of the Book, especially in Chapter 5, where it appears as Epigraph.

6 Another implication of the same dictum is discussed in 5.2.1.

7 Even if we don't take his words at face value, and go nitpicking and hair-splitting to say that he didn't really want to become a writer, but only **wanted to have wanted** to become one, the basic premise would stand, since his fellow-clerks would not have wanted to want to become "men of letters".

8 For discussions of the concept and methodology of the *implied spectator* see Kaynar 1997 and 2001.

9 Examples can be found in exceptional abundance; consider, for instance, the inner structure of Nína's last monologue in *The Seagull*; dialogues between Sónia and Yeléna or Ástrov in *Uncle Vania*; events surrounding the *absence* of marriage proposal by Lopákhin to Vária in Act 4 of *The Cherry Orchard*, to give just a few examples, and not necessarily the most striking ones, out of very many indeed.

10 As explained in the Preface, this French term is used in the absence of an English one to denote a *dramatic speech*, i.e., the text spoken by one personage until interrupted by another, usually as part of a dialogue.

CHAPTER

2

Basic Principles of Chekhovian Composition *(How?)*

2.0 Preliminary Remarks: 'Chekhov the *Structuralist*'?

*The Whole **at the Expense of** its Parts* is a crucial principle of Chekhov's composition and structuration techniques; it is just as typical, unique, and arguably exclusive to his art as principles of his thematics, presented in Chapter 1. Together they constitute the hallmark of *Chekhovism*, i.e., the *deep structure*[1] of Chekhov's unique artistic system.

Chekhov emphatically denied being a follower of any political, religious, or other school, group or persuasion;[2] similarly, he was not, nor ever claimed to be, identified with any *school, trend* or *movement* in drama, theatre or literature: *Realist, Naturalist, Symbolist, Impressionist*, etc. — none of these labels seems to do justice to his uniqueness, despite attempts to regiment him under the banner of this or that school in the arts.[3] However, the very act of composing a work of art results in making choices and decisions, selecting options while rejecting others. The overall picture of these creative actions, whether taken (partially or wholly) deliberately or intuitively, amounts to an author's *poetics*, which, in turn, is perforce characterisable as being closer to some schools or trends and farther from others. No author is a total island in this sense, though the argument presented here is that, comparatively, Chekhov is one of the most unique 'islands' in the history of the arts. Chapter 10 is dedicated to an elaboration of this idea.

If (and 'a big *if*' it is!) Chekhov can posthumously be recruited to any kind of *-ism*, only *Structuralism*, especially of the East European brand (as developed in Moscow, Prague, Tartu, and other academic centres in eastern Europe in the 20th century), comes close. Obviously, *Structuralism* denotes a school of thought in various academic disciplines in the humanities and social sciences, rather than a school of artistic creation. The term is often applied to the study of the arts, but never to the arts themselves; in other words, it is not analogous to such terms as *realism, cubism, impressionism*, etc., as discussed in Chapter 10. Therefore, claiming that Chekhov is a 'Structuralist' cannot be taken literally; rather, the contention is that his work, especially in drama, vindicates *Formalist–Structuralist* premises, theories and methodologies (or, at least, is compatible with them) more than the work of most other masters. Of course, Chekhov could not have recognised himself in *Structuralism* any more than Shakespeare or Sophocles could envisage, or indeed fully understand, what 20th and 21st centuries psychoanalysts, feminists, Marxists, post-colonialists, deconstructionists, etc., have said about them. However, there is a difference between these posthumous interpretations and what is attempted here. It is not argued that Chekhov was some kind of 'proto-Structuralist', or an intuitive harbinger of Structuralism through his social, ideological, political, or psychological attitude, philosophical thinking, or even that he heralded Structuralist schools in the study of literature or theatre. Rather, it is argued that his artistic **practice**, the way he constructed his texts through the very activity of writing them as he did, can be regarded as apt demonstrations of Structuralist ideology about the nature of texts in general, and artistic texts in particular, and their construction and perception (rather than about reality, humanity, society, politics etc.).

I am referring, first and foremost, to what is perhaps '**the** no. 1 banner-cry' of *Structuralism*: "the whole is greater than the sum-total of its parts"; this means, mainly, that in structured, composite wholes, the structure/composition as such has values of its own, above and beyond the cumulative values of the *parts*, or *components*,[4] which make up those wholes, regardless of the *semantic content*, and other qualities, of their parts.[5]

2.1 A Theoretical Complex of *Complexity*

2.1.1 The *Complex*, the *Simple*, and the *Complicated*

Complexity is one of the three *canons of aesthetic value* in western civilisation,[6] according to M.C. Beardsley (1958, 462–464).[7] The effect of a *whole* that is significantly greater than its *parts* (at least when that whole is a work of art in the western tradition) is closely linked to that whole's *complexity*.

Now it is a straightforward observation, indeed quite a simple one (adopted in all the dictionaries that I have consulted), that *complex* is the opposite of *simple*. This obvious dichotomy, however, is simplistic when it comes to the description and analysis of truly-complex works of art, and I propose to subsume it under a *trichotomy*, in which the term and concept *complicated* is added to *simple* and *complex*.[8] The term *complicated* implies a potentially indefinite expansion in the internal composition of the object characterised by it — the inclusion of more and more elements, more and more types of elements, and more and more connections and types of connections between them, potentially *ad infinitum*, regardless of limitations and constraints of the mind/brain, that may hinder the simultaneous cognitive processing of this object's *perception*. *Complex*, when contrasted with *complicated*, imposes the constraints of the 'humanly processable' on the latter: in other words, *complexity* amounts to maximum complicatedness that can be processed within the limitations of human perception and cognition. The dichotomy between *complex* and *complicated* is basically analogous to the dichotomies between *a few* and *few* and between *a little* and *little*, respectively: all these distinctions are based on the speaker's subjective attitude towards a given number or quantity, rather than on an objective size/amount of that number or quantity. Thus, if one's attitude towards the amount of free time (e.g., twenty minutes) that one has at a given moment is negative, one would say 'I have **little** time, therefore I cannot stay here any longer', whereas if one's attitude to the same amount of time is positive, one would say 'I have **a little** time, therefore I can stay a bit longer'. By analogy, one would say (or think) if one despairs of the intricacy of a work of art, '*this work is **complicated**; I will never be able to understand it/figure it out*', and would abandon it; if one is intensely intrigued by the same work, however, one would say/think: '*this work is **complex**; therefore I would like to get to know it better, to experience it repeatedly until I unravel its complexity and understand it*'.

The entire general–theoretical discussion here is conceived in terms of '*algebraic*' rather than '*arithmetical*' thinking (both terms used, of course, metaphorically): there is no actual number of elements, connections, combinations, subordinations, etc., beyond which the *simple* becomes *complex* or the latter becomes *complicated*. Moreover, thresholds vary not only for different individuals, but also for the same individual in different circumstances (depending, e.g., on tiredness, presence of mind/concentration, prior knowledge relevant to the specific text, etc.). Simply put, the point is that such a threshold exists, whatever its variable numerical values may be, and the distinction offered here is based on its existence.

Now since the *complicated* is characterised 'negatively', as a deterrent to engage in the perception of works characterised by it, authors would hardly ever create such works on purpose, communicability being a major concern of all artists, indeed of authors of texts in general.[9] That said, Beardsley is basically right that in western cultural consciousness *complexity* is held as a virtue that contributes to the appreciation and eventual canonisation of works of art.[10] Therefore, creative artists would often exercise brinkmanship, striving to test the limits of *complexity* by adding to its load up to, but not beyond, the threshold of the *complicated*. Indeed, upon crossing this threshold, virtues (of the *complex*) often turn into vices (of the *complicated*): the *complicated* and the *boring* often generate similar responses — one tends to avoid them both, but not in similar ways (as explained below in 2.5).

2.1.2 Two Types of *Complexity*

That said, I propose another distinction, within the realm of *complexity*, between two basic types thereof: *saturated* and *unsaturated*. These types are, once again, 'algebraic' abstractions, ideals hardly ever encountered in their 'pure' form in real texts. Theoretically and schematically, then, *saturated* complexity borders on the complicated but, ideally, without crossing that threshold; it applies to wholes whose parts, even if isolated from their contexts, are relatively meaningful, self-contained, striving towards potential autonomy/independence; conversely, *unsaturated* complexity applies to wholes whose parts are densely interwoven, but every one of them is relatively simple, even depleted.[11] In the former type, ideally, each and every single textual phrase is meaningful and interesting, possessing some degree of its own inner complexity; consequently, the larger units — from a short *réplique*, via a dialogue, a scene, an Act, to the full play — must be more meaningful and interesting than any single phrase within them.[12] On the other hand, if individual parts are insignificant and uninteresting, they can still join forces to produce meaningful, interesting wholes, provided that the forces that bind them together generate meaningful interest through their own operation, and even more so when these forces bring about a fresh look directed back at the individual parts, now no longer viewed in isolation. In the former type the wholes are inevitably 'strong': their strength results inescapably from the strength of the parts of which they are composed; in the latter type the wholes are also 'strong', but not obviously or inescapably so: their 'strength' results from the intricacy of the networks and structuration-mechanisms that bind and relate their *parts*, and *partial wholes*, to each other. Chekhov's typical practice in composing his plays results, indeed, in *unsaturated complexity*, in which the workings of the connections and interactions between and among the *parts* override the 'weakness' of these same parts as viewed in isolation.

In short: in Chekhov's art the 'strength' of a *macro* whole is not merely unrelated to the 'weakness' of its *micro* parts; the former comes **at the expense** of the latter: it is the very depletion and thinness of typical *parts* that propel our interest-seeking energies towards the *wholes*, via the networks of connections and interactions that join the former together to make up the latter; in short, what makes the *parts* 'weak' makes the *wholes* 'strong'.[13] For the *saturated* type, an aesthetic ideal is the potential ***independence*** of the parts (those that can carry meanings independently); for the *unsaturated* one, ***interdependence*** of parts within the wholes is the aesthetic ideal. As shorthand formula, the former can be characterised as *Micro+/Macro+*, whereas the latter would be *Micro-/Macro+*.

Another partial analogy may help to further clarify the issue: *saturated complexity* can be likened to a building made of solid, rock-like stones, cemented with large quantities of the best of materials into an unshakable structure; *unsaturated complexity* can be likened to an equally strong building, made of relatively hollow, soft bricks. In the latter case, the cementing materials must be exceptionally durable, with state-of-the-art supporting techniques, to achieve the desired results; at any rate, weaker bricks require stronger cementing to compensate for their weakness.[14]

2.2 *Saturated Complexity*: Shakespeare's Plays as Paradigm

For the purpose of the present discussion, Shakespeare's poetics serves as illustration for *saturated complexity*. Complexity reigns supreme everywhere in his work: from the smallest pre-semantic *micro* unit of prosody to the all-encompassing, crucially significant *macro* theme of an entire play, or even in the realms of groups of plays up to his entire *oeuvre*. To use his own words, the entire range from "the last syllable" (*Macbeth*, V, v, 21) to "the imperial theme" (*Macbeth*, I, iii, 129), and everything in between these extremes, tends to achieve complexity. This applies, of course, to all types of units and phenomena in the text: personages, ideas, events, etc. Here are two examples.

Consider lines from Hamlet's "To be or not to be" soliloquy:

[...] and by opposing END them? To die, to SLEEP
No more; and by a SLEEP to say we END
The heartache and the thousand natural shocks
That flesh is heir to [etc.] (*Hamlet* III, i, 60–63)

Each of the two capitalised words — END and SLEEP — is positioned, within the first two consecutive lines quoted, once at the end of a line and once in its middle (it is a known fact in the psychology of cognition and perception that, other things being equal, special prominence is assigned to beginnings and endings[15] of temporal or textual units). Thus, an almost perfect equilibrium is created between the two words (and what they refer to). The first SLEEP is ambiguous in terms of intonation: in principle, it can have two readings, one ending with a pause, the other without a pause. The former, end-stopped reading, would be: "to die, to sleep;/ No more", with "no more" referring to something unspecified in the text but inferable from it, like *living*. The latter reading would be a *run-on line*, or *enjambment* (see Golomb 1979): "to die, to sleep → no more", with "no more" referring directly to SLEEP. Needless to say, these two intonational readings produce diametrically opposed meanings: in the former *die* and *sleep* are synonymous, "to die" being an extension of "to sleep", whereas in the latter the two are juxtaposed, with death characterised, in this context, as the **absence**, or negation, of sleep (which is now viewed as a sign of life).[16] By analogy, the second END, at the end of the line, is likely to be taken as a *transitive verb*, signalling an *enjambment* that anticipates the direct object in the next line (in the final analysis, this proves to be the only syntactically legitimate reading of the line), but the same verb can also be interpreted as *intransitive*, followed by a pause at line-end, with "we END" meaning 'we are ended', i.e., 'we die'. Indeed, unlike the case of SLEEP, there is no real ambiguity here, since the *intransitive*, *end-stopped* option is not viable syntactically; however, for a split second, that option can be suggested to the spectator's mind through a properly vague intonation contour.[17] For the purpose of the present discussion, the main point is not the interpretation(s), potential or actual, but the ambiguity itself, as a text-enriching device, making the perceiver say to him/herself 'this "must give us pause"' (see the same soliloquy, line 68) in order to unravel the complexity and have a longer, harder look at the smallest of details. Only as a result of such slow, focused reading can the perceiver make the most of the subtlest complexities of the text, and its interactions of overt and covert meanings.

Now SLEEP and END are not only monosyllables, potentially subjected, as such, to intense prosodic care, but also words of high **thematic** significance. Dialectic relation between *sleep* and *death* are central not only to the soliloquy, but also to the play as a whole. Thus, the careful prosodic manipulation of tiniest *micro* units renders a valuable service to the play's central, comprehensive *macro* themes.

Similarly, consider *King Lear* I, i, 91–92:

<u>YOU</u> have begot me, bred me, lov'd me. <u>I</u>
Return those duties back as are right fit.

The line-division suggests an unexpected pause after the "**I**" at the end of the first line quoted. Here, too, Shakespeare is taking intensive care of single words and syllables as a means to an end: this particular line division juxtaposes the "**I**" at the end of the line with the preceding "**YOU**", at its beginning; the thematic and psychological gain from this juxtaposition is obvious once one considers the text attentively: much in *King Lear* is the result of clashes and confrontations between the *you* and the *I* of pairs of assertive personalities in general, and Lear and Cordelia in particular.[18]

Similar cases abound in the Shakespearean corpus.[19] Moreover, the principle of *saturated complexity* transcends the arena of prosodic–thematic interactions. It is typical of Shakespeare that single personages, scenes, events, *répliques*, etc., are also potentially independent: thus, a reasonably full view of a Shakespearean personage can often be reached from looking at the lines assigned to him/her, even if the lines assigned to others are ignored. The density and intensity of the text increase manifold when we consider all potentially relevant texts and contexts, including those that do not refer directly to the personage under examination.[20]

All the aforesaid only seems to apply to any complex artistic text: in fact, this is not the case. Shakespeare is exceptional in this context too, because in his plays, by and large, there is no reduction/relaxation in the load of emotional and intellectual content, or in structuration strategies operating on the highest *macro* levels (e.g., on the level of the play as a whole, and beyond): such reduction could perhaps counterbalance the enormous density and intensity of structuration strategies operating on *micro* levels (e.g., stress and syllable configurations). Indeed, he seems to have been oblivious, or mindless, of the cognitive limitations of normal mortals; his texts often require an amount of simultaneous mental processing that is above and beyond the cognitive capacities of most human brains. Many Shakespearean *répliques* can match an elaborate single, isolated poem in terms of textual *complexity*, rich *imagery*, inventive *figurative language*, and, most importantly, autonomous overall signification. Moreover, such a *réplique*, admittedly, falls short of a whole, autonomous work of art, simply because it is just part of one: it is included in, and subordinated to, *superordinate macro units* culminating in the entire play. Yet, in spite of their subordination to an artistic whole, single Shakespearean *répliques* are often, potentially, more complex than many single, really-autonomous poems. In short: in Shakespeare, the *strength/density/ complexity* of the *macro* whole is an **inevitable by-product** of the **same** qualities in its *parts*.[21]

2.3 *Unsaturated Complexity*: Chekhov's Plays as Paradigm

By contrast, Chekhov's texts — though virtually matching Shakespeare's in complexity — seem to reflect the author's mindfulness of cognitive limitations of ordinary humans and their difficulty to focus their undivided attention on all elements and levels within an intricate artistic text and the fictional world(s) that it creates. Chekhov seems to have taken a consistent decision (though, probably, a largely intuitive one) to favour *macro wholes*, and intricate networks operating within such wholes, in preference to their isolated *micro parts*. Consequently, his *parts* must be intensely contextualised; otherwise they are often reduced to apparent insignificance.[22]

This presentation of Chekhov's *micro* units as depleted or insignificant seems to be at odds with his reputation as a master of *detail* (he is very often hailed as such; see, for instance, the Chekhov-related discussions in Dóbin 1981, especially pp. 364–430). Indeed, Chekhov was very meticulous in choosing every single word and phrase, but he often invested his authorial effort precisely to create details that **feign *insignificance* in isolation**, and he was equally meticulous in placing those details in specific contexts, each consisting of comparable carefully-chosen details. Each such context activates intense interactions between details, which gain fresh significance from such interactions. In other words: Chekhov pays intense authorial attention to choosing *micro details* that appear at first as unworthy of the perceiver's attention. They earn the right to claim such attention only through contextualised interactions. This is a typical strategy whereby *wholes* are made to realise the potentials of *parts*.

To conclude: it may be by now a truism, that a structured *whole* is greater than the sum total of its *parts*; it is not at all a truism, however, that parts should be not merely lesser than wholes, but depleted, insignificant and uninteresting in isolation. After the mental pendulum between a given *subordinate part* and its *superordinate whole* has gone up and down at least once in each direction,[23] the *detail* (in this context, synonymous with *part*) is no longer isolated in the perceiver's mind, simply because it cannot be divorced from the structured whole once the latter, and its connection with the former, have been brought to the perceiver's attention. There is no going back to 'virginal' *tabula rasa*.

The process just described is not specific to Chekhov; it takes place in any artistic text worthy of the name. Yet, as we have seen, in Shakespeare the isolated *micro details* themselves are replete with significance; in Chekhov, conversely, typical details are devoid of comparable significance, at least by comparison, both to Shakespearean *details/parts* and to Chekhovian *wholes*. That is how Chekhov's *wholes* build their strength at the expense of the weakness of their *parts*, designed (as we have seen) to look and sound trivial, shallow, insignificant, uninteresting.[24] True, Chekhov's is an art of impeccable precision: little, if anything, is left to chance;[25] yet, potentially-autonomous, memorable, aphoristically quotable phrases are few and far between in his writing.[26] This, once again, is thrown into bold relief by the Shakespearean counter-example, where, typically, even the odd syllable[27] can have a life of its own within a poetics, whose hallmark is frequent memorability of single lines and phrases.

Indeed, Chekhov's art seems paradoxical in this context, as well in some others, as further characterised in 8.1 and elsewhere in the Book. Thus, one may be bewildered by the seeming contradiction between two equally-misleading qualities in his art: often-hidden precision and iron-clad architectural design, on the one hand,

and seeming accidentality, almost arbitrariness, of his chain of *répliques*, events, and their presentation and arrangement, on the other hand. This paradoxical mismatch between his artistic qualities is somehow resolved organically within his unified and unique poetics. In this context he can be described as someone who spends hours combing his hair in front of a mirror in order to look dishevelled.

2.4 A Third Ideal of *Complexity*: 'Strong' *Parts*, 'Weak' *Wholes*

2.4.1 *Saturated Complexity* Misplaced: Poe's "The Raven" as Paradigm

Chekhov's specific structuration technique can be illuminated from another angle, by contrasting it with a counter-example of a totally different nature, opposed more radically than Shakespeare's poetics to Chekhov's. Edgar Allan Poe's "The Raven"[28] is characterised by dense phonetic and prosodic networks of sound patterns, many of them expressive (see, for instance, Harshav 1980 and Tsur 1987). The complexity of this component of the text is *saturated*: it is a very difficult challenge to the reader's cognition to process everything that goes on simultaneously within the sound stratum of the poem. Here is a typical example:

And the silken, sad, uncertain rustling of each purple curtain
Thrilled me, filled me with fantastic terrors, never felt before.
So that now, to still the beating of my heart I stood repeating:
'Tis some visitor entreating entrance at my chamber door.

A mere slow, attentive and emphatic reading of this text (preferably through vocal, audible recitation) is enough to bring its exceptional density of sound and rhythm to the reader's attention: consider, for instance, the workings of the sounds (however spelled) of the consonants *s, f, silent th*, and *st*; *r-coloured vowels* (again, however spelled: *er, ur, or, ear*); overt and covert *rhymes*; *parallelisms* of *sound* and *syntax*; regular/expected/predictable and irregular/unexpected/surprising effects working prospectively and retrospectively;[29] intense, mutually subversive counterpoint between all the above, and conflicting options of pausing, retarding and accelerating while reading the text — these and other structural and textural organisations contribute to its density and to its genuinely artistic nature and effect (see Golomb 1979, 117–119, for a more detailed analysis of these aspects of the poem). However, in terms of *macro-semantic/thematic* content of the text, "The Raven" is "full of sound and (some) fury", yet almost '*signified* nothing': much ado in *micro* signifiers, about almost nothing in *macro* signifieds.[30] This text, then, represents another aesthetic ideal,[31] contrastable both with Chekhov's and Shakespeare's. For the latter two, the aesthetic ideal represented here by "The Raven" is clearly "the road not taken".

2.4.2 Chekhov's *Complexity vs.* Shakespeare's and "The Raven"'s

Chekhov's poetics in this context, then, occupies a special position in relation to Shakespeare's, in which both *micro* and *macro* levels achieve complexity, and

"The Raven"'s, in which only *micro* level does. The latter, in fact, is diametrically opposed to Chekhov's poetics, practically reversing the latter's preferences.[32] I argue elsewhere (Golomb 2014), that every art in particular (and every communication system, in general) has a 'natural' or 'default' inner hierarchy between its own basic components. In western tonal music this hierarchy foregrounds *pitch relationships* and **relatively** marginalises relationships of *duration* (rhythm), *loudness* and *timbre*; in *language*, and consequently in its artistic organisation through the various genres of *literature* (including *Drama*), *semantic–thematic* components are foregrounded, relegating other (including *prosodic*) phenomena and relationships to relative marginality (the latter hierarchy is typically challenged and refreshed in *poetry*, but hardly ever turned upside down). If *literary complexity* is intended, it cannot be achieved through a radical reversal of the basic hierarchy, i.e., by depleting its thematic–semantic component and subordinating it to extra-strong prosodic structuration. This, however, is precisely what "The Raven" is doing: despite its undoubtedly exceptional *prosodic complexity*, it is not complex **as a work of literary–poetic art**, since its complexity is limited to one component of the artistic whole (*prosody*), which is relatively marginal within the typical hierarchy of this art. Thus, Shakespeare's poetics of *saturated complexity*, which nurtures *micro textures* (mainly *prosodic* and *syntactic*) without sacrificing *macro* structures (mainly *thematic*), upholds and preserves the basic hierarchy of literary and dramatic art. Chekhov's poetics, which does sacrifice the potential independence of its *micro* components[33] to *macro* designs of thematic content and overall composition, certainly upholds the same basic hierarchy of literature and drama; in fact, it even fortifies this hierarchy.

2.5 Conclusion: Investment and Interest

The principle of *the whole **at the expense of** its parts* outlined in this Chapter is central not only to the understanding of Chekhov's poetics and its uniqueness; it is also crucial to the understanding of major issues in Chekhov reception and some of the effects that his plays are known to have made on professionals and lay audiences alike ever since their composition and first performances.

Chekhov is one of the most canonised, admired, even revered, writers and playwrights in history; his reputation among theatre practitioners of most professions, and among academic communities worldwide, is above reproach, and the adjective *Chekhovian* is one of the most coveted among writers and playwrights of generations after his death, to the present. Yet, there is a sort of *"The Emperor's New Clothes* effect" surrounding the reception of his works, particularly the plays, especially with new or young audiences, uninitiated students, lay spectators, etc.: those who experience his plays as unexciting, even boring (to call a spade a spade) fear to speak their minds, intimidated by a wide consensus of prestigious professionals, who are supposed to know better. Such novices (especially students) may experience cognitive dissonances between what they are told orally by their teachers and in writing by the secondary literature, on the one hand, and by their own minds and senses on the other hand. A student of theatre or literature, and even a reader or theatregoer, who wants to be 'cultured', has to be quite bold to say openly that s/he is bored by Chekhov's plays, or simply does not like them.

While 'liking'/'disliking' a play relates to the taste and psychology of a perceiver and cannot be properly addressed within the discipline dramatic, literary or theatrical scholarship/analysis, the 'boredom' claim resides in the interface between the personal and the textual, and should be addressed at least in its textual aspect.

Frankly, the claim that many *répliques* in Chekhov's plays are boring cannot be dismissed offhand. Let us think of *boredom* as a mental state of "weariness and despair of the hope for change",[34] or for the emergence, in the near textual/theatrical future, of a focus of interest, of something new, important, intriguing or engaging. I hope to have shown in this Chapter that a likely reason for *the boredom effect* in Chekhov is the relative depletion, indeed lack of interest, in several parts of his texts: individual *personages*,[35] single *répliques* (notably tedious "philosophising" speeches discussed in Chapter 8), single scenes, etc. Another likely reason for this effect is the *emotional restraint* so characteristic of Chekhov, as shown in Chapter 7. Both these typically Chekhovian phenomena are exponents of the basic interrelated principles of *presence through absence* and *unrealised potential*. The *potential* inherent in separate *parts* is realised through their interactions with comparable *parts*, and with *partial* and *complete wholes* relating to them through hierarchies, subordinations, and other types of interrelationships. As long as such interactions remain unnoticed, and consequently do not activate mental processes in the perceiver, this *potential* is functionally *absent* from the process of watching a play or reading its text; the result is boredom. The same applies to *Chekhovian restraint* and other instances of interplay between *present* and *seemingly absent* components of the plays' texts and worlds.

Boredom is a tricky phenomenon. Art abhors boredom: there is no *but* after a verdict of "it is boring". But in Chekhov's case, a major remedy, or antidote, to understandable but unjustified boredom lies in the perceiver's intense awareness of the text's *unsaturated complexity*, of the need to rise above the *parts*, to listen to the *potentials* yearning for *realisation*, to sense and experience the intricate ways in which parts are brought together to generate wholes. The fascination with such texts resides not only in the complex, structured wholes themselves, once they are noticed, discovered and experienced, but also in the **process** of discovering them; it resides, to use another metaphor, not only in the final edifice, to the extent that it exists, but also, and mainly, in the process of its construction, with its ups and downs, rewards and frustrations. Chekhov is a demanding, challenging author: he does not do his perceivers' work for them. The level of alertness, awareness, subtlety and sophistication, and the intensity of active cognitive processing, required from his audiences, is in all likelihood unprecedented in the history of drama. To be constantly alert to analogies and hierarchies is indeed a tiring process, but a fascinating and rewarding one.

True, *saturated complexity* of the Shakespearean type also requires sophistication and multi-channelled processing; but in Shakespeare's case it is not required as antidote to boredom, or in order to make integrative sense out of seemingly disconnected *répliques*. For *saturated complexity* such high-level processing is, in a way, a necessary luxury; for *unsaturated complexity* it is an indispensable necessity.

Shakespeare's texts impose their rich, sometimes overflowing complexities on their perceivers, who usually must make selections out of the bounty bestowed on them; the force applied by his plays is directed **from text to the audience**. Chekhov's texts work in the opposite direction: they open voids, active vacuums into which the perceiver is drawn, by suction, which is a kind of seduction, as it were, with a force directed **from audience to text**. There are gaps to be filled in: *absences* of content, of emotion, of interest; but the potential materials with which this filling process can be carried out are all *present*, in raw form, in and through the texts, via *textual absence*. The perceiver has to recognise and identify them, to pick them up so to speak, to enter the textual voids, fill in the gaps, integrate the disconnected and isolated *parts*, as if retracing and following the author's footsteps in composing the whole from them, and in constructing *surface realisations* of the *deep potentials*, to borrow a Chomskyan analogy. If such a process is anything short of fascinating, I doubt whether there is any meaning to that word.

The cognitive and emotional **investment** in a Chekhovian play is indeed formidable, but the **interest** it generates is bounteous. In addition to the structural aspects of this interest, as shown in this Chapter, another source of inexhaustible fascination is the *emotional restraint* and the powers bursting to break loose that it holds back: the powers of keeping frequent implosions and rare explosions in check and balance are also a source of enormous suspense.

The bored perceiver can be encouraged to make virtue out of necessity; to use the boredom and frustration[36] resulting from the depletion of the parts as motivation for constructing the hidden wholes and discovering the treasures of the Beardsleyan triad mentioned in Subsection 2.1.1 — *unity, intensity*, and *complexity* — in the construction of the texts and their inner and outer relationships (at this point, *outer* refers to the relationships that *present* elements generate with *absent* ones). It follows, then, that watching Chekhov's plays, or reading their texts while imagining their staging, can generate a never-a-dull-moment effect, contrary to the initial impression that they may produce, precisely because every potentially dull moment is a spring-board for hunting analogies, interactions, hierarchies, etc.[37]

As we have seen, the perception of art cannot tolerate boredom; shunning it can work in two opposite directions: abandoning the 'boring' text altogether, and clinging to it with even greater force, to look for antidotes within it. The former attitude would diagnose it as *complicated*, and leave it alone; the latter would diagnose it as *complex*, and try to vindicate this diagnosis by looking at the text more closely, *realising its potentialities*. A text that is genuinely boring would leave the searching perceiver empty-handed, offering no potentials to realise. The aim of this Chapter, and indeed of this Book, is to show that Chekhov's plays supply plenty of *realisable potentials* in the relationships between text and perceiver, often through exposing *unrealised potentials* within the staged fictional world.

The greater the effort invested in the quest, the richer the interest-generating rewards of the discovery.

Notes

1 The term *Deep Structure* is used here figuratively. Inspired, of course, by *generative linguistics*, it is applied and adapted to the study of the uniqueness of the individual poetics of authors of fictional–artistic texts. See below.

2 In a famous letter to A.N. Pleshchéïev (October 1889) Chekhov says: "I am not a liberal, not a conservative, not a believer in gradual progress, not a monk, not an indifferentist". See Friedland 1964, p. 63.

3 "*Chekhovism* and other -*isms*" is the subject of Chapter 10.

4 The terms *part, component,* and *(constituent) element,* are used here almost interchangeably, and admittedly loosely at that. *Part* refers to anything that joins together with comparable *part*s to compose a greater *whole*; a *partial whole* — e.g., a *scene*, whose parts in turn could be several dialogues — can be a part of a larger whole, like an *Act*, which in turn would be a part of an entire *play*. Likewise, a *personage* is part of a small *group* of personages sharing some traits, included in a larger group, up to a complete *cast list*, and then — especially in Chekhov — culminating in a list of everyone relevant to a play's human inventory, including *offstage personages*; etc. This Chapter deals with interactions between *wholes* and *parts, superordinate* and *subordinate* structures, *higher* and *lower orders,* etc., whatever their names.

5 This basic idea, variously worded and formulated, can be found in any basic book on *Structuralism*; see for instance, Culler 1975, 3–109. Earlier and later works, like Erlich 1965; Garvin 1964; the superb British series *Russian Poetics in Translation*; Matejka & Titunik 1976; Veltruský 1977. Other publications exposing the English-reading public to these East European scholarly traditions contain many additional relevant references.

6 The other two are *unity* and *intensity*, ignored at this point, but discussed below, in 10.4.1.

7 The notion (and phenomenon) of *complexity*, just as the other two Beardsleyan canons of artistic value, is applicable to all arts, and can serve as a useful tool in '*interart*' [=comparative art] studies. I gratefully acknowledge the impact that two senior colleagues have made on my thinking on the subject through their oral and written teachings: Benjamin Harshav in the study of literature, and Dalia Cohen in the study of music; I am of course solely responsible for any shortcomings in my study of the subject, including unquoted reference to their work.

8 Most dictionaries use similar rather than identical terms in defining *complex* and *complicated*; the nuanced, subtle differences between the respective definitions are compatible with the distinction offered here, though the distinction itself is not offered in regular dictionaries.

9 Rare exceptions — e.g., coded texts, designed on purpose to be cryptic and incomprehensible to all but a designated audience of one or more addressees — do not invalidate this point in principle, because they have their own mechanisms, or keys, to ensure their communicability to **that** audience.

10 I differ with Beardsley only about the totality of the canonisation of *complexity*, not about its existence or centrality, especially in European approaches to the arts in recent centuries.

11 These concepts and distinctions apply to all arts; however, in the present Chapter they are applied exclusively to the art of drama/theatre. Comparable applications to *music* are discussed in 10.4.2.

12 For the sake of this argument I ignore the risk of boredom-effect that results from the *complicated* and assume that steps are taken to prevent the creation of this effect.

13 On an absolutely different matter says Lady Macbeth: "That which hath made them

drunk hath made me bold:/What hath quenched them hath given me fire"... (*Macbeth* II, ii, 1–2).

14 This metaphor is designed, of course, to illustrate the theoretical point and merits no focus on its own details. The actual *complexity* of the phenomena and the theories that can explain them is greater than suggested so far, because the hierarchy proposed, of smaller units joining to generate bigger ones, is oversimplified. Signification units and their interrelations are often not congruent with discrete textual units: thus, a metaphorical meaning of a word can be both lesser and greater than that word (lesser, since the word has a literal meaning too; greater, since the metaphor can connect to ideas of an entire text, and beyond, radically transcending the limits of a single word). The subject figures prominently in literary theory (e.g., Lotman 1979; Harshav 2007, 113–127, 140–160.). However, even a simplified model as proposed here can illuminate Chekhov's uniqueness in this context.

15 *Primacy effect* and *recency effect* are terms associated with the prominence of *beginnings* and *endings*, respectively. See Herrnstein Smith, 1968, for an application of this conceptual framework to poetry, and Perry 1979a, especially pp. 50–61, for its pioneering application to the theory and analysis of fictional texts, and the References supplied therein for past work on the subject, mainly in *Gestalt* theories and the psychology of *cognition* and *perception*. More recent discussions abound in the relevant literature. In Chapters 3 and 9 these concepts are explicitly applied in analyses of Chekhov's plays.

16 This latter interpretation of *sleep* is compatible with "Sleep no more!" etc. in *Macbeth*, II, ii, 33–37.

17 Richard Burton's audio recording of the play is a rare demonstration of how the ambiguity can be preserved in a remarkably undecided oral reading of both SLEEP and END. Most other recordings resolve this ambiguity, thereby reducing the text's complexity. See Rimmon–Kenan 1977 about ambiguity and disambiguation; see also Perry and Sternberg 1986. See especially Tsur 1998, and numerous other studies by him.

18 A fuller analysis of this example can be found in Golomb 1979, 50–55. A similar prosodic–thematic interaction in Shakespeare is described in Smith 2009, 292.

19 For instance, consider the intense interplay between *metrical* and *phonological* patterns on the one hand and *semantic content* on the other in *Othello* I, iii, 57–59; *Julius Caesar*, III, ii, 65–66; and numerous other cases.

20 Extreme *saturated complexity*, as in Shakespeare and Bach, may border on the *complicated*; however, often there are checks and balances in place to offset over–complication. See Golomb 2011. The matter is elaborated in 10.4.2.

21 Of course, these statements do not apply to every single Shakespearean element (scene, character, theme, line, etc.). However, this kind of complexity is typical of Shakespeare, and its extent and prevalence are virtually unparalleled in any other great master. See Golomb 2001 for a more detailed juxtaposition between Shakespeare and Chekhov in the field of characterisation and the potential autonomy of individual personages.

22 For a more comprehensive view of *insignificance* in Chekhov, see Popkin 1993, 17–52; for a general discussion of (in)significance, on a level of theoretical principles, see pp. 1–16.

23 This is merely a schematic illustration of a general principle; in the actual texts it is usually and typically more complex, involving as it often does several strata of *super-ordination* and *subordination*, not just two.

24 I have deliberately imitated here the language–rhythm that Chekhov's personages, notably (but not exclusively) Vershínin and Andréï in *Three Sisters*, use in their generalised descriptions of Russians (or humans in general). Consider, for instance, Andréï's

long catalogue of adjectives in Act 4: "Why is it, that when we have just begun to live, we get boring, grey, uninteresting, lazy, indifferent, useless, unhappy?"

25 In this I beg to differ with one of the greatest Chekhov scholars of our time, the late A.P. Chudakóv; see his *Chekhov's Poetics*, 1971 (1983), and my comments in Chapter 4.

26 I am referring, e.g., to the words of Voïnítskiï [Vánia] "in such [fine] weather it's good to hang oneself", in *Uncle Vania*, Act 1, or to Trofímov's "We are above love" and Ranévskaïa's immediate rejoinder "and I am beneath it" in *The Cherry Orchard*, Act 3. Chekhov rarely grants such elegant, memorable and easily quotable phrases to his personages: most of his *répliques* are hard to memorise verbatim, even after many readings.

27 I mean *syllable* figuratively — as Shakespeare himself does in "To the last syllable of recorded time" (*Macbeth* V, v, 21). Sometimes, however, *syllable* is meant even literally, as in *Julius Cæsar*, III, ii, 65–66, *Hamlet*, III, ii, 261, and in many other instances, where Shakespeare nurtures interactions between textual elements on the syllable level.

28 I am not concerned with Poe's general aesthetics; my sole concern is one specific poem of his, in which certain aesthetic ideals can be shown with unique clarity.

29 Of course, everything becomes more predictable — i.e., works prospectively — with subsequent readings, when the text becomes more familiar; yet, one always reconstructs initial surprises in one's mind, just as in a second reading of a detective story the effect of a surprising turning point is not altogether lost.

30 I refrain from a detailed thematic–semantic analysis to corroborate these claims, to avert distorted proportion between central and marginal issues in this Chapter. "The Raven" is brought into the equation only for its paradigmatic value, while its intrinsic value is not the concern of this Book. I trust, however, that any careful analysis of the poem would find that its striking complexity in prosody is not matched by comparable complexity in its semantic–thematic content. The poet's own heroic attempt to claim otherwise (in his "The Philosophy of Composition") carries little persuasive weight.

31 I am not referring here to Poe's aesthetic ideals as expressed explicitly in his articles — notably, of course, "The Philosophy of Composition" (1846), dedicated expressly to "The Raven" — but to the ideals inferable from the text. The two sets of ideals are closely related, but not identical.

32 It is pointless to complement the scheme emerging from this analysis — *Macro+, Micro* + (Shakespeare), *Macro+, Micro-* (Chekhov), *Macro-, Micro+* ("The Raven") — with an example of *Macro-, Micro-* (i.e., total minus). Such examples, to be sure, are typical of works of poor value, which "richly deserve oblivion".

33 Not all such *parts* are 'potentially independent': single scenes or personages are more likely to gain independence than sound patterns, rhyme schemes, syntactic structures etc. In short, only semantic or 'semanticisable' textual elements can enjoy a certain status of isolated, context-free independence. However, the basic principle is one of investing structural energy in *parts* within *wholes*: if such a *part* possesses semantic content or potential, it also has a potential for some degree of independence or self sufficiency; if the part is blatantly non-semantic, there can still be an effect of density and textual 'strength', but not one of potential independence.

34 I learned this definition of *boredom* from my senior colleague and mentor, the late musicologist Prof. Dalia Cohen.

35 The famous dictum "there are no minor roles, only minor actors", attributed to Stanislávskiï and associated with Chekhov's poetics, does not contradict this point (characterising Chekhov's plays as *ensemble plays* does not and cannot mean that all personages are equally central). Granted, most of Chekhov's personages are not 'minor', but his poetics, compared to the great classics, is one of *reciprocal character-*

isation, whereby the centrality of personages is largely achieved not through their own makeup but through interaction with other personages and other elements in the text. This point is elaborated in Chapter 5, especially in 5.2.2.

36 Of course I am talking here about the perceivers' boredom and frustrations, not the personages'. The latter is a separate topic; yet, the *isomorphism* between the two is a meaningful, typically Chekhovian phenomenon.

37 Analogous theoretical claims, applied to major Hebrew poets, were made in 1979 in an article by Menakhem Perry, who explicitly used the term *Deep Structure* in an applied Chomskyan sense. Similarly, in current discourse in the field of *cognitive musicology*, it is argued that our mental perception and cognitive processing of music is enabled by *natural schemata* that humans are born with, as well as by *learned* [or rather, *acquired*] *schemata*, that are non-arbitrary, and the brain acquires them, consciously and/or intuitively, through exposure to types of musical organisation (e.g., rules of *tonality* and *functional harmony* in western tonal music); it can be said that one of the *natural schemata* is the brain's ability to internalise *acquired schemata*. Accordingly, the absence of the latter (in analogy to the absence of syntactic *deep structures* in the linguistic competence of a person's brain–mind) results in inability to appreciate music designed to activate such *schemata* and in experiencing it as boring (see Cohen 1998; Cohen & Wagner 2000). This is analogous, **in different ways**, to the inability to understand a language one never learned, and to the inability to respond to types of art without prior exposure to, and at least intuitive awareness of, its tenets and conventions. To borrow Chomskyan terminology, the present analyses can be described as aiming to instil Chekhov-enabled *learned schemata* (and *deep structures* of 'Chekhovese', or rather *Chekhovism*, as elaborated in Chapter 10), in those who were not exposed to them and could not develop them before, as well as to make these *schemata* explicit to those who have developed them intuitively.

PART

II

VIEWING

CHEKHOV'S DRAMATIC TEXT AND WORLD

3

Starts that Fit
The Curtain Rises
on a Chekhov Play
OPENING THE BOOK'S INNER CIRCLE

3.0 Truisms and Preliminary Theoretical Considerations[1]
3.0.1 *Frame/Text-Boundaries*: Starting Points

The functioning of a text's beginning, which activates *primacy effect*, can be regarded, in part, as mirror image of the functioning of its ending (discussed in Chapter 9), which activates *recency effect*: both effects share the quality of giving prominence to textual elements because of their location. Both constitute the *Frame*[2] (alias the *Boundaries*, discussed primarily in Chapter 10), which separates the '*inner*', *textual–artistic–aesthetic–fictional* '*world*', and the act of perceiving it, from the '*outer*', *extra-textual, extra-artistic, non-fictional world of reality/real life* (terms within each of the two groups are commonly used interchangeably). The latter 'world' includes of course all the acts that one performs in it, excluding those relating to the perception of the given work of art itself;[3] it constitutes the springboard from which a *perceiver/addressee* (*reader, listener* and/or *spectator*) embarks on his/her engagement with an artistic text, and into which s/he returns after this engagement is over.[4] Thus, each of these two outer *boundaries* of the text looks, as it were, both **inward** and **outward**. Their **inward** look is directed from the frame inside: the beginning looks forward, from the frame into the text that follows it, and the ending looks backward, into the text that precedes it. Their **outward** look works in the opposite direction, **in temporal terms**: the beginning looks backward into the past, towards whatever one was doing before starting the process of artistic perception, and the ending looks forward into the future, towards whatever one is going to do after finishing that process. This latter, 'outward look' is directed from the *frame* (or *framed text*) into the above-mentioned *extra-artistic, extra-textual, unfictionalised world of reality*, which, as a 'world', is radically different from the *framed text*, and operates in different, heterogeneous dimensions, whose study, by definition, transcends any discipline of textual analysis and is therefore out of bounds for the present study.[5] It was mentioned here merely to complete a theoretical overview.

An analysis of *primacy effect* must, in fact, be based on a hindsight view of the beginning, as taken from later stages of the text: the concept of *primacy* itself presupposes a longer stretch of text that relates to its own starting point. Such an analysis can artificially attempt to reconstruct a first exposure to the text on page or stage, pretending to re-create or relive a state of primal ignorance of its continuation when absorbing its beginning. Admittedly, such an attempt is psychologically questionable, for it is hard for the analyst to fake ignorance of what s/he knows. Moreover, the writer most probably knew from the start at least some, if not most or all, of what is to follow in the text even when writing its first words; it is very likely that those first words were not really the first to be actually written, let alone the first to be conceived in the author's mind. In this sense and context the analysis of *beginnings* and *primacy effect*, which is attempted in this Chapter, is radically different from the analysis of *endings* and *recency effect*, as proposed in Chapter 9: the latter is an act of remembering and reconstructing what is always supposed to be known, going back on one's tracks already trodden.

3.0.2 Authorial Presence: What's in a Name (Personal)?

How does a text begin, then? A truism that seems almost too obvious to merit mentioning is that an authored text, whether printed or staged, usually begins with *the author's name*, printed on top of the (first) page, or made present, one way or another, in the minds of the theatre audience. *The author's name* has, at least potentially, an autonomous *primacy effect* of its own: the initial knowledge that a famous author — a Chekhov/Shakespeare/Goethe/Ibsen/whoever — composed the text generates some kind of expectation from the very start.[6] Most important to the present argument is the question how the knowledge that Chekhov is the author of a text in general, and a play in particular, affects the nature of the temporal process of perceiving and experiencing that text. It is actually an interactive process, because the reputation and reception of a known author and the impressions and experiences gained from the perception process of the given work affect each other, reciprocally, in the perceiver's mind. The particular kind of expectations generated by the name *Chekhov* as a text's author will not be elaborated here, because, in a way, the entire Book is concerned with the 'what, why and how' of such initial expectations generated by the mere mention of Chekhov's name: see especially the Book's Epigraph by R.L. Jackson, a shining example of Chekhov reception.

3.0.3 Titles of Plays: What's in a Name (Textual)?

Next after the author's name[7] comes the *title*. The impact of a title is the epitome of *primacy effect*: it creates a text's very first impression, the earliest point where expectations for continuation are generated. In analogy to the syntactic–semantic matrix of a basic sentence, the title is a *subject* to the ensuing text's *predicate*: though this is often not borne out by a given instance's specific features, the very firstness of a text's name leads to a presumption of *predication-relationship* between title and text; in other words, there is an expectation that the two would say something explanatory and revelatory about each other. Moreover, there is *circularity* in the process of mutual vindication between the choice of a title and the choice of what and/or who is placed high in a *hierarchy of importance and centrality* in the text: on the one hand, the title's obvious function is to draw an audience's attention to something or someone central in the play, and on the other hand whatever is connected to the title later in the text is almost automatically perceived as central **because** it is connected to the title. As an inevitable complementary result of such processes, whatever is not perceived as connected to the title is relatively marginalised; however, such marginalisation is not final or irreversible: rather, an element that is unconnected to the title has to 'work harder' than one that is connected to it in order to become central to the play in the final analysis. For instance, if a play's title refers to a person or persons (e.g., *Uncle Vánia* or *Three Sisters*), this title gives these persons an automatic head-start in their way to centrality, whereas other persons (e.g., Ástrov in *Uncle Vánia* or Vershínin in *Three Sisters*) require extra 'support' from the author in order to achieve comparable prominence (e.g., by making them prominent in the eyes of others, and/or by giving them more significant text-lines, and/or connect them with memorable events, etc. etc.). In short, connection to the title does not secure prominence; it only contributes to it, and such contribution is unhindered only "other things being equal", which they very rarely, if ever, are.

The specific titles of each of Chekhov's four major plays will be discussed below, one by one, in their function as "the beginning of the beginning" of their respective texts. Suffice it to say at this point that no consistent pattern or method of naming emerges from looking at the titles of Chekhov's major plays: there is much more consistency in the way each of the titles relates to its respective play than within the list of titles as a sequence. Thus, a title like *Ivánov* or *Uncle Vánia*[8] establishes the expectation of centrality of one personage, whereas each of the other titles has its own *primacy-effect*-activation mechanism, as demonstrated below.

3.0.4 *Genre-Subtitles*

Much has been said in the literature about Chekhov's *genre-subtitles*, which are another conventional mechanism generating *primacy effect*. It has become customary to classify plays by *genre* in various contexts; thus, in "what's on" publicity notices the public is informed that a play staged at a specific point in time is a *comedy, drama, tragedy, farce* etc.; this is often the only information beside the *author's name* and the major *title*, as part of its marketing strategy: a theatre-goer is likely to form some initial expectations, however vague and indeterminate, based on such sketchy classifications. In this context Chekhov is not fundamentally different from any other playwright: in three out of the four major plays, and in all the earlier ones, he creates genre-expectations based on traditional practices and definitions of the terms *comedy* and *drama* (see however, Note 25).

3.0.5 Skipping the List of Personages

In the printed text of a play there is a permanent element that comes after the *author's name* and play's *title* (and optional *subtitle*), but before the *initial stage direction* (*ISD*; see next Subsection): the *List of Personages*, which includes their names, usually followed by a very brief account of basic characteristics of each, such as status, profession, relation to another personage (e.g., spouse, parent, child, sibling), etc. This is sometimes followed by a general statement of the time and place of the action (for the entire play, or at least for its first Act). This *List* will be ignored here, as it is hardly ever — and never in Chekhov — reflected in the staging.[9]

3.0.6 *Initial Stage Directions (ISD)*

3.0.6.1 Preliminary Remarks

What usually (and always in Chekhov) comes after the title and subtitle is the *initial stage directions* (*ISD*). Within Chekhov's poetics and theatre-language, *stage-directions* (*SD*) — being major exponents of the author's vision of the non-verbal aspects of the production[10] — are an integral part of the play as a work of art, both as a written text and as a mechanism designed to propel a theatrical event. Accordingly, the *ISD*, establishing a static and/or dynamic *tableau* visible to the audience before the first words are uttered, are the real beginning of the play on stage, rather than those first words.

It has to be borne in mind that writing a play in the modern era is an activity designed to set the entire theatrical machinery in motion — director, actors, stage and costume designers, etc. — and reading a play can thus be a process of imagining this machinery at work (see, for instance, Scolnicov & Holland 1991; Meisel 2007, especially pp. 1–11, and below). However, there is a difference between ways that the written text relates to the play's verbal and non-verbal components via the written *SD*. Basically, there is a 1:1 correspondence in terms of time, order and content within the former — i.e., the words written on the page are precisely the ones uttered by the actors, in the same order, and there is no substantial difference, in principle, between the time it takes to utter and to read them; no such correspondence, however, exists in the relation between the written *SD* and the physical reality on stage that they refer to, which is a-temporal in principle. This relation is largely analogous to the way in which a temporal–verbal description of a spatial–non-verbal object (e.g., painting, sculpture, building etc.) relates to that object: the description consists of words that come one after the other, whereas the objects to which these words refer are placed next to each other, with no consecutive time dimension governing their ordered perception.

In terms of the practical–theatrical function of *SD*, their actual wording is not supposed to be very important, and indeed it rarely is; yet, since a playwright is very often also a writer active in other *super-genres* of literature (which certainly applies to Chekhov), the wording of *SD* may be well designed as a verbal artefact in its own right and produce a pre-designed impact on its readers (this kind of literary merit of some *SD* works against regarding all plays as mere *playscripts*, inferior or "deficient" as literary texts, as argued in Notes 12 and 14). Even the choice and order of the specific words, which cannot affect the inventory of the visual–tangible props supposed to occupy the space of the stage, can still have an impact not only on readers of the play but also on its performers (directors, designers, even actors if they care to read these words, etc.), because it does control the order of impressions and affects attitudes towards the content of the *SD*. In a way, it may produce an effect closer to a film camera zooming in and out than to a static description of a painting, sculpture etc. This certainly applies to Chekhov, especially in his *ISD*, as we shall presently see in 3.1.3 and 3.4.3.

3.0.6.2 *ISD, Literariness,* and *Textual Complexity* of *Dramatic Texts*

In considering *ISD* on a general–theoretical level it is necessary to relate it to the concept of the potential *dual fictionality* of plays, realisable in the process of reading them, as part of the consideration of the status of *drama* between *literature* and *theatre*. As we shall see, *ISD* for Chekhov are addressed to both types of readers–addressees: explicitly to production teams, especially stage directors and designers, but implicitly to lay home-readers as well. Some of the instructions therein activate at first *textual* rather than *theatrical* mechanisms; they challenge the literary as well as the visual imaginations of their professional addressees and home-readers alike. Thus, their *primacy effect* works along both tracks of the *dual fictionality* specific to the reading-process of plays.

Indeed, the concept of *dual fictionality* is elaborated where it belongs in 4.3.2; however, it is necessary to pre-introduce it briefly here, in order to understand more fully Chekhov's ways of starting a play. A theoretical point should be made at this point concerning the **literariness** (see Harshav 2007, 161–173) — or, in this context, the textual–literary viability and potential autonomy — of plays as written texts of verbal art. Time-honoured traditions regard *drama* as a *super-genre* within literature, as argued in 4.0 and 4.3.1, and in such studies as Veltruský's (1977) *Drama as Literature*, whereas newer banner-cries for the autonomy of *Theatre Studies* aim at 'emancipating' play **analysis** from the 'clutches' of Literary Studies (as an inevitable complement to a plea for the 'emancipation' of plays from the 'clutches' of literature). Admittedly closer to the former than to the latter, a more pluralistic and relativistic approach is adopted here, which opposes any generalisation claiming applicability to **all** plays, indiscriminately characterising them as either autonomous works of literature or mere *playscripts* for the stage,[11] devoid of intrinsic value as readable fictional texts.[12] The point is that not all plays are created equal, and therefore they should be characterised differently in terms of their place within a continuum between the two poles — *non-dramatic literature* and *non-literary drama*. Indeed, certain plays are just *scripts*; their limited pretence is to function as mere prompters for directors, actors etc., while possessing and/or claiming no literary value. However, other plays throughout history, from ancient Greece to the present, are viable texts for a general public of home-readers, students etc., no less than for potential or actual stage-performers.[13] This approach, then, claims advantage over the purely-literary as well as purely-theatrical ones, because it is balanced, comprehensive and all-inclusive, treating and characterising different plays and different types and schools of poetics and artistic systems differently, to match their inherent differences. Thus, for instance, an inevitable consequence of principles advocated by proponents of the *playscript* approach would be the removal of the corpus of Shakespeare's *verse drama* from the canon of English literature in general, and English poetry in particular; this, of course, is quite preposterous, not only culturally–historically, but theoretically and analytically as well. Likewise, Chekhov's plays, no less than his stories, are pillars of 19th-century Russian **literature**; their texts are a permanent fixture of curricula of schools and universities, where they are read, studied, analysed, and treated as exemplary achievements of literary art. **This cultural–educational status is not the cause of the autonomous literary value of such plays, but its consequence.**

A crucial factor in assessing the degree of *literariness* of a play (in addition to social and even financial considerations)[14] is its textual complexity: the greater the author's investment in structuring *literary complexity* in a written fictional text as such (regardless of its status as potential to be realised in theatrical performance), the greater its viability as an autonomous work of literary art. As shown in 2.1, Shakespeare's plays are exceptionally complex as poetic texts, their *complexity* hardly surpassed by any literary work ever written, before or since, of whatever genre; in other words, the *specifically literary complexity* of most of Shakespeare's texts is unchallenged by the most complex **non-dramatic** literary texts. In such cases of literarily-complex plays, then, no single type of realisation, nor even all potential realisations together, can do justice to the full potential complexity of the author's art. Indeed, no reading, silent or audible, can provide the text with the presence of live actors and other elements (mainly non-verbal ones) that directly address an audience's senses in a live theatre event; yet, **equally**, no live performance can fully realise the text's verbal–literary complexity to its full extent, even if the inevitable partiality of any specific performance — being the interpretation of one director, one designer, one cast of actors, etc., — is ignored. It seems, then, that only repeated attentive readings of the text combined with repeated exposures to different stage-interpretations of it (the more the better) can come close to fuller understanding and realisation of its inherently inexhaustible complexity. It has to be borne in mind that a significant part of the complexity of Chekhov's plays is literary, at least whenever it has little to do with non-verbal components of a potential staging.[15]

It is argued and elaborated in 4.3.2 that the process of reading a play is designed to engender two simultaneous ***fictional*** *worlds* in the reader: a *reality-like* world, which is generated in plays just as in *narrative fiction*, and a *theatre-like* world. Now the substantial emancipation that Chekhov granted to the non-verbal components of his plays — to complement the unshakable centrality of their verbal components — is manifest in the nature and status of his *SD* in general;[16] the focus of the present discussion, as stated above, is a specific kind of *SD* — the *ISD*, which amounts to a *theatrical exposition* of the play. It must perforce be located at its beginning, to complement its *dramatic–literary exposition*, whose materials can be scattered in various ways throughout the entire play, even towards its ending.[17] The *ISD*, by definition and in principle, are designed to determine what the spectators in the auditorium actually see as the curtain rises; their text — being an instance of language, a string of *signifiers* — is presented temporally, and the items (words and phrases) comprising it have to be written and read one **after** the other.

Yet, the fabric of *signifieds* to which these signifiers refer is spatial and simultaneous, and the items that make it up exist on stage one **next to** the other. This of course applies to any verbal description of spatial phenomena; but the uniqueness, and perhaps paradoxicality, of *SD* texts is that they usually refer predominantly, if not exclusively, to the *theatre-like* component of the play's *dual fictionality*, though they often tend to look like a narrative text, at any rate not a dialogical one. The spoken dialogue often carries the *plot*, i.e., it functions partly as a storyteller, referring to events in the fictional world; *SD*, on the one hand, seem to be literary, because as texts they are meant to be processed by readers rather than spectators, but on the other hand they are more theatrical because they encourage their readers to imagine and visualise a theatre with its stage, actors, audience, set designs, etc., rather than a fictionalised reality. The theatre spectators are not the addressees of the *SD*' text; they perceive its non-verbal, predominantly visual realisation.

3.0.6.3 To sum up

In considering Chekhov's *opening-strategies* one has to take into account his intensive activation of *dual fictionality*. In shaping the precise wording and order of presentation, both within the *ISD* and in its interaction with the beginning of the dialogue and the rest of the text, Chekhov functioned both as a writer, with various types of professional and lay readers in mind, and as a kind of 'ghost-designer', 'ghost-director', etc., with actors and spectators in mind. In both, his *ISD* can be seen as an *expositional* presentation of the play's *deep structure*, or a substantial part of what can be figuratively described as its *DNA*. In this sense, an attentive reading can start an interactive back-and-forth movement of meanings between the *ISD* and the rest of the text. Such a reading can take its cue from the *ISD* and go on to glean from the unfolding text those materials that most significantly connect to whatever is mentioned, or referred to, in the *ISD*. At first, the *ISD* can misleadingly look like referring to a random aggregate of objects and props; however, the hindsight view gained from moving forward in the play while repeatedly looking back at the *ISD* from various later points in the text, makes the choice of items for the *ISD* appear to the perceiver less and less arbitrary, more and more carefully chosen and motivated.

In the initial reading of the *ISD*, any reader is usually (and a professional one is always) prompted to imagine a theatre stage, in addition to the reality-like fictionalised world that it represents: thus, reading *The Seagull*'s *ISD,* one imagines a dry, painted "lake" on stage rather than one with real–fictional water. In watching the actual–physical initial scenery on a real stage, somewhat paradoxically, something more complex can happen: when this staged reality literally "meets the eye", one may wonder beyond that and ask oneself what this array of props and object may mean and/or predict in whatever is to unfold in the rest of the play. In other words, a reader is likely to pose as a spectator, and vice versa. The processes described here in principle will be explored below in each play separately.

3.0.7 The Ending of the Beginning: The Spoken Dialogue Starts

The next step after discussing the *ISD* is to examine the very beginning of the spoken dialogue, up to a point where *primacy effect* begins to fade, and as far into the text as patterns and functions of shaping audience expectations can be usefully established and described. In principle, there is less to be gained from regarding the unfolding text as still being a part of a play's beginning beyond such a point. These initial expectations are integrated into the unfolding continuation of the actual text and its major components — e.g., exposition and characterisation of personages, presentation of events, attitudes and ideas; various interactions and interrelationships between them; etc.

The unfolding of the spoken dialogue is an ongoing process, and the variables of each play outweigh any constant features common to all texts. There seems to be no universally applicable yardstick — especially in texts like Chekhov's major plays, not divided into formal scenes — to identify the exact location of "the end of the beginning": any attempt to arrive at such an ever-valid criterion is likely to be questionable and debatable, in fact arbitrary. My practice in this Chapter is to follow the text of each play from its very beginning to a certain point, admittedly intuitively chosen, without claiming a theoretically viable principle governing this choice. Choosing "the beginning of the ending" in Chapter 9 works similarly.

3.1 The Beginning of *The Seagull*

3.1.1 The Title[18]

As a challenging exercise in faked ignorance, let us try to imagine a person reading/viewing *The Seagull*, without any prior information about the play other than its title and the author's name (this is not so far-fetched — all of us were probably in that position before our very first encounter with the play; actually, the same applies even to those who heard **about** the play without ever being exposed to it on page or stage). A title is often designed, first and foremost, to meet the challenge of such a *tabula rasa* perception-situation and such an 'ignorant' addressee. Later, readers have also the option of going back to the title after reading some, or all, of the text, pondering what they have just read, weighing it against the title, then resuming the reading, and repeating such a process as much and as often as they like. Theatre spectators do not really enjoy this privilege; they cannot interrupt the performance at will, like pushing a stop- or pause-button, look back at the title, and think for a while how the staged events relate to it, then release the button and resume watching (this is very possible, by the way, for DVD spectators, whom Chekhov could not envisage). Anyway, let us first think of what one can reasonably expect from a Chekhov play titled *The Seagull*. This is the "correct presentation of the problem" simply because the real title of this play (and all the rest of the plays) is not *The Seagull*, but "A. P. Chekhov: *The Seagull*, a Comedy in Four Acts"; therefore, an audience unfamiliar with this play can still take into account Chekhov's previous work, his reputation etc.[19] Anyway, the *primacy effect* generated by the title *The Seagull* would be first and foremost one of a special kind of curiosity: a 19th-century play, and by Chekhov at that, is not expected to be about the life of birds, and after such precedents as Ibsen's *The Wild Duck* an expectation that the bird would be an image or symbol connected with the lives and characterisations of the major personages is very likely. At any rate, if a title consists of the name of a personage (e.g., Ivánov, Uncle Vánia), it inevitably generates a simple expectation that the play is about that personage as the major protagonist (if that expectation is eventually frustrated, that does not invalidate its initial inevitability). "The Seagull" as a title, however, generates much more curiosity; there is a definite expectation that the unfolding play would include an explanation of its title. An alert perceiver would 'sit in ambush', waiting for any mention or suggestion of a seagull as part of the author's duty to account for this title. Thus, the very beginning of the play encourages its spectators to ascribe extra importance to 'seagull-tainted' materials. A hierarchy is generated, establishing the centrality of the seagull and everything that it represents, as analysed in 7.5.

3.1.2 The Subtitle

Out of the considerable literature published about Chekhov's *genre-subtitles*, curiously enough, the *Comedy* subtitle of *The Cherry Orchard* has been discussed more intensely than that of *The Seagull*, though the latter seems more problematic in this context. Even according to Chekhov's own humorous-yet-serious distinction between *comedy* and *tragedy* based on their respective endings,[20] *The Seagull* — ending with a protagonist's suicide — should have been subtitled *Tragedy*. To be sure, there are quite a few comic moments in the play, and somewhat comic personages (e.g., Shamráïev, Medvedénko, Polína Andréïevna — none of them as comic as *The Cherry Orchard*'s Semeónov-Píshchik or Yepikhódov); but the existence of these is not sufficient for the play as a whole to qualify as a *comedy*.[21] At any rate, then, one is likely to wonder why Chekhov chose this subtitle for this particular play. Indeed, that choice, to be honest, is likely to engender some uneasiness in anyone familiar with popular definitions and intuitive characterisations of the basic genres: the play as a whole cannot be regarded as a *comedy* in any conventional sense of the term, nor can most of its personages be regarded as *comic characters*. The general genre-problem in Chekhov's major plays is discussed at greater length in Chapter 10; here suffice it to say that the least the term *comedy* can be said to do, in terms of *primacy effect* for the entire play, is to inspire recurring thinking about it in the changing light of the unfolding text, highlighting any comic element in the play. A perceiver of this play, to the extent that s/he is aware of its subtitle, can be in constant state of bewilderment; the best way out of it (which is admittedly unsatisfactory) is perhaps to consider the hypothesis of Chekhov's *G-1 formula* (as elaborated in 10.2), supposedly governing his tendency to 'downgrade' his genre-labels from near-*tragedy* to *drama*, and from *drama* to *comedy*.

3.1.3 The *Initial Stage-Directions* and their Context in the Play

The Seagull has two focuses — in a way, in analogy to Pirandello's *Six Characters in Search of an Author* (whether or not it was influenced by Chekhov's play): (1) the 'human story', i.e., the romantic involvements and the personal and professional interrelationships between and among the play's personages, individually and variously grouped: men and women, young and old, parents and children, established professionals and unknown–upcoming novices, etc. (2) A self-referential content: it is a work of art about art, a piece of fiction about fictionality, a play about the theatre, etc. (see Appendix). Chekhov could have chosen to give prominence to the former, or evenly to both, through the *primacy effect* activated by the *ISD*, but he chose otherwise: the play's beginning laid the foundation for the centrality of the theatre-about-theatre theme.

The *ISD* are quite detailed in *The Seagull*. It is an outdoor scene: a park that is part of Sórin's estate, there are several chairs, a table, and some bushes here and there. There is also time indication: the sun has just set. Now *The Seagull*'s *ISD* text includes a seemingly strange instruction: it decrees a pathway stretching from the audience's view to an upstage lake, but the makeshift platform stage is supposed to block the lake view completely, making it invisible to the audience. Reading this instruction for the first time, it seems to be literary and almost anti-theatrical. The reader is encouraged to move to and fro between the two components of *dual fictionality*: in a *possible world* of fictional narrative (and, indeed, in reality!) a lake (real or imagined) can 'hide' from a spectator's view behind a stage platform and curtain, i.e., it can be invisible to anyone in front of that stage and visible to anyone behind it; however, in **the reality of a theatre**, there is no point for a designer to draw a lake, or any object, that would be invisible to the audience: either there is one, or there isn't… Only at a later point in the text of Act 1, in preparation for Nína's appearance on the stage, the inner curtain rises (or pulled sideways) and the audience is capable of seeing the lake (obviously, a painted one) that had been hidden up to that moment. Now the uniqueness of *The Seagull*, at least among Chekhov's plays, is in its focus on matters of art and theatre. Chekhov writes this *ISD* as a conscious introduction to this specific play; one of the first words that a reader of the play encounters is *stage*; more importantly, a stage is one of the first sights — arguably, the very first one — that a spectator encounters as the curtain rises and, as we know, *primacy effect* gives special importance and saliency to initial parts of a perception. In the reading process, the words of the *ISD* are the first to join the title (and subtitle, if there is one) in the temporal build-up of the text's impressions on its reader; in the viewing process in the theatre, the same *primacy effect* is generated by a static *tableau* of objects and props that precedes and surrounds the visible people (if there is one, before the first people start moving on, into and out of the stage), the audible words, and the events that take place on the stage. The transition between the *ISD* and the entrance of the first personages makes it clear that that static *tableau* precedes the first speakers and their words; it is up to the performers, mainly the Director, to determine how long the stage-upon-the-stage is allowed to make its silent impact on the audience until interrupted by the first words.

Let us go back to the *ISD* and the *primacy effect* that it generates and sum up what it can do to the perception of the play. An interesting time gap, a kind of delayed reaction, emerges when one considers the relation between the written text and its effect on the reader, on the one hand, and the order of perception of sights, sounds and objects on stage and its effect on the spectator. Whereas the reader, somewhat bewildered at the verbal presentation of the 'invisible' lake, can be curious as to its realisation later in the play (and curiosity is often a major factor in generating and sustaining the power of *primacy effect*), the spectator is simply ignorant of its existence until it becomes visible when the inner curtain rises. When that moment comes, both reader and spectator, in different yet similar processes, can understand and justify in their minds the existence of the delayed exposure of the initially-hidden lake: the centrality of the interaction between art and life, fiction and reality, in *The Seagull*, is given a powerful exposition in this view of the basic components of theatre and the world of art and fiction (stage, screen), capturing and encapsulating an aestheticised slice of reality (the lake), whose aesthetic quality resides not only in its own conventional beauty (lakes are universally considered beautiful) but also in its potentially capacity to **reflect**, which is also associated with art. This spatial fusion between elements of art/fiction and life/reality merges with the temporal double-take on the moment of the rising curtain (whether it is realised literally in two physical curtains or not), with its traditional as well as ever-renewable effect of 'the magic of theatre'. Thus, the *ISD* both anticipates and reflects an essential component of *The Seagull* as a whole, and its Act 1 in particular: with the progress of the text both reader and spectator are gradually made to realise the depth of *ISD*'s forward-oriented penetration into the play that follows it, and the relative prominence of the theme of art *vs.* life within the play's theme-hierarchy gets a powerful head-start.

This is arguably the most important contribution of the play's *ISD* and its anticipatory energy; however, virtually all the *ISD* text is worth noticing, and hardly a single element in it is superfluous or arbitrary. The time indication (just after sunset) is of course relevant to the precise timing of the planned 'premiere' of Konstantín's play: the lay home-reader can notice Konstantín's own remark (close to the beginning of Act 1) that the inner curtain should go up "precisely at 8:30, when the moon rises", otherwise "the entire effect will be lost", and relate it to the aforementioned time indication in the *ISD*. The professional readers (mainly director, scenery designer, lighting designer) — the immediate addressees of all *stage directions* — can take this time-indication as an instruction that can affect some visual elements of the scene, notably its lighting. As for the spectators, ignorant of the wording of the *ISD*, they can only see the results of this instruction, but to the extent that they notice the twilight as the outer curtain rises, and especially after they hear Konstantín's words, they can retrospectively realise the anticipatory nature of the initial non-verbal *tableau*.

I am now tempted to conclude this Subsection with "The rest is silence" — not in the *Hamlet* sense of this phrase, but in the sense that it is enough to point out the most significant function of the play's *ISD* and take a rest, committing the rest of its function to silent appreciation.

3.1.4 The Ending of the Beginning: The Spoken Dialogue Starts

One of *comedic*[22] features of *The Seagull* is that its first words are uttered in a dialogue between 'minor' personages engaged in seemingly marginal topics (in sharp contrast with *Three Sisters*) — a convention that, though not exclusive to *comedies*, is more typical to them than to other *genres*. The play opens with a kind of a quick "Q/A" — Medvedénko's first *réplique* asking Másha why she constantly wears black, and Másha's immediate rejoinder, saying that she is unhappy and "in mourning for her life".[23] This exchange, especially Másha's response, somehow challenges, even teases, *genre-boundaries*: the tone has increasingly funny traits, whereas the content is supposed to be sad. Thus, the beginning of the dialogue establishes expectations based on an immediate revelation of at least two skills that Chekhov really mastered, in his stories and plays alike: (a) a special kind of humour reflected in the presentation of a personage who is genuinely miserable, even heartbroken, yet talks about his situation in a pathetically funny way; (b) drawing a demarcation line between 'objective' *truth* and 'subjective' *sincerity*. In Chekhov's *oeuvre* there are many examples of both of these skills, separately or combined.

In terms of *primacy effect*, the expectations potentially generated by both *répliques*, and the ones following them by the same speakers, are reinforced by the positioning of this dialogue at the very opening of the play. These expectations function, *inter alia*, in characterising the two personages, and in drawing attention to potentially different hierarchies of priorities, which are not only theirs, but the play's — e.g., the relative importance of money, art, (un)happiness in love, etc. Specifically, the theme of art **as mentioned in this dialogue** has this evasive Chekhovian quality of fusion between the serious, almost hinting at the sublime, on the one hand, and the funny, almost bordering on the ludicrous, on the other; its centrality is also reinforced by the sheer presence of the inner stage (whose physicality addresses the senses of the spectator, and whose referentiality addresses the imagination of the reader) upon the 'real', outer stage. As we have just seen, the focus on that stage is automatic and unavoidable, and the convention of *stage-upon-a-stage* immediately creates expectations that a theatre production of some kind will be central to the play. *Self-reference* — regardless of its semantic content — is a powerful mental mechanism; it propels intense cognitive activity. The wording of this dialogue also generates the expectation that the other personages mentioned in it — Konstantín and Nína, yet unknown to the audience — are more central to the play than the two speakers who bring them to our attention.

Also activated by the opening dialogue is the *thematisation* of **colour**. Chekhov masterfully employs a seemingly very simple mechanism of relating verbal to non-verbal elements in all his plays; it is actually much subtler than it seems. Here, it is the *blackness* of Másha's dress that is brought to the spectator's attention: first and foremost directly, simply by its visual presence, then indirectly, reinforced by words relating to it. Thus, the reference to colours in general, and blackness in particular, opens up expectations that it should be thematically developed, being the first thing the words of the play refer to. In this case, the first *répliques* highlight at first some figurative connotations of *black*, making them more prominent than its directly visual impact; however, sight and sense are combined, and anticipations generated by their co-presence are subsequently picked up by the glaring *whiteness* of Nína's dress and, later, by the whiteness of the seagull itself, as bird and as symbolic image. Indeed, the Lady in Black Másha and the Lady in White Nína are contrasted on quite a few levels, and the contrast between the colours respectively associated with them is designed to work subtly, even clandestinely, in the spectators' minds, called upon to process the words and the sights simultaneously. Moreover, much simpler than all of that: the play's title, *The Seagull*, suggests whiteness (the suggestion in made by a word, but it works non-verbally), whereas the spoken text's first phrase refers directly to blackness. On a more abstract and sophisticated level, this contrast is integrated with the play's many contrasts, whatever the content of each of them. To sum up: the play can be characterised by its own start-section as a *comedy* ending in a protagonist's *suicide*, bearing a 'white' title and starting with a 'black' *réplique*. It's hard to think of opening up a 'world' of contrasts more condensed, more explicit, and more hidden, at the same time, than this: the stage is set from the very beginning for conflicting relationships all round.

One can go on, further into the rest of the text, to analyse how most other phrases near its beginning generate anticipations of various kinds and on various levels, and how later occurrences in the text, in all four Acts, relate to these early forerunners. As stated above, there is no way to determine "the end of the beginning" in such cases. Rather, some principles of identifying and analysing expectation-generating techniques and *primacy effect* have been presented here, and can be followed and applied to additional parts of the beginnings of this play and other ones.

3.2 The Beginning of *Uncle Vánia*

3.2.1 The Title

"Uncle Vánia", as a play's title, generates an initial expectation that a man named *Iván* (the official given name of all men nicknamed *Vánia*) is that play's major protagonist.[24] The main word in this title, however, is *uncle*. This establishes the centrality of a *nephew* or *niece* as another major protagonist, and, even more significantly, the relationship between these two as a focus of attention, in a way that the '*uncleness*' of Vánia is a defining feature of his. It **may**, perhaps, suggest a vague expectation that Vánia would not have children of his own (it is more customary to define people as parents than as uncles/aunts). In the same spirit, it is also reasonable to expect family relationships of *tripartite* nature to be a key topic for the play: whereas a reference to a relationship between spouses, parent and child, even siblings, can be *dyadic*, at least potentially (e.g., Tolstói's story "Two Brothers"), *uncle/aunt–nephew/niece* is a family relationships that cannot exist in a context of less than three, including a 'bridging' person — a sibling to that Vánia, and a parent to his *nephew/niece*. Above and beyond these specifics — more broadly speaking — the title *Uncle Vánia* generates expectations that the play under it would be focused on larger-family affairs and relationships, together with a certain tone of intimacy, of closeness beyond the most nuclear family.

In sum: the title *Uncle Vánia*, considered in isolation, fulfils at least the following functions relating to its named personages: it *anticipates* (in advance), and is expected *to highlight* (both in advance and in retrospect, where applicable) materials that relate to such topics and persons as: Vánia; his niece (Sónia), with an emphasis on viewing him through her eyes; the 'bridging' person, who turns out to be the deceased Véra Petróvna, Vánia's sister and Sónia's mother; any information about past and present relationships between and among these three person-ages; close family relationships in general (suggesting analogies with other family relationships). This is quite a lot of semantic load for a two-word title to carry; Humpty-Dumpty would have paid it extra.

3.2.2 The Subtitle

The *genre-subtitle* of *Uncle Vánia* — "Scenes from Country Life" — is unique among Chekhov's four major plays:[25] whereas the subtitles of the other three (*drama* and *comedy*) are taken from the limited stock of traditional genre-names. *Uncle Vánia*'s subtitle, in sharp contrast, has no commitment to tradition. *Scenes from Country Life*, as pointed out in the literature (see, for instance, Senelick 2005, p. 196) is also the subtitle of Turgénev's play *A Month in the Country* (published in 1855), but otherwise — especially against the background of Chekhov's usage — it is a rare, even odd choice for a subtitle. It faithfully describes the play itself, but does not label it as traditional subtitles in European drama do. In a way, it sounds like what a scholar or critic, rather than the author himself, would say to characterise such a play. Out of context it can also generate expectations that Uncle Vánia would be a benevolent elderly gentleman who is nicknamed 'uncle' by younger people without being anyone's real uncle; it can also anticipate amiable and tranquil family relationships, so far from what the actual play presents to its audience. Anyway, coming back to its Chekhovian context, the subtitle's major function is 'negative': it says what the play is **not**, indicating Chekhov's active refusal to relate it to the nomenclatural tradition, included in "the rules/tenets of dramatic art" (see Epigraph to Chapter 4), which Chekhov seems to have reproached himself for disobeying in *The Seagull*. For a brief duration of time — as long as *Uncle Vánia* was Chekhov's most recent play, i.e., between *The Seagull* and *Three Sisters* — he in fact 'rebelled' against the 'tyranny of genre-labels', before 'returning to the fold' with the last two plays, *Three Sisters* subtitled *drama*, and *The Cherry Orchard* subtitled *comedy*.

Indeed, it is a common (and consequently expected) practice in European play-writing to classify plays and label them using traditional nomenclature; therefore, in terms of expectations generated by the subtitle, this 'negative' effect of rejecting the traditional nomenclature is also its main impact: through it the playwright is saying to his audience that what they are about to watch/read is emphatically neither a *tragedy* nor a *comedy*, nor a *drama* in its narrower, specifically non-comic sense. This unconventional subtitle can arouse additional interest and curiosity in the audience because of the indeterminate nature of the expectations it generates, certainly if compared with *comedy* and *tragedy*. Thus, it is a tacit claim for newness, inseparably linked with some dissatisfaction with the existing nomen-clature; as if Chekhov is saying to his audience, '*I have written something unprecedented, which defies all existing labels*'. However, Chekhov seems to have been hesitant in his quest for emancipation from traditional genre nomenclature. We in the 21st century are entitled to say that subtitles as unprecedented as *Uncle Vánia*'s are more appropriate for all of Chekhov's major plays than the ones he actually chose for them, but Chekhov's own attitude to the subject was much more ambivalent and less assertive than the one adopted by "Uncle Vánia" [the personage], when he speaks of "realism, naturalism, and that sort of rubbish" (Epigraph to Chapter 10), or else he would not have felt the need to connect to the tradition by giving those traditional genre-names to his plays. Incidentally, it is probably no coincidence that a derogatory reference to traditional classifications in the history of drama is included in a play whose subtitle avoids such a classification, though the former refers to *movements/schools* (*-ism*s) and the latter refers to *genres*.

To sum up: in *Uncle Vánia*, more than in any other of his major plays, Chekhov uses the genre-subtitle to generate expectations that are actually borne out by the rest of the text, whereas using the traditional terms *comedy* and *drama* in the other plays creates subversive counterpoint between the subtitle and the actual play.

3.2.3 The *Initial Stage-Directions*

Uncle Vánia's *ISD* are admittedly less pregnant than the other major plays', in terms of generating significant expectations — regardless of whether they are eventually corroborated, frustrated, or modified by the rest of the unfolding text. There is nothing extraordinary in the stationary objects mentioned (table set for tea, benches, chairs, even the less obvious guitar and swing), nor in the weather (a cloudy afternoon). With time, as the play progresses, the motivation behind this selection is clarified: thus, the guitar is Telégin's, and he plays it at certain moments; Yeléna rocks herself on the swing (its very existence says something about the leisurely function of the Voïnítskiï estate garden); etc. In short, in this play the contribution of *ISD* to the rest of the text is quite conventional and predictable; they do not highlight multi-layered semantic structures nor modify hierarchies. Thus, there is little more that can be said about *Uncle Vánia*'s *ISD* in the context of the present discussion.

3.2.4 The Ending of the Beginning: The Spoken Dialogue Starts

As argued and implied above, the exposition of themes, personages and relationships, is an inevitably central part of any play's beginning, but plays differ in the ways in which this is carried out. In *Uncle Vánia* the opening scene is a dialogue between two personages, Marína and Ástrov; they soon enough turn out to be a relatively minor character and a decisively major one, respectively, but a hint of this difference between them is implied in the dialogue itself. It is remarkable in the Russian original that the two address each other using the familiar second-person-singular pronoun; of special significance is the fact that Marína, who is definitely lower than Ástrov in the social hierarchy, addresses him that way. This cannot be the result of the age difference between them, and must indicate their closeness. The form of address (singular or plural) is typically used with Chekhovian precision to indicate 'terms of endearment', or rather closeness and intimacy, between characters.[26] Placed at the beginning of the dialogue, such information can affect predictions, however indeterminate, about the nature of expected relationships between personages, both present and absent. Particular head-start and *primacy effect* prominence is given through the first dialogue to subjects of human ecology, including the negative effects of drinking, and to the characterisation of Ástrov as an overworked and conscientious doctor and as a human being aware of the waste of human potentials, in himself and in others. The tangle of relationships within the Voïnítskii household soon enough takes centre stage position, in the ensuing dialogue. General and personal subjects thus become focused on this shared theme of waste.

In conclusion: Chekhov's starting techniques seem to be less uniquely-Chekhovian in *Uncle Vánia* than in other major plays, and closer to those employed by other masters. By such comparison, this play's *ISD* as such, and the ways in which the beginning of the dialogue integrates into the rest of the play, are less significant or outstanding. One of the major differences seems to be that in *Uncle Vánia* the bonds that bind the materials of the beginning together with the rest of the text are made primarily of content, thematics, and 'chain of events', rather than of specifically Chekhovian strategies of analogy, composition and structuration; specifically, they are more linear and less contrapuntal. Personages begin the play by talking **about** a subject, and *primacy effect* gives this greater prominence, or head-start; it is simple as that. The perceiver's attention is continuously drawn to people's characters, relationships, themes and ideas — in short, to components of the play's fictional 'world' — while there is less reason (compared to the other major plays) to draw attention to Jakobson's (1960/1967) famous *poetic function*, i.e., to the ways in which the text of the play draws attention to **itself,** to the way it is structured.[27]

3.3 The Beginning of *Three Sisters*

3.3.1 The Title

As title, *Three Sisters* — like *Uncle Vánia* — predicts a play about family relationships focused on a *triad*. Indeed, the title of *Uncle Vánia* suggests its triad inevitably (as just pointed out) but **indirectly**, whereas in "Three Sisters" the number *three* is stated as clearly and unequivocally as possible. This focus is both 'positive' (the title simply says it) and 'negative': again, contrasted with *Uncle Vánia, the* absence of any names (not even a surname) stresses the universally sisterly focus of the play, as it is not about specific sisters, as it would have been if Chekhov had called it *The Prózorov Sisters* (an imaginary title reminiscent of Dostoïévskii's real title *The Brothers Karamázov*). True, the specific features of the Prózorov family are strongly emphasised in the play, but even more powerfully stressed are its universally-human traits. The fusion between the two groups of features is one of the play's most impressive feats.

It is admittedly through hindsight that one can read these central features of the play into its title, yet some of them — however vaguely — may be sensed even when the title is considered autonomously. Even if this early functioning of the title is debatable, it is undoubtedly certain that at later stages in perceiving the unfolding text, as moving back and forth between title and text becomes more and more possible, the title focuses attention on the three sisters, as a group, as the central protagonists of the play. This focus does not detract from the ultimate significance of others; it just means that the title gives the sisters automatic head-start over the others, so that more should be invested in the others to grant them the centrality that the sisters get 'for free'. The process of *mutual vindication* between title and text, mentioned earlier on, focuses audience attention on the three as a unified group; as a collection of three separate, even contrasted personalities; as a potential for any *two vs. one* configuration; as a group of the Prózorov women *vs.* others, particularly Andréï (the brother who could be more central had Chekhov chosen to call his play *The Four Siblings…*), and including actual and potential spouses, lovers (Másha's two men; Irína's suitors — imagined, accepted and rejected; Ól'ga's imagined 'husband', whom she "would have loved" if she had had one), and other significant persons.

The sisters are indeed very central to the play, in every respect. Theatrically, it is significant that only three times — in the beginning, at the end, and in the confession scene in Act 3 — the three, as a group, occupy the stage on their own. It is clear that they yearn for such moments, to be together just the three of them; but in all these moments they are not really left alone, and the presence of others (in very different dosages) seems to be superfluous or annoying from their standpoint. The uniqueness and prominence of these scenes are powerfully enhanced by the title. It is the effect of *mutual vindication* between text and title again.

Finally, the title as such mildly detracts from the importance of the universally-human materials by giving prominence to the family group and to the sisters within it; however, the play's exceptionally universal themes, relating to humanity-as-a-whole, are so powerful that they must be perceived as significant beyond any doubt. The point here is only that the significance of these all-embracing materials is not generated **by** the title, but **in spite of** it. As usual in Chekhov, a precarious balance between themes and ideas is created, metaphorically analogous to a *parallelogram of forces*: the title, as it were, draws the text in the direction of family and other relationships focusing on the three sisters, whereas explicit and implicit references to humanity, its destiny, the meaning of life, etc., draw the text in their all-embracing direction, focusing on the general rather than on the particular. The *resultant diagonal vector* — figuratively speaking, of course — would be some-where in between. Here, however, the effectiveness of the analogy with physics seems to weaken, since we are not talking about a precise diagonal; rather, the various forces keep pulling in different directions, but while the balance does tilt one way or another, they do not cancel each other out in favour of a compromise force. Moreover, from the perceiver's standpoint these resemble complementary perspectives, each focusing on different elements in the text, more than opposing forces. Be that as it may, the analogies can clarify the effect but not replace its direct analysis.

To sum up: one cannot overestimate the importance of any of Chekhov's titles, but in the case of *Three Sisters* the title should be "paid extra", in the unforgettable words of Humpty-Dumpty in *Alice through the Looking Glass*. This, then, has been a glimpse into the "extra work" that this title does for the play, its author, its perceivers, and the scholars who analyse it.

3.3.2 The Subtitle

The original *genre-subtitle* of *Three Sisters* is *Drama*. As mentioned often in the literature, including elsewhere in the Book, a theatrical tradition prevalent in and around Chekhov's time in general, and in Russia in particular, regarded this term as referring to serious plays only; thus, the term *Drama* was quite close to *tragedy*, and was used in various contexts (e.g., in Chekhov's correspondence) as opposed to *comedy*. That said, it should be emphasised that *drama* was **not** identical with *tragedy*. The subtitle, then, projects an expectation of a *mood* and *tone*, rather than a specific kind of plotline or events. Since the perceivers (whether readers or spectators) know from the start that the play is by Chekhov, those of them who have some knowledge of his work can expect something more specific from a *drama* by the author of *The Seagull* and *Uncle Vánia*, which were not thus defined.

3.3.3 The *Initial Stage Directions*

With *Three Sisters* Chekhov returns to highly significant *ISD*, whose impact on the play is powerful as well as complex. In this sense *Three Sisters' ISD* appear to be closer to *The Seagull*'s than to *Uncle Vánia*'s.

It may strike the reader that the first words of these *ISD* are "In the Prózorovs' home/house". Very much unlike the beginning of the text of *The Seagull*'s *ISD*, these words refer to the (fictionalised) reality-like world of the personages, rather than to the theatre-like world of the prospective performers of the play: *The Seagull*'s *ISD* begin with explicit reference to the spectators' point of view, in the most literal sense of these terms — i.e., to what they actually see on stage sitting in the theatre. The crucial centrality of the Prózorov family home for the play as a whole, in all its facets, cannot be over-estimated. For the spectator, who does not read the *ISD* words, the presence of the family home is supposed to be just as impressive from the start, if the *ISD* instructions are carried out with attention and precision: it is an impressive "drawing-room", separated by a row of columns from a "reception-room" behind it.[28] Both rooms are the public spaces of the late General Prózorov's private home, mainly designated for entertaining guests for a meal, a party, a get-together etc.; and indeed, an important prop on stage, as an integral part of these rooms, is a dining table, now set for late Sunday breakfast, which turns out to be Irína's birthday-party.[29] Undoubtedly Chekhov's intention was to produce an effect of an apartment with generous spaces. Consider the two spacious rooms and the imposing columns — the latter potentially reminiscent of Greek architecture, which in turn can connect *Three Sisters* with ancient Greek *tragedy*.[30] All of these spatial–visual elements on stage signal (especially to the spectator) the presence of authoritative owners or occupants: when the dialogue begins and we learn that this is the home of a deceased army general this should come as no surprise. Whereas the secondary-character status of the first speakers in *The Seagull* is clear from the start, and in *Uncle Vánia* the first speaker is a female servant, here — already at the *ISD* stage — we are introduced to the real occupants, three ladies (i.e., we see them before we hear them). Since readers are supposed to have read the play's title in the printed text before reading the *ISD*, and since spectators are supposed to have read the names of the author, the play and the actors in the programme notes before seeing the stage scenery in the theatre, both types of perceivers are likely to guess from the start that the three ladies on stage are the sisters in the title. The immediacy of the vindication of the title is indeed without precedence in Chekhov's two preceding plays: in *The Seagull* as well as in *Uncle Vánia* it takes quite a while to understand the title and to actually see who or what is the reason for choosing it; *ISD* in those plays do not contribute to this process.

Indeed, the very presence (albeit a silent one) of the three sisters produces an effect of almost *in medias res*: without much ado we are facing the very central protagonists. Now an effect of concentrated expectation and curiosity is generated. Their silence makes them blend in the visual background, or rather add a dynamic human presence to its static and inanimate one. Moreover, the three sisters add to the visual composition on stage an element of colour: Ól'ga, Másha and Irína are instructed to wear blue, black and white dresses respectively. The contrast between these colours, even without having a clue to decipher their meaning(s), generates an immediate contrapuntal effect in the audience. For a contemporaneous Russian audience, however, Ól'ga's dress betrays her profession: the *ISD* identifies the dress as the uniform of a teacher in a girls' school (gymnasium); in addition, she is instructed to correct her pupils' papers "standing and walking", which means that she is restless, nervous, even agitated: not only does she "bring work to home", but she does not have the peace of mind to correct those papers sitting down. Másha — sitting down almost motionless in black dress — is contrasted with her moving-about sisters; Irína, in white, standing but preoccupied with thinking, is also contrasted with Ól'ga who is preoccupied with working. The entire dynamic opening *tableau*, then, is exceptionally complex, much more than the colour-coded black/white dresses of Másha and Nína in *The Seagull* (which is quite complex, but not quite as complex as in *Three Sisters*). Here it is almost bursting with contrapuntal meaningfulness, but at the same time also unbelievably lucid and balanced with tense precision. Everything in this *tableau* is calculated and controlled by the author, and designed to encapsulate so much of the play that is about to unfold.

The sisters with their chamber-music-like contrapuntal dialogues of dress colours, of bodily movements and postures, of types and degrees of occupation and preoccupation, are thrown into bold relief against the inanimate background of the two cheerfully sunlit rooms that create unusual spatial breadth and depth on stage, but seem nonetheless to encroach on the sisters, because of their tense and nervous movements and states of mind. The latter elements, to be sure, highlight the contrasts between the sisters, as we have just seen, but they equally underline the fact that none of them seems to enjoy the advantages of the generously spacious house. In this way the *ISD* can predict some of the play's deepest and most significant human and ideational interactions: indeed, the nucleus of the play's main tensions, and its spoken and unspoken interactions and interrelationships, is deeply ingrained in the *ISD*. Of course, it is naïve and unrealistic to expect any reader or spectator to realise these hidden potentials in first or even repeated reading and watching the play's beginning, and be aware of the magnitude of the presence of these interactions, without the benefit of hindsight;[31] however, an attentive perceiver is likely to sense some of these pregnant potentials even during earliest exposures to the text. At any rate, Chekhov did plant these potentials in the text: they are there to be noticed, sooner or later.

To sum up: three major elements of the play are introduced in the *ISD*: (a) **the place**, i.e., the house, represented at this early stage by its two 'social' rooms; (b) **the time** — a sunny, "cheerful" midday "outside" (perhaps a courtyard)[32] — is connected with a late-breakfast birthday-party; (c) **the people** (the three sisters), whose presence and stage behaviour has just been described. Interactions between these three elements make up the intensely-complex 'world' of the opening *tableau*; the play's basic *DNA*, as it were, is deeply ingrained in its *ISD*, and the process of reading its text and/or watching it produced and performed on stage is, *inter alia*, a process of realising the potential bond between its beginning and continuation, by which, as we have seen, any later element whose roots can be traced back to the beginning becomes more prominent in a hierarchy of importance. Other factors can intervene to modify the end result, which also takes into account elements not connected with the *ISD*; however, the well-knit, tightly integrated nature of Chekhov's plays gains much from the powerful impact of the beginnings on the texts in their entirety.

3.3.4 The Ending of the Beginning: The Spoken Dialogue Starts

In *Three Sisters* Chekhov's art of well-integrated beginnings reaches new heights. Consider the very beginning, the first word of the play, "*Father*", which starts the first sentence "Father died exactly a year ago". With these words Chekhov achieves a *primacy effect* clearly emphasising the father's importance. The sisterly basis of the ensuing dialogue[33] continues to develop the process of investing much of 'the play's *DNA*' in its beginning by making the *ISD*, in preparation for the initial *répliques* of the dialogue, an exposition of a play's specific features — "specific" not only as opposed to practices of other masters, but also as opposed to those adopted in other Chekhov plays. The domineering figure of the dead father, his constant *presence through absence*, is crucially significant in the entire play; moreover, his afterlife in his offspring is made even more powerful after his death, arguably even because of it. The first spoken sentences also display Chekhov's art of *parallel functioning* of dialogues — i.e., functioning simultaneously on the *inner/fictional plane* (i.e., within the *fictional world* on stage) and the *outer/rhetorical plane* (i.e., along the axis author→text→audience). Within the former (addressing her sisters), Ól'ga's *réplique* seems to be unnecessary: she is not telling her sisters anything they do not know anyway, and indeed the immediate response by the youngest sister, Irína, is "why remember?", or "why reminisce?". Ól'ga's hidden message, however, is quite clear from the start, and is another instance of how the play's beginning builds up expectations for the rest of it. According to this message, memories of dead people and past events alike must stay alive and be repeatedly retold in order to keep the family flame burning: the living connection with the dead parents (especially the father) and their legacies can be crucial to the family's spirit in the present and the future, as shown in Chapters 8 and 11. Ól'ga also points out what must be sensed in the family as a fateful synchronisation between the dates of Irína's birth (or rather christening/name-giving) and the father's death-day. Addressing the real audience, none of this expositional information is superfluous; rather, all of it proves significant for the rest of the play, partly anticipating its development, but mainly gaining importance through the process of looking back from later points in the text. This includes the description of the father's funeral;[34] the military band (which reappears at the play's ending and closes a circle in its structure, as discussed in 9.2.4); the clock signalling the time (with all its potential significance, elaborated throughout the play); and even the weather. In short, every single detail, without exception, is pregnant with crucial meaningfulness for the rest of the play in its entirety; so much so, that sampling this material gives a fuller picture than an attempt to exhaust it, thus inevitably losing the wood for the trees.

Just as significant, in terms of thematics and play-writing technique alike, is the next textual event. The depth of the stage is now used very effectively to create a music-like structuration of the following scene, modelled after *polyphonic*, almost *antiphonal* prototypes:[35] while the dialogue between the sisters goes on in the front (in the "drawing room"), three men (Túsenbach, Chebutýkin and Soliónyï) appear in the back (the "reception-room"). The three are engaged in a dialogue supposed to have started earlier, offstage; now that they are onstage, the audience gets to hear snippets from that dialogue, interspersed between snippets from the sisters' dialogue in the foreground. Within each group, to be sure, there are some signs of limited communication, "*à la* Chekhov", but the two dialogues are supposed to be totally separate, each group being unaware of the other's very presence in the area, let alone the nature and content of the conversation between its members. To create this effect Chekhov needed the two big rooms on stage and the distance between them, which gives certain theatrical plausibility to the inaudibility of each of the two dialogues to the speakers in the other one. However, we as audience hear a selection from both dialogues, and combine them in our minds. Chekhov, unlike some of his successors (e.g., Beckett in *Play*), never instructs his actors to speak simultaneously; the two lines of dialogue are concurrent, but the audience can hear each word in its turn, when uttered, unhindered by a word spoken by another personage at the same time.

Thus, in our minds we construct two parallel–simultaneous lines — the conversations in the front room and in the back room — but each of them is audible only in part, while the other one is not. To make the illusion of simultaneity stick, Chekhov keeps the intervals within each conversation quite short while the other one is allowed to be audible, so that we can imagine that members of each group keep talking, though inaudibly to us. Thus we get three lines, each subdividable into the partly-disconnected lines of each of the two groups' three participants. The complex texture of this passage will be demonstrated as follows:

Front room dialogue is set in the regular (Times New Roman) font; within it, Ól'ga's text is in roman type; Másha's (and references to her in the *SD*) is in **bold** and Irína's is in *italic*. Back room dialogue is set in a sans serif font; within it Chebutýkin's text is in roman sans serif; Túsenbach's is in **bold sans serif**. The dialogue runs as follows (with slight omissions):

ÓL'GA: This morning I woke up, saw all that light pouring in, I saw the spring, my soul was full of joy, and I felt passionate longing for home.

CHEBUTÝKIN: **To hell with that rubbish of yours!**

TÚSENBACH: **Of course it's utter nonsense!**

[MÁSHA [...] quietly whistles a tune]

ÓL'GA: Don't whistle, Másha. How can you!

[*Pause*]

Because I am every day at school [...] I feel how my strength and my youth are draining from me drop by drop, and within me there grows stronger and stronger only one dream...

IRÍNA: *To go to Moscow! Sell the house, to finish everything here, and to Moscow...*

ÓL'GA: Yes, to Moscow! As soon as possible!

[CHEBUTÝKIN and TÚSENBACH **laugh**]

IRÍNA: *Andréï will become a professor* [...]

ÓL'GA: [...] If I were married and stayed home all day, it would have been better. [Pause] I would have loved my husband.

TÚSENBACH [to SOLIÓNYÏ]: **Such rubbish you are talking, sick and tired of listening to you!** [entering the drawing room, i.e., the front room and addressing the sisters] **Forgot to tell you [...]**

There are three major lines, interwoven polyphonically: (a) the sisters', (b) the men's (both within the *inner/fictional plane*), and (c) the composite line made out of the audible parts of the two previous lines (within the *outer/rhetorical plane*). (a) consists of talking about Moscow and other contrasts between the reality they describe and the wishes they dream about, but it is subdivided into Ól'ga's major line, Irína's echoing responses, and Másha's wordless whistling, which reflects her doubts and reservations without expressing them; (b) is unaware of (a) on the *fictional plane*, and consists of Túsenbach's and Chebutýkin's rejections of Soliónyï's (unheard) remarks as "rubbish" and "nonsense". At a certain point, within (b), the two men laugh, obviously also responding to something Soliónyï has just said.

Again, each of the two conversations is basically integrated and makes some sense, even if that sense includes, within the front group, Másha's dismissive whistling at her sisters' dialogue (which, in turn, has its own semi-communicative parts), and within the back group — branding the other's talk as "nonsense". However, (c), non-existent on the *inner/fictional plane*, is much more well-integrated on the *outer/rhetorical plane* — as a message from Chekhov directly to the audience — than (a) and (b) are within the *inner/fictional plane*. Within (c), then, the location of (b)'s interventions in the flow of (a) is well chosen and moti-vated. In fact, **Chekhov** is saying directly to **us**, without any personage's awareness, that Ól'ga's dreams of going to Moscow are "rubbish" and "utter nonsense, of course", that her reiteration of the wish to go to Moscow "as soon as possible" is laughable, and that her illusion that she "would have loved her [nonex-istent] husband" is worthy of the remark "such rubbish! [... I am] sick and tired of listening to you". Although the latter remark is visibly addressed to Soliónyï in the back room, it is nonetheless uttered within the polyphonic pattern just described. After that *réplique*, the other two men enter the front room, one by one, and join a single–(quasi)-integrated circle of communication, though, typically, communication remains erratic and intermittent.

One cannot overestimate the bold newness and utmost subtlety, complexity and precision of Chekhov's technique, as described here. This technique is obviously, though perhaps subconsciously and intuitively, inspired by *musical polyphony*, in spite of cardinal differences between the two arts. In terms of this particular Chapter, in this concentrated scene Chekhov forcefully activates mechanisms of prediction and *primacy effect*, in order to highlight themes and techniques throughout the entire play. *Thematically*, we have here a presentation of the unrealisability of the Moscow dream, with all its potential for clash between wishes and reality, together with other themes, e.g., the contrast between various attitudes towards love, marriage, work, loneliness, etc., discussed in various contexts throughout the Book. *Compositionally*, we are introduced to *polyphonic* techniques of simultaneous processing of various thematic data not only as a feat in its own right but also as a way of forcing the audience to grasp and to experience the inherently simultaneous and subversively contrapuntal web of interactions between various attitudes, themes, ideas, and people who generate them and respond to them.

In short, the lucid complexity of Chekhov's techniques here is a way to make us sense the infinite complexity of human existence, not least in the most crucial theme of all — the endless tension and reciprocal enrichment between the mental experiences of birth and death, of beginning and ending. One of the areas in which this technique operates most effectively is the mechanisms of prediction and anticipation that a beginning of a play can activate in an entire play following it; such mechanisms generate the anticipation of complementary mechanisms of memory, recognition and integration that an ending of a play can activate in an entire play preceding it. If Chekhov's feat in creating the *frame* of *Three Sisters* (comprising this beginning and the play's complementary ending, analysed in 9.2.4) were Chekhov's only contribution to world drama, he would have still made his unique and lasting mark on the historical poetics of this art.

3.4 The Beginning of *The Cherry Orchard*

3.4.1 The Title

In a famous memoir in his *My Life in Art* Stanislávskiï tells us about Chekhov's own view of *The Cherry Orchard*'s title (the episode is told and re-told numerous times in the literature; see for instance Senelick 2005, p. 323, n. 1). According to him, Chekhov made a distinction between two pronunciations of the first word of the title, *Cherry*, functioning as an adjective to *Orchard*'s noun: *víshnevyï* and *vishnióvyï*. The former, as Chekhov perceived and interpreted it, was "a market garden, […] a profitable orchard […]" whereas the latter "offers no profit, it does nothing but preserve within itself and its snow-white blossoms the poetry of the life of the masters of olden times". Chekhov preferred the latter pronunciation, with the difference between the two that it entails. In fact, for a reader/spectator whose native language is English this distinction could have been clarified by changing the second word of the title, the noun, replacing *Orchard* with *Garden* or *Park*; the former term stresses the fruit aspect, whereas the white blossoms can be better emphasised by the latter terms. But just as Senelick explains why he uses the title *The Seagull* though he prefers to call it *The Gull* in English, so I accept the unanimous tradition of naming this play *The Cherry Orchard* in English, though I would have preferred to call it *The Cherry Garden* or *The Cherry Park*, in accordance with the (correct!) distinction made by Chekhov himself (according to Stanislávskiï's memoir).

That said, what does *The Cherry Orchard*, as a title, do to a reader or spectator of this play in the initial stages of acquaintance with it? Again, the question should be re-phrased: what is one likely to expect from a play **by Chekhov** titled *The Cherry Orchard*? First of all, a 'negative' answer: it is not likely to be about the botany of cherry flowers, fruit or trees, nor even about the lives of cherry growers; otherwise, there is precious little the title can predict, if we try honestly to assume a state of ignorance of all matters but the names of the author and the play. Perhaps there is a likelihood of expecting some symbolic status to this orchard, based on traditions in literature and drama and on Chekhov's own practice in titles like "The Seagull".

The main function of this title, then, is not in its initial impact, which is admittedly unimpressive; it is one of the titles which generate sheer curiosity anticipating the continuation of the text much more than understanding of its own content or message. What remains is the initial anticipation (generated by all titles, as such) that somewhere down the road of the unfolding text *mutual vindication* between title and text will be activated. A complementary process, as we have seen, is the organisation of thematic materials in hierarchies, which give prominence to those that relate to the title, marginalising those that do not. In the case of *The Cherry Orchard* the centrality of the Orchard is so obvious that it hardly needs the 'support' of the title. An analogous situation would have been created in *Three Sisters* if Chekhov had decided to include *Moscow* in the title (e.g., 'Moscow!', 'To Moscow!', 'Dreaming about Moscow', 'Life without Moscow', etc.). It is not difficult to sense how, even without changing a single word in the text of *Three Sisters*, such a change of title would radically alter the nature of that play. A complementary argument would examine how *The Cherry Orchard* would change if it had been titled 'Liubóv' Andréïevna Ranévskaïa', or 'The Gáïevs'/'The Gáïev Estate', 'The New Owner', 'The Auction' — possibilities are many indeed. It is too tedious to examine how each such a hypothetical 'alternative' would change the nature of the play; yet, just as an intellectual exercise, comparing even a small number of "roads not taken" to the title Chekhov chose can provide us with a reasonable tool to assess the contribution of this specific title to the play. Whereas the title of *Three Sisters* contributes to the centrality of a core group of personages in the play — i.e., to the focus on *who* rather than *what* — the title of *The Cherry Orchard* does the reverse.

To conclude: a title does not merely reflect a hierarchy of centralities in a work of art; it also actively contributes to such a hierarchy. In the case of *The Cherry*

Orchard's title, its interaction with the body of the text encourages us to pay special attention to a 'miss-interpretation' of the play (i.e., an interpretation based on the notion of **missing** opportunities, **missing** goals and targets in life, etc.). The sheer beauty of the fruitless cherry blossoms, which the central family of the play temporarily owns, on borrowed time and money, and cannot save — neither as property nor as a productive enterprise — is a focus of an almost endless row of 'missings' in the play. The Orchard (or rather, the Garden/Park, if we take Chekhov's own view of the title into account) is also a silent but not altogether inanimate protagonist of the play, the ultimate victim of the Gáïev family's generations of negligence and irresponsibility — a central, if not **the** central, theme of the play.

3.4.2 The Subtitle

Again, the *genre* problem in Chekhov's plays has been discussed in the literature quite intensely. Despite tireless efforts and genuine insights of scholars from Chekhov's time to the present, the problem has remained basically unsolved. Neither the genres of drama nor Chekhov's poetics can claim to be an easy subject to discuss systematically. In Chekhov's case the question is challenging, because of his frequent insistence on giving conventional labels to such unconventional plays.

The subtitle *comedy* for *The Cherry Orchard* is somewhat less problematic than for *The Seagull*; to take our cue from Chekhov's half-joking half-serious remarks about endings of plays (Epigraph to Chapter 9), here we have an ending that defies the prescription, yet somehow almost obeys it: there are neither self-shootings (though, in a very roundabout way, there is a latent element of suicide in Firs's fate) nor marriages at the end of the play (on the contrary, there is a definite almost-marriage, or rather *missed marriage*). In short, if 'happy ending' and the sound of approaching wedding bells be the *distinctive feature* of *comedy* — *The Cherry Orchard* isn't one. However, if binary opposition between *comedy* and *tragedy* aspires to cover all possibilities, *The Cherry Orchard* is considerably closer to the former than to the latter, in spite of claims to the contrary — e.g., by Stanislávskiï's and many others in theatre practice, and by Dorothea Krook (1969, 119–145) and others in academic research. By the way, very few writers about *The Cherry Orchard* show awareness of the fact that the play — while indeed subtitled *comedy* in the original Marks edition (1904), whose authorial authenticity is unchallenged — "was denominated a drama [...] on the posters and publicity" (Senelick 2005, p. 323, and 2006, p. 979, note 2). There is no indication that this changed *genre*-subtitling ever got Chekhov's stamp of approval; it probably did not.

Anyway, the literature abounds in discussions of genre problem in Chekhov in general and in *The Cherry Orchard* in particular (thus, Shátin 1993 offers a thought-provoking perspective on the subject; Miles 2003, pp. 73–94, follows interesting changes and developments in the thinking of the late eminent scholar Mikhaíl Grómov on the subject). Senderovich 1994 is one of the most convincing pleas for the *comedic* (see Note 22) nature of the play, and, indeed, there are undoubtedly many *comic* elements in it, in terms of personages and scenes alike.[36] Another crucial factor in Chekhov's choice of *comedy* for a genre-subtitle for this play may have been the absolute absence of any *tragic protagonist*, while *comic characters* can be easily identified in it.

To conclude, let us remember that the proper question in this Section cannot relate to the subtitle alone; it should be 'What are the expectations generated by the subtitle *comedy* in a **1904 play by Chekhov**?' After the experience of *The Seagull*, the only certain expectation generated by such a subtitle is a 'negative' one: the play is not a *tragedy*. This is not much to go on; indeed, rather than predicting the nature of the play in advance, from the subtitle's vantage point, the reverse is what usually happens; i.e., after acquainting oneself with the entire play, and studying it thoroughly — i.e., only with hindsight — can one have a better view of what Chekhov could have meant by *comedy* when he gave that label to his last play, *The Cherry Orchard*.

3.4.3 The *Initial Stage Directions*

The Cherry Orchard can compete with *Three Sisters* in terms of the predictive powers of their respective *ISD*. It seems that the writer in Chekhov got the better of the playwright when he started his *ISD* with "A room, which is **still called** *the nursery*". In a story there is no technical problem with such a characterisation of a room, nor is there any problem for the **lay/home reader** of this *ISD*; the problem is for the primarily intended reader of *ISD*, i.e., the stage designer, probably consulting with the director: how can a designer 'translate' the first sentence in the *ISD*, especially the word "still" in it, into the language of stage-design? One can think of several options (e.g., a room with old children-furniture, even toys, that look untouched for decades), but none of them conveys the freshness and suggestiveness of the wording just quoted. Indeed, "a picture is worth a thousand words", but sometimes the reverse is true: no visual image can compete with the expositional power of Chekhov's concise, precise and intensely concentrated cluster of meanings inherent in the wording of the first sentence of the *ISD*. If a room is "**still called** *the nursery*" that means that no children inhabit it at the present, that the children who used it long before the beginning of the action have grown up and no children of newer generation have replaced them. Moreover, the youngest member of the family — 17-year-old Ánia — has a room of her own: Chekhov takes care to mention this fact in the second sentence within the same *ISD*. This tells us that there are no living children in the house to justify *the nursery*'s name; it is an uninhabited room, and has been so for quite a few years, at least, and there is doubt whether even Ánia had used it when she was a child. The same doubt applies also to the drowned child Grìsha's occupation of the room, because of Ranévskaïa's sheer delight when entering and identifying the room. Gáïev and Ranévskaïa themselves, then, are likely to have been the last child-occupants of the room, preceded most probably by their own parents and grandparents when they were children. It is indeed remarkable how much can be learned from these two first sentences about the room's role as a monument to generations of the family's long lost children.

It is a challenging task for stage designers, then, to physically–visually convey to a theatre spectator what a reader can easily imagine and understand, namely, that by their years of neglect of this room, and refusal to part from its outdated name, both siblings betray their unwillingness and inability to grow up; that even in their forties and fifties a significant part of their personalities is still that of the children of the family. All of that, and more, is captured in these amazingly powerful few 'simple' words. To be sure, in Chekhov's plays there are visual images galore, whose semanticised content cannot be rendered satisfactorily in words; however, in this particular case, words are invincible in their 'struggle' with the non-verbal components of *drama*.

Be that as it may, even if the designer's dilemmas are ignored, what strikes the reader from the start is the **present-presence of an absent past-childhood**: the *primacy effect* of this information prompts its addressees to grant special prominence to an acute presence and presentation of *childishness*. The tension between adulthood and childishness is a major hinge around which the entire play evolves: the fictional world of the play is largely populated by mental children who are only physically grown up, whose perception of themselves, of other people, and of the entire world of reality, is similar to a child's, and immune to assuming responsibility for anything.

This astounding first sentence is not spoken at all on stage and therefore not heard by the audience; it functions best, then, as an instance of *writer-to-reader communication*: it realises as fully as possible the potential of the play as an autonomous work of written fictional literature. Of course, practically Chekhov must have had his Director and Designers in mind when writing *The Cherry Orchard*'s *ISD* as well; yet, perhaps subconsciously, perhaps even against his own will, the fiction-writer in him is the one who wrote this sentence, which introduces the very first words that *The Cherry Orchard*'s **reader** reads on the page. Thus, Chekhov the fiction writer activates the most powerful *primacy effect* possible in capturing and highlighting the basic *DNA* of the entire play and most of its personages.[37] Since this effect, so crucial for the perception and understanding of the play, exists so clearly for the reader and so problematically for the spectator, it is definitely a formidable challenge for the performers — mainly, of course, for the stage designer and the director — to find and activate a stage-enabled equivalent.

The rest of the *ISD* is devoted mostly to the lighting, indicating a dawn in May, early sunrise and cold outdoors (incidentally, *Three Sisters* also begins in a May morning), which is of lesser significance for the rest of the play. However, the presence of cherry blossoms visible from the windows (on the borderline of the *backstage* area) is of utmost importance, and connects with the play's title. The *ISD* concludes with the entrance of Dunyásha and Lopákhin, holding a candle and a book, respectively. These instructions possess some introductory values, to be sure, but they are incomparably of lesser significance than the ones discussed earlier.

3.4.4 The Ending of the Beginning: The Spoken Dialogue Starts

The spoken dialogue starts, of course, with the first words actually heard by the audience in the theatre, which enjoy a *theatrical primacy effect*, as distinct from a *textual–literary* one.[38] Let us look, then, at those first words.

Almost the entire beginning of the dialogue appears to constitute a *comic*, even *farcical prologue*; this is so even if an expectation of a more serious continuation is not ruled out. Indeed, nothing in the very first minutes of the play looks or sounds important. First of all, the speakers appear to be secondary characters; secondly, even if the event they are discussing (the arrival of the lady of the house after a long stay abroad) is of potential importance, they seem to be engaged in technicalities and trivialities related to this event, rather than behaving like 'serious' people, aware of this importance and have something of value to say about it. However, soon enough — and certainly with the hindsight enabled at later stages of the play — even this beginning gradually gains significance by becoming well-integrated with the rest of the text, thus appearing less and less arbitrary, more and more carefully designed.

Indeed, the rest of the play realises its potential *primacy effect* to its full extent: the first impression generated by the beginning of the dialogue is a focus on *missing out*, on failing to reach any goal or purpose, however trivial. This, in itself, produces the *comic* effect of variations on a theme of petty failures and insignificant incompetence, a kind of barely hidden, barely sublimated slapstick. However, soon enough it becomes evident that they fail to realise the deep psychological significance of their negligence. One minor, seemingly harmless lapse, or one insignificant instance of negligence, follows the other, and their accumulation makes them, potentially, more and more of a major problem, harmful and significant.

Thus, Lopákhin complains, even chides himself for missing the arriving train that he was supposed to meet, because he fell asleep; Dunyásha had misunderstood him and thought he had already left for the railway station, which is why she failed to wake him up; then he confesses that he had been trying to read a book, failed to understand it, and fell asleep. He then complains also that he had missed the chance to be educated, and remained an ignorant peasant. Even his moving story about Ranévskaïa's kindness to him in his childhood is just a part of his curiosity about how she is at present, **having missed her** for many years. A genuinely comic character, Yepikhódov, joins the two speakers. His very being is an embodiment of *missing out*, misunderstanding, etc.: tripping, falling, hitting the wrong objects, dropping things, walking in squeaking shoes, finding the wrong words to say the wrong things at the wrong time to the wrong people, seldom able to speak plainly or intelligibly: he does not speak, he 'expresses himself'. People call him "twenty two disasters". His entrance changes the subject of the previous conversation, introduces a new focus for the audience, but the effect of comically failing to do anything properly, of missing any possible target, gathers momentum almost with every spoken word and every visible move on stage.

Later on in the text the theme of *missing out* gathers momentum and gradually but relentlessly reaches the dimensions of disastrous negligence, emerging as the single overall, superordinate theme of the entire play: we see people letting love, work, education, money, health and well-being, even life itself, "slip through their fingers", usually without realising it — i.e., people's capabilities to reach consciousness and awareness are also the victims of negligence, carelessness, and total irresponsibility.

Yet, as always, there is nothing irresponsible on Chekhov's part as an author: with textual hindsight, even the seemingly haphazard and just-funny beginnings prove to be meticulously designed and acquire serious significance. In this sense and in this way Chekhov creates his typical blend of seemingly arbitrary first impressions with iron clad motivation, on all levels. The same well integrated design governs his entire texts in general, and beginnings and endings in particular.

Chekhov's *oeuvre*, especially his plays, undergoes a process characterised by growing depth, complexity, subtlety, and integration — i.e., a process whereby parts and details are more and more motivated in relation to each other and to the wholes that they make up. This process can be regarded as the 'Chekhovisation' of Chekhov, in the sense that, by and large,[39] later texts contain more and more distinctively Chekhovian traits, and less and less elements shared with the work of other great masters. Consider, for instance, the diminishing role of *overt dramatic conflict*; the chronologically consistent tendency to change the nature and function of his plays' *endings*; and indeed the tendencies outlined in this Chapter as regards the changing shapes of his plays' beginnings. This development works not only on the intra-textual level of the beginnings themselves, but also, as we have just seen, on extra- and inter-textual levels, and on comparative–contrastive views of juxtaposing plays with each other, even beyond the Chekhov corpus. Of all plays, it is *The Cherry Orchard* that exhibits the greatest achievements of integration between the beginning, the 'body' of the play, and its ending.

As noted several times in the Book, Monroe C. Beardsley (1958) cites *Unity*, *Complexity*, and *Intensity* as the major three criteria for aesthetic value accepted in the western tradition (pp. 462–464). On all three counts the functioning of *The Cherry Orchard*'s *frame* (beginnings and endings) in some ways equals *Three Sisters*', in others surpasses it. If we accept Beardsley's view on the matter, the *artistic greatness* of Chekhov's plays can perhaps be objectively established, as attempted in 10.4; at any rate, discussing the beginnings of his plays is an appropriate way to start a larger-scale evaluation of this *greatness*, and to go on to examine other major components of his artistic system in this light.

Notes

1 This Chapter is concerned more specifically with beginnings of Chekhov's *plays*. Similarities and differences between his techniques in starting a story and a play are a subject for a separate study.

2 The concepts of *frame* and *boundary* — whose literal sense, in visual–plastic arts (especially in painting) will be henceforth ignored — are used figuratively so frequently in the analysis of temporal arts, that they have lost their original effect of trans-medium metaphors or analogies.

3 An intermediate position in this dichotomy is occupied by memories of past perceptions of works of art, in contradistinction with memories of past events in real life. Such memories — undoubtedly inseparable from the 'baggage' that any perceiver brings with him/her to the present process of perception — are extraneous-yet-analogous to the perception in the present.

4 This is a brief reference to the *beginning* and *ending* of a temporal act of engagement with a work of art, which does not **necessarily** begin with the text's beginning nor end

with its ending: it can start and/or end at some point in the middle, and can be interrupted and resumed at will. This further complication of the theoretical ramification of the *frame* concept will be henceforth ignored, because (a) the present argument is based on the presumption of pre-designed correspondence between order of presentation and order of perception, though, admittedly, it is not always the case in reality; (b) in staged plays in the theatre — unlike printed books, or video recordings for that matter — such correspondence is imposed willy-nilly on the perceiver, and therefore taken into account by the author.

5 The matter is discussed more thoroughly in 10.1.2.0, where the concepts of *Mimesis* and *Secondary Modelling Systems* are contrasted in detail.

6 In the case of an author unknown to the perceiver, this anonymity also generates some expectations; an author can be 'unknown' in different ways and degrees, e.g., known by name and reputation only, without actual prior exposure to a specific perceiver; known by nationality, historical period, style etc. (e.g., "restoration comedy"), but not personally; known in a different capacity (e.g., through biographical information, statements made by or about that author in an extra-artistic context, etc. etc.). Even when really unknown — being a beginner, writing under pseudonym, recently discovered, etc. — some vague initial expectations and curiosities are aroused. This point, noted here to complete a theoretical overview of the matter, is of course irrelevant to a famous writer like Chekhov in relation to an audience aware of his fame.

7 Sometimes the order of presentation is reversed, i.e., the author's name comes after rather than before the title and subtitle (e.g., in a sequence like "*The Seagull*, a Comedy in Four Acts by Anton Chekhov"). The common practice, however, is as described above, and the difference is not significant for the present argument, since the author's name and the title + subtitle actually constitute a single cohesive preambular unit in relation to everything that comes after it: the *initial stage directions* (*ISD*), the beginning of the dialogue and the rest of the text. The inner order within this initial unit, then, is of little consequence.

8 These two titles are not exactly identical in their structure: whereas the former is simply a surname, the latter includes two much more specific elements, indicating endearment and family-relation, as will be discussed below.

9 An interesting exception, the only one known to me, is a production of *Three Sisters* directed by Rina Yerushalmi with her "Itim" ensemble (Tel Aviv, 2004–2005). Before the beginning of the dialogue each actor said a couple of phrases in the first person about the personage s/he is going to impersonate. The text of these self-introductions was written by the director, and was not identical with Chekhov's explicit characterisations of his personages, whether in or out of the *List of Personages*, though it apparently aimed at making members of the audience aware of the *List* and familiarise themselves with each personage's significance.

10 Notwithstanding their predominantly *visual* function, *SD* occasionally include *auditory* instructions as well. These usually refer to non-verbal sounds, but they can also (very rarely) activate verbal ones, e.g., someone talking backstage, with the words functioning more as auditory background than as part of the spoken dialogue. In Chekhov there are interesting borderline cases, e.g., *SD* instructing Vária to call Ánia's name at the end of Act 2 of *The Cherry Orchard*, Arkádina's appearance in the window — the borderline between *stage* and *backstage* — calling Trigórin's name aloud (*The Seagull*, end of Act 2); there are similar cases elsewhere in the major plays.

11 The term *playscript* itself was conceived in analogy with cinema's *screenplay*, ignoring basic differences between the two: thus, whereas the tradition of printing and reading plays as autonomous fictional texts has been with us for centuries, no such tradition has

developed for *screenplays*. This difference is telling, and indeed very few screenplays are designed by their authors as texts for general reading, separately from watching the film for which they were written as a set of instructions, and by any readership other than the professional crew engaged in making the film. In terms of potential autonomy and self-sufficiency, then, *screenplays* are more similar to architect's designs for erecting a building than to written plays. Relevant to this contrastive comparison are also crucial differences between the roles and functions of *directors* in the two arts (a rather more *authorial* status in the cinema, compared to the theatre, as a general rule), but this is marginal to the present discussion.

12   See Eli Rozik's (2008) powerful presentation of the view (that I find debatable, to say the least) that plays (by obvious implication, **all** plays) are "deficient" as autonomous literary–fictional texts. See his entire chapter 6, especially 90–96, for what I regard as a well-argued but inherently partial (in both senses) theoretical view of the matter.

13   Another aspect of this comparison is the prominence of *stage directions* in the written text: their sheer length, and degree of interference with the verbal flow of dialogue, can be crucial for a play's literary readability, and therefore its autonomous literary value.

14   Rozik (see Note 12) and other advocates of the inherently "deficient" (his term) and non-literary nature of all plays, as such, ignore such relevant phenomena as the social–cultural fact (or at least the crucial significance of the fact) that for many centuries texts of plays have been printed, read, studied in schools, **and sold-and-bought for a price** by publishers and reading publics, and that playwrights, at least when preparing their texts for publishing in book-form, had an implied readership of lay home-readers in mind, in addition to potential professional performers. If plays had been intuitively perceived as so "deficient", playwrights would not have bothered to publish them in books for the general public; publishers — who have never been, nor should have been, philanthropists — would not have engaged in printing such books just for the limited readership of professional performers; lay readers would not have bought and read them; and the entire learning and educational systems of countries large and small would not have included them in mandatory curricula of national and international **literatures**.

15   This applies, notably, to various types of connection among parts of the spoken text, and most specifically to the very generation of meaning through analogies — a process that is inherently literary. For instance, consider the development of the symbolic image of the seagull in *The Seagull*, Moscow in *Three Sisters*, the cherry orchard in *The Cherry Orchard*, etc.; the constructive role of different references to education in *Three Sisters*; the build-up of the 'Medallion Scene' in *The Seagull*, as analysed in the Appendix; and a myriad of other examples of virtually unstageable artistic complexity generated by the verbal text and active in the process of reading. A stage director has less to do than a reader in realising potentialities inherent in such types of structuration.

16   The study of the nature and function of *SD* in Chekhov's plays is a worthy subject for thorough separate, autonomous research.

17   A famous paradigmatic case of delayed exposition is Sophocles' *Oedipus Rex*, but in fact the phenomenon is very frequent in detective stories and plays, as well as in numerous other texts, from time immemorial to the present (Ibsen's plays, for instance, are very often, and typically, characterised by the delayed presentation of vital expositional materials). For rich information and thorough analysis of relevant texts and problems, see Sternberg 1978.

18   Section 7.5 has a fuller view of the relation between *The Seagull*'s title and the play in its entirety. The scientifically correct name of the title-bird in English seems to be *gull*, rather than *seagull*. Thus, Senelick (2005, 135, n. 1) makes a reasonable comment:

"why do seagulls hover over an inland lake in Sorin's estate? In Russian *Chaika* [чайка, cháïka in this Book's transliteration] is simply a gull". Then he goes so far as to add: "*Sea* [italics supplied] has the connotation of distance and freedom, quite out of keeping with this play". Here I emphatically beg to differ, for reasons spelled out mainly in 7.5: these connotations have **everything** to do with this play (though Chekhov could not care less about their possible implications for translating his play into English). Senelick's conclusion of his note is: "In English, however, *The Seagull* has gained common currency as the play's title, so I have retained it here, but refer simply to the 'gull' in the text". To my mind, the whole discussion (having started long before the publication of Senelick's translation) gives too much weight to ornithological consid-erations and too little to poetic ones. The latter, however, are of much greater importance for the play — not only for its central personages, but also for its author: his very choice to grant centrality to this bird is primarily, if not exclusively, for its poetic and aesthetic values. From this angle, within the English-language context, even the harsh, thud-like monosyllabic sound of *gull* as opposed to the much softer disyllabic sound of *seagull*, whose trochaic rhythm resonates with the Russian original, is a valid point for prefer-ring the latter in English. The other sense if *gull*, from which the adjective *gullible* is derived, adds to its inappropriateness in the context of this play. For all these reasons I had no hesitation to adopt *Seagull* throughout the Book.

19 If we think of the original audience in St Petersburg in 1896, that reputation included only Chekhov's work published before *The Seagull*; for later (e.g., 21st century) audi-ences it may be much more complicated, since such an audience can of course get acquainted with Chekhov's works in any order, not necessarily the order of their compo-sition or publication.

20 In that famous 1892 letter to Suvórin (Chapter 9's Epigraph) Chekhov does not mention *comedy* and *tragedy* by name, but there is an obvious linkage between his reference to two types of ending and the popular distinction between these two genres.

21 Even the darkest of *tragedies* may have the odd comic personage or scene, e.g., the Porter and his famous soliloquy in Shakespeare's *Macbeth*, Act 3, and certain scenes and dialogues in his other major tragedies; the existence of such personages and scenes has never cast a shadow of a doubt on these plays' classification as *tragedies*.

22 I am using the terms *comedic* and *tragedic* (see Chapter 10) as adjectives derived from *comedy* and *tragedy*, respectively, referring to these *formal genres*, rather than to the characterisation of persons/personages, events, situations, etc., in life or in art, as *comic* or *tragic*. The *OED* has entries for *comedic* and *tragedical*, but no entries for *comed-ical* and *tragedic*. This seems to me sheer coincidence of usage, so I am taking the liberty to use the above mentioned terms, for symmetry's sake.

23 Rayfield 1999, 137–138, tells us that "The opening exchange between Masha and Medvedenko [...] comes directly from an episode in Maupassant's *Bel-Ami*", and supplies the source for the quotation in its entirety. Maupassant is also quoted — this time explicitly — in Act 2 of the play. This is one of the many overt and covert textual quotations and references to literary works, Russian and foreign, in a play, which has rightly earned the characterisation of being "Chekhov's most literary play".

24 In any reference to *Uncle Vánia* in this Book I have decided to ignore a fact which is very important in the genesis and nature of this play, namely — its great debt to a full-fledged, previously published prototype, *The Wood Demon* (or, in Senelick's English version *The Wood Goblin*). The name of Vánia's predecessor, a major personage in *The Wood Demon*, is Yegór (the Russian equivalent of *George*). Difference between the two plays and their respective parallel personages, including their changed names (where applicable), have been discussed intensely in the literature (in English one can mention,

inter alia, chapters devoted to the subject in Magarshack 1950 and Pitcher 1973). This fascinating subject in Chekhov studies is hardly relevant to the present argument.

25 In Chekhov's earlier work, and among his short plays (mainly one-acters), there is a number of unconventional *genre labels* — Senelick 2006 has an English version of the full list. A selection of these includes: just "A Play" and "A Joke" (several times each); "A Horribly-Dreadfully-Excitingly Desperate Trrragedy [sic!]" and "A Comic Oddity in Three Acts, Five Scenes, with a Prologue and Two Flops" (see Senelick 2006, p. 272 and p. 281, respectively); etc. However, the conventional subtitles *comedy* and *drama* are often used in the earlier plays too. *The Wood Demon* — *Uncle Vánia*'s prototype — is subtitled *comedy*. Radical differences between the two plays (see Magarshack 1980/1952, 121–156, 204–225; Pitcher 1973, 69–112) account for this change of subtitle.

26 In Russian social culture (as in other European languages — e.g., French, German, Italian and others, with peculiar differences between them), adults tend to use the formal/'respectful' plural when addressing each other; using the singular signifies closeness among adult peers (e.g., when a courting couple become engaged or married, or when strangers become friends), and/or an asymmetrical 'downward' form of address (e.g., when a superior/adult addresses an inferior/child); in the other ('upward') direction, the plural is commonly used. A form of address between two individuals can reflect their respective positions (e.g., adult and child, senior and junior) when they first met, even after these positions change (e.g., when the children who grew up together become adults). In certain families children use the plural addressing their parents (e.g., *The Seagull*'s *Másha* addresses both of them in the plural, whereas Konstantín addresses his mother and uncle in the singular); this reflects, and tells others (and/or an audience), something about the nature of parent–child relationship in that family and/or about that family's conception of social etiquette. However, *Uncle Vánia*'s first dialogue indicates that Ástrov and Marína had met eleven years before the time of speaking, when both were adults. Presumably, they must have used the plural at first, and with the passage of time they became closer and switched to the singular. Examining forms of address between Chekhov personages can be an interesting subject for research. In many cases using the singular is obvious (e.g., between spouses, close friends, members of a close family circle, etc.), but in other cases — like this one — an entire relationship can be suggested to the audience by an unexpected form of address. Nowadays, since the obsolescence of *thou* and its derivatives, this important socio-cultural aspect of Russian pragmatics has no equivalent in modern English usage, and has therefore become untranslatable. Thus, when Yeléna and Sónia propose to become closer friends (*Uncle Vánia*, Act 2), they seal their friendship by deciding to start using the singular between them. In other (admittedly rare) cases in Chekhov, the same two people are inconsistent in this matter, without any formal decision to change their form of address. At least in one case (Marína talking to the Professor, *Uncle Vánia*, Act 2) such inconsistency occurs within the same *réplique*, i.e., literally within a minute in stage-time (in that specific case, the change seems to result from her assuming the position of an adult mothering a child). In certain cases — e.g., the relationship between Arkádina and Trigórin in *The Seagull* — such fluctuations may reflect a difference between behaving within a closed dyad on the one hand and in the presence of others on the other; Arkádina, specifically, is portrayed once again, through this device, as the incessant actress in life, almost always 'performing' and controlling the outward appearance of her emotions, treating others as her 'audience'. Thus, if she does not want others to know that she addresses Trigórin in the singular, she will do so only when they are alone.

27 I am a bit hesitant to make this point in connection with *Uncle Vánia*. It may well be that the structural roles of the first dialogue(s) in this play are just as complex and as multi-functional as in the other major plays, and failing to notice it is simply an inadequacy of the present writer. In studying great works of art in general, and Chekhov's plays in particular, no matter how thoroughly and how often one tries to analyse them, there are always those subtle details and complex textual interactions that of course have always been there but remained "an undiscovered country" until one 'stumbles on them' for the first time, wondering how come one has not seen them before. The main hallmark of great art — as is well known — is its *inexhaustibility*.

28 Most English translations of *Three Sisters* render the names of these rooms this way; some of them use *living room* and *sitting room* for *drawing room* and *reception room*, respectively, and/or *parlour* or *hall* for either of the two rooms.

29 In the Russian original, her *name-day* or *Saint-day party*. The Pravoslav (Christian-Orthodox) tradition was to celebrate people's birthdays on the anniversary of their christening; normally the name of that day's Saint in the Orthodox calendar would be given to the newborn baby. The 5th of May, mentioned in the text, is Saint Irína's day (see Senelick 2005, p. 249, note 6). For all social–practical purposes, the function of an Orthodox *name-day* is identical with the function of *birthday* in the west.

30 My late teacher, Professor–Poet Lea Goldberg (1911–1970), said in class that *Three Sisters* was closer to the Greek than to the Shakespearean brand of *tragedy*. This idea can be supported by such loose associations as the *quasi-choric* nature and function of the sisters' (and particularly Ól'ga's) opening and closing statements, by the fateful turn of events in general and Soliónyï role in it in particular, and, indeed, by these columns (somewhat reminiscent of a Greek temple) in the General's place, that Chekhov took such care to mention in his instructions to the stage designer. Whether one agrees or disagrees with this contention, it is certainly thought-provoking.

31 By *hindsight* I mean both within the process of a single exposure to the text — i.e., looking back at the beginning from later points in the text one is reading/watching — and between subsequent repeated exposures to it, each with its own points of looking forward and looking back.

32 It is unclear, even to a reader, what this "cheerful outside" should precisely look like on an imagined stage; for a designer who tries to execute Chekhov's instructions faithfully it is a real 'headache'. Chekhov, with his proven capacity for precise *SD*, in this case seems to have deliberately left much to the designer's imagination.

33 It stands to reason that if Ól'ga had been talking to strangers she would have said "my father" or "our father", whereas her saying just "father" is another subtle proof, from the start, that the other two ladies on stage are her sisters.

34 In the production of the play in *Gesher Theatre* of Tel Aviv (1997–1998), directed by Yevgénii Arïë [Yevgeny Aryeh] and designed by Aleksándr Lisiïánskiï [Alexander Lisiyansky], the performance began with a wordless prologue, in which General Prózorov's funeral, as described by Ól'ga in the beginning of the play, took place on stage (with the military band, firing of salute etc.). After the few minutes' ceremony is over, the tombstones of the cemetery rise up and become the wall and furniture of the Prózorov home. This thought-provoking use of *stage-scenery* makes the audience tangibly sense (a) that the living presence of the dead father's legacy, reflected in his funeral, is the foundation of the family home, and (b) that the life in that home emanates from death. I am gratefully indebted to my senior student Tali Hecht for many insights, especially those connected with the birth–death imagery and thematics in Chekhov's plays in general and in *Three Sisters* in particular, with special reference to this thoughtful production of the play.

35   There is no evidence that Chekhov took his cue from any specific model in music; it is not a matter of influence, not even of inspiration, but of analogy.

36   Senelick, in both editions (2005, 315–322; 2006, 971–978), summarises the old yet never-ending debate about the play's *genre* and spirit, which is of crucial importance for its reception history. Chekhov's famous outspoken remarks in favour of a comic interpretation and against what he emphatically regarded as Stanislávskiï's distortion of it have naturally contributed to the tendency to prefer a *comedic* interpretation of the play.

37   Personages characterisable as 'childish' are a larger majority in *The Cherry Orchard* than in any other of Chekhov's major plays. Out of the play's 12 personages the only exceptions are Vária, Yásha and Firs, with Lopákhin as a borderline case.

38   The function of *ISD* texts, by definition, is predominantly theatrical, though technically they start the play's readable text; however, usually (even in Chekhov's other plays) it is mainly realisable through *stage design* rather than through fictional-world-generating *reading*. The first sentence of *The Cherry Orchard*'s *ISD* is unique in this sense, as we have seen.

39   Of course, such processes are never consistently schematic; thus, in all arts and in all great masters, there cannot be a strict 'dateline' separating early/immature from late/mature, and there are early works with mature characteristics, and vice versa.

4

Dramaticality, *'Dramaticalness'*, Theatricality, Dual Fictionality

I have finished with the play; the title is *The Seagull.* […]
generally speaking, as a dramatist I am minor-league.[1]
I began it *forte* and ended it *pianissimo*, contrary to all the rules
of dramatic art. […] It has turned into a *novella*.[2] […]
I am **not a dramatist at all**.

(Excerpts from two of Chekhov's letters, dated November 1895;
English version synthesised with minor stylistic changes from
Friedland 1965, p. 146, Senelick 2005, p. 413, and Hercher & Urban
2012, 180–81; emphases mine)

4.0 Introduction: Is Chekhov a Playwright?

Two mutually-complementary basic questions stand at the core of this Chapter's discussion of the distinctiveness of Chekhov's plays: (1) What is the uniqueness of **Drama** — i.e., the corpus of plays — within Chekhov's entire *oeuvre* (mainly as opposed to his *narrative prose fiction*)? (2) What is the uniqueness of **Chekhov** within a more comprehensive corpus of world (or, at least, European) *Drama*? These questions can be subsumed under an even more general one: What makes a play (in general, and a Chekhov play in particular) *dramatical* or *theatrical*?[3]

Such questions have been asked in various ways and forms before. Chekhov himself, at least in the early stages of his career as a playwright, shared some of his critics' views by regarding his dramatic works as 'non-plays'; it is significant that he hardly ever voiced such harsh criticism when evaluating himself as a story-teller.[4] In addressing these issues anew, this Chapter dwells on the interface between the specificity of Chekhov's poetics (as opposed to other masters) and the specificity of *Drama* as a whole (as opposed to other *literary super-genres*[5] and other arts). Although the express aim here is to contribute to Chekhov studies more than to a general theory of Drama and Theatre, some generalisations about the latter inevitably underlie the discussion.[6] Suffice it to say that, for the purpose of this study, (a) *Drama* is one of the three *super-genres* of literature, and (b) *theatre* is the art of presenting (and/or performing/interpreting/producing) *Drama* on stage. Derived from these basic two nouns are the adjectives *dramatic(al)* and *theatrical*, from which the self-explanatory abstract nouns *Dramaticality* and *Theatricality* are derived in turn.

The main question, then, is: Was Chekhov justified in branding himself as "not-at-all" a playwright (or at most a "minor-league"[7] one) — a view echoed by others throughout the decades? Are his plays 'non-*Dramatic*' fictional narratives, written only technically[8] as plays? Or, rather, perhaps theatre houses, with their performers and audiences, can benefit from staging these plays, not least because they are suitable precisely and emphatically to the theatre, irreducible to any other art or medium, and untellable as narratives without losing some of their crucial qualities?

These questions are, admittedly, rhetorical: readers can guess that my answer to the first two questions is negative, and to the last one is affirmative. However, they are not "it goes without saying" kind of answers, and they require substantiation.

4.1 Terminology: *Drama, Dramaticality, 'Dramaticalness' etc.*

4.1.0 Preliminary Considerations

The Chekhov-specific questions and the general–theoretical ones posed above should preferably be discussed together: only after clarifying what distinguishes *Drama* from other types of artistic–fictional writing can we have a more solid ground for determining whether Chekhov was the poor storyteller that struts and frets his writing for the stage that he claimed to be. To answer the general questions it is necessary first to distinguish between two separate ways in which the noun *Drama* and the adjective *dramatic(al)*, and their derivatives, are used: everyday usage, applied to real-life events and situations (henceforward, *Sense A* of the word), and technical–professional usage (*Sense B*), applying within the fields of literature and theatre. *Sense C* — *a single work of Drama*, i.e., a single play — is derived from *B*.

In this Chapter only, and only for the purpose of discussing different senses of the term *Drama*, the following graphical and terminological distinctions are strictly applied: *Sense A* is marked by small d and quotation marks (e.g., the "*drama*" in the courtroom); its abstract noun is *dramaticalness*. *Sense B* is marked by a capital D without quotation marks (e.g., Ibsen's *Drama*); its abstract noun is *Dramaticality*. *Sense C* is marked by small d without quotation marks, and preceded by an article, definite or indefinite as appropriate (e.g., '*Three Sisters* is a *drama*'); it can also take the *plural-s* as any other regular noun (e.g., '*Three Sisters* and *Ivanov* are *dramas* by Chekhov'). As elsewhere in the Book, the *drama/tic* word is often italicised to indicate its use in a dictionary–terminological capacity (as explained in the Preface).

This terminological practice is based on modern western usage, i.e. the way the term is defined and used in modern dictionaries[9] (see, for instance, the *OED* definitions). Chekhov's own use of this heavily-overloaded term, which was predominant in the Russian tradition of the time, according to which it referred to serious *Drama* only, and was thus closer to *Tragedy* and contrasted with *Comedy*, is deliberately ignored here, but discussed primarily in Chapter 10.

4.1.1 *Sense A* (*"Dramas"* in Real Life): Past and Present[10]

What, then, do we mean in everyday life when we use of the noun *Drama* and the adjective *dramatic* in *Sense A*?

Originally, in ancient Greek, *drama* meant something close to *action*, or even to *deed*; its application to the field of theatre, denoting a *play*, occurred already in the original Greek.[11] The strong, ancient bond between the concept of *action/activity* in life on the one hand and on the theatre stage[12] on the other hand is hardly observed in the use of *Drama* in modern European languages: each of them has its own word(s) for *action*, whereas the term *Drama*, unchanged and untranslated, universally applies to *verbal texts designed to be acted in a theatre*, while its original literal sense as *action* in reality has been practically lost in those languages.[13]

This imaginary semantic pendulum-movement can be recapitulated as follows:

Phase 1. In its ancient Greek beginning, the meaning of "*Drama*" was transferred from (1) *action* in the world of reality, via (2) the *mimetic imitation*, or 're-enactment' of such action in the *fictional world* of staged reality (and/or its literary preservation in writing) into (3) purely literary–theatrical meanings, 'forgetting' — or, at least, replacing — the original real-life sense (1). This way *Drama* has acquired two senses: the first — *the entire corpus of written, usually fictional, plays* (*Sense B*); the second — *a single play* (*Sense C*).

Phase 2. It is in these two latter senses that *Drama* has been accepted and adopted as an international term, functioning as the basic, literal usage of the word in most European languages, and many other languages as well.

Phase 3. Only in the aftermath of this process has the word been gradually re-used in modern languages to denote certain types of actions and events in reality (*Sense A*), which — though not taking place literally on the theatre stage — have certain qualities that make them, albeit indirectly and figuratively, **presentable** (or 'worthy' of being presented) on stage. These qualities include contrast and/or *conflict*; *intensity*/intensification; high concentration; immediacy and/or simultaneity (or, at least, proximity in time and place); suddenness; *climactic* effect, or at least a quick and relentless build-up, usually of suspense, culminating in such a climactic effect; and maybe first and foremost — in close connection to everything just said — an effect of crucial, extraordinary *importance, significance*, even fatefulness: it is highly improbable that anything experienced as mundane, negligible, trivial, ordinary, or insignificant, would be referred to as "*dramatic*".

And indeed, it is hardly conceivable that the term *dramatic* would be applied to relationships between people, events, or phenomena, if they are remote from each other in time and/or place, and are therefore unable to clash; likewise, a routine everyday event — e.g., having a daily meal or tying one's shoelaces — is unlikely to be labelled *dramatic*, unless a unique context justifies such a label, in which case it could be called a '*dramatic*' use of the term itself. By contrast, *dramatic* would be accepted as the most natural, even trivial, word to use, if applied to matters of life and death, sharp conflicts, and other intense, fateful events and phenomena. It has to be borne in mind, though, that this usage in everyday language (*Sense A*) is figurative, and perceived as such, whereas the *Dramatic–literary* usages (*Senses B* and *C*) are perceived as literal: this is a case where, contrary to the 'normal' state of affairs, reality borrows a sense from art, rather than the other way around.

4.1.2 *Senses B* and *C* in Relation to *Sense A*

Written *Drama*, then, in its literal senses, is characterised by the following two basic features: (a) in its construction and appearance on page, it predominantly consists of *direct speech* of *fictional personages*; it is divided between speeches (*répliques*) spoken by such personages;[14] and (b) in its purpose and *raison d'être*, it is designed to be spoken on stage by actors impersonating such personages.

Readers and theatre-goers are so accustomed to both modern usages of *Drama*(*tic*) — the literal and the figurative — that the link between them is taken for granted, as if it is trivially obvious that *Drama* (and *drama*s) ought to be "*dramatic*", i.e., intense, exciting, concentrated, focused, conflictual, etc. Yet, this is no foregone conclusion. The questions that present themselves here are: (1) Are there any "*drama*s" (i.e., "*dramatic*" phenomena) outside *Drama*? And (2) are there *drama*s (i.e., plays) devoid of "*drama*"?

As for question 1, the obvious answer is *yes*: there are "*drama*s" outside the super-genre of *Drama*, not only in real life (as borne out by the very existence of *Sense A*), but also in non-*Dramatic* literature: both *poetry* and *narrative fiction* abound in "*dramatic*" texts. Many poems (*ballads* and *Dramatic Monologues* come to mind first, but there are plenty of others) and novels (e.g., Dostoïévskii's, among numerous other examples) demonstrate that the formal division of a text between *répliques* is not a precondition for creating superbly-"*dramatic*" works of literary art. As for question 2, Chekhov's plays, in many important ways, pioneered a kind of *Drama* in which overt "*drama*s" are relatively few and far between, or at least hidden to the extent that their very existence is in doubt (the rest of the present Chapter is largely devoted to this issue).

To conclude: granted, "*drama*" is more typical of *Drama* than of the other *super-genre*s; it is in fact more typical of *Drama* than of any other type of text whatsoever. Yet the two are far from identical. Moreover, as we shall see below, *Drama* has at least one truly distinctive feature, but it is **not** "*drama*".

4.2 Chekhov's *Drama* and the Non-"*Dramatic*"

4.2.1 Preliminary Considerations

Indeed, the demonstrably incorrect theoretical generalisation that *Drama* and "*drama*" are inseparably linked is the basis for the allegation that the *drama*s (i.e., plays) of Chekhov are not a genuine part of the super-genre of *Drama*, because they are devoid of real "*drama*". This allegation, unjustifiably legitimised by the author himself, was also espoused by some of his compatriots and contemporaries,[15] as well as in later responses to his *oeuvre*. It is incontrovertible that Chekhov wrote *drama*s, technically speaking; the said allegation is based, then, on confusing *Senses A* and *B*, indiscriminately imposing the former on the latter.

At the time, this was understandable: the aesthetic ideal of fusion and confusion between the three senses of *drama* reigned supreme in pre-Chekhov writing on the subject. Indeed, this is the main reason for the critical canonisation of the famous *three Unities* (of time, place, and action) attributed to Aristotle as normative rules for writing and evaluating *drama*s. No rules of comparable strictness were ever imposed on *narrative fiction* or *poetry* (in the latter, norms of *prosody* and *genre* are different kinds of imposition on texts, based mainly on their formal and auditory properties while encroaching on thematic–semantic freedom of choice to a much lesser degree).

These *Unities* promote the cause of "*dramaticalness*"; more specifically, they facilitate the creation and functioning of intense *conflicts*, yielding climactic showdowns and/or resolutions. In most pre-Chekhov ('serious') Drama the artistic selection of personages and events was also motivated by preference for those who can generate more stark and focused *intensity*: personages in classical Drama were mostly 'important' people engaged almost exclusively in 'important' things; in pre-Chekhov *Realistic Drama* personages could already be 'unimportant' people, but still typically engaged in 'important' things.[16] They would not waste precious stage time on routine eating and drinking, humming a silly tune, reading mundane newspaper items, or having an idle conversation on what is regarded intuitively as trivialities and irrelevancies (all these actions are in fact performed on stage by Chekhov's personages). Rather, they would deal with matters that are crucial, or at least highly relevant, to their own fates and/or the fates of others, to the advancement of the plot, and/or to matters of importance for human collectives (societies, nations, generations, even humanity as a whole).[17]

To conclude: in *non-comic Drama*[18] before Chekhov there was little difference between "*drama*" (*Sense A*) and *Drama* (*B*): what fails to contribute to the former was not worthy of inclusion in the latter, or in a single play (*Sense C*).[19]

4.2.2 Balzac's Wedding in Berdíchev:
Integration and *(In)Significance*

Let us examine a short passage (with slight omissions) from Act 2 of *Three Sisters*, and check it for *Dramaticality/"Dramaticalness"*.

VERSHÍNIN: And yet, it's a pity that youth is gone…

MÁSHA: In Gógol' there's a saying: "It's boring to live in this world, Gentlemen!"

TÚSENBACH: And I say, it's hard to argue with you, Gentlemen. […]

CHEBUTÝKIN [*reading a newspaper*]: Balzac was married in Berdíchev.

[*Irína quietly hums a tune*]

CHEBUTÝKIN: Let me write it down in my notebook. [*writes*] Balzac was married in Berdíchev.

IRÍNA [*arranges cards for a game of Patience; pensively*]: Balzac was married in Berdíchev.

TÚSENBACH: Matter closed. I have retired.

MÁSHA: I have heard that, and see nothing good in it. I don't like civilians.

TÚSENBACH: It's all the same… [*gets up*] I am not handsome, what kind of a soldier am I? […] I will work […] Workers must sleep soundly!

FEDÓTIK [*To Irína*]: In Moskóvskaïa Street I have just bought for you coloured pencils, and this penknife.

IRÍNA: You are accustomed to treat me as a child. I am already grown-up! [*Takes the pencils and penknife, happily*]: Charming!

FEDÓTIK: And look what I bought for myself: a big penknife. Look, here's one blade, here another one, and a third one, this is to pick your ears, and here's scissors, to clean under your fingernails.

RODÉ [*To Chebutýkin*]: Doctor, how old are you?

CHEBUTÝKIN: Thirty-two. [*Laughter*]

FEDÓTIK: I will now show you another patience game.

Is there any "*drama*" here? Is the text intense, concentrated, or focused? Are there any sharp contrasts or conflicts in it, or condensed chains of events, leading to a climax? Or is this text highly significant, in any sense, at least for its speakers and staged listeners themselves? Out of its larger context, none of these questions can be answered in the affirmative. The passage is remarkably unremarkable; bluntly, it is quite tiresome (in a way, Másha's quote from Gógol' is reflexively self-referential). Most matters mentioned in it are not interconnected, and there is hardly any movement oriented towards a goal or destination, let alone leading to a climax.

Let us focus on the reference to Balzac's wedding: what can possibly connect this wedding to Irína, or Chebutýkin, or indeed anything 'important' in the play or in the lives of its personages? And if, as it seems, the answer is *nothing*, why is this sentence — "Balzac got married in Berdíchev" — uttered in the play, and on top of that double-echoed, repeated three consecutive times in the text? And what is the connection between Balzac's wedding and Túsenbach's retirement? Moreover, what does any of these topics have to do with the purchase and detailed descriptions of penknives? In short: why are these matters mentioned at all, and in such detail, and with such textual proximity at that?

Another feature of the quoted text is that personages seem to be queuing, or taking turns, to have their say, as if vying for attention, when actually they have nothing worth saying (see Popkin 1993, 3–15, and especially 213–217). A far cry from the 'ping-pong-like' exchange typical of *realistic* dialogue of the Ibsenian type — where *répliques* tend to be short and succeed each other in a **focused** talk between (usually) two speakers, each replying directly to the point made in the preceding *réplique*[20] — the 'conversation' quoted above occurs in a company of several people, in which very few listen, or reply, to each other "to the point". Furthermore, the shortness of the *répliques* here adds to the audience's anticipation of a 'ping-pong' dialogue as just described. Indeed, such anticipation is nurtured by Ibsen-type *realism*, to which the audience is conditioned and Chekhov subscribes in other matters. Chekhov's deviation from this type of dialogue, then, adds to the audience's frustration at its absence: the actual conversation has no continuity, and sounds arbitrary and meaningless. Some of its *répliques* do not require a reply; but those that do are hardly ever answered, and speakers and listeners alike do not seem to care one way or another whether a reply is forthcoming. It seems that people instantaneously forget not only what they have just heard from others, but even what they have just said.

It is tempting to explain this unfocused exchange away, as if every personage is too immersed and absorbed in his/her own world to care to listen to others, and indeed such explanations are often given in the secondary literature about Chekhov's dialogues; however, though this description can apply to some of them, it is not the case here (and in many other cases): it is highly unlikely that Balzac's wedding is on anybody's mind, or plays as much as an **in**significant role, not to speak of a significant one, in the life and inner world of any speaker. In short, the fact that personages dwell on this wedding cannot result from their preoccupation with it. Quite on the contrary, perhaps the personages' mental preoccupation with **something else** can somehow explain the automatic, thoughtless, dream-like repetition of the reference to Balzac's wedding, which is on nobody's mind. In short, all participants in this 'conversation' **hear without listening, and speak without thinking**. The same applies to the penknife that Fedótik had just bought: it is almost equally unimportant to him and to Irína, though she cares to respond to what he says about it, thus creating, almost paradoxically, the only seemingly conventional, to-the-point dialogic chain of *répliques* in the whole passage just quoted. The comic reference to Chebutýkin's age[21] adds to the quasi-arbitrary effect of this exchange. In short: the entire quote is almost the precise opposite of anything remotely "*dramatic*", at least when taken out of its original context, as has been deliberately done here.

Such passages in Chekhov are well designed and carefully planned — a far cry from the arbitrary impression that they initially make.[22] References to the game of patience[23] — and, indeed, to Balzac's wedding — are not as irrelevant and unconnected to the play's concerns as one might imagine at first. With reference to the wedding, (a) the idea of fulfilling one's dream of happiness in general, and marital bliss in particular, in a place remote from one's regular place of residence is all but foreign to the world of *Three Sisters* and its personages: this is a non-arbitrary motivation for the repeated invocation of this 'arbitrary' phrase; (b) on a more general level, the Balzac-wedding *motif* is a piece of deliberate authorial discourse, psychologically well motivated: in a typically precise and subtle way, Chekhov shows us the subconscious hierarchies that we make out of our sensual perceptions, selecting some and ignoring others; (c) specifically, the dreamy, pensive intonation of Irína's repetition of this text signals a state of wandering mind, but her unawareness underscores the psychological relevance of the text "Balzac got married in Berdíchev" to her deepest yearnings; (d) Chebutýkin's initial selection of this news item, copying it to his notebook, is not arbitrary either (granted, it is his habit to do that kind of thing to news items, but not to each and every one of them): it resonates with other aspects of his character and biography, to the limited extent that we know it; (e) the geographically remote wedding relates to the brigade's movements, first from Moscow to the provincial town and then from there to Poland, with the impact of those military migrations on the formation and dissolution of human contacts in general and romantic relationships in particular; (f) the wedding is definitely linked with the longing for Moscow, with telling references to the migration of birds in the play (and thus, with the idea of nesting away from home); etc. Indeed, Balzac's wedding in Berdíchev[24] touches many crucial concerns of the play.

The very choice of Balzac is also multi-functional while posing as accidental. First of all, it underscores the personages' interest in literature and its authors, or at least in trivia relating to them (i.e., once again, in the accidental that accompanies the well-designed); however, it probably does not make a cursory contribution to the dating of the play's fictional events, as it may appear at first sight. Chekhov did not engage in historical *Drama*, and his plays are roughly timed in the here-and-now — Russia of the transition between the 19th and 20th centuries — that he shared with his audiences; *Three Sisters* is not an exception. It is unlikely, then, that the reference to Balzac's wedding is meant to date the play's fictional events half a century before its writing (it was in 1850 that Balzac (1799–1850) married a Polish lady[25] in Berdíchev). It follows, then, that the newspaper that Chebutýkin is reading from chronicles Balzac's wedding and its location as an old item of trivia, rather than as a piece of today's news, and Chebutýkin makes a note of it — as part of his characterisation — as if it were a newsworthy event (this is a repetitive pattern: he picks up from the newspaper and jots down other types of useless trivial information). This reference may also allude to the difference between the poetics of Balzac's carefully designed works — *realistic novels* in the French tradition, that never pretend to be anything other than well-planned texts down to the smallest detail — on the one hand, and Chekhov's newly emerging poetics, in *Drama* and in *narrative fiction* alike, in which the carefully planned is often disguised as accidental and arbitrary, on the other hand.

The same multi-functionality applies to the connection between Balzac's wedding, Túsenbach's pending retirement, his talk about work, Irína's childishness, and other matters mentioned above. Thus, Túsenbach's retirement, later followed by his engagement to Irína, can be viewed, *inter alia*, as diversion from a pre-determined course in his life, and as relocation of the respective wedding venues he and Irína had dreamed about, separately, when they were youngsters, and without a specific potential spouse in mind. In this sense, it is analogous to Balzac's unexpected wedding venue.[26]

How much of this dense network of interconnections can work in fleeting moments in the theatre? One wonders; yet, similar questions can be asked in any case of complex interaction between heterogeneous elements in plays of great intricacy. The educated audience of compatriots and contemporaries that Chekhov probably had in mind must have known, at least roughly, who Balzac was, where and when he lived, and what kind of novels he wrote. This can enable at least part of these complex interconnections to work subliminally in the audience's minds. Moreover, it is a hallmark of great art that it is often characterised by 'wasted energy', manifest in networks of connections too complex to be cognitively processed under 'normal' conditions of communication.

The passage from *Three Sisters* was quoted here to demonstrate the dearth of "*Drama*" of the overt, actual type, occasionally compensated by its covert, poten-tial counterpart. The totally anti-"dramatic" effect generated by such seemingly-arbitrary passages in Chekhov is misleading: once the intense deliber-ateness of this text is duly recognised, it starts looking somewhat more "dramatic", through its focused intensity, though it lacks traditional "*dramaticalness*" and has no hint of **overt Dramatic Conflict** — a subject elaborated below.

Indeed, the reference to Balzac's wedding, and the number and nature of its repetitions, maintain a subtle counterpoint between the conflicting effects of the designed and the arbitrary. Such examples in Chekhov can be characterised as 'doubly subversive': even a genuine effect of arbitrariness is, almost by definition, subversive in an artistic text, since a work of art is perforce designed and organ-ised; faking it, as Chekhov does, makes the designed and the arbitrary undermine each other, barely hiding the clash between them.[27]

4.2.3 *Covert Dramatic Conflict* and Chekhovian '*Dramaticalness*'

It is largely the abundance of such seemingly disconnected dialogues as just discussed that has earned Chekhov the misleading reputation of a "non-Dramatist". This feature concerns mainly the *micro-textual* and *textural* dimension of his texts; however, on their *macro* level and overall structural and semantic–thematic makeup, the main reason for this reputation is the dearth of **overt** *Dramatic Conflict*. Considering both qualities together, Chekhov's *Drama* appears doubly non-"*dramatic*". Let us focus, then, on the concept of *Conflict in Drama*.

Major classical theories of *Drama* placed **overt** *Conflict*[28] high on the list of "*drama*"-generating factors; every serious play worthy of the name is deemed to focus on one major conflict, or at most very few conflicts, between personages and/or ideas. From this highly important angle there is little difference between classical or traditional *tragedy* (from the Greeks and/or Romans via Shakespeare to late 18th century, and beyond), on the one hand, and more recent serious *Drama* (by Chekhov's immediate predecessors, his contemporaries, and even many of his 20th-century successors), on the other hand. The centrality of *overt conflict* has been for centuries a hallmark of *Drama*, often pursued in late 19th-century *Realism* with greater tenacity than previously. Therefore, its absence is a highly marked deviation from the normally expected, for authors and audiences alike.[29]

In Chekhov's plays, however, there is a clear tendency to **avoid and evade** direct, overt *conflict*, occasionally to (and even beyond) the point of shunning it altogether. The word "tendency" is used here advisedly, since Chekhov applies a consistent, even relentless avoid-and-evade strategy *vis-à-vis* most potentially conflict-generating elements, refusing as it were to develop such a potential into a *dramatic conflict* of types and magnitude found frequently in his predecessors' plays. This is true within each single major play, and within Chekhov's artistic diachrony, i.e., his development as a playwright and the evolution of his Dramatic/theatrical system:[30] broadly speaking, in every major play this tendency is more powerful and consistent than in the play preceding it chronologically.

In *Ivanov* (1887) — *The Seagull*'s full-length predecessor — Chekhov still develops *overt conflicts*, whose consistency and centrality could have been recognised even by an Ibsen as his own.[31] However, in later stages of his development Chekhov shunned this type of overt conflict. *The Seagull* (1896) already marks a considerable departure from it: granted, there are still overt conflicts in the play, but also clear attempts to avoid/evade them: for instance, Konstantín's refusal to confront Trigórin for what would have been traditionally conflictual scenes, and the latter's refusal to confront the former in what would have been, probably, an offstage duel. In *Uncle Vánia* (1897) there are clearer conflict-evasions: Sónia, Yeléna and Serebriakóv evade a confrontation about **non**-playing the piano at the end of Act 2; Vánia's appearance with the flowers without confronting Yeléna or Ástrov in Act 3; Vánia's shoot-and-miss pursuit of the Professor, again Act 3; and one can regard Act 4 in its entirety as a masterpiece in conflict-evading. Examples in *Three Sisters* are even more striking in number and quality; thus, the sisters' refusal to confront Natásha is one of many cases in which **active non-conflict** is a major plot-propelling force. This process culminates in *The Cherry Orchard,* the last play Chekhov was to complete, where he manages to evade *overt dramatic conflict* almost totally: scenes of faint quasi-conflicts — few and far between — have little bearing on the plot's progress and structure.[32]

In all these cases, and many others, the "*dramatic*" situation among personages is loaded with suspense, thereby creating definite expectations in the audience for *overt conflict* on stage; such expectations are frustrated almost as a rule, and the audience is left with the growing weight of unreleased tensions and suppressed, unexpressed confrontations, with the withheld energies of words unsaid and deeds undone. Synchronised with the decrease in number and quality of ***overt** conflicts*, then, there is a complementary process of increase in number and intensity of ***covert** conflicts* in Chekhov's plays.

To conclude: if indeed *Drama* = "*drama*" also in the sense that the centrality of *overt conflict* is a prerequisite for the generic definition of plays, then Chekhov's plays gradually lose their claim to be considered *Dramatic*.[33] There are however two objections to this contention.

(1) As stated above in 1.5, elements in all arts are never annulled by being *hidden/covert/implicit*; moreover, in many cases in the arts in general, and in Chekhov's poetics in particular, *implicit potentials* are more potent and intense than their *explicit realisations*. Thus, it is simply incorrect to say that Chekhov's later plays lack conflict: on the contrary, they are replete with rich and central, even *"dramatic" conflicts*. These conflicts, however, are *typically covert* (taking place in the audience's minds), rather than *traditionally overt* (taking place on stage, with

tangible bones of contention between personages and/or ideas they express and/or represent). To sum up: Chekhov's plays — admittedly poor in *overt/explicit "drama"* — are rich in its *covert/implicit* variant.

(2) *"Drama"* — with its inherent focus on *conflict* — is not the distinctive features of *Drama* as such. It follows that even if the point just made in (1) above is denied, and the contestable statement that there is little *"drama"* in Chekhov's plays is temporarily accepted for the sake of argument, these plays can still be 'legitimately' admitted into the corpus of world *Drama* if they include the minimal requirements, the *differentia specifica*, of this *super-genre*.

In short, there is no case to exclude Chekhov's plays from *Drama*.

4.3 Chekhov and the *Differentia Specifica* of *Drama*

4.3.1 *Drama* between Written *Literature* and Live *Theatre*

A basic comparison between representative samples of the three *super-genres of literature* will show, that the real distinctiveness of *Drama* when viewed as written text[34] resides in its *multi-medium potentiality* (anticipating its staging in theatrical performance, for which it is designed in the first place): in other words, it is realised in the heterogeneity of perceptive and cognitive channels through which it is communicated to its addressees and in the ways its written form activates their imaginations.[35] Reference here is not to the visual impact of graphic signs printed on paper in the process of reading: this feature, in isolation, is of negligible importance in most types of written language, including, of course, the three super-genres of fictional literature;[36] in this context, the reading process activates a great deal of imagination and very little sensual perception, whereas watching a staged play does the reverse — the cognitive space occupied by sensual perception in the theatre allows for lesser preoccupation with the activation of imagination while watching a performance. The following discussion, then, focuses on the uniqueness of the **reading** of *Drama*, and the specific ways in which it activates the imagination and the senses of its readers.

With this in mind, we can indeed focus on *Dramaticality*, with a capital D, which derives from *Drama* (unlike *"dramaticalness"*, which derives from *"drama"*); it can also be labelled *potential theatricality*. It would refer to the activation of Drama's *differentia specifica*, its **imagining the activation of various senses** simultaneously in the theatre: **whereas poetry and prose fiction predominantly address the reader's imagination, and live theatre predominantly addresses the spectator's senses, *Drama* activates the reader's mind to imagine him/herself as being a theatre spectator, whose senses are being directly addressed.** Although *Dramaticality* thus characterised may represent an experience more complex than both reading narrative literature on the one hand and watching a theatre production on the other hand, it is still a secondary process, derived from the theatrical experience; it normally activates *Dual* or *Two-Tier Fictionality*.

Studying the *Dramaticality* of Chekhov's plays in this sense will undoubtedly disprove his own view of *The Seagull* as a piece of narrative, poorly designed for the stage; moreover, in this play, as well as in the three later ones, Chekhov created works of art designed specifically to affect their audiences only from the theatre stage (reading them as printed *drama*s, as just argued, is a viable option, but it is largely a derived experience; there is no way to re-create their specific qualities in non-Dramatic narrative prose). This statement does not detract from these plays' value as potentially autonomous literary texts; the derived nature of experiencing them through reading, as just described, is a value added, rather than a substitute, to their literary stature. Moreover, in this particular respect Chekhov surpassed some of his greatest predecessors, like Shakespeare or Ibsen, who enjoy a more solid reputation as dramatists (and understandably so, in terms of overt "*dramaticalness*"). To be more precise, the above does not apply to Chekhov's stage corpus in its entirety, but to selected, yet typical and conspicuous parts of it; however, these parts irrefutably establish Chekhov's status as a full-fledged dramatist, much more than he ever gave himself credit for.

4.3.2 *Dual (Two-Tier) Fictionality*: The Uniqueness of Play Reading

As argued briefly above (3.0 and 3.1), in the process of reading a play the reader's imagination can be activated to construct two types (or, rather, two phases/storeys/tiers) of *fictionality*. It is essential to understand them as types of reading *fictional* texts, particularly against the background of reading verbal texts in general (most of which belong to *non-fiction* genres). Some of the points made below are obvious truisms; however, making them in the present context may prove useful.[37]

Some mental processes are invoked in the cognitive response to any verbal text. Relevant to this discussion is the mental creation of *reality-like* images of people, objects, actions, events, concepts, etc., in the perceiver's mind. These images stand for the 'real things', and their mental creation is the core of any perception and cognitive processing of fiction, through reading or otherwise. The following discussion is focused on *reading*, but much of it is applicable to oral transmission as well.

4.3.2.1 Reading of *Non-Fiction* Texts

In *non-fiction* texts the verbal text denotes, and the mental images it produces relate to, components of the 'real world'. These images are *reality-like* (rather than *real*) only because they are mental, intangible, and exist in one's memory, imagination etc.; however, potentially and in principle, somewhere, some time, one could (if one would) match them with the reality they claim to relate (to), and test them for the amount of *factual-truth-value* that they possess (i.e., they are *true* or *false* to the extent that they pass or fail a *reality test*). Such actual or potential verification is unavailable for fictional texts.

4.3.2.2 Reading of *Fictional* Texts

Once again: in reading fiction we **know** that the *worlds* that the text denotes are only ***possible*** (rather than *real*) ones, or that their *fields of reference* are ***internal*** (in a different conceptual framework and terminology — see Harshav 1984 and 2007).[38] The present discussion is not concerned primarily with the theory and philosophy of fictionality in general, but with the distinction between two specific types of fictionality **in the reading of plays**, which is highly relevant to Chekhov's uniqueness.

Narrative Fictionality (NF). The *internal fields of reference (IFR)*, or *possible worlds*, mentally constructed by readers in *NF* are genuinely ***reality-like***. In Shakespeare's *King Lear,* for instance, the reader constructs an *IFR* in which Lear is really exposed to the storm, and Gloucester is physically blinded: in *NF* within plays people and events are **precisely** as real, and/or as fictional, as in *poetry* or *prose fiction*; in *NF*, then, there is nothing specifically *Dramatic*.

Theatrical Fictionality (TF). This type is unique to the reading of *Drama*. The *IFR [Internal Field of Reference]* constructed through *TF* is **a theatre**, rather than what is called in literary criticism "*a slice of life*"; within *TF* the reader's mind constructs a ***theatre-like*** (rather than *reality-like*) *Field of Reference*. It includes, *inter alia*, imagined stage and auditorium, with sets and props, actors imperson- ating fictional personages, a director supervising the staging process, and of course an audience of spectators. Therefore, coming back to the *Lear* example, when one reads the play with *TF* in mind, the imagined storm is a series of stage effects, doing no harm to the actor impersonating Lear, and the eyes of the actor imper- sonating Gloucester are being smeared with washable red liquid, not brutally blinded, and both actors go home after the show alive and well.

Interrelations between the Two Types of Fictionality. One can question the use of the term *fictionality* for *TF*: after all, a theatre (including, of course, its make- believe and illusion-generating devices) is a tangible part of the 'real world'; why, then, is *TF* not an instance of *non-fiction* reading? The answer is that, indeed, any one particular theatre is real, but imagining a potential theatrical production while reading is a process of creating a *fictional world* in one's mind. The words on the page of a play hardly ever denote a specific theatre in the 'real world'.[39] Reading a play is a far cry from reading a director's production book or a factual press report about a specific production (e.g., a first-night press review), where the words on the page do denote one single theatre and its physical space, named living actors and tangible objects onstage and offstage. The latter are, indeed, *non-fiction* texts, invoking non-fiction reading processes.

The *NF/TF* distinction is necessary at least for theoretical and methodological purposes. *TF* is a unique and distinctive feature of play reading. It need not replace *NF*; rather, in reading a play the two are as a rule mutually complementary. A stage interpreter (a director, actor, designer etc.) is bound to activate *TF* in reading the play in the course of preparing a production.[40] Conversely, a reader not involved in a production can read a play ignoring its *potential theatricality*, making a shortcut to *NF* while skipping *TF*; such a reader can of course freely oscillate between the two, ignore any of them at will — consciously or subconsciously, consistently or intermittently — for leisure/pleasure reading. In the final analysis, *NF* is invoked in the audience during the theatre production itself, at least within a theatre poetics of nonexistent *fourth wall* and *realistic illusion*: here *TF* does not exist, since the theatrical events are part of the tangible world perceived by the senses, having shed their reading-bound fictionality. *NF*, then, lives in the theatre; it is activated along the chain of theatrical communication (**Author → staged fictional reality → audience**), and usually ranks supreme among its aims. Whereas *TF* can be suspended in leisure/pleasure reading as well, *NF* can hardly ever be ignored. A comprehensive, fuller and more complex play reading, then, is two-phased: it invokes the image of a theatre which, in turn, invokes the fictional reality of the narrative in its spectators, with the important difference that they experience this *possible world* through their senses within a 'real' world. *TF* activates the reader's prior knowledge of facts about the theatre and some technicalities of stage production, just as *NF* activates prior knowledge of reality, and of written literature.

The complexity of play reading is even greater, and includes much larger variety than hitherto suggested. Thus, for instance, everything said so far has largely referred to 'realistic', or at least *mimetic*, Drama. Plays with fantastic or supernatural elements, or *absurd* ones, require finer distinctions. Other dimensions ignored here include differences in types of audience, aspects of the physical–tangible nature of the theatre itself, and other ontological, epistemological, perceptual and cognitive ramifications of the complex phenomenon of *fictionality* on stage.

The aim of the preceding discussion is to provide a theoretical background, necessary for understanding Chekhov's poetics in this regard. His realisation of theatre's multi-medium potentials, through the simultaneous activation of the audience's perceptual senses and verbal cognition, is an integral part of his Drama, not only of his Theatre. In reading a written play by Chekhov with the activation of *TF*, his new *Dramaticality* — i.e., his **potential** *theatricality* — is invoked as an integral part of the written play itself, simply because *dual-fictionality* is a quality inherent in all plays based on fictionalised reality. In Chekhov, the reading process reveals not only one of the greatest, but also one of the most **specifically Dramatic** playwrights in history. Indeed, *dual-fictionality* is a regular potential feature of any play reading, but Chekhov was a major 'realiser' of this potentiality, in both senses of *realising*: being aware of it and actualising it. It is mainly because of the multi-medium, multi-sensual aspect of his *TF* that his plays are irreducibly theatrical in their written *Dramatic* potentialities as well, as demonstrated in the next Subsection.

4.3.3 Chekhov's *Dramaticality* at Work: A Scene from *The Seagull*

4.3.3.1 Introducing the Scene

To demonstrate this point, consider the following example from *The Seagull*, the earliest of the four major plays, which Chekhov subjected to the self-critical remarks quoted in the Epigraph to this Chapter.

The scene is taken from Act 4. Characters present on stage are Konstantín (Kóstia), Másha, and her mother Polína Andréïevna.

> Polína Andréïevna [*Browsing the manuscript (of Konstantín's story)*]: Nobody could have guessed that you, Kóstia, would become a real writer [...]

[*stroking his hair with her hand*] and you have become so handsome... dear, good Kóstia, be a bit kinder to my Máshen'ka!

MÁSHA [*Making the bed*]: Leave him alone, Mama.

POLÍNA [*To Konstantín*]: She is a fine girl... All a woman needs, Kóstia, is a kind look. I know that from experience.

[*Konstantín gets up and leaves the room in silence*]

MÁSHA: You have upset him now. There's no need to pester him.

POLÍNA: I feel so sorry for you, Máshen'ka.

MÁSHA: A lot of good that does...

POLÍNA: My heart aches for you.... I see everything, understand everything.

MÁSHA: It's all nonsense. Hopeless, unrequited love is only for novels. It's nonsense. No use waiting forever in vain. If such love settles in, out with it! They said my husband will be transferred to another county; once we move there, I'll forget it all... take it out of my heart by the roots.

[*two rooms away a melancholy waltz is played*]

POLÍNA: Kóstia is playing; it means he is feeling gloomy longing.[41]

MÁSHA [*Quietly makes a couple of Waltz turns*]: The main thing, mother, is to get him out of my sight. Once my husband is transferred — believe me, I'll forget it in no time, in one month I will. It's all utter nonsense.

4.3.3.2 The Scene's *Dramaticality* (*Potential Theatricality*)

In this scene we can see Chekhov's sophisticated activation of a variety of medium components concurrently — mainly words, music and movement.

Personages, Present and Absent; the Audience as Implied Personage. At first glance, if we reduce *Drama* to its verbal component (i.e., only texts spoken by personages on stage), there are just two speakers here: mother Polína and daughter Másha. However, there is at least one additional presence, that of Konstantín: silently present as a direct addressee (spoken to) and an indirect one (spoken of); first present, later absent.[42] His 'thundering-silent' physical presence turns soon enough into *mental presence through physical absence*, accentuated by *auditory presence*: combining loaded silence, determined exit from the room, and "melancholy waltz" playing, he transmits loaded messages to Másha and Polína alike (their limited powers of observation and understanding notwithstanding) and to the audience (whose powers of understanding, consciousness and integration are supposed to be much superior to the personages', to match the author's). The audience, of course, is supposed to be aware of the nature of the message as transmitted to Másha and Polína, whether they get it or not.

Most importantly, there is a covert yet intense dialogue between two conflicting voices **within** Másha, i.e., between the explicit words she speaks to her mother, on the one hand, and her inner emotional self, non-verbally expressed through her waltz steps, on the other. The messages carried by these two voices are diametrically opposed, and it is doubtful whether Másha herself has the insight and self-awareness needed to identify this conflict within her. But unlike Másha, each of us, as readers/spectators, can say, with Polína, «Я ведь всё вижу, всё понимаю» ["I see everything, understand everything"]: we receive all the signals and messages coming to us from the stage; we can combine, juxtapose and integrate them in our minds, and construct the intricate and heterogeneous meanings generated by this exceptionally complex text. Arguably, then, the audience is more entitled than Polína to the awareness that she claims here.

As demonstrated often in this study, these processes are characteristic of the way Chekhov usually constructs meanings through analogies, juxtapositions and interactions. However, in this particular case the process becomes possible mainly because of the heterogeneous makeup of the *theatrical medium*, which Chekhov, being a true man of the theatre, knew inside out; it is totally immaterial whether, and to what extent, this knowledge of his was conscious or intuitive. This example is typical of Chekhov in showing how irreducibly *Dramatic* his plays are, regardless of what he said about himself in this regard.

Chekhov weaves here an intricate web of communication lines between **and within** the three present personages (Polína, Másha and Konstantín); more importantly, through these personages he does the same with another *implied personage*, but a crucial one — arguably, the most important personage in the world theatre and Drama: *The Audience*. Polína speaks directly to Másha and to Konstantín alike, but she hints at her inner emotions (covert internal dialogues with herself). Másha conducts an explicit dialogue with her mother, but much more interesting is her covert dialogue with Konstantín, and, once again, her hidden dialogue with herself is of even greater interest and significance. Konstantín, in turn, runs a kind of *anti-dialogue* (i.e., blatant **refusal** to communicate) with mother and daughter alike, whereas his inner dialogue with himself can be partly reconstructed by us, on the basis of his conduct, his piano-playing, and the words of other personages. Of course, on Chekhov's part this intricate dialogic web is woven with the audience in mind, to activate its senses, perception, cognition, and consciousness. In order to manage the *non-fiction* (Author→audience) transmission of this *fictional* communication complex to the audience (stage→auditorium), Chekhov uses diverse communication channels, addressing different senses in us.

The Verbal Component. The words spoken on stage behave as any other orally transmitted verbal message: technically they use an auditory–visual channel in the theatre, and a visual–graphic one in reading (with the added dimension of the imagined *TF*, i.e., the auditory–visual mentally embedded in the graphic–visual); yet they are not auditory in the way music is, but semantic–referential, and once they reach our conscious cognition, their auditory aspect is practically set aside, and they are processed and understood through the usual mechanisms that make verbal communication possible.

The Music, Semanticised. The music — in this case, the melancholy waltz played by Konstantín — works in ways typical of musical messages, i.e., it is more directly auditory; its emotional qualities interact with the verbal messages,[43] but here, as elsewhere in Chekhov's plays, the musical message is *semanticised* by a verbal one referring to it: the waltz sounds carry the meaning invested in them by Polína.[44]

Dance and Body Language. The dance (Másha's waltz rounds) works through body language, synchronised with the rhythms of the music; yet it is contrasted with the music's semanticised content as well as with the directly semantic content of the verbal text. The intersection and interaction of these three channels of communication, perceived through different sensory–cognitive channels in the audience's minds, constitute a case of truly *theatrical semiosis* and *synæsthetic reception* of meanings, irreducible to any other medium. It can work in the written *Dramatic* text too, even without staging, if readers activate *dual-fictionality* in reading (i.e., combine *TF* with *NF* in their minds).

Chekhov's Staged Simultaneity* vs. *Musical Polyphony. The simultaneous workings of the different medium components that we have seen in this example is in part similar to what happens in *polyphonic music*, where various potentially autonomous melodic lines, or voices, are heard simultaneously, while revealing and obeying a superordinate harmonic design, which in turn regulates the features of the separate lines to produce a unified though composite quality. This quality includes most of the cumulative qualities of the separate melodic lines, but it also possesses features of the whole — notably *counterpoint, harmony* and *tonality* — that transcend the cumulation of the separate melodic lines: as we have seen in Chapter 2, in art (unlike arithmetic) the whole is often greater than the sum-total of its parts. This dictum is particularly appropriate to Chekhov; arguably, even more than to some polyphonic works in music.

Polyphonic music is mentioned here only as an example, an imperfect analogy, compared to the interaction between various communication-channels in Chekhov's *Dramatic* text. It is well known that in music itself, when it leads its own autonomous life (unlike this case of the "melancholy waltz", where it is subordinated to its stage function), intelligible simultaneity of musical purport is possible: musically well-trained human cognition can find its way through the maze of simultaneous musical messages, especially if they are coordinated harmonically; such well-trained cognition can respond musically–intelligently to the whole as such, as well as to the combination of its separate yet coordinated parts. There is a major difference between such musical *polyphony* and its *Dramatic* counterpart, as created by Chekhov in the quoted scene: in the former, polyphony is generated by interactions between homogeneous messages (all auditory, all musical), whereas in the latter it is generated by interactions between genuinely heterogeneous components, variously encoded in language, music, and body movement (dance).

It is of utmost importance for the intelligibility and communicability of the whole that only one of its constituent elements (if any) is verbal; all other messages (music, dance, visual elements, etc.) can function (and be processed) simultaneously, both among themselves and with the verbal message, and yet remain intelligible. *Drama*, designed for multi-medium realisation in the theatre, occupies in this context a middle position between *music* and *theatre*. True, in the theatre — just as in literature — verbal simultaneity cannot be intelligible. However, verbal–non-verbal simultaneity — i.e., simultaneous processing of one verbal message with one, or even more, **non-verbal** ones — can be intelligible, since the latter is free from the limitations constraining the perception and intelligibility of verbal simultaneity.[45] Thus, the simultaneous transmission of a verbal message with a non-verbal one, even if the latter is semanticised, can be processed intelligibly: this can apply, for instance, to the combination of a verbal message with a visual one, especially (but not only) if the latter enjoys a static–durable presence (e.g., a significant use of set design, costumes, lighting etc.), or a musical one, or the simultaneous co-presence of two or more non-verbal messages of this kind.[46] *Drama*, then, can bypass the limitations hindering the perception and interpretation of verbal simultaneity by transmitting *semantic simultaneity* — i.e., the synchronisation of several meanings — through the activation of theatrical staging. Indeed, the theatre stage can be the meeting place of verbal and non-verbal messages, and the latter, *present* on stage, can have a *potentially verbalisable* content, that can be realised in a process of interpretation that is *absent* from the stage. Thus, in the foregoing analysis of the 'melancholy waltz scene' from *The Seagull* in this Section, the hidden meanings of the music and the dance (*present on stage*) were 'translated into' the words of analysis (*absent from stage*), which in turn purport to realise *the semantic potential* of these non-verbal elements. This can happen even if the non-verbal element creates an intense, concentrated experience of urgency, i.e., when the *semanticised non-verbal message* works as a kind of shorthand, whose immediate impact is irreproducible in the transmission of slower, single-channel verbal communication. The verbal analysis can explain this impact, but not reproduce it; it can work in retrospect, after the experience of the *verbal–non-verbal simultaneity*, or even before it, in preparation for it; but it cannot replace it in real time without producing *unintelligibility* all over again…

Chekhov knew these cognitive facts, albeit perhaps intuitively, better than most of his predecessors, as borne out by the nature of his art and theatre language. He handles and activates each medium component according to its typical characteristics: thus, indeed, he would never instruct two actors to speak simultaneously.[47] Even when his main concern is with situations of faulty communication (or total lack thereof) between personages on stage, he would never abandon communication, albeit **through** those ill-communicating personages, between himself (as author) and his audience. That said, it must be noted that Chekhov would often load his texts mercilessly, pushing them towards the upper limits of humanly processable complexity and simultaneity, but at the same time he would refrain from transcending those limits.[48] The text from *The Seagull* just discussed is a case in point.

4.3.3.3 An Overall View of the Scene

What happens in this text, *Dramatically (and theatrically) speaking*, beyond the realm of sensual perception?

Talking and Playing. As we have seen, mother and daughter have a dialogue **about** Konstantín, with other soundless presences in the background. Polína's attempt to talk Konstantín into falling in love with Másha backfires as expected: he leaves the room with thundering silence, and Másha is angry with her mother because of this unsolicited lobbying and its inevitable failure.

So far the explicit, verbal text; however, undercurrents of wordless dialogues are in motion between and within all relevant personages.

The clash between the two ladies' *répliques* and Konstantín's silence is irreducibly *Dramatic*, i.e., *potentially theatrical*; it is untranslatable into the language of *narrative fiction*. Konstantín appears as refusing to stoop to their level, exercising passive self-defence with poise and conviction, as it were, against what appears by comparison as tactless blabber, for all its subjective sincerity. From the audience's standpoint, it is a case of **divided** empathy, so typical of Chekhovian characterisation (and noticed so often in the secondary literature): that subtle, evasive quality of multiple psychological and even ethical points of view, all equally (un)sympathetic.

The rest of Konstantín's dialogue with the two ladies, after his exit, is certainly involuntary; it is even nonexistent as far as he is concerned. For the audience, though, it does exist, starting with his piano-playing from a distance backstage (Chekhov takes pains in his stage direction to place the waltz in the third room deep backstage).[49] It is clear that Konstantín wants to find solace in solitude with his piano, playing a melancholy waltz (of course, a deliberate choice on Chekhov's part). He must know enough about the nature of sound to realise, at least subconsciously, that his playing would be heard in the room he has just left behind, but it seems that he couldn't care less. Yet Chekhov, as it were, 'imposes' the continuation of their exchange on stage by making his own dialogue with us as audience — taking place, of course, in our minds — more significant than whatever happens between the three stage personages.

It is in our imagination that Konstantín's invisible–metaphorical *melodic line* within this metaphorical *polyphony* takes shape, stretching as it does between two 'anchors': the moment of his exit, perceived by our eyes, and the moment of the first sound of the piano, perceived by our ears from a distance. Thus, his line/voice continues its uninterrupted course even after his exit, while the other 'melodic lines' — the dialogue between Polína and Másha — are heard. It is another instance of Chekhovian *presence through absence*, intricately distributed between the senses.

When encountering *The Seagull* for the first time, before we hear the first piano sounds, and before identifying them (courtesy of Polína, as we have seen), we reasonably expect his exit to be a real one, until a possible reappearance on stage. When we hear the very first piano sounds, we have no way of knowing for sure that he is the player, until Polína identifies him and interprets his state of mind. Thus we learn that (a) Konstantín is the player of the sounds we hear; (b) he tends to play the piano when he is gloomy/longing; (c) the playing is a text-bound, integral part of the author's discourse (rather than a production-bound addition by a director).

Thus the scene presents a dense dynamic network of longings and movements of feelings and emotions: Másha is longing for Konstantín; Polína (at this particular moment!) is longing for communication with her daughter, not least as compensation for her own unrequited love for Dr. Dorn, which is constantly on her mind; and Konstantín himself is full of sad longing and frustration, but to the extent that a woman is the object of these emotions, it is not Másha (Nína, and even his mother Arkádina, are more likely candidates); and there may be other, not directly romantic, reasons for his sad longings (e.g., his frustrations as a writer). The three personages are on the same stage, and within the fictional world they are in the same room at the same time, but their wishes and yearnings are worlds apart. Moving in different orbits, they are doomed never to communicate, never to have an emotional reunion.[50]

This powerful emotional 'polyphony' is the direct result of Chekhov's *realisation of the potentials of the Dramatic medium*.[51] On stage, this is carried out simultaneously; but even on page, where the verbal and non-verbal messages must be read in succession, they are meant to regroup in our minds and give us the experience of simultaneity in *TF*. In fact, in this case *TF*'s capacity to produce tangible simultaneity is just an effective way to impress upon the spectators, and the *TF*-aware readers, a situation of *NF simultaneity*, as just described: the non-communicative tangle between the personages is part of their emotional lives within the *fictional world* to which they belong. It would have been just the same if they had been personages in a story; but a play has the potential, which Chekhov realises, to make a more focused, immediate impact on its audience. Thus, this scene is, in a way, not only an instance of *Dramaticality*, but also of *dramaticalness*, through its *intensity*.

Technically, we perceive the non-verbal messages as semanticised, potentially verbalisable ones; however, by encoding only one of them verbally Chekhov creates *intelligible simultaneity*, which enables us to perceive the entire interaction and witness how messages modify and/or subvert each other to yield, *inter alia*, a separation between elements of sincerity and fake in Másha's verbal and non-verbal behaviour. It is quite difficult, if not impossible, to reach comparable results in narrative prose fiction; at least not with the same urgency and effectiveness.

This does not suggest that *Drama* has a durable and unqualified advantage over *narrative prose*, or vice versa. Each art has its own relatively strong **and** weak features, when compared to other arts; and for each criterion according to which one of them (e.g., *Drama*) proves more effective than another (e.g., *narrative prose*) there is another one, according to which the reverse applies. The foregoing analysis has shown how Chekhov makes the most of the specific advantages of *Drama*. In an analysis of a story of his (e.g., "A Little Joke" in chapter 5) his mastery of *narrative fiction* can equally demonstrate his ability to make the most of the specific advantages of that art.

Talking, Playing and Waltzing. The most shining example of Chekhov's feat in this scene is the moment when Másha's talking and waltzing and Konstantín's playing occur **simultaneously**. This exemplary moment is rich and intricate, both because at least three synchronised messages interact in it and because the message itself has its intrinsic complexity as an inner dialogue within a personage's mind.

This ending of the short quote ties together, as it were, all the threads woven earlier on. When Konstantín is longing for something/someone away from Másha, the music he plays is a "*melancholy waltz*"; yet for him, arguably, the emphasis is on *melancholy* (compatible with Polína's characterisation of his mood as *gloomy longing*), whereas the *waltz* element can perhaps be immaterial (though he may be sadly longing for a waltz with Nína). As for Másha, however, she — though wearing black "in mourning for her life" in the beginning of the play — ignores *melancholy* and focuses on *waltz*, i.e., a potentially romantic dance, intended for a couple. Intuitively, in her subconscious mind and wishful thinking, she feels invited to waltz with him. The irony of the situation is heartbreakingly poignant: the very act of waltz-playing that functioned for Konstantín as an escape from Másha's presence — from her and her other's clutches, as far as his subjective feelings are concerned — is interpreted subliminally by her as a message of tender closeness. True, she hears her mother's words; she is fully aware, in her **conscious** mind, that neither sense of Konstantín's «тоска» (gloom and longing) is inspired by her. Yet the love she bears to Konstantín makes her wallow intuitively and subconsciously in her own gloom and longing. She combines Konstantín's playing with her mother's verbal interpretation to deep-down delude herself that the gloomy longing of his waltz is after all directed at her; and indeed, the sound that originates "two rooms away" reaches and almost touches her tangibly,[52] and she responds readily and wholeheartedly to that 'invitation', which she subconsciously attributes to him, to join him in a waltz of gloom and longing. Thus Másha, never before asked by Konstantín the "May I have this dance?" question, makes those rounds of waltz, synchronised with his playing, forgetting how and why this playing had just come into the world. There is something almost surrealistic and delirious in her dance of half-a-couple, while the other half has just now literally turned his back on her. Indeed, mentally speaking, the personages create parallel lines, never to meet; they even get farther away from each other. Physically, however, Másha turns Konstantín, without his knowledge, and to his potential dismay, into her imaginary dancing partner,[53] as well as into her/their accompanying pianist. His music imposes itself on her ears, penetrating walls, because this is how sound works; her dancing imposes the idea of partnership on him, but only in her tormented mind and in the audience's *presence*, but in his *absence*.

Of course, none of it is clear to Másha. Moreover, synchronised with those dancing steps, her words disown unrequited love, both in general and in her own life: once unable to lay her eyes on Konstantín, she says, she would forget him; kind of "out of sight — out of mind". However, even the literal sense of her statement is undermined when she does not **see** him (simply because he is in another room), and yet her entire being is attentive to him — or, rather, not to the real him, but to his imprint in her mind and heart, to the loving Kóstia that she invented and has nurtured in her inner life. It is clearly not sufficient just "not to see him" in order to tear the powerful presence of this love out "by the roots". On a more general and deeper level, this is also another demonstration of Chekhov's incessant preoccupation with the contest between life "as it is" and as experienced in (day)dreams and imagination, wishes and yearnings, and his adamant refusal to declare the winner in this contest. Konstantín himself, before the curtain rises on his play in Act 1, speaks in favour of showing dreamed/imagined life on stage; Chekhov, in *The Seagull* itself, shows inner–emotional life (including imaginative art) as really **embedded in** real life; but elsewhere his jury is often out on the more general and philosophical question of the fact–fantasy divide. Typically, he likes to "present correctly" this problem, without solving it. This crucial question for Chekhov's very being as an artist, then, is also present in this brief and unbelievably semantically and emotionally loaded 'Masha's melancholy waltz-scene'.

Coming back to Masha's actual words, the last remarks interpret them too literally: she must be referring to a much longer and permanent kind of "not seeing"

Konstantín. Yet, Chekhov's *implied, non-verbal message* to the audience says that often in the theatre — and, by the logic of *mimesis*, also in life — words and verbal messages may be lying, and non-semantic gestures may be meaningfully truthful. It is while she verbally renounces her love, and while she is literally unable to see her beloved, that Másha responds with every fibre of her body (and soul) to the falsely alluring call of an imaginary seductive invitation to waltz, vividly *present* in her mind while being *absent* in any other respect, in *NF* and *NF* alike. It is too clear which of the two messages — the overt–verbal and the covert–intuitive — is to be trusted.[54]

4.4 *Concluding Remarks*

"*Dramas*" and "*dramatic*" *conflicts* can be, have always been, and will always be, created outside *Drama* as well as within it; therefore, they are not its *differentia specifica*. That said, "*Dramatic*" *Conflict* has always been typical of *Drama* and closely linked with it. Chekhov's *Drama*, it has been demonstrated, is not devoid of poignant conflicts that can even earn the adjective "*dramatic*", in the traditional sense; it is their 'internal location' — covertly in the spectators' minds rather than overtly on stage, and often within a personage's mind rather than between staged rivals — which is new.

The *differentia specifica* of *Drama* is indeed the *medium-heterogeneity* of its *theatrical realisation*. Chekhov may have been unaware of the crucial historical role he was playing, through the actual activity of writing down his plays, in the 'emancipation' of the non-verbal components of theatre from their dependence on their verbal counterparts.

Indeed, Chekhov marginalised *overt conflict* and other aspects of the "*dramatic*" in his mature plays, while nurturing the *specifically Dramatic*, whereas most of his predecessors, including the greatest ones of all ages, almost ignored the non-verbal potentials of Drama **in their written texts** and nurtured the *overtly "dramatic"*. The foregoing argument refers, of course, to the written Dramatic texts, as handed down to us throughout the ages. There is no doubt that non-verbal elements played an important role in the theatre from time immemorial to the present; the point is that until Chekhov much of the *presence* of non-verbal elements in the productions turned into an *absence* from the written texts. Chekhov's predecessors could easily, technically speaking, write detailed *stage directions* determining the non-verbal parts of the production that they must have had in mind; they could, but they didn't.[55] By relegating these components of theatre to the performers the playwrights were saying, in effect, that as far as they were concerned the verbal dialogue constituted **what** the play is, which is the author's province, whereas the non-verbal elements constituted **how** it should be performed, which is the province of the stage interpreters (directors, actors etc.). By writing non-verbal elements down, in a virtually unprecedented way, Chekhov made the opposite statement, i.e., that much of the non-verbal in theatre is an integral part of the written work, the responsibility of the playwright rather than the licence of his theatrical interpreters. This change, as we now know, is of great historical magnitude, and as far as we can foretell is with us to stay (indeed, Chekhov's successors in the 20th century tended to follow in his footsteps in this respect, and some of them — e.g., Beckett — wrote plays in which more written lines on the page were devoted to *stage directions* than to spoken dialogue). In spite of that, however, pre-Chekhov classics were the ones who earned an unchallenged status as the pillars of *Drama* throughout the ages, whereas Chekhov is constantly challenged as a playwright, mainly because of his deviations from overt *dramaticalness*. It is often forgotten that Chekhov authored some of the most exceptionally *Dramatic* scenes ever created since the dawn of humanity to the present.

The final answers to the questions posed at the beginning of this Chapter are by now so clear that they hardly need re-stating. The uniqueness of ***Drama*** within Chekhov's entire oeuvre lies mainly in the here-and-now simultaneous activation of heterogeneous senses, each with its own *modus operandi* in our cognition. As always in *Drama*, the absence of a narrating voice — whether in the first or the third person — adds to the work's immediacy, and in Chekhov's case it encourages us to listen with equal, impartial initial attentiveness to the subtleties of every personage[56] and to their complex interrelationships. The *dual fictionality* of Dramatic texts works for the multiplicity of perspectives, often more precisely differentiated, and occasionally less nuanced, than in some comparable situations in his narrative prose.

The uniqueness of **Chekhov** in world *Drama* lies, *inter alia*, in his being a major harbinger of new medium-specific awareness; he realised for written Drama horizons of medium emancipation, which had been hidden potentials for his predecessors. He gave a new meaning to the phenomena of *Dramaticality*, *Theatricality* and *dramaticalness* (as characterised above) by unprecedented activation of *two-tier fictionality*, and by internalising traditionally external conflicts.

This assessment is explicitly and predominantly *medium-oriented*; much of Chekhov's greatness resides in other aspects of his art, some of which are discussed elsewhere in this Book. In many of these other aspects his uniqueness as a dramatist is not Drama-specific; it is similar, or at least comparable, to his uniqueness as a writer of narrative fiction, against the background of the work of other great masters of the latter *super-genre*. Chekhov's particular uniqueness as a playwright, however, is manifest mainly in his *medium-specific* contributions to this *super-genre*, in ways different from his contributions to narrative prose. The two contributions are comparable in value, but different in nature. This specifically *Dramatic* aspect of his greatness has not been emphasised enough in the secondary literature, and as stated in the Introduction it is a primary aim here to draw attention to this crucial and relatively neglected aspect of his genius as a Dramatist.[57]

Indeed, in terms of quantity, Chekhov's output as a playwright perhaps constitutes a mere tenth of his entire literary corpus; yet from the perspective of his innovative approach towards the basic features of *genre* and *medium*, his overall impact on *Drama* and its history is more radical and unique than his impact on *narrative fiction*, which constitutes the other nine tenths.

Notes

1 This is Senelick's version for the Russian original «Я драматург неважный»; I prefer it to all other translations I have come across, e.g., Friedland's "I am a poor dramatist".

2 In the original, «вышла повесть»; Senelick's *novella* sounds to me better than some alternatives (*novel*, *story*), suggested by other translators. Perhaps *a narrative* is even more preferable in this specific context.

3 The distinction between the interconnected concepts of *Drama* and *Theatre*, and their derivatives, is obvious; for now, though, they can be treated interchangeably, since both are opposed to *narrative fiction*, on the one hand, and to non-verbal staged–performative art (e.g., dance, mime) on the other.

4 This difference between Chekhov's self-evaluations as playwright *vs.* storyteller may result, *inter alia*, from the relative rigidity of time-honoured prescriptive norms, rules and conventions in the tradition of *Drama*, opposed to the relative flexibility of analogous norms in the traditions of *narrative fiction*. Chekhov, it seems, often disobeyed the former in practice, but rarely backed his own practices with statements of theory and artistic ideology. Chapters 8 and 10 elaborate the issue more thoroughly.

5 I use the term *super-genre* because if *tragedy*, the *sonnet*, and the *novel*, for instance, are *genres*, then *Drama*, *Poetry* and *Narrative Prose* are their respective *super-genres*.

6 I am indebted to many basic studies and text-books in the theory of Drama and Theatre, and particularly to the seminal book by Manfred Pfister (1988 [1977]), for comprehensive discussions of rudimentary theoretical issues discussed here.

7 It should be noted though, that Chekhov did not repeat such statements in later years. I am indebted to Laurence Senelick for drawing my attention to this fact.

8 That is, with the text divided between named speakers, and with *stage directions*.

9 Unless otherwise stated, the deliberate point of reference here is modern usage, rather than original or previous phases of etymological history, or the sense(s) in which Chekhov might or would have used one term or another within the conventions of his time and place. The discussion here is about a conceptual state of affairs from our contemporary standpoint, much in the way that a Shakespearean or ancient Greek tragedy, for instance, can be analysed in modern terms (e.g., psychoanalytical, [post-]structuralist, etc.). Such practices do not generate anachronisms as long as modern views are not ascribed to the writer.

10 The etymological and semantic discussion here is based on entries in several dictionaries, lexicons and encyclopaedias, as well as on verbal intuition.

11 An analogous example can be found in the etymology of *Opera*, which originally meant a *work* or *piece* (in the artistic sense of these words), and later gradually became more restricted to its present sense, referring exclusively to the art, and any work of that art, that we call today by that name. In English, as in the case of *Drama*, reference to *Opera* as a whole is made without an article, and to a single instance of it (work/piece) is made with an article, definite or indefinite.

12 One can think of the senses and uses of nouns and verbs derived from *act* and *play* in English (*to act, an actor, acting* [as a name of the theatrical profession]; *to play, a play, a player*; etc.) and similar phenomena in other languages, as additional evidence for this bond.

13 For a discussion of an intricate case of Art–Reality interactions in Chekhov see Golomb 2012 (reproduced as Appendix below).

14 The division of the text on the printed page between personages is as characteristic and distinctive of *Drama* as its division between verse-lines is characteristic of *Poetry*. As a result, the printed texts of *Verse-Drama* are divided both between personages and between verse-lines.

15 Many studies of Chekhov's biography and the history of his stage work quote such reactions of his contemporaries. Tolstói's was perhaps the most famous one: he reportedly expressed the idea, that Shakespeare's plays are bad enough, but Chekhov's are even worse... Negative responses to Chekhov can be found, *inter alia*, in an illuminating account by Simon Karlinsky (1984), and in various notes in Senelick (1997, 2005 and 2006).

16 The debatable concept of *importance* is used here admittedly loosely, consensually–intuitively, though not arbitrarily: 'important **people**' are **mainly** kings, leaders, rulers, army generals etc., who can do things of considerable historical, social, political, military (etc.) magnitude by activating others with words that they literally utter (*speech acts* with performative and commanding power); the term 'important **things**' loosely refers here to the potentiality or actuality of making a tangible difference, or impact, affecting major course of factual and/or mental events in the life of an *individual* or a *collective*, as elaborated below throughout the Book, especially in 8.0.

17 To a limited extent, daily trivialities are shown, or referred to, even in Shakespeare, and certainly in the periods between his plays and Chekhov's; but these tend to be marginalised as momentary diversions, and/or prove, in the final analysis, crucially and even tangibly important. It is a matter of proportion that becomes a matter of substance: virtually nowhere in *non-comic Drama* before Chekhov was so much precious theatre time spent on such seeming irrelevancies as the repetitive mention of Balzac's wedding in Act 2 of *Three Sisters* (whose sheer repetitiveness gives it an incantation-like effect), or reading out loud lotto numbers in Act 4 of *The Seagull*, whose importance never becomes as obvious as is in quasi-comparable cases in Ibsen, for instance.

18 *Comedy* as such is not discussed in this study at all; in this context it is largely a world of its own, characterised *inter alia* by total reversals (rather than Chekhov's typical explorations and modifications) of intuitive scales of 'importance', as shown , *inter alia*, in Note 16 above, and in Chapter 8.

19 Of course one can find borderline cases and exceptions to this rule, but these at most modify rather than invalidate it. As usual, such generalisations apply as polar, rather than binary oppositions, i.e., they operate in scales of grey 'more *vs.* less', rather than in clear-cut distinctions of black-and-white 'yes *vs.* no': subjecting a text to tests based on certain criteria, it can be 'admissible' to Drama *more* or *less* than another text.

20 See Pfister 1988, section 4.6, pp. 140–154; with special reference to Chekhov, pp. 148–150.

21 This part of the dialogue is connected to Irína's unanswered statement about her age: whereas she tries to make everyone ignore her young age, he fakes an attempt to do the opposite.

22 This effect of arbitrariness is a tricky pitfall in Chekhov: even some of the most sensitive and sophisticated Chekhov scholars — notably the late A. P. Chudakóv (1983; see especially his Conclusion, pp. 217–221) — sometimes seem to fall for it. See, however, Popkin 1993, especially 17–52, for a significant study of Chekhov's misleading "insignificance" in his narrative prose.

23 This game, too, is a hybrid metaphor for the fusion between the pre-ordained and the random. An association to the lotto game in Act 4 of *The Seagull* comes to mind.

24 Senelick (2005, p. 272; 2006, p. 913, n. 33) comments on the "incongruity" resulting from the fact that Berdíchev was at the time almost entirely populated by Jews. There is indeed a dissonance between a Jewish *shtetl* of the time, with its reputation for provincialism, commercial clamour, and lack of elegance, on the one hand, and the great Parisian novelist on the other. Moreover, it is a Catholic wedding (with its connotation of durability) between a French man and a Polish lady, in a small town full of Jews,

within the predominantly Pravoslav [Orthodox] Ukraine — too many contradictions for one event, especially bearing in mind that Balzac died a few months after celebrating his marriage, which gives an air of a bitter joke to its durability. Granted, regular theatre audiences are unlikely to be acquainted with some of these ramifications of the repeated sentence; however, even the meanings that come more directly to mind provide a complex web of motivations for it.

25 Of course this, too, is no accident in relation to *Three Sisters*: the brigade finally moves to Poland, and in Act 4 Kulýgin is joking about the likelihood that Rodè would marry a Polish lady, just as Balzac did. Even Rodè's French (or at least French-sounding) name — though never uttered on stage (!) — may be echoed in Balzac's 'Frenchness', as it were, though this is a bit far-fetched, especially in the theatre, where this kind of purely literary–textual connection can hardly work.

26 Indeed, any analysis of such unpredictable texts smacks of hindsight wisdom: once Chekhov wrote it, an analyst is tempted to find "method in the madness", almost at all costs; therefore, readers are cautioned to double-check every interpretation. Yet, in principle, this is how Chekhov's texts really work on page and stage alike: they make retrospective sense to an addressee, once s/he is receptive of his kind of poetics. Through the accumulation of such quasi-arbitrary devices Chekhov makes a powerful non-verbal statement, inferable by the addressee, about how the well-designed and the arbitrary, the pre-ordained and the random, are intertwined in art and life alike (see Appendix).

27 This example is indeed telling, but such cases are by no means unique, or even rare, in all the major plays. Typical examples include, for instance, the scene after the failure of Konstantín's play in *The Seagull*, Act 1, the first and last dialogues in *Uncle Vánia*, the scene immediately preceding the announcement of the sale of the estate in *The Cherry Orchard*, and many other scenes in all the plays. The analytical techniques proposed here can be used to analyse those and virtually all other relevant instances, while making the necessary adjustments emanating from the uniqueness of each case.

28 See Pfister 1988, especially pp. 140–141, for a survey of *conflict-oriented theories of Drama*, notably Hegel's. In fact, there is hardly any talk about the conflict being *overt/explicit* as opposed to *covert/implicit*: in discussion of pre-Chekhov plays such distinctions are really unnecessary. With such plays in mind, it goes without saying that a conflict should be *overt*. Moreover, the term *dramaticality* itself is rarely used, though the concept and phenomena denoted by it are discussed under other headings. Indeed, "What's in a name?"

29 The 20th century developed unprecedented diversity of forms, norms and content, in all arts, and therefore the expectation of conflict in modern plays is no longer a binding norm; yet, it has not been replaced by any other norm, so that a play with a 'good-old *central conflict*' still meets, and activates, a ready set of expectations. The same applies to traditional *figurative* styles, and even traditional *perspective*, in the visual arts, to *tonality* and even *functional harmony* in music, etc.: these 'basics' can be found in 20th-century works, alongside more innovative languages, in all arts, as shown in 10.4 .

30 The present study is indebted to many previous discussions of the *evolution of Chekhov's art* (Donald Rayfield's apt term) and *poetics* (mainly Chudakóv's term). See, for instance, Magarshack 1980 [1952] (especially pp. 159–173) and 1960; Rayfield 1975, especially pp. 201–229; all discussions of the plays in Rayfield 1999; Pitcher 1973 (especially pp. 69–112); Gilman 1995; Chudakóv 1983 [1973]; Bitsilli 1983, 115–123; Kataev 2002, and many other studies, for which Chekhov's development in play-writing is a major or side issue. They are too numerous to be given due credit for every single instance of closeness of thought or inspiration, agreement or disagreement.

31 Moreover, some of the personages, events and phenomena in *Ivanov* remotely resemble some of Ibsen's. Thus, for instance, Gregers Werle's ruthless, even callous pursuit of "Truth" at all costs, with its hypocritical, sanctimonious overtones and fatal consequences (in *The Wild Duck*, 1884) is quite comparable to an analogous combination of character traits with disastrous consequences, in the person of Dr. L'vov in *Ivanov*. The two playwrights even seem to detest these personages of theirs in analogous ways. This analogy is much more significant and thought-provoking than the obvious but comparatively superficial one, which some critics — from Chekhov's time (when he was explicitly accused of "Ibsenism" — see Henry 1965, 32; Seyler 1965, 168) to ours (see Seyler 1965's simplistic discussion) — have been tempted to draw between the two bird-plays, *The Wild Duck* and *The Seagull*. Most of these comparisons tend to ignore enormous differences between the two playwrights and their respective plays, that outweigh any similarities between them by far.

32 This process is closely linked to developments in other aspects and components of Chekhov's poetics, notably *characterisation*, as discussed in Chapter 5 and in Golomb 2001. Analogous developments in his *ending* techniques are discussed in Chapter 9.

33 This subject has been discussed widely in the literature, with different criteria and approaches applied, some similar to the present study's, but none, to my knowledge, identical with it (e.g., Magarshack 1952, Senelick 1997, Pitcher 1973; and this is an extremely partial list).

34 Some scholars and practitioners refer to written plays as *scripts*, *playtexts* or *playscripts*, by analogy to *screenplays* or *scripts* for films. This claim is discussed in 3.0.6.2 and its Notes 11, 12 and 14.

35 In a different context, this quality in *Drama* is also referred to as *syncretic* in terms of the fusion, or at least combination, of such complementary contraries as *spatial vs. temporal*, *auditory vs. visual*, *representational vs. non-representational*, etc. See, for instance, Žirmunskij [Zhirmúnskiï; Zhirmunsky] 1966 [1925], 19–21. The same term, *syncretic*, has also been applied directly and explicitly to Chekhov's art; see Winner 1977. The theoretical book by Manfred Pfister (1988 [1977]), once again, is a seminal study of this topic.

36 Exceptions — like graphic poetry, whose visual appearance and organisation on the page are designed to be significant to the eye, and languages (e.g., Chinese) whose written characters function graphically–pictorially rather than phonetically, and other systems of graphic visualisation in verbal texts — are irrelevant to the discussion of Chekhov's art, and therefore do not concern us here.

37 The following is a brief, condensed, admittedly simplified reminder of discussions of such concepts as *possible worlds* (vs. *real world*) in literary aesthetics, and *internal* vs. *external frames/fields of reference*, as developed in past decades by Benjamin Harshav (see especially his studies from 1982 and 1984, revised in 2007). See Appendix (Golomb 2012) for a more detailed application of the latter conceptual framework to the analysis of Chekhov's plays.

38 In my discussion of *fictionality* I am particularly indebted to Harshav 2007, especially pp. 1–31, 128–139, and 161–173. His "'double-decker'/'double-level' model of literary reference" is structurally similar to, though not identical with, my *dual fictionality* in this Subsection. One of the differences stems from the fact that Harshav's model is inspired by the process of reading literary (mainly narrative) texts, whereas my conceptual framework results from, and applies to, the peculiarities of reading plays.

39 The fact that Shakespeare, Molière, and indeed Chekhov, as most other playwrights, had a specific physical theatre and specific actors in mind when writing their plays is beside the point in principle, and even more so when we consider the actual reading

process of a reader separated from the author by miles and miles in space and years, sometimes centuries, in time. Whatever specific theatre space and players, if any, the playwright might have had in mind when writing the play, they are highly unlikely to play any role in future readers' minds, and are therefore not part of **the text's** referential mechanism.

40 In many cases, in such theatrically professional reading *TF* would merge with ***non-fiction*** reading, activating specific theatre space and other here-and-now details in the professional reader's mind; and, indeed, the mental images produced in such a reading process are verifiable and falsifiable against the real objects and components of the specific physical theatre that an individual performer is engaged in.

41 This is **not** what I would recommend as translation for a stage production of the play, nor even for a printed version of it in English. The Russian word Chekhov uses here — *москует* — invokes dual semantic fields, one related to *sadness* and the other to *longing*. All English translations I have consulted ignore the latter (using words like "sad", "depressed", "melancholy"). Avraham Shlonsky's translation into Hebrew, on the other hand, does the opposite — the word is rendered as *longing*, no sadness suggested. My English 'version', made exclusively for the purpose of this analysis, is admittedly clumsy; my sole purpose here is to serve the interpretation I am about to propose, in which *longing* and *sadness* are equally important. This is one of the cases where an adequate translation, especially for the stage, is impossible, and one of the two meanings probably has to go for the sake of reasonable flow of the dialogue. Even in a printed version I would reject the likes of the version printed here; at most, I would supply a footnote…

42 We have at least three additional personages whose background *presence through absence* is suggested via analogies: Medvedénko, Másha's unloved husband; Shamráïev, her father, unloved by his wife Polína and his daughter alike; and Dr. Dorn, Polína's beloved (Chekhov's evasiveness leaves it open whether he is her lover) and Másha's confidant. By similar, less direct analogy, the tacit presence of other unrequited lovers can be added, but these are less relevant to the present discussion.

43 The focus here is not the more frequent phenomenon (which is also more frequently discussed) of verbal–musical interaction as in vocal music, or in programme music. As we shall see, Chekhov created here a very specific kind of sophisticated and subversive verbal–musical interaction.

44 As a general rule, Chekhov hardly ever trusts his personages enough to make us take their words at face value; moreover, Polína is, in fact, one of his poorest mind readers. However, in this particular case, her point is corroborated by other evidence in the play. As argued in various contexts elsewhere in the Book, Chekhov often gives a *reliable statement* to an *unreliable personage*, or vice versa, as part of the system of audience-challenging techniques he employs, to sharpen our awareness and make it work overtime. In his poetics almost nothing is taken for granted; everyone must be double-checked for reliability, and everything must be tested for validity.

45 The cognitive reasons why non-verbal simultaneity can whereas verbal simultaneity cannot be intelligible are beyond the scope of this discussion. Suffice it to say, as a rough generalisation, that the informative nature of verbal communication, which is its very *raison d'être*, results in greater semantic load, and is largely responsible for the mind's need to give its undivided attention to each verbal message separately, whereas non-verbal messages occupy less cognitive space or volume in the mind, and need less attention span to be processed.

46 It is a matter for experimentation to determine how many such messages can be processed intelligibly, under what conditions, etc.; the present Section deals with prin-

ciples in theory, rather than with their applied experimental verification. I am not aware of experiments checking these matters in the perception of canonised, highly sophisticated *Drama*, reaching its peaks of complexity in plays by Shakespeare, Chekhov, and masters of comparable stature. The present discussion, then, is admittedly speculative in this respect, though it is compatible with many intuitive statements and practices in Chekhov studies and performance.

47 In this Chekhov radically differs from some 20th playwrights (for instance, Beckett in his *Play*), who deliberately create *verbal simultaneity*, inevitably leading to *staged unintelligibility*, as a serious critique of human communication and its limitations. Such unintelligibility used to be an exclusively comic effect in previous generations.

48 One of the most intriguing ways of comparing and contrasting various types of poetics in the arts is to analyse different *organisations of complexity*, typical of one author compared to another, or even one art compared to another: major similarities and differences between arts (e.g., music vs. literature), and between great creators of art, can be followed along these lines (e.g., Chekhov *vs.* Shakespeare, Bach *vs.* Palestrina, etc., are examples discussed in 10.4.2).

49 If I were to direct this scene, I would have the sound of Konstantín's footsteps gradually fade out during the mother–daughter dialogue until the beginning of the waltz, to make the stage-direction suggesting a piano located "two rooms away" — i.e., deep backstage — vividly audible.

50 This state of affairs is foreshadowed in the beginning of the play when Medvedénko says to Másha (Act 1): "My soul and yours have no mutual points of convergence" — Senelick's English version here (2005, p. 137; 2006, p. 744) captures Medvedénko's gratuitous choice of pompous vocabulary. Indeed, Chekhov often generates in his audience a precisely balanced fusion of empathy and distancing, e.g., when he lets the 'right' personage say the 'wrong' words, or vice versa, or when a serious or even sad situation is rendered in laughable words (for instance, at the play's opening, discussed in 3.1.4). The absence of ability to engage in human communication is no laughing matter, even if it is introduced at first as "no mutual points of convergence".

51 A musical analogy that can come to mind here is the *operatic ensemble*, as developed mainly from the 18th century and onwards, notably by Mozart: a group of personages sing simultaneously different words, set to different melodic and rhythmic lines, all harmonised according to the musical aesthetics of the age, but often retaining individual peculiarities of each line belonging to a different personage, to match the different, often contrasting, texts and emotional attitudes.

52 In *Uncle Vánia*, Act 2, there is another reference to the physicality of a voice, the potential synæsthetic fusion of sound and touch, in an emotionally analogous context: Sónia, another woman in unrequited love, a few seconds after the man she loves, Ástrov, has left the room, is saying: «Голос его дрожит, ласкает... вот я чувствую его в воздухе.» ["His voice throbs, caresses... there, I can still feel it in the air"]

53 If I were to direct this scene, I would have 'my' Másha hold one arm in a gesture of embrace around the body of an absent partner, whose *mode of existence* resembles that of the chairs in Ionesco's play, whereas the other arm is 'meeting' his nonexistent hand (as in a real waltz), while waltzing alone to the melancholy tune.

54 Yet, this is context-bound; one cannot generalise that Chekhov **always** makes non-verbal statements more reliable than verbal ones. A counter example is the communication among *Three Sisters'* title roles, analysed in 6.2.1.

55 Shakespeare, Molière, and other major playwrights of previous centuries were actively involved in the production of their texts, and may have thought that committing their oral instructions to paper was practically unnecessary. However, by the same token,

they could have relied on their actors' memory and refrained from publishing plays in the first place. Whatever their conscious thoughts of the matter might have been, the very act of writing/publishing has an element of addressing posterity, and in this context the demarcation line between present spoken text and absent stage directions is telling.

56 It is a separate project — which is anyway more problematic when the text is studied in translation — to analyse the subtleties of Chekhov's **verbal** characterisation of his personages. In certain cases one can sense the individual speech-rhythms of each. Thus, for instance, Konstantín in *The Seagull* tends to repeat the same word or phrase three times; it is amazing that this tendency of his is also heard through Nína's voice, when she recites **his** play: "cold, cold, cold" etc. (in the brief excerpt that constitutes the entire textual representation of 'Konstantín's play' there are four instances of three consecutive repetitions of the same word!). In performance, it may be a good idea to make the Nína actress subtly imitate his intonation in uttering these repetitions. Arkádina, his mother, has characteristic speech-rhythms of her own: for instance, she likes the phrase-construction "not X but Y". Trigórin — curiously, similarly to Konstantín — is also inclined to repetitions of the same word or phrase. There are of course other examples. Such speech patterns can provide invaluable guidance to actors working on a character — another evidence of the consummate *Dramatist* that Chekhov was.

57 A subject that is closely connected with Chekhov's play-writing is his attitude and practice in relation to *Tragedy* and *Comedy*, i.e., to the problem of *Dramatic Genres*. The *medium-oriented* focus of the discussion in this Chapter has left little room for a complementary focus on *genre* here; it is offered in Chapter 10.

CHAPTER

5

Character and Characterisation *(Who?)*

The very fact that a Chekhov character expresses an opinion
is reason enough to dissociate Chekhov from it.

(Nilly Mirsky[1])

5.0 Introductory Remarks

5.0.1 Preliminary Truisms[2]

All texts and all arts are — to use a Lincoln-inspired style — "of people, by people,
to people, from people"; that is, all their creators/authors/addressers, all their recip-
ients/addressees/perceivers/audiences, and all other agents involved in their
production, execution and perception–reception (for example, performers, where
applicable), are human beings. Moreover, all arts are also primarily **about** people;
at least indirectly, but more often explicitly and directly, especially where *reference, mimesis, fictionality* and *"aboutness"* are relevant.[3] The art of literature —
in all its facets, types and genres, including *fictional Drama* — usually produces
texts that create *fictional worlds*, referred to by such terms as *Possible Worlds,
Internal Frames/Fields of Reference*, and by any other relevant terminology prevalent in the academic literature (fuller discussions are offered in Chapters 4, 6 and
10). In literary texts, thus broadly viewed, the nature of *characters* and *characterisation* is a crucial factor in characterising the specificity of the texts themselves,
and in distinguishing between periods, trends, genres, and individual authors'
styles and artistic systems. In addition to people-like *fictional personages*, communication and *semiosis* in narrative and dramatic fiction include *implied*[4] persons,
rarely mentioned explicitly in the texts but inferable from them.

5.0.2 *Character vs. Characterisation*: Connections and Differences

Character and *characterisation* are two interconnected but distinct phenomena in
verbal–fictional texts.

    Character (=personage)[5] usually refers to a **static** entity — the type of fictionalised person(s) selected to inhabit a fictional world — and relates to the question *who?* (e.g., in phrases like "a typical Chekhov character" or "a Dickens type"). Thus, as a general rule, the fictional worlds of non-comic plays by Shakespeare and his predecessors are dominated by major personages of noble birth in positions of power. One can also make statements attempting to characterise the psychological profile of a typical personage created by Shakespeare, Ibsen, Chekhov, etc.; all such statements are basically static, referring to a fixed human– fictional entity. The term *static* itself refers to the final, hindsight perception of the character: the medium of *theatre* and *Drama*, especially its verbal component, is temporal by definition, whether on page or on stage; however, when this temporal unfolding adds up details and character-traits cumulatively, gradually completing some kind of pre-determined jigsaw puzzle, the end-product is 'assembled' and crystallised in our minds as a static anthropomorphic construct. Yet, when the same temporal nature of the medium is used to change a personage's character traits, attitudes etc., so that certain elements — usually, presented later in the text, and anyway referring to later stages in the temporal order of the fictional world — not merely add areas not covered previously in that temporal order, but rather modify, negate, replace or undermine those previous elements, we perceive the character as *dynamic*, as 'a different/changed person' from the one that inhabited earlier parts of the fictional world (usually, there is a correspondence between earlier and later stages in the temporal order in the fictional world and the order of presentation in the text (*fábula* and *siuzhét*, respectively, in *Russian-Formalist* parlance), but the reverse can also occur — typically, when *flashback* is involved). The present discussion is primarily concerned with the *dynamic unfolding of static characters*; *dynamic characters* — i.e. changing ones — are significant, but less frequent, especially in non-comic Drama; in Chekhov they are very rare indeed.[6] Another type of terms referring to the static aspect of *character* can further illustrate the art-specific nature of this concept: adjectives like *central* or *marginal*, extendable to *major* or *minor*, are typically applied to the noun *character* (or *personage*), whereas they are hardly applicable to real persons.

Such adjectives as *central/major* or *marginal/minor* imply the idea of a *frame*, which is an art-specific concept in this context:[7] *centrality* or *marginality* can have a meaning only within, and in relation to, a framed space, object or concept, whose frame focuses our attention on elements within it more than on ones that exist or operate across its *boundaries*. Even when terms such as *central* or *marginal* are applied to real persons, the literal or figurative image of a framed entity comes to mind: thus, if someone is 'central' within a group of people, an institution, a defined process, etc., that group, institution, or process is conceived of as enclosed within a frame — and therefore the metaphor of centrality or marginality can work in our minds. One cannot speak of a real person as 'central' or 'marginal' without referring to the framed entity within which these adjectives apply to that person; for that reason no one is 'marginal' in relation to his/her own life, which is a frame defined by that person's centrality in relation to it. In this context, it is of special interest to recall that in *Uncle Vánia*, at the end of Act 2, Yeléna Andréïevna characterises herself as an "episodic character" (i.e., a *minor*, *marginal* one) in her own life. This application to reality, and its (lack of) "dramas", of a term that belongs in *fictional Drama* is very clever, sarcastic, and subversive to the point of absurdity: Yeléna is definitely a major/central character within *Uncle Vánia,* who nonetheless claims to be a marginal/minor one in her own 'real life' — a 'life' that, in turn, exists only in Chekhov's fictional *Uncle Vánia*...[8]

Indeed, reality — unlike *possible worlds* of fiction — is experienced as unframed, or at least as having loose, fuzzy boundaries: thus, for instance, the entire human race at a certain point in time is connected, at least potentially, by an endless chain of acquaintances (A knows B who knows C who knows someone in China, whose links of acquaintances eventually, or at least potentially, embraces the entire Chinese people, etc.), whereas fictional personages in a play, or even in an epic novel or film, can be acquainted only with the other personages framed within that fictional world (borderline cases do not invalidate the principles of this distinction). In Chekhov's plays, as will be seen in Section 2 below, *centrality* is intensely based on intra-textual evidence, upholding the experience that the text is a framed, relatively self-contained, aesthetic object.

Unlike *character*, the concept of *characterisation* is usually connected with the question *how?* — of course, closely linked to *who?* — rather than with *who?* alone; in other words, it is related to techniques used by an author to create the distinctiveness of any given character (or groups of characters). *Characterisation* is therefore *dynamic* in nature, since such techniques are realised in processes unfolding in time, though the end-product — the *character* — is usually mentally reconstructed, with hindsight, as *static*.

Interconnectedness between the two concepts can also be illustrated through a major distinction between three ways of *characterisation*, based on three conceptions of *character*: (A) *individual*, (B) *collective*, and (C) *universal*.[9] (A) is self-explanatory: it refers to (combinations and clusters of) traits unique, or at least specific, to one single personage, distinguishing him/her from others; (B) refers to traits shared, in principle, by all, and only, members of a given group of humans;[10] (C) indeed refers to humanity as a whole, and applies to traits and features shared by all humans. It may seem surprising at first, that (A) and (C) tend to be closer to each other, and relatively distinct from (B): a thorough look at one human individual, even at his/her idiosyncratic traits, is likely to yield a view of universally human features more readily than a view of features typical of any partial group, however large, to the exclusion of other groups. Even an examination of that individual's group-related traits would often tell us more about the universal nature of group-related traits in individuals than about any particular group/collective and its exclusive characteristics. Differences between individuals are a universally-human phenomenon whereas focusing, or generalising, on differences between groups tends to blur the distinctiveness of individuals and the common traits of all humans alike.

In this context, Chekhov is a 'characteriser' concerned with (implicit as well as explicit) manifestations of (A) and (C) much more than with (B): this is one of **his** character-traits as a universally human and genuinely humanistic writer. The characterisation techniques employed by him, to which this Chapter is dedicated, are made (*inter alia* of course, and probably intuitively and inadvertently) to achieve a goal of characterising humanity as a whole largely through **its** character-trait as being reflected in/through the single individuals who make it up in the first place.

5.1 An Anatomy of Characterisation: No Joking Matter

5.1.1 "A Little Joke" — an Epitome of Chekhovian Poetics

My discussion of characterisation in Chekhov's plays starts with a reading of "A Little Joke" (1886/1899),[11] one of his short stories, and the only Chekhov story discussed in detail in this Book. This brief story is in many ways "*Chekhovism* in a nutshell": there are few texts in Chekhov's oeuvre that match it in displaying so much of his poetics with such brevity, clarity, intensity and concentration. From this angle the story is a rare gift that Chekhov, of course unwittingly, gave to future analysts of his work; it is an enigma why it has received so little critical and scholarly attention, to the best of my knowledge.[12]

"A Little Joke" epitomises Chekhov's art in some of its crucial aspects, observable more extensively in much longer works of fiction and drama that he authored. ***Thematically***, it focuses on the precarious balance and interaction between delusion (sometimes bordering on illusion),[13] fantasy and wishful thinking on the one hand, and factual reality on the other; ***psychologically***, it focuses, through its characters, on the clash between two diametrically opposed exclusively-human needs: on the one hand, to indulge in self-deception and self-delusion, especially in conjunction with the need for love, and, on the other hand, to expose the truth and reject delusion and deception; in its ***tone***, it has the elusive, quasi-pardoxical blend of humour and seriousness, of light-hearted jest and agonising poignancy — another hallmark of Chekhov's art; in its ***composition***, it has the no less specifically-Chekhovian blend of iron-clad planning and design with an occasional misleading effect of a loose, somewhat arbitrary collection of details; in its choice of ***characters***, it demonstrates Chekhov's almost permanent focus on people who, despite enormous differences between them, share a severely limited ability for self-awareness; in its ***characterisation*** (the major subject of this Chapter), it manifests Chekhov's preference for *reciprocal* techniques, whereby different personages are made to characterise each other, mainly through (*implicit* and *explicit*) *analogy*, at least as much as they characterise themselves, and to place each other in perspective from complementary angles; and in its ***overall effect*** it displays Chekhov's adamant refusal to meet the needs of naïve or simple-minded readers[14] by resolving ambiguities, dispelling doubts deliberately infused into the text, or detracting from its open-endedness by answering questions that are inherently unanswerable. In short, the story epitomises Chekhov's treatment of humans — whether fictional personages or real readers and audiences.

5.1.2 Chekhov's Poetics and *Dramatic Irony*: Interplay between *Author, Perceiver/Addressee*, and *Personage/Character*

In juxtaposing *perceivers* and *personages*, and in seemingly bonding with the former behind the backs of the latter, Chekhov creates an effect similar to the time-honoured rhetorical device of *dramatic irony*; however, this device functions in special ways within Chekhov's unique artistic system. Traditional *dramatic irony* usually applies to gaps in privileged information: the *perceiver*, at a given moment, knows facts unknown to the *personages* about their situation; normally, such knowledge has little, if anything, to do with the perceivers' circumstances, thus encouraging them to feel superior to the personages. In Chekhov,[15] conversely, the knowledge granted to the perceivers and withheld from the personages is psychological rather than factual; it is withheld from the latter not because it is inaccessible to them, but because of basic flaws in their ability for self-awareness. In other words, this type of knowledge is about universals of the human psyche; these, by definition, have everything to do with any perceiver's innermost world as a human being. Indeed, in Chekhov too, granting this type of knowledge to the perceivers while exposing its absence in the personages creates in the former some sense of superiority towards the latter, which is checked and balanced by being part of a complex and highly elusive combination of empathy, sympathy, identification, detachment, estrangement, and other conflicting emotions. The process just described takes place because the 'we-know-better' type of superiority in the perceivers soon enough proves no less self-deceptive than any of the mental tricks that the personages play on themselves and on each other. The mental process in the perceivers comes full circle, then: once they realise that, at least potentially, they are as gullible as the personages, they can sense their shared humanity with them. This is in fact part of a significant feature of Chekhov's brand of *Mimesis* (this concept is discussed from different perspectives elsewhere in the Book). Indeed, to the extent that the fictional world in a play or a story serves as a model for the world of human reality, Chekhov's model characterises this world by abundance of personages deficient in capability for self-awareness; but to the extent that the entire chain of theatrical *semiosis* and communication (from *author* via *fictional world* to the *end-perceiver*) is the model for human reality, then the two *outer, non-fictional* links in this chain that are still embedded in the text — ***implied author (IAu)*** and ***implied** perceiver/addressee reader/spectator/audience* — are deemed to possess superior psychological awareness (though, significantly, their ability for **self**-awareness cannot be tested through the fictional work — a fact that once again undermines their claim for superiority). Thus Chekhov's world of humans is at the same time inferior and superior in this respect.

How does this *semiotic–communicational chain/process* work? At first, indeed, we may feel superior to Chekhovian personages when we see what they fail to see **about themselves**; we tend to say to ourselves: it is 'under their noses', how come they don't see it? However, this is precisely the convincing point Chekhov is making: one's own faults and problems, especially mental ones, are often the hardest to observe, identify, and be aware of. Now Chekhov encourages us to put ourselves "in the personages' shoes" (while retaining our identity) and **to doubt** whether we would possess more self-awareness in those circumstances. The question is real, not rhetorical: it is typical of Chekhov to inspire doubts and questions in his addressees, rather than to affirm or negate outright an assertion, embedded implicitly or explicitly in a text or situation. In this case, Chekhov does not imply unequivocally that we either would, or would not, be more self-aware than the personages if we were in their shoes; he just poses the question implicitly but emphatically. In fact, Chekhov makes us think something like *"there but for the grace of God go I"*, or he is saying to us, as it were, that only those who have never daydreamed or deluded themselves have the right to throw the first stone of supe-riority at these personages. Such an effect is achieved — simply, truthfully and artfully at the same time — by the sheer universally-human emotional nature of the subject-matter. It is likewise the result of things that the personages are unaware of, and the cognitive processes of attentively perceiving a fictional world on page or stage.

Thus, in exposing delusions and internal conflicts around his personages, Chekhov displays another exclusively-human trait: the clash between two conflicting needs, the temptation to evade the truth and the commitment to pursue it, which is just as universally human as the two needs themselves (though humans vary considerably in the nature and magnitude of such a clash, in its makeup, in the balance of power between the clashing forces, and in its outcome, if any). Our awareness of the need for delusion is part of the truth that we uncover in us, just as our denial of this need is in itself part of our delusion. Perhaps the major, final conclusion is that these two mental forces are doomed to coexist perpetually; that the exposure of delusion keeps it in check, but does not cancel it out. This is how, in our relationships with Chekhov's personages, empathy and sympathy on the one hand and detachment, dissociation and a sense of superiority on the other hand cohabit in our minds; moreover, these two emotional clusters even generate, enhance and perpetuate each other, to the point of becoming inseparable, albeit seemingly opposite, sides of the same attitudinal coin.

Granted, the situation in this story is extreme, and lacks *"slice of life"* verisimil-itude on a superficial level. Thus, it is hard for ordinary readers to put themselves "in the shoes" of the personages, asking themselves, for instance, how they would respond to a deliberately muffled declaration of love (the challenge facing Nádia, the story's 'heroine'): the question itself looks contrived, virtually absurd. However, it is precisely the extremity of the specific events of this story which lays bare basic, almost raw emotions checked by a subtle web of highly artistic struc-turation; it throws into bold relief what amounts to a Chomskyan *deep structure* of a human universal — that powerful yet subtle link between the quests for love, delusion, and truth. This link, essential to Chekhov's world, is the very essence of "A Little Joke", and as such it creates an intuitive and immediate bond with the innermost worlds of its readers, as will be presently shown.

5.1.3 The First-Person *Narrator*'s Function: Preliminary Considerations

The story unfolds mainly as an exercise, or a study, in the 'anatomy' of the self-delusion-dominated[16] clusters of needs and clashes just discussed. While it manages to develop several other themes and thematic clusters (e.g., different images of the quest for love in men and women, fickleness *vs.* determination, almost sadistic callousness *vs.* compassion, and some others), its overriding super-ordinate thematic cluster focuses on (self-) delusion: a cluster that organises the entire story and motivates its sequence of events, while other themes can be subsumed under it.

Obviously, there are two major personages: Nádia[17] and the Narrator (since he is nameless, in what follows the term *narrator* will be used both as a name and as a literary function, the former usually capitalised, and the latter usually italicised). He assumes several roles: a *narrator* in the present, an active personage in the past, and a past and present observer, of himself and of Nádia, in the past and in the present (though this is not an exhaustive list of his roles). Since the story is told in the first person, all we know about Nádia comes to us through his prism. But, being the epitome of an *unreliable first-person narrator*,[18] he unwittingly exposes his weaknesses throughout the entire story, most of which are subsumed under the general weakness of extremely deficient self-awareness. We tend at first to believe whatever he tells us, simply because he is our sole source of information, and generally narrators in fictional stories enjoy a head-start in gaining their readers trust. However, soon enough we cannot ignore elements of inconsistency and improbability in his account, which encourage us to doubt and scrutinise everything he is saying. As always with *unreliable narrators*, what he says (here, mainly about Nádia) can be viewed along an axis of credibility and reasonability — ranging from undisputable solid fictional facts (e.g., that the two protagonists went tobogganing in the winter), via plausible, and subsequent less-and-less plausible, expressions and interpretations of events, to the most unlikely conjectures and speculations about thoughts and feelings, hers or his own. I shall return to the analysis of the Narrator in 5.1.5 below.

5.1.4 Nádia: Inheriting the Wind?

Bearing this caveat in mind, let us look at Nádia, as we see her through him, and beyond. In her attitude there is a basic line of development from the story's beginning to its end. A surprising analogy comes to mind: in the nature and intensity of the clash between clinging to delusion and pursuing truth she is reminiscent of Sophocles' Oedipus. A closer analogy is Chekhovian: Sónia in *Uncle Vánia*, in whom Chekhov exposes a largely conscious conflict between these two emotional needs.[19] Nádia is caught in a similar tangle; but, unlike Sónia who soliloquises about her feelings, Nádia's thoughts and feelings known to us are only those that the *Narrator* chooses to verbalise, to report, or to speculate about. Of course, these choices of his are also part of how Chekhov characterises him.

Nádia's growing need for preserving her delusion/illusion is emphasised by the Narrator time and again; half-way through the story he even uses the analogy of addiction to alcohol or morphine. However, up to a point the young lady does not behave even remotely like an addict. She is sober enough to conduct a scientifically valid step-by-step test or experiment: first, she repeats the previous procedure in order to check whether its inconclusive results are reproduced. When this fails and the results are again inconclusive, she tries to isolate the variable that precludes conclusiveness most crucially: she focuses her look on his mouth and lips, but he manages to make this inconclusive again. Now comes her next, unexpectedly bold step: she goes tobogganing on her own, further isolating a highly relevant variable, namely his presence. This, according to him,[20] proves inconclusive again: it seems that he manages to gain *presence* even through his *absence*. Throughout these stages we witness a battle of wits between the two: she is committed to fact-finding just as he is committed to evading and deluding her, pre-empting her every move.

However, the last stage in this battle is a turning point (henceforward the story's *watershed*). Unexpectedly in terms of his unfolding characterisation, the Narrator respects her boldness and resolve, and risks his entire delusion-enterprise by allowing her this solo-tobogganing (which he could easily have pre-empted by making her aware of his presence — e.g., by waving at her and/or calling her name — and joining her for the slide). As for her, from this *watershed* moment on, she no longer cares that much for reality, and consciously indulges in 'controlled delusion': she is less and less surprised, her anticipations becoming more and more routine and repetitive. Excitement is probably still there, but it takes the form of self-fulfilling prophesy. At any rate, she is now more and more in control, thus overturning his short-lived *presence-through-absence* victory. Thus, his presence gradually loses its emotional relevance, not only because she is discouraged by her previous failures to discover the truth, but also, and mainly, because the sounds that she herself regards (albeit erroneously[21]) as delusion, or even illusion, become a subjectively psychological truth for her. As a result, factual truth is of much lesser interest to her. Indeed, from her standpoint it is quite a valid reality-test to conclude that the sounds are produced by "the wind", not only because of her successive failures to establish their origin, but mainly because she reasonably assumes that the Narrator's plan to depart from town and part company with her for good means that he just could not be the one who uttered the words of love.

Notwithstanding initial indications to the contrary, Nádia's tenacity in search of factual truth in the earlier part of the story, prior to its *watershed*, is compatible with her subsequent resolve to indulge in the delusion/illusion, since all these actions and attitudes are the result of her conscious decision, and she does not allow any of them to obstruct the course of her life. This resoluteness is incompatible only with her image as a 'romantic dreamer' — a fragile, delicate, stereotyped feminine creature, addicted to the sweet sound of words of love, as suggested by the *Narrator* (in the earlier, 1886 version of the story, this image is explicitly associated with generalisations about women; in the later, 1899 version, it is implicitly suggested as an individual character trait of this specific young woman, without any hint that she represents all women in any way).[22] The Narrator is unaware that he is creating a contradiction, in spite of himself, between this image and the determined young lady emerging from his own reporting of the facts.[23] Nádia's resolve to dispel the mystery once and for all is more powerful than her fears of tobogganing, and even than her need for love-words at this stage, as she proceeds "doggedly" to climb the stairs to carry out this new stage in her 'fact-finding mission'. Her failure to get results does not diminish the impact of her resolve on the reader, especially as this constitutes a turning point (*watershed*) in her entire attitude.

It is first and foremost through Nádia's character that Chekhov raises the question whether factual truth is invariably and unconditionally preferable to an emotional truth emanating from controlled, conscious self-deception.[24] In

Chekhov's world this is not a rhetorical question, but a real and crucial one; it is also genuinely unanswerable, but Chekhov seems to have insisted on asking himself and his addressees this type of questions, regardless of their inherent unanswerability.[25] It is also typical of Chekhov that this question is never asked in a fully verbalised manner, but it is clearly inferable from the texts: '*Is factual truth* **invariably** *preferable and superior to wishes, dreams, delusions?*' In terms of the story's world, the question can be re-phrased: '*Is being loved and wooed by "the wind" decidedly worse for Nádia than being wooed and loved by any man in general, and the Narrator in particular?*'

The answer is not unequivocal. Indeed, Nádia can think to herself — privately, and probably subconsciously and intuitively — something like '*Millions of women since time immemorial have been wooed by men with declarations of love; how many women have been wooed by the wind?*' In a roundabout way, though a convincing one, switching her orientation from the Narrator to "the wind" is an act of self-esteem and self-generated assertiveness. The Narrator, unwittingly and in a convoluted way, now seems to grant her more than his own real love (which he is anyway incapable of giving to anyone — see below); or rather, thanks to him she can give these rare emotional gifts **to herself**: this sweet delusion of being so special that she is wooed and beloved by the universe and its elements, through the sensory pleasure of hearing a man's voice, carried to her with the wind, confessing love to her.[26]

Thus the real, crucial, but banal question of whether a certain male mortal is confessing his love for her and is expected to propose to her is marginalised. She is past that stage. She may not believe her own ears, but she loves the sweet sound they bring to her. In this way the anonymity of these sounds' origin is transformed from a source of torment and exasperation to a source of strange and private contentment and gratification. This turning point within her is evident even in the *Narrator*'s explicit text: at first — ostensibly echoing Nádia's own thoughts and reproducing, as it were, their abrupt, agitated rhythms — he says: "Were those words said or not? Yes or no? Yes or no? It is a question of pride, honour, life, happiness — a very important question, the most important question in the world". This perfect example of *Free Indirect Speech*[27] retains the *Narrator*'s third-person voice while suggesting Chekhov's subtlest, most evasive irony at the expense of the Narrator's hierarchy of values, behind his back of course. Subsequently, the Narrator verbalises directly, as it were, Nádia's own thoughts about the words of love, this time supposedly quoting her verbatim in the first-person direct speech: "It can't be the wind that said them! And I don't want it to be the wind that said them!" For the moment let us ignore the *narrator*'s reliability problem, and accept his report of her thoughts at face value[28] (the fact is that later on in the story even he does not ascribe **such** thoughts to her, thus upholding the *watershed*-status of this scene). That said, it is significant that her abandonment of fact-finding coincides with accepting "the wind" as her secret lover, actually preferring it to him. The Narrator tells us: "Which one of us [i.e., he or the wind] is declaring love for her she does not know, but she clearly no longer cares; it does not matter what vessel one drinks out of, when the only goal is to get drunk". Thus, pleasure and frustration merge in her, complementing each other in what finally becomes gratifying fusion.

The final stage of her emancipation from the need to connect the Narrator's presence with hearing the words of love comes, of course, after the thaw. Now she does not see him, and the extraordinary description of her response to hearing the confession of love that he utters for the last time carried by the gentle spring wind has elements of sublimated orgasm,[29] of delusional blending with an essence of intensely sensual and yet uplifting and spiritual experience of being one, as it were, with the wind and the world. More consciously, she may think that she is blessed with hearing declarations of love in very special and rare moments, and this rarity is a safeguard against going literally and clinically insane. She must think, reasonably though erroneously, that he is not physically around, so that for her the matter is settled once and for all: it is indeed "the wind", a code-name for *illusion*, even *hallucination*,[30] or a peculiar auditory auto-erotic skill that she has developed. Whatever it is, one thing is clear to her: it is not the real man (while all the rest of the world — Chekhov, the *Narrator*, and the readers — know that it is no one but the real man).[31]

This factually false but intrinsically true knowledge, then, does her a world of good: in fact, she is better off without the Narrator. The wind is her secret, intimate, sensual and spiritual lover; yet, she does not "inherit the wind", because she goes on with her life.[32] In this context, then, Chekhov seems to make a substantive case for the superiority of controlled fantasy over fact. However, there are other contexts that counterbalance such a conclusion.

Indeed, the simultaneous development of the two complementary points of view, his and hers, is extraordinarily subtle and evasive: we, the readers, know that (a) the *Narrator* is right on a factual level — he knows that he is present and his words were really uttered — yet this looks technical, arguably unimportant; (b) Nádia is right on a deep psychological level by concluding that "the wind" is her secret lover, and this erroneous conclusion, somewhat paradoxically, indicates that she can distinguish between fantasy and reality (which, once again, puts mental–subjective *sincerity* above factual–objective *truth*, or on the same level); (c) obviously Chekhov is right in showing us such a persuasive and sophisticated tangle of human emotions, and (d) readers are right to sense and internalise it all, with measured 'dosages' and proportions of empathy, understanding and (dis)belief towards both personages, and to appreciate Chekhov's feat in combining acute precision with elusive openness.[33]

The tense balance between the needs for fact and fantasy is a major driving force in love, art, science, and in almost every human experience and endeavour. Chekhov for one devoted a major part of his efforts as an artist to observe, to study, and — in his restrained way — to celebrate this uniquely human dualism.

5.1.5 The Narrator: A Deluding Windbag?

Creating an *unreliable narrator* is a challenging endeavour for writers, since all the 'incriminating evidence' to establish unreliability comes from the *narrator*'s own text; in other words, an *unreliable narrator* is usually an unwittingly self-incriminating personage, that cannot "claim the fifth"; the challenge is especially formidable if that *narrator* is a major personage in the narrative. In "A Little Joke" this is done mainly by undermining the conflicting images that the Narrator tries to create for himself and for Nádia: rather than being the active deluding subject while she is the passive deluded object, rather than being dispassionate, calculating, clear-sighted, scientific, and analytical, whereas she is naïve, 'romantic', sentimental, gullible, almost hysterical, as he would have us believe, in fact the opposite is often the case (often, though not always; in Chekhov there is hardly ever an 'always' in such matters). Thus, he is the one really obsessed with delusion, with arousing hers and ignoring his own: the whole game of delusion that he is playing with her was his idea, and he does not realise to what extent he is the one who needs it: who but a man obsessed with the need to engage in delusion would invent such a strange "joke", not to say a sick one, and stick to it the way he does? His characterisation is achieved through Chekhov's perspectival, reciprocal and structured techniques, as we have seen. The blatant errors in judgement that he makes about himself and about her are keys to understanding him and Chekhov's art alike.

In examining his words and silences, his actions and inactions, his cruel, almost sadistic trait cannot be ignored: he tells us how he callously let her agonise to the point of tears over the gratuitous enigma which he had created by design, without ever budging from his indifference and evasion, regardless of the mental suffering that it inflicts on her. It is also remarkable that he exposes this behaviour of his, betraying the sadistic streak within his personality many years later, without a word of hindsight reservation, second thoughts or heart-searching. He even seems to enjoy this suffering, but up to a point. Therefore, to characterise him as 'sadistic' is simplistic and half-true, since he is much more interested in controlling her emotions through provoking her delusion than in making her suffer. Granted, this is also callous on his part, but it is not sadism plain and simple. Indeed, his choice of forms of presence or absence, action or inaction, is motivated by their expected impact on her delusion and on his dominating it, regardless of whether this delusion is agonising or pleasurable to her. The analogy of cat-and-mouse game comes to mind, but within the rules of this game the 'cat' grants the 'mouse' fair chance of self-defence, even some degree of respect, as seen when he lets her go tobogganing on her own (the story's *watershed*).

The Narrator is not aware of his own motives; moreover, except for the last sentence (which will be discussed presently), he never asks any questions about these motives, with the implication that he considers himself 'normal', ignoring having a lot of explaining to do. This, in turn, sharpens his characterisation as divorced from reality and in all likelihood unaware of the normative rules of social behaviour, which he violates, probably unknowingly.[34] Factually, but only factually, he is in total control: he starts the entire manipulation; he decides where, when and how to utter the love words; his actions and manner of speaking are "dispassionate", says he; and, in conclusion, he dismisses the entire events, which he cares to relate in such intensive and selective detail, as a trifle, "a little joke" indeed. It goes without saying, as it were, that the *narrator* of the 1899 version (unlike his 1886 precursor) is not in love with her: he is "above love".[35] Or is he? It is Chekhov's masterstroke that when the Narrator's words and actions are considered in perspective, almost everything belies his self-characterisation. Indeed,

Nádia, at least as long as she prefers the wind to him, may be more "above love" than he can ever be; certainly she is above **his** love.

Thus, in a deeper sense, he is of course not at all in control: he is manipulated by his own unconscious need for delusion; and the way he tells the story, his very need to tell it,[36] his obsessive preoccupation with her delusions, all betray his own self-delusional needs. Even what is ostensibly his 'scientific' experiment in controlling her emotions and delusions is in fact inferior to her much more genuinely scientific experiment of isolating variables, as pointed out above.

In terms of Chekhov's art of characterisation, then, we learn about this *Narrator* largely through Nádia's function within his discourse. This is a typical Chekhovian technique, used widely also in the plays: personages serve as each other's partial mirrors for reciprocal reflection, and the external perspectives provided for each personage complement internal ones, that can be gathered from thoughts, words and actions of the personage him/herself. In addition, non-personal materials, such as events and themes extractable from reading the text in depth, contribute to Chekhovian characterisation alongside reciprocal and self-generated materials.

When these perspectives are considered in relation to the *Narrator*, it is clear that he is in love with saying "I love you", no less than she is in love with hearing this phrase; that he is deluding himself that he couldn't care less about the whole matter, and that it is all a trifle to him, no less than she is ever deluded by him, or by herself. Moreover, in his neurotic way he **is** in love with Nádia (that is, once again, to the very limited extent that he is capable of loving anyone); or, at the very least, that she is the female relationship closest to love that he ever experienced in his loveless and self-centred life.

Consider the tiny, subtle vignettes of his tender descriptions of her, dwelling with apparent affection on her more as well as less endearing external qualities — e.g., the down on her lip, the smallness of her figure, her "little galoshes", etc. It is of special interest to note that the young lady is formally–properly addressed — with her name-plus-patronymic (as explained in *Guide* 3, especially 3.2), *Nadézhda Petróvna* [Надежда Петровна] — only once in the story, when the Narrator reports to the reader about his own direct address to her, in the second-person. The double-diminutive, endearing–affectionate *Náden'ka* [Наденька] is used by him consistently when speaking about her, in the third person, while the muffled love confessions (uttered, as it were, by "the wind") are addressed to *Nádia* [Надя], the single-diminutive form, somewhat occupying middle-ground between the former two. This is very subtle, but starkly telling: the Narrator's subconscious but con-sistent practice betrays his affections. Just as he is scared stiff of exposing (to her, or to anyone) any genuine romantic feelings he might have for her, he takes care never to utter any affectionate or endearing nickname-version of her name **in her presence**; but when he manipulates his *alter ego*, "the wind", to utter a muffled love confession to her, in a kind of *half-present, half-absent* relationship between them, he chooses the single-diminutive, moderately-affectionate form *Nádia*; but it's only the truly-endearing double-diminutive *Náden'ka* for him when he is off his guard, telling the story many years later, in the third person and in her *absence*. Thus, an extreme case of genuinely Chekhovian love confession is created: without any con-scious awareness of any active personage, addresser or addressee, the former betrays his surprisingly true feelings, however clandestine, mentally distorted and convoluted they may be. Chekhov achieves this precisely controlled and balanced result, *inter alia*, through a twist of the Russian language's hierarchy of endearing diminutives (it is, again, very Chekhovian that this tripartite usage of the diminutives is not 100% consistent: to avert neat schematicism, there is a couple of exceptions to the rules formulated here, but they do apply in a large majority of the cases, so that the mental process is clear). To this we can add his patronising yet affectionate reference to her as "the poor girl", and other heart-warming expressions, and, above all, his description of her radiant beauty in their last encounter after the thaw: this is the way a man in love looks at the woman he loves (though, of course, his is not the way a man in love **treats** the woman he loves).

In addition, consider his intense interest in her, bordering on the obsessive: he must have made every effort to inquire about all the important stations in her life; without such inquiries he would not have known about her marriage and children. Thus, he could for instance write to friends and relatives in his native town after having left it for the capital St Petersburg; on the other hand, there is no indication that she showed any parallel interest in him and his life. One must conclude, then, that in a strange and unexpected way he is the one who harboured unrequited love for her, rather than the other way around. She is the secret love of his life; so secret that even he does not know it... but Chekhov and the readers do.

Last but not least, it does not stand to reason that one would repeat the words "I love you" so obsessively unless the idea itself has at least crossed one's mind. Moreover, the Narrator did not plan only evading her and his parting from her for good; he also planned the words "I love you Nádia" to be the focus of the delusion he inspired in her. He is quite obsessed with the tangible oral physicality of almost tasting these words spoken in his mouth time and again. Even at the end of the story he cannot refrain from saying the entire phrase once again in full, within a subordinate clause which does not require it grammatically, rather than relying on the reader's short-term memory and just referring to the phrase. In short, he lied to himself in thinking that he was lying when he spoke those words.[37] Here, once again, the difference between the two versions of the story is striking: there is no doubt in the earlier version about his love for her, in spite of the brief manipulative trick that he is playing on her, with its short-lived cruel component; but in the later version his delusional needs, his lack of self-awareness and the totally unconscious need to engage in the verbal materials of love, make him, rather than her, the most self-denying and self-deceiving character of the story.

Indeed, one can say that what Chekhov does to the Narrator behind his back is largely analogous to what the latter does to Nádia in provoking and teasing her delusional needs; that said, one must be aware of the obvious difference between personage-to-personage relationships within a fictional world, on the one hand, and author-to-personage relationship across the fictional boundary, on the other hand. However, Chekhov does something similar even to us as readers, by the sheer subtlety and elusiveness of his strategies: he leads us on as well, but he also provides us with the tools to see beyond that, to "call his bluff" and to realise what he is up to, as a writer. These manipulations in relation to the reader are not a game, or "a little joke"; they are scrupulous strategies meant to sharpen our tools of observation, to experience the full extent of the irreducible complexity of evasive mental processes.

To conclude: the superordinate, overarching feature of the Narrator's motivation is not sadistic, but manipulative–deluding. If deluding her makes her suffer, fine with him; if it makes her happy, as in the thaw scene, fine with him too, as long as he deludes himself that he is in control of deluding her. To the extent that the whole story has a barely hidden erotic element, it can additionally, rather than alternatively, be analysed in terms of sexual *vs.* auto-erotic behaviour: he does not even get close to sexual, or even sex-like activity **with** her; rather, he imposes on her something that becomes more and more analogous to masturbation, and his own auto-erotic satisfaction comes from watching it in her before his eyes. In this context, the triumph of "the wind" over him fulfils his deeply unconscious preference for secluded, uncommunicated masturbation over mutually communicated intercourse, in all senses of that word.

Indeed, once again, why does the *Narrator* have to tell the story in the first place? Why does he bother to inquire, even spy, after her so many years after their separation, so that he knows about her marriage and children, in the obvious absence of direct communication between them? And above all, how dare he say with such conviction and self-persuasion that it was "irrelevant", "all the same"[38] whether Nádia married her husband of her own volition or was married off? Or that her having three children has no significance in comparison to the reminiscences of the tobogganing accompanied by the words of delusion? Let us consider the matter: a woman gets married and bears three children. This means, probably, courtship, proposal, wedding, sex and intimacy, happy and unhappy times with a husband; it certainly means three pregnancies, three births, three times bringing up a child. All of this can give a wife and a mother some opportunity for emotional experience, good and bad, but significant: at least, one can assume so with some certainty, unless proven otherwise. But not the *Narrator*. He says that **for her** [sic!] the most moving and wonderful experience in **her** entire life was the tobogganing and the words of love heard then. Moreover, those words were the epitome of evasiveness in the first place; they were barely heard, literally "gone with the wind", literally "airy nothing". Upon what authority, then, does he make his speculative assumption that those words, doubted by Nádia and disowned by the Narrator, are more significant for Nádia than her marriage, family and children?

Doubtless, the only possible basis for this preposterous assumption is projection: i.e., that the tobogganing and the words of love are **for the Narrator** the most wonderful and moving experience of his life. He, one can assume with high degree of plausibility, never got married, never had children (otherwise he would mention them, presumably). For him, unconsciously, those events were all-important. But just as he could not come forward to Nádia and tell her that he really loved her — i.e., tell her that it was a fake that his love declaration had been a fake — he could never have the courage to check with her how she felt about the matter in the years that had passed since. And just as his entire mind-reading activity in the past had been nothing more than guesswork, so in the present time of the story-telling he just guessed that it remained so important to her, so much more important than her marriage, children and family.

Moreover, there is a lot of vanity and condescending arrogance in the way he mentions her husband — a bureaucrat of sorts[39] — and even her children.[40] His implied rhetorical question is: '*How can a marriage to this clerk,*[41] *and giving birth and education to their children, overshadow, or measure up to, any experience with me?*' It is to him, not to her, then, that those words of love were so crucially significant. It is only within his unfounded reading of her mind that she can possibly share his view of these words' significance (moreover, a significance that he does not admit attributing to these words in **his** life!), even though she believes that the words were never really spoken by him; as far as she is concerned — so he thinks, after all these years — his mere presence inspired, almost fertilised her with these words, enough to be much more important to her than her whole life as a person, a wife and a mother. He makes these absurd assumptions with great conviction, without any hesitation (which he does show with some of his other observations), as if they are unquestionable. Indeed, in preferring sweet delusion to this man Nádia chose the wind over the windbag.

So, indeed, the trick that he thinks he played on her is the trick that Chekhov plays on him, by divorcing him from a reasonable perception of reality: in the absence of any evidence to the contrary, Nádia seems to have a better deal in life. He is probably lonely, without love or humanly significant relationship, and has only those memories to cling to, memories of words that he took care to conceal, and never took any responsibility for. A raw deal indeed, for which he has but himself to blame.

In this context it is instructive to have a hard look at the very last sentence of the story, where Chekhov seems to have selected every single word and its position in the sentence very carefully, even beyond his usually meticulous choice of words. «А мне теперь, когда я стал старше, уже не понятно, зачем я говорил те слова, для чего шутил...» or, in a more literal version, aimed at preserving the original word order and rhythms for the sake of analysis (and admittedly much less successful in terms of the requirements of English style): "But as for me, now that I have grown older, I can no longer understand, why I uttered those words, what ever for I made/played that joke [or: What was my purpose in making/playing that joke]". The sentence begins with a *but*, or *yet*, and the obvious contrast implied is between the Narrator and Nádia; as for her, so he claims, the tobogganing and the love-words whispered in the wind were the most cherished memory in **her** life; but as for him — well, after a *but* one would expect a statement to the contrary, i.e., that for him these events of the past are not so important; however, Chekhov makes his Narrator say that he no longer understands his actions, which is not the opposite of what he ascribes to her. The asymmetrical contrast created is astounding, bringing his unreliability to new heights: he claims full knowledge of what Nádia has been feeling, and remembering, all these years, whereas he "no longer" understands or remembers his own feelings and motivations.

One could assume that this is an expression of self-awareness, of the psychologically reliable combination of being more aware of the other than of oneself; however, this is not the case, since there is no sign of any admission of the lack of self-awareness, in the past or in the present, and since it is unreliable that the Narrator should know so much about Nádia and so little about himself. In short, he tries to be omniscient and ignorant at the same time, which is doubly unreliable. The clear implication of the phrase "no longer" is that the Narrator had understood himself in the past, when he was an active agent, but now at the time of telling the story he remembers the events but not their meaning, reason, and especially purpose. From everything that we read in this story, and from the blatant unreliability pointed out here, we can conclude that this observation, too, is invalid; that in the past the Narrator's true understanding of his own motives was not better than years later, when he narrates the story. Moreover, he is deluding himself when he removes the element of loving her, in the past and in the present, from the equation: this is what he did not, does not, and never will, understand.

The *frame* of the story — its title and its very last word — is highly significant not only because of the usual importance of beginnings' *primacy effect* and endings' *recency effect*, but mainly because both words are from the same root — the noun *joke* in the title, and the verb *to joke,* or *to play a joke* in the last word. This *framing* effect adds to the story a sense of powerful *aesthetic motivation* and *structuration*; a sense of closure. It also makes the reader wonder with intense curiosity who plays the "joke", when and how it is played, and at whose expense. The Narrator at Nádia's? (And/or) at himself, with hindsight? (And/or) with or without awareness? (And/or) even Nádia, at his expense? (And/or) Chekhov, at his expense, and hers? And perhaps, on a subtler lever, the mature 1899 Chekhov at the expense of his own younger *alter ego*, the relatively shallow 1886 Chekhonte?[42] And finally, is it a joke at all? What kind of a joke? Isn't it, as he says, "the happiest, most touching, and beautiful memory" in her life, and/or indeed in his? Isn't his very reference to it as something that was very serious for her but a mere joke for him a sad sarcastic joke that Chekhov plays at the expense of his Narrator's delusional lack of self-awareness? And since some lack of self-awareness is a universal human trait, isn't it, to some extent, a joke at our expense, and at Chekhov's? And isn't asking ourselves about the nature and point of the joke a disillusioning process, getting nearer to **a truth**[43] behind the delusion's back?

It would undermine, even desecrate, Chekhov's entire project to attempt an answer to these questions. As he said in that famous letter, the artist's role is not to answer questions, but to present them correctly. An analyst's role may be different, though; but let us remember once again, that when Chekhov, as an artist, "presents the questions correctly", he does not use explicit words to formulate them. For him "to present the question correctly" means — to use the parlance of 20th-century Anglo-American literary–narrative criticism — *showing* rather than *telling*: he creates *internal fields of reference*, i.e., *fictional worlds*, and within them he shows situations, emotions, relationships, interactions, etc., to audiences of readers and spectators, and these fictional worlds are made to "beg questions", or rather suggest them to those audiences, who in turn are supposed to ask (for) themselves, or at least to think about them and concern themselves with them. According to Chekhov, then, it is not for the artist to give answers, nor even to formulate the questions in so many words, but merely to "present them correctly", so that the addressees would be prompted to ask them, with or without words.

The scholar, i.e., the academic analyst, however, is not an artist, and might not be exempted by a Chekhov from giving answers, or at least from being concerned with them as part of his/her role and responsibility; but the analyst's province is not the real human world, but its (re)presentation in a fictional text created by an artist. To personalise this point, Chekhov's province is humanity, its life and world, whereas mine is Chekhov's art, poetics and fictional world. And indeed, as an analyst, I am trying in this Book to ask **and answer** questions about 'my province'; moreover, when I, using my own explicit words, formulate **questions** about life, the human condition etc., that Chekhov (in my humble opinion) insisted on leaving implicit and unanswered, I am trying to **answer** questions about his fictional world and other aspects of his poetics. As for answering questions about human life and the real world — this is neither Chekhov's business (as an artist, according to his views) nor mine (in analysing his world). In short, **the verbalisation of his unverbalised questions about life is my answer to questions about his poetics.**

5.1.6 Conclusion

Beside its uniquely lucid demonstration of Chekhov's characterisation, "A Little Joke" has important bearing on his "realm of ideas", to use Chudakóv's (1983) phrase [«сфера идей», in the original Russian].

By leaving all questions open Chekhov seems, after all, to give some credence to the Narrator's claim about the supreme importance of the muffled love-declaration in Nádia's life. This may be so, but with a crucial proviso: there is a world of difference between what the *Narrator* is saying, or 'has the right to say', to his addressee,[44] on the one hand, and what Chekhov (as the story's *IAu*) is saying to us (through the *narrator* as a vehicle, yet behind his back as a character) on the other. The former's assertions are indeed unfounded, vain and arrogant, and Chekhov provides us with every perspective we need to evaluate them as such. The latter, however, on a higher level of *author-to-perceiver communication*, manages to turn these **assertions** into implicit existential **questions** about the human condition; and whereas the Narrator is unqualified to make his 'unshakable' cut and dry assertions, every person is fully entitled to ask these existential questions, and no person is ever equipped to answer them fully. Having negated the Narrator's right to make those assertions — how should **he** know? — the story as a whole (i.e., Chekhov as *IAu*) says to us that we actually have no way of knowing the opposite either. The unlikely is not impossible; perhaps, just perhaps, the Narrator happens to be (unknowingly) right after all, and the story's events, mainly the barely heard love declarations, were indeed so significant in Nádia's life? It is Chekhov's practice to release such implied questions 'into the air' of a text, into its cognitive–communicational space, and let them do their work in our minds: we can totally oppose the Narrator's shaky and unlikely assertions, or 'certainties', but we cannot reject the *implied author*'s doubts and questions. As seen repeatedly in these analyses, it is a Chekhovian strategy, in stories and plays alike, to create an elusive balance of checks and balances when a valid statement is made by the person least qualified to make it.

The story as a whole, then, poses and leaves open not only questions concerning the emotional experiences and attitudes of its personages; through those fictionally circumscribed questions it asks incomparably broader, eternal, non-fictional ones about the relative roles, functions and significance of *fact* and *fantasy*[45] in the world and lives of human beings, where the unresolved tension between them is a major component of the human condition. This additional, genuinely universal type of questions is a direct (though implicit) consequence of the story, though its events lend intense urgency and poignancy to such questions, shifting them from the realm of abstract contemplation into the realm of the reader's immediate emotional experience, where art is in its own element, and has a clear edge over philosophy. These general questions, then, are contextualised and intensified, without losing their universality.

Chekhov's *unresolved doubts* and *unanswerable questions* enjoy such solid credibility not only because the authority of the *IAu* is the highest one in a text, but precisely because they are questions rather than assertions, and because the optional role of answering them, or refusing to answer them,[46] is given to us, the ultimate jury of mankind sitting in self-oriented judgement. It is very likely that Chekhov expected his readers to conclude that they, too, cannot answer these questions. Actually, he leads us into such a conclusion by the sheer complexity of his "correct presentation" of the problem; by the tense and precarious balance that he creates between such elements as (the need for) factual truth, delusion, fantasy, imagination, reality, communication, and love. This is the essence of his inescapably **truthful** treatment of **humans** — personages, audiences, and himself; it is also the essence of his intensely **human** treatment of **truth**, within a text of unsurpassed art and artistry; a text that is — by Shakespearean definition of a poet's work — "of imagination all compact", and "gives to airy nothing a local habitation and a name" (*A Midsummer Night's Dream*, V, i). Arguably, if anyone can rise to such challenges, it is Chekhov; however, by charting this map of human strengths and weaknesses the way he does, he also exposes his own strengths and limitations, never attempting the super-human, which is inhuman: "I dare do all that may become a man;/Who dares do more is none" (*Macbeth*, I, vii, 47–48).

5.2 Characterisation in the Major Plays

5.2.1 Two Interrelated Analytical Tools

Whereas the discussion of "A Little Joke" focused on characterisation techniques shared by stories and plays alike in Chekhov's *oeuvre* and poetics (notably principles of *reciprocity* and perspectivity in characterisation), the remainder of the Chapter is dedicated to the plays alone; moreover, this discussion is based on viewing the Dramatic text as potential for staging and theatrical performance within a *TF* [*Theatrical Fictionality*]-oriented approach. Exploring the subject of Chekhovian characterisation from these two mutually complementary angles is designed to provide a more comprehensive and integrated view of this crucial aspect of any playwright's poetics.

The analytical strategy offered here is based on two interrelated constructs: (1) *Implied Actor/Actress*[47] (*IAc*) — i.e., the potential/hypothetical/virtual/imaginary actor for whom a personage-text is written, and whose tacit presence is implicit in every personage in any dramatic text (the term was introduced in Note

4 above); (2) The *Part-Play* (*PP*) — i.e., a play's text as viewed from the stand-point of such an *IAc*, organised and hierarchised around one role, with a single *IAc* in mind. Within the term *Part-Play*, "*part*" has two senses: (a) *role/personage/character* (as in "the part of Desdemona"), and (b) *segment/section/component* (as opposed to *whole*).

IAc is not a person, not even a personage; it is a unit of *Dramaticality* (in its *sense B*), in general, and a unit of *TF* (*Theatrical Fictionality*) in particular (these terms were presented and discussed in 4.3.2). In other words, it is part of reading a play as a text referring to a theatrical situation, to a potentially concrete world of stage, auditorium, directors, actors, audiences etc. Moreover, *IAc* is not about ways in which real actors (should) work on their parts; rather, it is about hierarchies and perspectives within the written text itself, regulated by *the implied presence of potential actors,* each with the specific focus dictated by his *part*.

As explained above, the concept of *Part-Play* also means a **partial** reading of the play; again, both senses of this adjective — i.e., *incomplete* and *biased* — are relevant, the latter because of the actual selection of the chosen *part*, regardless of its 'objective' centrality or marginality in the play. Any text of a whole play can be viewed, ***partially*** (notably, ignoring its *stage directions*), as the sum-total of its *PP*s.[48] Of course, in its relationship to complete plays, *PP* constitutes a subordinate particular species of the superordinate general genus of *part–whole* relationships. The idea of *constructing ('strong') wholes at the expense of their ('weak') parts* is elaborated in Chapter 2 as a purely structural, semantically neutral principle in Chekhov's poetics (though the reason for labelling an element as 'strong' or 'weak' in the first place is usually semantic–thematic).

Indeed, Chekhov's reciprocal characterisation is based, as it were, on the principle of '*Tell me how other personages and their wishes (and other relevant materials) interact with you and your wishes, and I shall tell you who you are*' — an exceptionally awkward paraphrase of the elegant dictum "Tell me what you want, and I shall tell you who you are" of Chekhov's Professor Nikoláï Stepánovich, the *first-person-narrator* and the major protagonist of the story "A Dreary Tale" (this dictum is also discussed in 1.3). Wills and wishes, much more than deeds and actions, are the major stuff Chekhov's texts (not only his characters) are made on. Thus, Chekhovian *IAc*s should ask themselves how the wishes of their personages — i.e., of the *parts* they are to play — interact with the wishes of the other *parts*.

It is the major theme and contention of this Book that Chekhov's poetics leans heavily on *unrealised potentials* and *present absences*. In the context of the present Chapter, these terms refer mainly to a variety of *offstage* phenomena,[49] i.e., inter-relationships between whatever is literally *present* on the stage, on the one hand, and *absent* from it, on the other. They include (1) technically-absent but significantly 'present' personages;[50] (2) situations and relationships, non-existent in a play's explicit text and world, but suggested by it as active absences (e.g., marital happiness or self-fulfilment in work — *absent* constructs thrown into bold relief by their *present* opposites); (3) unsaid/withheld statements, anticipated in vain at certain points in the text (e.g., the sisters' thundering silence in response to Andréï's confession at the end of Act 3 in *Three Sisters*); etc. (The point is elaborated in greater detail in Golomb and Heskia 1990). Chekhov-*IAc*s, then, take *absences* into account no less than *presences*; their *PP*s consist of 'hovering potentials' as well as 'hard facts'. They are obliged to do that,[51] not least because the materials supplied in their explicit texts and actions are inadequate to some extent or other, if isolated from their contexts.

5.2.2 *Character-Centrality*; *Reciprocal Characterisation*

5.2.2.1 Tests for *Character-Centrality*: Literary and Theatrical

In view of the aforesaid, *character-centrality* — anyway not a clearly definable concept, on the theoretical level — is particularly problematic in Chekhov. His poetics in drama is famous for requiring *ensemble acting*, necessitated by an *ensemble group* of leading personages, alien to the traditional concept of just one or two major protagonists;[52] yet, of course, there is no art without hierarchies, and even in Chekhov some personages are more central than others:[53] indeed, if "all elements are equally important", then all elements are (equally) unimportant. Granted that *character-centrality* is a 'Chekhov-enabled' phenomenon, the question is how it is signalled in Chekhov's texts.

A telling example is Másha, the middle sister in *Three Sisters*. There is a universal, intuitive consensus among virtually everyone that has been exposed to this play, professionals and amateurs alike, that she is its very central character, even within the title-supported core ensemble of the three sisters, or the four Prózorov siblings.[54] The fact that this role was written for, and premiered by, Ól'ga Knipper-Chekhova, Antón Chekhov's wife, does not create its centrality, but adds a factual–biographical aura to it.

How can a Másha-*IAc* (i.e., an *implied* Másha-actress) create this centrality on stage? What are the tools provided by Chekhov, which she can use to make herself prominent? If we read the text through the eyes of a Másha-*IAc* (i.e., a *potential* Másha-actress) — starting, as a probable first step, with a careful examination of her own explicit *part* (i.e., what she says and does on stage) — there is little reason to attribute extra centrality to her. True, one can construct a profile, a kind of character-silhouette, based on the sharpness and terseness of her typical verbal statements, her non-verbal or non-semantic sound utterances (e.g., whistling, "tra-ta-ta", as discussed in 6.2.5.2 and its Note 32) and body movements inscribed in the stage directions. She is radically different from most other personages in these and other respects. Yet, some of the intuitively obvious criteria for establishing character-centrality in a play are conspicuously absent from her *part*, or, at least, poorly represented in it. I am referring mainly to two types of such criteria, which I shall term the *theatrical test* and the *literary test* of character-centrality.

The *theatrical test* regards *centrality* as emanating from a character's actual, quantifiable presence on stage (number of entrances; duration of stage presence; nature and intensity of observable physical activity; number, length and frequency of *réplique*s, etc.). Másha definitely 'fails' this kind of *theatrical test*: **physically**, she is the most static and restrained among all major personages, as she moves about the stage much less than most of them (the text explicitly instructs her to sit or lie down motionless much of the time, in contrast to virtually all others);

verbally, her lines are few and far between, compared to other personages: a simple word and line count would bear that out; moreover, **outwardly** there are little changes in her life during the play's action, and she is neither seen nor talked-to or talked-about considerably more, or more often, than other major characters. In all these respects, other major characters' claim to *centrality* is more (or, at the very least, equally) justified, compared to Másha's.

By contrast, the *literary test* of centrality is intrinsically unquantifiable. It draws on such resources as the depth and intensity of a personage's involvement in crucial events in the plot, and the importance and significance, rather than length or frequency, of what a personage is saying or doing. By this test, Másha is definitely **at least** the others' equal. However, even equality is incompatible with the universal intuition that she is more central than others. This begs the question of why and how it is so. A possible answer, albeit a partial one, can be given by using the *Part-Play* (*PP*) construct.

5.2.2.2 Plays and *Part-Plays*

A useful way to achieve a fuller understanding of a play, almost any play, is to re-read its text at least as many times as there are (major) personages in it, one reading per *part*, so that each reading would assume the standpoint of a different *IAc* and create a different *PP*. Each such *PP* has its own beginning and ending, as well as its own curves of plotlines, climaxes and anti-climaxes, with its own personage as its central protagonist. Obviously relevant texts to any *PP* are the words spoken by, or directly connected to, its *defining personage* (or *core-personage*). In addition, *PP*s also include everything else in the play (stage-directions, other personages' utterances, analogies, etc.) that has relevance to that *core-personage* and its construction, including 'voids' or *absences* (i.e., **specific, delimited** things unsaid or undone) inasmuch as, and to the extent that, they are relevant to that personage.

The last point is particularly relevant to Chekhov. In his plays, once again, personages as well as actions and events are often *present through their absence*, and heard mainly through their silence. Schematically, there are four degrees of such present absences in a (potentially) staged play: (a) *nearby offstage*, perhaps best termed *backstage* — often audible and almost-visible to the audience, e.g., the way the Orchard is supposed to function visually according to *The Cherry Orchard*'s stage directions, or when gradually weakening footsteps of an exiting personage are still audible to the audience, clearly marking the virtual boundaries of a *backstage* space; (b) *remote offstage* — a personage or event whose presence is reported but not perceived by the audience's senses because of its distance from the stage space; (c) *permanent offstage* — something or someone that, albeit almost tangibly experienced by the audience, is absent from the entire play, e.g., an *offstage personage* like Véra Petróvna (Vánia's sister and Sónia's mother in *Uncle Vánia*), General Prózorov, the sisters' and Andréï's father in *Three Sisters*, or an *offstage event*, like the auction in which the Orchard is sold in *The Cherry Orchard*;[55] (d) *fantasised offstage*, e.g., the idealised imaginary husbands of Ól'ga and Irína in *Three Sisters*, Sórin's wished-for career as a writer in *The Seagull*, etc. Additional categories can be proposed based on finer nuanced differences, and borderlines between the ones proposed can be a bit fuzzy, but the basic distinctions are valid.

PP, however, is an analytical construct, which is not as well-defined as a Chekhovian *present absence*, or frustrated expectation. It does not possess a finite number of words and *répliques* and clearly identifiable beginning and ending. Its textually fuzzy boundaries notwithstanding, *PP* is a hierarchised construct, resembling a set of concentric circles, whose boundaries gradually blur inasmuch as they get farther away from its centre, like circles caused by a stone thrown into water. Indeed, it would be simple (or rather simplistic) to start and end the *PP* with the first and last points of stage-presence of its *defining personage* in the text of the play. In a deeper sense, however, *PP* is a more effective tool of description and analysis if it is deemed to be coextensive with the duration of its personage's impact or significance in the play. This view is more literary than theatrical; it is complex, making considerations subtle and boundaries blurred, but it goes to the heart of the matter of characterisation. A model of concentric circles is indeed appropriate: *PP*'s inner circle is drawn around a core, consisting of elements most crucial for determining a personage's "who am I?" question, while its widening outer circles around that core have lessening relevance to this question. It is typical of Chekhovian characterisation that what seems to be less relevant — e.g., something said by someone else, even without mentioning the personage — is often crucial to the understanding and characterisation of that personage, and can belong to a central inner circle of its *PP*.

Thus, for instance, the above mentioned total silence of Ól'ga and Irína, attentively but speechlessly listening to the confession of their brother Andréï towards the end of *Three Sisters'*, Act 3, is an *absence* that lies at the very core of the characterisation of all three siblings. When the drunk Chebutýkin refers to Natásha's "[sordid] little affair" ["романчик"][56] with Protopópov (Act 3) he contributes to the characterisation of Másha and Vershínin, by **not** mentioning them, though they, too, have an extra-marital affair. By his choice to mention only one of these two affairs that are going on at this point in the plot he reveals his contempt for Natásha and Protopópov and respect for Másha and Vershínin (both attitudes are compatible with the basic norms of the play).[57] Thus, Chebutýkin's monologue is a genuine contribution to at least four, maybe five *PP*s: (1) Másha's and (2) Vershínin's, who are **not** mentioned in it; (3) Natásha's, who is; (4) Protopópov's, to the extent that an *offstage personage* can have a *part-play* in the first place;[58] (5) Andréï's, albeit indirectly, by an optional link-through-analogy to his Act 4 reference to the falsehood of husbands who ignore their wives' infidelities, and by the very fact that he is the betrayed husband in Natásha's "[sordid] little love affair".

This example, one out of many, illustrates some of the indirect ways by which Chekhov builds characters and their *PP*s. The principles just exposed can be applied to other Chekhovian texts.

5.2.2.3 Indirect Characterisation in Másha's *PP*

Másha's *PP* in *Three Sisters* is a case in point. Its initial exposition is inactive for a first-time spectator when she is simply seen onstage on a sofa, silent and motionless, reading a book, with a hat on her lap, but it definitely begins with the first reference to her in the text, in the opening talk between her two sisters. Then she is typically presented to us through a contrast between some *absence* in her that is synchronised with some *presence* in others: while her sisters talk, she remains silent (except for a conspicuous whistle, which, *inter alia*, underscores her verbal silence). Now whereas Ól'ga and Irína are talking, the former while walking restlessly and the latter while standing, Másha says nothing while sitting down, probably reclining. At any rate, she is more static than everyone else on stage. She begins to talk surprisingly late, and with seeming irrelevance (a quote from Pushkin, without any overt connection to the dialogue just heard). Soon enough, though, her silent immobility becomes more dynamic than others' runnings-around, and her silence speaks louder and clearer than much of the talk (as uttered by others, or even by her — i.e., her silences often speak louder than her own words). This is achieved typically indirectly. Silent and immobile Másha whistles a tune, almost scornfully, as it were, appearing to ignore her sisters' Moscow longing. This in itself is part of her direct characterisation, but much of the job of characterising her and building her centrality is carried out by other characters. Ól'ga, keenly aware of Másha's presence, is irritated by the latter's silence and responds to her whistling with indignation. Both Ól'ga and Irína explicitly refer to Másha's presence in the room and regret her anticipated absence from the Moscow of their imaginary future. The same pattern continues with Irína's annoyance at Másha's decision to leave before breakfast, and with Ól'ga's pathetic, futile attempt to show understanding and sympathy for her sister. Másha's sisters, then, react to a presence of personality in her, unaccountable so far by anything Másha says or does; something that makes her so valued and important for them. As her character unfolds, direct and indirect characterisation strategies begin to complement and reinforce each other.

A Másha *IAc* is confronted, then, from the very start with the problem of how to bridge the gap between the dearth of explicit materials at her disposal, on the one hand, and the other characters' responses to her presence, which convey their high appreciation for her, on the other hand. Her initial verbal silence and immobility on stage (in theatrical terms, only a stage-prop can be more lifeless) goes on for well over a hundred prose-lines of dialogue by others. Therefore, a Másha-*IAc* can ask herself: '*What kind of a person am I, if I inspire that kind of attitude in others? How can I make my detachment involved, my silence articulate, my immobility dynamic, my whistling meaningful?*' There are no ready answers to such questions: as far as the analyst of the dramatic text is concerned, what matters is only the **type** of questions relevant to the situation, whereas the questions themselves belong in the province of theatrical interpretation, in other words, to actors and directors.

Indeed, if a Másha-*IAc* would like to answer such questions for herself, she would find precious little by simply resorting to her own explicit part for constructing her character, or personality. Asking how and why the others view her as they do, and looking everywhere for material outside the explicit *part* for relevant information is not a luxury, nor an added dimension enriching that *part*; it is the barest of necessities for making any sense at all of this scene, and of her *part* in general.[59]

The unfolding of Másha's character is much slower, more gradual, and more emotionally loaded than any other major personage's. This aspect of the play can thus be described as a grand polyphonic structure, comprising a large number of *parts* (=voices). They are *mutually-interdependent*, each of them having its own curves of rhythms and tempi, emphases, climaxes etc., and each of these resonates with analogous features in the other *parts*; thus, each point in stage-time is made out of different moments in the individual curve of each personage (i.e., in each *PP*), and the perceiver can relate such composite temporal points to each other, and/or to trace the position of each of them within its own *PP* curve — quite a complex assignment, but a rewarding one. Thus, Irína's outburst monologue in Act 3 is arguably the climax, the highest point in her own *PP curve*, whereas at that moment Másha's *PP curve* is just about to go up, but more moderately, in her own confession (when that is heard, Irína's curve is already going down), whereas Másha's own climax is definitely in Act 4, at the moments of her final farewell from Vershínin. The analogy between such synchronisation of different *parts/lines/curves* and the texture of musical polyphony — e.g., a *fugue* by Bach — is thought-provoking, even strikingly mind-boggling. This analogy is further developed in 10.4.2.

5.2.2.4 Másha's *PP* vs. Kulýgin's and Andréï's[60]

Two types of examples in *Three Sisters* demonstrate Chekhov's techniques of *reciprocal–perspectival characterisation* most effectively.

1. On two separate occasions Kulýgin equates his wife with her sisters — Ól'ga and Irína. Once (Act 3) he says to Ól'ga that she is "just like" Másha, and that he could marry her if he were not already married to Másha; and on another occasion (Act 4) he equates between Irína and Másha in a similar manner.[61] The strategy of reciprocal characterisation is most effective here: by failing to distinguish between his wife — undoubtedly the most individuated among the Prózorovs — and her sisters, whose highly distinct personalities are also clearly delineated, Kulýgin obviously and directly characterises his banal self, but indirectly he also characterises the others. First of all Másha is characterised, through her sharp contrast with him, but in fact, all three sisters are characterised here. Thus, we are encouraged to test his indiscriminate statements against our own impressions of the three: Másha *vs.* Ól'ga, Másha *vs.* Irína, but also Ól'ga *vs.* Irína, and each of them against Kulýgin, and then a more general implicit statement can emerge in our minds, about being sensitive *vs.* thick, profound *vs.* shallow, etc. as general human traits in observing and characterising oneself and others. All of these are demonstrated in Kulýgin's observations here. Reading the play carefully, then, a Másha-*IAc* can take another cue for building her character from Kulýgin's indirect characterisation: she can work on the individual traits that make her similar as well as dissimilar to each and both of her sisters, and the traits that make her, and all three of them, so diametrically opposed to her husband, whose tendency to see *sameness* in all people and all things makes him blind to the blatant differences in character and personality between his wife and her sisters.[62] Chekhov, as we are repeatedly reminded, abhors such *sameness*.

This is especially thrown into bold relief when in Act 3 Másha characterises Kulýgin's love for her by sarcastically reciting to him the entire conjugation of the verb *to love* in Latin, or when Andréï, in Act 4, characterises the inhabitants of the provincial township as "living corpses" precisely because they totally resemble each other. Thus, as we have seen in Chapter 1, an implied analogy is drawn between 'Individuality *vs.* Uniformity' and 'Being Alive *vs.* Being Dead', respectively. This view (undoubtedly shared by Chekhov and the norms of his texts) makes immobile but highly individuated Másha one of the most genuinely vibrant persons in the play, while Kulýgin is shown as bringing death into her life. The irony of the matter is that Vershínin, too, tends to apply banal characterisations to Másha (unlike Túsenbach, who always describes his beloved Irína in specific and individuated terms, inapplicable to any other character: contrasting them is another gem of Chekhovian *reciprocal characterisation*). It goes without saying that Vershínin's banality is a far cry from Kulýgin's: though the former uses stereo-typed clichés borrowed from conventional discourse (literary/poetic confessions of love, etc.), it would never cross his mind to equate his ladylove Másha with anyone else in the universe. Thus, the said Chekhovian analogies between dichotomies around 'deadliness/aliveness' and around 'sameness/uniqueness' (respectively) endow the seemingly trite 'romantic triangle' Másha–Kulýgin–Vershínin with an exceptionally loaded imagery of *life/death* significance. Of all the men in the play, Túsenbach is the one truly individuated and individuating lover in his relation to Irína: his love statements are removed from the **relative** banality of Vershínin's almost to the same extent that the latter's are removed from Kulýgin's **absolute** banality. It is of poignant urgency that he is the one whose love is emphatically unrequited, and the only one who is finally "permitted", as he so painfully implores Irína, to give his life for her, or more precisely for their never-to-be-realised love.

2. There is similar example in Act 4. In a moment of truth and frustrated lone-liness, Andréï cries out loud in desperation for help; quite typically, there is no one within hearing range (and he knows it!), except deaf Ferapónt and Natásha — the person least appropriate to hear his cry for help. The actual words used are: "My sisters! My splendid, wonderful sisters! Másha, sister mine!" Thus, Andréï, the brother who compromised his principles and his father's legacy more than any of his sisters is crying for the one sister who is most uncompromising among them in her relentless pursuit of truth, the one whose view of him is most critical, judge-mental, even unforgiving, unprepared to smooth over her bitter disappointment with him.[63] A Másha-*IAc* would be advised take this instance of *reciprocal characterisation* into account as well, asking herself how her acting can contribute to the plausibility of Andréï's desperate plea for her harsh sympathy, in her absence, singling her out among her equally absent sisters, in spite (or rather because) of her outspoken rejection of his behaviour.[64]

5.2.2.5 Másha's *PP* vs. Vershínin's

Másha's part is particularly intertwined with Vershínin's. A Másha-*IAc* is likely to ask herself what kind of a person she is to have such a relationship with this particular man, with his unique biography, character traits, compulsive urge for "philosophising", etc. Her love for him is greater in scope and intensity than he can ever reciprocate; it is enough to compare what he says to her and about her with what she says to him and about him to realise that. While he addresses her with the most banal expressions of love (e.g., "splendid, wonderful woman", Act 2), her confession of love for him, spoken to her sisters in his absence (Act 3), is exceptionally specific to him, his situation and his traits: it is so genuinely unlike anything that could be said about any other personage in the play, so different from what one can read in any other work of literature or drama, that these two personages, Másha and Vershínin, too — while reciprocally characterising each other — emphasise Chekhov's intense preoccupation with the contrast between *individuality* and *sameness*. Yet, even banality is not uniform, and there is a hierarchy between its various manifestations: the very presence of Kulýgin in the play indeed makes Vershínin look less trite and banal, especially as the latter 'enlivens' Másha's life, 'deadened' by Kulýgin and her marriage to him. The contrast between Másha and Vershínin becomes even sharper in Act 4. At the moment of their final farewell he still has the time, and more importantly the need, for blah-blah "philosophising", which he delivers with fluent, easy-going, and syntactically composed manner, whereas she, who up to this moment never wore her heart upon her sleeve, is utterly shaken, crying loud with uncontrolled sobbing (Chekhov's *stage directions* are quite explicit on this point), reciting her garbled misquote from Pushkin. By comparing him with her the text creates around him a void, in fact a vacuum, precisely because it is filled to capacity by her alone, whereas his *potential* share in filling it is *unrealised*, which means that he never had such a potential to begin with. Thus, a Vershínin-*IAc* can ask himself what, in spite of his platitudes, makes a Másha fall so passionately and desperately in love with him. Again, the point here is the type of questions that the text begs, rather than possible answers to them (the farewell scene is analysed in detail in 7.4).

In the final analysis, then, a Chekhovian personage is largely defined by interactions with 'extraneous' elements expressed in the text and/or implied by it, associated with other personages and/or with impersonal thematic materials. This general principle is especially applicable to the case of Másha: any *IAc* charged with playing her part must resort to a lot of such 'extra-character' materials in order to build her own character and establish her centrality, not least because of the **relative** 'weakness' of her own direct, explicit materials. It is specifically Chekhovian that a personage so economical in words, so restricted in movement, and so actively-passive in detaching herself from direct confrontation and conflict, should be so central in a drama. Indeed, Chekhov's revolutionary impact on the history of Drama largely draws on the radical changes that he introduced into the nature and centrality of *Dramatic conflict*. The centrality of a character like Másha epitomises Chekhov's contribution to this historical change: previously, playwrights were reluctant to present on stage a personage who evades *direct conflict* so consistently, to begin with; and if such a personage would be 'allowed to exist' in a play, it would rarely, if ever, be granted *character centrality*.

5.2.2.6 Liubóv' Andréïevna Ranévskaïa: An Outline for a *Part* Reading

To further illustrate the all-Chekhov scope of the techniques and strategies described above, I am turning now to a personage from a different play, Liubov' Andréïevna Ranévskaïa from *The Cherry Orchard*. Out of the many things that can be said about her character and characterisation, I shall focus on one aspect only (this analytical practice admittedly oversimplifies her personality and character, but the purpose of this discussion is to illustrate Chekhov's characterisation techniques rather than to provide full, rounded view of individual characters). I am referring to the way Chekhov juxtaposes her negligence and irresponsibility with the loving response that she elicits from others; this is a shining example of his technique of *reciprocal–perspectival characterisation*.

A hard look at major facts in Ranévskaïa's life and behaviour can yield a long list of actions and inactions indicative of carelessness and irresponsibility of awesome dimensions, bordering in certain cases on fraud and criminal negligence, if viewed strictly and without empathy to her and to those surrounding her. A likely sheet of indictment drawn up against her would include, for instance, careless neglect of Ánia, Vária and the servants; complicity in the mismanagement of the family's estate and finances; near-fraudulent misuse of money — originally earmarked by the old grand-aunt to buy the estate back for Ánia's sake — to finance her 'sinful' reunion with her drunk lover in Paris; acts of extravagant spending of money that she anyway owed to creditors, while failing to secure the financial future of her immediate dependents; etc. So far the financial component of the 'indictment', but there is more, and more severe, to follow. The very existence of the *absent, offstage character* Grísha — her son who had drowned at the age of seven before the action of the play started — is designed to show that careless and complacent negligence can be fatal: there is no other reason for the *presence* of this *absent, offstage personage* in the play.[65] A similar point, from a different angle, is made at the end of the play through the fate of Firs: the real culprit here is of course villainous Yásha, but Ranévskaïa, too, is responsible, or rather irresponsible, for taking Yásha's word at face value, when there is plenty of evidence that he cannot be trusted, especially with this kind of mission. Criminal negligence can be the result of passive inaction, not only of active action.[66]

Ranévskaïa's irresponsibility affects everyone: young and old, rich and poor, men and women, relatives and strangers; it causes damage to money and property, physical and mental health, and even life itself. However, no one in the play — neither her direct victims nor any of the onlookers — calls her to task, or shows any signs of awareness that an indictment, at least a moral one, is in order. On the contrary: all characters — regardless of age, gender, status etc. — feel only love and affection for her.[67] She is so engaging and lovable, and generates so much empathy, that at least within the close circle of her family and friends (who inhabit the play) she can almost literally get away with murder.

An *implied, potential actress* (*IAc*) working on the role of Ranévskaïa cannot convincingly account for this absolutely disarming quality of hers by resorting to her own words and actions alone (though it goes without saying that these words and actions must serve as a primary tool for portraying her, as any other character, on stage). The nature and extent of Ranévskaïa's lovability, just as the nature and extent of *Three Sisters'* Másha's centrality, cannot be established on the basis of their respective explicit *part-texts*. A significant component of the challenge of a Ranévskaïa *IAc*, then, is to look at her image as reflected in the slanted mirrors supplied by the other *parts/personages*, as well as additional extra-character materials, in order to have a more comprehensive view of her own character. An integrative view of the play's text requires emphasising her endearing qualities — spontaneity, sincerity, humanity, generosity, femininity, etc. — to make the one-sided, affectionate responses of other personages plausible. Such character traits, to be sure, do exist in her own *répliques* on the page and actions on the stage, but not always explicitly, and not to the extent that accounts for the universal love that she elicits from everyone.

Thus, a truly indignant Vária, rather than the exasperated but loving–forgiving one as created by Chekhov, would have made Ranévskaïa's irresponsibilities look much more damning than they do; likewise, if it were Ánia, rather than the prudish and ridiculous Gáïev, who expressed indignation at Ranévskaïa's 'corrupt' or 'depraved' quality (Act 1 — the only truly-negative view of her ever explicitly uttered in the play), she would have looked altogether less lovable. Indeed, Gáïev's criticism of his sister at the end of Act 1 — of course, yet another instance of reciprocal characterisation — is not altogether unfounded. Yet, coming from him of all people, and with the wrong moral emphasis, it is hard to accept his comment, even its correct parts: he seems to have her sexual promiscuity in mind (as clearly suggested by the immediate context and by his reference to the way she moves), rather than her personal and social irresponsibility, carelessness and negligence, i.e., faults that he exceedingly shares with her. Yet, the things are said on stage; and once turned loose into our minds they cannot be erased and ignored, no matter who had uttered them. In such cases Chekhov creates a precarious balance whereby the partial correctness of statements is filtered through the morally slippery ground on which the person uttering them stands. Chekhov has developed the art of the elusive mixture of factual truth checked by moral injustice to perfection.[68]

Obviously, there is some sort of charm, almost magic, about Ranévskaïa, effectively neutralising almost anything bad that can be said or even thought of her. People's trust in her, often ill founded, is almost unshakable — observable facts of her behaviour, actions and inactions notwithstanding. Indeed, while she — hardly ever capable of harbouring ill feelings to anyone — brings out the best in the people around her, they fail to realise that she too often brings the worst to them. She is always genuinely candid, warm, compassionate, well-wishing, and totally without malice; she is absolutely sincere and authentic in everything she says, even if it is at odds with what she said just a few stage-minutes before. There is something heart-warming in such child-like naïve subjective honesty (not to be mistaken for objective, genuine truthfulness). No one in the play, least of all Ranévskaïa herself, is capable of seeing the destruction that her carelessness spreads around her (no one says to her, or even about her, something similar to what Ástrov says to Yeléna Andréïevna in *Uncle Vánia*, Act 4, about the devastating effect that she and her husband bring to the human environment around them); and even if someone sees that, it is only for a fleeting moment (e.g., Vária's or Ánia's reactions to recurring moments of Ranévskaïa's spending spree), immediately followed by kind-hearted forgiveness, stemming from an automatic mental mechanism, which accepts her as she is — in spite, or even because, of all her faults — with unconditional love. To make her *part* plausible, a Ranévskaïa-*IAc* would draw on the resources of her personage's genuinely endearing qualities and match them with the attitudes of others.

This type of characterisation, then, puts us — the audience — in a spot. We possess the information for the 'indictment', but have no 'standing' in the 'court' of the play. After all, she has done no harm **to us**... Thus, we have no right to 'sue' her for punitive damages, while those who have earned that right to do so never contemplate exercising it.

This is another typical feature of the *semiotic and communicational system* of Chekhov's theatre: the audience assumes roles and responsibilities that used to be assumed by fictional characters on stage in the poetics of previous generations of playwrights. This difference is at the core of the typical nature of direct conflict — or, rather, lack thereof — in Chekhov's plays, when the personages on stage 'refuse' to engage in confrontation with each other.

One can cite numerous additional examples of reciprocal characterisation in the plays. Thus, for instance, in *The Seagull*, it is by the contrastive analogy between Konstantín's preference for death over life (through suicide) and Nína's preference for life over death (despite the objectively harder conditions she is facing in life, compared to him) that the two characters shed light on each other, and on the more general theme of bearing the whips and scorns of life *versus* flying from them. Similarly, in *The Cherry Orchard*, Lopákhin's resourcefulness in matters of money and property, contrasted with his child-like helplessness in matters human and romantic, is mirrored by a partial reversal of these traits in Ranévskaïa. Though in Chekhov nothing is as neatly schematic — the two personages are not totally and symmetrically opposed — partial analogies of this kind abound, and enrich most characters with added depth and complexity. An *implied Chekhov actor* looking for resources of material relevant for building his/her character can find them almost everywhere in the texts: they are just there for grabs; one just has to look hard enough.

5.2.2.7 'I Might Have Been a Dostoïévskiï/a Schopenhauer': A Brief Survey of Cases of Reciprocal Characterisation in *Uncle Vánia* and *The Seagull*

In the heat of the overt clash between Iván [Vánia] Voïnítskiï and Professor Serebriakóv, the former hurls at the latter: "If I had lived a normal life, a Schopenhauer or a Dostoïévskiï could have come out of me!" (Act 3).[69] Much earlier on in the play, in Act 1, the former speaks with total contempt about the latter's professional achievements. The more closely one looks at these statements, the more they look as an epitome of *reciprocal characterisation*; in other words, the speaker (here — Iván Voïnítskiï) is typically unaware of the fact that by these words he is characterising himself at least as much as his opponent. Voïnítskiï unwittingly exposes his own total lack of professional credentials to evaluate Serebriakóv's (who, after all, is a recognised professor in a state university): who is he to pass such unsubstantiated judgement in a matter of professional expertise? Without going into his conscious and subconscious motives (which is a separate subject, worthy of analysis), it is clear that he exposes them, and his own character, by his attempt to characterise the Professor. Milder cases of reciprocal characterisation can be found in *The Seagull*, in which a thick as well as subtle network of *reciprocal characterisations* among almost all personages — Konstantín, Trigórin, Dorn, Nína, Másha, Arkádina, and others (even Shamráïev and Polína) — serves to characterise speakers and referents alike, each providing '*slated mirrors*' for the others.

5.2.3 In Conclusion: *Character Centrality* and Chekhov's Poetics

The theoretical and methodological points of this Chapter are consistent with other components of Chekhov's world and poetics, as proposed in the rest of this Book, especially its opening and concluding Chapters. The later Chekhov's poetics of *unrealised potentials and present absences*, in which the indirect and the implicit often signify more than the direct and the explicit, is consistent with Másha's centrality: it is no accident that a personage characterised by potentially bursting yet powerfully suppressed emotions, someone rough, even coarse on the outside ("around the edges") and "boiling" inside (Másha's explicitly self-characterising phrase, Act 4, is Chapter 7's Epigraph), should be granted centrality in a Chekhov play. Indeed, it is through her that Chekhov calls into doubt the almost-obvious correlations between centrality, dynamic activity, duration of stage-presence, etc.; yet not by physical immobility or by short and infrequent *répliques* alone can a Chekhov character become central: Chekhov's dramatic world abounds in counter-examples to any generalisation automatically linking centrality with (im)mobility, or with talking much, or little. In Másha's case, centrality is achieved by a combination of heterogeneous, even contradictory characteristics — e.g., the overt co-presence of immobile passivity and 'anti-"philosophising"' reluctance to engage in idle talk with a covert mental hyper-activity, marked by uncompromising passion for truth. Indeed, this combination is unique, genuinely individuating its bearer; yet much of it, as pointed out above, cannot be retrieved from Másha's own text, but from seeing her in perspective supplied by other characters and some non-verbal and impersonal thematic material. Similar analyses are applicable to most personages in Chekhov, as has been demonstrated by the foregoing analyses of a larger sample, including Vershínin and Ranévskaïa.

Let me also reiterate that the analytical procedures offered here are not intended as blueprint for any real actor or director, nor do they claim to describe what any real actor or director has done, is doing, or will be doing in working on a Chekhov play. These procedures may pose as theatrical, but they are essentially dramatic and textual, even literary. *Implied Actor* and *Part-Play* are constructs derived from reading a text, rather than from observing any actual rehearsal, or even from imagining a potential one.[70]

As explained in Chapter 2, once the entire process of creating powerful *wholes* out of feeble *parts* has taken place in a perceiver's mind, those single *parts* no longer appear thin and depleted for that perceiver. Thus, static, immobile and painfully restrained Másha becomes much more vibrant, bursting to near-explosion with barely controllable energies; likewise, Ranévskaïa, mirrored by her loving environment, hardly ever fails to charm audiences, often in spite of her own words and actions. These seeming contradictions are part of the evasive and powerful arsenal of Chekhov's disarming rhetoric, which never fails to convince; not least because he gives us every reason and every tool to doubt his actions as a writer, and to be aesthetically and even humanly content with questions that are genuinely and eternally unanswerable. It is largely because he is so inherently truthful, and because he is courageous enough as a writer — his typical elusiveness notwithstanding — to be exposed *vis-à-vis* his addressees, inviting them to constantly test his authorial infallibility, that he finally passes almost every test with flying colours.

In principle, characterising statements can be divided into four categories: *characterisations of self* and *characterisations of others*, each of which can be *direct/explicit* or *indirect/implicit*. For Chekhov, direct/explicit statements are non-starters in terms of reliability, for two complementary reasons: (a) as noted in the analysis of "A Little Joke", Chekhov rarely trusts his personages to possess the necessary insight and awareness (especially with regard to themselves, but also with regard to others) to characterise human beings with the required amount of balance, subtlety, sophistication, and fairness; (b) as a sophisticated user of language through his writings, he regards most direct statements as a shallow, simplistic technique that 'cannot deliver' the qualities necessary for a 'rounded', truthful characterisation of human beings. Thus, his characterisation relies on *indirectness* and *reciprocity* in plays and stories alike, where personages characterise each other more significantly than themselves; likewise, indirect statements and situational perspectives usually characterise personages more effectively than direct statements, whoever utters them. Chekhov's main structural tool is creating *analogies* of various kinds, as a *superordinate* strategy that coordinates between *subordinate* partial statements and components, thus creating composite wholes which, in turn, can get nearer to the goal of truly characterising the infinite variety and complexity of human beings.

Bearing in mind how *anti-schematic* the entire Chekhov phenomenon is, one would regard any attempt to schematise his system as a contradiction in terms; yet, some purely structural principles governing the way he constructs his largely anti-schematic world seem to be schematisable, to a point. Thus, personage A makes a statement of direct characterisation (of self or other); personage B makes another statement of similar nature; these statements, even in their initial stage, are multi-functional, since they can, and usually do, characterise the speaker, the object of observation, the addressee (if different), and others, and contribute to a general picture of characterisation-capabilities and the conditions that enhance or curtail it, etc.

In parallel, Chekhov **shows** us personage A, in situations that vindicate and/or undermine the validity of statements made about him/her, usually by personage B (this, of course, is indirect and reciprocal characterisation). Again in parallel, Chekhov creates an analogous confrontation between what we hear about personage B and what we are shown about him/her. Now we are in a position to contrast not only the two personages, but also the statements (direct and indirect,

implicit and explicit), each statement with each object and with the other statement, and also to generalise about the validity of such statements **on a level of
principle** (i.e., if characterising statements are refuted by evidence, the validity of
such statements in principle, beyond the value of the specific statements just
negated, is being **questioned**, though not necessarily totally, or always, negated).
Out of such processes of statements and events partially vindicating, and/or undermining, and/or negating each other, the picture becomes fuller and more and more
intricate, and — as a result — complex, balanced views of the world and humanity
emerge.

This schematic skeleton of Chekhov's basic techniques of characterisation
relates to the entirety of his characterising texts just as a skeleton relates to the full
body, not to speak of the spirit, of a human being: an initial point of departure for
understanding the structure; perhaps no less, certainly no more. Academic analytical procedures, then, can hardly grasp and capture the incredible density and
intricacy of a project of human characterisation as undertaken by a Chekhov; their
ability to capture the spirit and soul of that project is even poorer. That said, there
is something basically clear, that looks even simple, as has been shown in this
Chapter and in Chapter 2: Chekhov's *wholes* are complex **at the expense of** their
constituent *parts*; the latter, in turn, are connected and contrasted with each other,
juxtaposed and aligned, creating subtle and intricate networks. Yet in the field of
characterisation this is even much more complex on the level of the parts as well,
because the separate parts themselves can be characterised as complexity incar-
nate, since every single personage is supposed to embody one of the world's most
complex and evasive creations — the individual human being. Once again, the
model of *reversible hierarchies* (see Harshav 2007, 178) is at work here: the individual is a complex superordinate structure consisting of *subordinate parts* like
(his or her) love, work, education, friendship, communication etc., just as each of
these themes is a *complex superordinate structure* consisting of subordinate parts
like personage A, B and C, each functioning in love, work, etc. In the analytical
discourse, then, one can oscillate and choose between looking at this complex in
different ways, configuring mutually complementary hierarchies between the
superordinate and the subordinate in sequence, one after the other, since it is impossible to activate such processes simultaneously. In the work of art itself, however,
all of these relationships and hierarchies do co-exist simultaneously and perpetually, never diminishing in their infinite intricacy.

Exempt from Chekhov's 'rules of conduct' for creative artists — supposed
according to him only to "present questions correctly" rather than answer them —
I am concluding this Chapter with a statement rather than a question. Out of the
Chekhovian techniques described above emerge some of the truest, most adequate,
fulfilling, convincing, complex, and — above all — some of the most humanly-
correct presentations of the world of human beings ever created, in any art, by a
human being.[71]

Appendix to Chapter 5*
A Little Joke — version published in *Sverchók*, 1886

A clear winter midday... The frost is so hard and crisp that Nadenka, who is holding my hand, has a silvery layer coating the little curls on her temples and the barely noticeable down on her upper lip... Nadenka and I are standing on top of a big hill. From our feet down to the ground below stretches a sloping icy run, which the flirtatious sun is looking at as if it was a mirror. Near us are little sledges upholstered in bright red cloth.

"Let's go down, Nadezhda Petrovna!" I beg her. "Just once! I promise you, we won't come to any harm, we'll be fine."

But Nadenka is faint-hearted. As far as she is concerned, the entire slope from her little galoshes edged with lambskin down to the bottom of the toboggan run is an awful and unbelievably deep abyss. She is struck with fear and holding her breath just from gazing down, because if she were to risk flying off into the abyss on such a flimsy vehicle as a fragile sledge, it seems she might die or go mad. But, ladies and gentlemen, women are capable of making sacrifices. I'm ready to swear to this a thousand times, either in court, or in front of the author of the new book which is called "About Women". Fearing for her life, Nadenka eventually gives in to my entreaties. I settle her into the sledge, all pale and trembling, put my arm firmly round her waist and then push off with her into the depths.

The sledge flies like a bullet at breakneck speed... The air we cut through hits our faces, roars and whistles in our ears, frenziedly grabs at our coat-tails, and seems to want to tear our heads from our shoulders. The wind is so strong we can barely breathe... It seems as if the devil has caught us in his clutches and is dragging us down to hell with a roar... Everything around us melts into one long strip that is tearing along at great speed... Any moment now we will be overturned!

"I love you, Nadya!" I say in a low voice when the roar of the wind and the humming of the runners reach their *forte*.

But now the sledge starts to go much more slowly, it becomes easier to breathe, and we finally come to a halt. Nadenka is neither dead nor alive. She is pale and can scarcely breathe... I help her to stand up...

"Nothing in the world will make me do that again," she says, looking at me with wide eyes full of terror. "I promise you, I almost died!"

A little later she recovers and looks inquiringly into my eyes: did I really utter *those* four words or did she just hear them in the noise of the wind whooshing past? And I, as if nothing had happened, am standing beside her smoking, carefully examining a spot on my glove. She takes my arm and we spend a long time walking round the hill... The mystery is clearly bothering her... Were *those* words said or not? Yes or no? It is a question of pride, honour... and not something to be joked about! Nadenka keeps looking at my face and answering distractedly, pursing her lips with impatience... One moment her face lights up with happiness and the next

---

*The two versions of "A Little Joke" are reprinted by permission from Bartlett (2008, pp. 41–45 and 96–99). See Note 11 to this Chapter.

it clouds over with dejection... I soon begin to notice that there is a fight going on inside her; it is the female spirit hesitating... She stops and obviously wants to say something, and ask something, but she just cannot summon up the courage...

"You know what?" she says without looking at me. "I think... I mean..."

"What?" I ask.

"Let's do it again... go down in the toboggan...."

We walk up the steps to the top of the hill... Once more I settle the pale and trembling Nadenka into the sledge, and once again we hurtle off at breakneck speed; and once again at the fastest and noisiest point of our ride, I say in a low voice: "I love you, Nadenka!"

When the sledge stops, Nadenka looks back at the path which we have just taken, then looks intently at my impartial face, and listens to my indifferent voice, and the whole of her little figure is an expression of utter bewilderment...

"What is going on?" is written on her face. "Those words again! And again it is impossible to understand: did he say them, or did I just hear them?" The lack of an answer is bringing her almost to stupefaction, and taxing her patience... The poor girl does not answer my questions, is frowning and tapping her little foot nervously.

"Should we go home now?" I ask with a forced yawn...

But — oh, you women! Nadenka again wants to hear those words which are sweet to a woman's ear...

"Actually... I like this tobogganing," she says, going red. "Shall we go down again?"

She "likes" the tobogganing, and yet as she gets into the sledge she is pale, barely able to breathe she is so scared, and shaking like a leaf... To hear those words again, though, she is prepared to go flying into a hundred abysses.

We go down a third time, and I can see her watching my lips to see if they will move. But I put my handkerchief to my lips, cough and blow my nose, although I still manage to utter:

"I love you, Nadya!"

So the mystery remains a mystery! ... Nadenka is almost in tears...

When I am accompanying her home after the tobogganing, she dawdles the whole way, looking inquisitively at my impartial expression, and waiting impatiently to see whether I will say those words to her.

"It can't be the wind that said them!" says the expression on her face. "It's you, my friend, who said, them! You!"

But as we come to her house, I begin to say goodbye in the most impartial way possible... She holds out her hand to me slowly, unwillingly, as if she is still expecting something; then after thinking for a minute she pulls it back and says in a firm voice:

"Come for dinner with us!"

I love going out for dinner, so I accept her invitation with alacrity... The dinner is simple but elegant. A glass of vodka, a bowl of steaming soup with macaroni, rissoles and mashed potato and puff-pastry pies for dessert, which sigh under one's spoon... Add to that a long, searching look from a pair of large black eyes, which keep watch on my face throughout the meal, and you will agree it is a magnificent menu... After dinner, when we are alone for a *tête-à-tête*, Nadenka ??... She is even pale with impatience, while I... I am Bismarck! I continue to pretend that I do not know what is going on... I leave her without hinting at love, and not even pronouncing a single word beginning with the letter "l".

The next morning I get a little note: "If you are going tobogganing today, come by and pick me up. N." And from then on I punctiliously start going tobogganing every day with Nadenka, and as we fly down in the sledge, I punctiliously say in a low voice the same words: "I love you, Nadya!".

Soon Nadenka becomes as addicted to this phrase as if it was opium or morphine. She cannot live without it. She is just as terrified going down the run as before, of course, but what place does danger have now? Take away the toboggan from Nadenka, and she will go down on her knees... As long as she hears those words, she does not care about anything else...

But the words of love still remain a mystery... There are two suspects — the wind and I... Which one of us is guilty Nadenka does not know. Having set off decide to go tobogganing solo one midday, and losing myself amongst the crowd I see Nadenka approaching the hill and looking out for me... Then she goes timidly up the steps... It is scary for her being on her own, but she has to put it to the test finally: will she hear those wonderfully sweet words when I am not there? I see her getting into the sledge, all pale, her mouth open with terror, then shutting her eyes, parting with the world forever and pushing off... "Zzzz!" go the runners. Whether Nadenka hears those words I do not know... All I see is her getting up from the sledge looking exhausted and flushed... And one can tell from her face that she herself cannot tell whether she heard anything or not... Her heart has sunk into her boots from the terror of it all, and with it has gone her hearing, her vision and her brain...

But here comes the spring month of March... The sun becomes more affectionate, but the earth greyer and gloomier... Our toboggan run grows dark, loses its sparkle and begins to disintegrate... We have given up going tobogganing. There is nowhere for poor Nadenka to hear those words now. Whoever has given up smoking or kicked a morphine habit will know what that yearning feels like.

One day at dusk I am sitting in my garden, which is next to the house that Nadenka lives in. It is still quite cold, there is snow on the ground, and the trees are leafless, but there is already a whiff of spring in the air... I see Nadenka coming out on to the porch and looking sadly and longingly at the bare trees... The spring wind is blowing straight into her pale, sorrowful face... It reminds her of the wind, whose roar on the toboggan run brought her those four words, and her face becomes sad and tearful, as if asking the wind to bring her those sweet words... I steal up to the bushes, hide behind them, and when a gust of wind blows over to Nadenka over my head, I say in a low voice:

"I love you, Nadya!"

Good gracious, look at what is happening to Nadenka! She gives a cry, a smile lights up her face, and she holds out her arms to the wind... That is all I need... I come out from behind the bushes, and without giving Nadenka the chance to lower her hands and open her mouth wide with astonishment, I run over to her and...

But now allow me to get married.

A Little Joke, as revised for *Collected Works*, 1899

A clear winter midday... The frost is hard and crisp, and Nadenka, who is holding my hand, has a silvery layer coating the curls on her temples and the down on her upper lip. We are standing on top of a big hill. From our feet down to the ground below stretches a sloping run, which the sun is looking at, as if it was a mirror. Near us are little toboggans upholstered in bright red cloth.

"Let's toboggan down, Nadezhda Petrovna!" I beg her. "Just once! I promise you, we won't come to any harm, we'll be fine."

But Nadenka is scared. As far as she is concerned, the entire slope from her little galoshes to the bottom of the tobbogan run is an awful and unbelievably deep abyss. She is struck with fear and holding her breath as she gazes down, when I am merely suggesting that she sit down on a toboggan, but just think what might happen if she were to risk flying off into the abyss! She might die or go mad.

"Please say yes!" I say. "You don't need to be scared! Come on, don't be such a coward!"

Nadenka finally gives in, and from her face I can see that she is giving in while fearing for her life. I sit her down on the toboggan, all pale and trembling, put my arm round her and then push off with her into the depths. The toboggan flies like a bullet. The air we cut through hits our faces and roars, whistles in our ears and roars, pinches us spitefully and painfully, and seems to want to tear our heads from our shoulders. The wind is so strong we can barely breathe. It seems as if the devil himself has grabbed us with his claws and is dragging us down to hell with a roar. Everything around us melts into one long strip that is tearing along at great speed... One moment more and it seems that we will perish!

"I love you, Nadya!" I say in a low voice. The toboggan starts travelling more and more quietly, the roar of the wind and the humming of the runners are no longer so frightening, it becomes easier to breathe, and then finally we are at the bottom. Nadenka is neither dead nor alive. She is pale and can scarcely breathe... I help her to stand up.

"Nothing in the world will make me do that again," she says, looking at me with wide eyes full of terror. "I promise you, I almost died!"

A little later she has recovered and already looking beseechingly at me: did I really utter those four words or did she just hear them in the noise of the wind whooshing past? But I just stand there next to her, smoking and carefully examining my glove.

She takes my arm and we spend a long time walking around the hill. The mystery is clearly bothering her... Were those words said or not? Yes or no? Yes or no? It is a question of dignity, honour, life, happiness, a very important question, the most important in the whole world. Nadenka is impatiently and sorrowfully looking into my eyes and answering distractedly, while she waits to see whether I am going to start talking. Oh, the play of emotions on that sweet face, my goodness me! I can see that she is battling with herself, that she needs to say something, and ask some questions, but she cannot find the words, she feels awkward and scared, and it is getting in the way of her happiness...

"You know what?" she says without looking at me.

"What?" I ask.

"Let's do it again… go down in the toboggan."

We walk up the steps to the top of the hill. Once more I settle the pale and trembling Nadenka on to the toboggan, and once again we fly into the terrible abyss; once again the wind roars and the runners start throbbing, and again at the fastest and noisiest point of our ride, I say in a low voice: "I love you, Nadenka!" When the toboggan comes to a halt, Nadenka looks up at the hill which we have just come down, then looks intently at me while listening to my indifferent and dispassionate voice, and the whole of her little figure — every bit of it, even her muff and her hood — is an expression of utter bewilderment. On her face is written:

"What is going on? Who said *those* words? "Was it him, or did I just hear them?"

The lack of an answer is annoying her and taxing her patience. The poor girl does not answer my questions, is frowning and on the point of tears.

"Should we go home now?" I ask.

"Actually… I like this tobogganing," she says, going red. "Shall we go down again?"

She "likes" doing these runs, and yet as she gets on to the toboggan she is pale and trembling like the other times, and barely able to breathe she is so scared.

We go down a third time, and I can see her watching my face and following my lips. I put my handkerchief to my lips and cough, but when we are halfway down the run manage to utter:

"I love you, Nadya!"

So the mystery remains a mystery! Nadenka is silent, thinking about something… I take her home, and she tries to dawdle and walk slowly, waiting to see whether I will say those words to her. And I can see that she is suffering, and has to make an effort to stop herself from saying "It can't be the wind that said them! And I don't want it to be the wind that said them!"

The next morning I get a little note: "If you are going tobogganing today, come by and pick me up. N." And from then on I start going on runs every day with Nadenka, and as we fly down in the toboggan, I say in a low voice the same words: "I love you, Nadya!".

Soon Nadenka becomes as addicted to this phrase as if it was alchohol or morphine. She cannot live without it. She is just as terrified going down the run as before, of course, but now the fear and danger lend a peculiar charm to the declaration of love — a declaration which is a mystery, and causes heartache just like before. There are also the same two suspects — the wind and I… Which one of us is declaring their love for her she does not know, but she clearly no longer cares; it does not matter what vessel one drinks out of when the only goal is to be drunk.

One day I decide to go tobogganing in the middle of the day by myself; amongst the crowd I see Nadenka approaching the hill and looking out for me… Then she goes timidly up the steps… It is scary for her being on her own, really scary! She is white as snow as she climbs up, and trembling as if she going to her execution, but she goes up doggedly, without looking back. She has obviously decided to carry out the ultimate test: will she hear those wonderfully sweet words when I am not there? I see her sitting down on the toboggan, all pale, her mouth open with terror, then shutting her eyes, parting with the world forever and pushing off... "Zzzzzz!" go the runners. Whether Nadenka hears those words I do not know... All I see is her getting up from the toboggan looking weak and exhausted. And one can tell from her face that she herself cannot tell whether she heard anything or not. The terror of going down took away her ability to hear, distinguish sounds or understand...

But then March arrives... The sun becomes more affectionate... Our slope goes dark, loses its sparkle and finally melts. We give up tobogganing. There is nowhere for poor Nadenka to hear those words now, and in fact there is no one to say them, because there is no wind, and I am about to go to Petersburg — for a long time, probably for good.

About two days before my departure I find myself sitting in my garden in the dusk, and it so happens that my garden is separated from the grounds of Nadenka's house by a high fence studded with nails... It is still quite cold, there is still snow under the manure, and the trees are leafless, but there is already a whiff of spring and the rooks are cawing loudly as they settle for the night. I go up to the fence and spend a long while peering through the gap. I see Nadenka coming out on to the porch and looking sadly and longingly up at the sky... The spring wind is blowing straight into her pale, sorrowful face... It reminds her of the wind which used to roar on the toboggan run when she heard those four words, and her face becomes ever so forlorn, and a tear trickles down her cheek... The poor girl holds out both arms, as if entreating the wind to bring her those words again. And when the wind does start blowing, I say in a low voice: "I love you, Nadya!"

Good gracious, look at what is happening to Nadenka! She gives a cry, a smile lights up her face, and and she holds out her arms to the wind, looking radiant, happy and beautiful.

Meanwhile, I go off to pack...

That was a long time ago. Nadenka is now already married (whether she wed by choice or not is irrelevant) to a secretary of the Board of Trustees for the Nobility, and she aleady has three children now. She has not forgotten that we used to go tobogganing together, or that the wind carried the words "I love you, Nadenka". That is the happiest, most touching, and beautiful memory in her life...

As for me, I can no longer understand, now that I am older, why I uttered those words, and for what purpose I played that little joke...

Notes

1 Bibliographical data for this quote are supplied in Chapter 1, Note 5.
2 This Subsection has no claim to originality or innovation, and is focused on general–theoretical matters, rather than Chekhov-specific ones. Its sole aim is to offer a theoretically-oriented baseline for the ensuing discussion of Chekhovian characterisation.
3 This caveat refers primarily to music, a non-referential art, whose omission — deliberate and self-explanatory — is not a subject for the present discussion.
4 *Implied* is used here as in Booth 1961 (especially pp. 71–76). In this Book Chekhov's name, as a rule, denotes the *implied author* (*IAu*) of his work; the biographical, 'real' man Chekhov is hardly ever discussed, and local contexts keep clarifying the distinction between the two. I am also indebted to Wolfgang Iser's (e.g., 1974) development

of the concept of *implied reader* and to Gad Kaynar's (1997 and 2001) development of *Implied Spectator*, specifically applicable to *Drama* and *Theatre*.

5   The Book's treatment of the terms *character*, *personage* and *protagonist* is explained in the Preface.

6   A notable exception is Nina in *The Seagull*, whose changing personality unfolds concurrently with the play's progress on stage; analogous changes are reported about other personages, with varying degrees of reliability, as *expositional materials* — i.e., taking place in a play's past (see Sternberg 1978). A dynamic change in another Chekhov personage — Nádia from the story "A Little Joke" — is analysed in the present Chapter.

7   *Frame* is borrowed from painting, where it is used literally, but it is seamlessly extended to all other arts, where its use is figurative, stressing the beginnings, endings, and boundaries that separate between the 'framed', autonomous work/text/aesthetic object (in all arts), on the one hand, and the external/extra-textual world outside that frame, on the other. Frame-boundaries can be fuzzy; they can be challenged, blurred, subverted etc., but cannot really be annulled or obliterated in any art.

8   This contradiction in terms apparently intrigued Chekhov; it is actually the central theme in his story «Душечка» (1898) ["The Darling" is the common English translation of its title], whose central personage — Ól'ga Semiónovna Plemiánnikova — is a woman whose major character trait is a personality-vacuum: the absence of character traits, opinions, 'backbone' — of her own; an absolutely extreme case of character-less personage (by the way, her funny surname is derived from the Russian for *niece* or *nephew*, a 'derivative' status in a family).

9   I am indebted to Sternberg 1985 for a presentation of an analogous distinction in the context of Biblical narrative (see especially pp. 253–255, 344–364).

10 In this context a *group* is any collective of people (larger than one individual and smaller than humanity as a whole) sharing a common trait: e.g., belonging to a gender (i.e., all men or all women), race, class, nation, profession, generation, age-group, historical period, etc.

11 In the Russian original, "Шуточка". The story has been published in English several times, *inter alia* under such titles as "A/The (Little) Joke/Jest/Trick", and perhaps other English titles have been offered in translations unknown to me. I am gratefully indebted to Dr. Rosamund Bartlett for her generous contribution to this Book by allowing me to use her new translations for the two significantly distinct texts, published under the same title by Chekhov first in 1886 and later in 1899. To the best of my knowledge, Dr. Bartlett's is the first English-language publication of the former. Both her translations are published in Bartlett 2008. My discussion is focused on the 1899 text, unless otherwise stated.

12 I am particularly indebted to Robert Louis Jackson's (1999) discussion of this story, and through it to the few previous studies that he cites, notably a historical–textual study by the late Russian scholar Èmma Artém'ïevna Pólotskaïa (2006). Some of Jackson's points are integrated into my discussion, though it was difficult to acknowledge them separately. Kataev (2006, 195–196) illuminates Chekhov's decision to make a radical change in the story's ending from a different perspective, which complements mine. An autonomous version of 5.1 is published in Golomb (2012a).

13 There is a fine line between the terms *delusion*, *illusion*, and *hallucination* (even a look at dictionary definitions can bear that out); the distinctions are mainly based on differences in the degree of *physicality* of false or deceptive perceptions, and in the degree of *awareness* of their deceptiveness. I sometimes use these terms interchangeably, since Chekhov, typically paradoxically, is a master of combining sharp precision with blurred vagueness in drawing such fine lines and subtle distinctions. Thus, in this story, Nádia

tends to *delude herself* that she has an *illusion*, and at a certain point there is even a *delusion of hallucination*, when she fails to realise that the sounds she hears are acoustically real (Note 21 provides a complementary perspective). A rich variety of interactions and interrelations between *fact/reality* and *fantasy/fiction* preoccupied Chekhov in quite a few of his works: consider, for instance, how radically differently Chekhov presents and treats cognate phenomena in "The Black Monk" (its date, 1894, is between the two versions of "A Little Joke"), where the term *hallucination* figures prominently and explicitly in the text. A related theme in *The Seagull* is analysed in Golomb 2012, revised as Appendix in this Book.

14 Such naïve readers are occasionally the authors of scholarly studies; see, for instance, Johnson (1993) for an extremely simplistic view of this story: he takes the Narrator's account at face value, ignoring his blatant *unreliability*; it goes without saying that such a gullible reader ignores the striking difference between the two versions of the story, mismatching the later text with the earlier date. To be fair, it must be noted that the same error-of-judgement is made in the dating of the story even in the most authorised scholarly editions of Chekhov's stories in their Russian original.

15 Chekhov is not unique in his tendency to create gaps in knowledge between personage and perceiver that are mental–psychological rather than factual–informative; this seems to be more typical of modern literature in general. However, as will be shown here, his **way** of doing it was quite new, even unique.

16 Arguably, Nádia is more deluded by the Narrator than deluding herself, but she practises "*willing suspension of disbelief*", and the main term here is *willing*. This, indeed, is part of the conflict. Through her consent, or complicity, she can be seen as *self-deluding* in addition to being on the 'receiving end' of his constant and consistent efforts to delude her.

17 *Nádia* — the name used for this personage in this Chapter — is a diminutive form of *Nadézhda*. Chekhov occasionally resorts in his oeuvre to the old, somewhat hackneyed and *non-realistic* (i.e., incompatible with the edicts of *Realism* in literature) practice of giving his personages 'symbolic' names (going to a certain extent in the direction of *nomen-omen*). Thus, for instance, *Nadézhda* means *hope*; *Liubóv'* — *The Cherry Orchard*'s Ranévskaïa's full Christian name — means *love*. Both names are very common given names in Russia(n), with automatic–traditional diminutive nicknames (Nádia and Liúba, respectively), so that in real life one would easily ignore their lexical meanings; however, it is difficult to ignore it in a fictional text, where everything is supposed to be motivated (this has been challenged specifically in relation to Chekhov, though in my view not too convincingly, in the seminal book by Chudakóv 1983 [1971] and other studies). This practice weakens the usually consistent 'realistic' component of Chekhov's poetics, and, in my humble opinion, is not one of his numerous strengths as a writer. Yet in cases as the ones just mentioned the *nomen-omen* element is weakened considerably by the frequent use of diminutives and the rare use of the full Christian names in the texts themselves: in *Náden'ka* one does not hear *hope* as clearly and explicitly as in *Nadézhda*.

18 For theoretical discussions of *narrators'* (un)reliability, see Yacobi 2001 and 2005.

19 We see this conscious conflict in Sónia at least twice: in her ambivalence towards Yeléna's plan to find out Ástrov's intentions, and in her own attempt to test the ground by talking about a hypothetical girl-friend who would be in love with him. Ástrov's failure to take the latter hint exposes his own lack of emotional awareness; this is one of numerous examples of Chekhov's *reciprocal characterisation*.

20 Granted, he is an *unreliable narrator* in many ways, but on this particular point his account is largely vindicated by the story's plotline.

21 Unlike her, the reader and the Narrator know that she is hearing real sounds; in other words, in terms of factual reality, but not psychologically, it is precisely her subjectively plausible assessment that the sounds are illusory that is delusional, or at least mistaken.

22 Chekhov's conscious, consistent deletions of every reference to stereotyped group-images attributed to all women are most telling, and represent his later-acquired preference for individual and universal, rather than collective, type of characterisation. Note that in the earlier version this *group-characterisation* of all women is **not** accompanied by a complementary group-characterisation of all men (e.g., through the character of the *Narrator* himself). The implication, then — following the rhythm of the first sentence of *Anna Karenina* — is that every man is an individual, whereas all women are similar. All these gender stereotypes, explicit and implicit, are wiped out of the later version. Yet, even the later version is gender-asymmetrical: the chain of events of this story would just fall apart if the genders of the two protagonists were reversed. It has to be borne in mind, though, that even in the earlier version the *first-person narrator* is clearly distinct and distanced from the *IAu*, and certainly from Chekhov the man. This may again call for a *feministic* reading of the story, as complementing other readings; I am not aware of any such study, and it cannot be undertaken here.

23 This contradiction between Nádia's *narrator*-generated image and her fictional reality contributes to his own characterisation as a questionable characteriser of self and others.

24 A set of broader questions about hierarchies of reality and fantasy, implicitly and powerfully posed by the entire story, is discussed below.

25 The intrinsic value of unanswerable questions, and of the **urge** to ask them, is one of Chekhov's deeply held convictions about mankind; it is the very essence of some of his open endings, notably that of *Three Sisters*, but also of several stories: e.g., "A Dreary Tale", "The Lady with a Little Dog", and "A Little Joke" itself. See Winner 1966 (especially p. 5). I return to this subject in the Book's last Chapter.

26 An instance of another auditory manifestation of a Chekhovian unrequited love comes to mind — Sónia's monologue after Ástrov leaves the room in Act 2 of *Uncle Vánia*: "his voice vibrates, caresses… I can still feel it in the air".

27 The fusion between the voices of two or three speakers (here: the *Narrator*, Nádia, and perhaps *IAu* Chekhov himself) — characteristically suggesting rhythms of thought or imagined speech of covert speakers through the direct speech of the overt speaker — is a famous literary and dramatic device, discussed often in the literature. The prevalent term in English is *Free Indirect Speech*; the Russian term is *несобственно прямая речь*; its theory was also elaborated in the 1970s in Hebrew studies by Menakhem Perry and me. My initial (1970) term, rendered in English as *Combined Speech*, was subsequently elaborated by Perry (1979) as *Combined Discourse*, both terms referring to the effect of fusion between *narrator* and *personage*, or between two personages, combining their voices in one utterance. A striking use of this device by Chekhov is the opening of his story "Rothschild's Fiddle".

28 One of this *narrator*'s inconsistencies, establishing his unreliability, is that at some points, as in this quote, he claims near-omniscient capabilities to quote Nádia's thoughts verbatim, and at some other points — e.g., in his account of the *watershed* events — he concedes inability to read her mind.

29 In his discussion of this story R.L. Jackson (1999) lays special and convincing stress on its erotic aspects, most of which are typically implicit.

30 *Hallucination* is the explicit focus of Chekhov's famous story "The Black Monk" (1894). Thus, it is potentially relevant both to the present analysis and to the study of *art–life* interactions in the Appendix. At this stage, however, I have decided to avoid the added complication and hierarchy-reversal inherent in a further analysis of connec-

tions between "The Black Monk" and matters discussed in the Book. This potentially intricate subject is worthy of separate research, which cannot be carried out here.

31 In the earlier version Chekhov makes the Narrator quote Nádia's thoughts verbatim, as he reads them from her facial expression: "It can't be the wind [...] It's you, my friend, who said them! You!" In the later version this sentence (from the pre-*watershed* section of the story) is gone without a trace.

32 Did Nádia get over the Narrator by getting married and having children? The answer to this question is beside the point, not only because of its absence: the question itself, and the doubt that it represents, are enough for Chekhov's purposes. The more general question, whether having a marriage and a family is a solution to this type of situations and problems, also stays open, typically raised but not answered. For the story's purpose, casting serious doubts on the credibility of the Narrator's assertions at the end of the text is sufficient. *The Seagull*'s Másha's failure to make her marriage to Medvedénko get over her unrequited love for Konstantín may come to mind, but the analogy is wrong: Másha was indeed in love with Konstantín, whereas in "A Little Joke" there is no evidence that Nádia reached the point of falling in love with the Narrator. Marriage definitely failed in the former case, but could (or could not!) work in the latter. Chekhov's jury, once out, is seldom recalled in such cases.

33 This is a major reason for the blatant inferiority of the earlier version to the later one: once the mystery of the source of the voice is dispelled, admitted by him and revealed to her, and once, consequently, "'the wind' option' is ruled out, there is hardly anything complex, or even interesting, in the "joke", which is neither funny nor poignant or sarcastic. The 1899 revision, involving as it does changing a small number of words in a single-digit number of lines, turned a work characteristic of a gifted but quite shallow young writer of 1886 into a masterpiece of an 1899 genius.

34 In this he is diametrically opposed to classical (notably Shakespearean) villains, typically aware of their villainy through awareness of the norms they violate.

35 The analogy is of course to Pétia Trofímov's self-characterisation as being "above love" (*The Cherry Orchard*, Act 3). Ranévskaïa's immediate rejoinder, "and I am probably beneath it", would conform to the way the Narrator here would characterise Nádia, especially in the earlier version of the story. Of course he is simplistic in both these characterisations.

36 One of the open questions in "A Little Joke" is the nature and status of the act of telling the story itself, bearing in mind that it is a *first-person narration*: there is no personalised addressee to whom the story is being told, nor is there a dramatised or fictionalised act of writing. Thus *the reader* has to stand for the *addressee* of both texts: the *narrator*'s as well as Chekhov's. This point is further elaborated in Note 44.

37 In the unforgettable words of Jack/Ernest towards the end of Oscar Wilde's *The Importance of Being Earnest*: "It is a terrible thing for a man to find out suddenly that all his life he has been speaking nothing but the truth".

38 «Это всё равно» in the original — the same indifferent, nihilistic phrase with which Chebutýkin counterbalances the sisters' quest for knowledge at the ending of *Three Sisters* as shown in 9.2.4.

39 There is no hint of the Narrator's profession, occupation, origin, name, etc.; in fact he is defined in the story only in terms of his relationship (such as it was) with Nádia.

40 Thus, he does not mention Nádia's children's sex — a subtle vignette: it is very likely that when he kept inquiring about her for years, and was told of the three births, each in its time, the sex of each baby was mentioned to him in passing; however, his generalising statement "three children" implies that her motherhood was insignificant, not only for him, but — the way he saw it — for her too.

41 One can remember Chekhov's story "The Lady with a Little Dog", in which Ánna Sergéïevna refers to her bureaucrat husband's occupation as being "a lackey". It is significant though that in "A Little Joke" there is no such explicit statement, and the implicit one is made by the Narrator, not by Nádia.

42 The 1886 publication was not signed by Chekhonte, but by a rarer pseudonym that Chekhov used at the time, "Man without Spleen", but Chekhonte is an umbrella-name for Chekhov's early period.

43 Chekhov's poetics, with its *abhorrence of dogmatism* (see Chudakóv 1983, 204) indicates a disbelief in **the truth**, the one and only absolutely correct opinion or answer, but it smacks of a constant, uncompromising pursuit of **a truth** (though Chekhov himself could not have made this distinction **in these terms**, in the absence of articles in Russian), which in turn is different from subjective *sincerity*, as explained in 8.2.6.

44 Again, the storytelling situation is unclear. The earlier version ends when the *Narrator* explicitly addresses his readers, in the second person plural. No trace of this device is left in the later version, so the only *addressee* of the *narrator* is *the reader*, who is also Chekhov's own addressee, in his capacity as *IAu*. The result is asymmetrical: on the authorial side of the textual transmission, the *implied author* is certainly distinct from the *narrator*, whereas the *reader* is on the receiving end for both. This may (though need not necessarily) be regarded as a single minor flaw in a story whose writing technique, by and large, is an epitome of perfection.

45 Of course, these two terms hardly cover the entire gamut of phenomena, which is incomparably more varied and intricate: thus, for instance, such loaded concepts as *truth* and *art*, to mention two out of many, deepen and complicate the issues considerably. However, to conclude the discussion of the story this admittedly simplified dichotomy seems to illustrate the basic issues.

46 In "A Dreary Tale", arguably the most heart-breaking moment — the final farewell between Nikoláï Stepánovich and Kátia — occurs when he refuses to pretend that he has a solution to an existential problem of hers. What she asks him is to tell her, indeed to instruct her, what to do and how to salvage her life's emotional wreckage. It is clear that at this point she would accept **any** answer coming **from him**. This does not necessarily mean that she would really implement any advice of his, and they both know it, but this is not the point. Rather, the point is that his conscience — in this context, the conscience of a Chekhov-like doctor and scientist — forces him to leave her heartbroken rather than to fake a false answer when there is none to give. This is another powerful instance of the potentially crushing force of *presence through absence*. This scene is discussed in greater detail in 7.1.

47 To avoid clumsiness, henceforth *actor* also stands for *actress*, and *he* and its derivatives also stand for *she* and its derivatives. The term *Implied Actor (IAc)* is modelled after Booth 1961's *Implied Author (IAu)* and Kaynar's (1997, 2001) *Implied Spectator*.

48 Thus, for instance, Tom Stoppard's *Rosencrantz and Guildenstern are Dead* is an exceptionally rich blow-up elaboration on Rosencrantz's and Guildenstern's *PPs* within Shakespeare's *Hamlet*.

49 I am indebted to my colleagues Karin Heskia and Prof. Shimon Levy for part of the conceptual framework and the actual discussions of the *offstage* phenomenon. See also Golomb and Heskia (1990).

50 For instance, *Three Sisters*' late General Prózorov (the father of the three sisters and their brother Andréï), powerfully present, *inter alia*, in his children's lives and in the play's system of values; *The Cherry Orchard*'s Grísha (Ranévskaïa's drowned son, see below); and many others.

51 Once again, all the *implied* agents (*IAu*s, *IAc*s etc.) are mental constructs inferable from

the text rather than real or even fictional persons; saying that an *IAc* is "obliged to do something" means, in this restrictive context, that the hierarchies in a *PP* imply that he should be doing that 'something'.

52 Plays' titles come to mind in this context: thus, titles from the Greeks to the present are often names of one protagonist, or two (e.g., *Oedipus Rex*, *Macbeth*, *Romeo and Juliet*, *Hedda Gabler*). Among Chekhov's four major plays, only one — *Uncle Vánia* — has a single personage for a title. Of course, *Ivánov* comes to mind as a Chekhov play named after one personage, but it is not one of his posthumously canonised "Four Major Plays"; *Platónov* is a name posthumously given to Chekhov's first, unfinished and unnamed play, called in scholarly editions simply *Untitled Play*).

53 The Stanislávskiïan dictum "there are no minor parts, only minor actors" is witty, but if taken literally it is simply incorrect.

54 To the best of my knowledge, this centrality has been regarded by tacit consensus as an obvious feature of the play, so obvious that it has hardly ever been challenged, questioned, or even systematically studied with the aim of establishing and corroborating it.

55 The general nature of such phenomena in Chekhov's poetics was discussed in Chapters 1 and 2, also in conjunction with the time-honoured concept of *Subtext* in Chekhov studies.

56 The Russian word for *sordid* is not there, but is implied by the derogatory use of this diminutive; even the sheer sound of it — /ramánchik/ — in a Russian context, has a demeaning effect.

57 If Chebutýkin (or most other personages) had mentioned the Másha-Vershínin love-affair, the derogatory term *románchik* would not have even crossed their minds to refer to it; but Chebutýkin chooses here to ignore this affair altogether, thus showing confidentiality and restraint, an impressive attitude especially in this scene, marked by his drunkenness, to which Kulýgin, in his typical Latin, responds with *in vino veritas* ["in wine there is truth", roughly, or rather "drinking brings out truth"].

58 Since *PP* is a construct introduced solely for the purpose of this discussion, this question can be decided by me as its inventor. My sole consideration whether or not to allow the concept of an *offstage character*'s *PP* is whether such a concept contributes to a better understanding of Chekhov's poetics; and since offstage, absent personages are an important part of this poetics, the answer should have been *yes*. This results in a split between the constructs of *PP* and *IAc*, since there can be no actor, real or implied, who potentially works on the part of an absent, text-less personage.

59 Indeed, concepts of *aesthetic motivation* have been with us for quite a few decades, and in some forms for centuries; yet, it is perhaps not superfluous to reiterate, that such "making sense" is legitimately sought and required in works of fiction in general, and in this theatrical context in particular, much more than in real life. This is so at least because a creator of a fictional world is our human peer, and as such accountable to us for his/her authorial decisions in a way that the presumably divine creator of the real world (or, for an atheist, the laws and forces of nature) cannot be. Thus, whereas a real person dies, Andréï Bolkónskiï was 'killed' by Tolstóï in *War and Peace*, and Chekhov was the one who both 'begot' and 'killed' Túsenbach in *Three Sisters* and the fictionally-stillborn Grísha in *The Cherry Orchard*. We, then, are entitled to ask the writer 'why', holding him accountable to us (of course, this type of 'why' is answerable in aesthetic–artistic rather than legal or moral terms). Usually (depending on genre and tradition), unlike real-life events, fictional ones have to persuade perceivers of their authors' choices; these choices are expected to make sense, at least within the terms and conventions of genre, time and tradition.

60 The exceptional complexity of the materials discussed here seems to resist the intended

neatness of some of the distinctions governing the Subsection-division in this Chapter, so that some types of characterisation techniques may coincide and overlap; the examples, however, are designed do demonstrate dominance of certain aspects over others.

61 One of the comic aspects of these comparisons is that Kulýgin is unaware that "it's not done" for a husband — especially a conventional husband like him, so concerned with keeping up appearances and keeping telling everyone who cares to listen that he and his wife love each other as they should — to confess so explicitly that he does not regard his wife as unique. In Act 3, shortly after equating Ól'ga with Másha (addressing the former), he addresses the latter as "my one and only", totally unaware of the flagrant contradiction, which prompts Másha's sarcastic response in conjugating the verb *to love* in Latin at him. Complementary aspects of the function of Latin in the play are discussed in 6.2.5.1.

62 Indirectly, though, Kulýgin may have a point: notwithstanding his preference for *individual* and *universal* characterisation, Chekhov does characterise groups here and there. Thus, all the play's *Muscovites* differ in certain respects from all the residents of the provincial township. Even obtuse Kulýgin, unable to understand the full significance of this *collective characterisation*, can still sense it (as does his townswoman Natásha). Indeed, contrasted with Kulýgin, all the Prózorovs, and especially the three sisters, do have some traits in common; yet Kulýgin misses the point in the way he says it.

63 We know about her opinion of Andréï from her explicit statements in Act 3, made in his absence; Andréï knows about it simply because he knows her: she does not have to give him a piece of her mind in so many words to make him know what she thinks of him. His own conscience and self-reproach are experienced as the voice of 'the Másha within him'.

64 It should be noted that Másha is absent from the last scene in Act 3, where Andréï breaks down in tears confessing the depth of his failures, his betrayal of the family values, to the other two sisters there present (but invisible to him and to us, behind their bed-screens). Andréï's desperate calling for her in Act 4, then, is a continuation of his previous confession to the other two sisters. Andréï shouts Másha's name only when he knows that she cannot hear him, just as he admits speaking to Ferapónt precisely because he knows that the old servant can neither hear nor understand him. Thus, he is destined never to tell Másha how much she means to him, and never to tell anyone who can understand him how frustrated he is. This, of course, compounds his frustration.

65 The *raison d'être* of fictional personages is a theoretical question that comes up time and again in the literature. In *The Cherry Orchard* this question is raised explicitly by Charlótta at the beginning of Act 2, where she simply asks not only **who** but also **why** she is, she wonders about the reason and purpose of her very existence. By implication the question is asked not only by her, on the play's *inner/fictional plane*, but also by Chekhov, within the tacit dialogue between him as *implied author* and us as *implied spectators*, and it can of course be expanded to other personages: indeed, why Charlótta? Why Gáïev? Why any personage, onstage or offstage? Once the question is brought up, it cannot be annulled, and we are invited to ask it, i.e., to question Chekhov himself, not to take anything, even his authorial decisions, for granted.

66 Similar in many ways is the case of the woman killed by Chebutýkin's maltreatment, mentioned in Act 3 of *Three Sisters*. This tragedy was the result of his false pretence to know and remember the relevant information from his medical studies. He mentions this incident in conjunction with his behaviour at the club, where he pretended to have read Shakespeare and Voltaire. The latter pretence can be taken lightly — "so what" if someone pretends to have read some author, without having really read him, during a social occasion? — but through the analogy with the deadly results of medical ignorance

Chekhov tells us that lying about one's ignorance can betray a habit of irresponsibility, which, at the end of the day, can have fatal consequences.

67 Professional Chekhov scholars over the decades, present writer included, are no exception: few seem immune to her charms on page or stage; personally, it took me years of research and teaching under her spell to notice incriminating evidence against her that has been right there in the text ever since Chekhov committed it to paper.

68 An analogous case (one of quite a few) is Arkádina's hurling at Konstantín "parasite! Kiev *petit bourgeois!*" (*The Seagull*, Act 3). There is more than a grain of truth in what she is saying, but she is the last person on earth entitled to chide him, since she is a major cause for his turning out the way he did: she is the one who had chosen a "Kiev *petit bourgeois*" for his father, and whose presence and absence had a crucial impact on his upbringing; it is almost like the story about the son who murdered his parents and begged for the court's clemency because he is an orphan...

69 This is a more precise rendition of the original phrase; most English translations, however, render it as "I might have been a Schopenhauer! A Dostoïévskiï!" — which is much smoother in English.

70 For book-length studies of reading plays see Meisel 2007, especially 1–11; Scolnicov & Holland 1989.

71 A complementary view of *character and characterisation* in Chekhov, from a predominantly historical perspective, is offered below in 10.3, within a proposed model of *The Descent of the Stature of Man*, initially presented in 6.0

CHAPTER

6

Communicating
(in) Chekhov

I don't understand you;
you don't understand me;
what else do we have in common?

(Text on a card sold on a London street; unattributed)

6.0 Communication and the *'Descent of Man's Stature'*

Characterising Chekhov as a major, if not **the** major, communicator of the experience of *non-communication* among fictional human beings (i.e., personages),[1] is
so prevalent in the relevant secondary literature that lack of communication has
become almost synonymous with his name. Terms like *Chekhovian dialogue,*
Chekhovian situation, Chekhovian scene, especially when applied figuratively to
real-life situations or events, or to fictional texts authored by others, usually mean
'dialogue between the inattentive (or 'mentally deaf')', 'situation of mutual misunderstanding', 'scene of faulty communication', etc. Indeed, Chekhov's is an
undeniably crucial contribution to a historical process in western literature of the
last two centuries, marked by gradual increase in faulty communication between
personages in fictional literature, and, naturally, by growing awareness of this
phenomenon in the secondary literature of textual analysis, scholarship and criticism.[2] However, this Chapter will show that Chekhov's view of human
communication is incomparably subtler and more intricate and heterogeneous than
just suggested; that in treating this crucial component of human life (as well as
other ones) he was committed to showing its variety, complexity and diversity, and
its dependence on a host of objective and subjective variables. Thus, despite superficial impressions to the contrary, he seems to have had little interest in generalising
about the totality of existence, or non-existence, of human communication. In his
typical way, he tends to refrain from telling his audience directly, or even from
showing them indirectly, that people, when relating to each other, are either always,
or never, mutually understanding, attentive, communicative, etc. As with regard to
other major components of Chekhov's poetics discussed in the previous Chapters,

so with regard to *communication*, he supplants such potential **assertions** with a set of implicit **questions**, never explicitly asked (let alone answered), such as: What is communicated? Who is communicating, and with whom? When? Where? How? In what circumstances/context? In what order/sequence? What enhances communication and what hinders or undermines it, in general, and/or for a particular individual person, and/or for a particular case in point? Such questions, and potential answers to them, are inferred from what we hear and see in a play, in a variety of indirect ways. Thus, highly differentiated and heterogeneous conditions radically affect the nature and 'amount' or 'volume' of communication achieved in each instance. Chekhov shows human communication, then, as an ever-changing and constantly flexible phenomenon, contingent on a myriad of variables. In short: Chekhov's system of communication is preoccupied with the intricacy, heterogeneity and infinite variety of the phenomenon, rather than with indiscriminately affirming or negating its existence.

In order to study communication in Chekhov's plays — as indeed in *fictional worlds* in general, and dramatic/theatrical ones in particular — a working distinction is proposed here between two types or areas of communication, operating simultaneously. The first type · – the *inner,* or *fictional plane* of communication — operates within the confines of the fictional world, i.e., between/among personages (and, to a lesser extent, among other components of the fictional text and world); the second — the *outer,* or *rhetorical plane*[3] — operates within the 'real world', i.e., between the non-fiction participants in the process of communication — the author/addresser on the one hand and the audience of recipients/perceivers/addressees on the other — **through** the *inner plane* of fictional personages, or even 'behind their backs'. Of course, when it comes to Drama, the *inner plane* is the *staged* (or potentially staged) fictional world. This distinction is needed, *inter alia*, to present both possibilities of discrepancy between these two planes of communication: (1) a text that maintains reasonable communication with its addressees, by conveying its meanings coherently and lucidly, while depicting lack of such communication among its characters, and (2) a text that does the reverse: the personages are reciprocally attentive and understanding, whereas the audience is left 'in the dark', so to speak, out of this communication. The former type of communication, functional on the *outer* plane and dysfunctional on the *inner*, can be illustrated by typical (though not all-pervasive) parts of Chekhov's plays, where the audience is provided with all the necessary clues to understand what the characters say and mean, while they fail the tests of mutual attentiveness and understanding among them; the latter, functional on the *inner* plane and dysfunctional on the *outer*, is typical of many dialogues in "*absurd*" plays such as Beckett's *Waiting for Godot* or Ionesco's *The Chairs*, where the personages seem to respond coherently to each other's points — the very points, which the audience is likely to find incoherent, enigmatic, or even *non sequitur* (a complementary perspective of *historical poetics* on the latter point is given in 10.3).

In this sense, even if Chekhov's plays had displayed exclusively and one-sidedly situations of lack of communication among personages (which is hardly the case, as will be shown below), this would not have amounted to characterising his entire world as non-communicative, since on the *outer plane* he is still communicating with/to **us**, his audience of addressees, which implies the existence of some kind of human communication within the theatrical semiotic system as a whole. This of course is part of a more general question of the traditional concept of artistic *mimesis* (see for instance Auerbach 1953) or Lotman's (1977 [1971]) concept of *modelling*. The modelling/mimetic/representational[4] relationships between a 'real' world on the one hand and its *fictional representation* on the other hand[5] can be viewed in two ways. Thus, reality is analogous to, or modelled by, either (a) a well-framed, autonomous *fictional world* (in theatre it is the world on stage), functioning as an integral closed set, or (b) the *theatrical semiotic-communicative process* in its entirety, which includes the *outer* participating factors — (*implied*)[6] author and perceiver/audience — **in addition to** the *fictional 'world'*. According to the former approach — i.e., if we look at the *staged fictional world* as claiming *representation of reality* — the apparent steady historical process of gradual decline in the human, intellectual and verbal stature of most stage personages is deemed to represent a process of human decline in the real world, or at the very least it reflects the authors' strong belief in such a gradual process of such decline; in other words, this approach focuses on the declining stature of personages in European drama in the course of the past four or five centuries[7] to reach the conclusion that later playwrights have a much poorer view of humanity than earlier ones. According to the latter approach, however, the (*implied*) *audience* is an integral part of the equation, no less than the fictional world and its personages; and since in most Chekhovian and post-Chekhovian models of reality the *implied* perceivers, or audience members, share the towering stature of the author himself, with whom they are supposed to converse on virtually equal terms 'behind the backs' of the comparatively inferior fictional personages, the overall stature of humanity is not in historical decline. Put more simply, the process of decline in the stature of personages is accompanied by a complementary process of rise in the stature of *implied spectators*. Schematically,[8] then, there is inverse proportion between the respective statures of fictional personages on the one hand, and audiences on the other: *semiotic responsibilities* of various voices and agents (e.g., authors, performers, perceivers) can switch roles and places, while the basic, overall *semiotic–communicational process* remains intact. Thus, if the personages on stage are deficient in their verbal and intellectual capabilities, and/or if the text is boring or depleted, the implied audience is deemed to have superior intellectual and integrational capabilities to fill in the semiotic-communicational vacuum.

To conclude: by taking into account the entire *semiotic–communicational process* (which includes real-human and fictional elements alike), the latter approach is superior to the former one (which takes into account only the *fictional* elements) in viewing ways in which reality is reflected in Drama; and according to this comprehensive approach *Chekhovian persons* are not inferior to *persons* in earlier and classical Drama, if this term refers not only to the fictional personages Chekhov created but also to the real persons whom he addressed (albeit **through** those fictional ones), and to the person of the writer himself. Moreover, it takes an intellectually active and sophisticated person — in possession of perspectives gained through one's experience as reader of literature, spectator in the theatre, and human being in the 'real world' — to perceive, integrate and evaluate the 'inferior' aspects of Chekhovian fictional personages. The model of the '*Descent of Man*' (or rather, *the Descent of Man's Stature*) in the history of drama, then, is misleadingly partial, because it does not examine the complementary 'ascending' stature of the implied audience.

6.1 Chekhov and Staged Communication: 'Public Images'

Chekhov has been regarded a pioneer of presenting lack of communication on stage; this is one of the main reasons for hailing him as a major precursor of the *absurd* (this hindsight view of Chekhov's image and legacy is a matter of almost universal consent). To substantiate this point both stories and plays are frequently cited; and, indeed, most of his later stories and all of the major plays stress faulty communication: misunderstood, misdelivered, ill-timed, and wrongly-addressed messages abound in these works and charge them with a heavy load of *unrealised potentials* of communicational energy, of potentially communicable, yet actually uncommunicated messages and meanings. The result is a very powerful *presence* of clearly identifiable and precisely delineated *absences* — the unspoken, the undone and the unfulfilled can usually be acutely sensed, and often reasonably formulated by the perceiver, as something that is **almost** tangible in the text, but not quite, because it is specifically absent.

As shown throughout the Book, Chekhov has a real passion for plurality, diversity and heterogeneity, manifest in his treatment of all strata and components of his 'world' — themes, personages, events, etc. In this sense, his treatment of *communication* is analogous to his treatment of many other themes and human phenomena, particularly those that are comparable to it in magnitude (being central to the human condition), such as *love, art, work, education*, etc. In all of these cases a striking degree of plurality and diversity characterises the selection of textual events through which the given theme is presented. As shown in Chapter 2, all themes — indeed, all significant information data — are communicated to us through structuration, i.e., through relationships and interactions between at least two, but usually many more, such relevant elements. As for the specific theme of human communication, a heterogeneous inventory of communication-relationships between and among personages should also be viewed as yet another set of relationships between and among textual segments. In this sense, basically the same structuration technique discussed above as communicating Chekhov's pluralistic view of *love, work, art*, etc. is at work in communicating his view of *communication* to his audience.

Indeed, no thematic point is ever made in Chekhov through an isolated element in the text. This applies especially to plays, where all statements are made by personages, who hardly ever function as Chekhov's mouthpiece (see Epigraph to Chapter 5), and no single event embodies a conclusive view of any subject. Only a composite view of all different, often conflicting, materials deemed relevant to the presentation of a subject has a legitimate claim to be considered Chekhov's.

The two planes (*inner* and *outer*) exist in the presentation of all themes, but the status of the theme of *communication* is unique among them, because *the outer/rhetorical plane* always constitutes the **communication** of the author, through textual relationships, with us, his audience/perceivers/addressees. Thus, in the case of themes like *love, work*, or *education*, for instance, we can watch them as phenomena in the lives of the personages (i.e., on *the inner/fictional plane*), but obviously, the text as a whole — as an act of *outer plane* communication — does not love, work, or educate in relation to us; rather, it **communicates** to us a view of love, work or education. Only in the case of *communication* itself, operating on the *inner plane*, can we trace *isomorphism*, whereby the text's (*implied*) *author*, on the *outer plane*, communicates to us a view of communication, constructed from the interplay between the diverse communication-events that take place among personages on the *inner plane*, and, in the final analysis, also from the ways in which **it** does or does not make itself communicable to us on the *outer plane*. The latter, of course, is just another act of communication: it goes without saying that the play as a whole, as any text and any work of art, is an act of communication from addresser to addressee.[9]

Finally, in parallel to the distinction between direct/indirect characterisation proposed in 5.2, one can find in Chekhov's plays direct and indirect presentations of the presence and/or absence of communication and mutual understanding.

6.2 Communication at Work: *Three Sisters* as a Case Study[10]

Discussion in this section is based primarily on analyses of scenes and relationships from *Three Sisters*, in which Chekhov reached an unprecedented peak in the process of developing his poetics in the field of communication.

6.2.1 Sisterly Communication: *Voluntary/Involuntary, Explicit/Implicit*

The communication relationships in the innermost circle of personages within the play's *inner/fictional plane* between members of the Prózorov family, and particularly between the three sisters and within any pair of them, are saturated with direct/indirect (explicit/implicit) networks. I shall start with a few examples from the Ól'ga–Másha relationship.

The first explicit reference to communication between the two elder sisters appears in Act 1, soon after the curtain rises on the celebration of Irína's birthday (or *name-day*, in the *Pravoslav* [Christian–Orthodox] tradition, explained in Chapter 3, Note 29, and in the *Guide*, Note 30; see also Senelick 2005, p. 249, note 6). Chekhov unfolds their respective moods.

Másha's role in this scene, and this scene's role in the construction of her character, are discussed in 5.2. Her whistling, as well as her seeming *non sequitur* quote from Pushkin (these are her first **words** in the play), indicate her demonstrable aloofness of the conversation, of which she is of course keenly aware. This is a case of ***involuntary*** one-sided communication — i.e., Másha cannot help being privy to her sisters' conversation, though she clearly would prefer to be left alone to her own thoughts. Subsequently, when she takes her leave of Irína and the others, her gloomy, distracted mood is also reflected in the inadvertent contradiction between saying that she is going "home" and, immediately afterwards, that she is going "somewhere". This entire chain of verbal and non-verbal behaviour is the unfolding of a coherent, though puzzling, mood-complex in Másha, that changes only in the wake of Vershínin's entrance.

Ól'ga's reaction to this mood is a process of communicational trial-and-error. She moves from reprimanding Másha outright for her whistling ("Don't whistle, Másha! How can you!") to ignoring Másha's defiant, second whistling; then she moves further on, through an attempt at characterising Másha's mood ("You are not cheerful today, Másha") till she makes the explicit claim (the accompanying *stage-direction* is *through tears*)[11] "I understand you, Másha" — apparently, partly in response to Irína's and Túsenbach's unsympathetic responses to Másha immi- nent departure. In this particular scene, Ól'ga's stance towards Másha is almost one of unrequited wooing: Másha, in a carefully orchestrated delayed response[12] to Ól'ga's "I understand you", reacts both to the content and to the tone (*"through tears"*) of the latter's message, with what appears in the text as "Másha [*to Ól'ga, angrily*]: Don't howl!".[13]

This detailed account of the scene shows the subtlety of Chekhov's technique. He builds up, step by step, Ól'ga's attempt at reaching communication and empa- thy. The attempt appears doomed to failure from the start, not least because an act of communication, by definition, must be reciprocal, while this one looks as if it is taking place in its entirety in Ól'ga's mind: after this seemingly 'intra-Ól'ga' process culminates with her announcement of success — now that she finally "understands" Másha, as it were — comes Másha's response, which exposes the hollowness of Ól'ga's pretence to "understand" her sister, and shows how futile and unrealistic the entire effort had been from the start.[14] Másha, on her part, is char- acterised here for the first time as possessing a keen sense of observation and a total impatience with, and intolerance for, any form of sentimental pretence. At this point she is clearly bewildered by the strangeness of her own conduct, of which she is keenly aware, making no attempt to smooth over it. There is no reason for her to accept that Ól'ga understands her better than she herself does (beyond stating the obvious, that Másha is "not cheerful"). The outspoken, candid disapproval of her behaviour, as expressed by Túsenbach and Irína, does not bother her at all, but she is almost incensed by Ól'ga's unfounded and affected, though genuinely well-wish- ing, offer and declaration of understanding.

However, Chekhov's composite, "correct presentation of the problem", through the *outer plane*, is even subtler and more complex: beyond and through the verbal exchange between the two sisters one can sense an undercurrent of sensi- tive communication that runs stronger and deeper than the momentary misunderstanding between them. Ól'ga's angry reaction to Másha's whistling is not merely the intolerant response of an elder sister (and a teacher by profession at that) to her younger sister's apparent display of bad manners; it shows her genuine, intuitive **understanding** of this whistling as an expression of Másha's scepticism towards the naïve and oversimplified manner in which her two sisters have just presented the family's Moscow plans and Másha's own role in them.

Másha's silence, her demonstration of disengagement from her sisters' dialogue, puts her from the play's beginning in a position of solitude and, more important, of reservation and even dissent towards her sisters; in addition, she is also cast in the role of a yardstick by which the amount of naked truth in her sisters' dreams is measured (Andréï, too, is keenly aware of Másha's truthfulness, as shown in 5.2.2.4). Thus, Ól'ga — from her subjectively justified standpoint — is angry at Másha for the 'right' reasons, and has understood Másha more than she herself has realised, but not at the moment, and not in the sense, that she claims to possess such an understanding. Similarly, by exposing the hollowness of Ól'ga 'understanding', Másha is responding on a deeper level to Ól'ga's permanent desire to smooth over differences and unpleasantnesses, even at the price of evading and ignoring a truth because it is unpleasant. It is a formidable challenge for the creative team of a production (director, actors etc.), especially so early in the play, to make use of non-verbal channels in order to bring this undercurrent of indirect, hardly noticeable communication-subtleties to the subliminal attention of an audience. If they manage to do that, the role of these channels of communication in the reciprocal characterisation of the two sisters can become apparent.

Thus, the two sisters can be seen as sensitively communicating with each other on a deep level of responsiveness — as a dialogue between basic character traits, that is all the more convincing when occurring between two siblings sharing heredity as well as a history that goes back to childhood. At any rate, a significant point is that communication is shown as deeper and more genuine when it seems to be missing ("don't whistle"/"don't howl!"), while it almost stops functioning when its triumph is explicitly boasted (with Ól'ga's "I understand you"). This is a striking example of Chekhov's frequent (though not permanent!) disbelief in explicit statements, especially when interpreted literally, and deep belief in undercurrents of subliminal emotions, that **may** be expressed verbally through their opposites. It is of course an instance of the celebrated *subtext* in Chekhov; however, that intuitive term is often a mixed bag of vague generalities, in need of corroboration through focused observations of detailed subtleties.

Chekhov's tendency to give us conflicting viewpoints of themes and phenomena can be demonstrated by juxtaposing the scene just discussed with Másha's confession-scene in Act 3 (the scene occurs against the background of the town fire). Just as Ól'ga's declaration that she 'understands' Másha is pronounced when she understands next to nothing, almost the reverse happens in Act 3: at the very moment when Másha, after a short and agonising hesitation, finally names Vershínin's as her lover, Ól'ga reacts with an explicitly declared refusal to listen to her sister. Here is the dialogue between the two (with slight omissions of subtleties somewhat irrelevant to the point made here, though intrinsically very significant, as always in Chekhov):

> MÁSHA: I love, I love . . . I love that man … you have just seen him … well, there it is … in a word, I love Vershínin.
> ÓL'GA [*goes behind her screen*]: Stop that. Anyway, I don't hear you.
> MÁSHA: What am I to do! [...] At first I thought him strange, then I felt sorry for him . . . then I began to love him [...]

ÓL'GA [*behind the screen*]: I don't hear you anyway. Whatever silly things you may be saying, I don't hear them anyway.
MÁSHA: Ah, you're silly, Ólia. I love him — that must be my fate [...]

When Ól'ga says that she "does not hear" her sister's confession, she is in fact "all ears": she hears, listens, and understands; and her choice of *hear* (rather than *listen*) further undermines her credibility. Her moving behind the screen, ostrich-like,[15] is pathetic, even ridiculous, yet it is too serious and emotionally loaded to be funny; it is a desperate attempt to "see no evil, hear no evil, speak no evil", like the famous statuette (or relief) of the three monkeys. But Chekhov makes a precise and effective distinction between the operations of the two senses: she can block the voluntary visual channel between her and her sisters, but not the involuntary auditory one; and it is the latter that carries the cognitive message of communication. Yet, if we take the two sisters' words at face-value, we are left with a combination of Ól'ga refusing to listen, and Másha — neither trying to make her listen, nor making any apparent effort to understand Ól'ga's refusal — branding her elder sister as "silly". One of the implications of this adjective, if taken literally, would suggest that Másha regards any effort to communicate with Ól'ga as a waste of time; however, it is clear that it must not be taken literally here.

Indeed, these explicit exchanges must be understood and filtered through the relevant semantic and thematic networks in which the two sisters take part and which, in turn, place them within a complex, balanced perspective. Thus, Ól'ga's proclaimed refusal to listen to Másha's confession must be understood in connection with the former's strongly held prudish, old-maid convictions about marriage — convictions that she is trying to 'sell' to Irína in this scene. She has spoken about the subject several times in the play, always with self-persuasion, always betraying her total lack of life experience by being pathetically abstract and bookish: "I **would have loved** my husband", she says in Act 1, referring to an imaginary spouse in a hypothetical marriage, which she would have preferred to her position as a schoolteacher.[16] It is clear, then, that Másha's falling in love with Vershínin, and on top of that disclosing this fact at this very moment in front of Irína, can be sensed as a 'stab in the back' from Ól'ga's standpoint. Here she is, the eldest sister, the 'Greek chorus' of the family and the play as a whole, trying to do and say 'the right things', to unite and conciliate, to cement the cracks within the family, and mainly to provide the 'correct' answers by upholding the 'right' values that have passed on, posing as *heritage*, from generation to generation. She, the spinster sister, advocates a Másha-Kulýgin-type marriage, both for herself ("God willing") and for Irína, as she has just said a few minutes earlier in the very same Act 3 confession-scene: "One doesn't marry[17] for love, but to do one's duty [...] and I would marry without love [...] so long as he was a decent man". Thus, Ól'ga is actually, though implicitly, preaching to Irína to avoid her own lot of spinsterhood by following Másha's example, implying something like '*If you don't follow Másha's example by marrying a decent man without love, you would actually be following my example, and end up an old maid*'.

Now Másha — a silent, but actively attentive, witness to this conversation between her two sisters, culminating in Ól'ga's explicit advice to Irína to agree to marry Túsenbach —does not respond directly. When Natásha — unexpectedly, and totally ignoring the sisters' presence — crosses the room silently and resolutely with a candle,[18] Másha remarks sarcastically that Natásha is walking as if she started the fire herself, to which Ól'ga retorts: "You, Másha, are silly. The silliest one in our family is you. Forgive me please". Of course, she cannot mean it literally (not any more than Másha had just been literal in branding Ól'ga as "silly");[19] here, as in many cases in Chekhov, a personage's words cannot be taken at face value. But Ól'ga is clearly irritated — as with Másha's whistling in Act 1 — because she knows her sister and senses intuitively the 'vibrations' emanating from her. Indeed, Másha's presence and personality make it difficult for Ól'ga to preach her platitudes to Irína. It is Másha's tone of voice and sharpness of tongue, giving out her personality (as characterised in 5.2.2), which must have triggered Ól'ga's response, rather than her words about Natásha.

Now comes Másha's confession of her love for Vershínin, which makes Ól'ga's views — advocating, in fact, loveless marriage — sound very hollow indeed. From Ól'ga's standpoint, Másha must be doubly guilty: both through her infidelity and by 'spoiling the child', setting an unhidden immoral example for Irína. Indirectly, then, Másha's confession is a powerful rebuttal of Ól'ga's argument in favour of Irína's marrying Túsenbach.

This is the main reason why Ól'ga does not want to hear or to witness Másha's confession; and when she says it explicitly, Másha hurls the same word — "silly" — back at her, though undoubtedly with a different intonation. Then, almost ignoring Ól'ga, She turns to Irína directly and says to her:

> When you[20] read some novel or other, it appears that everything is so old and understandable; but when you fall in love yourself, you realise that nobody knows anything, and everyone has to decide for himself.

Thus Másha is answering Ól'ga through addressing Irína, to complement and reverse what happened in the previously mentioned exchanges between the two older sisters, where Irína was very much the *implied* addressee. Moreover, this is one of many examples of *répliques* that say quite the opposite of what the speakers mean, not because of any deliberate reversal of meaning, let alone a wish to conceal or mislead, but because of various kinds of counterpoint between inner emotions and outward expressions. In such cases Chekhov often deliberately suggests that the *speaking personage* can be partly aware of this counterpoint, and of analogous awareness in the *fictional addressee* (the staged listener, to whom the message is addressed). Thus, Ól'ga is most attentive when saying that she "does not hear" Másha's confession; in fact, all three sisters — addresser Ól'ga, addressee Másha, and witness-listener Irína — know full well that "not hearing" in these circumstances means anything but its literal sense. Likewise, just as no one present took Ól'ga's saying "silly" to Másha at face value, so it is when Másha hurls "silly" back at Ól'ga that she **does** answer her, very seriously and sincerely, with mutual respect and understanding. By addressing Irína the way she does, Másha shows that at this moment communication between her and Ól'ga is at its highest, and it is a typically Chekhovian presentation of human communication that this climax of mutual understanding is conveyed though an indirect dialogue between the two elder sisters through the younger one: IRína is, so to speak, the **arena** for the conflict of messages between her two elder sisters. Needless to add, this is also a moment of powerful *reciprocal characterisation* between all three sisters.

Thus, while Ól'ga's message to IRína can be paraphrased as proposed above (i.e., offering IRína a choice between a 'decent' loveless marriage and spinsterhood), Másha's message to IRína implies something like '*You have **heard** Ól'ga; you have **seen** my marriage — custom-made according to Ól'ga's specifications — leading to a hopeless extra-marital love; but neither of us can teach you. You have to decide for yourself*'. Másha's message to Ól'ga is (as it were, of course) as follows: '*Here, in the family context, you are no teacher, and no one can be. My marriage could vindicate your convictions, but my love for Vershínin has disproved them. So don't you preach to IRína, let her decide for herself*'. Such thoughts are largely subliminal; they are unspoken, and remain so, but — with Chekhov's poetics of *unrealised potentials* and *present absences* — they are subtly, poignantly and powerfully communicated among the three sisters: above, behind, and beyond their spoken words. And the entire process, one should remember, takes place under the guise of total, proclaimed 'deafness' and, partly, through explicit refusal to communicate. Chekhov is justly reputed for his skills in showing deafness disguised by false attentiveness; here, however, he at least equally skilfully does the opposite.

One can conclude from the aforesaid that Chekhov is presenting us with a schematic model of inversions, whereby whenever someone says that s/he understands someone else s/he actually doesn't, and vice versa. Things are not that simple, however. To cite just two counter-examples: when Natásha and Ól'ga in Act 3 say to each other "I don't understand you", and when Natásha concludes "It's either I don't understand, or else you don't want to understand me", they **really** do not communicate with each other. Similarly, when Ól'ga says to IRína (in the same Act) "I understand everything" in the limited context of understanding the link between Túsenbach's plain looks and unattractiveness as a man and IRína's reluctance to marry him, she **really** understands her sister on that particular point.

In fact, theoretically, we have here four combination-possibilities, and in *Three Sisters* there are actual instances of all four: people saying, both correctly and incorrectly, that they do, or do not, understand others. This four-way inventory yields a very typically Chekhovian "presentation of the problem",[21] namely, that nothing can be taken for granted and that each case must be understood on its own merits. Indeed, Chekhov has an almost innate uncontrollable impulse to discredit his characters' explicit pronouncements (see Epigraph to Chapter 5), particularly on matters of communication and self-awareness. Yet his aversion to **any** schematicism is much stronger. He would hardly ever refute an *always* with a *never*, or vice versa, when he can do it with a *sometimes* or a *contingent on circumstances*: as Chudakóv (1983, 204) puts it, "The single dogmatic feature in Chekhov is his condemnation of dogmatism" (in 1.5, where this dictum is quoted for the first time in the Book, I suggested replacing *condemnation* with *abhorrence, negation* etc). This usually applies even to Chekhov's own 'dogmas': his aversion to any 'dogma' is uncompromising; it makes no allowances and tolerates no exceptions, except for exposing a dogmatic trait even in an 'anti-dogmatic dogma'. It is the side-by-side existence of apparent contradictions that is so typical of his poetics; yet, in fact, they are hardly ever real contradictions: rather, they are manifestations of diversity and complexity, of variable effects resulting from variable causes, as shown throughout this Book. Taking one's cue from Chudakóv's dictum, one can probably say that one of the only constant things in Chekhov is ever-changing, ever-contingent variability.

6.2.2 Turning the Other Ear: Attentive 'Deafness'

So far *communication* has been discussed only in cases when Chekhov's dramatic text itself made explicit references to its presence or absence. However, most communication-events in literature and Drama — in Chekhov and elsewhere — simply happen (or do not happen), without such explicit verbal–textual references to their (non-)existence. And indeed, Chekhov's depiction of communication varieties is even more impressively heterogeneous where the subject is not explicitly discussed. Thus, we have in *Three Sisters* a whole gamut of communication-types and communication-effects, ranging from (few) straight 'Ibsen-like', 'ping-pong-like' dialogical chains of replies-to-the-point to 'disintegrated' dialogues with no apparent connection between what the various characters are saying (ostensibly, to each other). The latter type, in numerous forms and degrees, is basically Chekhov's elaboration of the *dialogue of the deaf* device.

This device — whether *staged deafness* was real or metaphorical — had been an old, hackneyed feature of Drama and theatre long before Chekhov; however, it used to be employed almost exclusively for comic effects. Chekhov is an innovator here too, because he made pathbreaking use of the old device for totally non-comic purposes.[22]

However, one instance in *Three Sisters* seems to constitute a totally comic use of the device, activating the old technique: I am referring to the seemingly irrelevant and pointless argument in Act 2 between Soliónyï and Chebutýkin, ostensibly about a meaning of one word, while each of them, without being aware of it, is saying, and defining correctly, a different word (the two words — черемша [*cheremshá*] and чехартма [*chekhartmá*] — sound alike but are not identical). The argument as such has little relevance to anything else in the play, but it does play important roles in its network of communication types and effects. Among these roles I would like to mention three: (a) supplying a comic pole, essential to the balanced and diversified presentation of the predominantly serious, even gloomy picture of *communicational deafness* in the play; (b) demonstrating Chekhov's ability to create a scene in the old comic tradition, tantamount to *verbal slapstick*, made prominent by its sheer rarity in the Chekhovian context, and — through this contrast — throwing the other instances of 'deafness' into bold relief; (c) fitting (together with other scenes) into an interaction-pattern that plays a variety of physical and mental deafness-instances against each other: Chebutýkin and Soliónyï are not reported to have any hearing problems, but they prefer to have a silly and irrelevant row rather than to make the slightest effort simply to lend an attentive ear to each other and literally hear what the other one is saying. Thus this exchange is a crude, unsophisticated counterpart of the subtle disconnected dialogues, more typical of Chekhov's poetics.[23] Unlike the *cheremshá–chekhartmá* 'argument', in the subtler examples there is no 'communicational showdown'; people spin out their separate threads of thought, which occasionally form a pattern, and are hardly aware of the discontinuous nature of their conversation. The latter, in turn, functions more as part of the *outer plane* discourse, by which Chekhov is telling and showing us something both about how to write plays and about how people often communicate in real life, than as part of the *inner plane* enclosed within the play's fictional world.

At the other polar extreme in terms of subtlety and meaningfulness are Andréï's '*monologic dialogues*' with the nearly-deaf Ferapónt (Zviniatskovsky 2006 provides a relevant complementary analysis of these exchanges). Both personages, in diametrical opposition to Soliónyï and Chebutýkin, are aware of the type of 'dialogue' they are having; thus in Act 2, during their first conversation, we have the following exchange:

> ANDRÉÏ: [...] My God! I am the secretary of the local council [...] I, who dreams every night that I'm a professor [...] the pride of all Russia![24]
> FERAPÓNT: I couldn't tell... Don't hear well...
> ANDRÉÏ: If you could hear well, I probably wouldn't be talking to you.

Ferapónt is, literally, almost deaf; moreover, he could not properly communicate with Andréï on these matters even if he could hear, because some of the words Andréï is using are not within Ferapónt's vocabulary, and the problems that the former is referring to are far beyond the intellectual and even the informational reach of the latter. Yet in the 'dialogues' between the two, in all the last three Acts of the play, one can sense genuine though frustrating attempts to communicate, and subtle, sensitive attentiveness that goes beyond the physical deafness. Ferapónt does his limited best to listen, and he picks a familiar word (naturally, *Moscow* is more familiar to him than *professor*), and makes a naïve, well-meaning and hopeless attempt to say something useful about it; but, of course, he cannot say anything that Andréï can find comforting, or even relevant. Andréï, on his part, is looking for a way out of his loneliness, and willingly suspends his disbelief in Ferapónt's ability to be a partner to a meaningful conversation with him. On the *outer plane*, Chekhov uses Ferapónt as a device to bypass the hurdle of contemporaneous sensibility's uneasiness with *dramatic soliloquy* (i.e., the negative attitude of *Realistic* theatre — as characterised in the Book, notably 10.1.2.1 — towards this time-honoured device): a character genuinely confessing his innermost thoughts to another character who is partly deaf, though somewhat attentive, with a limited ability to understand the content of the confession is an innovation in drama, an ingenious combination of *dialogue* and *monologue*.

At any rate, in a typically Chekhovian structuration-strategy, we have interactions between those who are deaf but listen; those who hear and refuse to listen, with or without being aware of it; those who listen while declaring their refusal to hear; etc. Each case is highly functional and motivated, both on the localised *micro* level of the specific scene and on the global *macro* level, coextensive with the play as a whole. Once again, the infinite variety is demonstrated, a variety where the presence and the absence of **willingness** as well as **capacity** to listen are shown to be stronger than the physical capabilities or limitations of hearing. Even the axiomatically involuntary nature of the sense of hearing is questioned, and its automatic acceptance is presented as oversimplified.

6.2.3 Confessions: Unrequited Communication

Three Sisters has a relatively large number of highly significant *confessions* (whether or not referred to as such in the text). Their centrality to the construction of the theme of *communication* is self-evident, since confessions, by definition, are pleas for communication. It is highly characteristic of Chekhov that something often goes astray in the way leading from the addresser of the confession to its addressee's and/or listener's response (the latter two are not necessarily identical; see below). More often than not, there is a conventionally expected response (e.g., a *yes* or a *no*, worded one way or another, as a response to a direct love-confession; or analogous responses of acceptance or rejection to other types of confessions). However, in Chekhov this expectation is almost invariably frustrated: the typically Chekhovian response neither welcomes the confession with acceptance or sympathy, nor repels or rejects it head-on, but rather ignores, evades or misunderstands it, as if pushing it aside (rather than away), refraining from noticing it, without gracing it with a relevant response. A typically Chekhovian confession, then, is a *potential unrealised*; it is somewhat defused and keeps hovering, 'hanging in the air'. Paradoxically, it is often made more powerful by remaining forever emasculated through the lack of response. The effect may range from comic (e.g., the interruption of Andréï's love confession to Natásha at the end of Act 1 by the entrance of the two officers) to the most movingly heartbreaking — e.g., Andréï's confession at the end of Act 3, culminating with his crying out loud "Don't believe me!", broken in turn by the sisters' thundering silence and Kulýgin's entrance; or Túsenbach's final departure, broken by his own ordering of a cup of coffee and the immediate entrance of Andréï and Ferapónt in Act 4. Some feats of irreducible combination of the comic with the heartbreaking are unmistakably Chekhovian, e.g., Kulýgin's masquerading as the "German teacher" with the confiscated beard and moustache between the inescapably tear-jerking farewell of Másha and Vershínin and the news about the death of Túsenbach in the duel (the brief "German teacher" episode is a 'comic relief' may surpass even *Macbeth*'s 'Porter scene', Act 3 — Shakespeare relegates the comic effect to an outside agent, the porter, whereas in Chekhov it is the same people who are involved in crying and laughing at the same time).[25] Yet, the basic principle, which is both *thematic* and *structural*, is largely the same: it is the building up of a *potential* and then preventing, or rather obstructing, its *realisation*, creating ever-growing quantities and qualities of *present absences* through interactions between the conventionally expected response (that is absent from the text) and the frustration of that expectation (that is present in it). In other words: the principle is that a substantive **presence** (an expected response) is **absent**, whereas a substantive **absence** (a frustration of such an expectation) is **present**. A specific, perhaps unique Chekhovian effect, then, is the *neutralisation of the dichotomy between the 'positive' and the 'negative'*: both look similar in being equally supplanted by the seemingly irrelevant. Such cases, however, are not a permanent occurrence in Chekhov; they are typical, characteristic, unmistakably Chekhovian, but not all-pervasive. Other types of responses, some of which are much more conventional, definitely exist in Chekhov's texts. It is the combination of an enormous variety of emotional and communicational patterns of behaviour — or, in other words, of the uniquely-Chekhovian and the more conventional or traditional ones — that is, in the final analysis, truly Chekhovian. **Chekhov would not be Chekhov if his works consisted exclusively of the typically-Chekhovian**.

That said, it should also be stressed that the typically-Chekhovian type of the *irrelevant* — i.e., the diagonally or sideways-oriented response — is hardly ever accidental or truly irrelevant. It is almost invariably amply motivated in many ways; it is a junction of heterogeneous motivations — to borrow B. Harshav's (1976) term — functioning simultaneously in connection with individual characterisation, scene-construction, global thematic presentation of communication in the play and other contexts.

For the purpose of the present analysis of a selected number of confessions it seems useful and convenient to distinguish between *confessions of love* and *confessions on other subjects*, and within the former between *second-person* and *third-person confessions* — i.e., those spoken directly to the loved person and those spoken to others about him or her.

Vershínin's confession of love to Másha (Act 2) is a masterpiece of semantic loading: interaction between semantic elements charges them with meanings that they could never have had on their own. What Vershínin himself has to say, here and in several other places in the play, is 'remarkably unremarkable':

> VERSHÍNIN: I love, I love, I love . . . I love your eyes [...] You splendid, wonderful woman! It is dark here, but I see the sparkle of your eyes.

The first part of this quote could have been said to thousands of women by thousands of wooing men: there is nothing in it that is specific to the addressee Másha (or to the addresser Vershínin, for that matter). The sheer banality of the choice of words is made perhaps even more obvious by the platitude of the 'poetic diction' of light-in-the-darkness in the second part of the quotation. It is not Vershínin's sincerity that is called into doubt here, but the communicative power of his love-clichés. Judged by result — winning Másha's love — he does seem to communicate satisfactorily within the *inner plane* of the fictional world; however, on the *outer plane*, it is actually Másha's genuinely personal and highly unpredictable reaction to these clichés that makes the scene so full of meaning and so saturated with communication. With the pointed and subtle irony so typical of her, Másha moves to another chair, saying: "There's more light here". In terms of communication we have here an interesting variant: Másha's coquettishly pseudo-naïve, mock-literal understanding of Vershínin's words betrays a true understanding of his real meaning and rhetoric, which she **chooses** to pretend to ignore or misunderstand. Vershínin, on his part, ignores her irony — which he most

probably understands, and loves — and goes on with his confession, unimagina-
tive as before: "I love, I love, I love your eyes..." and then, again, the same
adjectives ("splendid, wonderful woman"). Másha's reaction again exposes a
complex mixture: a growing responsiveness to his love; a growing fear of that
responsiveness and its inescapable, menacing consequences for a married woman;
a resignation to her fate; and an inability to say plainly *yes* or *no*, let alone to speak
with the same platitudes as he does. She uses everyday words, not poetic ones, yet
they are loaded with much more meaning and emotional complexity than all his
poetic clichés:

> When you talk to me like that, I laugh for some reason, although I am frightened.
> Please don't repeat it, I beg you ... Well, maybe you'd better go on talking, it's all
> the same to me... Someone's coming, talk about something else...

The banality of Vershínin's confession does not prevent him from communicating with Másha even during that scene; nor, indeed, from finally winning her
love. In a complementary manner, the relatively much more individuated and
genuine nature of Túsenbach's love-confessions to Irína does not guarantee instantaneous communication, nor indeed does it secure the achievement of **his** ultimate
goal — Irína's love. In Chekhov's world — saturated as it is with highly intense
and heavily charged potentials that remain forever unrealised — Túsenbach's
potential for love and communication is one of the most powerful instances.
Vershínin's case is just the opposite: the realisation, in terms of Másha's love and
attentiveness, is far greater than the potential. The typically Chekhovian effect of
unrealised potential is achieved here only when the relationship is viewed from
Másha's standpoint: her love potential is too great for a Vershínin to realise.

However, Túsenbach, too, has his moments of inattentiveness. The other side
of the coin of love — its potentially uncommunicative self-centredness — is
demonstrated in a nutshell in his first love-confession in Act 1:

> TÚSENBACH: So many years lie before us, a long, long succession of days, full
> of my love for you...
> IRÍNA: Nikoláï L'vóvich, don't talk to me of love.
> TÚSENBACH [*not listening*]: I have a passionate thirst for life [...]

Here Irína listens to him and understands him, but would not (because she cannot)
communicate on the plane of his choice — the plane of love. But it is he, who is
supposed to be much more in need of communication with her, who goes on
talking, without listening to her upsetting and disappointing reaction. It is remarkable that Chekhov provides us here, explicitly, with such an unequivocal
stage-direction as "*not listening*".

From this instance one could draw a hasty conclusion, as if Chekhov is
presenting here a conflict between love and communication. This proves not to be
the case, however, both in *Three Sisters* in general, and the Irína-Túsenbach relationship in particular. One has to remember the tender, suspenseful and extremely
sensitive scene of their farewell (Act 4) in order to see that both the loving-and-

unloved Túsenbach and the loved-and-unloving Iŕina are most impressively capable of attentive, deep communication with each other. Thus the confession of non-love between them is a masterpiece of attentiveness and empathy. This scene includes the most direct plea for communication. It comes right after that tender confession of non-love by Iŕina and its total understanding by Túsenbach (the scene is analysed from a different angle in Golomb 1984, 183–186):

> TÚSENBACH: Say to me something.
> IRÍNA: What? What should I say? What?
> TÚSENBACH: Something [or: Just anything].
> IRÍNA: Enough, enough!

The scene concludes with his last words — asking Iŕina to make coffee for him — which follow a stage-direction "*not knowing what to say*". These two examples seem to suggest lack of communication; but, again, one should keep in mind Chekhov's mechanism of contrasting different elements in a given structure. Looking at the scene in its appropriate context, one can be convinced that Iŕina's refusal to say **"something"** (or **just anything at all**) and Túsenbach's *not knowing what to say* are products of mutual attentiveness: she senses that nothing she — or anyone else, for that matter — can possibly say could be that particular "something" that he needs at this very tense, intense, suspenseful and loaded moment; except, perhaps, the words *I love you*, which she cannot utter and he is doomed never to hear.[26] He, on his part, feels her tension and is genuinely helpless; in order not to dramatise his final exit he opts for the banal order of that cup of coffee that he is doomed never to drink. Once again, then, what looks like a flagrant and obvious case of crippled communication proves to be almost the opposite.

As a digression within the subject, I would like to draw attention to the analogy between Túsenbach's cup of coffee and Vershínin's never-to-be-drunk cup of tea that is a centre of so much attention in Act 2; but this analogy serves in a context different from the one discussed here. Vershínin's light-hearted nature is manifest in his constant willingness and readiness to "philosophise" instead of drinking tea and even while waiting for his final farewell with Másha (creating an almost comic analogy between tea/philosophising/final farewell); Túsenbach, on the other hand, is much more serious, and his farewell is really final: he is knowingly going to die; and instead of hollow "philosophising" analogous to tea, in Túsenbach's case that coffee-order is the result of *not knowing what to say*. Thus, Túsenbach's loaded silence, and seemingly trivialised order of coffee, are much more communicative and meaningful than Vershínin's ever-ready "philosophising", as shown in 8.3.2.

6.2.4 Multiple ('Criss-cross') Communication

So far dialogues and confessions involving basically two persons have been discussed. The following is a more complex example, consisting partly of love-confessions or love-statements, but activating criss-cross communication patterns involving four persons.

One of the streaks that run across Act 3 of *Three Sisters* is the sisters' persistent effort, though apparently a subconscious one, to remain together alone, just the three of them — a privilege denied them again and again throughout the play (The play's title serves, *inter alia,* to focus our attention on this streak).[27] The very urge to be together alone is indicative of both a need and a capability to communicate with each other, realising the potential sibling intimacy that the presence of others can only spoil. And indeed, a strong need and a considerable capability for communication are intensely displayed in those brief, rare and precious moments that they are left alone in this Act — the moments of their most sincere and self-exposing confessions.

This subconsciously concerted effort to push outsiders out begins with Irína's flat order to Solióny, who has just entered, to leave the room. But after both he (under protest) and Vershínin (taking the hint with grace) leave the room comes Túsenbach's turn. He is asleep and Irína wakes him up. He mumbles a mixture of work-plans and love-confessions. But even in this moment of disorientation, having just woken up, Túsenbach's words of love, unlike Vershínin's, are very specific to the woman he loves, Irína, and totally inapplicable to any other woman. However, it is Másha, not Irína, who responds. To her, probably, Túsenbach's confessions sound like Kulýgin's (unfair to the former as this may be), and her attentiveness to, and identification with, her younger sister makes her second-guess the latter's unspoken response. Therefore she says to Túsenbach: "Nikolái L'vóvich, do get out". Túsenbach cannot control his emotional build-up and makes perhaps his most heartbreaking love confession to Irína, which he concludes with a prayer that proves ominous: "If only it were granted to me to give my life for you!"

This moving expression of love is even more poignant because it gets no apparent response from the addressee, Irína, while Másha responds impatiently: "Nikolái L'vóvich, do go away, what is it, really?!" The two sisters' behaviour seems to indicate that neither of them really heard what Túsenbach had just said, or at least that they did not care to listen carefully enough to be able to process the full emotional weight of his words. It is indeed unfortunate for Túsenbach that his most tender confession is uttered at the wrong moment, which shows that he, too, is now insensitive and inattentive to the people around him and what is going on with them. This confession, then, is doomed to join other unspoken, unanswered, unacknowledged and unrequited statements and emotional gestures which form the long list of unrealised communication-potentials of the play and to add exceptional weight to its heavy load. Irína's urge to confess her emotional distress to her sisters, and to no one else, makes her quite deaf to what must sound to her like yet another tiresome love-confession from Túsenbach (this seems to be the most likely explanation of her silence). She may not have really listened to it, then; but the most striking fact at this moment is the deep and subtle wordless communication between the sisters, that coincides with their almost callous inattentiveness to others: it is Másha who intuitively does Irína's work for her, telling Túsenbach to leave. Soon enough, Irína returns this favour in kind: when Másha wakes Kulýgin up and he begins to pour his love-clichés on her, it is Irína who first tries to implore him to leave. Each of them, without conscious collusion, speaks her sister's mind.

The most important *third-person love confession* is undoubtedly Másha's declaration of love for Vershínin to her sisters in Act 3, discussed above. Másha's ever-individuated and unpredictable way of speaking serves here to highlight the poor performance of Vershínin as a 'verbaliser' of love back in Act 2 as well. Once again, the simple, everyday, but succinct and precise words of Másha have the power of the concrete and specific, conspicuously absent from Vershínin's confession: when she describes how she finally fell in love with him as a 'package', *in toto* — including his voice, his words, his misfortunes and his two daughters — one can sense the individuality of Vershínin through these words; they could not have been said about anybody else in the play.

Thus we have banal, unspecific love-confessions from Andréï (Act 1) and Vershínin, and individuated, specific ones from Másha and Túsenbach; but the communication achieved is very specific to each case. Two cases of *hypothetical third-person love statements* are worth mentioning here: the two spinster sisters, Ól'ga and Irína, speak about the love they would bear to imaginary men (the former in Act 1, speaking about the husband she would have married and loved, "God willing", and the latter in Act 3, speaking about the man she would have been destined to meet and love if the family had moved to Moscow). Now Chekhov's artistic system, characterised as it is by utmost subtlety and flexibility, hardly ever allows or accommodates simplistic, symmetrical formulas of direct or inverse proportion. Rather than providing us with a 'teach-yourself-how-to-communicate-and-succeed-in-love' manual, Chekhov enables us to sense the *inexhaustible complexity* and *heterogeneity* of love and communication. The two are correlated, but the key to the rules governing this correlation has been lost (to paraphrase what Irína says about the piano that she likens to her soul in Act 4).

6.2.5 Communication and Language(s)

Out of the confessions[28] on subjects other than love in *Three Sisters* I would like to mention two, both in the confession-packed Act 3: Irína's confession in the middle of the Act, and Andréï's towards its end. Both are concerned with communication itself as a theme, and with the phenomenon of *language*, which is man's chief means of communication. This phenomenon is indirectly but powerfully explored in these confessions in two different contexts. Irína's confession is indeed focused on the theme of **language**: explicitly, in its literal sense — one's native language and foreign languages — and implicitly, in its figurative senses, i.e., the 'languages' of all arts, sciences, religions, ideologies etc. (the latter is subsumed under Lotman 1977's term *secondary modelling systems*, discussed elsewhere in the Book). All of these are means of human *communication*. Andréï's confession is differently, but just as powerfully, at the forefront of the play's treatment of the communicative power of language in general (as opposed to its total absence, i.e. silence), and of its *reductio ad absurdum* through meaningless and non-referential *potentially-verbal* sounds ('gibberish' vowels and consonants).

6.2.5.1 Languages (Native and Foreign): An End or a Means?

In her confession or outburst in Act 3, Irína views her entire life as wasted, and it is remarkable that her despair is epitomised for her, as it were, in having forgotten some Italian words:

> IRÍNA: Where has it all gone? Where is it? [...] I have forgotten everything [...]
> I don't remember what's the Italian for window, or for ceiling.

Now it is clear that at this juncture in her life Irína couldn't care less about the Italian words for *window* or *ceiling*. Why, then, is this what comes to her mind there and then?

Chekhov prepared this confession for the spectator well in advance, in Act 1, when Andréï tells us that their father had made Irína study Italian in addition to the three foreign languages (French, German and English) that her siblings had also studied. Somewhat later in the same Act Másha adds the observation that in the provincial town the knowledge of three foreign languages is at best an unnecessary luxury, or even something harmfully superfluous, "like a sixth finger". This is a powerful pathological analogy; however, coming as it does from an involved personage, at an early stage in the play's development, it requires some evidence to validate or invalidate it. It is only here, in Act 3, that it acquires such direct substantiation, when we see the degenerating process at work in Irína's mind.

Why did General Prózorov Senior insist that his children should learn these foreign languages? Why does Irína bemoan so bitterly the loss of that specific faculty — the knowledge to say something in her fourth foreign language? The answer to these questions lies in the potential function of the knowledge of foreign languages as a tool for broadening one's horizons through communication with other peoples and cultures. Within the late General Prózorov's world of values, foreign language, music and science were definitely seen in these terms, and all constituted part of an education designed to produce enlightened, well-read and open-minded persons.[29] It is precisely the communicative function of foreign languages that is most important for the Prózorovs — for the sisters, and even for Andréï; once this function is not fulfilled, the knowledge of the foreign language itself degenerates because of disuse, and even becomes a liability ("a sixth finger"), as happens to all the languages, literal and figurative, that the late General imposed on his children. As illustration of this degenerative process, the text singles out Andréï's English, science and music (violin playing), Másha's music, and Irína's Italian. The comprehensive significance of this approach to languages, culture and learning is corroborated by its vindication in all these instances; as we have seen, Chekhov's poetics supplies time and again this type of analogies, and encourages us to look for them as a crucial part of generating significant overall meanings out of what appears as trivialities if viewed in isolation.

Now this attitude to a foreign language as a tool, as a means to an end, is sharply contrasted with the attitudes represented by the two major provincial personages in the play — Natásha and Kulýgin. Although the Prózorovs are reliably described as having good command of several foreign languages, none of them ever utters as much as a single non-Russian word[30] throughout the entire play. On the other hand, the kind-hearted Kulýgin and the callous Natásha, who equally epitomise the narrow-minded provinciality of the local population, have a special liking for speaking foreign languages. In this ingenious way Chekhov questions (though does not reverse) the cliché that dwellers of metropolitan centres, being "people of the world", speak foreign languages, whereas provincial people can speak only their native tongue. The real question for Chekhov, then, is not technical but functional: **how** a language — whether native or foreign — is used, and **what for**.

For Natásha, speaking French (and funny French at that, as pointed out by some critics) is a means to an end; yet not to the end of communicating with French culture, God forbid — she would probably have difficulties in spelling the word — but to the end of making an impression and showing off. The Prózorovs' genuine knowledge of foreign languages is beyond this stage: they do not need this kind of showing off and get along perfectly well in their native Russian; Natásha's provinciality is underlined by her affected 'internationalism', and it acquires grotesque proportions when she, in her ridiculous French, scolds Másha for her bad manners (Act 2). Natásha's French is an anti-communicative employment of a foreign language; instead of serving as a window or binoculars enabling one to look at the outer world, it is designed to serve as a flattering mirror — Snow-White's stepmother style — to impress upon her in-laws how educated she is. No wonder that Túsenbach can hardly refrain laughing at this moment.

As for Kulýgin, the function of Latin in his life and world-view is even more diametrically opposed to that of foreign languages in the world of the Prózorovs. For him Latin is an end in itself; not even Latin as a whole, but its grammar, its *ut consecutivum* (Act 4). It is a subtle and significant act of selection on Chekhov's part to choose, of all languages, to contrast Latin and Italian. On the one hand, the formalised, self-sufficient, grammar-oriented Latin is a barren language that has lost its communicative vitality, but thorough knowledge and vivid memory of its fossilised rules are a source of pride and contentment for Kulýgin. On the other hand, Latin's living descendant, Italian, is a language that long ago, in Irína's childhood, had been earmarked for living communication with brave new worlds; and now, having forgotten this language is a source of pain, disillusionment and hopelessness to her. It should be stressed in this context, that the late General Prózorov had his children study living languages of Western Europe, rather than classical Greek or Latin — the former are keys to ever-broadening horizons in the present and the future, whereas the latter are culturally dead end, a closed set leading only to texts and worlds of the past. This choice is indicative of the General's hierarchy of values and the priorities in his perception of the purpose of learning and education.

Thus, typically, Chekhov's presentation is thoroughly non-schematic: the knowledge of foreign languages, as such, neither guarantees nor precludes the opening of new avenues for broader and richer human communication. A foreign language is no more and no less than a tool; and, like all tools, it can be used well or badly, efficiently or counter-productively. Thus, the sophisticated and diverse presence of the theme of foreign languages in *Three Sisters* lends to the play's communication-system an explicitly general, universally-human dimension.

6.2.5.2 Language, Silence, *Non-Language*[31]

Andréï's confession at the end of Act 3 is almost an uninterrupted single *réplique*. He is talking and talking, against a backdrop of active silence on the part of his addressees, Ól'ga and Irína. The extraordinary thing about this confession is that it makes a complete reversal of attitude, a 'U-turn', in its speaker, without any apparent reason within the text itself, on the page or on the stage, without any contradictory arguments being made. Technically, it is a monologue, since the addressees remain silent; it even appears to be a soliloquy, because its onstage addressees are invisible to the audience. However, this monologue is an act of communication **on stage**, placed firmly within the *inner/fictional plane* (of course, in addition to its function within the ever-present *outer/rhetorical plane*). The sisters' thoughts and attitudes are known to the audience; moreover, they are known to Andréï himself perfectly well. This is so not only because life-long intimate acquaintance enables him to form much more than an educated guess of what his sisters are thinking, but also, and mainly, because they represent his other self, his "better half" (in Hamlet terms) through their own conversations and confessions just heard, and their intense silence speaks loud and clear. In his torn, split being there is a voice, heard aloud in his one-way conversations with the deaf Ferapónt and dialogues with Chebutýkin, and that is the voice of 'Moscow', of the sisters, of the dead father's values, legacy and education. The sisters need not talk back to him in order to make that voice resonate in his mind's ears; moreover, talking back is not their strongest point throughout the play. It is their beings, rather than their words or actions, that are in conflict with the Natáshas and Protopópovs of the play. In this specific scene there is no conceivable thing that the sisters could have said that could be so powerfully meaningful and communicative as their silence.

On the *inner plane*, they are silent because they are tired, because they know that Andréï is mentally cornered and cannot really pursue his untenable self-defence, because they see no point in arguing with him, and because the main emotion he evokes in them is pity, rather than verbal sabre rattling. Had they talked back, Andréï would have probably entrenched himself more deeply in his stubborn defences; but it is their silence, the powerful mental and communicative *presence* of their visual and verbal *absence*, which softens him up by activating his inner voice that resonates with their unspoken thoughts. It is that voice which brings the cathartic process within him to its culmination with his final breakdown, crying with tears: "My sisters, my dear sisters, don't believe me!"

On the *outer plane*, this scene is a very important element in the thematic mechanism designed to question, but not to deny, the communicative powers of **any** language, native or foreign, as compared to those of language-negating systems such as silence or non-semantic sounds. In this context one can contrast the pseudo-philosophical ("philosophising") deliberations between Túsenbach and Vershínin throughout the play with the nonsense dialogues ("Tram-tam-tam/tra-ta-ta") between Másha and Vershínin. The semantic weight and referential power of the former are of course incomparably greater than those of the latter. On the one hand, we have a few Russian sentences as *signifiers*, while the *signified* is almost infinity, the entire future of humanity in the universe of posterity; on the other hand, we have a meaningless gibberish, "*signified* nothing". Yet, in this case, there is inverse proportion between the semantic power of the words and the communicative power of the respective messages conveyed through them. The 'philosophies' of Vershínin and Túsenbach are quite shallow generalisations, sometimes reduced to '*bla-bla*', uttered more for the very pleasure of pastime and conversation-making than for genuine communication. The idle small-talk nature of this 'talking big' is emphasised when Vershínin, in Act 2, waiting in vain for his cup of tea, says: "If they are not going to give us any tea, let's at least philosophise"; and even when he is waiting for his final heartbreaking farewell with Másha, he cannot refrain from irrelevant "philosophising", though with some measure of self-irony (as discussed elsewhere in the Book). The 'big words', as such, ring hollow both because they are full of second-rate platitudes and because the speakers do not care much for what they are saying about humanity anyway. It is not their lives, or even their own worlds and emotional beings, which are at stake here. Both Vershínin and Túsenbach (especially the latter) are much more men of their words when they speak about their own lives, loves and loved ones.

Now the entire "philosophising"-dialogues communicate considerably less than the meaningless *reductio ad absurdum* of language in the dialogues between Másha and Vershínin consisting of "tram-tam-tam" and similar sounds (which Chekhov, at one point in Act 3, carefully instructs his actors to utter with question-and-answer intonation, followed by laughter).[32] We know from life experience that close friendships, and particularly intimate relationships between partners to a couple, tend to produce private languages that may include funny nonsense sounds. Usually, much is said, felt and communicated between the two partners before they reach this degree of intuitive mutual understanding. This dialogue is non-referential nonsense only as far as the outside world is concerned; yet to Másha and Vershínin, on the *inner plane*, and to us, on the *outer plane*, it means much more than the "philosophising" dialogues. The former refer to a whole universe and mean little; the "tram-tam" refers to nothing and means a world of love and communication. We don't know what they are saying here; even Chekhov, who created the scene, has no idea "what the hell they are talking about"; but Másha and Vershínin do know, perfectly well, what they are saying to each other. Thus, in the *inner plane* there is perfect communication between the two; in the *outer plane* Chekhov perfectly communicates to us the very fact that there is perfect intimate communication between them; but in order to sense and experience it, it is essential that the content of their communication would be theirs alone, unknown to anyone else, not even to the audience, not even to the author. Even the fact that they and the world they inhabit are not factual but fictional is irrelevant in this context; their communication, once released through Chekhov's text into the real world, is more real than they are.

Technically, this is reminiscent of the "*absurd*": in both cases there is a sense of collusion between personages on stage 'against' the audience, leaving the latter out of the communication among the former. However, there is a significant differ-ence. In Beckett's *Waiting for Godot*, Ionesco's *The Chairs*, and in many other plays nicknamed *absurd*, the dialogue is carried out in real language, using words from the dictionary; in this scene from *Three Sisters* the whole point is that the 'talk' consists of wordless, non-lexical sounds. This inevitably means that Chekhov's personages **know** that they are talking gibberish, which is **for them** meaningful (based on some offstage communication that must have taken place before this dialogue, the latter referring to the former in ways known only to them); Beckett's and Ionesco's personages imagine that they are 'normally' communicating, in real language. The audience, then, is placed in quite different positions in these two cases. Ironically, of course, it is the conscious gibberish of Chekhov's personages which is undoubtedly communicative, whereas in the *absurd* type communication is in doubt, at best: it is the former which reaffirms the rules of coherent verbal communication by violating them deliberately and momentarily, whereas the latter subverts them by adhering to their external frame while being unaware of violating their inherent content.

When Chekhov's personages "philosophise", though, they hardly ever perform a subversive act; their communication is basically normative, verbally–linguistically speaking, though frequently shallow. Yet, not all the verbally explicit generalisations in Chekhov in general, or in *Three Sisters* in particular, are shallow. When Másha says in Act 2 that people should know the reasons and purposes of things that happen in the world, or when Vershínin says that happiness, once attained, becomes unnoticed, Chekhov shows us that language does have the *potential* (proven by its momentary *realisation* in these few cases) for genuinely effective communicative power. Such examples are few and far between in the talk of Chekhov's personages, but their very existence is further proof of his passion for diversity, complexity, relativity and heterogeneity in his persistent effort to reach "a correct presentation of the problem".

6.2.6 Communicational *Polyphony*: *Absent Deep* and *Present Surface*

The final type of communication technique to be discussed in this Chapter can be illustrated by the following short excerpt *Three Sisters*, Act 4.

> MÁSHA: Did you love my mother?
> CHEBUTÝKIN: Very much.
> MÁSHA: And did she love you?
> CHEBUTÝKIN [*After a pause*]: I don't remember that.

On the surface, it is a normative, straightforward dialogue of questions and answers to-the-point, of the type that abounds in Ibsen's realistic plays. But the explicit spoken dialogue stands for an entirely different dialogue that motivates it deep below that surface, of the kind that gave rise to the prevalence of the time-honoured notion of *subtext* in the literature about Chekhov (a similar device is used in the confessions-scene in Act 3). The indication on the *surface* that we should look *deep* is embodied in Chebutýkin's reply, **after a pause of hesitation**: it simply does not stand to reason that he remembers that he loved the late Mrs. Prózorov but does not remember whether his love was reciprocated or rejected. The pause that Chekhov chooses to insert here adds to our conviction that Chebutýkin quickly considers his answer to Másha and deliberately chooses 'to forget'. In other words, he subtly, but transparently and resolutely, **refuses** to elaborate on the subject; it may well be a perfect example of a 'white lie', but some kind of lie it definitely is. What is the reason for it?

One can think of several answers to this question. One of them is undoubtedly related to Másha's motivation in this short exchange: Chebutýkin's love for the late mother had become common knowledge through his own repeated confessions (he probably started uttering them only after the deaths of the General and his wife), so there must be a reason for her to ask what she already knows; moreover, even if she does not know the answer to her second question, there is a reason why she is asking it now, rather than years before. A plausible explanation is that she is trying, perhaps subconsciously, to draw an analogy between herself and her mother, somehow to find comfort in sharing her agonising pangs of conscience (for violating her marriage vows) with her late mother through being part of a pattern, a link in a family-destiny chain, etc. In fact, she is trying to do the opposite of what she told Irína in her Act 3 confession, when she said that there is no resemblance between reading about love affairs in novels and experiencing them in real life, since the latter inescapably involve taking responsibility for a personal decision. Now she is trying to use her mother's case as a kind of fictitious novel, as it were, to help her to face her own decision. Chebutýkin gets this unsaid message and responds to it by refusing to take part in the game. Másha accepts and respects this refusal, subliminally realising that Chebutýkin's attitude is genuinely the one she so recently preached to her sister, and should re-adopt according to her own values.[33] Thus, she moves on to a direct reference to the subject that motivated the whole dialogue: Vershínin. It is very rare to encounter examples of such a neat distinction between a *surface-* and a *deep* (or *underlying*) dialogue,[34] with both partners communicating on both levels.

To clarify the matter further, the latter, 'real' dialogue, could be something like this:

> 'Másha: *I know that you loved my mother when she was already married, and now I am in love with someone other than my husband. It is important for me to know whether my mother loved you too.*'
>
> 'Chebutýkin: *I refuse to answer your question and to let you use my love for your mother for your own purposes. Let bygones be bygones, and make your decision without reference to what happened in my generation.*'

Of course, Chekhov could not have written something so raw and pedestrian, something so clumsily direct and explicit; but a very sophisticated communication system is needed to make the dialogue that he did write actually mean this one. The indirect innuendoes are very subtle, but they are readily perceived and interpreted with remarkable precision by both participants in the dialogue. This example is even neater than the confession-scene: here both the *surface structure* (textually *present*) dialogue, and the *deep structure* (textually *absent*) dialogue (alternatively, *text* and *subtext*, respectively) constitute complete and coherent texts. The choice of the two personages enhances the effect of conscious, calculated restraint and of *polyphonic*, simultaneous communication of two fully developed lines. This subtle mutual awareness on stage is what makes this scene the ultimate opposite of strict 'deaf-dialogues', such as the *chekhartmá–cheremshá* argument between Chebutýkin and Soliónyï in Act 2.

6.3 Concluding Remarks

Nothing short of an analysis of the entire text of Chekhov's plays is likely to do justice to the inexhaustible richness and diversity of his types of dramatic and theatrical communication.[35] Such comprehensiveness has not been attempted here; rather, the purpose of the present Chapter has been twofold — thematic and compositional. *Thematically*, to demonstrate Chekhov's presentation of human communication in his plays, with *Three Sisters* as a representative test-case; *compositionally*, using this theme as illustration, to provide a further demonstration of his principles and strategies of thematic structuration and theme-construction in general, as proposed in Chapters 1 and 2.

To recapitulate the latter: the major principle of Chekhov's theme-construction can be described through a *three-storeyed model* for every major theme (e.g., *communication*). In such a model *the lowest storey* consists of textual instances in isolation; *the middle storey* consists of the interactions, mutual modifications and other relationships that obtain between them and make them modify each other's meanings; and *the upper storey* is the overall "presentation of the problem" by Chekhov, in his capacity as *implied author*. This *upper storey*, being Chekhov's composite view of the given theme, is invariably and inevitably irreducible to a philosophically or ideologically coherent dictum. Now this *upper storey* in the construction of a theme, in turn, is the *lowest storey* in an isomorphous three-storey construction on a higher order of generalisation, where the composite view of *communication* is analogous to similarly constructed views of work, love, education, etc.; these, in turn, interact with each other on a higher-order *second storey* and create — on a third, higher one — composite views of Chekhov's views of major facets of human life and mankind, on the one hand, and of his compositional techniques, on the other hand. These generalisations can serve us, in turn, in doing a better job at analysing the isolated scenes and details in the text, making the most general overview of the entire work subordinate, at least for the purpose of analysis, to the subtlest of textual details.

This generalisation about Chekhov's thematic and compositional structuration is tightly linked, in its tripartite conception, to the *trichotomic principle* proposed in 1.2. These are attempts to facilitate the systematic conceptualisation of a schematicism-resistant artistic system, that is highly structured yet flexible and anti-dogmatic to the core. Academic writing strives to be systematic in applying rational and consistent methodologies to all objects of investigation, and Chekhov's art, as an object of research and analysis, is of course no exception. But the process here is *tripartite* as well: *first*, reading and experiencing the work of art; *second*, trying to analyse it methodically, with results and conclusions; and *third*, returning to the text with the hope of gaining a broader and deeper experience with the application of the analytical methods to the artistic text. The models proposed here are supposed to emanate from the specific nature of the Chekhov phenomenon, rather than being imposed on it from the outside.

Chekhov's later work is indeed representative of very central features of literary and dramatic art: by communicating themes through structuration at the expense of the isolated elements, he has made one of his own unique contributions to the never-ending endeavour to realise the potentialities inherent in the literary and dramatic modelling of the world.

Notes

1 By this formulation I would like to communicate to this Book's readers that Chekhov was hardly ever 'guilty' of faulty communication with his addressees/audiences, though the message **supposedly** communicated by him to them was that humans tend to fail in their attempts to communicate with each other (and sometimes fail even to make such attempts in the first place); in other words, the idea (implied, but rarely spelled out) in large sections of Chekhov criticism and scholarship was that there is a lack of *isomorphism* between the ways Chekhov, as author, communicated with his addressees and audiences and the ways in which his personages communicated with each other. In what follows I will try to modify (though not to refute or reverse) this characterisation of his poetics.

2 It goes without saying that such processes in *fictional literature* betray a vision of *reality*, marked by faulty communication between human beings: without growing awareness of communication problems in modern societies no author would have portrayed such problems in his/her fictional writings. However, presentation and analysis of real life situation is outside the province of the textual study of drama, theatre and literature.

3 The terms *fictional* and *rhetorical* are used here in a restricted sense, for the purpose of the working distinction just proposed; the former is self-explanatory, and latter emphasises the addressee-targeting function of the text (related to the "conative function" in Jakobson 1967, 300–302); however, to avoid the broader range of meanings and cultural and historical associations connected with the terms *fictional* and *rhetorical*, the simpler and comparatively neatly-structural terms *inner* and *outer* are more frequently used, often together with the terms *fictional* and *rhetorical*, respectively. There is some affinity between this distinction and the one between *mimetic* and *diegetic* as used in Issacharoff 1981, but they are not identical.

4 Important differences between these conceptual systems are deliberately ignored here, since these, too, are differences in modelling the same cluster of phenomena. These differences are central in other contexts of discussion (e.g., in 10.1.2 below), and in other (neighbouring) disciplines; here the actual phenomena, however modelled, viewed, characterised or defined, are the focus of discussion, so that in the present context these differences are marginalised.

5 In the present context the latter refers to *staged* representation, with its *dual fictionality*, as explained in 4.3.2.

6 The term *implied* is given in parentheses advisedly, since it is a borderline/interface case between real persons and theoretical constructs: the two extreme edges of the communicational chain, on both sides, are indeed the real persons, but they are accessible only through their textual representations, i.e., their *implied* presences therein. Moreover, the matter is more complex, because of the asymmetry between one named and identified author (in this case, of course, Chekhov) and many nameless, unidentifiable perceivers/addressees/audiences (past, present and future).

7   Of course this does not mean a calculable diagonal slope in which the location of every single play down the road of decline is determined with precision according to its date of composition or publication. Like all historical processes of this kind, this is a general '*macro*' trend, which accommodates '*micro*' ups and downs, zigzags, conflicting undercurrents and counter-examples.

8   Schematicism here, as virtually anywhere else, is admittedly simplistic and superficial, and genuinely anti-Chekhovian in its spirit; however, it can clarify the basic nature of rules, tendencies and processes, which can, and indeed should, be subsequently modified, to match the complexity of the real phenomena.

9   An analogous *isomorphism* is evident specifically in *The Seagull* when Chekhov simply cannot, technically speaking, refrain from communicating his own views about the nature of art and theatre, or about how one should write a play — subjects that are explicitly, even vociferously, debated between personages in the play — to his addressees. By the very act of writing *The Seagull* he perforce makes a stand, for instance, against the poetics of Konstantín's fragment-play, simply through the radical difference between that poetics and the one practised by Chekhov in *The Seagull* itself. No other Chekhov play is forced to make such an unequivocal stand, simply because the arguments and the "philosophising" in the other plays are not about how to write a play.

10 I am using *Three Sisters* in this Chapter as a major source of illustrations of Chekhov's techniques and principles in communicating to his audiences the variety of human communication phenomena; however, analogous (though, of course, never identical) examples in the other major plays abound. The principles outlined here are applicable to all Chekhov's plays, and can generate analyses of communication relationships in all of them. Consider, for example, instances and conditions of communication (or lack thereof) between the major personages of each of the other major plays: Konstantín–Arkádina–Nína–Trigórin–Másha and others, in *The Seagull*; Serebriakóv–Vánia–Ástrov–Sónia–Yeléna in *Uncle Vánia*; Ranévskaïa–Gáïev–Lopákhin–Vária–Ánia–Trofímov in *The Cherry Orchard*. In each of these plays additional personages, perhaps less central, communicate with each other in numerous subtle ways and degrees; and, of course, Chekhov communicates with his audiences in an infinite variety of ways through the personages' thickets of communication. However, there seems to be little that is genuinely different from *Three Sisters* in the other plays in terms of basic types and principles of communicating relationships, so that the analytical strategies of this Chapter can be applied to the other major plays, with minor modifications resulting from the specificity of each individual case.

11 As Chekhov remarked, this stage-direction does not mean literally bursting into tears, but a mood, presumably reflected in actors' intonation (and possibly facial expression).

12 The delay is created by a seemingly untimely and bizarre *réplique* by Soliónyï, that looks like an out-of-joint wedge that has no business in the middle of the sisters' conversation. Of course, Chekhov always carefully designs such 'wedges', in content and location alike.

13 In the Russian, the *morpho-phonemic structure* of the imperative of the two verbs makes Másha's "Don't howl" [не реви = *ne reví*] — echo through the half-rhyme, or assonance, of the identical last stressed vowel, with Ól'ga's initial reprimand to Másha, "*Don't whistle*" [не свисти = *ne svistí*]

14 Some analysts — e.g., Styan (1971, 168), and Magarshack (1972, 133 — miss this point entirely: they take Ól'ga's statement at face value and credit her for understanding her sister, while ignoring or downplaying Másha's response; Chekhov, however, does not fall into this trap (that he himself designed for naïve audiences), neither does any of the characters on stage, nor should we.

15 This brings to mind the pathetic attempt of another Chekhovian Másha to evade an uneasy situation by physically hiding from it: in *The Seagull*, Act 4, after Konstantín has just left the room, Másha says that "not seeing him" would end her unrequited love for him, and everything she does in that scene belies this statement, as shown in 4.3.3.

16 She seems unable to contemplate bridging the gap between the two, by becoming a married schoolteacher, as her sister Irína planned to be before the duel that made her a widow before becoming a wife.

17 There is an untranslatable subtlety here in the original: in Russian, two different verbs (or verb-phrases) denote *to marry* when applied to a man and to a woman. Ól'ga uses the impersonal construction *one does not marry*, but with the verb applying to women (something like *one does not marry a husband*), so that while stressing the marital duties of women, she may also imply, albeit faintly, that this applies to both sexes, though more to women than to men. Some English translations stress the unequal attitude towards the two sexes is (e.g., "women don't marry for love", etc.), whereas others tend to ignore it (e.g., "people don't/one doesn't marry for love", etc.). There are other variants in the vast literature of Chekhov's plays in English translation.

18 She walks "*à la* Lady Macbeth", as Chekhov suggested a letter to his wife, Ól'ga Knípper-Chekhova, from January 1901 (this is, of course, a famous quote; see Senelick 2006, p. 936, note 59).

19 The word "silly" is repeated twice more between the sisters. It is interesting to quote Chekhov's instruction to his wife, Ól'ga Knipper — the first Másha, for whom the role had been created — about this very scene: "behave [...] so that one can feel that you are more intelligent than your sisters, you think yourself more intelligent, at least" (quoted from Senelick 2006, p. 936, note 60).

20 The *you* here is not vocative but impersonal (i.e., Másha's "when you read" means *When one reads*). What makes it clear that Másha is addressing Irína here is the stage directions, not the spoken text.

21 I am alluding here, as elsewhere in the Book, to Chekhov's much-quoted 1888 letter to Suvórin; for English versions see Friedland (1965, 60) and Chudakóv (1983, 194).

22 Variants of such clashes do exist in classical tragedy (Greek, Shakespearean etc.); these, however, are largely conflictual. Not least for this reason they are even more different from Chekhov's types of 'deafness' than those of the comic convention.

23 Such as the Act 2 reference to Balzac's wedding in Berdíchev (4.2.2), or the lotto scene in Act 4 of *The Seagull*, or even instances of real semi-deafness such as the dialogues between half-deaf Firs and several other personages in *The Cherry Orchard*, notably Ranévskaïa. The Ferapónt–Andréï dialogues in *Three Sisters* are, of course, cases in point, and they are discussed more fully here and elsewhere in the Book.

24 A wry view of the notion of a "professor who is the pride of Russia" begins the story "A Dreary Tale" (1889), with the sarcastic self-characterisation of Nikoláï Stepánovich, the story's first-person narrator. While Andréï is saying these words without a shred of irony or sarcasm, a 'Chekhov-well-informed' reader/spectator may remember the similarity between the two texts. Moreover, it is of significance that a sarcastic view of being "the pride of Russia" is adopted by the personage who has attained distinguished professorship, whereas the one who only dreams about it is capable of looking sarcastically at quite a few things, but this is not one of them.

25 In other Chekhov plays there are plenty of no less comic and poignant examples, or moments of utter sadness comically structured (e.g., Vánia's famous appearance with the bouquet of flowers at the very moment when Yeléna and Ástrov have their momentary kiss in Act 3 of *Uncle Vánia*, or Lopákhin's misquotes from *The **Tragedy** of Hamlet* in Act 2 of *The Cherry Orchard*, "Okhméliïa, to a nunnery!", hurled with callously comic delight at vulnerable Vária). The variety of *unrealised communicational poten-*

tials, doubly stifled, tragically and comically at the same time, is indeed infinite; even a book-length study cannot possibly enumerate and analyse them all, let alone a single Chapter devoted to this inexhaustibly significant component of Chekhov's poetics.

26 Another Chekhovian moment of loaded communication expressed through apparent lack of it occurs towards the end of the story "A Dreary Tale". Emotionally, there is much in common between these two heart-breaking farewell scenes.

27 The three of them are on stage alone three times in the play: in the opening and closing scenes and in the confession-scene in Act 3. On all three occasions they are not left alone long enough to communicate satisfactorily: there are always intrusions from outsiders — the three men in the back room behind the pillars in the beginning, Kulýgin, Andréï and Natasha (separately) in the confession-scene, and Chebutýkin at the end (with the silent background-presence of Kulýgin and Andréï).

28 Here I use the term *confession* in a broader sense — a highly personal statement that allows a glimpse into one's inner world and private thoughts and feelings.

29 The inner contradiction between this end and the means of coercion that the General used to achieve it are discussed above, in 1.2.1.

30 There is only one exception to this rule: Másha's angry recitation of the entire conjugation of the verb *love* in Latin (Act 3). In context, this is clearly designed to characterise sarcastically Kulýgin's love as failing to transcend his horizons, circumscribed as they are by Latin conjugations, and as being as lifeless and as devoid of passion and imagination as verb conjugations in a dead foreign language. Thus, Másha is not using here a foreign language, but rather mocks its use by Kulýgin.

31 In this Subsection, the term *non-language* does not refer to genuinely non-verbal systems and elements operating in Drama and theatre (music, stage-props and sets, costumes, etc., discussed elsewhere); rather, the term refers here to **verbal** gibberish: meaningless vowels and consonants that, in their specific context, fail to realise their potential to become part of a phonological system of a natural language. These invariably function as language substitutes and as negations of the use of language.

32 In a letter to Ól'ga Knipper from January 1901 Chekhov wrote: "Vershínin pronounces 'tram-tam-tam' in the form of a question, while you [i.e. Másha, whose role Knipper was playing] reply in the form of an answer, and you think it's such an original idea that you pronounce this 'tram-tam' with a grin... You utter 'tram-tam' and laugh, but not loudly, rather — barely audibly [...] Remember, you are easily given to laughter and to anger". See Magarshack 1972, 163. These explicit authorial instructions, fully compatible with the written text, disprove interpretations by some scholars, who use the proximity between this exchange and a previous musical quote from Chaïkóvskiï's Opera *Yevgéniï Onégin* as an indication that the non-verbal exchange should be sung to a tune from that opera.

33 In fact, she unknowingly reciprocates the respect that Chebutýkin, being drunk in Act 3, had shown her and Vershínin, in their absence, by refraining from naming them alongside Natasha and Protopópov as having a "[sordid] little love affair".

34 The terms *surface* and *deep/underlying* are used here in an applied sense, borrowed from their original use in Chomskyan theory of *generative–transformational grammar*

35 Different and complementary aspects of Chekhovian communication are discussed in a book-length study by Andréï D. Stepánov (2005). For a review of this important book, see Levitan and Golomb 2007. Other recent thought-provoking views of Chekhovian communication can be found, *inter alia*, in Zviniatskovsky 2006 and in Tiupa 2006.

CHAPTER

7

"Restraining Order"
Repression of Expression as Pressurised Explosiveness

«Вот тут у меня кипит»
["Here it is boiling"]
Másha, pointing at her chest,
(*Three Sisters*, Act 4)

7.0 Focusing on *Chekhovian Restraint*

Chekhovian Restraint is primarily a major 'species' within the 'genus' of *unrealised potential* (as presented in Chapter 1 and discussed throughout the Book); it is also inseparably linked with other topics, notably the lack of *dramaticalness* and the dearth of *overt conflict* as hallmarks of Chekhov's art. It is being singled out here as worthy of a separate Chapter because it is one of the most typically-Chekhovian emotional qualities and effects, that anyone exposed to a Chekhov text is likely to sense almost instantaneously, whether intuitively or consciously, whether labelling it *restraint* or "by any other name". In other words, this Chapter offers a perspective, within which this specific feature of Chekhov's poetics functions as *superordinate*, while other features are *subordinated* to it, to complement other perspectives, based on different hierarchies.

7.1 Major Features of *Restraint* and Basic Distinctions

Chekhovian restraint, then, is *unrealised **emotional** potential*. It is viewed here as a three-phase process, modelled on the *trichotomic principle* presented in Chapter 1, whereby (a) some content of emotionally highly-charged potential — absent from the text but inferable from it — is repressed, or prevented from being explicitly expressed, by (b) some form, process or mechanism of holding back/withholding, and/or belittling that content's significance, magnitude and potency, resulting in (c) a text in which emotions are expressed (if at all) less freely and in a fashion more subdued, contained, or suppressed, at least as compared with what is expected or accepted as 'normal' in the given situation. I propose to name these three phases (a) the *unrestrained potential*, (b) the *restrainer* and (c) the *restrained* (or the *restrained text*), respectively.[1] As in most other Chekhovian *trichotomies*, the tangible text actually printed on the page and/or heard from the stage usually consists of the *restrained*, i.e., the third phase of the process; the *restrainer* is also often (but not always) present in the text; the *unrestrained potential*, however, is by definition absent from the text, being a construct inferable from it — as a rule, it can be characterised as "the road not taken". Yet, the cognitive activity of inferring what the absent, unrestrained alternative of the text could or would have been (that is, if it had not been authored by a Chekhov) is an integral and inevitable part of the process whereby the text, as handed down by Chekhov, can be understood, in the most elementary sense of *understanding*, of 'making sense':[2] without considering, or at least sensing, the perspective of that absent "road not taken", major parts of this text would often be trite and shallow, almost meaningless, and much of its overall significance could be lost. This is so mainly because the unrestrained alternative is what we sense as *unmarked*, conventional, or straightforward norm of verbal or non-verbal behaviour expected in the given situation; the appreciation of the uniquely Chekhovian deviation from that norm cannot be understood without inferring or reconstructing it from its negation and substitution in Chekhov's actual text.

In principle, the specific emotional effect of any instance of *Chekhovian restraint* is produced by the nature and intensity of the tension between its three phases–components. One would expect that a powerful *unrestrained potential*[3] would require a *restrainer* with a comparably powerful restraining force in order to produce the effect of a *restrained text*. However, things are less neat and schematic: a *restrainer* is a contextualised phenomenon; it is usually made of weaker stuff than the *unrestrained potential* that it restrains, so that if taken out of context it is often unimpressive. Indeed, when two opposing forces are comparably powerful, creating a tense balance or symmetry of contraries, the result is likely to be a clash, or *conflict*, rather than *restraint*. A typical Chekhovian *restrainer*[4] gains its force from its surrounding context; it risks being 'wasted' (i.e., rendered ineffective) if its *unrestrained potential* is weak or insignificant. *Chekhovian restraint*, then, is usually characterised by *asymmetry* — e.g., between a 'strong cause' (*unrestrained potential*) and a 'weak effect' (*restrained text*) — produced with the essential presence of a 'weak' *restrainer* that generates a 'strong' effect of mismatch, of withholding, of *presence through absence*; it is closely related to the 'sideways-oriented' type of interaction or communication (as presented in 1.4 and discussed elsewhere), so typical in Chekhov as substitute for an expected direct clash or *overt conflict*. Of special importance in this context are two specific techniques: the typical use of *stage-directions*, which instruct directors and actors to create various non-verbal restraining environments that preclude the 'eruption' of emotional outbursts (examples abound), and strategies of restrained ending, in stories and plays alike. Of course, there are also examples of *restraint* produced by sheer verbal means.

Additional distinctions can help in clarifying relevant issues: one can speak of *restraint* as *inward-* vs. *outward-directed* (or *-oriented*); as *verbal* vs. *non-verbal*, and *'micro'/textual* vs. *'macro'/compositional* (there are borderline and half-way cases, but the basic distinctions are quite clear).[5] The term *inward* means here anything self-imposed or self-oriented; alternatively, it can also be called *mono-logic*. *Outward*, by the same token, refers to anything directed by someone, or through something, to someone/something else; alternatively, it can also be called *dialogic*. The distinction between *verbal* and *non-verbal* is self-explanatory, whereas the one between *'micro'/textual* and *'macro'/compositional* is basically a matter of scope, and is *polar* (rather than *binary*), i.e., the smaller the scope of the particular instance the closer it is to the former pole, and the larger its scope — the closer it is to the latter.

7.2 *Restraint* in Stories: A Moment in "A Dreary Tale"

Though the Book's primary concern is with Chekhov's major plays, discussions and analyses of stories are sometimes helpful in focusing our attention on relevant aspects of Chekhov's poetics in general; thus, an analysis of a story in 5.1 was proposed as an introduction to Chekhov's *characterisation*, and a brief look at *restraint* in another story is proposed in this Chapter as an additional eye-opener in discovering Chekhov's emotional strategies in general. It has to be reiterated, then, that most features of Chekhov's poetics as presented in this Book charac-terise his plays and stories alike, though the Book's concern is mainly with the former. Indeed, *restraint* is exceptionally prevalent in the stories; yet, it is perhaps more striking in his plays, because it is, by definition, at odds with phenomena like *conflict* and *'dramaticalness'*, normally associated with *drama* (as discussed in Chapter 4). Thus, Chekhov's typical *ending* strategies, discussed throughout Chapter 9, can also be regarded and analysed, complementarily, as instances of *restraint*.

The story "A Dreary Tale" (mentioned several times throughout the Book) is an exceptionally powerful case in point. Towards its ending the two main protag-onists — the narrator, Professor of Medical Science Nikoláï Stepánovich, and his ex-ward Kátia — face each other, unable to verbally discharge the unbearable emotional load of what they feel for each other. Kátia, a failed actress, is heart-broken after being abandoned by her lover, the father of her dead illegitimate baby; on the verge of succumbing to an even more disastrous love-affair, she is desper-ately longing for some kind of guidance, even 'gospel truth', from Nikoláï, who had been a mentor and father-figure for her since childhood. He loves her more than anyone in the world, and feels much closer to her than to his own wife and grown-up children. However, he is duty-bound to reject her desperate plea and frustrate this urgent need of hers — not least because of his high standards of truth-fulness. These standards were developed through life-long dedication to scientific ethics, as well as through personal integrity as a human being: he cannot pretend to have an answer for her existential plight when he has none. For him, to fake soothing words that he knows to be false is tantamount to falsifying the results of a crucial scientific experiment. These two people, as genuine soul-mates as one can find in world literature, face each other dumbfounded, choked to their very throats by the magnitude of the selfless love they bear to each other, confounded by their inability to verbalise it and to reach out to each other. At this moment Nikoláï Stepánovich is torn between two conflicting forces, both generated by his innermost being: emotions of love and powerfully helpless desire to help the person dearest to him, and the ethical and constitutive *DNA* of his own personality. Kátia, on her part, would accept **any** guidance coming **from him**; but he is genuinely unable to give her such advice and solve her problems for her. Yet she finds it very hard to empathise with his emotional plight; rather, she is the child who expects the adult, especially parent or teacher (she explicitly appeals to him in these terms), to be omniscient and omnipotent and the ultimate problem-solver. She is crushed by his refusal–rejection, which she at first must experience as betrayal. Yet, deep down she must know that his real betrayal would have been if he had compromised his own deeply held convictions, the principles of conduct that make him what he is. He would not have been "to his own self true" if he had given her what she seems to want, the inevitably false palliative answer that she is craving for. If he had done that he would not have been the kind of person she is looking up to with such intensity in the first place; it is in that case that he would have betrayed his own trust in himself, and would have made him unworthy of her trust either. Thus, the disappointment and frustration that both of them feel, towards themselves and towards each other, are inevitable, and inescapably produce that 'choking' effect that is generated in the fictional situation but weighs on the perceivers–readers with crushing force. This kind of intense tangle is the very heart and soul of *Chekhovian restraint*.

7.3 Some '*Micro*'-*Level* Examples

Examples of *self-imposed/monologic restraint on the micro level* can be found in several instances. A representative sample is offered here. (1) In her final mono-logue (*The Seagull*, Act 4) Nína repeats several times the statement "I'm a/the (sea)gull";[6] but every time, without fail, she follows it by the restraining disclaimer «не то» ["no, not so" (or: "not that", or "that's not it")][7]. (2) In Act 4 of *Three Sisters* Chebutýkin surprises everyone present, including himself, by delivering what amounts to an out-of-control, almost out-of-the-blue declaration/confession of love for the three sisters (or perhaps just for Irína in particular);[8] this confession is further intensified emotionally with his self-characterisation as an old migratory bird left behind while the young one(s) can spread wings and soar to the horizon.[9] After a couple of sentences, though, he interrupts himself by surprisingly turning to Kulýgin, chiding him for shaving his moustache. The restraining function of the last remark is very clear: it is an obvious though hopeless face-saving attempt by Chebutýkin to put a lid on his own emotional outburst and to minimise the embar-rassment of having exposed his emotions to others. (3) Throughout *The Cherry Orchard*, Gáïev has an almost uncontrollable tendency to make eloquent, senti-mental and irrelevant speeches, causing embarrassment to him and those close to him. As a rule, he soon enough makes an awkward attempt to change the subject (often pretending to play an imaginary game of billiards) as a way out of his embarrassment. These attempts are usually prompted by the explicit irritation of his captive audience, notably Ánia and Vária; therefore, these are borderline cases, halfway between *inward-* and *outward-oriented* (or *monologic* and *dialogic*) types of restraint.

Examples of *outward-oriented restraint on the micro level* can be found, for instance, in the ingenious interweaving of two brief series of love confessions: Vershínin confessing to Másha and Túsenbach confessing to Irína in Act 2 of *Three Sisters*. In each pair, the woman restrains the man's confession and curbs his enthusiasm, preventing him from being carried away verbally–emotionally, whereupon the restraining action is transferred from the 'intra-couple' to the 'inter-couple' arena: instead of two separate and problematic couples there is one friendly foursome, and instead of two emotionally charged intimate talks about forbidden or unrequited love there is one talk shared by all four, dominated by the theme of Irína's frustration **at work** — undoubtedly an uneasy subject, but one that is much less loaded and 'dangerous' emotionally than the love-confessions. Thus, the unexpected encounter between the two couples redoubles the effect of *restraint*, with the audience's realisation that the about-to-be-said intimately is doomed never to be said socially. In this specific instance, the stratified, or rather reciprocal, structure of dual (two-tiered) restraint can also demonstrate the strategy of *micro-* and *macro-levels* analogies; it can also be viewed as yet another instance of *three-storeyed structuration*: the lower storey consists of each love dialogue/confession separately; the middle one consists of the interaction between the two dialogues, and the upper one consists of implied generalisations that the audience is led to infer from the lower two, both about human communication and about Chekhov's strategies. Once again, many textual instances analysed in other parts of the Book can be also studied with the *restraint* perspective serving as a superordinate mechanism that subordinates other, complementary ones.

Another example of such multi-layered restraint can be found in Act 3 of *The Seagull*. Several scenes within this Act are intricately interwoven, without clear-cut demarcation lines between them: (1) the 'Medallion Scene' between Nína and Trigórin, with Arkádina in the background, is discontinuous, split by other scenes into two non-consecutive parts (see Appendix); (2) the two thematically symmetrical scenes focusing on Arkádina's stinginess, one (2a) with Sórin pleading with her for Konstantín, exacerbated by Sórin's fainting, and the other (2b) with Konstantín pleading with her for Sórin; (3) the 'Bandage Scene' between Konstantín and Arkádina; and (4) the scene between Arkádina and Trigórin, that can be termed "Arkádina's (temporary) 'Conquest'", which is the most overtly "dramatical" of all, i.e., the most heavily charged with "*dramaticalness*" (as characterised in Chapter 4). A close look at detailed timings of the various *répliques* and, more significantly, at the precise distribution and configuration of exits and entrances, can yield an analysis of yet another case of carefully planned series of events that restrain each other; the effect generated by such strategies is that everything happens, as it were, by accident from the personages' standpoint, but all is pre-designed to the subtlest detail by an authorial master-plan. A typical example is the seam between the Bandage (3) and the 'Conquest' (4) Scenes, when Trigórin enters barely before Konstantín, manages to pick up the bandage and exit the stage. Similarly designed series of restraints can be found in *Uncle Vánia*'s Act 3, in the dialogue between Yeléna and Sónia leading up to Yeléna's uncalled-for intervention, volunteering to ascertain Ástrov's emotional attitude toward Sónia: here, too, most *répliques* function as each other's *outward-oriented restraint*. Analogous examples in the other plays abound, and some of them are analysed elsewhere in the Book under different headings.

7.4 An Illustration: Structuring Restraint in *Three Sisters*

A particularly masterly activation of a multi-layered complex of *restraint* strategies can be found towards the end of *Three Sisters*. Typically, several lines of development along the temporal axis of the play, especially in its plotline and characterisation of major personages, are intricately and polyphonically intertwoven to culminate towards its ending.

First, Chekhov builds up the character of Másha as the play's outwardly most static, motionless, and taciturn major personage (as analysed in 5.2.2). Then, gradually, the attentive spectator can see through her silence how powerful her emotions are, precisely because they are suppressed rather than expressed, to the extent that controlled *emotional restraint* has become her hallmark in the eyes of the audience. Ultimately, during the final farewell scene between her and Vershínin, she loses control, and Chekhov instructs the actress with an unusual, almost non-Chekhovian stage-direction: "**sobs vehemently**". This unexpected and unprecedented *fortissimo* is a climax in the aural fabric of the play as a whole, and all the more so in the character of Másha: her entire being as a restrained stage-presence looks now — with hindsight, as the play and her part in it draw to a close — as preparation for this climactic, blatantly *unrestrained* moment. This climax is juxtaposed, however, not only with preceding Másha scenes and moments, most of them in the text's relatively distant past; it is also sharply contrasted with the restraining action of the immediate entrance of Kulýgin, a person particularly unwelcome at this moment. This, in turn, elicits an immediate response in Másha, who is now instructed by an explicit stage direction to "restrain her sobbing". However, perhaps even more masterly is the interweaving of the Másha–Vershínin farewell with Irína's response to the news of Túsenbach's death, soon afterwards.

Chekhov creates here an incessant, relentless chain of diverse restraining strategies, in which each link 'pours' its own type of 'cold water' on what could otherwise be the 'boiling, steaming pot' of the link preceding it. Másha's "vehement sobbing" occurs while she powerfully clings to Vershínin, unable to let go of him, until he asks for Ól'ga's help in physically tearing her sister from his embrace; once released from her loving clutches, he still embraces her briefly and exits ("in haste", as Chekhov takes care to instruct his actor). This precise moment is the cue for the aforementioned entrance of Kulýgin — so ill-timed for Másha and her sisters, and so perfectly timed by Chekhov the master of designed *restraint* — whose well-meaning and insensitive clichés produce a unique blend of overwhelming subjective kindness and affection with striking objective inattentiveness, bordering on totally unintended callousness. This is one of those seemingly self-subverting blends, so typical of life's complexities, that perhaps only Chekhov is capable of creating in writing. Crushed by this unbearable emotional load, Másha is almost out of her mind, reciting incorrectly (and of course out of any rationally relevant context) the Pushkin lines she had recited absent-mindedly when Vershínin appeared for the first time in the family's provincial home (Act 1). Thus, through the return of this Pushkin allusion, she inadvertently closes a circle: like a recurring musical motif,[10] the repetition of these phrases signals her **subconscious awareness** that her relationship with Vershínin has come to an end — an end, which is just as poetical, and just as mysteriously connected with her Moscow childhood and early school years,[11] as its beginning. She collects herself, restrains her sobbing, and commands enough presence of mind to state her adamant refusal to ever again set foot in the Natásha-dominated house that used to be her family home.[12]

It is in the middle of all this emotional turmoil that yet another perfectly timed stage-direction tells us that "a muffled shot is heard in the distance" offstage; an attentive audience should be aware of it (the precise audible strength of this "muffled shot" is left, of course, to the discretion of directors and their production teams), but the personages on stage are apparently so involved in their shattered emotions that they manage to ignore it, or even subconsciously refuse to be aware of it, though the duel had been mentioned in the dialogue, just a few minutes before (see Magarshack 1972, 181). A brief comic interlude is introduced, focusing on an artificial beard, which Kulýgin had confiscated from a pupil, and the resemblance that it creates between him and the German teacher in his school; this interlude is allowed to bring fleeting moments of smiles through tears to Másha and her sisters,[13] whereupon in comes Natásha, provincial narrow-mindedness and indi-vidual malice personified — the one person whose entrance is even less welcome to the sisters, and to Másha in particular, than Kulýgin's. The characteristic manner and content of her last *répliques* is even more chilling, especially in the dramatic context, when she speaks so ruthlessly about chopping the tree that the about-to-die Túsenbach has just regarded as his posthumous monument on earth. These last spoken words of the two provincial personages, Kulýgin and Natásha,[14] function as powerful *restrainers*, as wedges between two particularly emotional scenes, each with its own inner mechanisms of *restraint* — the Másha-Vershínin farewell and the moment that Irína and her sisters (and the audience) learn about Túsenbach's death in the duel.

> CHEBUTÝKIN: Ól'ga Sergéïevna!
> ÓL'GA: What is it? [*a pause*] What?
> CHEBUTÝKIN: Nothing… I don't know how to tell you… [*whispers in her ear*]
> ÓL'GA [*Aghast*]: It cannot be!
> CHEBUTÝKIN: Yes… that's how it is… I am tired, exhausted, don't want to say any more… [*annoyed*] anyway, it's all the same…
> MÁSHA: What happened?
> ÓL'GA [*embraces Irína*]: Terrible day today… I don't know how to tell you, my precious…

IRÍNA: What? Tell me quickly, what? For God's sake! [*weeps*]
CHEBUTÝKIN: Just now in the duel the Baron was killed.[15]
IRÍNA [*weeps quietly*]: I knew, I knew…

Of vital importance is the precision with which Chekhov creates hierarchies of *emotional restraint* through stage directions that control the level of relative loudness: the gamut is ranging between *fortissimo* and *pianissimo*.[16] It starts with Másha's **"sobbing vehemently"** (*fortissimo*), then the stage-direction is **restraining her sobbing** (*mezzo forte*), then going up again to another brief outburst (*forte*): the stage direction is "sobbing, but stops abruptly". A few seconds later Másha's instruction is **"weeping"** (down to *mezzo piano*). This is Irína's first sound-level instruction: she is "weeping" (i.e., *mezzo piano*, creating a kind of loudness-plateau between the two sisters), when she asks the fatal question, urging to be told what had happened. However, when she hears the news of Túsenbach's death she is "weeping **quietly**" (*piano*, or *pianissimo*), as response to the expected answer, fatal and fateful.[17] It is of utmost importance, then, that Irína is "weeping" when asking the question, and **"weeping quietly"** when hearing the answer (rather than vice versa). This reversal of 'normal' behaviour is an epitome of *restraint*. Again, there is a *restraining order* here; emotions and their effects are hierarchised with utmost precision; they are set free or held back in controlled dosage, timing, and relation to each other.

7.5 A '*Macro*'-Level Example: The Seagull in *The Seagull*

One of the ways to demonstrate the centrality of *restraint* to Chekhov's poetics is to survey the close links between it and such central symbolic themes as the seagull and the cherry orchard in the plays bearing these names, or Moscow in *Three Sisters*. By activating a technique similar to a computer search-command[18] one can follow the development of each of these symbols throughout their respective plays and see how they exhibit patterns of *Chekhovian restraint*. The following discussion will be restricted to a partial account of the seagull in *The Seagull*, but other symbolic themes and images can be analysed similarly.

It is young Nína Zaréchnaïa who is the first to bring up the image of the seagull. After reporting to Konstantín that her family objects to the "bohemian" nature of the life that awaits her, according to them, if she realises her dream to become an actress, she says: "but I am drawn here, to the lake, like a seagull. My heart is full of you". From the very beginning it is clear that the seagull part of this statement cannot be taken literally: Nína is a native inhabitant of the lake-shore,[19] and if indeed it were the lake that she was drawn to, she could easily access it to her heart's content from her lakeside home just as well as from the Sórin estate. Once "the lake", taken literally, is ruled out as a cause of her attraction, the context clarifies its real cause: her parents oppose her attraction to the theatre, **"but"**, she says, she is drawn to the lake like a seagull. This "but" says it all: her attraction is not really "to the lake"; rather, it is precisely to the "bohemian" milieu of artists that dominates the Sórin estate, and to fulfil her wish to "become an actress", defying her parents' narrow-minded objection to that wish.[20]

Viewed from Nína's home perspective, then, the lake has nothing to do with art; but in the neighbouring estate the two are inseparable: it is only there that the lake's view is blocked by a theatre curtain and then enclosed within the frame of a makeshift stage (this is stipulated explicitly in the *initial stage directions*; it is only there that she can share her love of art with the young writer and playwright whom she cares about, and sincerely believes that she loves at this point in the plot-line[21] (differences between their approaches to the theatre notwithstanding); it is only there that she can meet the famous actress, who at this stage is not yet her rival in love, and hear her encouraging words; and it is only there, on the Sórin shore, that the lake is set for the fishing rod of the writer whom she really adores, and with whom she is destined to fall in love.

At this moment, then, her mind produces the seagull as representation of her love for the lake (literally), for art and the theatre, for fame as an actress, for mingling with famous artists, and for the young writer and playwright who harnesses or mobilises nature, and as it were subordinates the lake itself, to be at the service of a theatre stage, on which she is about to perform in front of those famous artists. The four-way homology suggested here can be schematised as $A \rightarrow B \parallel C \rightarrow D$ ($\rightarrow$ signifies attraction, and $\parallel$ signifies analogy): Nína (A) is figuratively drawn to the 'art-infused' lake (B), in a way parallel or analogous to the way in which a real seagull (C) is literally drawn to the real lake (D). By implication, this means that Nína's need for the theatre is nothing less than existential hunger: it is basic to her nature, and she cannot live without it just as seagulls need the natural habitat of the lake (and the fish in it) for their survival. The image of the beautiful white bird capable of soaring upwards above the lake, then, is instantaneously linked for Nína — but in a way also for the audience through her — with love, art, theatre, and fame.

Young Nína simply refuses to be confused by facts: in spite of her knowledge of the realities of seagulls' lives and the true reason for their 'attraction' to lakes, Nína the would-be actress and the avid reader of romantic literature gets the better of Nína the native lake-shore girl. For her, seagulls are poetic, not ornithological; the bird's whiteness (associated by human cultural consent with beauty and purity) and its upward flight (similarly associated with freedom of spirit, and with everything lofty and sublime) supplant the realities of its existential behaviour.[22] In this sense she is a typical Chekhovian personage, for whom the world of dreams and imagination is not only more valuable, but, in a profound sense, more real than the world of facts and actions.[23] This complex of meanings is experienced and shared by Nína, who generates it subliminally when bringing up the image of the seagull, and by Konstantín who perceives it as her addressee.

Next, the seagull appears as a stage prop — the bird that Konstantín had shot in Act 2, before "laying it at Nína's feet", literally. His shooting adds a powerfully tangible and restraining imagery to Nína's initial figurative use of the bird as an idea: the stage-prop (with its presentation by Konstantín to Nína) not only concretises the idea of the seagull's flight and plight for the audience, but also brings to mind an upward surge of a beautiful white bird abruptly and violently turned into a sudden fall at the hands of a human killer–hunter. The flight of the seagull — representative of love, beauty, art, and the urge to perceive, achieve and experience them — turns into the fall of the seagull, which is the violent end of these values and aspirations. The latter meanings are perhaps only intuitively sensed by the personages, but they are of paramount importance in the message conveyed implicitly from author to audience.

The actual dialogue between Nína and Konstantín is concerned with their personal, private worlds, rather than with the universal implications just proposed; yet Nína, somewhat wryly, introduces a derogatory hint at the obscurity of *symbolism* into her talk about communication between her and Konstantín. By doing that the way she does, her text occupies a borderline-space between the *inner/fictional plane*, where it formally belongs, and the *outer/rhetorical plane*, activated by the explicit mention of the word *symbol*. At the same time her words evoke the aura of meanings associated with the seagull for these two specific personages in the former plane and for the audience in the latter.

By shooting the seagull Konstantín is saying to Nína as it were — as often in Chekhov, totally implicitly, but powerfully — something like *'when you fell out of love with me you killed 'our' seagull, our love, our common aspirations and ideals, and the love of art, beauty and the theatre that we used to share; I killed a real bird, in the most tangible way, to make you realise the full extent of your betrayal, and* **you** *should know better, because you are the one who verbalised the inseparable link between the seagull, our love, and the love of art, beauty, and the theatre'*. The image of the white seagull flying freely upward, then, is the *unrestrained potential*; Konstantín's act of shooting the bird functions as *restrainer*; whereas the final image of the slain, fallen bird is the *restrained text*: the flight of the seagull was held back, brought down, and thus remained a potential violently killed, never allowed to live and witness its realisation. A powerfully emotional type of *unrealised potential*, this is an extreme instance of *Chekhovian restraint*.

Next, at the end of Act 2, Trigórin outlines his "idea for a short story", featuring a tripartite analogy between (a) a fictional girl-protagonist, (b) the real seagull just killed, and (c) the real Nína. At this point the imagery of the fallen seagull — having acquired the meanings enumerated above — recurs, with the three components of the tripartite analogy sharing the fate of curbed soar (literally and/or metaphorically). In Act 4, Konstantín's mention of Nína's habit of signing her letter to him as "The Seagull" can evoke another process of *restraint* in the audience, now in possession of all the information that this signature can convey. For Nína, then, this self-identifying signature, specifically in messages addressed to Konstantín, is a clear act of restraining, holding back a world of emotions desperately looking for ways of expression. It is a substitute for crying out loud. Nína's life story being what it is, she experiences the seagull as a persistently ominous presence in her life; the fact that she is the one who started her 'fatal relationship' with the seagull image, and therefore has "no one but herself to blame", does not mitigate this experience of seagull-related doom; it just adds a dimension of frustration and inescapable responsibility to this experience. Whether she likes it or not, she must perforce realise that at most significant junctures in her life there is some inescapable presence of a seagull — real or figurative, dead or alive, explicitly verbalised or intuitively sensed. 'That damned bird' just wouldn't let her be: it is always with her, whether she is on her own, or in the company of one or more of the most important factors in her life — Konstantín, Trigórin, or the theatre. Her somewhat unexpected expression of death wish in her final monologue ("I should be killed") — quite out of character, and inconsistent with most of the rest of the monologue — can also be understood in this context. It can be taken as a pre-Joycean instance of stream of consciousness: fed by the analogy between her and the slain seagull, an association comes to her mind, leading to this remark (as if she is saying to Konstantín, or thinking to herself with him in mind, *'you killed a seagull, you said you would also kill yourself, but you should have just as well killed me too, or instead'*).

In her final monologue, then, her self-reference as "seagull" and retracting from it is a sign of an internal struggle within her. One part of her wants to acquire a ready-made self-definition provided, as it were, by fate. Thus, sticking a stereotyped label on her person is an easy way to relieve herself of the responsibility of thought-through self-characterisation, of unwavering soul-searching aimed at ascertaining her "own self" to whom she should "be true". This part of her, then, is saying to herself, as well as to the outside world, as it were, something like *'this is me, this is what and who I am; like it or not, understand it or not — I am a seagull,*[24] *whatever this means!'* The other part of Nína, however, cannot be satisfied with such a simplistic label, however understandable in the mental and biographical circumstances, and prefers no label at all to a shallow and profoundly meaningless label.[25] Through her and through what she is saying to Konstantín, on the *inner/fictional plane*, then, it is Chekhov who is making us aware, on the *outer/rhetorical plane*, of a profound generalisation about human individuality. According to his implied message, any attempt to define a person by an image, an analogy, or a label, even an appropriate and well-motivated one, is at best correct and incorrect at the same time: thus, Nína is a seagull, in the senses developed throughout the text, but she is also not all of that: she is more, and less. More, because Chekhov's world in *The Seagull* (unlike Ibsen's in *The Wild Duck*) is incompatible with reducing a human being to such a definition, and even in this particular case there is much more to Nína than her analogy with the seagull. Less, because the seagull in *The Seagull* is much more than one person: it stands, as we have seen, not only for other personages as well (Konstantín, Trigórin, and others, in different dosages and meanings — see also Rozik 1988), but also, and perhaps mainly, for ideas and values, some of them relating to humanity as a whole. In short, the question is not only "**who** is 'the seagull'?" (or "**whom** does 'the seagull' stand for?"), but also, and mainly, "**what** is 'the seagull'?" (or "**what** does 'the seagull' stand for?"). Of course, being Chekhov, the author gives no explicit answer to this question, however formulated, but he does give us clues to a possible answer, however partial, as long as it does not falsely pretend to be complete.

The physical seagull's final destiny is to become a stuffed bird, ordered by Trigórin (see Jackson 1967a and Chances 1977).[26] It is not very difficult, taking everything said so far into account, to identify the semantic field of the stuffed bird.

The idea of divorcing beauty from life/reality by perpetuating lifeless beauty resonates with the different approaches to art, literature, and play-writing as expressed both explicitly and implicitly in, and by, Chekhov's play *The Seagull* as a whole, not only by its personages. An analogy is brought to mind between Nína's ready retracting from her self-reference as a seagull and Trigórin's denial of his earlier order to stuff the seagull, but this is a technical, partial, and partly misleading analogy, which needs to be stated and retracted at the same time… Suffice it to say that whereas Nína's retracting from her self-definition is a sign of pursuing a truth about herself, Trigórin's denial, conversely, is a sign of running away from any kind of truth. Nína attempts the flight **of** the seagull and whatever it represents, whereas Trigórin attempts the flight **from** it. His approach to art, love, work, literature, let alone fishing — in short, to everything significant in his life, even according to his own hierarchies of importance — is characterised by this duality. Indeed, he creates life (as a writer, but also, briefly and disastrously, as a father), and destroys it; he wishes to nurture and perpetuate beauty at the expense of life, and denies this very wish. He turns "*a thing of beauty*" (the seagull that he himself calls "a beautiful bird") into *a beautiful **thing***: a stuffed bird is, at best, a **thing**, a far cry from "joy forever". He is aware and unaware, remembers and forgets at the same time. Thus, the two personages, mainly through their contrasting qualities, reflect each other in so many ways, within a play in which *reflection* is a crucial idea and central image. The seagull soaring in the sky is also reflected in the deep of the lake. The inexhaustible wealth of potential meanings is just hinted here; it is boundless.

A close look at other personages, almost without exception, reveals similar features of affirming and negating the same traits in the same person, though each of them differs from the others in what s/he affirms and negates. Here is just one additional example: in Act 4 Sórin speaks of suggesting to Konstantín "an idea for a story" (the wording of this suggestion of course resonates with Trigórin's "idea for a short story", inspired by the fate of the shot seagull at the end of Act 2). Sórin's idea is for a story to be titled "The Man who Wanted", and he gives himself as an example: he wanted to get married and remained single; he wanted to become a man of letters, and didn't; he wanted to be an eloquent speaker, and is a clumsy one; etc. This "idea for a story" is exceptionally significant in many respects: thus, specifically in *The Seagull*, it is relevant in a context of art–life interactions. However, at this point I would like to point out how it fits in with a whole array of affirmations and negations in the play. Thus, the same basic rhythm of statements and retractions connects at least the following elements in the play: Sórin's suggested short story; Nína's affirming and negating her self-definition as a seagull; Konstantín's (and Trigórin's) frequent contradictory statements; Arkádina's typical "not X, but Y" or "Y, but not X" statements (e.g., "It is not a matter of new forms, but of bad character" in Act 1, or "I am an actress, not a banker" in Act 3); Trigórin's ordering the stuffed bird and "forgetting" it; his urge to write as an escape from fishing and to fish as an escape from writing (without realising how similar these two activities are in his case; see also Rozik 1988); etc. Indeed each of these has its own specific meanings, very different from the others, but they share this deeply Chekhovian refusal to formulate any significant characterisation of a person, or an idea, by way of simplistic equation: indeed, $X=Y$ may perhaps work well in some mathematical contexts, but never in an attempt to capture the true meaning and character of a person, an idea, a significant event in human life, etc. This forward-and-backward movement is genuinely a pattern of reciprocal *restraint*.

In short, through the central theme of the seagull, one can follow up some of the techniques by which Chekhov creates an overall effect of *restrained emotion* in the play. Indeed, on the one hand, this effect is not confined to the seagull image itself, and on the other hand there are matters related to the seagull image that are not related to restrained emotions. Moreover, *restraint* does not define the seagull image exhaustively any more than being a seagull is an exhaustive definition of Nína. Yet, this Chapter has shown that *restraint* is one of the most general, persistent, and — above all — characteristic, qualities of Chekhov's uniqueness. Viewing it through the image of the seagull, which (once again) works intensely in our minds not least because of the play's title, is an effective way of demonstrating its centrality in this play; its centrality to Chekhov's other plays is just as striking, perhaps even more.[27]

7.6 Conclusion: A Survey of the Other Major Plays

Uncle Vánia, Chekhov's next play, is so full of effects of restrained emotions, that one does not know where to begin. It is an overwhelming effect, dominating almost all individual personages, relationships (where the superiority of the unsaid/unspoken over the said/spoken is occasionally more overwhelming than in the later plays), themes that are suggested rather than fully presented, etc. The movement of the play as a whole is marked by *Chekhovian restraint* from start to end: it is replete of unfulfilled dreams. Thus, to mention two of many, consider Ástrov's hardly-realisable dreams of saving Russia's forests'; Vánia's almost ridiculously-unrealisable dream of being capable of becoming "a Dostoïévskiï, a Schopenhauer"); unrealised loves (of most personages, each with its unique features); and, above all, the unspeakable sadness of the play's "back-to-normal" ending, after the entire turmoil has subsided and come to nothing. Thus, at the end everything is much more hopeless than ever before. The rare but significant moments of outburst — notably in the abortive shooting scene in Act 3 — gain much of their saliency from the contrast between them and the persistent *restraint* that characterises most of the other moments. By the same token, the play's ending has a crushing effect of restraint mainly because of its contrast with the shooting scene. Of course, there are many *micro* ups and downs, which in the poetics of a master of subtlety like Chekhov are at least as significant as the *macro* ups and downs outlined here.

In *Three Sisters* we have seen how Chekhov's poetics comes to full fruition, how trends and streaks present in his earlier work mature and reach their ultimate peak. This applies with added emphasis to the principle of *Chekhovian restraint*, which is carried out in this play with iron clad relentlessness. Reading *Three Sisters'* text with *Chekhovian restraint* in mind can yield the conclusion that there are very few moments in the play that are devoid of this quality. The play's text in its entirety is a series of repeated attempts to ignite a fire of emotional outburst and squash it mercilessly and almost immediately, by the speaker him/herself, by another speaker, by an entrance of yet another personage, by silence or lack of response, or by some other type of non-verbal theatrical event signalled by a *stage direction* (sight, sound etc.). Perhaps nowhere else is the ultimate effect of *Chekhovian restraint* so powerful in conveying powerlessness as in *Three Sisters*; perhaps in no other Chekhov play is the stifling experience of almost literal throat-choking in withholding an almost inevitable sob so intensely experienced by a perceptive audience, as shown above in this Chapter.

In *The Cherry Orchard* the effect may not be so total and all-pervasive as in *Three Sisters* (this is mainly due to the relatively comic nature[28] of Chekhov's last play), but it is certainly powerfully present: consider the build-up of the characters of Vária and Lopákhin and the lame relationship between them, culminating in the 'non-marriage-proposal' in Act 4; Gáïev's speeches and the responses that they elicit; the structure of the dialogues between Ranévskaïa and Trofímov, especially in Act 3; the latter's 'revolutionary' tirades practically stifled by their irresponsive textual vicinity; the interaction between Lopákhin's triumphant speech announcing his purchase of the cherry orchard and the mechanisms that restrain it, mainly through silent responses of other people present; and, of course, the entire sequence of the play's ending.

To conclude: the major aim of the present Chapter is to draw attention to the **centrality** of *Chekhovian restraint* within the general poetics of Chekhov's art, especially in the plays: in fact, the stories are characterised by it just as much (as demonstrated in the few stories mentioned and analysed in the Book), but there is something more intense and immediate in this specific mechanism when our interactions with the fictional world take place in the arena of the theatre, experienced through the tangible presence of real people on stage, their words, actions, gestures and behaviour. *Chekhovian restraint* is an integral part of the basic principle of *unrealised potential*, being its most salient manifestation. To stress this connection I would like to repeat here almost verbatim, with minor changes, some of my final words about the general principle, as formulated above in Chapter 1. What I say there about Chekhov's potentials in general is applicable with special force to **emotional** potentials, prevented from realisation through restraint, in particular.

Indeed, Chekhov's potentials on all planes gain potency **because** of being unrealised. They are forever held back, almost exploding with potential energy, which they are doomed never to release. The clouds over the terrain of his world keep gathering, ever greyer, ever denser, yet rains rarely fall, and storms hardly ever break out. It is erroneous to describe this quality as *understatement*; rather, it is comparable to violently boiling water in a pressure cooker covered with a hermetically sealed lid, hardly emitting any vapour. From the perspective of an outside observer it may look similar to a cold pot; yet, just try to remove the lid lightly, for a split second, and you'll be alarmed by the difference. And, indeed, Chekhov gives us hints, though often hardly noticeable, to the existence of the controlled explosives.

It is precisely this type of 'pressurised explosiveness' that generates Másha's centrality in the play, as explained in 5.2.2. The choice of this particular quote as Epigraph to this Chapter, then, results from the characterising quality of Másha's uniqueness.

The simmering embers of the surface of Chekhov's texts can hardly hide the boiling explosive emotions underneath, which really propel the action in his plays. Generally speaking, in Chekhov's plays *present through absence* agents and elements play an unprecedentedly crucial role in propelling the plot. The "restraining order" in these plays, by which an imminent outburst of bare emotion of some kind is hinted, suggested, expected, and then undermined and frustrated (or frustrated even in advance, before the outburst was suggested in the first place) is a general *regulating principle* (see Harshav 2007, esp. pp. 10–11, 82, 187) in Chekhov's poetics. The tension between the various implicit and explicit components of these plays, and particularly the tension inherent in the process by which an *unrestrained potential*, through its interaction with a *restrainer* yields a *restrained text*, may well be the main hallmark of Chekhov's uniqueness.

Notes

1 Terminologically, this distinction is inspired (respectively) by the *signified–signifier–sign* model in semiotic theory, though the analogy is based on verbal–rhythmical association only; in substance the two distinctions are quite different.

2 The structure of this statement is largely a Chekhov-specific application of procedures of understanding texts as proposed by Harshav 2007, 76–112.

3 For instance: sharp, overt conflict; intense manifestation of love; the death of a major personage, especially if untimely, violent, or otherwise 'irregular', and particularly if a vociferous response to it is suggested or anticipated; an incident provoking extreme, barely containable emotions like anger, fear, joy, sadness, hope, despair; etc.

4 For instance, responses betraying misunderstanding or indifference *vis-à-vis* emotionally charged materials; an ill-timed or 'strange' non-verbal behaviour (e.g., Fedótik's laugh when announcing the burning of all his possessions in Act 3 of *Three Sisters*, or Másha's tendency to smile, laugh and whistle 'inappropriately', in the same play); the choice of words that create 'cognitive dissonances' with a situation (e.g., Trigórin's characterisation of Konstantín's attempted suicide as "tactless"); the entrance/presence of an outsider, or otherwise undesirable person, within an intimate situation (e.g., Natásha's walking with a candle "*à la* Lady Macbeth" — according to Chekhov's own instruction —when the three sisters try to have a heart-searching conversation, or Vánia's famous entrance with a bouquet upon Ástrov's and Yeléna's embrace, *Uncle Vánia*, Act 3); or, conversely, the exit/absence of someone needed for such an intimate situation (e.g., the sisters' out-of-sight presence during Andréï's painful monologue, *Three Sisters*, Act 3, and their total absence during his monologue in Act 4); etc.

5 Other distinctions can be added (e.g., between *personal* vs. *impersonal*, *onstage* vs. *offstage* sources of elements that make up the restraining process), but for brevity's and clarity's sake they will not be addressed here: they can blur the picture without affecting the argument as presented in this Chapter. For similar reasons, various composites of these distinctions (*outward–verbal–'micro'*, *non-verbal–'macro'–inward,* etc.) will be ignored; moreover, not all of these potentials are realised by Chekhov, and no theoretical point in this discussion is an aim in itself, if it does not serve a purpose in characterising Chekhov's poetics.

6   Several translators into English — notably Laurence Senelick in his monumental
     Norton editions (2005, 2006) — make two points relevant to this statement by Nína,
     and to the play as a whole, from the translation perspective. (1) There is an argument
     concerning the best way to render the play's title in English, whether *The Seagull* or
     The Gull. Senelick makes a case for the latter, which he uses in his text, but still uses
     the former for a title, because of well established tradition in English (a fuller discus-
     sion of the matter is provided in Chapter 3, Note 18). (2) Again, several
     scholars/translators (e.g., by implication, Senelick 2005, p. 174, n. 1) make the point
     that in the absence of articles in Russian it is unclear whether the correct English version
     of Nína's words is "I'm **a** (sea)gull" (which is much more prevalent in English versions
     of the play) or "I'm **the** (sea)gull", the latter referring, of course, to the specific seagull
     that Konstantín killed and whose image haunted Nína throughout her life. The point is
     worth making, but the fine change of nuance between these two versions does not make
     a substantial difference, one way or the other, to arguments presented in this Chapter.
     Bearing these two points in mind, my preference is to uphold the tradition in English
     and have Nína say "I'm a seagull" in her final monologue, but "The Seagull" in
     Konstantín's reference to the signature in her letters to him (Act 4). The matter is further
     pursued in Note 24 below.

7   Senelick (2005, 2006) translates this disclaimer of Nína's as "That's wrong", which, in
     my opinion, is wrong: the moral undertone of *wrong* in English is gratuitous here.
     Rhythmically, too, a pensive two-word or even three-word version ("not so", "not that",
     even "that's not it" or "that's not right") renders the original's resolutely-hesitant tone
     more effectively and attentively than a determined monosyllable like "wrong".

8   Both interpretations, which do not contradict each other, are possible: the second-
     person-plural pronoun in Russian (as used here) — just as its only English equivalent,
     you — can refer to any number of addressed persons, from one to infinity. This *réplique*
     responds to Irína's, making her the probable addressee; yet, the reference to an old
     migratory bird observing (a) young one(s) — which makes more sense if the latter is
     in the plural — speaks for the entire *réplique* being addressed to all three. Luckily for
     translators into English, in this case both interpretations yield the same translated text.
     In other languages, like my own native Hebrew, the second person has to be identified
     in gender and number, so that in this case an inescapable decision is imposed on the
     translator.

9   This is bitterly ironic, considering that the sisters are presented, and regard themselves,
     as wingless birds (without using this metaphor explicitly), who will never soar to the
     Moscow horizon; see especially Túsenbach's and Másha's dialogue in Act 2, where they
     "philosophise" about the migration of birds in analogy with the meaning of life, and
     Másha's affectionate yet envious look at the birds in Act 4. These two moments are
     subtly though obviously connected, and take major part in the formation of the birds-
     Leitmotiv in the play (a subject worthy of separate discussion).

10   A musical analogy is offered here by free association: at the end of Schumann's *Lied*-
     cycle *Frauenliebe und Leben* [*A Woman's Love and Life*], after the last song dedicated
     to the heroine's mourning her husband's death, the piano's first bars — originally
     describing the excitement of her first meeting with him — return without words,
     signalling her sad and silent reminiscing, thus bringing the magical moments of her
     falling in love with him back to the audience.

11   The quote is the very first words that Másha utters on stage; at first, in the beginning of
     the play, it is probably brought to her mind by the Moscow- and childhood-related remi-
     niscences of her sisters. The text is the opening lines from Pushkin's famous
     fairytale–poem *Ruslán and Liudmíla*; every educated Russian knows these lines by

heart, because every Russian child memorises them as an integral part of good schooling that nurtures a shared national–cultural heritage, to which Pushkin's oeuvre is central in ways comparable to Shakespeare's centrality to the heritage of the English-speaking world. The actual words, though, are somewhat enigmatic (at least for Russians of generations later than Pushkin's), and their nebulous meaning is part of their hypnotic charm; quite a few educated Russians have much less of a problem reciting them with a sing-song intonation than understanding them fully, in the elementary sense of understanding words from the dictionary. Chekhov skilfully manipulates his audience's thorough acquaintance with this text and uncertainty about its precise meaning — a combination that enhances a Russian audience's subconscious identification with Másha at this point, based on a vague sense of shared childhood and upbringing (see Magarshack 1972, 113, 181; Senelick 2005, 253 n. 1, 303 n. 3). By the way, in his translation of *Three Sisters* David Magarshack replaced it with the opening lines of Coleridge's "Kubla Khan", whose combination of fame with vagueness of meaning, he believed, would function in the minds of an educated English audience similarly to the ways in which the original Pushkin quote affects a comparably educated Russian audience.

12 This refusal echoes with her refusal to play the piano after her father's death, as reported in Act 3. See also Golomb 1984, 178–183.

13 This interlude, as it functions at this precise moment, is a stroke of genius; enormous differences notwithstanding, it is perhaps comparable in world drama only to "the Porter Scene" in Shakespeare's *Macbeth*, Act 3, with its hopeless attempt to momentarily divert the audience's attention from the traumatic presence of the murder just committed and the words and deeds directly connected with it. The pre-destined failure of this attempt in *Macbeth* actually results in reinforcing the emotional effect of the murder, rather than weakening it, just as here, in the Chekhov example, Kulýgin's moving attempt to make the sisters smile, even laugh, does not make anyone on stage or in the audience even momentarily forget the fateful events surrounding this comic interlude. The laugh perhaps glitters through the tears, but does not dry them.

14 The two comparably narrow-minded representatives of the provincial township in the play — kind-hearted Kulýgin and callous Natásha — make their final exits in respectively characteristic ways: while the former tries his limited best to defuse the tension and ease the burden of Másha and her sisters, the latter's words exacerbate the sisters' emotional plight (she couldn't care less about this effect of her words if she knew it, but she is obtuse enough not to notice it in the first place). The effects on the audience are comparable: a momentary partial relief, then increased, stifling oppression.

15 The English version of the text as written here is designed to illustrate a point in the analysis; it violates normal English usage, and cannot work in a published book or on the stage. Here it is an attempt to come closer to the well-designed word-order, which is, grammatically, a standard option in the Russian original (this version's accidental metrical regularity in *amphibrach*, gratuitous and annoying, is another reason for its unacceptability as a real English translation of this text). In fact, the original is even less compatible with English word-order; it is, literally, "just now in the duel was killed the Baron", which reserves the disclosure of the duel's victim's identity to the end of the sentence, as the final blow that crushes Irína.

16 This suggested musical terminology **must not** be taken in any literal sense; it is only an illustration for the up-and-down curve of relative loudness and voice intensity, as implied by the *stage directions*.

17 One cannot ignore the connection that Chekhov creates between Irína's "I knew",

Ól'ga's final "If we/one could know", and other uses of the verb "to know" and its derivatives in the play.

18 This technique — simply searching for each instance of a key word or term, as if compiling an index, in an attempt to analyse and contextualise its developing meanings and functions throughout the text — serves here as a model, but it is not applied verbatim; rather than dwelling, literally, on every single instance, step by step, general principles are discovered by discussing a partial representative sample.

19 This is stressed several times in the play; for the Sórin estate residents, and especially for Konstantín, she is indeed "the girl next door". Nína herself emphasises her 'native status' at the end of Act 2, when she literally points her family home and estate across the lake to Trigórin, saying that she spent her entire life on the lake-shore where she had been born, and knows "every little island" in the lake.

20 In *Three Sisters*, the headmaster of Kulýgin's school is also reported to dislike art and artists, presumably regarding them as unrespectable. Alongside Protopópov, this personage is an offstage epitome of provincial narrow-mindedness, in parallel to the onstage presence of Kulýgin and Natásha.

21 In typically Chekhovian feat of elusiveness it is not absolutely certain whether she loves Konstantín at this point, evidence being inconclusive. Two statements addressed directly to Konstantín must not be forgotten, however: in Act 1 "my heart is full of you", in the present tense, and in the Act 4 monologue "I loved you", in the past tense.

22 To this there is a sideline with a very subtle, hardly noticeable olfactory streak: in Act 2 Nína gives Dorn a bouquet of flowers she has just picked (soon afterwards destroyed by Polína Andréïevna); there is a hint of contrast between the 'fishy business' that goes on around the lake (fishing being Trigórin's hobby and the real seagulls' non-poetic preoccupation — see Rozik 1988) and the poetic, potentially romantic and fragrant act of picking flowers, though the latter has also an element of destroying life for the sake of (temporary) perpetuation of beauty, partly analogous to the stuffing of the seagull towards the ending of the play. Flowers are also connected to Konstantín's demonstrative attempt to ascertain his mother's love for him by plucking out petals ("she loves me — she loves me not"; Act 1). Note that the lake-native Nína likes fragrant flowers and has nothing at all to do with fishing — neither as an economically viable activity nor as a hobby — whereas the town-dwelling Trigórin is enthusiastically fond of it. This is just one example of the finely woven webs of imagery that Chekhov's texts almost secretively cast before us.

23 In assigning comparable reality-values to fact and fantasy *à la* Chekhov there is not even a shred of psychosis: it simply means that people's inner lives and emotional worlds, including their fantasies, are mental **facts**; the contrast for Chekhov, then, is not between reality-values of facts on the one hand and fantasies/dreams/wishes etc., on the other hand, but between the reality-values of **two types of real facts**: tangible–physical and mental–psychological. In some personages, though — e.g., in the narrator of "A Little Joke", and, to a much lesser extent, in the Prózorovs (in *Three Sisters*) — there is an element of reality-denial, that can be described as neurotic, and in the former case as bordering on the psychotic. For an individual person(age), it is crucial to know fact from fiction and to treat them differently; for humanity as a whole, as observed by Chekhov from the vantage point of a creator of fictional worlds, fantasies are one type of significant facts. We, as his audience, are made to share both points of view: the personages' from within, and the author's from above.

24 See Note 6 above. Whether the definite or indefinite article is chosen here for an English rendition of Nína's seagull-refrain, she must be referring to her personal perspective of the seagull. However, if the definite article is used, it makes sense that "*I*" should be

more emphasised than *"seagull"*, as an answer to the question "who is the (real) seagull?", whereas the use of the indefinite article suggests stronger emphasis on *"seagull"*, as an answer to the question "who/what am I?" (in other words, the roles of *logical–psychological subject* and *logical–psychological predicate* are reversed in these two options for an English translation). The former interpretation may look attractive, but is not convincing, because it would imply that Nína is consciously competing with Konstantín for the title of "the real seagull". Indeed, at the beginning of Act 2 Konstantín made an explicit reference to himself as analogous to the seagull he had just killed, and this analogy proves ominously correct at the end of the play; however, there is no shred of evidence that he had ever challenged Nína with saying or writing to her *'I'm the real seagull, not you!'*, to which she could have replied *'no, I am the one'*. In short, the more reasonable emphasis is on "seagull", rather than on "I am", because Nína is making here a failed effort to define and characterise her own identity, rather than to quibble about the seagull's (the latter option, incidentally, is more appropriate to Ibsen's *The Wild Duck* than to Chekhov's play). Being a matter of translation into English (and other languages with articles), this is one question that never crossed Chekhov's mind.

25 Indeed, Chekhov usually has a 'soft spot' for characters who at least honestly try to expose or to face a truth, however painful, and refuse to whitewash a situation and pretend to have found an answer where there is none, whatever the emotional cost.

26 It is difficult to trust Trigórin's recurring denial, as if he forgot that he had ordered the stuffing of the bird. Chekhov prefers not to make it clear whether he really had a sudden and convenient 'amnesia' or was lying about it. At any rate, there are no other instances of such forgetfulness in him, and in both cases he comes out extremely insensitive. At any rate, the stuffing contributes to the crucially significant theme of art–reality interactions in this play more than to its effect of *restraint*. See Appendix.

27 It was my deliberate decision to focus so much of the discussion of *Chekhovian restraint* on *The Seagull*. This is the earliest of Chekhov's "Four Major Plays"; in many ways it is relatively more conventional and less 'Chekhovian' than the other three, especially when compared to the last two (e.g., in its **comparatively** clearer patterns of plotline, conflict, and romantic relationships); see also Hingley 1968, Vol. 1, p. 7. *Chekhovian restraint*, too, is more immediately striking and intuitively perceived in the other late plays. Showing its impressive centrality in *The Seagull*, then, is an *a fortiori* argument; it emphasises this quality's centrality to Chekhov's uniqueness, to his basic *DNA*.

28 The problematic *genre classification* of Chekhov's plays is very widely discussed in the literature (see especially Senderovich 1994), but is outside the scope of the discussion in this Chapter; it is addressed especially in Chapters 3 and 10.

8

"Tea or 'Philosophising'?"
Hierarchising Ideas and Values

They don't give us tea — let's at least philosophise.
(Vershinin, *Three Sisters,* Act 2)

You have chosen your subject from the realm of abstract
ideas, which is just as well; because a work of art must
express some great thought [...] What's beautiful has to be
serious. [...] Describe only the significant and the eternal.
(From Dr. Dorn's advice to Konstantin, *The Seagull*, Act 1)

8.0 The Importance of Being Specific:
Hierarchising, Referentiality and Organisation
in Literary and Dramatic Art

8.0.1 General Theoretical Considerations

The intuitive distinction between the 'important' and the 'unimportant' (alias 'significant/insignificant') in human life is rather clear 'around the edges', i.e., in extreme cases, and much more blurred 'in the middle': there would be a general consent that such events as the birth or death of a human being, passionate love with crises and (un)happiness, matters of personal success/fulfilment or failure/frustration on a grand scale, etc. (on the level of the individual), and a path-breaking invention or discovery, war, revolution, natural disaster etc. (in the lives of nations and societies, which of course affect multiple individual fates), are 'important'. By contrast, such mundane events as the very act of reading a daily newspaper (whether the news printed in it is 'important' or not), an uneventful routine day spent at home or work, getting dressed in the morning or preparing for bed in the evening, tying one's shoelaces, or, indeed, drinking a cup of tea or coffee[1] — are all 'unimportant' by the same token. Only exceptional circumstances — e.g., grappling with a disability that prevents a person from performing this kind of mundane activities — can make such events 'important'. Other types of events and occurrences in life are less clear-cut and more debatable in this respect, and the assessment of their 'importance' brings up questions of individual, social and cultural conventions, values, norms and criteria, determining what is 'important' for/to whom, under what circumstances, in what context, etc. The matter is so complex, so contingent on numerous variables, that no rules with universal validity can be formulated, and most people would not even bother to try establishing such rules; yet, intuitively and routinely, we keep saying to ourselves and to others 'this is (un)important', 'X is more/less important than Y', often without explaining why, and with no explicit hierarchies of relative values or consistent priorities in mind.

As a writer, Chekhov was intensely preoccupied with questions of hierarchies and priorities in life and in art.[2] One can learn of this preoccupation from attentively analysing his work, and drawing explicit conclusions from its implicit features; typically, he did not engage in authorial/authoritative statements about such questions in his fictional writings, but shaped and moulded them in ways that inspire his readers and audiences to explore and ponder questions of 'importance'/'significance'.[3] This brings us back to Chekhov's much-quoted 1888 letter to Suvórin discussed above, where Chekhov contends that an *artist*'s job is only to "present correctly" questions/problems, rather than to answer/solve them. In other words, it is through the creation of *fictional worlds* with events, personages and their words and deeds, and (arguably, above all) through the way he structures these fictional worlds in/and his texts as verbal artefacts, that an artist undertakes the self-imposed task of "presenting questions/problems correctly". As argued above, in this context the concept of "correct presentation" implies the artistic realisation, within a *fictional world*, of the potential for depth and complexity inherent in given human situations and relationships in the 'real' world. Failing to do that — usually through shallow, simplistic platitudes, be they explicit or implicit — amounts to 'incorrect', reductive presentation of the human condition, even if they are not literally false or mistaken; undoubtedly, such platitudes were anathema to Chekhov. Thus, for him, the "correct presentation of the questions" of *unrealised potentials* of/in the human condition is largely achieved through **textual** *unrealised potentials/present absences*; however, seemingly paradoxically, such *unrealised potentials* constitute the only way for the *artistic **realisation** of the potential for complexity* inherent in the human world. As shown throughout the Book, paradoxes of comparable magnitude are typical of Chekhov's unique poetics.

Once again, in this letter explicitly, and in his actual artistic work implicitly, Chekhov defined himself as an *artist* — i.e., in this context, a creator of fictional worlds through plays and stories — as distinct from other types of people who "do things with words" in creating verbal texts and communicating them to addressees (e.g., philosophers, politicians, teachers, preachers, journalists, etc., or even, by implication, critics, scholars and analysts of works/texts created by artists). This calls attention to two interrelated but distinct matters in any art, and particularly in verbal art: (a) what is *specific* or *distinctive* to (an) art, and (b) what is *important* to/in/about it. At first, intuitively, one would tend to regard the two categories at least as closely related, if not identical; in various contexts we are trained and encouraged to search, identify and characterise *distinctive features* of/in whatever we are observing or exploring, and naturally tend to attach utmost importance to the unique/specific.[4]

In the case of verbal–fictional art (whether *narrative prose*, *poetry* or *Drama*), however, the *unique/specific* and the *important/significant* are not necessarily identical.[5] If the *importance* of an object, phenomenon etc., is judged by its purpose, or *raison d'être*, as perceived by most of its (active and passive) users, then the way to establish the importance of verbal–literary art resides primarily in its *semantic–thematic content* i.e., in the *fictional 'world'* that its language conveys to its addressees — first and foremost by activating its *referential* capacities — rather than in structural–compositional features of textual organisation. In other words, the importance/significance of texts of verbal art resides in the interactions and interrelationships between *units of the reality-like fictional world* rather than between *units of the text* as such. This line of argument is based on the observation that, by and large, what motivates most writers/authors, on the one hand, and most perceivers/addressees, on the other hand, to be involved in literary or theatrical communication is to engage in 'the *what*' (i.e., focusing attention on a human story, situation or message, conveyed by the text) rather than in 'the *how*' (i.e., focusing attention on a compositional–rhetorical trick, technique, strategy, etc., and/or pure formal–structural properties of a text, all attesting to the active presence of an author).[6] Put as simply as possible, the focus on '*What does he tell us?*' is replaced by a focus on '*How he does it?*'. However, it is an incontestable fact that human stories, messages, or situations, can be discussed, conveyed, related, transmitted, etc., through language that is not organised artistically (e.g., in articles, reports, personal letters, and other non-fictional types of verbal texts), and in texts in which the *poetic function* (*à la* Jakobson 1960/1967) is not dominant.[7] In short, the 'important' aspect of verbal–artistic fiction (narrative, dramatic or poetic) resides in the semantic–thematic capacity of its language, which it shares with non-artistic types of language.

The interrelation between the *important* and the *specific* is, however, more complex. It is easily demonstrable that the semantic–thematic content of works of fiction, especially complex ones, cannot be reduced or viably 'translated', re-stated or paraphrased by non-artistic means: this has been demonstrated in centuries of theoretical and analytical studies of fictional–artistic texts. Indeed, the attempted analysis of Chekhov's texts in this Book is a case in point: such analyses try to explain the creative processes of *an author's production* and *a perceiver's perception*, but not to replace or even emulate them. In terms of the present discussion, then, a concluding argument can be formulated as follows: artistic verbal texts are (a) *unique* among the *arts* in having *verbal raw material* (i.e., their pre-artistic raw material is *language*), which endows them with *referential* powers, but, of course, are (b) *not unique* among *verbal texts* in sharing *verbal signification and referentiality* with non-artistic usages of language; consequently, they are (c) *unique* among *verbal texts* in their *artistry*, and, of course, (d) *not unique* among the other (*non-verbal*) arts (such as music, painting, sculpture, etc.) in their shared *artistry*, but they are (e) *unique* among them in their *verbality* and *referentiality*.[8] What is more crucial for the purpose of this discussion, however, is the way in which the above distinctions affect the dichotomy between *important* and *unimportant*, and, in the final analysis, how all of this relates to the uniqueness of Chekhov's poetics and artistic system. In this context, then, the following conclusion (*quasi-syllogism*) can be drawn: (a) *Literature's* main claim for *importance* lies in its *semantic–thematic* component, which is *not unique* to it; (b) its main claim for *uniqueness* lies in its *artistry*, which is unique to it only among *verbal texts*, but not among the *arts*; (c) its *uniqueness* enables it to exercise its *important* function in ways that excel above all other types of verbal texts. In other words, the *message* or *content* of a work of literary art — which is conveyed through the *referential* features that it shares with other types of verbal texts and not with other arts — is served by its *unique* features, which it shares with other arts, but not with other types of verbal texts. This 'service' rendered by the *unique* to the *important* is manifest mainly in the way that the latter is experienced, rather than merely understood, in the process of perception and cognitive internalisation. The hierarchy presented here does not imply in any way whatsoever that the unique is unimportant; on the contrary, it is absolutely necessary for artistic communication and experience. This hierarchy only means that there is a relation of *subordination* at work here: the *unique/specific* is usually at the service of the *important/significant*, rather than vice versa. Both, however — the *what* and the *how* — are equally indispensable.

Consider the following trivial analogy: in syntax, as a rule, *subordinate clauses* can be just as meaningful as *principal* ones (depending on the content of the specific sentence); a clause is called *principal* or *subordinate* for structural–functional reasons only:[9] because the former can, at least potentially, function on its own, whereas the latter cannot. By the same token, *artistic mechanisms* (compositional, rhetorical etc.) cannot function on their own, divorced from *content and signification*, whereas the latter — though liable to become trite, lifeless etc., if deprived of the former — can still function autonomously.

8.0.2 Typical Hierarchies in Four 19th-Century Russian Classics

As a more concrete illustration of the above general–theoretical discussion, Chekhov will be contrasted with the three other great 19th-century Russian writers (Tolstóï, Dostoïévskiï and Gógol') through their four respective hierarchies of the *significant/insignificant* dichotomy. The following four-way presentation is unusually brief and admittedly superficial, in the absence of any textual analysis and examples to corroborate its declarative statements. Readers are requested, then, to take these statements on trust, and/or check them against their own views and intuitions, bearing in mind that the major, if not the sole, purpose of the entire exercise is to shed additional light on Chekhov's poetics and clarify its uniqueness in constructing hierarchies of *important/unimportant and superordinate/subordinate*. The generalisations about these great writers are crude, then, deliberately leaving out fine subtleties that would be crucial in other contexts, but they do claim to capture major features of their artistic systems, especially in the context of contrasting them with each other. In a way, this is also an exercise in *reciprocal characterisation of authors*, somewhat analogous to Chekhov's *reciprocal characterisation of personages*. A major difference between the two is that for Chekhov this *reciprocity* is a tool in the actual creation of his personages, whereas the authors contrasted here were real people and writers, who are being merely viewed (rather than created) through a reciprocal–contrastive perspective.

Radical differences between the artistic systems of the three major 19th-century Russian authors will be broadly outlined, but comparatively marginalised when contrasted with Chekhov: as will be shown below, each of these writers presents his own versions and hierarchies of *important/unimportant*, but all three tacitly agree that there is such a dichotomy in the first place, which can be stated, re-stated, over-stated, under-stated, maximised, minimised, reversed, etc., without negating its existence and basic characteristics. Chekhov, conversely — as shown throughout the Book and will be shown from a different angle in this Subsection — typically questions (or, rather, **makes us** question) its very existence and the basic principles governing its meanings and construction. In this subversive technique, it must be reiterated, Chekhov docs not intend to obliterate the dichotomy forever; perhaps such techniques can even reinforce it, if it proves resilient enough to withstand doubts and questions. The order of presentation of the three writers is determined by the extent of contrast between each of them on the one hand and Chekhov on the other.

8.0.2.1 Dostoïévskiï [Dosto(y)evski] (1821–1881)

The poetics of this great master of narrative prose upholds and reaffirms the tacit hierarchy "with a vengeance": his novels make the impression that nothing interests him but the incontestably 'important', which is for him mainly matters of life and death, fateful events in the lives of his personages, deep soul-searching, matters of philosophy and ideology, exposing the deepest and darkest parts of the human soul and its most powerful emotions, etc. He does engage in descriptions of nature and scenery, "the weather", etc., but marginalises anything that is not closely related to matters crucial at least for the personages themselves, especially to their souls and the meaning of their (often miserable) lives. There is hardly any idle talk, and to the extent that 'trivial, unimportant' things gain entrance to the text they are quite often under-developed, even unconvincing, and seem to be forced upon the writer by some rules and conventions of writing that he hardly cares for, the kind of concession to the reader that a Gógol' narrator would blabber about; as if saying to himself *'Readers look for landscape descriptions, idle talk, etc., in novels; OK, I will condescend to give them what they want, but I won't be caught dead investing in those superfluous parts of my writing time and effort that I should invest in things that really matter, in art or in life'*. For Dostoïévskiï, then, there seems to be precious little in between the crucially significant and the totally negligible; in his view time and space are in short supply,[10] and must not be wasted on trifles.[11]

8.0.2.2 Tolstóï [Tolstoy] (1828–1910)

This master of narrative prose upholds traditional hierarchies, with clear, though implicit, discrimination between what is more or less 'important', but unlike Dostoïévskiï he makes use of the generosity of the Novel as a genre that can afford hundreds of pages, and manages to tackle the *important/unimportant* hierarchy adopting a more balanced approach: thus, in his major novels (especially

War and Peace and *Anna Karenina*) the broad epic rhythm of the flow of his story-lines and the opulence of his human and natural universe include a wealth of details, many of which are 'unimportant' by most standards, including of course the author's (implicit) own. Tolstói often carefully cultivates and elaborates the kind of details, which by most standards of 'significance' are considered doubly or triply marginal.[12] Indeed, he can dwell on such details for a while, investing in them aesthetic energy that a Dostoïévskiï would consider wasteful and a Gógol' would consider insufficient. However, the point is that he gives even more attention to the 'important' personages, events, ideas etc. His hierarchies are clear, then, but he does not care for the 'important' exclusively: its centrality can even be served by perspectives that enable one to appreciate it from the perspective of its periphery. In short: for a Tolstói there are no high peaks without low planes, plateaus, and even ravines. Nurturing the 'marginal' does not detract from the significance of the 'central'; on the contrary, the former provides the background indispensable for appreciating the latter.

8.0.2.3 Gógol' (1809–1852)

As pointed out by many Gógol' specialists and scholars, this master likes to have it upside-down, so to speak: he seems to revel in *superordinating–fore-grounding* what is conventionally considered 'unimportant'/'insignificant', at the expense of the 'important'/'significant', which is given the role of *subordinate background*. Thus, as pointed out in the literature — e.g., in Boris Eichenbaum's (1963 [1919]) seminal study of "The Overcoat" and in other scholars' studies of other works — Gógol' was in the habit of intentionally exaggerating the authorial (or rather narratory) attention given to flagrantly marginal matters, of no apparent significance to anything in the text by any standard, while glossing over matters of (at least comparatively) greater significance. In other words, he explicitly reverses 'normal', or 'traditional', hierarchies, seemingly undermining them. The effect of such procedures, as activated by Gógol', is usually *comic*, even *grotesque*, because he is fully aware of his readers' almost innate emulation of those 'normal' hierarchies, as acquired through living in a civilised human society and internal-ising its norms and formative texts (in the broadest sense of this word). He knows all that, but his narrator chooses to 'play dumb' and pretend to be ignorant of it, for the sake of the desired effect (including the characterisation of the narrator himself as a character). In short, to characterise his practice in a deliberately convo-luted way: Gógol' readers know that he himself knows that they know that in his narrative a conventional hierarchy is undermined and consciously reversed, turned upside down. *Comic effects* result primarily from this mutual awareness, whose function resembles communication between persons who openly wink at each other. An appropriate metaphor to clarify Gógol''s strategy is that he makes the hierarchy itself "stand on its head", as it were, for the duration of a reading session, perhaps also when recalled in a reader's memory after reading, but not for much longer: one cannot stand on one's head for too long… Thus, the hierarchy and its reversal are **both** ridiculed in a process which 'calls its own bluff', as it were, but this effect's temporariness is built-in: no reader believes, or believes that the author believes (as his naïve–foolish wise-guy of a narrator does), that absolute trifles unconnected to the basic plotline, and/or to a major personage, are important enough to justify the amount of attention and narrative space that they are granted in the text, in contradistinction to, and at the expense of, matters that are obviously more significant.[13] The 'importance-hierarchy' is exposed, but not irrevocably undermined, not even seriously shaken or challenged. The comic effect itself depends on the simmering tension between two clashing forces that permanently counterbalance each other in the readers' minds; the effect would be lost if the narrator's reverse hierarchy were accepted at face value by the readers: it derives its very viability from the experience of standing back on one's feet while remembering how it felt to stand on one's head.

8.0.2.4 Chekhov (1860–1904)

In a way, to clarify Chekhov's uniqueness in contrast to his three great predecessors in 19th-century Russian literature as just characterised, the entire Book should be cited here. In this concise Subsection, though, it is enough to point out that Chekhov's subversiveness *vis-à-vis* conventional 'hierarchies of importance' is more radical than any of the other three. Paradoxically, this applies even to Gógol', whose negation of the hierarchy, as just described, is faked: 'turned on its head', a hierarchy stays, in essence, intact. Chekhov, on the other hand, does not even pretend to negate the hierarchy: he neither accepts nor rejects it; he 'simply' **questions** or **doubts** it, and the effect is not comic at all. Extremely often — occasionally explicitly,[14] but more often implicitly — he makes his addressees pause and 'think again' whether the hierarchy, as presented in the previous Section, is "a correct presentation of the problem" of whether and how to hierarchise '(un)importance'/'(in)significance'. When Vershínin fails to get his famous cup of tea in Act 2 of *Three Sisters*, and exclaims *Richard III*-like, "My kingdom for a cup of tea"; or when the overtly nonsense "tra-ta-ta" dialogue between Másha and Vershínin in Act 3 of the same play is clearly presented as more significant than the "philosophising" tirades about the destiny of mankind uttered by Vershínin and Túsenbach; or when Yepikhódov makes one of his ridiculous acts or remarks throughout *The Cherry Orchard*; or in literally countless other instances in all the plays — Chekhov may appear to suggest that meaningless trifles are more 'important' than what is usually accepted as such, but this is just a first impression. Indeed, especially if contrasted with millennia of stage history, Chekhov's plays seem (just seem) to glorify the insignificant (see Popkin 1993 for a systematic refutation of this idea, applied to Chekhov's narrative prose); however, a closer and more attentive reading of the texts would show that Chekhov, typically, "to his own self is true": he abhors simplistic presentations of the human condition in all its facets. Outright acceptance and outright rejection of 'hierarchies of importance' are equally simplistic; that is why Chekhov rejects them both. We have seen throughout the Book how he revels in the uncompromising presentation of complexities anywhere; he uses similar techniques in approaching the conventional hierarchies "sideways", rather than embracing them with open arms or turning his back on them in their entirety. Thus, an undrunk cup of tea is something that (a) a Dostoïévskiï would omit altogether, or pay little attention to; (b) a Tolstóï would relegate to the background, immersing it in an array of comparably-trivial details, all subordinated to the 'really' important stuff, throwing the latter into bold relief; (c) a Gógol' would pretend considering most worthy of attention, as if ignoring its irrelevance. Chekhov, however, does neither of these. Rather, he makes well-chosen trivialities assume a role of *reflection*, in both senses: they encourage us to reflect on the ways in which the 'insignificant' is analogous to the 'significant', contextually becoming mentally-interchangeable, and, perhaps more importantly, how 'significance' shines, as it were, through a cloud of 'insignificance', assuming *isomorphism* and analogous functioning with it. An undrunk cup of tea is on the one hand important to the fictional personage (in this case, Vershínin), because he is simply very thirsty: Chekhov hardly ever forgets to grant full 'realistic' motivation, mundane within the confines of the *inner/fictional plane*, even to the most potentially symbolic events, acts, and verbal expressions. However, on the other hand, through his multi-functional strategy within the *outer/rhetorical plane*, he creates subtle analogies between this never-to-be-drunk cup of tea and other events and phenomena that are isomorphous with it — i.e., all sorts of mismatches in life, love, work etc. By all of these, taken together, Chekhov manages to make an implicit point: the cup of tea itself may be an insignificant trifle (for humanity of course, but even for Vershínin himself, with later hindsight, within his *inner/fictional plane*); yet, within the *outer/rhetorical plane*, the cumulative weight of such trifles is generalisable as a representative, highly significant feature of life. Indeed, it calls attention to such crucial, most profound and insoluble philosophical problems as the relation between the predetermined and the arbitrary in reality. Similarly, Yepikhódov's squeaking boots are, slapstick-like, ludicrous and insignificant trifles, but they are analogous to so many things that go wrong while making noises (literally and figuratively) in *The Cherry Orchard*; these include, for instance, Yepikhódov's own ridiculous way of speech, Trofímov's galoshes, etc., but also the more serious mishaps of the loss of the estate, the Lopákhin–Vária failed marriage proposal, the drowning of Grísha, and Firs's final fate. In all of these Chekhov never negates differences between important and unimportant things, in (a) life or in a text; as we have repeatedly seen, he abhors the idea that everything is equally important, which is tantamount to everything being equally unimportant and nothing being important. Indeed, we have seen how intensely Chekhov detests the notion of *sameness*, the "it's all the same — it makes no difference" attitude, almost under any circumstances; hierarchies, by definition, are diametrically opposed to such an attitude, so the very idea of hierarchising, as such, must be acceptable to him. Rather than uphold or negate hierarchies *in toto*, then, he encourages us **to suspect in order to inspect rather than to readily accept or reject**: he never absolves us of the responsibility to think for ourselves. In the final analysis, we usually end up with refined and modified versions of the same hierarchy: love and work are still more important, 'even for Chekhov' — indeed, particularly for him — than a cup of tea, drunk or undrunk, or a pair of shoes, whether squeaking or not. In the absence of Gógol''s tone that suggests a conscious pretence to the contrary, Chekhov lets us resort to our restored hierarchy of values, with sobriety. However, his masterful strategies of *analogy* and *isomorphism* teach us that **sometimes** trifles can be endowed with utmost importance (as Túsenbach says in his final words in Act 4 of *Three Sisters*), that

sometimes a drop of water reflects the composition of an ocean of which it is part. Hierarchies are essential, both for cognitive convenience and efficiency and as a safeguard against deadly *sameness*, but they must not be taken for granted; nothing is immune from our right, which for Chekhov is our duty, to ask questions of *why, when, how, under what circumstances, for how long*, etc.

A valid hierarchy is one that can withstand such questions.

8.1 "Sheer Indifferentism":[15] Does Chekhov Really Care?

> To be an artist, he [Chekhov] felt, was to be primarily an observer. Yet, […] it was difficult for him to remain neutral. It was equally difficult for him to take sides.
>
> (Valency 1966, 65)

Chekhov's *artistry* and personal poetics — characterised, *inter alia*, by all-pervasive, deliberate preference for the indirect and the implicit over the direct and explicit, as shown throughout the Book — may be a major cause for his alleged "indifference", unengaged/uncommitted stance *vis-à-vis* human concerns and sufferings, especially those connected with values, ideologies, moral principles and emotions. He was often accused by critics, both during his lifetime and posthumously, of shirking what they regarded as a writer's or an intellectual's duties and responsibilities. These were, for them, taking sides in controversial moral, ideological, social and political controversies, adopting the stance of a mentor, even a preacher, in relation to his readers, upholding a set of values while rejecting others, in short — being committed, engaged, identified, even mobilised and regimented, morally, ideologically, even politically.[16] Specifically as a writer, he was often described as treating his characters in a detached, dispassionate, even callous manner, as part of his alleged uncaring attitude towards human beings and their suffering.[17] As in many other topics in Chekhov criticism, here, too, one encounters simplistic generalisations, which sometimes do possess a negligible shred of truth (based on partial[18] reading of the texts); moreover, these half-truths are often accompanied by methodological errors, notably failing to distinguish between Chekhov the man and his *persona* as an *implied author*, and even between any of these and specific fictional personages, erroneously regarding them as the writer's mouthpiece. Such a methodological mix-up is inescapably misleading in principle, whether the actual views about Chekhov, as a person, are correct, and to what extent.

A truism hardly worth mentioning is that a text's attitude towards a person, or towards values and ideas, need not be verbalised explicitly in direct statements expressing support, opposition, affection, dislike etc.; such an attitude is part of a dialogue between that text's (implied) author and its (implied) recipient, and it activates the views and attitudes formed in the latter prior to the beginning of the process of perceiving that text. No reader or spectator comes to a text *tabula rasa*, and an author can, and usually does, rely on certain values and attitudes of his/her addressees being part of the emotional, intellectual, educational and ideological 'baggage' that they inevitably bring into that dialogue. This applies invariably to all authors, texts and audiences; Chekhov's typical uniqueness here, as elsewhere, lies in the extent of his reluctance to spell out attitudes, values, ideologies, etc. in explicit authorial statements. In his work the balance between the author's and the audience's respective responsibilities for generating the text's overall meanings, attitudes and opinions, is tilted more heavily to the latter, if we compare him to many other major authors, especially his predecessors. Simplistic readings tend to interpret the dearth of judgemental statements[19] about personages or ideas as neutrality, indifference etc., as if the author "couldn't care less"; however, it is precisely the vacuum created by the *absence* of Chekhov's explicitly verbalised opinions and attitudes that enhances the *presence* of such opinions and attitudes in his audiences, often after the delaying effect of soul-searching questioning that he nurtures with such dedicated precision.

Elsewhere in the Book, especially in 5.1, we have encountered Chekhov's precision and meticulousness as an artist, and particularly his insistence on revealing the innermost truth of his personages' hidden motives, thoughts and feelings, and above all **his** acute awareness of **their** lack of self-awareness, the relentless hide-and-seek by which he goes after them into their deepest and far-thest mental hideouts, exposing their self-delusions relentlessly: indeed, they can manage to run away from themselves, but not from him (and therefore not from us). This quality of his art has also contributed to his image as an uninvolved observer; my colleague Nilly Mirsky (see Epigraph to Chapter 5) goes so far as to propose an analogy between Chekhov's attitude to the sufferings of his per-sonages and the stance of a detached scientist, who nonchalantly observes the nervous reflexes of the legs of frogs he has just dissected. Such views of Chekhov's art, though extremely exaggerated in my opinion, are not without foundation, and cannot be dismissed offhand; personally, I even prefer them to diametrically opposed views, romanticising and idealising him as overflowing with the milk of human kindness, almost crying his eyes out commiserating with the personages whom he (let us not forget) created in the first place — them, their fates and their miseries. Indeed, between the wishy-washy tearful type and the cold, unmoved observer the latter is relatively truer to Chekhov's character as a writer. Yet, there is no compulsion to adhere to this clear-cut, unbearably sim-plistic choice; on the contrary, it is precisely through his immaculate precision and unyielding pursuit of an evasive yet definite truth, forcing it down the throats of his addressees even against the wishes of his personages, that Chekhov acti-vates the innate and intuitive compassion of his audiences. Chekhov's nature as a writer is complex, subtle and evasive, often bordering on the paradoxical and self-contradictory; it is therefore difficult, perhaps even impossible, to describe and characterise him in words without some inconsistencies and subversive con-tradictions in the process of analysis (the analogy of the 'dishevelled pedant' from 2.3 comes to mind). Be that as it may, as we have seen, only through such inconsistencies can one get nearer to a balanced, persuasive, all-round character-isation of his art — a goal that one can spend a lifetime aspiring to, without deluding oneself that it is ever fully attainable.

In sum: most texts generated by Chekhov are typically **interactive**, enabling a genuinely two-sided author-perceiver dialogue. An instance of this general quality, in the present context, is an *implied presence* of an audience, whose mental mechanisms of caring, compassion and commitment — generated by value-infused education from early childhood — are willy-nilly activated by components of the text, designed to propel this activation. Such basic, intuitive, almost instinctive, automatically-expected audience-attitudes are manifest in regarding freedom, compassion, love, kindness, wisdom, knowledge/education, and many others, as 'good', and oppression, callousness, hate, cruelty, stupidity, ignorance, and many others, as 'bad'. They may be hard to define (and, anyway, defining them is outside the disciplinary province of any theory and analysis of texts), yet impossible to suppress or ignore in any 'normal' or 'normative' human being; they are an integral part of a person's upbringing in any civilised society. Chekhov's textual strategies are designed to question and challenge many aspects of these 'innate' attitudes towards ideals of right and wrong, good and evil. More than anything else, these strategies are designed to undermine these attitudes' concomitant distortions in education and society — whether these distortions smack of hypocrisy, oversimplification, partiality, or whatever — but not their innermost core, which Chekhov does not seek to undermine. While seriously doubting the realisability of such ideals in our imperfect human world, his texts never obliterate or undermine them. In Chekhov's work and world these values and attitudes tend to operate covertly within complex networks; they often modify and counterbalance each other, subtly re-shaping, but not dismantling, the home-made 'baggage' that audiences bring to a dialogue with an artistic text and its (implied) author. Thus, in the final analysis, the mental process of ever-testing and rethinking the 'obvious' often yields a qualified and distilled reaffirmation of that very same 'obvious', which even gains force and credibility after passing such tests: the 'injection' of doubt-antidotes keeps the 'obvious' ideals in check, immunising them against mindless gullible belief and cynical negation alike. Such a process is a far cry from neutrality and indifference in matters of human values, emotions and attitudes.[20]

8.2 Perspectives on "Philosophising" in Chekhov's Plays

8.2.1 Personages' *Partiality*, Authorial–Textual *Wholeness*

What has been said with a focus on emotional "indifference", lack of involvement and compassion, etc., can be applied to *values* in a broader perspective. Obviously, specific value-judgements in a play's text are voiced by the personages whose views and opinions, as a general rule, are a far cry from Chekhov's — both as a person (which is not our concern here) and in his capacity as *implied author* (which is). As we shall see, a very significant part of personages' statements on matters of *value* comes to us in the form of tirades, and shorter statements, that can be subsumed under the term "philosophising". In other words, such explicit statements are usually disproved — either as simply incorrect or, at least, as narrow, shallow and partial — by the composite overview of the text and the entirety of its 'world'. Of course, it is only through such an overview that any conclusion about

Chekhov's own overview of a theme can be reached (to the extent that such a conclusion can be reached at all).

8.2.2 Thematic *vs.* Structural Perspective[21]

This discrepancy between characters' statements and the text's overview manifests itself first and foremost *thematically* (i.e., there is a marked difference between the *semantic content* of the two). Thus, for instance, in *The Cherry Orchard*, explicit self-characterisations by Trofímov (as being "above love") and Ranévskaïa (as being "below love") — undoubtedly wittily put — are both simplistic, falling short of any Chekhovian "correct presentation" of a complex and heavily charged theme, that emerges from juxtaposing them with each other as well as from integrating other relevant materials with them. However, beyond these *thematic* differences, the same discrepancy reflects Chekhov's ways of addressing such problems *structurally*: the perceiver of these shallow statements is encouraged, not least by their aphoristic and thought-provoking shallowness, to check them out against a broader array of relevant materials, directly supplied and indirectly implied by the text. Thus, the treatment of *love* and *self-* and *reciprocal-characterisation* (in this specific case) match Chekhov's treatment of a large variety of other major themes (elsewhere in the play, and in other plays). Governed by the same structural principles (with preference for *trichotomic* organisation, as shown in 1.2), themes are hardly ever stated fully and explicitly; their comprehensive presentation can be elicited only by the addressees carrying out procedures of *analogy* and *inference*. It is through such interactions between partial views that distortions can be mentally neutralised and eliminated, and composite overviews are created and substantiated.

An attentive scrutiny of the relevant material, then, would yield a complex picture of Chekhov's attitudes to the subject, based on the centrality of *unrealised potentials* and *unfulfilled wishes* to his overall view of the human condition. Moreover, as we have seen, Chekhov not only prefers structured wholes and relationships to their isolated constituent elements as carriers of messages and meanings, but he **actively depletes the latter in order to strengthen and deepen the former,** regardless of the actual semantic content in any given instance (be it "human, animal, vegetable, mineral, or abstract"). In this way, his view of human nature and the human condition blends with aesthetic principles governing the artistic organisation of his texts. This blend amounts to a crucial part of a *deep structure* (in the Chomskyan sense) or 'mental *DNA*' of Chekhov's poetics.

Therefore, in the context of the present argument, there is ample reason to reject claims that Chekhov's *value-system* stems from his (alleged) attitude of 'condescending contempt' towards human beings (whether real persons or his own fictional creation) and regard them as misleadingly partial: such a rejection can be based on structural grounds, in addition to the thematic grounds discussed in the previous Section: indeed, the very same compositional techniques are used by Chekhov in totally different thematic contexts, that have nothing to do with 'emotional indifference', the presence or absence of empathy, etc.

As we have seen above in this Chapter and in previous ones, it is a typical feature of Chekhov's poetics that *thematic structures* are organised in a *tripartite* or *three-storeyed model*: a *superordinate thematic cluster* subordinates the partial components that contribute to its composition and balances between them, whether they contradict and undermine or complement and reinforce each other. Thus, Chekhov's *value system* is the result of a *network of analogies and interactions* ('middle storey') between and among its components (located in the 'lower storey'); this network, in turn, works in the perceivers' minds to generate general-isations of higher orders — usually principles deductable implicitly rather than verbalised explicitly — providing overarching, superordinate overviews ('upper storey'). The latter, as a rule, are very rarely, if ever, explicitly verbalised in the text as authorial–authoritative statements, ascribable to Chekhov himself. The perceiver's cognitive processes can generate them as intuitions, but trying to verbalise them proves frustrating, because words typically fail the subtlety, complexity and (paradoxically) even the precision[22] of Chekhov's presentation, which can be deeply and acutely sensed in a state of pre-verbal awareness.

Examples to make these vague statements more concrete can be found in many analyses in this Book and elsewhere in Chekhov scholarship; thus, several isolated instances of love relationships, whether realised or not ('lower storey'), connect in analogies and other significant reciprocal interactions relating to the theme of love and produce complex pictures ('middle storey'); these in turn, 'aspire to' interact with each other on a higher level of abstraction and generalisation ('upper storey') in order to yield a formulation of 'Chekhov's ultimate view of *love*' (the same of course applies to any other theme of comparable magnitude, evasiveness, subtlety and complexity — work, learning, parenthood, friendship, art, etc. etc.). Now this 'ultimate view' is of course never verbalised by Chekhov himself; more-over, it poses an enormous challenge to anyone who dares such a verbal formulation 'for Chekhov', as it were. Our sense of 'Chekhovian love' can be balanced, acute and precise, with many instances coming to mind, endlessly modi-fying each other to reach ever-higher degrees of balanced precision; indeed, in all these attempts, verbal descriptions try their best, but typically fail, to meet the chal-lenge of capturing and rendering verbally, "in so many words", what is inherently pre-verbal (or maybe post-verbal).

Such tense and precarious balance between the simplest and the most complex is often a hallmark of great art, especially great verbal art; however, in Chekhov this balance is more typical, more evasive and more powerful than in most if not all other great writers. The fact that, being verbal art, Chekhov's *oeuvre* is encoded in language — and does its work in our minds through arrays of words that we read, remember, weigh in our minds, try to understand, etc. — does not make it less word-repellent, as it were: his art is indeed exceptionally resistant to attempts to capture its substance in words. The "philosophising" speeches are a formidable obstacle to any such attempt, precisely because they, superficially, appear like one: they try **to reduce complexities to platitudes**, and their very existence in the text is a temptation to regard them as a real statement of the overall meaning of a major theme, perhaps of the play as a whole, and beyond that — of human destiny and the meaning of life. Of course, they never qualify as such; rather than an urge to adopt them as 'Chekhov's overall view' of anything, their raw oversimplifications should elicit the opposite response, i.e., almost automatic rejection of their pretence to be the play's truth, while regarding them as a mere contribution, often a minor one at that, to a process of interactive clashes between various verbalised and unverbalised statements and attitudes. A partial view of a truth with pretence to be the whole truth is even more partial and distorted than without such pretence.

8.2.3 "Philosophising" and the (Un)Reliability of Chekhov's Personages

Explicit generalisations presented with inevitable partiality by personages on stage in Chekhov's plays, then, can never be taken at face value, their chief function being just to draw initial attention to a topic and its centrality to the play, rather than to make a complete statement of that topic. Thus, for instance, the subjectively sincere, though pitifully superficial, slogan of "new forms" in art, as voiced by Konstantín in *The Seagull*, as well as its equally superficial (and less sincere) dismissal by Trigórin and Arkádina, are both incomparably inferior — in depth, complexity, and sophistication (and hence also in truth-value *à la* Chekhov, see below) — to the way in which Chekhov himself presents the same theme through his actions and choices as the author of the actual text of *The Seagull* (as especially apparent in his skilful manipulations of dramatic structure and of art–reality thematic interrelationships). The personages' statements are sharply distinguished from Chekhov's views at least for two reasons: first, automatically, because they are uttered by personages, and as such — as we have repeatedly seen — hardly ever represent Chekhov's views; second, because the statements themselves are simplistic, explicit and one-sided. A third reason can be added when a personage "philosophises" by voicing a generalisation about life and the human condition (most statements about values can be described as such): here a Chekhov-informed addressee is trained to distrust any pretence to pronounce valid generalisations of that kind, regardless of the identity of its author or source. This distrust, then, is added to an analogous distrust of the capabilities of personages to achieve high degree of awareness even about themselves; **their** abilities to be the authors or even carriers of "gospel truths" about humanity and its destiny, then, are stripped of any credibility and reliability, and the statements themselves, at best, beg questions and refutations. The whole of Chekhov's presentation, then, with its fusion of explicit and implicit materials, is perforce and by definition truer than the partial presentation of any personage, or even of all personages collectively, because the authorial view also includes unverbalised, often unverbalisable components that the personages can be ignorant of, or incapable of experiencing, let alone verbally expressing. Once again, the old 'Structuralist banner-cry' applies to all the central themes in all the plays: the whole is much greater than the sum-total of its parts.

Thus, the "philosophising"-mechanism is especially effective being double-edged, prompting two contrapuntally complementary responses: it draws our attention to a theme and its centrality, and at the same time it exposes its own simplistic quality and undermines the credibility of the speaker who voices it. We are then encouraged to stay with the theme itself and its intrinsic significance, yet without being content with its presenter and presentation, and to look for any materials that would reconcile the two responses, as an inevitable result of view-ing the entire process through a fuller, more balanced and comprehensive perspective.

This process repeats itself with every 'philosophised' theme. It is not coinci-dental, then, that in *The Seagull* "philosophising" revolves mainly around the theme of art/fiction *vs.* life/reality, in *Uncle Vánia* — mainly about waste and futility (in the life of individuals, society and the environment alike), in *Three Sisters* — mainly about humanity's values, future and destiny (as shown at some length in a following Section and in Chapter 11), and in *The Cherry Orchard* — about the missing of targets and opportunities, mainly in the social arena. In short, there is a correspondence in theme — though not in the level of expression, complexity and sophistication — between what is central to a play's 'world' and its personages' "philosophising".

8.2.4 Why "Philosophise"? A Question of Motivation

Chekhovian "philosophising" is a peculiar type of personages' **oral–verbal** activity, communication and psychological behaviour; it is also, and significantly, a peculiar **stage-action** in Chekhov's plays, where it is not a universal character trait shared by all or even most personages: rather, only a small number of them, hardly two or at most three per play, tend to engage in "philosophising". Therefore, in a way, it begs 'why-questions' more than types of behaviour and stage-action that are more widespread, and/or perceived as 'common', 'normal' or 'natural' in the plays and in life. In general, as well known and elaborated above, questions about *motivation* of actions and events in drama can be asked and answered within two complementary frameworks: the *outer/rhetorical plane* and the *inner/fictional plane*. The former is the framework for discussing the author's motivation as a text-composing artist; the latter is the framework for discussing the personage's psychological motivation as if s/he were a real human being. Of course, a personage is merely a figment of the author's imagination, but centuries of inter-nalising the conventions of *reality-like fictional worlds* make us perceive personages as real persons within the process of our considered response to a fictional text, thus expecting their words and actions to be motivated by convincing psychological logic and consistency. Thus, there is a point in drawing a demarca-tion line between the author's own motivations in constructing his texts and the motivations that s/he grants a personage.[23] These general truisms apply to Chekhov with special force. There is hardly a single scene, moment, event, *réplique*, hardly even as much as a single phrase in the spoken text of his plays, that is not moti-vated on both planes, simultaneously and autonomously.[24]

The elementary questions regarding the motivation for "philosophising" in Chekhov, then, are two. (a) Within the *outer/rhetorical plane*: What motivates Chekhov to characterise certain personages as "philosophisers", and to assign to them "philosophising" tirades or *répliques*? (b) Within the *inner/fictional plane*: What motivates the *fictional* "philosophisers" to "philosophise"?

The answer to (a) has been given several times in this Book, and more intensely throughout this Chapter: the "philosophisers" are Chekhov's 'agents' (which does not mean that they represent his views) in drawing the audience's attention to the centrality of a theme in a play; the shallow and simplistic way in which they address that theme interacts with Chekhov's complex and profound way of presenting it, partly non-verbally, and his techniques and strategies serve to highlight thematic, personal and structural networks.

Before discussing question (b), it is worth re-emphasising that quite often (a) and (b) appear to work at cross purposes. Thus, for instance (one out of numerous cases), Konstantín's motivation for "philosophising" about art and "new forms" — deeply anchored in his relationships with his mother and Nína, even with his uncle and Dr. Dorn — is far from Chekhov's motivations in characterising him and in having these views reverberate in *The Seagull*. Such counterpoint techniques broaden and deepen the thematic scope of the play and enhance the complexity of its characterisations and ideological perspectives alike.

As for possible answers to (b), they cannot be identical for all cases; they must differ from each other inasmuch as the "philosophisers" themselves, the points they make, and the staged circumstances in which they "philosophise", differ from each other. Indeed, beside the tendency to "philosophise", there is little in common between Konstantín from *The Seagull*, Ástrov from *Uncle Vánia*, Trofímov and Gáïev from *The Cherry Orchard*, and Vershínin and Túsenbach (and partly Andréï) from *Three Sisters*. There is something in common though between all of them — shared, by the way, also by some "philosophisers" in the stories (examples abound) — in spite of the marked individuality of each of them: they all seem to be motivated by two mental driving forces, 'negative' and 'positive', that complement and reinforce each other.

These forces can be termed, respectively, as (1) 'The escape from'; (2) 'The escape to'.[25] (1) 'Negatively', resorting to "philosophising" nearly always serves as an alternative to addressing something else, which is undesirable at the moment; in other words, it is a course of action and route of escape that seems the most appropriate for the specific speaker, as a potential character-trait that is realised at a given moment. Whatever "philosophisers" run away from, specifically, is different in each case, but "philosophising" is virtually always a sign of an acute but usually subconscious feeling that something is missing in their personal lives, and/or interpersonal relationships (e.g., the absence of love or personal calling, or a problematic entanglement in either, or both); in any case, it is almost invariably something that they do not want to speak or even think about, least of all at the given moment. Their subconscious awareness of the imminent 'danger' that this unwanted stuff may be exposed, and force them to acknowledge it and respond to it, is triggered by something said by others, in a conversation that may signal to them that a psychologically threatening turn is about to take place. This 'danger' propels a mechanism of fear that produces the need to escape. (2) 'Positively', the "philosophisers" choose abstract and impersonal themes/ideas as the best route of escape. This is not a foregone conclusion: there are all sorts of alternatives to it;[26] moreover, there are lots of potential abstract and impersonal themes out there, so that choosing a specific one, rather than others, and expressing an opinion about it, are an integral part of the individual characterisation of a given "philosophiser" (Who?), and of the given moment and situation (When?).

The thematic and characterising structural strategy is analogous to the one analysed in 1.3 above: Sórin in *The Seagull* — the example discussed there — is different from numerous others who did not become writers in that he **wanted** to become one; by the same token, out of the many routes of escape from embarrassing situations and conversations open to Chekhov personages,[27] the "philosophisers" prefer resorting to the abstract, eternal and impersonal.[28] For them, then, being intensely interested in abstract ideas and generalisations is something to aspire to and be proud of: they like to show off — to themselves as well as to others — that they embrace a hierarchy of values that makes them care about 'spiritual' and 'altruistic' subjects as art, society, ecology, the destiny and future of the planet and/or humanity that lives on it, etc., more intensely than about anything 'petty', 'self-centred', 'material', or 'mundane' as their own lives, loves, fates and welfare.[29] The latter point — characterising the 'positive' aspect of "philosophising" 'negatively', by what it is **not** — is perhaps the most crucial feature of this Chekhovian phenomenon: *a principle of seeming irrelevance* decrees that the content of "philosophising" has hardly any bearing on what **really** matters in the lives of the "philosophisers" themselves, inasmuch as these lives are characterised by observable facts, events, etc. Arguably, the word *really* is the trickiest in the previous sentence, since the content of "philosophising" often matters a great deal in the **inner** lives of the "philosophisers" — their mental worlds, wishes and yearnings, dreams and fantasies, etc., even if this is not certain in all cases.

In conclusion: the 'positive' motivation of "philosophisers" seems to stem mainly from their need to show and prove to everyone, often mainly to themselves, that they are intensely preoccupied with "the significant and the eternal", in Dr. Dorn's words (see Epigraph to this Chapter).[30] This common denominator operates in addition to the individual psychologies and life circumstances of each "philosophiser", and to the local reasons inherent in a certain moment, scene etc., that work together to motivate a specific "philosophising" speech at a specific moment by a specific "philosophiser".

Here, it seems, the similarity between the various cases and moments of "philosophising" ends, and individual differences between them begin: not only every individual character, but each individual moment on stage, and each separate *réplique*, must be explored and analysed if a fuller understanding of the specific motivation for every single case of "philosophising" is sought. However, such a meticulous, detailed analysis need not be carried out at this point: for an analysis to make a valid point it may be enough to unearth the underlying basic principles involved, as has been attempted above. Perhaps Chekhov scholars and text-analysts may be well advised for once to step back and leave the fuller exploration of each isolated case to the creative and imaginative intuitions of practitioners — actors and directors — engaged time and again in the never-ending process of giving stage-life to these precious moments.

The challenge is quite formidable, because — as we have seen — texts of most "philosophising", often shallow and simplistic, may produce an effect of plain boredom on stage if not placed within proper performative, structural and thematic perspectives. It is one of the evasive paradoxes of Chekhov's art that a breathtakingly fascinating edifice may be erected from almost dull building blocks. This is made possible only because of the compositional strategies discussed in Chapter 2.

8.2.5 "Philosophising", "Philo-Sophistry", and the Gender Perspective

There is also a gender aspect to Chekhovian "philosophising": every one of the "philosophisers", in all plays, are men; by the way, this observation largely applies to 19th-century Russian literature in general.[31] Chekhov's women are, at best, good and appreciative listeners to the men's tirades, sometimes too much so: Chekhov occasionally uses their sounding-board status as another means to distance himself, his text and his audience, from his "philosophisers", their (often) tiresome tirades, and their content, to the point of ridiculing them. Thus, for instance, in Act 1 of *Three Sisters* we are introduced for the first time to Vershínin's tendency to "philosophise". His points at that theatrical moment are arguably worth making more than some of his later ones, and Chekhov subtly signals this moment to us as the point in time when Másha begins to fall in love with him (having heard him, she reverses her previous decision to go home, saying "I'm staying for breakfast", eliciting a kind audible smile in the audience in many productions that I witnessed). Yet, Irína's naïve response to the same "philosophising" — "Really, all of this is worth writing down…"[32] — cannot be taken seriously at face value. More unequivocally comic is Ánia's response to a ridiculously impassioned 'revolutionary' speech by Trofímov at the end of *The Cherry Orchard*'s Act 2. Addressing an imaginary audience of 'working-class masses', he shouts 'at them' enthusiastically: "Forward, comrades! Don't stay behind! March towards the bright star shining at us from the distance!" — while his real audience consists of one teenage Ánia, who, lifting her adoring eyes up to him, says "admiringly" (Chekhov's explicit stage-direction): "How well you put it! How beautifully you speak!"[33] Of course her naïvely-funny response makes the anyway-laughable aspects of his speeches even more ridiculous; what adds even further to their ludicrous nature is his own remark, just after one of them (Act 2), that he dislikes "serious faces and serious talks" and is frightened by them, and that "it's better to shut up"… The audience can hardly refrain from thinking 'You are a fine one to talk'; yet — as always in Chekhov — Trofímov's words themselves, in counterpoint with these comic filters, can inspire serious and critical consideration in the audience: these words are there to stay in our minds and take part in a mental process of checks and balances that places so much of the text in complementary simultaneous perspectives.

A more seriously thought- and doubt-provoking effect is generated in *Uncle Vánia*'s Act 3, when Yeléna Andréïevna is evidently bored by Ástrov's "philosophising" about the ecology of Russian forests. His speeches about the subject (there are a few of them) are interwoven into a more significant network of actions and reactions, which cannot be extensively elaborated here (thus, Yeléna's boredom is caused not only by her indifference to Ástrov's subject-matter, but also by its irrelevance to the real reasons that prompted her to initiate this conversation). Suffice it to say that here, too, responses by women to a man-

"philosophiser" (Yeléna Andréïevna and Sónia, here and elsewhere in the play) assume a crucial role in creating the above-mentioned perspectival mechanism that enables a balanced appreciation of the "philosophiser" and his message alike.

Audience attention to "philosophising" and to its gender aspect is also drawn, in a peculiarly Chekhovian oblique way, in Act 1 of *Three Sisters*: Soliónyï, seemingly out of the blue — introducing an uncalled-for wedge between *réplique*s in a non-"philosophising" dialogue between Ól'ga and Másha (analysed in 6.2.1) — says something blatantly nonsensical (Magarshack 1972, p. 133, has a point in referring to it as "idiotic") about the difference between men and women as "philosophisers". This *réplique* is weird by any reasonable standard (as is much of what this enigmatic and deliberately annoying personage has to say throughout the play); beside being an unfair challenge to any translator (no two of the six English translations I have checked attempt a similar solution to the translation problem), it strikes a reader or spectator as superfluous, serving no recognisable purpose, and the temptation simply to ignore it in analysing the play,[34] and even to cut it altogether in production,[35] seems too justified to resist: one can easily get annoyed at Chekhov himself for having ever written this text in the first place. The following English version of this *réplique*, in David Magarshack's translation, reads as follows: "If a man philosophises, it is philosophistry, or, if you like, sophistry; but if a woman or a couple of women start philosophising, it's all a lot of nonsense".[36] In addition to its obvious (and bewildering) function in contributing to Soliónyï's characterisation, this unpleasant and unfathomable *réplique* throws its dark light on at least two aspects of Chekhovian "philosophising" in general, and on the way it is practised by Túsenbach and Vershínin in particular: (a) its relation to *Sophistry*, whose reputation from ancient Greece to the present is described as "specious but fallacious reasoning; the use or practice of specious reasoning as an art or dialectic exercise" (*OED* definition); (b) its gender dimension.

As for (a), Chekhov's "philosophisers" are often closer to *sophistry*'s debating, just for argument's sake, than to the relentless pursuit of a truth, so characteristic of Chekhov himself as an author, let alone certain leading trends in *Philosophy*, which believe in the existence of **the truth** and the philosopher's duty to pursue it. As for (b), maybe Chekhov himself, as an *implied author*,[37] wanted to convey an intuition that men and women do differ (in general, or in Russian society/culture in particular) in their tendencies (or lack thereof) to "philosophise" and in the nature of their "philosophising". However, since it was just an intuition, he chose this roundabout way to convey it: having an irritating character make an annoying statement at an inappropriate moment (when no "philosophising" is heard in the vicinity); yet, the message itself, stripped from its alienating environment, is heard loud and clear, and suggests to an attentive audience the idea that the question whether men and women differ in this respect is worth thinking about. Annoyance is of course unpleasant, but memorable; so is Soliónyï's deliberately nonsensical presence in *Three Sisters* in general and this remark of his in particular. Here, in addition, his expression of mindless misogyny, as well as his misuse of the term "philosophising" itself, serve not only as another reason for totally discrediting his judgement but also as a reason to question this term and its meaning, though its use by Vershínin and others is more consistent and makes much more sense.

Finally, the most authorially-credible responses by women to men's "philosophising" are the ones expressing reservation and criticism, e.g., Ranévskaïa's "why drink so much? Why eat so much? Why talk so much?" (*The Cherry Orchard*, Act 2); or the repeated annoyance of three women in the same play — Ánia, Vária and Ranévskaïa, individually and/or together — at Gáïev's invariably ill-timed and embarrassingly inappropriate "philosophising".

Másha's "they just talk and talk the whole day" (*Three Sisters*, Act 4) is much more significant, probably the most significant response by a woman to a man's "philosophising", not because of what the *réplique* literally says or even means in isolation, but because it is a response to Chebutýkin's quasi-abstract "philosophising", which offers a nihilistic vision of doubt about the existence and significance of everything and everyone, a vision of absolute **indifference** (literally, i.e., the absolute lack of **differentiation** between people, things, ideas, actions, etc., because they are «всё равно», i.e., "all the same", an expression of the *sameness* that Chekhov abhorred). Chebutýkin's stance is an epitome of irresponsibility: if no one exists, anyone can get away with murder, almost literally, and certainly no one is responsible for anything. Másha responds to Chebutýkin's quasi-"philosophising" so angrily because the latter is spoken while the real-life-existence of Túsenbach is ominously threatened, and subsequently terminated in the duel. Again, here the author's (Chekhov's) and the personage's (Chebutýkin's) respective motivations for making these remarks, specifically at this moment, are radically different. A powerful self-referential point is made by Chekhov with utmost care and precision, because the content of this specific instance of "philosophising" brings up, *inter alia*, dichotomies between *purposefulness* and *arbitrariness*, *existence* and *non-existence* (the latter designed to make death itself meaningless, as it were). While Chekhov celebrates here another feat of perfect planning and functionality and a total aliveness of his *authorial presence* in his text, it is within the *inner/fictional plane* that Chekhov activates his *outer/rhetorical plane* presence, when he uses Chebutýkin's irresponsible nihilism as antidote, to inspire the audience's mental realisation that matters of life and death are not to be idly "philosophised-about". Thus, through a non-communicational dialogue and through the lives and fates of his *fictional personages* within the *fictional plane*, he perfectly communicates to the audience the painful poignancy of the *non-fictional* distinction between real life and real death.[38] Chebutýkin's shallow "Philosophising" is a mockery of this distinction.

In sum: almost everything about "philosophising" is idle talk. Even criticising idle talk is idle talk; even **self**-criticism about idle talk is idle talk, since it usually is no more than lip-service, not leading to any action or change. Yet, idle talk is not always worthless, even within the *fictional plane*; much depends on its content, circumstances, speakers, listeners, and whether it has any advantage over a potential alternative of total silence (if and when this is a viable alternative), and in what sense one can think or speak of *advantage* in a given situation in the first place. Moreover, it is not idle to reiterate that no 'Chekhovian idle talk' is **Chekhov's own** idle talk; the personages' idle talking is **always** meaningfully functional within *the outer/rhetorical plane*, where the communication thread between author and audience is spun.

8.2.6 "Philosophising" *vs. Philosophy*; (*A/The*) *Truth vs. Sincerity*

Real *philosophy* and Chekhovian "philosophising" are not only different; in many significant ways they are diametrically opposed. A far cry from profound thought and relentless quest for truth and knowledge — a hallmark of true *philosophy* — Chekhovian "philosophising" is usually a skin-deep form of social pastime (especially in *Three Sisters*, maybe precisely because it is the closest to true *philosophy* among Chekhov's plays): its aim seems to be the sheer oral pleasure of talking for talking's sake. Superficial, non-committal, its *modus operandi* is not the communicative dialogue, but the socialising monologue, which is often manifest in uncalled-for lecturing to a present or even absent audience, not necessarily an appropriate or attentive one.[39]

Another crucial distinction for Chekhov's world is between *truth* and *sincerity*: the latter, of course, is more subjective than the former. Thus, for instance, Iván Petróvich Voïnítskiï (the title role in *Uncle Vánia*) is one of the most sincere personages in Chekhov's plays; however, when he, with no professional credentials and no proven standing or understanding in the discipline of art history and analysis, vilifies a retired University Professor in this discipline as a total nonentity in his profession (Act 1), there is a definite cognitive dissonance in our minds between his evident subjective sincerity and the lack of any objective basis for his 'professionally-guilty' verdict.[40] The clash between sincerity and a potential truth is even more acute when Voïnítskiï exclaims (Act 3) that he could have been a Schopenhauer or a Dostoïévskiï. It is laughable and touching at the same time that a provincial estate accountant, with no literary, academic or philosophical text to his name, should believe, with pathetic emotional sincerity, that but for his brother in law's interference with his life (by his own invitation at that!) he could have become no less than a literary or philosophical genius. That said, it is also a remarkable truth that he ever wanted, and still aspires, to achieve greatness **as an artist or intellectual** (rather than in any other field), and that he chooses precisely these specific geniuses as role models. *The Seagull*'s Sórin's "the man who wanted" (Act 4) is analogous, though radically different. Unlike Iván Voïnítskiï, Sórin is unassuming in his literary aspirations: it would please him to have become a minor writer, a "man of letters" of sorts («литератор», in the original Russian), and he blames no one (neither himself nor others) for failing to achieve this goal.[41] Other finer distinctions — e.g., between *truth* and *fact*, and their synonyms, "by any other name" — have been discussed above in analysing the story "A Little Joke" (5.1) and scenes from the plays.

In short, Chekhov's view of *truth* and related concepts is marked by exceptional subtlety, complexity and infinite variety. Dispelling some of the thick conceptual fog surrounding the representation of these concepts in Chekhov's world has been the modest goal of the present discussion. Much still remains to be clarified and elucidated by further research.

8.3 Value Structuration: The Case of *Three Sisters*

In an attempt to elaborate points made above, especially about Chekhov's complex treatment of *values*, without oversimplifying them, this Section will focus mainly on one play, *Three Sisters* — arguably, the clearest as well as the most complex Chekhov play in the presentation and treatment of value-charged materials; yet, a claim is made for a more comprehensive validity and applicability of basic principles found in this play to most of Chekhov's later work, in drama and in narrative fiction alike — of course, with the necessary adjustments for each individual case and text.

8.3.1 The Specific Centrality of "Philosophising" in *Three Sisters*

Three Sisters is a play largely concerned with problems of value, arguably more intensely so than other Chekhov plays. Explicitly, in the personages' discourse, people and events are repeatedly subjected to value-judgements. Moreover, value-charged topics of the grandest scale possible, encompassing the history of humanity as a whole and life's broadest significance, are (as shown above) the subject of a lot of explicit "philosophising". The present Section will focus on specific features of "philosophising" in *Three Sisters*.[42]

Túsenbach and Vershínin (and, to a much lesser degree, Andréï) tend to hold lengthy discussions about the prospects of improving the moral and spiritual standards of mankind in the future. Andréï (in Act 4) explicitly juxtaposes truth and deceit, humanity and bestiality, individuality and uniformity, vitality and death-in-life, clearly-yet-implicitly correlating members in each pair respectively. Other personages address similar broad, all-embracing value-charged subjects. Each of these explicit pronouncements, without exception, is surrounded in the text by an intricate network, consisting of various heterogeneous elements that add to, and/or detract from, its validity in varying degrees. Thus, when Andréï generalises about the deceit of husbands who choose to turn a blind eye to their wives' infidelities, without referring to anyone in particular (Act 4), his statement is juxtaposed not only with his own behaviour as a betrayed husband, but also with other facts and phenomena in the text, such as: Kulýgin's behaviour under seemingly analogous circumstances; drunk Chebutýkin's speech in Act 3 about the affair between Natásha and Protopópov, contrasted with his silence about the affair between Másha and Vershínin; manifestations of (self-) illusions and delusions in other matters in which *Three Sisters*, like most Chekhovian texts, abounds; etc. Similarly, when Vershínin and Túsenbach have their fruitless discussions about whether human happiness can exist, there are numerous events and *répliques* in the play that have direct as well as indirect bearing on their statements: while each of the two personages gives a flat *yes* or *no* to this question, Chekhov's text shows us how each of them actually deprives himself, and others, of prospects for happiness (however defined), without the slightest capacity for self-awareness and realisation of the unbridgeable gap between what they abstractly say and what they actually do. As always in Chekhov, we ultimately have a fuller presentation of conditions and perspectives that affect the possibility to get nearer to the goal of happiness, rather than a total vindication or refutation of one of the conflicting (and comparably shallow) views expressed by the various personages. What is substantiated by Chekhov's text time and again, therefore, is the breadth, depth, conditionality and perspectivity of crucial phenomena in life, and what is negated by it is a universally human inclination to oversimplify them, which can be exposed and challenged, but not totally eliminated.

8.3.2 "Philosophising" and Reciprocal Characterisation in *Three Sisters*

Another human inclination — by no means a universal one — is exposed in *Three Sisters* more than in any other Chekhov play: it is an urge to "philosophise" in the first place. Thus, the play's '№ 1 "philosophiser"', Vershínin, explicitly (though, as usual, humorously) equates his 'spiritual' "philosophising" with the 'material' cup of tea that his hosts fail to serve him to quench his thirst (see Epigraph to this Chapter) — a substitution that actually makes fun of both, stripping the former of its spiritual–intellectual pretence, its ostensible advantage over the latter. Much more telling is a moment in Act 4, when he is waiting for Másha in order to part from her forever. Their farewell is an event of incomparable significance, supposed to be an emotionally shattering blow to both of them;[43] however, just before that most moving scene, he says to Ól'ga that he feels like "philosophising" — as if it were the most natural thing to do at such a moment — but does not know what to "philosophise" about (Act 4); actually, he consults her about the choice of a theme. In short, he feels the urge to "philosophise" even when this activity is balanced against a fateful farewell, not a cup of tea. Consider this tripartite analogy: in Act 2 he is saying, as it were, '*I am waiting for tea — in the meantime, I'd like to "philosophise" instead*'; in Act 4 he is saying, as it were, '*I am waiting for Másha my beloved, to say goodbye to her forever — in the meantime, I'd like to "philosophise" instead*'. The almost perfect analogy between these two instances, then, shows clearly that he has no specific message, and certainly no specific truth, that he just cannot hold back at a given moment. In the first instance, the oral satisfaction and the feeling of time well spent that he can gain from babbling some platitudes are commensurate with the oral satisfaction and the feeling of time well spent gained from consuming a cup of tea (especially if one is thirsty); in the second — a moment of truth for Vershínin — Chekhov's characterisation is even subtler and more sophisticated: indeed, the analogy can almost be stated in terms of simple mathematical equations. It has been established in Act 2, that — for Vershínin —**"Philosophising"=(unconsumed) cup of tea**; here, in Act 4 he offers the equation **"Philosophising"=farewell to Másha forever**. Elementary algebra tells us, then, that for Vershínin **farewell to Másha forever=(unconsumed) cup of tea**... Of course, the materials Chekhov is dealing with are not algebraic, but the almost-explicit equations do serve Chekhov in his showing the serious limitations of Vershínin's emotional range. In this he is contrasted not only with Másha, who is emotionally shaken to her foundation in this very scene, but — implicitly, subtly yet effectively — also with Túsenbach (another feat of *contrastive–reciprocal characterisation*): whereas for Vershínin, in all probability, life will go on with tea and "philosophising" opportunities, Másha would live on, heartbroken, and Túsenbach will literally die. As he prophesies in Act 3, he will finally be allowed "to give his life" for Irína and his love for her.

Thus, Túsenbach's **subconscious** state of mind when he is about to make his final exit, knowingly, from his beloved Irína and from life itself, is characterised by an explicit stage-direction "not knowing what to say", which is Chekhov's message to the audience within the *outer/rhetorical plane*. Túsenbach's embarrassment makes him "say something", or "just anything", to Irína (as he has most recently desperately begged her to say to him — a plea for communication that has just failed in both its participants). However, at this moment of truth, Túsenbach's character — unlike Vershínin's, in **his** moment of truth — leads him not to resort to "philosophising" (which he enjoys in other circumstances); rather, he breaks the silence by saying something much more mundane, asking Irína to prepare a cup of coffee for him.[44] These are his "famous last words": it is so appropriate that Túsenbach, his inclination to "philosophise" notwithstanding, should end his role (and his life on the *inner/fictional plane*) with this simple request (an analogy with Chekhov's own last words is analysed in 9.3). Vershínin, by sharp contrast, feels the urge to "philosophise" in order to break what would otherwise have been a moment of pregnant, suspenseful silence — something that he seems to find intolerably embarrassing, much more than hollow "philosophising". Not-knowing-what-to-say, subconscious in Túsenbach, is Vershínin's **conscious** state of mind: he is fully aware of his uncontrollable urge to blah-blah; his only hesitation is what to blah-blah **about**, which actually means that for him it makes no difference one way or the other, it's all the same (sic! — Chekhov's *sameness*-anathema) as long as what he is saying means little **to him**, maybe even less than his Act 2's cup of tea.

In sum: both Vershínin and Túsenbach, faced with a final farewell from a beloved woman, feel an urge to say just something to escape an emotionally unbearable silence, but the difference between their individuated character traits, especially as lovers to their respective ladies, is starkly reflected in the way each of them responds intuitively to emotional needs and embarrassments, their own and their ladies'. This contrast is further emphasised by the difference between their fates: Vershínin is destined to live, and Túsenbach is destined to die. Chekhov's way of presenting the contrast between them — each with his hierarchy of embarrassment and his way of avoiding it — is an incomparable feat.

On the *outer/rhetorical plane*, however, the specific content of Vershínin's "philosophising" is far from arbitrary (nothing is "all the same" for Chekhov): this content is carefully chosen to signal crucially significant themes, whose importance may escape the personages' own notice, but is not supposed to escape ours. Vershínin's "famous last words" of "philosophising" (again: just before the emotionally loaded farewell with Másha) are: "if only industry[45] could be complemented by learning, and learning by industry!" Indeed, for Vershínin himself, as a fictional personage, these words are quite hollow: he is neither exceptionally industrious nor exceptionally learned (Chekhov takes care to make us aware of both); more importantly, as we have repeatedly seen, his platitudes have little to do with what really concerns him in general, and at a given moment of speaking in particular.[46] For Chekhov, however, the choice of this phrase at this particular moment is highly significant in terms of what he wants to convey to the audience, both in content (Chekhov, to be sure, is genuinely preoccupied with the themes of work and learning, central specifically to *Three Sisters*) and in showing the crucial importance of differences between individual human beings as an indispensable part of their shared humanity. A world in which a Túsenbach and a Vershínin would be really similar is a dull world of **indifference**; it is a world of lesser humanity, according to Chekhov's hierarchy of values, which celebrates the humanness and aliveness of *difference* and *uniqueness* and abhors the bestiality and deadliness of *border-blurring similarity* and *sameness* between human beings. "Philosophising" debates and arguments, for all their *sophistry*, tend to work in the opposite direction.

Therefore, rather than addressing these often-tedious "philosophising" tirades at unnecessary length, and with unearned reverence, the present discussion has tried to consider some of the more significant ways, or rather principles of poetics, by which Chekhov signals structures of values in the play. These, in summary, usually involve supplying us with implicitly value-charged materials that interact both with each other and with explicitly verbalised value-judgements. Moreover, it is only through the logic of these interactions that we can realise the value-potentialities of these materials. As we have repeatedly seen in analogous cases, the composite end result of such interpretative operations is always genuinely different not only from each of the interacting elements viewed in isolation, but also from anything that may result from technically adding them up.

The semantic patterns in the play that fit this description are very large indeed: they are so many that their sheer number makes it impossible to analyse all of them in the Book. Out of these, the next Subsections are confined to one complex: signalling *value* meanings by the semantisation of *time* and *place*.

8.3.3 Correlations between *Values*, *Time* and *Place*

Three Sisters is organised, *inter alia*, along three interrelated axes: of *time*, *place*, and *values*. *The axis of time* is represented (again: *inter alia*) in the generation-patterns within the central family, the Prózorovs, and in constant references to (usually idealised) times of past and future, contrasted with the (degraded, or at least negated) present. *The axis of place*, then, is virtually stretched between two opposing poles — Moscow *vs.* the provincial township — but it is also present in other spatial images and ideas, so varied as to include the cyclic migration of birds, the distant Polish town where the brigade is heading at the end of the play, differently functioning rooms in the Prózorovs' household, its courtyard, Ól'ga's school, etc.[47] As for *the axis of values*, in a typically Chekhovian way it is much more powerfully present when inferred from indirect materials (i.e., an **implicit** *potential-realisation*) than when directly stated (i.e., an **explicit** one). One example of how such indirect material is activated can be found in the way in which value-content is projected through human agents (who of course, within the *inner/fictional plane*, cannot be aware of their role in implicit projections of a *value-axis*).

As we have just seen, the play's main *value-axis* is stretched between two poles: the dead father at one extreme and Protopópov at the other. Once the play is seen through this prism, the basic correlations become obvious: the father is strongly linked with Moscow and everything that it represents for the family; Protopópov is equally linked with the provincial town (and even more organically so, being the Chairman of its Local Council). Most of the other personages, especially those who belong to the Prózorov family nucleus, can be placed on the *value-axis* between these two extremes, gravitating towards one or both of them with different and changing proportions and emphases. On the whole, their order, from the Father to Protopópov, would be: (1) the Father (General Prózorov); (2) Másha; (3) Irína; (4) Ól'ga; (5) Andréï; (6) Kulýgin; (7) Natásha; (8) Protopópov. It must be noted that the two extremes on this list — (1) and (8) — are technically-absent but otherwise powerfully-present *offstage personages*; "present absences".

8.3.3.1 Correlations between Systems of *Value* and *Place*

The *place axis* is correlated with the *value-axis* in more ways than one. The family's father, the late General Prózorov, had come from Moscow; his death, before the beginning of the action, constitutes vitally significant *expositional material* (see Sternberg 1978), which is powerfully underlined by Chekhov's decision to start the spoken text of the play with the most direct reference to it possible, the first two words (uttered by the *choric character* Ól'ga) being "Father died". The offstage father functions as the embodiment of Moscow, and his values are experienced as "the Moscow values", which were implanted in his children through his strict and highly motivated education, and inspired as well as crippled them throughout their lives. These children — all four siblings, in varying degrees — are "caught in the middle": their individual differences notwithstanding, they were all born in Moscow, and they carry in them an emasculated version of their father's values. Kulýgin, Natásha and Protopópov (again, their individual differences notwithstanding), are all genuine members of the provincial community and represent its values through their personalities and behaviour. Moreover, the individual differences within each of the two latter groups serve to underscore these value-similarities and their 'geographical' correlatives: if two persons as diametrically opposed in terms of human kindness and decency as Natásha and Kulýgin share certain traits and attitudes absent from **all** the Muscovites, it follows (at least within the play's logic and value-system) that the correlation between the two axes — of values and place/geography — has at least some validity. The intricate interrelationships between and around these axes are part of a whole network of multiple perspectivity, through which a tense, precarious and carefully controlled balance between various value-charged elements is maintained. Thus, the Prózorovs' obvious tendency to assign value-judgement to the *place-axis* (i.e., Moscow vs. the provincial township) is both corroborated and counterbalanced by more authoritative evidence, drawn from sources (verbal and non-verbal) other than their own discourse. Moreover, Chekhov activates various audience-responses, heterogeneously motivated, in order to further doubt and question — but not necessarily to contradict — the direct and indirect value judgements adopted by personages in the play.

Thus, for instance, the attitudes of different members of the family are juxta-posed with each other and with those of 'outsiders' — both within the play (extra-family characters) and outside it (the audience). The typically Chekhovian effect resulting from such procedures is one of a constant call for reconsidering, rather than reaffirming or disproving, many of the automatically accepted or expected pronouncements, values, beliefs, etc.

The composite nature of the value-patterns that emerge in the play is manifest in the genuine difficulty to determine Chekhov's own attitude (of course, as *Implied Author*) towards the validity of the analogies and/or correlations, so strongly suggested by the text, between the deictic axes of *time* (the past of the dead father, the present of the siblings *vs.* the future of Natásha's children) and *place* (Moscow vs. provincial town), on the one hand, and the axis of *value*, on the other. Thus, the sisters — especially Irína, but also Ól'ga, to a certain extent — are demonstrably divorced from any sense of reality in much of their 'pro-Moscow' rhetoric; however, this is to a great extent counterbalanced by much of what we, as audience, are made to see, which does grant some demonstrable value-superi-ority to Moscow, compared with the provincial township.

Other value questions are similarly structured. At the same time, the very nature and credibility of the play's proclaimed value system (e.g., assigning high posi-tions to such values as learning, work, and even love) are called into question, even if we disregard the shakiness of the 'geographical' and 'temporal' analogies that the text both suggests and undermines. Much depends on what we can assume as *the Implied Spectator*'s views, i.e., the audience-views, which we can reliably assume that Chekhov designed his texts to interact with. For the purpose of this discussion, there is no need (and there may be no possibility) to spell out those views; as we have repeatedly seen, Chekhov's role, as he saw it, is to provide us with "correct presentations of questions" rather than with answers. As to the present discussion's role, it is to show and analyse the mechanisms, which enable Chekhov to "present the question correctly". No more, no less.

8.3.3.2 *Value Structuration* and Chekhov's *Thematic Deep Structure*

Hardly ever in Chekhov, then, can something explicit be taken on trust. Again, Chekhov's approach to values is inseparably linked with his almost obsessive preoccupation with interrelationships and interactions between *potentials* and their *(non)realisations*, and between *presences* and *absences*. As a general rule — inas-much as any general rule can be elicited from the work of this schematicism-repellent master — 'positively-judged' values reside in *absent* ('there and/or then') entities, while 'negatively-judged' values reside in *present* ('here and/or now') ones. A pattern of *partial isomorphism* is thus formed between the structures of the three *axes*. However, even this complex conception is not applied schematically, but with generous allowance for deviations, accommo-dating differences between time and place, between various personages, etc. Without specifying all of these deviations in detail, suffice it to say, by way of illus-tration, that the *place-axis* is basically binary (Moscow vs. the provincial town), whereas the human carriers of values fall into a larger number of basic groups (e.g., father vs. several siblings-subgroups vs. Natásha and Protopópov) and many more sub-groups, while the *generation axis* has three basic components (father, siblings, grandchildren). Correlations between all are partial and complex, but basic patterns do exist along the lines proposed above. The most powerful value-statements are non-verbal and subliminal, rather than verbalised and explicit. Even seemingly technical decisions —such as *stage-directions* or *stage-design (scenery) instructions* — are often correlated with values, thus functioning as carriers of value messages. For instance, the four Acts' locations invariably reflect the sisters' *point of view*, both in the literal–visual and in the figurative–attitudinal senses of this term: we are literally 'made to see' things their way; and this in itself is part of the play's intricate value-system correlating in this case the actually-visible space of the stage with a clear, though not dogmatic, value-preference.

8.3.3.3 Correlations between Systems of *Value* and *Time*

Similarly subliminal-yet-effective is the analogy between the *time-axis* and the *value-axis*. Chekhov made a clear selection, whereby values inherent in learning and education, science and music, and certain degrees of refinement and sophistication, are most powerfully represented in the dead father, who had felt strongly enough about them to be able to pass them on to the next generation. The same values are diluted to the point of impotence in the four siblings (in varying degrees, of course), who experience them very strongly in their hearts and minds, but cannot act on them or pass them on to others (e.g., to offspring that the sisters do not have anyway, or to pupils, whom Ól'ga is too tired to teach anything of her father's world of values, yet whom Kulýgin is all too eager to teach his value-less lore of Latin grammar). It is crystal clear from the logic of the play, though merely speculative as far as the explicit textual evidence is concerned, that these values are deemed and doomed to be non-existent in the third generation. Even the very fact that the only reproductive member of the Prózorov family is Andréï (and by Natasha at that) is part of a subliminal-yet-powerful statement embodied in the linkage between the axes of time and value (this is even more powerful if we consider the insinuations, suggested yet unsubstantiated textually, that both of Natasha's children, or at least Sófochka, are biologically not Andréï's but Protopópov's). This selection is not a logical imperative, nor is it in any way corroborated by the laws of reality: there is no 'real-life' correlation — positive or negative, direct or inverse — between people's values and their power of reproduction. Yet, in the play this act of authorial selection acquires a force of persuasion as if it were the inescapable product of the harsh laws of reality. This effect is produced precisely because it is shown on stage as raw material for optional interpretation by the audience, rather than proclaimed in some explicit dictum about inescapable degeneration from generation to generation.

8.3.4 *Value Structuration* and Chekhov's *Presence/Absence* Dichotomy

In Chekhov's world, as we have seen, truest values in human life reside in wishes, dreams and yearnings; they are *unrealised potentials*, yet there is much more to their *presence* than meets the Chekhov-inexperienced eye. Their ostensible *absence* is misleading, because they are powerfully present in motivating people's actions and inactions that doom their lives to destruction, usually without their being aware of how and why it all happens. The infinite complexity of this view of values in Chekhov's world is largely responsible for much of the futile contro- versy in Chekhov criticism since its inception, based on two opposing equally reductionist and one-sided views ('optimistic' *vs.* 'pessimistic', or 'humanistic' *vs.* 'misanthropic') of the place and function of value in his work and view of the world and mankind. A structurally-oriented, multi-perspectival approach, however, can do some justice to the subject, by unfolding basic principles of constructing its loaded complexity. Chekhov, as shown above, is by no means neutral to all values, just as he is not indifferent to all his personages. Thus, for instance, he hates *Three Sisters'* Natasha and *The Cherry Orchard'*s Yásha and what they stand for; he loves *Uncle Vánia'*s Sónia, sides with quite a few other personages, and espouses the values passed on from the father to the siblings in the former play, though he shows how problematic and precarious they are in themselves and in the ways in which they had been passed on from father to children.

Chekhov, then, conveys his likes and dislikes to his addressees; however, he does that not through direct pronouncements, but through patterns and structured relationships, often interacting with the audience's expected norms. Thus, by linking the audience's visual point-of-view to the sisters' visual and attitudinal point-of-view Chekhov is, *inter alia*, subliminally signalling to us his preference for their value hierarchy, at least as compared to the provincial characters' hier- archy. This device is especially effective if we consider Protopópov's position in relation to this point of view. In Act 1 the sisters dominate the house from its central parlour, and Protopópov, uninvited, sneaks into its space vicariously, by way of the cake he sends in for Irína's party. The sisters are thereupon gradually pushed out of the house. In Act 2 Protopópov, still outside and uninvited, lures Natásha out after she has proven her domination of its interior. In Act 3, we move with the two sisters into the room which Natásha had forced them to share; now the parlour is out of bounds, both for us and for the sisters. In Act 4 the last vestiges of the sisters' presence in the house have been eliminated, and we are with them outside, while Natásha openly entertains Protopópov inside. This deserves special notice: in Act 1 she was a last-moment guest from the outside, while Protopópov remained there; however, by Act 4 the scene is almost schematically reversed: it is set outside, and Natasha appears at the window from inside, while Protopópov's presence inside is so well-established that no one comments about it. As far as the house is concerned, it is sisters-and-audience in, Protopópov out, in Act 1; exit sisters-and- audience, enter Protopópov, in Act 4. Thus Chekhov makes us sense that Protopópov is the lurking danger from the outside, who finally, in an act analo- gous to hostile takeover, occupies the heart of the house, but is always alien not only to the sisters' value-system, but also to the play's, the author's, and ours. Chekhov causes the dramatic–theatrical spatial system itself to "take sides", adopting the sisters' standpoint and imposing it on the audience. This, by the way, is another instance of Chekhov's skilful craftsmanship as a playwright: in narra- tive fiction there is no parallel to such a technique.

Another example — quite different in nature and thematic content, but similar in structural technique — is the way Chekhov takes care to make us place Natásha where she belongs at the bottom of the play's hierarchy of moral values. It seems at first that the only saving grace of this callous woman is that she is a caring mother to her children: thus, for instance, it is presumably for her Bóbik's sake that she disrupts the preparations for the masked guests in Act 2. However, after barring those guests from entering the house, she goes off for a *tróïka*-ride with her lover Protopópov, leaving her allegedly sick child in the nurse-maid's hands (Chekhov's stage-directions imply that the nurse's lullaby, heard for the first time soon after the beginning of the Act, should be heard from time to time as background, and once again at the Act's ending, after Natásha has gone to spend the evening with Protopópov). More conspicuous is the fact that Natásha's expansionist policy, taking over the house room by room, is also supposedly motivated by motherly care: actually, the factual data of the entire story of the Prózorovs' house in the play can be misread as the story of a mother who, naturally, takes care of her children and prefers their real needs to the imaginary fantasies of their childless aunts. Of course, one can sense intuitively and instantaneously that such a view is a misrepresentation of *Three Sisters*, distorting the play irreparably; but the most impressive piece of explicitly verbalised textual evidence substantiating this audience-impression comes from Andréï's speech in Act 4, where he speaks of the prospects of children doomed to grow up in the stifling atmosphere of the provincial township. At this point in the play's development, any perceiver can construct a spiritual profile of a child whose horizons and value hierarchies are shaped by a Natásha as a mother and by a Kulýgin as a teacher. By saying "a Natásha" and "a Kulýgin" I am taking my cue once again from the same speech by Andréï, stressing as he does the total resemblance between the inhabitants of the provincial town, making them virtually indistinguishable from one another. Andréï says point blank that such children grow up to be living corpses, not really human (this statement echoes his description of Natásha, in a dialogue with Chebutýkin earlier on in the same Act, as an inhuman animal). The thematic content of this *réplique*, with its powerfully value-charged message, is conveyed once again as a patterned relationship: it is the structurally-organised dichotomy between *deceit*, *bestiality*, *uniformity/sameness* and *death-in-life* on the one hand and *truthfulness*, *humanity/humaneness*, *individuality* and *aliveness*, on the other hand, that carries the relevant implicit message. This message, according to the play's value-hierarchy, is the de-automatisation of our automatic tendency to prefer a child to an adult when it comes to granting conditions for growth and development. Using these indirect but powerful means, the play suggests that an Irína, for instance, can make much more valuable use of a good room than a Bóbik, since her potential is worthy of greater realisation, in the deepest sense of the word, than his (analogous points are made in complementary discussions, especially in Chapter 1).

8.4 Conclusion

To end this Chapter, closing the circle begun in its beginning is called for. In his treatment of value, just as in his treatment of other central themes and components of human life, Chekhov is a true artist–writer, in contradistinction to a philosopher or thinker. He shows a composite view of values-in-interaction, which can be conveyed and experienced only through artistic structure and organisation. His, then, are some of the most genuinely artistic, literary–dramatic ways of coping with problems of presenting values in and through fiction, whether narrative or dramatic.

Notes

1 The latter example is not hypothetical, but literally refers to explicit preoccupations of Chekhov's personages — Vershínin's Act 2 tea and Túsenbach's Act 4 coffee, both typically not consumed, in *Three Sisters*. Similar 'mundane' preoccupations of Chekhov's personages abound.

2 Hierarchies and priorities are an integral part of an artist's work: much of what an artist does, **as an artist**, is the organisation of various types of raw material in forms and structures governed by various types and orders of hierarchies. Chekhov, however, is outstanding in the intensity of his preoccupation with such problems, and in the *isomorphism* between its applications to art on the one hand and to reality on the other.

3 This Chapter is intended, *inter alia*, as complementary discussion to Cathy Popkin's (1993) seminal exploration of 'insignificance' in Chekhov's poetics.

4 By analogy, it is pertinent to recall Chekhov's negation, even abhorrence, of *uniformity/sameness* and complementary preoccupation and fascination with *distinctiveness/uniqueness/individuality* in human beings as reflecting their humanness and even their very aliveness. The centrality of this theme in Chekhov's world and poetics is discussed repeatedly in the Book.

5 The points proposed here are admittedly intuitive and cannot be readily corroborated by any kind of systematic methodology; yet, this does not invalidate them. Readers can judge whether they match their own intuitions.

6 It is, in a way, a 'professional deformity' of scholars and analysts of fictional texts (present company included) to reverse this hierarchy, and focus primary attention on the author's strategies. This preference was given a powerful boost with the advent of various *formalist*, *structuralist*, and cognate *movements*, *schools* and *trends* in 20th-century scholarship, whose predominantly East European pioneers had a considerable impact in other parts of the academic world as well. This, however, should not be allowed to blur the basic, almost ontological hierarchy of most fictional texts, as perceived and experienced by most authors and recipients alike.

7 The approach adopted here is largely inspired by the idea of *Literariness* [*литературность*] and related concepts (whatever their lexical labels), as expounded by Russian Formalists and later *trends/movements* of East European structuralists and semioticians (e.g., the schools of Moscow, Prague and Tartu), and by 'the Tel Aviv School of Poetics', especially in the 1970s, and in articles variously published in the first volumes of the journals edited by Benjamin Harshav: *Hasifrut* in Hebrew, and subsequently *PTL* and *Poetics Today* in English. For most recent accounts, see Harshav 2007, especially 1–31 and 161–173.

8 The symmetry presented here is a bit too 'neat' in its *micro* details, because some major types of visual art — notably *figurative* painting and sculpture — can be described and characterised as *non-verbal* but *referential*. This, however, does not invalidate the binary symmetry proposed here on the *macro* level. Basic semiotic distinctions, mainly between *iconic* and *symbolic*, can successfully address the question of different types of *referentiality*, so that the present dichotomy is concerned with *verbal* vs. *non-verbal*, and *artistic* vs. *non-artistic*.

9   This has absolutely nothing to do with the relative 'importance' of the **content** of each type of clause (*principal* or *subordinate*). In the sentence "I had just eaten a sandwich when the world war broke out" the subordinate clause's content (the beginning of the world war) is incomparably more important, by any standard, than the principal clause's (eating a sandwich).

10 This is not really true in the novel as it is in drama/theatre: the former can afford pages and pages of 'marginal' materials. Dostoïévskiï just refused to take advantage of them: to him, they are a liability rather than an asset.

11 The analogy between this model and 'Classical *Realism*' in *Drama*, as characterised in 10.1.2.1, is too striking to overlook. Indeed, the two models — represented, *inter alia*, by Dostoïévskiï in the novel and Ibsen in drama — share a significant trait, describable as 'impatience with trivialities'. Otherwise they are quite different.

12 This may be reminiscent of Gógol''s seeming irrelevancies (see next Subsection), but the practice of the two masters are radically different, because of the difference in the way these details function within their respective artistic systems.

13 Eichenbaum 1974 [1924] cites, *inter alia*, the example of a ridiculously detailed description of a general's portrait on a tobacco case of a minor personage that has no apparent relevance to anything or anyone in the story (p. 289).

14 A rare example of explicit reference to this matter can be found in Túsenbach's last *réplique* of farewell, addressed to his beloved Irína, just before the duel from which he is doomed never to return. He speaks to her about life's "silly trifles" that one is used to ignore, or laugh at, which suddenly become exceptionally meaningful, to the extent that one cannot stop thinking of them.

15 The quote is from Medvedénko's words to Másha (*The Seagull*, Act 1): he contrasts the intensity of his love for her with her emotional indifference towards him. Chekhov makes him use the Latinised form *indifferentism*, though there is a perfect genuine word in Russian to convey the same meaning (in English, the difference between *indifference* and *indifferentism* would roughly convey the nuance). The effect of this choice is typically partly comic, characterising the speaker as a teacher who likes to use affectatious platitudes with Latinised forms (in many ways, he is a prototype of *Three Sisters'* Kulýgin), and partly emotionally moving, since the affectatious words that he uses, and even the blatantly funny aspects of his personality, do not detract from the genuine agony that he feels because of his unrequited love for Másha.

16 Chekhov's famous, almost mythological journey to the penal colony in the Island of Sakhalín and the report that he wrote in its wake (1890), the way he conducted his often voluntary medical practice, and his stand on other public issues (all Chekhov biographies profusely refer to these activities), and even opinions on controversial issues that he did express in private communications with friends and acquaintances, are a formidable challenge to such allegations so far as Chekhov the 'real', private person — rather than the author of plays and stories — is concerned. He was acutely aware of the difference between the two types of activity and expression, adamantly refusing to blur demarcation lines between them (the point is elaborated many times elsewhere throughout the Book).

17 Such allegations, especially by Chekhov's contemporaries–compatriots (see some studies in Chekhov reception — e.g., Karlinsky 1984, Tabachnikova 2010, Urbanski 1979 — for quotes and discussions), have, as one would expect, fallen into disrepute throughout the decades, in view of Chekhov's established reputation, reaching near-unanimity over a century, as a great artist–humanist. Indeed, an overwhelming majority of writers about him oppose the interpretation of such typical Chekhovian features as *emotional restraint* (the subject of Chapter 7) as callousness, and refusal to make

explicitly authorial ideological statements in his fictional writing, as (im)moral neutrality, i.e., indifference to right and wrong, to human suffering, and to human values in general. See for instance Booth 1961, 68–69.

18 This word has two meanings here: the opposite of *whole/complete*, and the opposite of *impartial/equitable*.

19 A clear distinction between plays and stories is relevant here. Statements in plays are as a rule made by personages, who — especially in Chekhov — rarely represent the author's opinion (see Epigraph to Chapter 5); therefore, Chekhov does not avoid writing judgemental statements about people and ideas in his plays, as long as assigning them to personages keeps him safe from appearing as espousing them. In narrative fiction, however, an authoritative (*omniscient*) *narrator* is often equated with the author, whether rightly or wrongly. Yet, even in plays, spectators — activating their own norms and beliefs — can look for the author's opinion between the lines, partly by looking for personages who seem, more than others, to represent his views. At any rate, Chekhov's stories and plays usually manage to hide their author's opinions more often and more effectively than the fictional texts of his compatriots and contemporaries. The latter often do not aspire to hide their opinions in first place; see R. L. Jackson's Epigraph to the Book.

20 Textual examples of such processes in Chekhov's texts are so prevalent, that almost any play or story that comes freely to mind can amply supply corroborating evidence. Think, for instance, as randomly chosen illustrations, of stories like "In the Ravine" or "The Grasshopper", and of course of "A Dreary Tale", or plays like *Ivánov* and *Uncle Vánia*, or almost any other, in the light of the general statements just proposed. However, see the next Section for a more focused illustration, where some of these generalisations are examined in the context of a single work.

21 The content of this Subsection is largely a re-statement of principles presented above, especially in the Book's opening *Part I: Previewing*, which comprises its first two Chapters. This content is however an integral part of the ensuing argument, indispensable for its presentation in an autonomous manner in the context of the present Chapter. Thus, it is possible to skip this Subsection — especially its last four paragraphs — as long as the content of *Part I* is borne in mind.

22 This appears paradoxical, because words (well-chosen ones, of course), and the process of selecting them, are supposed to facilitate precision and undermine vagueness; a process that Shakespeare, in undoubtedly well-chosen words, describes as giving "to airy nothing a local habitation and a name" (*A Midsummer Night's Dream*, V, i, 16–17). Pinpointing Chekhov's "airy nothing" — which is neither *airy* nor *nothing*, yet an epitome of evasiveness — is a challenge this Section is trying to meet.

23 This argument — a reformulation of the basic tenets of Formalist and Structuralist schools — especially applies to the perception of *realistic drama* in particular and *referential art* in general since the dawn of history.

24 Most playwrights aspire to achieve such degree of persuasiveness (some try to delude themselves, and/or their audiences, that their own manipulative motivations in the *outer/rhetorical plane* can be denied, ignored or dispensed with, as required by *dramatic illusion*); as an ideal, then, this aspiration is not specifically Chekhovian. Chekhov's greatness lies in his recurring feats in achieving this goal, i.e., in the persuasiveness of his personages as *reality-like persons* and as invented *fictional personages* alike: we can view them as 'the person next door' and as Chekhov's marionettes with equal reliability.

25 An analogical dichotomy between "the flight **of** the seagull" and "the flight **from** the seagull" (both, of course, within *The Seagull*) is offered in 7.5.

26 *The Cherry Orchard*'s Gáïev is a borderline case, since he chooses two different types of escape routes on different occasions: sometimes he is a "philosophiser" (his address to the bookcase, Act 1, is a shining example), but more often he uses an imaginary billiard game as antidote to embarrassment (both are totally ineffective — his addressees usually see through him, and their responses prolong his embarrassment).

27 Evading the issue and changing the subject is a 'specialty' of many a Chekhov character, e.g., *The Seagull*'s Másha reading lotto numbers in Act 4, *Three Sisters* personages' talk about Balzac's Berdíchev wedding in Act 2, to choose random examples out of numerous instances. Admittedly, it is a very well known mechanism in real life as well; those who never use it should throw the first stone…

28 Konstantín's case in *The Seagull* is both an exception to these rules and their revalidation. It is an exception, *inter alia*, because (a) whereas Chekhovian "philosophising" is defined as an exclusively **oral** activity, Konstantín's **writing** is a major and integral part of his "philosophising", which is not a response to the course of a conversation; (b) his plea for "new forms" and other "philosophising" expressions of his artistic ideology do seem, after all, to touch on something of vital importance **to him**, at least to his inner world. Yet, it revalidates the rules, *inter alia*, because (a) he ideologises his abstract, impersonal writing and his unconventional views ignoring their psychological roots; (b) there are indications that deep down, subconsciously, the abstract ideological themes and arguments are not **that** important to him, that his major motivation to engage in various forms of "philosophising" — both in general and at a particular moment — is **to make an impression** (on himself, his mother, Nína and others) **rather than to make a point** (very partly analogous, in this respect, are the motivations of *Uncle Vánia*'s Ástrov, who undoubtedly does care about the environment, but maybe cares more about impressing Yeléna). Some inner inconsistencies between my various arguments in this Section are deliberate, and attest to the pregnant many-sidedness of Chekhov's "correct presentations".

29 For some other people, however — e.g., Nína's parents in *The Seagull*; Ástrov's critics, as quoted by him in *Uncle Vánia*, Act 2; personages responding to Gáïev's and to Trofímov's "philosophising" throughout *The Cherry Orchard* — these very hierarchies are odd, even a cause for ridicule.

30 Indeed, Dr. Dorn's response to Konstantín's play in Act 1 of *The Seagull* gives the latter the serious appreciation of his written "philosophising" that he so badly needs. However, Chekhov's tangled web of actions, inactions and reactions — which in *The Seagull* is largely focused on artistic creativity, its production and its reception — puts this response in contrapuntal perspective, which, in turn, subverts our potential identification with it. Thus, most other onstage spectators are much less sympathetic to the play (different as they are from each other); the only other favourable opinion is Másha's, whose love for Konstantín, as well as her personal limitations, shake her credibility. Moreover, Konstantín himself is rather impatient to hear what Dorn has to say, being at that moment concerned with Nína's whereabouts more than with the message of his own play and its impact on an intelligent and disinterested spectator. Moreover, our access to the play-fragment itself gives us tools to judge and doubt Dorn's assessment: he may be a benevolent and unconventional consumer of art, but not necessarily a trusted connoisseur.

31 Thus, novels by the greatest 19th-century Russian novelists, Tolstói and Dostoïévskii, include quite a lot of "philosophising"-speeches spoken by men, and incomparably less, if any, spoken by women (the latter are more inclined to witty, aphoristic one-liners, and rare ones at that). "Philosophising", then, is 'a man's thing' by social–cultural consent, at least in 19th-century Russian literature; it is an accepted norm that seems so

natural that it is hardly ever discussed (note that in *Love and War*, Woody Allen's film-parody on 19th-century Russian literature, "philosophising" is almost equally uttered by male and female characters, which is one of the signs that this film is an American parody rather than 'the real Russian thing'). In the present context, though, another difference between Chekhov and these great novelists is highly relevant: whereas both of them take their "philosophisers" seriously, granting them the authors' own gifts of profound thinking and eloquent expression, and investing "philosophising"-tirades with their own thoughts and opinions, Chekhov keeps his distance — often an ironic one — from the "philosophisers" that he created and their opinions that he worded. Thus, the speeches of *War and Peace*'s Pierre and Prince Andréï, or of many of Dostoïévskiï's major protagonists, are closer to *Philosophy* itself in their quest for truth, whereas very little in Chekhovian "philosophising" (termed as such by Chekhov's personages themselves) resembles genuine *Philosophy*, even to the limited extent that Chekhov had one. This distinction in the realm of writing strategies is closely related to a more philosophical–ideological distinction pointed out admirably by Robert Louis Jackson (and chosen as an Epigraph to the entire Book), whereby Tolstóï and Dostoïévskiï tried to liberate their readers, whereas Chekhov left his readers free to liberate themselves.

32 Note the three dots that Chekhov writes at the end of her response, as a suggestion for actress intonation and audience notice; more important, note the subtle mechanism of self-reference activated here: Vershínin's points at this moment are arguably not "really" worth writing down, but Chekhov himself, as the author of *Three Sisters*, did write them down forever... The complexity and multi-perspectivity generated by such self-referential mechanisms are astounding, not least because they are so subliminal, hardly noticed by a reader, let alone a spectator.

33 Quotations in this paragraph are concocted from various English translations and from separate *répliques* that are so adjacent in the text that they are usually printed on the same page.

34 Styan 1971 and Magarshack 1972 in their close, scene-by-scene readings of Chekhov's major plays, hardly mention this *réplique* (pp. 168 and 133, respectively), apparently unaware of its significance.

35 Thus, for instance, it was cut in the 1970 BBC-TV production, adapted by Elisaveta Fen and directed by Cedric Messina, available on DVD within BBC–VIDEO's *The Anton Chekhov Collection* (2008). This *réplique* is, understandably, one of the first to go when there are cuts in productions, especially non-Russian ones.

36 This version by Magarshack (London: Unwin Books, 1969, p. 122) clearly evades the translational challenge by substituting the term "nonsense" itself for the actual barely-translatable nonsense of the original; however, it is precisely this avoidance that determined my choice of his version here, since the specific nonsensical content of the original is irrelevant to the present argument.

37 Another case of Chekhov's subtle handling of a latent gender issue is discussed in Chapter 5, Note 22.

38 The fact that Chekhov does that within *Three Sisters*, which is a fictional text, does not detract from the acute intensity of his real-life message.

39 The embarrassing effect of mismatch between "philosophising" and its audience is more explicitly addressed in *The Cherry Orchard*, when Ranévskaïa chides her brother Gáïev for his offstage lecturing about the 1870s and the "decadents" to a captive, and obviously uninterested, audience of restaurant waiters (Act 2); this is in a way a further development of the onstage speeches by Andréï (about his dreams of Moscow and academic career there) to Ferapónt in *Three Sisters* — where the near-deaf addressee

could not have understood the speaker even if he could hear him. In all the plays there are other instances and kinds of mismatch between "philosophiser", message and addressee(s).

40 In fact, this dissonance is not created in perceivers unfamiliar with the academic *via dolorosa* on the way to professorship and other aspects of institutionalised scholarship; but this reservation applies to the partial functioning of all allusions, references, and other forms of activating assumed previous knowledge, in audiences and addressees of texts. Just as someone ignorant of Shakespeare's works, for instance, would not recognise and appreciate Shakespearean allusions in a modern text, in this case Chekhov's subtle strategy just described would be lost on anyone who lacks the tools to appreciate it. In terms of communication with an audience, this is a professional hazard of authorial sophistication.

41 In the textual environment of *The Seagull* this modest self-appreciation of Sórin's enters into a network of analogies with other personages who weigh potential artistic talent (of themselves or others) against actual achievement (or lack thereof) in art. This applies with different degrees to the way the play's four artists — Arkádina, Trigórin, Nína and Konstantín — appreciate themselves, each other, and others, and to the way Shamráïev, Medvedénko, Dorn and Másha (who have no artistic aspirations of their own) view artistic talent in others (be they personages in the play or offstage characters). The text of the play, very much *à la* Chekhov, supplies more questions than answers about the talents of all its four artists, giving vague and even contradictory indications about the subject: how 'really' talented are Nína, Konstantín, Trigórin and Arkádina? In the final analysis the audience is led to wonder and to realise the difficulty inherent in any attempt to appreciate talent unequivocally and authoritatively.

42 The term is used, always with some degree of humour, also by other personages and in other plays; it implicitly applies to quite a few moments of 'speeching' and debating not explicitly labelled as such.

43 In fact, it is only **supposed** to be so heartbreaking for both of them; the difference between their responses — another Chekhovian feat of *contrastive–reciprocal characterisation* — shows how immune Vershínin is to emotionally shattering experiences: he is obviously saddened, but departs standing firmly on his feet (figuratively speaking) leaving the Másha chapter in his life behind him, whereas the same scene leaves Másha an emotional wreck. His "philosophising" is part of the mental equipment that builds up his immunity.

44 Of course, there is an analogy between two cups destined never to be drunk: Vershínin's tea in Act 2 and Túsenbach's coffee in Act 4.

45 The Russian word that Chekhov uses here, *трудолюбие*, can be rendered in English as *diligence* or *industry* (or, rather, *industriousness*, which is perhaps more precise but sounds a bit awkward); literally–etymologically, however, it is a compound word, derived from *the love of work/labour/toil*. In Chekhov's original text, then, this word resonates with other references to work and "philosophisings" about it (and about the urge and love that it inspires in some personages) that figure prominently throughout the text of *Three Sisters*.

46 Granted, the topics of his "philosophising" do occupy his mind from time to time and to a certain extent; they are somehow chosen by his internal filters to become stock subjects for his frequent "philosophising", out of literally endless potential topics, and Chekhov does provide us with some reasons that account for Vershínin's (and Túsenbach's) choices of topics, that are valid in terms of their respective characterisations within the *inner/fictional plane*; yet, the reasons for choosing them within the *outer/rhetorical plane* are much more significant.

47 Analogous *axes of place* exist in the other major plays as well. The *axis of place* includes such offstage locations as "the town" as well as specific towns (e.g., Khár'kov) in *The Seagull*; Finland, St. Petersburg and Africa in *Uncle Vánia* (about the latter, see Marsh 2012); Paris, "the town", the auction hall, an offstage restaurant, etc., in *The Cherry Orchard*. It would be a worthwhile project, even a fascinating one, to analyse each of these in detail. It has been established for many years in Chekhov scholarship, that all the major plays include a clash between "locals" and "outsiders"; *Three Sisters* differs from the other late plays in this respect in assigning a relatively 'positive value' to the 'outsiders' and 'negative value' to the 'locals', whereas the reverse is roughly true in the other plays. In order to make *Three Sisters* conform to the general pattern, one has to regard the Muscovites as 'locals', which would turn the real locals into 'outsiders'. This is indeed so within the worldview and mentality of the Prózorovs, which the audience (particularly the originally-intended audience of the **Moscow** Art Theatre!) is made to share; however, from strictly geographical standpoint, the 'real' provincial town is 'local', whereas distant and unattainable Moscow is simply outside the play's frame. Thus, the Muscovites are 'outsiders' to the local town and its inhabitants.

CHAPTER

9

The End(ing)s Justify the Mean(ing)s
The Curtain Falls on a Chekhov Play
CLOSING THE BOOK'S INNER CIRCLE

I have an interesting idea for a comedy, but haven't devised its ending. **Whoever devises new endings for plays, will open a new era** [emphasis added]. Those damn endings just don't come out: the protagonist has either to get married or to shoot himself, there is no other way out. […] I will not start writing it [the comedy] until I have devised for it an ending as ingenious as its beginning. Once I come up with the ending, I will write it in two weeks.

Chekhov in a letter to Suvórin, June 1892[1]

9.0 Preliminary Remarks

It is by now a truism that, all other things being equal, a text's beginning and ending are perceived as more conspicuous than its middle, producing *primacy effect* and *recency effect*, respectively.[2] It is a study of how Chekhov uses *endings* to make his artistic–compositional *means* suit his artistic–thematic *ends* (here, in the sense of *goals*), and how these endings **justify** (in both senses, *vindicate/substantiate* and *adjust/align*, even *reorganise*) the meanings of an entire text.

Thomas Winner (1966, p. 5), discussing the composition of Chekhov's short stories, makes a distinction between "*surprise* (or *pointe-*) *ending*" and "*zero ending*" (the latter is Víktor Shklóvskiï's term, and the device itself is described by Winner as "a Chekhovian innovation"). Using this distinction as a point of departure, I am talking about stories and plays with two-phased or multiple-phased endings, that combine *surprises*, *climaxes*, *zeroes*, and other types of closure as successive segments, that follow each other along the temporal axis of the text's continuum. In other words, such endings constitute *syntagmatic combinations* (i.e., 'strong' *surprises/climaxes*[3] plus 'weak' *zeroes*), rather than *paradigmatic selections* (i.e., either 'strong' or 'weak'). In several European languages the term *pointe* (or *pointe-ending*) applies to most *climaxes*, and virtually all *surprises*; consequently, the *zero* that follows such a *pointe* can be termed '*post-pointe*' ending. From a strictly structural viewpoint, this composite type of ending is partially analogous, on a *micro* level, to a feminine ending of a verse-line (a sequence of *accented+unaccented*, or 'heavy+light' syllables), or to a sequence of *downbeat+upbeat* in metred music; on the *macro* level in western tonal music, it is partially analogous to an ending consisting of a 'strong' or 'heavy' *cadenza* and a 'weak', 'lighter-weight' *coda*.[4] Such analogies are, once again, admittedly partial, mainly because of the non-referential nature of music; yet when considered with proper caution they can be illuminating and help in clarifying the issues.

9.1 Double-Phased Endings in Three Stories[5]

The *post-pointe ending* is a common feature of a considerable number of Chekhov's stories, and the phenomenon could have been demonstrated by any one of them individually. The three stories discussed below, then, indeed illustrate this Chekhovian technique effectively, but other stories could have been chosen for this purpose just as well.

9.1.1 The Concept of *Skeleton Plot*

The term/concept *skeleton plot* is offered here as a tool for assessing the type and extent of indispensability of an ending in relation to the text preceding it, and for monitoring the process of *retroactive penetration* of an ending into that preceding text. It is related to the Aristotelian *argument* and to kindred concepts developed by scholars over the centuries in their quest for criteria for determining what makes an element in a text more 'important' (alias 'significant'/'crucial'/'indispensable'/'prominent' etc. — see 8.0), at least when contrasted with other elements that have not 'earned' such characterisations to similar extent; in other words, criteria that would determine what, by universal (albeit usually intuitive) consensus, aught to appear in any paraphrase, recapitulation or summary of that text. Complementing structural–compositional criteria of importance that have been suggested (e.g., repetition, analogy/parallelism, *primacy effect* and *recency effect*, etc.), stress is laid here on extra-literary, extra-textual, largely culture-bound hierarchical scales of values, that assign *a priori* centrality to certain types of thematic materials (and, of course, assign complementary *a priori* marginality to other thematic materials), regardless of how they are structured or organised within the text's composition. The higher an element (e.g., an event, a saying, etc.) ranks on such a scale, the more indispensable it is as a component of the *skeleton plot*; which comprises the events, sayings, attitudes etc. that cannot be omitted from any schematic representation of the text, because of their intrinsic, text-free value.

Granted, the actual criteria that determine the 'right of entry' into a *skeleton plot* are largely intuitive and therefore contestable; the phenomenon itself, though, undoubtedly exists, and functions effectively, at least in obvious cases. Thus, matters of love, other significant relationships (e.g., between parents and children, best friends and sworn enemies), work, war and peace, sharp conflict, health and sickness, life and death, etc. — especially when related to a central personage — are part of any *skeleton plot* of a narrative/fictional/Dramatic text, and their inclusion in it is consensually accepted as trivially true.[6]

9.1.2 The Ending of "Ván'ka" (1886)

The basic *skeleton-plot* of "Ván'ka" can be told in a couple of sentences: Ván'ka Zhúkov, a nine-year-old orphan, is an apprentice at a shoemaker's household, where he is constantly abused, virtually enslaved. Out of his intolerable misery he writes a letter to his grandfather, imploring him to come to his rescue (most of the story consists of the full text of this letter, written in reliably naïve style). On the envelope he writes the only address he knows: "To Grandpa, in the village", adding for clarity the Grandfather's forename and patronymic (Konstantín Makárovich), to make sure that the letter is delivered to the right person and destination. Indeed, the *skeleton plot* ends with a *pointe*, which is the surprising last event in the *skeleton* narrative; but the actual text of the story ends with a Chekhovian *post-pointe*, i.e. the description of Ván'ka's inquiring about how letters reach their destinations and his going to bed to dream happily about his "grandpa in the village" reading his letter and showing it off to friends. This composite ending is truly multifunctional: it functions first and foremost within the confines of the story itself, subtly yet significantly modifying its thematic hierarchies, as compared with the hypothetical alternative, "the road not taken" by Chekhov, of placing the *pointe* — the *surprise ending* of the pathetically dead-end address — at the very end of the text. However, for now it is sufficient to skip discussing the ending's role in the story itself and confine discussion to two out of its many functions, which transcend the story's limits and operate primarily on the level of Chekhov's overall poetics and artistic credo. (1) *Compositionally*, this ending reflects a contrapuntal conception of how to organise literary texts: it plays *thematics* and *composition* against each other, placing as it does the thematically most powerful moment (the address on the envelope) at a compositionally relatively weak point (somewhat removed from the very end of the story), and of course vice versa — placing the relatively insignificant event (the child's return home and his dream) at a compositionally strong point (the very end of the story). This mutually-subversive juxtaposition, as we have seen repeatedly in previous Chapters, is typically Chekhovian. (2) *Thematically*, this amounts to an implicit, yet crystal-clear statement of *the importance of the conventionally unimportant*, of 'the "philosophical" dimension of drinking tea' (reference here is obviously to Vershínin's joking remark in Act 2 of *Three Sisters*, juxtaposing tea with "philosophising", Chapter 8's Epigraph. However, all these manoeuvres counterbalance, rather than overturn, the basic thematic hierarchy. By being removed from the ending, the address on Ván'ka's envelope is embedded in a complex, heterogeneous perspective, but does

not lose its impact. This impact emanates from the intrinsic, extra-textual significance of the event, the clash between the child's hope and its cruel shattering
through his own innocent ignorance. It is a powerful case of *unrealised potential*
and *presence through absence* on all levels — of events, narrative, and text composition. However, there is a subversive relationship between the strength of the
ending of the *skeleton plot* and Chekhov's obvious refusal to place it at the very
end of his text. The compositionally highlighted ending of the text and the narra-
tively highlighted ending of the *skeleton plot* undermine each other and produce a
typically-Chekhovian *'post-pointe' ending*.

9.1.3 The Ending of "Sleepy" (1890)[7]

> To die, to sleep
> No more; and by a sleep to say we end
> (Shakespeare, *Hamlet*, III, i, 60–61)

> Sleep no more
> [...] murder sleep, the innocent sleep
> (Shakespeare, *Macbeth*, II, ii, 32–33)

The contrapuntal clash between thematically- and compositionally-determined
emphases is my main reason for choosing the short story "Sleepy"[8] as the next
example. The *skeleton plot* is once again short and simple, summarisable in a
couple of sentences. Var'ka, a twelve year-old girl — in many ways like Ván'ka in
the story discussed in the preceding Subsection[9] — is abused and bullied, virtually enslaved, in a household where she spends day after day without a moment's
rest, doing all the house chores. When everyone goes to sleep, her major task is to
watch over the insomniac crying baby of the host family. A detailed account of
how she literally goes out of her mind with sleeplessness culminates with the
story's last, chilling sentence (which is rendered here in a functional English
version): "Having strangled him, she quickly lies down on the floor, laughing
happily now that she can sleep, and in a minute she is sleeping deeply as [if she
were] dead." In order to fully appreciate the effect of Chekhov's calculated
ordering of the material, let us imagine a reversal of the sequence of components
in this sentence; this would be something like *'She lies down on the floor, laughing
happily now that she can sleep, and in a moment she is sleeping deeply as [if she
were] dead, after she has strangled the baby'*. This would have been a 'strong',
pointe-ending, untypical of the late Chekhov; a *surprise* and a *climax*, an ending
with a bang.

In shaping to end the story the way he did, Chekhov makes masterly use of the
deeply rooted, almost innate hierarchies of values, which make the mental process
of constructing *skeleton-plots* possible. Such universal hierarchies automatically
assign the greatest importance to an extraordinary and unspeakable event like a
child strangling a baby, making it a central part of any *skeleton-plot* imaginable:
under no circumstances can it be skipped or ignored. However, Chekhov does
everything in his authorial power to undermine this absolute thematic dominance

by mobilising, as it were, every resource of compositional organisation against it. Quantitatively, the entire story — amounting to about four pages in most editions — is placed on one scale, weighed against just two words in the Russian original («задушив его», which I have rendered in English as the three words *having strangled him*)[10] on the other scale. Moreover, these two words are even further weakened by their syntactic subordination and compositional distance from the very end of the text. Thus, in terms of thematic and narrative structure, the story is marked by a gradual, constant build-up, paving the way for the ultimate horrifying event, whereas in terms of compositional organisation it shrinks this central event to the minimum, as if enclosing or embedding it within a cushioning, shock-absorbing frame dominated by the effects of drowsiness and sleeplessness (see a discussion of these descriptions in Struve 1961). It takes such flagrant disproportion and imbalance between quantities to produce some semblance of balance between the cause (sleeplessness and its impact on Var'ka's mind) and the effect (the child-nanny strangling the baby). However, Chekhov knows well that the horror of the event cannot be diminished as a result of his technique; on the contrary, it is bound to gain force from this obviously and deliberately futile attempt to hold back its impact and water it down. A far cry from subdued understatement, this instance of *Chekhovian restraint* is like a loud scream whose impact grows stronger with every futile attempt to stifle it. Thus, the employment of compositional manipulations is a device laid bare, to use good-old Russian Formalist parlance.[11]

Gleb Struve (1961, p. 475) writes: "It is strange to think now that in the story as printed originally in the newspaper the last sentence was missing. It occurs first in the version, otherwise almost unrevised, included in the volume *Хмурые люди* [*Gloomy People*]". Strange indeed: the entire story seems to spring from its last sentence, which sheds its light, or rather its darkness, on the entire text, from its very first to its very last word, and seems to be a major *raison d'être*, inspiration and motivation for Chekhov's decision to write the story in the first place. Granted, the prospect of killing the baby is strongly suggested by the penultimate sentence even without the ultimate one; it appears as a voice that the girl protagonist hears in her mind's ear. However, it becomes a (fictional) fact only in the later version, which makes the balance between the various forces operating in the story tenser and more precarious. The baby is indeed killed, but the way the last sentence is proportioned internally and functions externally (in relation to the rest of the story) creates an epitome of *Chekhovian restraint* and *unrealised potential*: the killing is stated tersely, as a matter-of-fact report indifferent to its harrowing meaning, with utmost economy, muffled by syntactic subordination and suppressed, as it were, by the network of direct and indirect expressions of (the *absence* of) *sleep* and *rest*, as opposed to *killing* and *death*.[12] In short, the last sentence adds enormous concentrated power to all the conflicting forces operating throughout the story; it provides the entire story with awe born of the clash between the shocking event and what appears to be a failed attempt to minimise its magnitude. This may well be the story's most memorable sentence.

Be that as it may — i.e., regardless whether this key final sentence was written, then omitted, and later restored (a highly unlikely sequence of events) or whether it had occurred to Chekhov only when he prepared the story for the later publication — the case of the ending of "Sleepy" is clear evidence that Chekhov's conscious preoccupation with endings was no less apparent in his practice as a writer of fictional texts than in explicit remarks in his letters (see Epigraph at the beginning of the Chapter).

The *recency effect* produced by this last sentence is indeed subversive–contrapuntal: its textually–compositionally–structurally determined hierarchy and its thematics undermine each other. Let us focus on the story's very final simile — «как мёртвая» (literally, "like dead", or "dead-like", or "as if [she were] dead") — which almost miraculously reinforces both poles of the story, by referring explicitly to the concept of *death* on the one hand, and by doing it through the veil of a simile on the other hand. Thus one single word, «мёртвая» ["dead"] — so charged thematically–semantically, subordinated syntactically–figuratively, yet foregrounded structurally–compositionally — is made to function as an Archimedean point of leverage and balance for the entire story. It is this word that is primarily responsible for the powerful, though implicit, analogy — stronger than anything that the text explicitly spells out — between the killer-child and the killed baby as two murdered victims. This effect of presenting two parallel victims is achieved to a very large extent by the technique of post-pointe ending, and its meticulous application by Chekhov, weighing every single word very carefully in the balance, to produce the desired effect with utmost precision.[13]

9.1.4 The Ending of "A Little Joke" (1899)

A story comparable to "Sleepy" in the force, efficiency and retrospective action of its ending is "A Little Joke", analysed in great detail in 5.1 above; I shall confine myself here only to observations about the function of its ending:[14] whereas in 5.1 it was discussed in the context of the story as a whole, here it is discussed in the context of endings of other works.

At least three major factors make this ending's role so radical. (1) In terms of *plot* and *characterisation*, the entire chain of actions by the two protagonists, as well as their characters, are retrospectively reinterpreted after the *pointe* of the protagonist-narrator's departure from town and Nádia's marriage to someone else, rather than the conventionally expected *happy ending* of the two marrying each other (as Chekhov indeed ended the 1886 story; see 5.1, and the full 1886 text of the story). (2) The *reliability* of the narrator and his narrative is both corroborated and undermined by the complex, ambivalent relationship that the ending, more than any other part of the story's text, creates between his three roles (as active protagonist, seemingly disinterested witness-observer, and reminiscing narrator). (3) Structurally, of special importance is the very last sentence, also analysed more fully in 5.1.

In a different Chekhovian context, M. A. Petróvskiï (1927) said: "Every story is, finally, a story about the meaning of its title". One need not take sides, one way or the other, on this statement's claim to general validity in order to subscribe to its applicability to this story. As stated previously in Section 5.1, it is precisely and literally "**finally**" (i.e., at its ending) that the last word — "I joked", or "I played/made that joke" — is "**about** the meaning of the story's title", "A Little Joke", with its *primacy effect* and the ending's *recency effect* significantly providing a superordinate frame for the story as a whole (fuller discussions of these matters can be found in 5.1.5 and 5.1.6 above). Moreover, if, and inasmuch as, the mature Chekhov of 1900 may be subconsciously playing his own "little joke" at the expense of the young Chekhonte of 1886 (as suggested in 5.1.5), this "joke" is about the *absence* of the *pointe* as well as the *post-pointe* from the 1886 story. This of course is another type of a *presence-through-absence* game, that Chekhov so typically likes to play. Thus, this is an additional meaning of the story's last sentence: when the narrator says, in the first person, "Now that I have grown older" he obviously refers to the time that has passed between the present of telling the story and the past when its events 'really' happened. Possibly, though, 'behind his back' stands the 1899 Chekhov as *the implied author* and the real author of the later story and says to us, as it were, '*now that I have grown older as a writer, I can no longer understand why I wrote that little trifle of a crude joke*'. Indeed, whether this suggested additional interpretation is valid or not, the meaning of the entire text is radically changed by the last paragraph, the last sentence, and the last word.

9.2 Endings in the Plays

9.2.0 Six Lines of Development in Chekhov's Construction of Endings

It seems that in his conscious pursuit of new types of ending for his texts Chekhov was much more persistent and consistent as a playwright than as a writer of short stories (indeed, as the Epigraph at the beginning of the Chapter clearly indicates, he was consciously preoccupied with the specific problem of how to end **plays**). While a study of how his stories end can hardly yield any chronological pattern indicating a clear trend or trajectory, his development as an 'ender of plays' is marked by amazing consistency in pursuit of constant goals, identifiable at least with hindsight. These endeavours of his reflect at least six major lines of development, which can be traced and followed from play to play, each later work being a step in the same direction compared with its predecessor. These lines of development can be characterised as follows:

1. The end of the *skeleton plot* becomes less and less identifiable as a single event.
2. It is less and less *climactic* in its thematic material.
3. It is more and more removed from the ending of the text.
4. Consequently, the text's actual ending is more and more subdued — i.e., less "*dramatic*" (in the popular sense of the word, see 4.1) — in its tone (of course, this is another way of characterising Chekhov's *dual, two-phased* or *post*-pointe *ending*).
5. Structurally, endings become more and more polyphonic–simultaneous.
6. The ending of every later play retroactively penetrates into the entire text preceding it more deeply than the ending a play written previously. Thus,

the ending of every later play changes the text ended by it increasingly radically, compared to what it would have been without this ending.

These claims will be demonstrated by analysis of the endings of the last five full-length plays written by Chekhov. This process can also be characterised as a relentless quest for being "to his own self true", especially as a playwright; a consistent process of the 'Chekhovisation of Chekhov'. This does not mean that in earlier stages of his play-writing he was not "true to himself", in terms of his artistic conscience. It does mean, however, that his later work, in many respects, becomes less and less comparable to the work of other great masters; that, as we shall see below, specifically the endings of his plays are more and more inimitable in their rhetorical strategy as well as in their deepest thematic implications.

9.2.1 The Ending of *Ivánov* (1889)

This play ends conventionally on all counts; it is the 'least Chekhovian' of Chekhov's last five play-endings. Let us check its position in relation to the six criteria just proposed.

1. Its final *skeleton plot* event — the protagonist's suicide — is clearly identifiable.
2. It is definitely *climactic* (see the status of suicide in the Epigraph to this Chapter).
3. It perfectly coincides with the ending of the play's text.
4. It is certainly "*dramatic*" in the sense of 4.1
5. It is *linear* rather than *polyphonic*: there are no significant lines of information running concurrently with the suicide; everything on stage at that moment is focused on this central event.
6. While shedding some light on previous events, the ending does not change their meaning radically. It is a result of a chain of preceding events, rather than a point of reflection on, or reassessment of, those events.

9.2.2 The Ending of *The Seagull* (1896)

The Seagull considerably differs from *Ivánov* almost in all these respects.

Granted, the *skeleton plot* still ends with a suicide, which is almost by definition a single identifiable climactic event; but —

The complexity of the chain of events leading up to Konstantín's suicide, which includes quite a few tentative potential climaxes, weakens the climactic effect of this ending, at least as compared to *Ivánov*.

The same suicide is quite significantly removed from the ending of the play's text, since the curtain falls on Dr. Dorn's restrained, 'in passing' account of the event, rather than on the shot itself.

No grand "*dramatic/theatrical*" gestures are made in connection with the news of the suicide (this is remarkable also because Arkádina is on stage, but her *potential* for such gestures is *unrealised*, as she is yet unaware of the fatal news).

The virtually simultaneous, *quasi-polyphonic* co-presence of quite a few lines of thought and action towards the end of the play (e.g., the lotto game and the dialogue around it; the stuffed seagull as dialogue-topic and as symbolic **and** physical presence — see Jackson 1967a); Nína's appearance and departure; the ever-changing subjects of almost all conversations, and particularly continued references to art) weakens the effect of the ending as a culmination of a single straight, ascending line.

The suicide does throw a retrospective light on the play as a whole, changing interpretative hierarchies in comparison to what they would have been without it. The least that can be said in this context about *The Seagull*'s ending is that in comparison with *Ivánov*'s it reinterprets and rearranges more elements in the entire play, when viewed in retrospect.

9.2.3 The Ending of *Uncle Vánia* (1897)

The ending of *Uncle Vánia* is another step in the same direction.

1. There is no clearly-defined ending to the *skeleton-plot*: several events have comparably justifiable claims to this status.
2. The only event that has some *climactic* ingredients in it — Vánia shooting Prof. Serebriakóv — is clearly mock-climactic, while the ending of the text of the play, if tested against pre-Chekhovian dramatic convention, is *anti-climactic*.
3. Any event describable as some kind of potential climax is much further removed from the play's ending than in *The Seagull*.
4. As regards the tone of the final episode — Sónia's last monologue — it is very low key, simulating Winner's *zero ending*. I shall return to this remarkable monologue below.
5. The very same last speech is synchronised to coincide with Telégin's playing, Máriïa Vasíl'ïevna's reading and Marína's knitting — a simultaneous orchestration of verbal and nonverbal signs, the latter highly semanticised (see discussions of parallel phenomena in Golomb 1984).
6. Retrospectively, the ending of *Uncle Vánia* serves (for the first time in Chekhov's plays) a *cyclic* function, showing at the same time that **nothing** has changed — as if none of the play's events ever happened — and that **everything** has changed: everything is even more hopeless, precisely because the old routine is back in spite, and regardless, of the play's events.

Thus, at least two thematic purposes are served: (1) several central Chekhovian themes — e.g., *unrealised potentials*, and the typical combination of failed hopes with the powerful urge to engage in hopes and aspirations regardless of their *unrealisability* (as elaborated above) — are all highlighted by this ending, and through it, retrospectively, in the play as a whole. (2) More specifically, the thematic complex of *work*, *idleness* and *rest* — as exponents of the basic life/death dichotomy — is made to call into question the extent to which it is a dichotomy in the first place. This introverted, self-reflective ending radically challenges the pre-existing, expectation-generating conventions of "*dramatic*" ending, making *Uncle Vánia* herald the "new era": whereas in *The Wood Demon* one protagonist gets married and another one shoots himself, neither event occurs in *Uncle Vánia*. Thus, Chekhov the playwright answers the joking remark of Chekhov the letter-writer (quoted in the Epigraph), in all seriousness: there **are** ways out, after all, and Chekhov the playwright has discovered at least one of them.

9.2.4 The Ending of *Three Sisters* (1901)

The ending of *Three Sisters* is a large step in the direction outlined so far.

1. Identifying the end of the *skeleton plot* here is at least as difficult as in *Uncle Vánia*: the duel offstage, the various exits and final farewells of the various characters — all have a claim to this label, and thus undermine and disintegrate any potential crystallisation of a single focus that would qualify as the one and only ending.
2. Care is taken to suppress — or at least to restrain — any sense of *climax*, even where it potentially exists (e.g., the duel, Másha's and Vershínin's final farewell).
3. The final *tableau*, virtually tantamount to a formally separate epilogue, is more clearly removed from the end of the *skeleton-plot* (whatever its precise identification) than in any previous Chekhov play. In fact, Dr. Chebutýkin's report of Túsenbach's death is, both psychologically and in terms of Dramatic functionality, an elaboration on Dr. Dorn's report of Konstantín's death at the end of *The Seagull* (this is not the last time that, at some point in the course of a later play, Chekhov alludes to an ending-technique he had used in an earlier one, **as if** to assess his development as a playwright; see 9.2.5. below).
4. The tone is introverted and reflective — all speakers thinking out loud.
5. A genuinely contrapuntal conception characterises this *finale*, since the carefully synchronised verbal and nonverbal (visual and auditory) lines — each with its own message — create a definite simulation of musical polyphony: the last spoken words of each sister and Chebutýkin take turn alternately and sound almost simultaneously with the semantically loaded visual stimuli of happily-smiling Kulýgin and of Andréï pushing the baby pram, and with the auditory stimuli produced by the military band dying in the distance. This contrapuntal polyphony, displaying multi-dimensional, multi-sensory and multi-medium heterogeneous *tableau*, conveys a complex though unified vision, a unique fusion of closure and openness. All the verbal, visual and auditory elements in this ending are highly semanticised, and each of them closes a circle that consists of several points of reference throughout the play. Thus, Kulýgin's almost triumphant happiness (while trying his pathetic best to be of some help to Másha in carrying her hat and cape) is, *inter alia*, a wordless reminder of the painful discord between the radically different ways in which he and Másha experience their marriage and the crisis that it has just barely withstood (it is also a reminder

of Andréï's explicit remark about Kulýgin's contentment with the departure of the brigade and the collapse of his own marriage); the music played by the military band obviously closes the circle begun at the beginning of the play with the mention of the band playing at the father's funeral, thus constituting a nonverbal reminder of the late General Prózorov's *presence through absence*; Andréï's pushing the baby pram also serves as a silent reminder of his subordinate role in his marriage, and the powerful *presence through absence* of Natásha at this moment (elsewhere this is often reversed: the sisters are more related to *absence* whereas Natásha is more *present*); and similar observations can be applied to every single detail in this unusually dense and delicate ending of the play.

6. Thus, the retrospective function of the ending is unprecedentedly radical, subtle and complex, blending as it does **conclusive finality** with **inconclusive openness**: it is, *inter alia*, a very powerful, though implicit, statement about the conclusiveness of the inconclusive in human life, which is one of the reasons for its crucial role in the retrospective re-interpretation of the entire play.

Indeed, the play's ending requires a more detailed analysis. Its vital importance is epitomised in the combination of the sisters' quest for meaning-and-knowledge, brought to a head with Ól'ga's very last sentence, with Chebutýkin's nonsensical refrain — "Ta-ra-ra-búmbiïa" etc. — followed by the significantly meaningless "it's all the same". The former is still further distilled and crystallised in Ól'ga's (and the whole play's) very last sentence, «Если бы знать», usually rendered in English as "If only we knew", or "If only we could know" (The latter is the English title given by Harvey Pitcher to his translation of Vladímir Katáïev's collection of papers on Chekhov — see Kataev 2002). This may be just for the best for English; yet, for the purpose of the specific verbal subtlety discussed here perhaps a cumbersome '*If (only) it were possible to know*', or '*If (only) one could know*' — i.e., without the pronoun *we* — would be more precise and functional. When Ól'ga utters this sentence, which is a fluent and colloquially credible turn-of-phrase in Russian, she is indeed referring to the private and family situation in which she and her sisters find themselves towards the end of the play (i.e., there is an implicit *we* throughout all the sisters' last *répliques*. Moreover, in the preceding sentences Ól'ga uses the pronoun *we* **explicitly** several times, which means that the family-*we* is what (and who) she has in mind. However, when Chekhov makes her use the more impersonal form for the very last sentence, omitting the first-person-plural pronoun, he retains the credibility of her family-centred point of view, but at the same time he provides his audience with the broadest perspective humanly possible. The two perspectives — the Prózorov-specific and the universally-human — complement each other to produce an ending that crowns the entire play with awe-inspiring magnitude on the *outer plane*, namely in the discourse between Chekhov (author/addresser) and us (audience/addressees), beyond the consciousnesses of the staged speakers. This ending highlights the duality of the narrowest and broadest perspectives, that is so typical of this play: thus, "*philosophising*" speeches, as well as seemingly cursory remarks elsewhere, keep suggesting to the audience that this specific 19ᵗʰ-century Russian family scene is indeed just that — i.e., a specific 19ᵗʰ-century Russian family scene — but at the same time it is also a parable about human history, destiny and existential meaning (this point is elaborated throughout the Book). The ending's blend of **closed infinity and finite openness** encapsulates this quality in the play as a whole, whose deep oxymoronic structure is not designed to display intellectual ingenuity, but to reflect the boundless complexity of the subject-matter as fully and as honestly as possible.

With extreme economy this last sentence manages to convey the human thirst to understand and to know, to make sense of life — a thirst that forever remains powerful and unquenchable, in spite, or even because, of the poignant realisation that it is doomed to remain unquenched. The images, auditory and visual, that are simultaneously projected at the theatre spectators (concurrently with this multiply meaningful combination of the texts spoken by Chebutýkin and Ól'ga), function as samples of the unexplainable absurdities that one desperately **wants** to know and understand. The last word, «знать» — "[to] know" — manages to tie together numerous thematic threads in the entire play, whether subtle and subliminal or obvious and explicit.[15]

The common denominator of these is either the overt presence of the verb *to know* and its derivatives, or its covert presence through words and/or phrases evoking its semantic field. The monosyllable «бы», which precedes the mono-syllabic «знать» ("[to] know") is untranslatable as such into English.[16] It is indeed a minimal meaningful unit, but it serves as shorthand for the quintessence of much of the broadest semantic load of the entire play. Thus, these two last monosyllabic words join forces in the production of the described composite semantic effect: absolute, finite knowledge is the object of powerful wishes and burning desires of humanity, encapsulated in the verb "to know"; however, this knowledge resides in the sphere of 'the unattainable would-be' of life, properly expressed in language through a *conditional-hypothetical* tense, encapsulated in the Russian language through this monosyllabic particle, «бы» (pronounced /by/ as these graphical characters are realised phonetically according to the *Guide*, 2.1 and 2.2, §29 and Note 21).

The entire play is saying to us, then — primarily through its ending — that the human need, the desire, and the thirst for knowledge (in the broadest sense and applicability of that word) is unquenchable in spite, or perhaps because, of our knowledge that it will never be satisfied. We know for sure that we do not know; moreover, we know for sure that we are doomed never to know in the future what we do not know now; but, regardless, being human, we also know that we are eter-nally doomed to **want to know**. In short, the knowledge that we won't know does not quench the desire to know, and the desire to know, however strong, does not detract from the knowledge that we will never know. Thus Chekhov offers the most complete knowledge of the human condition; no one, it seems, will ever know better.

Coming back to the compositional aspect of this ending: it is through the play as a whole that the ending acquires its final meanings; but it is the ending that retrospectively establishes the ultimate balances and hierarchies in the play. The "new era" in the history of Drama, introduced through Chekhov's "devising new endings for plays" (see Epigraph to this Chapter), is firmly established with *Three Sisters*.

9.2.5 The Ending of *The Cherry Orchard* (1904):[17] Exit Chekhov the Writer

Since *The Cherry Orchard* is the last work of fiction that Chekhov ever committed to paper, it is often considered, with hindsight and sometimes without proper corroboration, his own literary ending, his artistic 'last will and testament' in many respects (for a critical and sober view of this tradition, see Senderovich 1994); however, simply because of its date, it cannot be denied the status of his last demonstration of how "to devise new endings for plays". And, indeed, *The Cherry Orchard*'s ending is innovative even in strictly Chekhovian terms, let alone in the historical context of Chekhov's predecessors. It is easy to examine this ending according to the 'six lines of development' proposed earlier on in this Chapter; such a procedure is bound to yield results similar to the ones just shown in previous plays, namely, that on all six counts Chekhov has made further steps in the same direction in which he had moved from play to play until — and including — *Three Sisters* in a process termed above as *The 'Chekhovisation' of Chekhov*, because it is characterised by moving further away from pre-Chekhov traditions of ending plays and developing a more unique, unprecedented types of endings (and, indeed, of writing plays in other significant respects, notably the building of *conflicts* — as shown above, especially 4.2.3). Yet, the procedure will not be repeated here, in order to stress the fact that in *The Cherry Orchard* alone Chekhov has covered such a distance in that very same direction, that a difference in degree has become a difference in kind. I shall concentrate, then, on the most unique features of this particular ending.

In a conventional, pre-Chekhovian sense, this ending is singularly *static* and *non-climactic*. The play itself provides an unprecedented number of alternative *skeleton-plot* endings, and they are increasingly removed from the end of the text. A case can be made for a much more far-reaching claim — namely, that the *skeleton-plot* ends with the auction in which Lopákhin buys the estate offstage, an event reported as early as somewhat before the end of Act 3. According to such an analysis, then, the very end of Act 3 and the entire Act 4 function as *post-pointe codas*, beyond the limits of the *skeleton plot*. This view of the play can be corroborated by the striking resemblance in tone and function between Ánia's monologue addressed to her mother Ranévskaïa at the very end of Act 3 and Sónia's monologue addressed to her uncle Vánia at the very end of *Uncle Vánia*. Indeed, in *The Cherry Orchard*'s Act 3 (!) Chekhov supplies us with an *Uncle Vánia*-like ending — once again, as if alluding to his previous achievement, only to contrast it with the significantly subtler and more sophisticated ending that he has in store for us at the end of the present text.[18] And, indeed, within this last *coda* at the end of Act 4 there are several further '*cadenza/coda* relationships', embedded within each other.

It is my contention that, prior to the play's real ending — i.e., the very last words in this play, which happen to be the very last words in his very last fictional text — there are at least eleven[19] **Potential Endings** (I am using here a different font for structural clarity of my argument) that Chekhov suggests to us, one after the other, in the last two-or-so pages of the actual text of *The Cherry Orchard* (in fact, there are several more than eleven; yet, to avoid hair-splitting, not all will he specified here). These Potential Endings are unique manifestations of Chekhov's principle of *unrealised potential*: each of them is "a road not taken", an option for an ending that Chekhov decided to adopt, but he does leave the tracks visible on the entire trail, so that we can follow all his moves. These *present absences* of abandoned endings are milestones in Chekhov's road to accomplishment on stage. **Retrospectively, each of these *Potential Endings* turns the play into a different one.**

This is possible specifically in *The Cherry Orchard*, more than in any Chekhov play written previously, mainly because of one of its unique characteristics: *The Cherry Orchard* has several carefully balanced, equally central themes — e.g., changes in social and economic conditions and hierarchies in Russia (with specific emphasis on interrelationships between classes in Russian society and the changing role of land ownership in establishing a person's social standing); clashes, contrasts, analogies, interactions and interrelationships between (a) generations (parents and offspring onstage, past and future generations offstage) and ages (childishness and adulthood/maturity), (b) members of families, (c) human types and character traits, (d) men and women, (e) old and new, (f) old and young, (g) indigenous and foreign, (h) the predetermined and the arbitrary, (i) the real and the imaginary, (j) the comic and the serious, etc. etc. (these pairs of opposites have been given here in arbitrary order, and quite a few additional themes, not mentioned here, can also be found in this play). No other Chekhov play has such a variety of themes with comparable equilibrium between them, without any predominant theme, or even cluster of themes, over and above any other one(s). Thus, this radical retroactive penetration of the ending into the text preceding it is potentially — and, in the final analysis, also factually — a way to determine and reorganise hierarchies of significance between various themes that vie, as it were, for prominence: all other things being equal, a theme that is foregrounded by the text's ending becomes much more central in the play as a whole, compared with a theme that is ignored or played down by/in the ending. Thus the ending, far from being arbitrary, plays the part of an 'arbitrator' that assigns each theme its place in the final hierarchy of centrality.

Indeed, a major reason for the uniqueness of *The Cherry Orchard* among Chekhov's plays is that it ends with a long series of *potential endings*, each of which could reasonably fulfil the position of the final ending, and each of which is connected organically with previous elements in the text. Each of the endings provided at the end of the play is related to a different theme or aspect, and lends its *recency-effect*-generating support to one (or more) of them, thereby contributing to its foregrounding at the expense of one or more of the other, comparable ones: when the balance between themes is so delicate and precarious, the ending could be decisive in tilting it one way or the other.

Before offering a detailed analysis of *Potential Endings* (*PEs*) supplied at the end of Act 4, I would like to stress that Act 3 provides several *PEs* of its own: one can just imagine what a play *The Cherry Orchard* would have been if it had ended with Lopákhin's triumphant return from the auction (there are several *PEs* even within that scene, within his speech and the reaction to it), or with Ánia's monologue addressed to Ranévskaïa. Act 4 in its entirety, then, can be seen as a *post-pointe ending*, introducing the longest and most radical wedge between the ending of the *skeleton plot* at the end of Act 3 and the ending of the text at the end of Act 4.

In the following analysis each *Potential Ending* (*PE*) of the play's Act 4 is identified by its number, as provided in the Appendix to this Chapter. The analysis aims at assessing the hypothetical contribution of each such *PE* to the play as a whole, assuming that this was the play's real ending. Of course, these *PEs* do not supplant each other; each of them is a hypothetical ending that appears after the previous ones, interacting with them, so that later *PEs* are always inclusive of earlier ones. The final, actual ending, is of course all-inclusive.

PE 1 stresses the childishness and helplessness of Gáïev and Ranévskaïa. It is enough to imagine what a play *The Cherry orchard* would have been if the curtain had been down on *PE* 1, even without changing as much as a single word in the entire text that precedes this ending: it would establish the factual–practical change of ownership of the orchard as the central point or theme of the play as a whole (reinforcing its centrality as established at the end of Act 3), and, by comparison, would play down all its other aspects — psychological, emotional, even social (etc.). It would have made a decisive contribution to making *The Cherry Orchard* a play about the emergence of the new class of money-aristocracy as the most central theme.

PEs 2 & 4 (each in its own way, *PE* 4's effect modified by the prior presence of *PE* 3) stress Lopákhin's status as the new owner, and his decisiveness is opposed to the aristocrats' childish and dreamy helplessness.[20] In *PE* 4 Chekhov makes Lopákhin distort the standard Russian word for *see you later* to give it a comic, slang-like twist, perhaps also a silly one; this subtlety is ignored in most translations (I have made an attempt to preserve it by translating *see-ye-later*). Obviously, *PE* 4 thus relates to the play's generic subtitle, *comedy*: if it had been allowed to finish the text, the play's comic elements would have been more predominant, and the nostalgic weeping of Gáïev and Ranévskaïa would have been seen through a comic reflection.

PE 3 foregrounds the young generation's point of view, and — like the preceding and following *PEs* — it is loaded with the semantic weight that would have enabled it to penetrate the preceding text and change hierarchies there, retroactively, if Chekhov had decided to use it as the play's real ending. Let us just imagine what a play would *The Cherry Orchard* have been, if it had ended with "Good bye, old life! [*Curtain*]" and/or with "Welcome, new life! [*Curtain*]". Even without changing an iota in the preceding four Acts, *The Cherry Orchard* ending with these words would have been a play primarily and predominantly about social–historical change. *The Cherry Orchard* as we know it, to be sure, includes important references to changes in Russian society; moreover, these social and economic themes are more prominent in *The Cherry Orchard* than in any other Chekhov play. Yet, this play is definitely not **primarily and predominantly** about the social topic. This statement is valid only because Chekhov did not end the play at *PE 3*, which means that he **refused** to assign the role of the play's ending to *PE 3*.

PE 5 brings out the touching and credibly nostalgic aspect of the previous owners' attitude. If ended here, *The Cherry Orchard* would have given the final word to the sentiments of this vanishing breed of people, and their point of view, and their sorrow — genuinely sincere, and yet affected at the same time, in an inimitable Chekhovian blend — would have counterbalanced, or even outweighed, the approaches of Lopákhin and the two youngsters. In such a hypothetical case — again, without changing anything in the preceding text of the entire play up to this point — *The Cherry Orchard* would have been much closer to a tear-jerker; it would have still been focused on social change, but the emotional balance would have tilted heavily towards the Gáïev siblings, mourning their lost childhood and values, their family's spiritual *heritage* (not only their material *inheritance*; see Chapter 11). If *PE 5* had been the real ending, it would have also served Chekhov's poetics in exercising *emotional restraint*: the stage directions are clear in instructing the actors to quell their emotions, too embarrassed to wear their heart upon their sleeves and show them for what they are. *PE 5* would have made quite a powerful ending in a play designed to highlight the sentiments of the siblings' generation, filtered effectively through the aristocratic decorum of *emotional restraint*, above and beyond all its other themes and components. *The Cherry Orchard*, however, is not such a play: to be sure, these sentiments exist in it, alongside others; but if they had been granted the status of shaping the play's ending, their partial prominence would have turned into superordinate predominance. Obviously, this is not what Chekhov had in mind.

PE 6 adds Ranévskaïa's words to the silent *tableau* of *PE 5*. These words are definitely much more sentimental and less restrained than *PE 5*, so that Chekhov was much less likely to allow this *PE* to become a tear-jerking real ending. Its very *presence*, then, underscores its status as "the road not taken", i.e., its *absence* from the real ending of the play. In other words, Chekhov's refusal to give it the status of ending casts it into the role of *unrealised potential ending*. True, the same applies to all the *PE*s; however, in this particular case the *potential/non-realisation* balance is unusually tense because of the restraining power required to counterbalance this momentary outlet to sentimentality that Chekhov grants here to Ranévskaïa. Indeed, he goes out of his usual ways as an extremely restrained artist to humour this unrestrained character.

In short, *PE 6* throws into bold relief the substantially different road that Chekhov did take. If this had been the real ending, nostalgic sentimentality, with it subjective frankness and sincerity, is allowed into Chekhov's characterisation of characters, but it cannot be allowed to dominate his composition of texts: Chekhov is also a master in presenting emotions seemingly dispassionately. Ranévskaïa, then — unrestrained though she is as a personage — is eventually restrained by her textual context. Indeed, the sentimentality of this *réplique* is both a *realised* and an *unrealised potential*: *realised*, because it is allowed into the text; *unrealised*, because it remains a *PE* that is not allowed to be realised in the role of the ending of the play.

*PE*s 7–8, appearing as they do after all six preceding *PE*s, *polyphonically* and *antiphonally* contrast the two generations' outlooks (with different emphases and dosages). If the play had ended here, no one acquainted with Chekhov's plays until (and including) *Three Sisters* would have suggested that anything is missing or deficient at this point. Indeed, in terms of ending technique, *PE 8*, inclusive of *PE 7*, reflects the mature phase that Chekhov had reached in *Three Sisters*: the phase of the *'polyphonic' thematic recapitulation*, rounding off the entire text and tying up all the threads. *PE 7–8*, then, represents his *'Three Sisters* phase', just as Ánia's monologue after the auction at the end of Act 3, with its resemblance to Sónia's last monologue, represented his *'Uncle Vánia* phase' in the process of perfecting his play-endings. The point is that Sónia's monologue comes at the end of the entire play, ending its Act 4, whereas Ánia's comes at the end of Act 3 and precedes an entire Act. In other words, Act 4 of *The Cherry Orchard* in its entirety — in this context of Chekhov's development as creator of plays' endings — is beyond the reach of the *'Uncle Vánia* phase'. The *'Three Sisters*-like' polyphonic exchange within *The Cherry Orchard* comes much later, towards the end (but not at the very end) of Act 4 of that last play of Chekhov's. Thus, by his refusal to 'copy and paste' his ending technique from previous plays, by just pausing for a short while to reminisce, retracing and recalling his previous endings and then moving on, he is, as it were, saying to the audience, *'Look here at the journey I have made: this is how I ended a play seven years ago, now this is how I did it six and three years ago; that's good and fine, but look at what I am capable of doing **now**; you can compare and see the difference for yourselves'*.[21] There is no better way to appreciate the innovation of *The Cherry Orchard*'s ending than to contrast it so tangibly with Chekhov's previous attempts to "devise new endings for plays".

And indeed, *PE*s 8–11 plus the real ending of the play are the specific invention/innovation of *The Cherry Orchard,* carrying it beyond all Chekhov's previous work and giving a new meaning, more radical than ever, to his premonition of *opening a new era through devising new endings for plays*. *PE 10* — the option of ending the play with a **silent** appearance of Firs — already does the trick of a radically new type of play-ending (it is carefully balanced with *PE 5*, both being silent, yet highly semanticised *tableaux* that make an impact even before words are added to them). The very presence of Firs in the locked-up house is a total surprise; it would have been an effective, innovating ending, which, to be sure, could earn Chekhov the acclaim of the "deviser of new endings" that "opens a new era". Indeed, it is hard for anyone acquainted with the play to imagine being ignorant of it, and evaluate *PE 10* as if we do not know that this is, once again, "the road not taken". Firs's silent presence is indeed a powerful twist, and Chekhov, as clearly implied in his stage directions, allows it time to sink in within the audience's minds before letting Firs speak.

But now Firs speaks; one can listen to every single word he is saying and see how well-chosen and functional it is; how, true to character, this old, dying breed of servants-with-dignity embodies the death of *decorum* as well as responsibility and commitment, among people of all ages and classes in whom these qualities are sorely missed. His worry about Gáïev's choice of wrong coat for the road is sharply contrasted, through poignant lack of reciprocity, with everybody's (and mainly the masters') irresponsibility and carelessness towards Firs. His quiet, acquiescent lament of life not lived, can be applied, in very different ways, to every personage, and thus, by implication, to humanity as a whole (of course, this is Chekhov's discourse behind Firs's back).

Chekhov's endings of the late plays have much in common, but *The Cherry Orchard* is undoubtedly the most radically different from anything written before (and, actually, also since) in world Drama; it is, in short, the most Chekhovian of all endings. Looking at the succession of **Potential Endings** in the play, one can evaluate this 'parade' of multiple endings and characterise their uniqueness. A far cry from merely rounding-off and recapitulating, these endings' retroactive function lies mainly in the reshuffling of previous hierarchies: through their accumulation they foreground and underscore a pervasive, but latent thematic streak in the play, namely, the theme of mundane, everyday metaphorical misfiring-without-shooting;[22] of missing targets and opportunities in life through carelessness and indefensible-yet-non-malicious negligence, through the irresponsibility that makes life itself and everything in it slip through one's fingers. By his very presence at the end, as well as by everything that he says in this last *réplique* of his, Firs embodies and epitomises this theme, retrospectively throwing into bold relief almost everything in the play — whether central or peripheral, farcical or sombre — as being organised around it. Consider, for instance, the loss of the estate and its circumstances; Lopákhin's missing Ranévskaïa's arrival-train by falling asleep; his failure to propose to Vária (or at least to reject or refuse this idea explicitly); money as a nonsensical lost-and-found commodity as personified in Píshchik; practically everything about the character of Charlótta, especially her monologue opening Act 2);[23] the family's losing the formula or recipe for making cherry comfiture; Yepikhódov's slapstick-like "twenty two disasters";[24] the lack of proper attention that must have been instrumental in the drowning of the child Grísha; and, last but by no means least, leaving Firs in the locked-up house — the latter two showing us that even the most benevolent negligence can prove criminal through its potentially fatal consequences (by the way, the general validity of this principle is stressed by the fact that of the two helpless victims one is very young and the other is very old). Thus, the trusting and trustworthy Firs is the one who ends up as the final victim of his masters' irresponsibility: it is he — rather than the theatrical, incorrigibly unreliable Ranévskaïa — who pays the price of being "sold with the orchard", in the most literal sense, while making no grand gestures or theatrical declarations to this effect. She exclaims "Sell me with the orchard!" without any genuine commitment to this declaration, which rings particularly hollow once we have the benefit of hindsight at the end of the play: at that point "selling Firs with the orchard" can be contrasted with Ranévskaïa's leaving all her responsibilities behind, using Ánia's money to join her nonentity of a lover in Paris. And perhaps the most elusive slip and missing-of-the-target of them all is the absolute failure of **all** characters to deplore, even to properly notice, this irresponsibility.

Thus the structurally 'strategic' position of Firs's last appearance in the final *coda*, producing the play's *recency effect*, makes its contribution to the recognition of this complex of missed-opportunities-and-goals–targets as a central, *super-ordinate organising theme*. The most comprehensive and consistent understanding of the play can be called in English its 'miss-interpretation', an interpretation that focuses on the theme of *missing*. All social, family, interpersonal and psychological relationships are at least partly subsumed under it, whereas it is not subsumed under them. The overall centrality of this theme, then, is firmly established by the play's composition and clinched by its ending.

Typically of the later Chekhov, the very last word uttered on stage — the quintessence of the ultimate *recency effect* with which the audience takes its farewell from the play — is carefully chosen and multiply functional. This word — «недотёпа»[25] — is prepared in advance both as part of Firs's characterisation and as part of the entire household's vocabulary (for which they give him credit). Typically once again, no one of the users of this word is aware of how appropriate and totally applicable it is to him/herself and his/her type of people: a case can be made for most of the play's personages (curiously, with the possible exception of Firs himself) to be labelled *good-for-nothing, gawk, nincompoop*, etc. But the closural function of this word's end-position lies first and foremost in its ability to skilfully and subliminally epitomise this central theme of the play's. It is obviously made to resonate in the ears of the audience, simultaneously with the semanticised nonverbal sounds of the breaking string and the axe cutting the trees. Thus, once again, Chekhov gives a misleading air of coincidence and randomness (as part of the old Firs's mumblings) to the carefully designed, meticulously planned ultimate emphasis on coincidence, randomness, negligence and carelessness as a central theme in the play. In short: practically nothing is missed in an interpretation that focuses on this theme of *missing*.

In other words, *the inner/fictional plane* (what happens among characters within the confines of a work's fictional world) interacts with *the outer/rhetorical plane* (what happens along the axis author ➞ text ➞ audience, as explained previously) in a typically Chekhovian way (see similar cases in Golomb 1987). On the former plane, of course, it is entirely by accident on Firs's part that he ends this particular soliloquy with this word, that he is so used to uttering anyway. In this sense Firs — far from being a "duffer" or "gawk" in the way he discharges his duties in the Gáïev household — has partly become one (through old age and partial deafness) in the use of words, and thus this particular word is self-characterising in more ways than one. Yet, on the latter plane, here as in many other places in Chekhov's work, it is hard not to fall into the trap of his image as a creator of random, unmotivated details. Chekhov is far from being a *gawk* in the *paradigmatic* and *syntagmatic* planning of the positioning of every chosen word in its chosen place); as far as his work is concerned, his targets and opportunities are hardly ever missed through careless irresponsibility; everything happens by design, and very little, if anything, slips through his authorial fingers.

The conscientious responsibility and the controlled planning of Chekhov the artist in organising his texts is diametrically opposed to the inactions of the *duffer*s and *gawk*s that inhabit *The Cherry Orchard*. Thematically as well as compositionally, the final exit of Chekhov the writer — the ending of his last written work — is a powerful demonstration of how unbridgeable this gap is. It is a gap analogous to that between Chekhov as an ultimate **realiser of his own potentials**, on the one hand, and his insistence on creating fictional personages doomed to *unrealised potentials*, on the other hand. These are two sides of one of the paradoxical coins of the inexhaustibly complex nature of the Chekhov phenomenon.

9.3 Exit Chekhov the Man, Or: How to End a Life and *A Life*?[26]

> I have a disease:
> 'Autobiographophobia'.
> (Chekhov in a letter to Rossolimo, 1899)

Although such statements as the one quoted as Epigraph to this Section should be taken with a grain of salt, such a declaration of "disease" should at least help to caution us against drawing hasty analogies between Chekhov's work and events in his life. Moreover, it is both inhuman — and in the case of Chekhov also out of character — to even remotely imply that he staged his own death to conform to the *post-pointe coda*s typical of his poetics in ending stories and plays, or that such an analogy was created by some fatalistic or providential force. However, coincidences do happen. Chekhov's 'famous last words' — the final *cadenza* of his life — were, by all accounts, *Ich sterbe* (in German "I am dying"), which he is reported to have said to the German doctor who treated him on his death bed in Badenweiler, a small resort-town in the German Black Forest, in July 1904. This is easily and correctly describable as true to character: the insistence on factual precision in a diagnosis made by a man trained to be a physician; the absolute and relentless commitment to the naked truth and lack of any attempt to whitewash the harsh situation; the terseness and economy of expression; the conscious control and presence-of-mind that led him to speak in German (which he hardly knew, see below) to the German doctor — all of these are typical character-traits of Chekhov the writer and the man.

The need for 'famous last words' — marking a conventional, climactic and rounded closure — must have led at least two biographers, David Magarshack and Borís Záitsev to describe Chekhov's last moments as follows:

> His last words were "I am dying";[27] then, in a very low voice, to the doctor in German: *"Ich sterbe"*. (Magarshack 1952, 388)

Both biographers (Záitsev's similar description, in Russian, is not quoted here) have acted like numerous Chekhovian personages in deluding both themselves and others. For them, indeed, "those damn endings just don't come out" (see Epigraph to this Chapter) because, apparently, the real end of Chekhov's life happened to resemble the *post-pointe 'zero'-endings*, as one can learn from the only two eye-witness accounts — by Ól'ga Leonárdovna Knipper-Chekhova, Chekhov's wife, and the Russian student Rabeneck — which are, in this point, dovetailed in the way they complement and corroborate each other. Thus, Ól'ga Knipper-Chekhova (1972, 62):

Antón Pávlovich sat up, and somehow in a **loud, clear voice** [emphasis added] said to the doctor in German (he knew very little German): *"Ich sterbe"* [...] then he picked up the glass [of champagne], turned his face to me, [...] and said: "it's long time since I last had champagne" [...] and soon enough was silent forever.

This account of the turn of events, corroborated by Rabeneck's (1958) eye-witness evidence, is adopted in most major biographies (e.g., Hingley 1950, 247, and 1976, 314–315; Simmons 1963, 638; Troyat 1986, 332; Rayfield 1997, 596; Callow 1998, 402–403). The picture that comes out of Ól'ga Knipper-Chekhova's and Rabeneck's accounts, then, is a reversal of the order of events as recited by Záïtsev and Magarshack. Of course, the facts of the matter are by now, more than a hundred years since, of little consequence; but the psychological need to invent illusory 'proper' *recency effects*, even if reality fails to supply them, is significant: it is an epitome of that quest for (self-) delusion, that Chekhov dedicated his life as a writer to expose. Likewise, the two biographers' insistence that Chekhov uttered the last German words "in a very low voice", despite explicit evidence to the contrary — presumably, because 'famous last words' on a consumptive patient's death-bed are not supposed to be loud — is probably similarly motivated. It seems that psychological necessity, even in professional biographers, is the mother of invention... By taking the liberty, so typical of Chekhov's characters and so opposed to his own character, to twist the order of events in order to serve 'elegance' at the expense of truth, the two biographers have quite unwittingly shown how — admittedly by accident — genuinely Chekhovian were Chekhov's last moments and his death. Troyat (1986, 332) apparently could not help winding up his description with the remark "[Chekhov] had passed from life to death with characteristic simplicity". Indeed, Záïtsev and Magarshack seem to have behaved in a way that vindicates Chekhov's observations of human beings.

Chekhov's real last words were an everyday sentence, devoid of any closural grandeur. The Chekhovian double-ending had its ultimate, sad, and genuinely coincidental and 'undevised' triumph on the 16th of July 2004 in Badenweiler.

Прощай, Чеховская эра! [Good bye, Chekhov's Era!]

Appendix to Chapter 9:
Potential Ending(s) of *The Cherry Orchard*[28]

GÁÏEV [*overcome with emotion, afraid that he is going to cry*]: The train... the station... Shot to the centre, the white into the corner...[29]

RANÉVSKAÏA: Let's go! {*PE* 1}

LOPÁKHIN: Is everyone here? No one left behind? [*Locking the left door.*] There are things stored there. I must lock up. Let's go! {*PE* 2}

ÁNIA: Good bye, house! Good bye, old life!

TROFÍMOV: Welcome, new life! [*Exits with Ánia*] {*PE* 3}

[*Vária looks around the room, and exits slowly. Exit Yásha*
and Charlótta, with her lapdog]

    LOPÁKHIN: Till spring, then. Go on, everybody. Bye-bye,
               see-ye-later   {*PE* 4}

    [*exits*]

[*Ranévskaïa and Gáïev remain alone. As if they have been waiting*
for this moment, they throw their arms round each other's necks
and sob with restraint, quietly, afraid of being overheard]   {*PE* 5}

    GÁÏEV [*in despair*]: My sister, my dear sister…
    RANÉVSKAÏA: Oh, my dearest, lovely orchard! My beautiful orchard!
My life, my youth, my happiness! Good bye! Good-bye!   {*PE* 6}
    ÁNIA'S VOICE [*calling gaily*]: Mother!
    TROFÍMOV'S VOICE [*gaily, with excitement*]: Hey there!   {*PE* 7}
    RANÉVSKAÏA: One last look at the walls, the windows! Our dear
mother used to walk in this room…
    GÁÏEV: My sister, my dear sister…   {*PE* 8}
    ÁNIA'S VOICE: Mother!
    TROFÍMOV'S VOICE: Hey there!
    RANÉVSKAÏA: Coming! [*They exit*]   {*PE* 9}
The stage is empty. There is the sound of the doors being locked up,
and the carriages driving away. It grows quiet. Through the silence
one can hear the dull and lonely thud of an axe on a tree. Footsteps
are heard. Firs appears in the doorway on the right. He is dressed,
as always, in his long coat and white waistcoat, with slippers
on his feet. He is ill.   {*PE* 10}

    FIRS [*Going to the door and trying the handle*]: Locked. They've gone.
[*Sitting down on the sofa*] They've forgotten about me. Never mind… I'll
just sit here a bit… And it seems that Leoníd Andréich did not put on his
overcoat, went away in his cloth jacket. [*sighs worriedly*]. And I was off
guard… Young wood, green wood! [*mumbles incoherently*] Life has gone
by as if I'd never lived. [*Lying down*] I'll lie down a bit. There's no strength
left in you, none at all, nothing. Ah, you …
nincompoop [*lies motionless*]   {*PE* 11}

[*A distant sound is heard that seems to come from the sky, like that of a*
breaking string, dying away, melancholy. All is still again, but far away in
the orchard one can hear the thud of an axe against a tree.]

    Curtain

THE PLAY'S REAL ENDING

Notes

1 English version primarily based on Senelick 2005, p. 411; this Epigraph, in a slightly

different English version, appears in Kataev [Katáïev] 2006, p. 193. Hercher and Urban 2012, p. 93's version is much less accurate.

2 The present Chapter complements earlier discussions of this matter, especially in Chapter 3, which opened the Book's 'Inner Circle' with a focus on beginnings of Chekhov's texts. Now the present Chapter offers a complementary focus on their endings. The two Chapters tend to reflect each other quasi-symmetrically, focusing on these *effects* of beginnings and endings. The present Chapter is partly indebted to Gornfel'd 1939, especially its focus on Chekhov's calculated design of the misleadingly 'endless' endings (especially p. 288).

3 At this point in the discussion a rough binary opposition contrasting '*strong*' and '*weak*' types of ending is functional enough. I am fully aware of differences between *surprise* and *climax* (the former need not be climactic, and the latter need not be surprising), yet at this stage the basic distinction between the 'strength' of both of them, on the one hand, and the 'weakness' of *zero-endings*, on the other hand, is the focus of the argument: *climaxes* as well as *surprises* are 'strong' for thematic and compositional reasons alike, i.e., their *recency effect* derives from their position at the end of the text as well as from their inner content, whereas 'weak' endings produce *recency effect* through their final position only; yet, paradoxically, 'weak' endings are often surprising because they frustrate a universal expectation in readers and spectators for a 'strong' ending, for a final 'bang' rather than a '*whimper*'. Besides, at least at first encounter with a story or play, all endings interact with one's curiosity regarding 'how will it end?', which of course adds to the strength of any ending as such, whether it satisfies or frustrates the expectations leading up to it. The terms *syntagmatic* and *paradigmatic* are used as in Jakobson 1960.

4 In music, to be sure, *codas* are not always 'weak' (consider, for instance, the powerful *codas* that end Beethoven's symphonies № 5 and 8). The term 'Light-weight *codas*' refers here to an ending like the two last bars of Mozart's *Violin Concerto no. 5 in A Major*. Highly relevant to this discussion is the etymology of *coda* — the Italian for *tail*, implying something added-on rather than an integral, organic part of the 'body' (of course, this is a distorted anthropomorphic view of the nature and [lack of] function of animals' tails). A major aim of this Chapter is to demonstrate how misleading it is to equate the late Chekhov's endings with a *coda* in music: indeed, Chekhov's development, notably as a playwright, is reflected — *inter alia*, of course — in endings that retroactively penetrate more deeply into the texts preceding them, producing crucial intra-textual impact.

5 The stories discussed in this Section are very well known in Chekhov's corpus, and have been translated into English several times; they can be found in more than one collection of Chekhov's stories in translation, and are free to read on the web (e.g., "Ván'ka" on http://www.online-literature.com/anton_chekhov/1196/; "Sleepy" on http://www.online-literature.com/anton_chekhov/1248/); as for "A Little Joke", new translations into English of its two versions are printed as Appendix to Chapter 5.

6 In all matters of Chekhovian (in)significance Cathy Popkin's 1993 study is of utmost significance.

7 The story is usually dated 1888, which is the year of its first publication in the newspaper *Rússkaïa Gazéta*. However, its revised ending, prepared for subsequent publication in the 1890 volume *Khmúrye Liúdi* [*Gloomy People*], gives the story its definitive form; therefore 1890 is the correct date of the final text of the story, especially its ending.

8 Here, as in many other cases, Chekhov's title is a challenge to translators. The original Russian title, «Спать хочется», means roughly "feel(s) like sleepy/sleeping", or

"want(s) to sleep", none of which sounds right in English. "Sleepy", then, is a reasonable option, embraced by all translators known to me; however, it does not reproduce the rhythmic–grammatical effect of the original, which also has a child-like ring to it, or the subtlety of effect produced by Chekhov's use of the infinitive *to sleep* (the first word in the original title).

9   There is also a remarkable similarity between the names that Chekhov chose for these two ill-fated child-protagonists; in fact, they can be told apart only by one single consonant. There is hardly any similarity between their full Christian names (*Iván* and *Varvára*), but the Russian mechanisms of diminution yield almost-identical diminutives for these different formal names: *Vánia* and *Vária*, which in turn produce the more familiarised nicknames *Ván'ka* and *Vár'ka*. Even the *palatalisation* — the softening of a consonant, marked in Russian by the graphic character ь and transliterated here as ' (see *Guide*, 1.2, 2.1, and §30) — is identically placed in both nicknames. Another instance of Chekhov's treatment of name-diminutions is pointed out in Chapter 5, Note 17.

10   In most English translations the phrase is quite longer than in the original. Thus, in a translation supplied anonymously on the web, the equivalent phrase consists of five words: "when she has strangled him"; granted, this may be preferable as an English phrase, but it does not aim to preserve the extreme brevity of the original. The translation offered above does not claim any artistic merit; its sole purpose is to reflect the rhythms and tensions of the original, almost at all costs in ignoring the requirements of English style.

11   See Erlich 1965 for relevant *Russian Formalist* terminology and its meanings.

12   Chekhov inadvertently echoes here Shakespeare's dialectical presentation of the inter-relationship between *sleep* and *death* being synonymous and contradictory at the same time. See 2.2 and Epigraph to this subsection.

13   For an illuminating discussion of the Grammatical aspects of this ending in particular, and of the relevant Russian verb constructions and their use by Chekhov in general see Chvany 1985.

14   For a more reception-oriented approach to Chekhov's change of this story's ending see Kataev 2006, 195–6.

15   It is an enlightening exercise to search the play's text for all occurrences of the verb *to know*, its derivatives and synonyms; the results are illuminating and highlight the crucial importance of various ideas and manifestations of *knowledge* in the play — e.g., Másha's entrance to the stage in Act 2 with the words "I don't know", or, more importantly, Chebutýkin's admission in Act 3 how his false pretence to have (medical) knowledge leads him to malpractice resulting in death of a patient. The subject of *knowledge* is central in all of Chekhov's plays (in *The Cherry Orchard*, for instance, it includes the practical knowledge, now forgotten, how to make cherry preserve, as well as 'philosophical' knowledge of truth and love), but in *Three Sisters* it is most ingeniously interwoven into the fabric of the entire play.

16   It is the Russian grammatical particle marking the *hypothetical-conditional*, converting, e.g., '*if we know*' into '*if we had known*', or '*you knew*' into '*you would have known*'.

17   This ending has been analysed from different angles in the literature; see, for instance, a recent attentive analysis of interactions between the dramatic text and its potential realisation on stage, with special reference to potential intonations, in Dománskiï 2012.

18   A musical association can come to mind: in Beethoven's *Symphony No. 9 in d minor* the last (fourth) movement begins with brief, abruptly interrupted quotes from thematic ideas suggested (and developed quite fully) in the preceding three movements, one by one; these earlier thematic materials are 'rejected' only to pave the way to the 'right'

one, as "happy prologues to the swelling act/ Of the imperial theme" (*Macbeth* I, iii, 128–129). This interpretation of Beethoven's practice here is corroborated by the words with which **he** chose to start the vocal part of the movement: "*O Freunde, nicht dieser Töne!*" [Oh friends, not these sounds!]. This is a structural rather than semantic analogy: I am not suggesting that Chekhov makes here an explicit rhetorical gesture of rejecting his previous endings as Beethoven 'rejects' his previous materials (of course, he does not really reject them, he keeps all previous three movements intact… but the rhetorical gesture is one of rejection all the same); rather, Chekhov does offer his audience, probably unwittingly, an account of how previous techniques and practices led to new ones, as if retracking his former moves.

19 According to this reading, there are eleven Potential Endings that precede the actual ending, which (by the same token) is № 12; but rather than adding it to the eleven it is better not to give it a number at all: this one is not another **Potential** Ending; rather, it is the "road taken" by Chekhov in establishing the play's real ending.

20 It can also be contrasted with his own childish helplessness in erotic and matrimonial matters, when he fails either to propose to Vária, or to tell himself and others that he does not want to propose to her, just before this ending, as shown in 5.2.1 and 5.2.2.

21 Of course I am not suggesting, not even remotely, that Chekhov was really thinking that way, but this is what his practice is saying to us, regardless of his actual thoughts, verbalised or subliminal.

22 Contrasted, for instance, with *Uncle Vánia*'s literal misfiring **while** shooting (and in Act 3, rather than at the very end, at that), and with *The Seagull*'s and *Three Sisters*' literal well-aimed shooting

23 Much has been said, and argued, about the crucial centrality of this personage. See for instance Senderovich 1994, Rayfield 1994 and 1999, Senelick 1997, and Loehlin 2006; see also Pólotskaïa 2003 (a very partial list). There is no doubt that Chekhov himself attached crucial centrality to Charlótta, but many interpretations and productions since Stanislávskiï have marginalised her, to a greater or lesser extent (see discussions of stage interpretations in Senelick 1997).

24 Of course, it is ironic as well as ridiculous that Lopákhin — who understands so much about money and so little about human nature — hires him, of all people, to look after the estate in his absence. This is almost as absurd as Gáïev's new job as a banker.

25 The word has been translated into English in numerous ways; e.g., *nincompoop, good-for-nothing, muff, duffer, gawk, half-baked bungler*, etc.

26 "*A Life*" [in *italics*] — a biography; "a life" — the real life of a real person.

27 Magarshack, in his English-language biography, writes these words in English; of course, Chekhov must have said them in Russian.

28 As usual in this book, the English text of the last pages of *The Cherry Orchard* is concocted from a number of English translations of the play. I have numbered the potential endings of the play in {} brackets. The foregoing analysis in 9.2.5 refers to these numbers.

29 This is not the first time that Gáïev utters or mumbles words related to the game of billiard as a sign of uncontrollable embarrassment. Precision in rendering the actual words and terms seems to be of much lesser importance in a translation.

PART

III

OVERVIEWING

A COMPREHENSIVE LOOK

1 Act 3. An emotional showdown between mother–Arkádina and son–Konstantín, with the production's lighting-ladder as arena.

Opposite page:

2 Act 1. "Satan's red eyes" towards the interruption of Konstantín's play; Sórin on the right and Arkádina from above are watching.

3 Act 1. After the play's fiasco, Dr. Dorn gives Konstantín words of encouragement and advice.

4 Act 2. A cheerful moment with Sórin and Nína.

This page:

5 Act 1. Opening a circle in Nína–Konstantín art–life relationship. Hardly visible on the far left as a red dot, the Konstantín-operated camera captures Nína's appearance in his play on video, her projected image facing the real audience, while the real actress, back to the real audience, faces the stage audience. In the background (right to left) are Trigórin and Dr. Dorn.

6 Act 2. Arkádina takes turns with Dr. Dorn reading Maupassant's travelogue *Sur l'eau (On the Water)*, with Nína (left) and Másha (right).

7 Act 2. Trigórin shares his ordeals as a writer with attentive Nína.

Main photo:

8 Act 1. Another moment in Konstantín's play; Nína seen from the back through smoke (ostensibly, of sulphur) lit by red projectors.

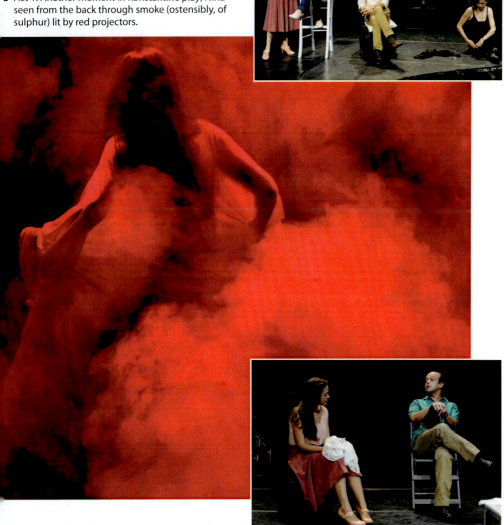

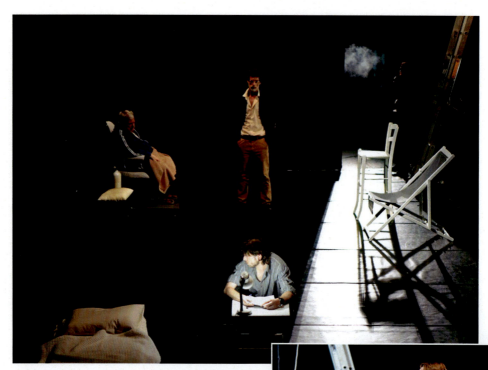

9 Act 4. Konstantín revising his own story, with Sórin and Dr. Dorn watching. On the left, a bed made for Sórin.

10 Act 4. Closing the Nína–Konstantín art–life circle: Konstantín reminisces Nína's acting in his play by projecting her video image on his wall, while the real Nína re-enters the scene. Sórin's empty wheelchair complements this game of presences and absences.

Inset:

11 Act 4. Nína's reunion with Konstantín.

CHAPTER

10

Chekhovism Viewed from Beyond its Boundaries
Comparative–Contrastive Perspectives

10.0 Structural Preamble[1]

After *Part I*, which is concerned with *Previewing* Chekhov's art from a **close outer perspective** and *Part II* — the heart of the Book, concerned with *Viewing* major components of his poetics from **inner perspectives** — the present Chapter starts the Book's 'way back' to an even more distant outer perspective, *Overviewing* Chekhov's art from a **remote outer perspective** (*Part III*). Put in metaphorical terms — borrowed from the world of photographing/cinema — *Part I* views Chekhov's plays through a kind of *middle shot*, *Part II* enters the heart of the object, *zooming in* to achieve a series of *close ups* on aspects of Chekhov's poetics, and *Part III* is *zooming out* more radically and taking *long shots* from a farther perimeter, away and above, so that relevant non-Chekhov objects are included in the background of the 'frame' and set Chekhov's art in bold relief.

This *Overview* is divided into four Sections, providing four mutually-complementary perspectives on *Chekhovism*, as elaborated below. Each of these examines *Chekhovism* and tries to characterise it from a different angle, asking, and trying to answer, its own questions about it. These are: (a) the perspectives of *Theoretical* and *Descriptive Poetics*, i.e., in the present context, contrasting *Chekhovism* with *Trends*, *Movements* or *Schools* (whose names, usually, end with the suffix *-ism*), viewed *pan-chronically* or *a-chronically* (10.1);[2] (b) the perspectives of *Genre* — a cursory survey of the topic (10.2);[3] (c) to complement (a), the perspective of *historical poetics*, i.e., the *diachronic* study of the autonomous history of an art from within (10.3); (d) the perspectives of *Aesthetic Evaluation* and *Interart Studies* (alias *Comparative Art*), here focusing on *music* as another external perspective on the uniqueness of *Chekhovism* (10.4). In all of these I occasionally resort to re-formulated definitions, gathered and synthesised from various sources — entries in authorised encyclopaedias, lexicons, dictionaries etc.,[4] and from other studies in the relevant fields and disciplines — in an attempt to view *Chekhovism* within a network of relevant concepts. Admittedly, this Chapter offers only general outlines for these broad subjects, each deserving a separate book-length study.

10.1 *Chekhovism* among Other *-isms*: A Pan-Chronic View

10.1.0 Chekhov's Personal (?) Attitude to *Groupings/-isms*

> For twenty-five years he has been chewing over other people's ideas about realism, naturalism, and all that other sort of rubbish [...] things that intelligent people have known for ages, and fools are not interested in.
>
> (Iván Petróvich Voïnítskiï [Vánia] in *Uncle Vánia*, Act 1)

The above Epigraph shows, *inter alia*, that Chekhov was one of those great writers and playwrights who were keenly aware of the metalanguage of their trade. Beyond this easily demonstrable general statement, it is more difficult to establish his attitude towards the accepted terminology and what it stands for. Looking more closely at this quote, it is the personage Iván Petróvich Voïnítskiï (alias Uncle Vánia; henceforward 'Vánia'), rather than the playwright Chekhov,[5] who says that *-isms* in the arts are the "sort of rubbish" that has been known to the wise for ages and fools couldn't care less about. He mentions only *Realism* and *Naturalism* by name,[6] but his sarcastic tone must apply to the scholarly discourse about *trends/schools/movements* in the arts (and comparable nomenclatures, groupings and classifications, like *genres*) in its entirety: for Vánia the lot of them are "rubbish". In other words, by implication — of which he, unlike Chekhov and the audience, is unaware — he takes no notice of a distinction between **knowledge** of a matter and **interest** in it. However, as a more objectively-logical inference, such fusion or confusion between the two is hardly a foregone conclusion (regardless of whether Vánia's observation is factually correct or not), because of the *asymmetry* ingrained in the argument: according to his wording, fools have no *interest* in these matters, but may have *knowledge* of them, whereas intelligent people have had *knowledge* of these concepts for ages, yet may (or may not) find *interest* in them. The speaker himself, in the heat of argument, can hardly notice these implications of his words.

Arguably, this quibble about *interest* vs. *knowledge* adds little, if any, *knowledge* or *interest* to the present argument; however, Chekhov has rightly earned a reputation of choosing his words consciously and cautiously, and this quality is especially apparent, somewhat paradoxically, when his carefully designed wording **as an author** produces an effect of loose thinking, resulting in sloppy use of words, **in a personage**. In this instance, the '*knowledge* vs. *interest* asymmetry' adds to the more substantive reasons for understanding the subversive nature Chekhov's presentation of Vánia's argument. Indeed, the personage Iván Petróvich Voïnítskiï has every subjective reason to discredit Professor Serebriakóv — whom he regards as his mortal enemy — and show him disrespect in every possible respect, including the latter's professional–professorial qualities; but objectively the former is unqualified to evaluate his opponent's scholarly standing.[7] In fact — as argued also in 5.2.2.7 — in characterising the Professor's academic stature as an art-historian the way he does, Vánia exposes his own academic ignorance much more than the Professor's incompetence. Moreover, Vánia's point is subversive also *vis-à-vis* an audience of theatre-goers and play-readers, Chekhov's intended addressees, for whom "*Realism, Naturalism*", and some other *-ism*s, are a far cry from "rubbish"; rather, these concepts are object of desired *knowledge* as well as genuine *interest* for such people, as well as for Chekhov himself.[8] In short, Chekhov's presentation of Vánia's sarcastic remark is designed to produce a subversive effect of doubt, ambivalence and uneasiness, directed at **all** 'parties' involved: the Professor (first and foremost, being the explicit target of Vánia's remarks); the playwright and Vánia (thereby sharply dissociating them from each other); and, most significantly, the audience's own self-esteem and intuitive convictions, thus questioning the (in)significance of *-ism*s, and other labels and classifications in literature and drama, as such. Moreover, since Vánia is unreliable as an evaluator of the Professor's personal–professional standing, he is even more unreliable as an evaluator of concepts and terminologies of disciplines in which he is, at best, an unqualified amateur. Thus, Chekhov reverses the operation of the rhetorical mechanism that Vánia tries to activate. The latter's implied rhetoric can sound somewhat like '*take it from me — I understand all about art, and when I claim that Prof. Serebriakóv is a charlatan, and his conceptual framework is rubbish, I know what I am talking about*'; however, after examining the evidence, we can say to ourselves something like '*Iván Petróvich Voïnítskiï has no professional credentials in the study of art, and thus has no valid cause, other than personal spite, to discredit the Professor; he is unqualified to judge* **what** — not only **who** — is "rubbish", and what or who is not*'.

Yet not only Vánia's, but even Chekhov's own attitude to such classifications is a side issue here: rather than what he said (or even what he thought and sensed), it is what he actually **did**, as writer and playwright, that is the focus of discussion.[9] The major topic, then, is the interrelationship between Chekhov's unique art of writing — the artistic system and poetics of his *oeuvre* — on the one hand, and the very idea of assigning him, and his works, to groups that include some other, comparable works and authors, on the other hand.

10.1.1 Chekhov's Art and the '*-isms*': Reasoning the Need for *Grouping*

> Reason Not the Need!
>
> (Shakespeare, *King Lear*, II, iv, 263)

10.1.1.0 The 'Cognitive Need' for *Groupings* and their Indispensability for Establishing Chekhov's Uniqueness

Indeed, Chekhov's uniqueness, the Book's major theme, cannot be meaningfully and comprehensively characterised and understood, without a comparative–contrastive perspective: only against the background of the work of other masters, taking the distinctive traits of the individual poetics of each of them into account, can a single master's uniqueness be established. It is one thing to discover the existence, or even centrality, of certain traits and qualities in the poetics of a given author, viewed in isolation, and another thing to claim that these traits are also unique to that author rather than shared with others. Finding such shared features is at the heart of the process of grouping individual people and/or texts under a common 'umbrella'.

As a universal tendency, one of the ways used to characterise individual people (mainly others, but often even oneself), and other individual items, objects and phenomena (e.g., texts and works of art), is to assign them to groups. Such groups are the result of a process of comparing–contrasting such items with each other and identifying their shared/common vs. distinctive features. The reason for this inclination is primarily *cognitive*: the human brain — a tireless generator of *models* and *modelling systems* — can manage a smaller number of groups or clusters, emphasising their common features, much more easily than a larger number of separate items, considered in isolation with common features hidden or non-existent; it is also the brain that is prompted to doubt and question the basis for such groupings (in other words, there is an element of built-in subversiveness in this process). Creative artists and the works of art that they produce are a case in point: for many centuries they have been assigned to groups, with common denominators ('umbrellas') to justify such groupings under headings like *genre*, *period*, *movement*, *school*, etc., and this process has also been questioned and debated time and again.

The creation of such *groupings*, then, is admittedly inescapable, and their use in professional discourse is even helpful — at least inasmuch as it clarifies the conceptual scene and facilitates its discussion; however, this should be exercised with extra caution, to avoid oversimplified, stereotyped generalisations that do injustice to the specificity of individuals: it is indeed too easy and potentially shallow to label a person or a text as a characteristic type defined by *trend, period, genre, movement* etc. (e.g., "He is a *mannerist*", "this is a *bedroom-farce*"), instead of addressing his/her/its individuality head-on.[10]

This caveat applies with special force to specific creative artists, and Chekhov is undoubtedly one of them. As asserted in 2.0 above,

> Chekhov emphatically denied being a follower of any political, religious, or other school, group or persuasion; similarly, he was not, nor ever claimed to be, identified with any *school, movement* or *trend* in drama, theatre or literature: *Realist, Naturalist, Symbolist, Impressionist*, etc. — none of these labels seems to do justice to his uniqueness, despite attempts to regiment him under the banner of this or that school in the arts.

His intuitive, almost automatic sense of distaste in the face of such attempts is, of course, a matter of personal self-defence against invasion of his cherished individuality, even his guarded privacy, and what he must have experienced as a repulsive mismatch, a forced attempt to group him together with "strange bedfellows"; however, over a century after his death, it is now much more pertinent to view this sense of distaste in terms of objective features of his poetics, which indeed intrinsically resist most attempts at such 'regimentation'. An overview of the relevant groupings in the 'vicinity' of Chekhov's poetics is, then, an indispensable step on the way to a fuller view of his uniqueness.

In conclusion, another concept should be considered in the context of *grouping–labelling*; I am referring to *partial systematicity*, as offered and used in Harshav 2007, p. 172. All *groupings* constitute structured clusters of heterogeneous features and components, some of which are more crucial than others to the very identity and *raison d'être* of the *grouping* as such, and for being the 'label-of-choice' to characterise (a) specific text(s). In other words, such clusters are formed with a solid and unshakable *core*, or *backbone*, at their centre and more fuzzy and flexible margins around their periphery, in associative visual analogy to the concentric ripples that gradually vanish, in time and space, around the point where a stone hit the water. Thus, for instance, the demise of the protagonist is a *sine qua non* for *tragedy*, a defining *core-feature*, without which this label cannot be meaningfully applied to a specific play. Some other features — e.g., the protagonist's status being a national or local ruler (king, prince, governor, etc.) — are typically frequent, but their presence and importance are less consistently required, thus being more flexible, possibly varying from play to play. Additional features — e.g., the division into five Acts — are frequently chosen, but not essential for the basic characterisation of the *genre*: there can be *tragedies* whose inner division is different, though they are undoubtedly identified as such by their *core-features*. The *partial systematicity* principle, of course, is valid for most kinds of *groupings*.

10.1.1.1 'Passing/Failing a Test': The *Superordinate* and the *Subordinate*

When trying to define or characterise an individual artist or an individual text by labelling him/her/it as belonging to a *grouping* or *-ism* of any kind, we tend to forget that such labelling/grouping, however cognitively indispensable, is a means to an end, rather than an end in its own right. Thus, for instance, the literature abounds in discussions/debates about whether *The Cherry Orchard*'s most appropriate *genre*-label is *tragedy*/*comedy*/*drama*, and/or about whether the play (whatever its *genre*) is *realistic*/*impressionistic*/*symbolistic*, and/or whether Chekhov is (predominantly) a *Realist*/*Naturalist*/*Impressionist*/*Symbolist*,[11] etc. The usual way to conduct this type of discussion is to try to match the characteristics of the *oeuvre* of the given author (and/or of the given text) with an existing definition and/or accepted characterisation of the *grouping*. If the two reasonably match, the individual author or text can indeed be reliably assigned to the group. If not, a mismatch is diagnosed, and the text/author is found unsuitable or disqualified to join the *grouping*. Such a procedure, willy-nilly, has about it an aura of 'passing a test', typically activated in one direction: the given individual (author/text) passes, or fails to pass, the test of conforming to the group's requirements.[12] The test is rarely, if ever, applied in the opposite direction, i.e., to 'flunk' the validity of a *grouping* because it fails to accommodate an individual instance (text or author).

In fact, the situation is more complex: a definition of *tragedy*, for instance, that would leave out major exponents of the genre, like *Oedipus Rex* or *Hamlet*, would indeed fail its basic test, as would a definition of *comedy* that excludes

Shakespeare's or Molière's plays universally known as comedies. Likewise, a definition of the *novel* that would leave *Madame Bovary* or *War and Peace* out, a definition of *realistic drama* that would not apply to Ibsen's *Hedda Gabler*, etc., would fail the test posed by these individual texts, accepted by universal consent as paradigmatic for these groupings. Admittedly, indeed, there is some *inevitable circularity*[13] here: the definition/characterisation of a group (e.g., *tragedies, realistic drama*) cannot be effectively clinched without citing names of defining members of that group as paradigmatic examples of it, while a characterisation of paradigmatic authors and texts cannot be effectively clinched without resorting to authors' (and texts') 'home-group', so to speak: the two define, characterise and represent each other.[14] The symmetry between the two sides of the 'equation' as just suggested, however, gives an oversimplified picture of the situation, because it ignores a *hierarchical* relation that exists between them, a relation between a *means to an end* and an end *in itself* (or *in its own right*); in other words, a relation between the *subordinate* and the *superordinate* (respectively, of course).

Indeed, if the individual case (person or text) is 'tested' against the requirements of the group, the former is subordinated to the latter, at least mentally. The reverse, however, usually makes more sense, as just claimed, because these group categories and the terms/labels that denote them are merely **tools**, whose *raison d'être* is to serve **us** in our quest for understanding the nature of a work of art and/or the poetics of its author, rather than the other way around: no text and no author can be said to exist in order to meet the requirements of any *grouping/classification*. Yet, since some of these labels/terms (notably *tragedy* and *comedy*) and the categories they denote have been with us from time immemorial and have naturally acquired high prestige that overshadows the reputation of most single plays, they have assumed tyrannical status as yardsticks to judge plays by, and some people have forgotten their role as mere tools. It should be remembered, then, that tools are never evaluative criteria; rather, they are constantly the object of evaluation. The criterion to evaluate or judge a tool is the degree of its usefulness, its effectiveness in performing the job for which it was created. Therefore, the 'blame' for any mismatch between such a group's requirement and a given text, in principle, rests neither with the text, nor with us in characterising or analysing it, nor even with the *grouping*/label itself (e.g., *tragedy, Realism*) and its claim to usefulness, but in the occasional wrong-headed attempt to match a specific label with an individual case, and even more so in a doubly erroneous attempt to judge the value of the latter by the extent of its conformity to the former. If, for instance, *The Seagull* does not qualify as belonging to any of the established *genres,* no one is 'to blame': neither the play itself, nor any *genre*-label and its traditional definitions, nor anyone trying to check its suitability to this label or that, nor even Chekhov for writing it the way he did. Indeed, he may be somewhat 'to blame' for subtitling it *comedy*, but only if a credible definition and characterisation of this *genre* can be established in a way that contradicts Chekhov's use of it; especially 'to blame', then, is anyone who insists on pinning a label on a play, ignoring or defying their mutual incompatibility, reading the group's characteristics into the play (if that is the case).

To clarify this point, still on a general–theoretical level of discussion, I would like to propose the following *three-storeyed* or *three-tier model*:[15] (a) certain play-wrights, whether aware or unaware of each other, whether close or distant in time and place (e.g., Sophocles, Shakespeare, Racine), composed plays;[16] (b) subse-quently, critics, scholars, and other readers examined these plays, and noticed (whether consciously–analytically or subconsciously–intuitively) some common features (e.g., *formal structure*, *thematics*, *models of reality*, etc.) that these plays have in common, considering these shared features **similar and significant enough** to justify grouping the plays under a common 'umbrella'-term (e.g., *tragedy*);[17] (c) again subsequently, aestheticians, theorists, scholars and analysts can look back at the process that had generated (b) out of (a), and ask themselves (this time, consciously–analytically **rather than** subconsciously–intuitively) why and how the conclusion in (b) could be reached; or, in other words, what are the features of (a) that could give rise to the conclusions in (b). (c), then, is a process of consistent–systematic analysis and examination, by which later observers and analysts try to reconstruct, understand and account for earlier probably-intuitive observations.[18] An important point here is that (c), in which the present discussion is engaged, amounts to an attempt to understand and reconstruct the (intuitive) logic that motivated people 'like us',[19] after examining and experiencing artefacts also produced by people 'like us', to group them together under a specific 'umbrella'-term. The theoretical point — obvious, though worth re-stating — is that humanistic disciplines (e.g., the systematic study of the arts) differ from other disciplines (notably exact and natural sciences), *inter alia*, in that we are auto-matically qualified, by our 'birthright' as humans, to ascertain the principles governing the brain-children of other humans by putting ourselves 'in their shoes'.[20] In this case, we can mentally trace every step of the way from (a) via (b) to (c) inclusive, primarily because we possess human brains/minds which enable us to check and question every premise, and call everyone who proposes it to account. Thus, more specifically, we can demand satisfactory explanations for labelling Chekhov, or his plays, under a known *trend/school/movement* (in other words, *-ism*) or *genre* (or, more significantly, for **refraining** from labelling him this way) as well as for the validity/usefulness of these terms/tools in the first place.

In principle, relating the *subordinate* to the *superordinate* amounts to asking whether an A (here, the poetics of an author, e.g., Chekhov, or the characteristics of a text, e.g. *Three Sisters*) is at the service of a B (here, the characteristics of a *genre* or an *-ism*), or vice versa.[21] Since we have already established that the latter answer — B is at the service of A — is the "correct presentation of the problem", it is time to question the importance, or the very necessity and *raison d'être*, of the kind of classifications we are talking here about. Indeed, we are at the service of the *labelled groupings* only if they, their characterisations and definitions, are the major subject and object of our investigation, which is not usually the case:[22] it is clearly not the case in this Book.

To sum up: if a *group-label* fails to account for the *important* and/or the *distinc-tive* features of a text (or even a group of texts), and/or of the poetics of an individual author, such a 'failure' does not seriously undermine the validity of the label, as long as it is demonstrably applicable to other authors/texts. It is simply misused in a certain case. Of course the reverse is doubly true: nothing is detracted from the value of an author or a text because it 'fails' to conform to a group which it had never been intended to join in the first place. The tool *tragedy*, or the tool *Realism*, is good — i.e., effective/efficient — in/for some cases, and not so in/for others. Chekhov, as a rule (which defies other rules), is one of the "others".

10.1.1.2 *Chekhovism*: What's in a Name-Based -*ism*?

Any poetics of a single artist, especially a great and canonised one, has unique distinctive features, manifest in the entire range between isolated *micro* elements and overall *macro* structuration. There is no logical reason why the suffix -*ism* cannot be attached to an artist's name to denote such a unique poetics, as accepted in other fields (e.g., *Marxism*, *Freudianism*, *Darwinism*, *Stalinism*, and in more recent decades even *Thatcherism*); yet rarely, if at all, can one encounter surname-based -*ism*s in the literature discussing or characterising the work of great creative artists (thus, there is hardly any talk of *Shakespearism*, *Mozartism*, *Flaubertism*, *Da Vincism*, *Chaplinism*, etc.). In fact, when appended to names of creative artists, such -*ism*s seldom refer to a quintessence of their art; rather, they often denote highly characteristic and easily identifiable stylistic features, likely to be parodied, even ridiculed, as mannerisms *à la* the named author, that serve as models for second-rate imitators. In short, such usage underscores an epigone's lack of originality rather than creativity and innovation in an original artist. Thus, in 1896, "Ibsenism" was mentioned as one of *The Seagull*'s shortcomings by the Literary Committee of the St Petersburg Aleksandrínskiï Theatre.[23] Be that as it may, I suggest that in Chekhov's particular case, and specifically in the plays, there is room for the term *Chekhovism*,[24] if applied to a quintessence and uniqueness of his poetics, because Chekhov's dramatic corpus is *sui generis* in very crucial ways. That said — taking into account the prevalent usage of *Author's name* + -*ism* as just described — I am **not** advocating, certainly not campaigning for, the introduction of *Chekhovism* into the academic discourse on Chekhov in operational terms, unless there is an unforeseeable change in that usage; I am just explaining its use in this Book and for the purpose of the present discussion.

In this context it is worth noting that just as some authors are predominantly "archaists" whereas others are "innovators",[25] an analogous distinction can be made between *group models* and *mavericks* (or whatever suitable terminology is found to make such a distinction work — it is the distinction rather than the terminology that matters). The former are more paradigmatic, mainstream representatives of a *grouping*, those whose work exhibits that grouping's characteristic features; typically, that work served as the initial model for the very creation of the *grouping* in the first place (with the inescapable *circularity* just described). The latter authors are more unique, 'unlike anyone else', sharing less crucial features with their contemporaries, predecessors, and/or successors. In fact, these *mavericks* are a group only by intellectual exercise; otherwise, by definition, they are a **non-group**: the only feature that *mavericks* inherently share is the **dearth** of major features describable as common denominator shared by any of them with any others, including any other *maverick*.[26] At this stage it will come as no surprise to this Book's readers that Chekhov belongs to the latter group; yet, his uniqueness is not autarkic or insular. Thus, the term *Chekhovism* would be used most effectively if it did not apply exclusively to all and only works by Chekhov, but to the specific blend of traits and features characteristic of his poetics and artistic system. In principle, the term could have referred to *Chekhovism* in the work of other authors, just as the St Petersburg Committee (rightly or wrongly is beside the present point) ascribed *Ibsenism* to a play by Chekhov; *Chekhovism* outside the Chekhov corpus, however, is rare almost to the point of non-existence, and this rarity is telling.

10.1.2 *Chekhovism* and Specific *-isms*[27]

10.1.2.0 *-isms as/and Secondary Modelling Systems*

How does Chekhov's poetics relate to well established *-isms*? Can any of them account for its uniqueness, or, at least, is any of them compatible with this uniqueness?

In an attempt to answer such questions, let us look at definitions of some of those relevant groupings and *-isms*, synthesised from various authoritative sources (see Note 4). These definitions are rarely quoted here verbatim; mentioning a specific source indicates that it serves as a major basis for a largely-paraphrased wording. Yet, before getting to the actual materials, a theoretical preamble is in order.

All the *groupings* discussed in this Chapter are considered here as *secondary modelling systems*[28] (*à la* Lotman 1977, especially pp. 7–31) and as *regulating principles* (*à la* Harshav 2007, especially pp. 10–11).[29] In short, the concept of *modelling* (and *modelling system*) complements and conceptually reverses the hierarchies inherent in the concept of *Mimesis*:[30] whereas the latter regards art as a virtually **passive** *reflection* (see Appendix) and/or *imitation* of reality, the former regards it as an **active** system that creates/generates/produces *models of reality*. Thus, *mimesis*-oriented studies explore *verisimilitude* — i.e., whether, and to what extent, reality/life/the 'real world' (however defined/described/characterised) is correctly **represented/reflected in** the work of art; by contrast, the *secondary modelling systems* conceptual framework is not concerned with *verisimilitude*. Focusing as it does on the description, analysis and/or interpretation of type(s) of *reality-models*, **created by/in** the work of art. This is done, in principle, while deliberately ignoring the 'real-life' or 'real-world' side of the equation. The latter procedure is much 'cleaner' or 'neater' methodologically–disciplinarily: it relieves text-analysts — trained and specialised, by definition, in the study of **texts** (of literature, drama etc.) — from the burden of faking the expert examination of **reality** (i.e., pretending to do it as professionals). Of course, text-specialists are entitled to their views about life, 'the real world', society, history, human nature etc.; they may hypothesise, even "philosophise" *à la* Chekhov, about such matters. Yet, in doing so they are no more and no less qualified than any other human being. Their professional expertise in text analysis does not add an iota to their credentials as 'reality-analysts'. Moreover, major aspects of 'the real world' can indeed be studied professionally, but within other disciplines (e.g., *philosophy, psychology, history, sociology, medicine*, some *natural sciences*, etc.) rather than within disciplines of textual analysis.

Specifically, a Chekhov scholar working in a *mimesis*-oriented conceptual framework would go about answering a question like 'Was Chekhov a *realist*?' by trying to check whether his portrayal of 19th-century Russian society in particular, or even the human condition in general, generated a credible '*slice of life*' effect (however defined). Thus, such a framework would make the analyst ask him/herself, and answer, questions about 'real life' in general and 19th-century Russian life in particular, and then compare/contrast them with the way these realities are depicted in Chekhov's world. On the other hand, if one views *Realism* as a *secondary modelling system*, one can just 'forget about' reality, focusing one's investigation on the kind of *reality-models* that Chekhov **created** and his texts generate. Of course, one cannot pretend to be *tabula rasa* and avoid drawing upon one's experience as an inhabitant of the world, who was previously exposed to one's past life and to other texts, and is capable of subjecting a text to cognitive processes of understanding, analysing, observing etc., on the basis of such past experiences. However, the least such a scholar can do is to be aware of the difference between the expert text analysis and the lay life-expertise that s/he brings into the process of exploring the text at hand. Indeed, the demarcation lines between the various *intra-* and *extra-textual* mechanisms that must operate in such a process may be thin, but they exist and should be consciously observed.

Bearing in mind all these caveats and reservations, let us examine the compatibility of Chekhov's poetics with the major *movements/schools* that could potentially be relevant to it. In all of them *secondary modelling system* is the conceptual framework of preference in the present discussion. Thus, for instance, if a crucial aesthetic ideal of *Impressionism* is the blurring of boundaries and demarcation lines in a visual or verbal description, and if we try to check whether Chekhov's plays are *impressionistic*, a *mimesis*-inspired approach would use *extra-textual* procedures in order to check whether and to what extent such boundaries are blurred in a Chekhov play **more than** in 'real life' in general, or in Russia in his time in particular; so we are back to *reality check* again. Within a *secondary modelling system* approach, however, we are limited to checking the manner and extent of blurring boundaries *intra-textually* only, leaving 'real life' aside. With regard to *Symbolism*, the choice would be between the impossible task of contrasting *symbols* in reality and in fiction (if inspired by *mimesis*), and analysing *symbols*, their nature and function, only within the confines of a text (if inspired by *secondary modelling systems*). The same principles apply to all other -*isms*.

10.1.2.1 *Realism*

Out of the -*isms* to be surveyed here, *Realism* is a natural choice for a major focus of attention: for historical–chronological reasons as well as intrinsic–substantive ones, this is the main -*ism* often attributed to Chekhov and the one more genuinely relevant to his art.

Is Chekhov a *Realist*, then? What is *Realism*, in this context?

Let me say from the outset that all dictionaries and encyclopaedias that I have managed to consult are implicitly inspired by the conceptual framework of *mimesis* rather than *secondary modelling systems* in their attempts to define/characterise various -*isms*; it seems that the authors are not even aware of the latter option.[31]

Thus, *Realism* (in the arts generally) is defined (*OED*) as having "Close resemblance" to "the real"; it is characterised by "fidelity of representation", rendering precise details of "real things". *Britannica* stresses "The accurate, detailed, unembellished presentation of nature or of contemporary life", as well as precision and vividness of detail, objectivity and impartiality; focusing on "the unexceptional", "the ordinary" and "the humble". In the context of theatre, dictionaries and encyclopaedias add "dispensing with" verse and poetic diction in the dialogue (the latter point — the replacement of *verse* by *prose* in staged dialogue — will be also highlighted in 10.3 below). Reading these formulations, and their likes elsewhere, one cannot help noticing the seemingly inevitable recourse to intuitive, *unfalsifiable* arguments, smacking of *circularity* and bordering on *tautology*, which beg questions rather than answer them:[32] what is meant by "precise", "fidelity", "vivid", "impartial", etc.? How can such criteria be defined, and then applied to a text and used as a yardstick in measuring the extent of its *Realism*? Another, though closely related, set of questions applies, especially in the present context, to the degree of applicability of such terminology to Chekhov's poetics, or *Chekhovism*, and most particularly to the nature of potential *interface* between it and *Realism*.

I am leaving these questions open, as a conceptual challenge to this *interface* and its components, since any attempt to answer them within their *mimesis*-oriented framework requires lengthy examinations of 'the real world', then and now, there and here, which need not be undertaken in the present discussion. Rather, a *secondary modelling system* approach to the entire problem is offered here; this is done while keeping in mind that the Book's business is to characterise Chekhov's poetics, so that theoretical discussions are offered only as a means to serve this Chekhovian end.

All definitions I have encountered in the established encyclopaedias, then, are deficient in structural thinking: thus, for instance, subjects like the mutually-complementary activities of *selection* from reality-materials and cognitively *modelling* them — crucial to the creation and formation of any *-ism* — are rarely mentioned in these dictionary/encyclopaedia entries. Reading those definitions one does not have a sense of what a typical *Realistic* **text** would look like on the page, and, more importantly, what a **play** based on it would look like on the stage (the same applies of course to the way other *-isms* are characterised in such definitions). Focusing on *modelling systems* inevitably leads one to deal with such questions.

It is a truism that no art — however 'true to life' and generating *verisimilitude* it aims to be — can function like a video camera that is switched on indefinitely and captures, without any selection or editing, everything said and done within its range (even such a camera, of course, has *frame* limitations). After all, in reality, too, we make selections out of the 360° of the world around us; we turn our heads to face a given direction, choosing where to look, what to see, for how long etc. All the more so in **any** art, where *organised selectivity*[33] is the name of the game, and *Modelling* is an expression of it: an author makes a selection from an endless number of potential options, and the nature of this selection constitutes his/her *model of reality*. The main differences between various *groupings* in general, and *-isms* in particular, are manifest in these processes of *selection* and *modelling*.

Now an anecdotal memoir told by Meyerhold (1978 [1913], p. 30) is very much to the point at this juncture. In September 1898 — he tells us — Chekhov attended a rehearsal of *The Seagull* at the Moscow Art Theatre, and was told that offstage noises of croaking frogs and barking dogs were intended to accompany some scenes. Chekhov asked "Why?" with dissatisfaction, and the answer was "because it is realistic". Chekhov retorted, sarcastically: "realistic?" and laughed; then, referring to a famous portrait-artist who specialised in perfectly-'realistic' painting of faces, he asked: "What would happen if you cut the nose out of one of the paintings and substituted a real one? The **nose** would be 'realistic', but the picture would be ruined". Chekhov went on to insist that "the stage is art", which "demands **a degree of artifice**"; it "reflects **the quintessence of life**, and there is no need to introduce anything superfluous on to it". [34]

In fact, Chekhov's apt remarks, for all their wit, beg several questions, some of which concern his own poetics: the matter is more subtle and complex than meets the eye at first glance. In an imaginary argument between (advocates of) the respective poetics of 'Classical *Realism*' on the one hand and *Chekhovism* on the other, each would blame the other for failing to capture 'life as it is' on stage. (1) The former (roughly, the model typical of Ibsen's *A Doll's House, Hedda Gabler*, etc.) would argue that it is no other than *Chekhovism* that 'adds a real nose to the portrait', by having so much precious stage-time 'wasted' on 'blatantly unimportant' materials and other typically Chekhovian forms of *presence through absence and unrealised potentials*.[35] (2) The latter (i.e., *Chekhovism*) would equally blame the former for distorting real life's proportions and hierarchies by placing the 'important', exclusively, at the centre and pushing the 'unimportant' away, to near-extinction out of the *frame*, as if it were illegitimate to take the existence of the 'unimportant' in reality into account. '*It is unnatural and unreal for a person to talk **only** about the most significant things in (his/her) life*' the 'Chekhovites' would say; to which the 'Ibsenites' would retort: '*Yes, but time in the theatre is precious: not everything is equally important or interesting; granted, all people have to eat, drink and sleep, even go to the toilet, but it is plain boring to show it or talk about it on stage*'. As repeatedly shown, Chekhov would be the first to subscribe to the proposition that all things are **not** created equal in importance/significance. His secret gift is that he just has a way of showing the contingent importance of some seemingly unimportant things, making them significant and exceedingly interesting under certain circumstances and in certain contexts. It all boils down, then, to questions of **proportion** (extent, relativity, perspectivity, contingency etc.). Different artistic ideologies, represented in the actual practice of the various -*isms* no less than in whatever proclaimed manifestos they may have, have different respective answers to such questions as '*What is "superfluous"?*' '*How do you identify "the quintessence of life"?*', etc. A Chekhov and an Ibsen have different answers to such questions, and these answers are reflected implicitly, in their respective practices, rather than explicitly in treatises or analytical studies. Thus, of course, it is the pitfall of *mimesis*, that Chekhov himself, in this incident told by Meyerhold, fell into in his comments; it is however the exact pitfall that he stayed away from it in his creative practice (as most creative authors do), by actively *modelling* his own *staged reality*, whose tests of reasonability are basically intrinsic and autonomous.

Additionally, there is an elementary point that Chekhov ignored in connection with his "real-nose" analogy, though he must have been aware of it: in reality, a real nose and a real face are three-dimensional whereas a 'realistic' portrait (including everything in it) is two-dimensional. There are *rules of perspective* and other conventions that 'tell' a painter how to make the conversion, how to project an object of three dimensions onto a surface of two. As experienced viewers of such two-dimensional portraits, we have developed *cognitive schemata* (of which the figurative–'realistic' painter is aware, whether consciously or intuitively) that enable us to convert the two-dimension image that we actually see back into a mental image of three dimensions and to add the 'missing' dimension in our minds (while knowing full well that it's not really there!). Structurally–functionally, this process is analogous to communication in language: speakers *encode* their thoughts and ideas into language-structures manifest in language-sounds that they utter, and listeners *decode* the language-sounds that they hear back into language-structures and ultimately into thoughts and ideas. In both cases one has to be consciously, or at least intuitively, acquainted with the system of *conversion* (alias *encoding–decoding*) that operates in this process.

It is therefore impossible to transfer an arbitrarily chosen detail from either one of them — two- or three-dimensional objects — into the other, without paying the price of what Chekhov called "ruining" the perceptual experience: this kind of *Gestalt* can be either accepted–emulated, or challenged–negated, **but *in toto***.[36] A real nose is "realistic", in Chekhov's words, only in its correct 'native' context — i.e., in real life, which has its own rules of perceiving three-dimensional objects; replaced by a two-dimensional nose (displaced, in turn, from a 'realistic' portrait), the latter would undermine those rules of reality, and be perceived as *unrealistic*, perhaps *grotesque*, as a mirror-image of the reverse combination (three-dimensional nose in a two-dimensional context) brought up by Chekhov. An effect of *verisimilitude*, then, is context- and *Gestalt*-specific.

That said, the argument borrowed from painting is just an illustration, and it is the theatre analogy that concerns us (as it concerned Chekhov in this incident). The art of the stage has its own conventions, functionally–historically analogous to the rules of *perspective* in painting, to create *models of reality* — argues, in fact, Chekhov (without using this jargon). The undoubtedly obvious (though implied) analogy is that, indeed, in the reality of the Russian countryside there are usually croaking frogs and barking dogs; but once a country scene is set on stage, it has to obey the latter's constraints, tenets etc., which in this case boil down to *rules of selection* that generate *models of **stageable** reality*. Different systems of aesthetic ideology, explicit or implicit, interpret differently the notion of *stageability*, but **some** selection is absolutely unavoidable. *Realism*, by the implications of the word itself, tries, or in fact pretends, to minimise this *selectivity*. It tries to give the *slice-of-life* illusion, which is of course a bogus in reality, but not so in the cognitive perception of it. Even the *slice-of-life* metaphor itself implies *selectivity*: slicing something leaves out other slices… but the metaphor is misleading beyond that: each and every *slice*, in the applied sense, is not just arbitrarily carved out of the boundless whole of life, regardless of its inner structure and relationships between its own components; rather, it is a carefully designed artefact, with its outer *frame* and inner structure, an autonomous micro-universe that is extremely rare, if not totally non-existent, in *unframed* reality.

It is precisely here that the main difference between *Chekhovism* and *Realism* is located: the rules and selections that generate *models of reality* in each are partly different. Most writers **about** *trends*, *movements* and *schools* in the history of drama would concur that the exceptionally historically-resilient *model of reality* that started (roughly) with Ibsen's social prose plays, and can be gleaned and abstracted from them, represents an epitome of *Realism* **on stage**. This *model* is still viable in the present: since its inception in the second half of the 19th century it has been active in inspiring and moulding an ever-growing number of plays the world over. A majority, or at least a large number, of new plays produced in any Western cultural centre (New York's Broadway, London's West End, theatre and art Festivals the world over, etc. etc.) at any given time are, broadly speaking, *realistic* in this sense.[37]

Very concisely, this highly resilient, seemingly viable-forever model can be characterised as follows: (a) typical audience members would recognise the personages on stage as their own peers — e.g., the past school-mate, the neighbour next-door, the colleague from work, etc. — because they are neither kings/princes/rulers who live in palaces nor homeless ruffians from the gutter; (b) they speak 'educated prose' rather than versified poetry or sub-standard idioms;[38] (c) they answer each other to-the-point in short, efficient *répliques* ('ping-pong'-like dialogue); (d) they confine their talk to subjects of **significance** (at least for them personally) and **interest**: they wouldn't waste their time (which is, in fact, the theatre-time of the spectators) on such boring subjects as daily activities of eating, drinking, getting dressed etc.; (e) they communicate mainly through language, and the purpose of communication is primarily to share social–psychological content; etc.

Without falling into the *mimesis* trap by starting or pretending to research reality, it is intuitively apparent that the model just summarised does not correspond to hierarchies and proportions of most people's real lives. Granted, all manners of staged representation of reality are *models* that result from *selection*; choosing to speak only about things 'that matter' (to whom? why?), and to answer a previous *réplique* always immediately and to the point, is just as selective and as remote from 'unselective' reality as speaking in verse; however the effect of the former is much more 'realistic', and deviating from it may have the effect of "sticking a real nose onto a portrait". We have seen that this *model* — only partly compatible with *Chekhovism* — is still accepted as the 'proper' way to represent reality on stage, just as adhering to *the rules of perspective* is the 'proper' way to represent three-dimensional reality on a two-dimensional canvas. The proof of the pudding is that millions of brains, for many decades, have been accepting *perspective*, *stage-Realism*, *tonality* and *functional harmony*, etc., as *default*; and millions of brains cannot be wrong. It is a matter for different disciplines to research the whys and wherefores of these phenomena, but facts cannot be denied. The genius of Ibsen and other founders of '*Classical Realism*' (as well as the genius of the pioneers of *default models* in other arts) is that they managed to 'strike gold', whether consciously or intuitively; that they discovered the 'recipe' for creating models that conform to the requirements of basic *cognitive schemata*, which secure their longevity for decades, if not centuries, to come.

A word about *Realism* as a word, in a terminological context, is called for at this point. Most of the verbal labels under discussion are identical with, or at least clearly derived from, regular words in the dictionary, but context-specific usage endows such a regular word with a specific sense that may restrict, and/or broaden, and/or alter, its original meaning: thus, *Impressionism* does not mean all, or only, things that make, or are affected by, an *impression*; not even in the context of the arts: the term refers to a specific *school/trend/movement/period in* the history of the arts, though *impressions*, in the 'normal' dictionary sense, have much to do with works of art associated with other schools or periods (thus, a *cubistic* or *Romanesque* painting can be described as *impressive*). Similarly, *modernism* is neither all, nor only, things that are modern/new/innovative in general or even in the arts in particular; again, the term refers to a specific *school/trend/movement/period*. By the same token, *Realism* definitely suggests some conceptual relation to *reality*, but as far as this goes it is a very vague concept indeed: the dictionary origins of such *-ism*-terms are almost irrelevant to understanding them in the proper cultural–historical context.

Thus, Roman Jakobson (1971 [1921]) has a valid point when he exposes the "uncritical use of this word [*Realism*], so very elusive in meaning" (p. 38). After analysing its various senses systematically, he arrives, *inter alia*, at his "meaning C", which is the "sum total of the features characteristic of one specific artistic current of the nineteenth century" (p. 39). This specific meaning is the result of the belief of many "literary historians" that "the realistic works of the last [i.e., 19th] century represent the highest degree of verisimilitude, the maximum faithfulness to life" (p. 39). At this point Jakobson describes a paradox: to some followers of *Realism*,

> [...] a description based on unessential details seems more real than the petrified tradition of their predecessors. But the perception of those of a more conservative persuasion continues to be determined by the old canons; they will accordingly interpret any deformation of these canons by a new movement as a rejection of the principle of verisimilitude, as a deviation from Realism. They will therefore uphold the old canons as the only realistic ones. (p. 41)

Here Jakobson — probably unwittingly — roughly draws a line between *Chekhovism* and *Realism*. Indeed, these two *-isms* differ mainly in their attitude to the identification of "unessential details" and to whether they are "more real", or less, than "essential" ones; consequently, they would differ about the admissibility of certain types of details as suitable for presentation on stage. Within Jakobson's scheme, then, *Realism* (in the sense adopted here) would be identified with "those of a more conservative persuasion", whereas *Chekhovism* would be "a new movement", though, once again, I doubt very much whether this is what he had in mind.

Jakobson sums up his argument drawing attention to the predominantly subjective and even arbitrary nature of the debate, by emulating, as it were, the attitude of a typical participant in it, using the rhetorical device of "Combined Speech" (alias "Free Indirect Speech" — see Perry 1979, 93–105) for the ironic–sarcastic effect:

> Only those artistic facts which do not contradict my artistic values may be called realistic. [...] I find in [... other] traditions only a partial, embryonic, immature, or decadent Realism. I declare that the only genuine Realism is the one on which I was brought up. (p. 41)[39]

In this Chapter, too, *Realism* refers to a specific *modelling system*, though this label has been associated with other *modelling systems* as well (*inter alia*, by including Chekhov in it); the present choice does not imply preference for this *model* because it is 'truer to life', 'more genuine' or simply intrinsically 'better', for whatever reason. Rather, this preference is based on terminological efficiency: since terminologies and nomenclatures are merely tools designed to serve us, the sense chosen here for the term *Realism* is the sense that serves its users more efficiently than others, given the situation 'in the field', i.e., (a) the nature and number of texts that the *Realism-model* adopted here can be compatible with, and (b) the aforementioned historical resilience of this *model*, viable from Ibsen to the present, and most probably into the future. This type of *Realism* shares some important feature with *Chekhovism*, but the latter has its own *core* ('backbone'), its typical cluster of central and marginal features that constitute its *partial systematicity*, that are not identical with *Realism*'s, as defined here.[40] Thus, to restrict the applicability of *Realism* to the *Ibsen model*, and its adherents to the present, as proposed here, means to create out of it a powerful and efficient terminological tool, capable of referring inclusively–exclusively to a large body of texts over the past 120–150 years or so.[41] In order to incorporate *Chekhovism* into it, some of its crucial components have to be removed, replaced, modified etc., thereby reducing its applicability to other plays and playwrights that genuinely share the basic *realistic model*. Such a methodological loss to *Realism* is not balanced by a comparable gain to *Chekhovism*.

In sum: it is methodologically preferable to assign the label *Realism* to the *modelling system* that is most resilient historically; that has *distinctive features* applicable to a large yet characterisable body of texts; and, above all, that has a coherent, solid yet flexible mechanism of relating its various components to each other within a general design of *concentric circles*, solid in the centre and loose around the edges, as described in 10.1.1.0 in relation to the notion of *partial systematicity*. A concise table offering a fuller contrastive comparison between *Chekhovism* and other -*isms*, notably *Realism*, is provided in the context of *historical poetics* in 10.3.2 below.

At this stage let us return to the relevant authorised definitions, in an attempt to give a more conclusive answer to the question whether Chekhov was a '*Realist*'. Naturally, all encyclopaedias provide names of artists and works providing typical examples for each -*ism*. Chekhov — as expected, being a *maverick* — is very rarely cited as example; and when he is (e.g., in *Encyclopaedia Britannica*, where he is untypically mentioned in connection with *Naturalism* in the theatre) — matching him with a particular *grouping* is highly problematic, to say the least. Clearly,

Chekhov's aesthetic ideal was 'realistic', in the 'normal', everyday sense[42] (when denoting this sense, 'Realism' and its derivatives are written in Roman type and in single quotation marks; otherwise, when referring to the *model* presented here, they are *italicised*); it is much less clearly *realistic* if we understand the term in a narrower, more precise professional–terminological sense, as often used in academic discourse, and even less so in the further restricted sense adopted here. In other words, Chekhov is obviously a 'realist' if the term functions 'negatively' as opposed to (a) 'classical' drama from ancient Greece and on (notably Shakespeare), in which verse is spoken on stage as 'default', and the plotline may (and often does) include flagrantly super-natural events (gods, ghosts, miracles etc.): the poetics of these authors does not pretend, or aspire, to be *mimetic*, in the sense of resembling reality as perceived by our senses,[43] (b) '*absurd*' drama and theatre of the late 20th century, which does not refrain from using *supernatural* devices, though they function totally differently from their use in 'Classical' drama; (c) overtly *symbolistic* or *fantastic* plays (differences between them ignored in the present context) etc. In the controversy (*The Seagull*, Act 1) between Nína, who insists that "live characters" and love must be part of any play, and Konstantín, who rejects, almost scorns her attitude and prefers "life as it appears in dreams/visions",[44] Chekhov is much closer to the former's aesthetic ideals, as borne out by his own play, i.e., *The Seagull* itself. That said, **his** brand of reality, the selections that he made, the *reality model* that he created, cannot be characterised as *realistic* if compared to such paradigmatically *realistic* artists as Tolstóï [Tolstoy] or Flaubert (enormous differences between these two, and others that can be mentioned in this context, notwithstanding) in the novel, or Ibsen in his social prose plays in drama (e.g., *Ghosts, Hedda Gabler*). The artistic model of 'classical' *Realism* in drama has pursued a policy of *aesthetic censorship*, foregrounding the directly functional, the 'important' and 'relevant', and shunning the overtly 'trivial', the blatantly unmotivated and the *prima facie* irrelevant to the plot and to the life and fate of the major personages. The bans imposed by this type of *censorship* are not motivated by political, religious, moral, or any other ideological doctrine, but by artistic–aesthetic abhorrence of *boredom*: much of what Chekhov considers essential for his *model of stageable reality* would be considered by *Realism* too boring and trivial to be eligible to stage life.

In spite of everything said to the contrary, one can still try to see in Chekhov's plays a paradigmatic model of *Realism*; yet, as we have seen, significant parts of the basic *model of Realism* should be revised in order to enable Chekhov's inclusion in it. Clearly, without such revisions, he was not a *realist*, or else he was *a realist sui generis*: sharing some traits with *Realism* as defined, rejecting others, and questioning almost everything.

10.1.2.2 *Naturalism*

Was Chekhov a *Naturalist*? The present Section is concerned, of course, with *Naturalism* only in the arts (and in theatre/drama in particular), though the term has also other senses. Historically and intrinsically, *Naturalism* is closely related to *Realism*, and some dictionaries and encyclopaedias have a point in blurring the boundary between them, often explicitly. Some authors are listed in various studies under either heading, or both; some single plays are cited to characterise the same author (e.g., Ibsen, Strindberg) as predominantly, or characteristically, of *realistic* and/or *naturalistic* 'persuasion'.[45] When Leonid Grossman (1967 [1914]), however, writes about "The Naturalism of Chekhov", he has in mind mainly one of the non-artistic senses of the word — i.e., the centrality of *nature* and its phenomena in Chekhov's 'world' and *oeuvre* — rather than the name of a *movement/trend/school* in the history of the arts, which is the sense that Chekhov's own Vánia had in mind when he made the remark quoted as Epigraph to this Section.

The relevant entry in the *Encyclopaedia Britannica* (other sources basically concurring) says that *Naturalism*'s assumption of scientific determinism is one of the features that distinguish it from *Realism*; this assumption led *naturalistic* authors to emphasise the accidental, physiological nature of human beings rather than their moral or rational qualities. Individual characters were seen as helpless products of *heredity* and *environment*, motivated by strong instinctual drives from within, and harassed by social and economic pressures from without. As such, they had little will or responsibility for their fates, and the prognosis for their lives was pessimistic at the outset. These authors' views on *heredity* gave them a predilection for simple characters dominated by strong, elemental passions. Their views on the overpowering effects of environment led them to select for subjects the most oppressive environments — the slums or the underworld — and they documented these *milieu*s, often in dreary and sordid detail. So far a summary of the *Britannica* entry.

The entire Book is full of evidence that shows how un-*naturalistic* (in these senses) Chekhov's poetics is, and there is no point in repeating the entire statement of his poetics just to refute his *Naturalism* blow by blow. Chekhov's, or rather *Chekhovism*'s, response to *Naturalism* would be one of *balance* and *complexity*: one can sense the contrast between the two by simply reading carefully the catalogue of *distinctive features* of *Naturalism* (as clearly formulated above), on the one hand, while keeping the respective features of *Chekhovism* (as spelled out throughout the Book) in the back of one's mind, on the other hand. Chekhov's entire system is based on complex interactions and tense, precarious balances between *potentials* and *(non)-realisations*, *presences* and *absences*; *Naturalism*'s world-view may (or may not) be more powerful, more intense, certainly more goal-oriented, but less balanced and blatantly less complex. More specifically, it is enough to look closely at Chekhov's approach to *heredity* (detailed in Chapter 11), to *science* (consider, for instance, the story "A Dreary Tale"), to the type of *environment* in which personages are placed, etc., in order to experience the striking difference. It is bewildering that *Britannica* — the major source for the lucid and coherent statement of *Naturalism* just summarised — is also the only encyclopaedia known to me whose *Naturalism*-entry mentions Chekhov as an illustration: to the extent that Chekhov deviates from strict *Realism*, and he does, his deviation is not in the direction of *Naturalism* (Ibsen, by the way, though cited here mainly as *realist*, is also inclined to *Naturalism*, at least in the way he portrays the inescapability of the impact of *heredity* on people; indeed, this is a *naturalistic* trait in his personal poetics).

To sum up: Chekhov is not a *Naturalist* in the senses presented above; in fact he was as remote from this kind of *Naturalism* as anyone could be, within a general 'realistic' outlook. For one thing, his perception and cherishment of the *individuality* of human beings, manifest in a myriad of analogies between characters and events, demonstrates how different people make different choices even if their life conditions and environments are similar (e.g., Konstantín *vs.* Nína in *The Seagull*, the Prózorov siblings in *Three Sisters*, etc. etc.). Moreover, whereas *naturalists* viewed *science* and *Darwinism*[46] in deterministic terms, as major, or even only, statements of **cause**s to life's effects, Chekhov was much more interested in how, and to what extent, science is the **result** of **human creativity**. In other words, for Chekhov science is the product of the individual human mind, whereas a *naturalist* would see man as the product of mindless science (though figuratively); hence the faint rays of optimism that rarely but definitely shine through the fog of Chekhov's outlook — however guarded and subversive, checked by doubt and balanced by scepticism — in assessing and anticipating the role of *science* and *scientific progress* in the life of humanity, as opposed to the predominantly negative and gloomy view of this progress prevalent in *naturalistic* writings. Chekhov could not reject any *optimism* outright, not because he was an optimist, but because rejecting or accepting outright any *-ism*, almost any outlook whatever, was too simplistic for him. Thus, he rejected *totality*, or *dogmatism*, of any kind; see Chudakóv 1983 [1973], p. 204 (quoted more fully in 1.5).

10.1.2.3 *Symbolism*

Was Chekhov a *Symbolist*? A synthesised definition of *Symbolism* would characterise it as the practice of representing things by *symbols*, giving a *symbolic* character or dimension to a text (or parts thereof), with its events, objects or actions. In short, *Symbolism* in the arts is not merely the actual employment of *symbols* in an artistic text; it implies the **systematic–consistent** presence and function of *symbols*, and their paramount, predominant status and function in artistic texts. It is a crucial feature of truly *symbolistic* literature that the text, or at least important parts of it, cannot be understood, in the most elementary sense of *understanding*, without recourse to *symbolic* interpretation. In many instances it is precisely the cryptic–enigmatic and/or incoherent effect of a straightforward, *realistic* reading, that 'sends' a recipient of the text to look for sorely-missed coherence elsewhere, through interpreting the text *symbolically*. If such a procedure is successful — i.e., if a *symbolic* interpretation turns an otherwise inexplicable or incoherent text into a more communicative and comprehensible one — this is a clinching argument for characterising a text as *symbolistic*.

Indeed, as shown repeatedly in the literature (including this Book), Chekhov often uses *symbols* and elements endowed with symbolic meanings and functions in his plays (e.g., the seagull in *The Seagull*, Moscow in *Three Sisters*, the orchard in *The Cherry Orchard*), and in this his practice is just as consistent and systematic as in everything else. Yet, he introduces symbols to his plays by careful design, selectively and sparingly, and — more importantly — always with 'realistic' motivation in terms of character psychology and textual consistency. No text of his is incomprehensible on its elementary, 'realistic'–*fictional* level. Indeed, a Chekhov play's *inner/fictional plane* is almost 'symbol-free': the personages conduct the business of their lives 'realistically', hardly bothering with anything *symbolic*,[47] beyond their own lives and relationships.[48] The various *symbols* and *symbolic meanings*, then, belong in the *outer/rhetorical plane*, i.e., through the personages as well as 'behind their backs'. One can understand a Chekhov play on its 'realistic' level, without recourse to any additional layer of *symbolic* interpretation, however rewarding it may prove to be. Moreover, such a reading would not miss much in terms of the inner integration and cohesiveness of the text; even in terms of complexity of messages and their presentation, Chekhov's plays provide a solid basis for autonomous, coherent 'realistic' comprehension, without recourse to a *symbolic* layer of interpretation: there are very few exceptions to the rule that in Chekhov every *symbol* has a 'realistic' motivation and explanation,[49] whereas the reverse is simply false: there are many instances of 'realistic' meanings that make no hint at *symbolic* ones.

That said, adding a *symbolic* layer, which is so well integrated into the play's 'realistic' texture, to the process of understanding the text, obviously and undoubtedly deepens and enriches its overall impact, even radically so. Yet, a clear hierarchy always prevails, whereby *symbol*s are subordinate to 'realistic' considerations, not vice versa. Looking from this perspective, then, *Chekhovism* is partly describable as a unique blend of *Realism* and *Symbolism*: more precisely, it is both, **and** neither: its *Realism* is optionally enriched by its *Symbolism*, and its *Symbolism* is checked by its *Realism*. Moreover, if *Symbolism* means *decadent* literature[50] — whatever that means in a French, Russian, or any other cultural context — or specifically the poetics that inspired Konstantín's play in *The Seagull*, then Chekhov is certainly not a *symbolist*.

10.1.2.4 *Impressionism*

Was Chekhov an *Impressionist*? Dictionaries characterise *Impressionism* in literature as the literary presentation of some scene or emotion in its salient features, done in a few strokes. Referring to *Impressionism* in painting, the *OED* stresses the **lack** of detail. Chekhov — by almost unanimous consent, a master of detail, and precision in its presentation — seems an exceptionally unlikely contender to gain an *impressionist* label, if the latter is so defined.

However, the matter is not so clear-cut. Senderovich 1977 discusses "Chekhov's *Impressionism*", focusing on the master's narrative prose rather than his drama. He starts by quoting Chizhévskiï, who characterises *Literary Impressionism* as follows [below is my summary of Senderovich's summary of Chizhévskiï's argument, with my comments printed in **bold type** and enclosed in 'braces' { }]: (1) vagueness of the total picture {**which is diametrically opposed to Chekhov's renowned *clarity* and *precision***}; (2) (in apparent opposition to point 1) prominence of details and trivia {**this feature is much more inconclusive and ambivalent in Chekhov, because of his exceptionally complex treatment of 'hierarchies of importance' presented in 8.0.2**}; (3) renunciation of such elements of "didactic" art as the use of *aphorisms* and *maxims* supposed to communicate to the reader the intent, the "tendency" of the work {**Chekhov's plays are full of such *didactic* and "tendentious" statements, some of them as part of "philosophising", yet his total work is devoid of them: they are attrib-**

uted to the personages who utter them, thereby guaranteeing Chekhov's dissociation from their content}.

Next, while insisting that any talk of *Impressionism* must relate to its original context in French painting, Senderovich stresses the following characteristics of this highly significant *school/movement*: (1) Imprint of reality captured by an instantaneous impression, free from all traces of prior observation, without mental processes such as *identification, comparison* etc. {**Chekhov revels in mental processes, identification and comparison — his complexity is primarily built on analogies and comparisons — so at least in this sense he is not an *impressionist*}.** (2) Objects function as 'negative' elements in the milieu, and much is based on shading, thickening and thinning etc. {**especially in the plays** (hardly mentioned in Senderovich's article), **Chekhov nurtures the interplay between *fusion* and *distinctness* of verbal and non-verbal components of the theatrical medium, often *semanticising* the latter to interact with the former on analogous grounds:**[51] **this is much more complex and varied than *Impressionism* as characterised here}.** (3) *Impressionists* are also renowned for their technical achievements, use of colour, etc. {**Chekhov's *technical* achievements in *narrative fiction* and in *drama* alike have been analysed above, producing *inter alia* incomparable fusions of distinctness, precision, and careful–meticulous design with a misleading effects of vagueness and arbitrariness**[52]}. (4) Creatively new treatment of *space*, the negation of *perspective* {**Chekhov shares the spirit of *Impressionists* as innovators, but the nature of his innovations is largely different: as we have repeatedly seen, he rarely negates previous techniques — rather, he prefers to re-evaluate them, adding angles and shedding new light on them, and his manipulation of *space* and *stage design* for *semanticising* the stage's visual components (e.g., the function of set-designs of the four Acts in *Three Sisters*) is a case in point.**} (5) Senderovich also makes a distinction between *"gloomy" Impressionism* and the celebration of colour in some prominent *Impressionist* paintings. {**This ostensible contrast between instances of *Impressionism* is also analogous to contrasts between contradictory characterisations of Chekhov's art (e.g., the *tragic* and the *comic*, the aforementioned *precision* vs. ostensible *vagueness, compassion* and *emotional detachment*, similar/different treatments of *micro* and *macro*, *onstage* and *offstage*, and other manifestations of the major features of Chekhov's poetics: *presence vs. absence* and *unrealised potentials*)}.**

In sum: as with other *-isms*, Chekhov shares part of the typical features of *Impressionism* while differing from it in other significant respects. For reasons of terminological economy, then, in addition to other considerations, it is more efficient not to group him together with members of this group either.

10.1.2.5 Conclusion

It has been established in this Section that Chekhov's refusal to be 'recruited' to join the ranks of any *-ism* is not just a matter of subjective whim or fastidiousness, but, genuinely, a matter of the objectively-unique nature of his art. Clusters of features that bind individual instances of every such *-ism* together within models of *partial systematicity* are valid, but so are differences between such clusters on the one hand and *Chekhovism* on the other hand: Chekhov's distinctness *vis-à-vis* masters of any potentially relevant *-ism* is greater than the distinctness of most of these masters, within the respective *-ism* of each of them, from each other. This inherent uniqueness, in addition to the universal consent about the supreme *greatness* of his work and its significance — both intrinsically–textually and historically (as shown in 10.4 below) — can justify using a term like *Chekhovism*, which implies that this single author may be treated on a par with a whole grouping (*trend/school* or *period*) of authors, in the history of his art.[53] Yet, this term has its drawbacks too, and there is no imperative need to use a single word to celebrate Chekhov's uniqueness: terms like *Chekhov's art, Chekhov's Poetics, Chekhov's uniqueness*, etc., may be preferable in certain contexts, as long as the extent of his distinctness is clearly recognised.[54] The fact that *Chekhovism* has been useful and functional for the foregoing discussions does not necessarily mean that it should be preferred in other contexts.

Perhaps in spite of his conscious self, then, Chekhov was a *Chekhovist*; the first, last and only genuine exponent of *Chekhovism*.

10.2 Chekhov and Major *Genres* of *Drama*: A Survey

> Tragedy, comedy, history, pastoral, pastoral–comical, historical–pastoral, tragical–historical, tragical–comical–historical–pastoral
>
> (Polonius in Shakespeare's *Hamlet*, II, ii)

Despite an initial–superficial impression to the contrary, this Epigraph does not show us that Shakespeare was dismissive of terms, concepts, distinctions and terminologies relating to the major *genres* of *Drama* (of which he was certainly aware). Rather, it is quite clear from this quote that academical–aesthetical–theo-retical–terminological–methodological thinking was not altogether foreign to him, just as it was not foreign to Chekhov (as the Epigraph to 10.1.0 clearly shows). Indeed, there is some affinity between Vánia's derisive attitude towards major -*isms* in the history of drama and Polonius's **seemingly** similar attitude towards its major *genres*. Thus, in both cases — sharp differences between them notwith-standing — the authors dissociate themselves from the disparaging texts by assigning them to *unreliable personages*, yet in both cases the actual words, regardless of who utters them, are designed to do their subversive work in the audi-ence's minds. Shakespeare and Chekhov could not, and in all likelihood did not want to, distance themselves from the world of drama/theatre, where these concepts, terms and classifications are no joking matter. Thus, both of them create a carefully designed subversive effect, targeted, first and foremost, at themselves (begging, as it were, questions like '*if genre-labelled plays are so ridiculous, why do you go on writing them?*'), but also at others: e.g., the two speakers, Polonius and Vánia,[55] other personages present on stage (and some absent from it), and the audience's own attitudes.

Major *genres* of *drama* have been with us for many centuries, actually even millennia (unlike the major -*isms,* whose presence in the literature is measurable in decades, hardly more than one century), and it is unnecessary to dwell on their definitions here; however, checking the poetics of Chekhov's plays against common views of such phenomena as *tragedy*, *comedy*, *farce*, *tragicomedy*,[56] *melodrama*, etc., yields similar results: each play of his has its own blend and combination of features shared with a number of these established *genres*, but no single *genre* is compatible with the features of any play of his, or any combination of plays.[57] In short, in the realm of *genre*, *Chekhovism* is neither *tragism*, nor *comism* (or should cumbersome *tragedism* and *comedism* be coined in this context?), nor any other potential *-ism* (it is noteworthy that the suffix *-ism* is not normally appended to names of *genres*).

Indeed, in all its facets, *Chekhovism* is largely a blend of elements that can be found separately elsewhere, but within it their original specific features are barely recognisable. The bottom line, then, is that *Chekhovism*'s relentless prism, or filter, of *unrealised potentials* and *presence through absence* — to which Chekhov subjects almost invariably any material that his system processes — is incompatible with any of the *-isms* and the *genres*, originally shaped and moulded on the creative terrain of other masters; this, in the final analysis, is a major obstacle facing any attempt to absorb/integrate Chekhov's *oeuvre* into any of the systems underlying pre-existing text-groupings, or, complementarily, to absorb/integrate any of these pre-existing systems into Chekhov's unique poetics.

It should be emphasised that this is not a normative–evaluative statement, but a descriptive–analytical one: some major creative artists, whose *greatness* is uncontested, can be quite easily grouped together with others. Indeed, such artists are often *paradigmatic* and exemplary in forming textual groupings in the first place — e.g., Ibsen (in part of his *oeuvre*) for *Realism*, Zola for *Naturalism*, Beckett for "*absurd*", Maeterlinck for *Symbolism*, etc.,[58] — whereas others are less susceptible to such adaptive operations.

It is clear that this Book joins a consensus that regards Chekhov as one of the greatest writers and playwrights ever, but it is not his specific kind of incompatibility with all groupings, defying their distinctive features, that makes him greater than others. He just 'happens to be' great as well as unique in this specific way. It is of course remarkable (and, again, not logically-inescapably connected to his own type of uniqueness) that, thematically–ideologically, Chekhov so passionately cherished and treasured *individuality* and so vehemently abhorred *sameness* in human beings, as shown repeatedly in the Book.

It is easy to demonstrate that no major play of Chekhov's complies with any consensus characterisation of any of the major *genres*. Yet, he did give three out of his four major plays traditional *genre subtitles*, all of which — to a greater or lesser extent — appear problematic, even bewildering: returning to the *three storeyed model* offered above (in 10.1.1.1) as a tool that may help us, while in stage (c), understand what prompted Chekhov, who both created and later perceived the texts, in stage (a), to give them the subtitles that he did when he assumed the (b) position. In other and simpler words, how could Chekhov match and reconciled the plays that he had designed, then wrote, then read and probably characterised **to himself**, with the subtitles that he gave them? I venture to assume that virtually no one trained and educated in *literature*, *drama* or *theatre*

— in Russia or anywhere else, in the late 19th century, before or ever since — other than Chekhov himself, would characterise either *The Seagull* or *The Cherry Orchard* as a *comedy* upon reading its text. *Three Sisters* is more compatible with *drama*, its original *genre*-subtitle, but no one would have frowned at a *Tragedy* subtitle, if Chekhov had chosen to give it to this play. To the best of my knowledge, no persuasive simple, unequivocal answer to these misgivings has been suggested so far, though the subject has been discussed time and again in the literature.[59] As Gáïev says in *The Cherry Orchard*, Act 1, if many cures are suggested for a disease, that means that it is incurable; likewise here, if many (mutually-contradictory and equally unsettling) explanations–interpretations are suggested to the problem of Chekhov's *genre-labels*, it is a sign that the problem is, in the final analysis, insoluble.

That said, another attempt will be made here to offer a modest contribution towards 'containing' this problem, without presuming to solve it "once and for all". The sketchy ideas proposed here are admittedly tentative and provisional; they are offered as a complementary addition, rather than as a substitute replacement, in relation to some other attempts that have been made to tackle this problem.

Two additional considerations may partly account for Chekhov's problematic choice of *comedy* as *genre*-subtitle for *The Seagull* and *The Cherry Orchard*.

Chekhov was self-conscious as a playwright, and was reluctant to claim the status of innovator that he had justifiably earned through the practice of his playwriting. Thus, he adopted (in theory, and arguably subconsciously) the time-honoured hierarchy, whereby *tragedy* is the 'highest' among the genres of *drama*; further down in this hierarchy comes *drama* itself, whose nature and status are less strictly defined, and then, still 'lower down the ladder', comes *comedy*. Against this background he adopted a personal hierarchy (again, most probably subconsciously), based, as it were, on the simple formula *G-1* [= *G minus one*], where *G* stands for the *genre label* that should have been 'correctly' assigned to the play under consideration, i.e., the label most appropriate to its nature and distinctive features, whereas the *minus-one* signifies the *demoting* operation performed on it to generate the subtitle as actually given by Chekhov. Thus, *The Seagull* and *The Cherry Orchard*, subtitled *comedy* by Chekhov, should or at least could have been subtitled *drama*, which is the general term that denotes neither *tragedy* nor *comedy* in a conventional pre-Chekhovian sense;[60] however, activating the *G-1 formula* seems at least partly to account for Chekhov's preference to append the subtitle *comedy* to both plays. *Three Sisters* is undoubtedly closest to *tragedy* in the entire Chekhov corpus,[61] but the *G-1 formula* yielded *drama* as its characterising subtitle (in other words, *G* in this case could have been *tragedy*, with some reservation; *G-1* makes it *drama*, the next step on the downward ladder of genres). In *Uncle Vánia* Chekhov gave up any conventional *genre subtitle*, and called it (as we all know) "Scenes from Country Life" — a subtitle that reflects his apparent need to dissociate this play from any *traditional genre* and defuse any *primacy effect* that a subtitle indicating such a *genre* may generate. The fact that he did not opt for a similar solution in the other plays shows that he was unhappy with these traditional subtitles and with avoiding them alike.

More specifically, Chekhov's refusal to apply the subtitle *tragedy* to any of his plays may also stem from the absence of any *tragic protagonist* [=‘*hero*’] from all his plays, including even ‘*tragedy*-like’ *Three Sisters*. Indeed, no Chekhov personage has the appropriate ‘greater than life’ stature; moreover, almost none of them possesses any **capacity**[62] for self-awareness and introspection that some authorities, from Aristotle on (e.g., Krook 1967), regard as a central quality of *tragic protagonists*. This is another reason why Chekhov’s intuitive caution regarding the application of the term *tragedy* to his plays makes sense; it is as if he was saying to himself, and/or indirectly to us, something like ‘*If Sophocles’* Œdipus Rex, *or Shakespeare’s* Hamlet, *are* tragedies, *then whatever I am writing is not*’. He seems to have been keenly aware of the difficulty to match his art — so different from older traditions and defying older terminologies — with *genre*-terms ‘born and bred’ in a different historical–cultural–artistic era and context. Yet he did not feel free to adopt a Vánia-like openly disrespectful attitude to such terms, which really did a disservice to his innovative art. Rather, he felt the need to cling to a terminology that would connect him to “the conventions/tenets/rules of dramatic art” that he once admitted sinning against, without realising that in his relation to these rules/conventions he was more sinned against than sinning; rather, he seems to have respected those tenets in theory while rejecting them in his play-writing practice.

Indeed, he apparently did not have the ‘audacity’ to realise the extent of his innovation in inventing new terms for new phenomena. Under these circumstances, Chekhov scholars and critics find themselves time and again checking his texts against those pre-existing terms as traditionally defined, with the inevitable result that the merits of his works are somehow evaluated by the extent of their conformity to rules and characteristics formulated under different — and, arguably, irrelevant — historical, cultural and aesthetic–artistic circumstances. Rather, a case could be made for reversing this practice: Chekhov’s work (and the work of any other innovative master’s, by the same token) should serve as yard-stick to evaluate the relevance of those pre-existing genre-terms, terminologies, rules etc.; if they fail this test, they should be replaced with other ones that meet the requirements of the new poetics’ specificness, or discarded altogether: it is better to have no descriptive labels at all than to have misleading, confusing and misplaced ones. Chekhov did not come to this conclusion, but he did sense the awkwardness of applying the old nomenclature to his new art; the resulting compromise that he reached, intuitively, seems to have been this *G-1 formula*. By this he practised as a playwright, within the *outer/rhetorical plane*, one of the kinds of behaviour so typical of personages within the *inner/fictional plane*: the avoidance, downplaying or sidetracking of *dramatic conflict*.

In sum, Chekhov’s *genre*-subtitles are the result of his own (conscious or subconscious) internal conflict, of unresolved ambivalence, a difficulty to choose between tradition and innovation. He did extremely well in practice, in carving out his unique genre-poetics for himself; his success in theorising about what he did was much more limited. His genre-subtitles, then, should be taken with a grain of salt. It is the analysis of what he actually did as a writer–playwright, rather than quibbling about the labels that he chose to characterise what he thought he did, that should be the focus of studying his work.

10.3 A Perspective of *Historical Poetics*: A Diachronic View

> He had no precursors, and his successors do not
> know how to do anything *à la* Chekhov.
>
> (Aleksándr Blok [quoted from Senelick 1985, p. 137])

10.3.1 *Isomorphism* of *Diachronic* and *Pan-Chronic* Perspectives

The *pan-chronic* approach adopted so far in this Chapter is complemented in this Section by a *diachronic* one. It is remarkable, though not altogether surprising, that the same kind of uniqueness that *Chekhovism* displays within the pan-chronic perspective, which ignores the historical–temporal aspects of the subject, is also apparent in the historical perspective added by this Section.

The discussion is going to be brief and cursory; it will just establish the basic principles of such a perspective, without resorting to textual examples to corroborate the declarative claims. The main point of this Section, then, is that there is a basic *isomorphism* between the way *Chekhovism* relates to comparable -*ism*-phenomena, whether viewed as a *school/trend/movement*, on the one hand, or as a *period* in history, on the other. Indeed, the greatest individual creative artists in all arts — e.g., Shakespeare, Chekhov, Bach, Beethoven, Michelangelo, and others, but not too many of them — can be regarded as a *school/trend*, even as a *historical period*, on their own. This is so mainly because they incomparably tower above everything and everyone else, by creating **defining** *models* of interaction between *form*, *content*, and/or other fundamental properties of art (wherever applicable), to the extent that they literally "make history". "Men at some time are masters of their" art: the impact of very few individuals on the history of (their) art(s) equals, and even exceeds, the impact of a whole group or an entire period. There is a difference though between those who are outstanding in relation to the group/period/school which they define, and those who define no group but themselves. As argued above, especially in 10.1.1, Chekhov belongs to the later group of *mavericks*, which is by definition a *non-group*, the group of *group-resistant* creative artists.

That said, Chekhov's chronological position in the history of European drama matches his position among otherwise-determined groupings (*Realism* and other kinds of -*isms*). More specifically though, his position can be considered along a historical process of *The Descent of Man's Stature*, as presented and discussed in 6.0, in conjunction with changes in the nature and function of *language* in the plays of various periods.

In seeming contradiction to the aforesaid, it has to be reiterated that all the creators of the greatest works of art, whether *group-models* or *mavericks*, play a *defining* role in the historical–diachronic as well as the theoretical–panchronic characterisation of their arts. In other words, even those *mavericks* who "define no group but themselves", as just stated, do explore and ultimately define, or re-define, the substance as well as the boundaries of their respective arts in their entireties. Thus, a hallmark of *greatness* is a combination of its *inexhaustibility* (as stated repeatedly above) and its *self-defining* power. The model of defining the *individual case* and the *universal whole*, skipping the *partial–collective group*, operates (by analogy) also in other fields, e.g., *characterisation*, as shown in 5.0.2.

10.3.2 Chekhov's Plays in a *Diachronic* Scheme of European Drama[63]

In this Subsection the uniqueness of Chekhov's poetics in drama is viewed *diachronically*, with *Chekhovism* being considered as a 'period' on its own. On the one hand, *Chekhovism* is a significant part in 'the *realistic revolution*' of the late 19th century. On the other hand, he did not share some of its central traits. The following table is designed to summarise and clarify Chekhov's position in the history of European drama, tested by major parameters that enable a comparative–contrastive perspective of crucial periods in this history. This scheme/table (overleaf), as the rest of the Book, focuses on 'serious' *drama*, deliberately ignoring infinite varieties of *comic* plays throughout history. The picture presented here, then, is not only schematic and generalised (in this sense, anti-Chekhovian), but also blatantly incomplete. However, it has to be borne in mind that its major purpose is contributing to the understanding of *Chekhovism*'s uniqueness, rather than presenting a complete *historical poetics* of European play-writing.

10.4 Assessing Chekhov's *Greatness*, with an *Interart* View

10.4.1 Evaluating *Chekhovism*: An 'Objective' Assessment?

10.4.1.1 A General–Theoretical Perspective

Towards the conclusion of the Book's project of studying and analysing the Chekhov phenomenon in drama and theatre, there is room for an attempt to take another step back to gain a broader perspective and ask the most basic *it-goes-without-saying* question: What is such a project good for? Why **and how** is it worthwhile to engage in an attempt to formulate (or, perhaps, re-formulate) Chekhov's poetics?

Certain premises underlying any project of this kind are inescapably destined to be *axiomatic*, hopelessly ridden with *circularity*, even *tautology*; one such premise is that *great art* is worth dealing with, in a various ways — experiencing, discussing, analysing, etc. etc.: it is part of the human condition to engage in such activities, though not every single human being would actually be concerned with them. What perhaps requires at least a short discussion is the question of *greatness*, and whether (and how and why) Chekhov's art meets the requirements of this elusive concept.

Another premise related to *greatness* is also taken here for granted, as an axiom: as just stated, the greatest works of any art play a *defining role* in establishing and characterising the nature and boundaries of that art. In other words, *distinctive features* of an art are not imposed on its corpus (e.g., the world's plays for *drama/theatre*, the world's sculptures for the art of *sculpture*, etc.) deductively, from 'above' and/or from the outside; rather, they are inferred, inductively, from 'within', from the existing greatest feats achieved by human creators of that art. Whatever the greatest minds in an art have achieved is tantamount to the realisa-

Parameters for comparison	Periods			
	From Antiquity to 18th Century[64]	'Classical' Realism (from Ibsen till now)	Chekhov/ Chekhovism	Absurd and Other Trends in Late 20th Century[65]
1. Presence or Absence of the Supernatural (personages and events)[66]	Present	Absent	Absent	Inconsistent[67]
2. Major personages–protagonists: Social stature	Rulers of countries, cities etc. (e.g., Kings, Governors, Military Chiefs)	Mostly middle classes	Broad spectrum around a middle classes core	Broad spectrum, typically low classes
3. Major personages–protagonists: verbal/ mental/ intellectual stature[68]	High level (comparable to author's)	Mid-level (comparable to audience's)	Broad spectrum, typically much lower than author's	Broad spectrum, typically lower than the audience's
4. Presence/Absence of Self-Awareness	Present, but usually too late	Often too late	Presence rare; absence frequent, often remains to the end of the play	Broad spectrum, often absent
5. Audience Attitude to Personages	Looking up to them	On same plateau	Changing: looking down, then often on same plateau	Typically looking down on them
6. 'Important' vs. 'Unimportant' hierarchy	Clear though 'mild' hierarchy	Strict hierarchy: hardly any room for the 'unimportant'	Hierarchy present, but questioned and manipulated	Hierarchy upset, hardly recognisable

7. Language organisation: poetry vs. prose	Mostly poetry (verse)	'Educated prose'	**Broad spectrum, mostly 'educated prose'**	Broad spectrum; typically lower than 'educated prose', sometimes verse and song[69]
8. Language: centrality, nature of, functions[70]	Most central, communicative, often self-oriented	Most central, communicative, functional, goal-oriented	**Less central, less communicative; non-verbal elements functional**	Often marginalised, non-verbal elements highlighted
9. Soliloquies	Present, typical, quite frequent	Absent	**Rare, calculated, disguised**	Occasional
10. *Réplique* autonomy in dialogue[71]	High	Low	**Broad spectrum, quite higher than in *Realism***	Broad spectrum
11. Communication *Inner/fictional plane* [onstage]	High level	Focused, very high level	**Broad spectrum, typically low level of communication**	Broad spectrum, typically high level
12. Communication *outer/rhetorical plane* [stage to audience][72]	High level	High level	**High level**	Typically low level
13. Stature of Implied Audience/Spectator[73]	Capable of interpretation/reception of verse and prose texts	Capable of reception of 'normal' prose communication	**Requiring high level of textual integration, recognition of analogies etc., above the personages' level**	Exceptionally high level of decoding, integration and interpretation, is required
14. Dramatic Conflict	Overt–external	Overt–external	**Covert–internal, transferred to audience**	Extremely varied; often absent or covert

tion of that art's potential. New feats are bound to be achieved and challenge pre-existing ones in an endless process. They may be *different* in nature, realising the art's potentials in unprecedented ways, perhaps re-defining some of these potentials themselves in the process; however, they will not surpass the very scope of greatness of the towering giants of the past. They can be differently great, but not greater. Of course, this statement is genuinely unprovable, which does not detract from its axiomatic validity.

10.4.1.2 Subjecting Chekhov's *Greatness* to Beardsley's Tests

M.C. Beardsley's attempt to answer the general question of aesthetic–artistic value (without specific reference to Chekhov or to any individual in particular) is mentioned in 2.1.1 in a slightly different context, and it is well worth coming back to at this point. Unlike most other discussions of the "*good*" and the "*bad*" in works of art (e.g., Lotman 1976 [1972]; Herrnstein Smith 1979), Beardsley's discussion is not an attempt to evaluate any specific work of art and/or to corroborate such an evaluation, even by way of offering new criteria for it. Rather, he examined a large number of evaluative statements made (within the context of Western/European culture) about art — i.e., statements expressing judgemental opinions about the *good* and *bad* in the arts in general, and in specific works, performances and productions, etc., in particular. Based on this examination, he synthesised three *canons/criteria of aesthetic value*: **unity**, **intensity** and **complexity**. According to him, these are the major criteria, which have been guiding scholars and critics (whether consciously or intuitively) in their assessment of the aesthetic value (merits and faults) of works of art. One can safely assume that *great* is an augmentation/intensification of *good*, in this context. In short, within the western tradition, a work of art's *value* (and, of course, its greatness) is directly proportionate with its *unity*, *intensity* and *complexity*. For the present argument Beardsley's view is accepted, by and large, axiomatically; neither do I tackle here the theoretically challenging question of the balance, inter-relations and interactions between these three criteria. Arguing about these problems is indeed a subject for theoretical studies in aesthetics and art theory, rather than for a study of the poetics of a single author.

As for the *objectivity* of Beardsley's claim, it can be substantiated on two levels: (a) according to his research, it is an *objective fact* that most scholars and critics indeed activate these criteria, whether explicitly or implicitly, in their evaluations of aesthetic merits of works of art;[74] (b) the three criteria themselves are '*objective*' in nature, i.e., hardly susceptible to arbitrary individual whims. Taking these assumptions for granted (i.e., adopting Beardsley's view axiomatically, as a point of departure), it is clear that this Book's descriptions and detailed analyses of Chekhov's major plays substantiate a valid claim to *greatness* made on these plays' behalf. Thus, **Unity** is shown and demonstrated almost throughout the entire Book as a quality that characterises Chekhov's plays to a remarkable extent: (a) in their *outer frame*, the plays' *beginnings* and *endings* (discussed in Chapters 3 and 9, respectively) provide a sense of well-designed *opening* and *closure*, which enhance a powerful effect of *unity*; (b) inside the text proper, each play is characterised by a dense and intricate network of *analogies* on all levels (between personages, events, ideas, and other components of the plays), as well as other unifying strategies unearthed or thrown into bold relief throughout the Book. All of these measures and strategies create an overarching *architectural unity* of the highest order, and its frequent disguise as randomness only adds to its impressive design. *Complexity* is also shown countless times in the Book, often in collaborative interaction with *unity*, and its typically-Chekhovian disguise as *simplicity* provides, in the final analysis, an added dimension to its intricacy. Emotional *intensity*, Beardsley's third canon of artistic–aesthetic value — typically checked and counterbalanced in Chekhov by *restraint* — is likewise a hallmark of Chekhov's art, and its occasional false disguise as *understatement* adds to its relentless force.

Attaching the evaluative quality of *greatness* to Chekhov's *oeuvre* is a matter of wide, virtually axiomatic consent; yet, in his particular case, recipients (readers, spectators, professional analysts) are encouraged by the ethos of his work not to take any consensus for granted and to keep questioning even what seems to be a most elementary truism. His own work or status should not be immune from this imperative, from which, by definition, nothing should be exempt. In this Chekhovian spirit, then, this Subsection's aim is to subject the consensus about Chekhov's *greatness* to scrutiny based on universal criteria, whose universality requires an outside perspective and renders them extraneous to his own system. These criteria, in turn, are of course potentially subject to further questioning and doubting, undermining previous consensuses and rendering them provisional and contingent on further verification *ad infinitum*; however, for the present discussion this is where this subversive process stops: its purpose here is to characterise Chekhov by using theoretical tools as provisional *axioms*; these, in turn, can indeed be questioned in a discussion focusing on theoretical considerations, **but not here**. Here they must retain their axiomatic function, as a solid ground to walk on.

This, anyway, is an attempt to provide the conviction of Chekhov's *greatness*, largely based on intuition, with an 'objective grounding'; in other words, this is another extra-textual vindication, from an additional perspective, of Chekhov's towering presence in our cultural consciousness.

10.4.2 *Chekhovism* and Music-like *Complexity*: An Interart Perspective

In 2.1.1 distinctions were proposed between the *complicated* and the *complex*, and within the latter — between *saturated* and *unsaturated complexity*. These concepts were presented in the context of *drama/theatre* in general, and Chekhov's plays in particular; however, they are applicable to all arts, and indeed the understanding of Chekhov's specific poetics can be served, and perhaps be made accessible to additional audiences, if light is shed on its basic principles from additional angles.

I am proposing here very briefly, then, an *interart perspective* based on *music analogies*.[75] Complementing the juxtaposition of Shakespeare's *saturated complexity* with Chekhov's *unsaturated complexity*, I am proposing to consider **strictly-structural** parallels whereby *Baroque polyphony*, especially Bach's, is analogous to Shakespeare's *saturated* complexity, and *Renaissance polyphony*, especially

Palestrina's, is analogous to Chekhov's *unsaturated complexity*. It was argued in 2.1.2, with reference to the artistic organisation of verbal–fictional (literary–dramatic) texts, that the aesthetic ideal of the former is potential *independence* of constituent elements of the whole, whereas the aesthetic ideal of the latter is *interdependence* of the same. By analogy, the same can be claimed with reference to music: the ideal of a *Baroque fugue*, for instance, can be formulated 'positively': it is the *potential independence* of its separate voices, so that each voice, ideally, has 'a life of its own' as a full-fledged *melody*. If, out of a polyphonic texture of several voices designed to be heard simultaneously, we isolate just one while the others are muted, such a voice is supposed to be self-contained, with a measure of inner *complexity* that makes it interesting enough without recourse to a simultaneous presence of the other voices. Thus, ideally, such voices are all **equally strong**, and the total *complexity* of their simultaneous co-presence is **the result of** the strength and *potential autonomy* of each of them separately. It is this quality that accounts for the *saturated complexity* of the entire whole.[76] In *Renaissance polyphony*, however, the ideal itself is different, and it can be stated 'negatively': no single voice out of simultaneous *polyphony* is supposed to be more interesting, to possess greater *potential autonomy* (i.e., to have a more self-contained 'life of its own' as a separate melody), **than the others**; yet, there is no requirement for any of them to have such a potential independence of its own.[77] Thus, in this ideal model the voices are **equally weak,** and the total *complexity* of such a whole is *unsaturated*.[78]

The analogy with Chapter 2's 'Shakespeare *vs.* Chekhov' comparison is clear. It has to be re-emphasised though that the analogy between Chekhov and Palestrina, as suggested here, is **purely and merely** *structural*, relating as it does to techniques of composition of *wholes* out of *parts*. In any other context, the nature and effect of the styles of Chekhov and Palestrina are as different, even opposed, as they can be. Thus, for instance, the emotional effect of *Chekhovian Restraint*, as presented in Chapter 7, is much closer to the restrained intensity of Bach's music, whereas the effect of Palestrina's music is typically designed — in practice as well as in its aesthetic ideal — to be calm and unexcited (see Cohen 1971 and 1983). Therefore, the latter has very little need for *restraint*, in the absence of 'bursting' emotions to be restrained. This comparison, then, serves as demonstration of the potential autonomy of structural analysis *vis-à-vis* other types of analysis.

Additional parallels and interactions between music and Chekhov's *oeuvre* can be found in Golomb 1984, where music in *Three Sisters* is discussed in great detail, with quite a few examples analysed. That article analyses music in the play (a) as a sound system activated in the *stage directions*, to be literally heard in performance, in interaction with comparable systems (mainly addressing other senses); (b) as a central theme; (c) as a *structural model* for structuration techniques that Chekhov employs. The present Subsection is focused on (c), because it is of greater significance to Chekhov's poetics, but there is room for extensive research into other aspects of interrelation between Chekhov's art and music.

10.5 In Conclusion

There is basic *isomorphism* between *Part II*'s internal, local, *micro* analyses of specific aspects and instances in Chekhov's plays and this Chapter's attempt to provide complementary external, overall *macro* analyses of the same corpus. Whether *zooming in* or *out*, whether practising *long shot, middle shot* or *close up* — i.e., regardless of analytical and methodological techniques and strategies — the results and conclusions finally reached are remarkably similar: all these routes lead to almost identical conclusions displaying Chekhov's *uniqueness* and *greatness*, as two separate but often interrelated qualities: not only stating them, but also describing and analysing their specificness, telling us **how** he is *unique* as well as *great*.

So far, everything has been said from interrelated standpoints of *past* and *present* (Chekhov's as well as ours, in various configurations). It is just right, then, to end the Book with the ultimate complementary perspective: Chekhov's view of the *future*, and the *future*'s view of Chekhov: our own *past* and *present* seen as **his** *future*, and the endless *future* lying ahead of all of us, viewed from integrated perspectives shared by Chekhov, his personages and us. This is the focus of the next, concluding Chapter, bringing the exploratory journey of the entire Book to a close.

Notes

1 A small portion of this Chapter is based on a lecture delivered at an international symposium dedicated to Chekhov's art (*Poetics • Thematics • Hermeneutics*), held at the University of Ottawa (Ontario, Canada) in December 2004 at the initiative of Prof. Douglas Clayton. This Symposium concluded an eventful year worldwide, marking the centenary of Chekhov's death (1904–2004). Printed versions of most of the papers presented at that symposium are published in two parallel volumes: in English (Clayton 2006) and in Russian. Regrettably I could not take part in these volumes because of time-consuming prior commitments. I am gratefully indebted to Prof. Clayton and his colleagues for commissioning that lecture and for oral comments that contributed to the final version of this Chapter.

2 In other words, within this perspective, *diachronic–historical* dimensions of the phenomena under consideration are explicitly ignored and reduced to a *synchronic* view, placing, as it were, all items **next to** each other, quasi-spatially, though in reality they appeared one **after** the other, temporally. This is done for methodological reasons, for the sake of clarity and convenience of argument, bearing in mind the existence of a complementary, temporal–historical perspective (i.e., *Historical Poetics*), presentable separately (as done below, in 10.3). See Harshav 2007, 215–249, especially p. 231. Miles 2003, engaging with Mikhaíl Grómov's Chekhov scholarship, discusses panchronic dimension in the plays (especially *The Cherry Orchard*).

3 *Genres* and the usually-*ism*-suffixed *trends/schools/movements* are different types of text-groupings. Broadly speaking, *genres* are defined and distinguished from each other in terms of intersections between *semantic–thematic* content, *emotional effect* and *structural designs/schemes*, including *plot construction*s (*genres* — especially *tragedy* — have been extensively discussed from Aristotle to the present; for a late 20th-century view, see Krook 1969), whereas the '-*isms*' are largely characterisable as *modelling systems* of realities (see Lotman 1977, especially pp. 1–31) and as *Regulating Principles*

in the process of perceiving artistic texts (see Harshav 2007, especially pp. 3, 10–11, 187; both concepts are elaborated in 10.1.2.0 below). However, these phenomena are not the focus of interest in their own right; rather, they are used here as additional–complementary perspectives from which more light can be shed on the Chekhov phenomenon (alias *Chekhovism*).

4 General ones, like the *OED*, the *Encyclopaedia Britannica*, etc., and specialised ones, like Kelly 1998, Pavis 1982, Pfister 1988 [1977], Preminger 1988, etc. It goes without saying that I am solely responsible for gathering, selecting, synthesising and summarising these materials in my words.

5 Chekhov's consistent refusal to grant the role of 'the author's mouthpiece' to any of his personages is a matter of widespread knowledge that has often been mentioned in the literature, and in the Book, especially in Chapter 5 and its Epigraph. His careful portrayal of the Voïnítskiï–Serebriakóv confrontation is a case in point; see below.

6 Looking at Vánia's remarks from a 21st-century perspective, one tends to regard *Realism* and *Naturalism* as spirits of the past, suitable for a catalogue that would include *Classicism*, *Romanticism*, etc.; one must remember though that Chekhov, writing in the late 1890s, was talking about the most contemporaneous -*isms* around: at that time even his own writings of the most recent past, immediate present and nearest foreseeable future would be described by scholars and critics of the time in these very terms. Moreover, by naming these specific -*isms* as the Professor's topics of study Vánia is unwittingly characterising his opponent as someone engaged in the most updated, 'burning' issues in his profession, a far cry from the fossilised image that he is trying to attach to him.

7 Chekhov challenges his addressees to overcome their expected spontaneous inclination to side with Vánia against the Professor. Such an inclination is based mainly on intuitive *Schadenfreude*, generally at the expense of anyone being ridiculed, as well as on more specific readiness to make fun of the slightest hint of pomposity, especially if based on unfounded intellectual pretence. Here this tendency is also fuelled by some genuinely negative traits of the Professor's character, actually shown on stage: the antipathy that he generates in the audience is indeed well earned. However, even if he is the repulsive old grumbler whom we seem to know, these traits are totally irrelevant to his professional stature, about which we know almost nothing (beside the highly relevant fact that he made his way up to professorship without a social head-start — a point that Vánia tries to raise against him, without realising that it actually works for him and against Vánia's argument). In short: *Uncle Vánia* (the play), unlike "Uncle Vánia" (the personage), provides no valid case against the Professor's academic–professional credentials. Richard Peace (1983, 155–156) speaks of the Professor as "the false man of science, the bogus authority [… of] the barren aestheticism […] of his time-serving academic career". Earlier on in his book (especially pp. 60–65) Peace supplies interesting circumstantial corroboration of this view, which might have intuitively influenced an original audience of Chekhov's compatriots and contemporaries more than a comparable audience nowadays. However, even if Chekhov intended such arguments to have an impact on his audience, they are *extra-textual*, i.e., not realised in the play itself; thus, they work, perhaps, only for a well-informed, mainly scholarly audience, and if they do (which is debatable), the powerful potential for subversive irony pointed out here, which is genuinely Chekhovian, is lost. The jury must be forever out on such interpretative dilemmas; I for one tend to grant more prominence, even credibility, to considerations of Chekhov's unique personal poetics and 'tone' than to general cultural–sociological ones.

8 As evident, *inter alia*, from the Epigraph to Chapter 4, and from his thoughtful and

meticulous (though sometimes bewildering) choice of *genre-labels* for his plays, discussed later on in this Chapter.

9 Chekhov's personal attitudes would have been more relevant in hybrid biographical–textual research (of the *X's life and work* genre) than in this Book, focusing as it does on the nature and characterisation of his poetics. Thus, it is claimed here that Chekhov's art itself defies most classifications more radically than the work of most other great masters. That this is also compatible with his personal attitudes is some kind of a side benefit, reinforcing the claim rather than substantiating it.

10 Thus, in Act 2 of *Uncle Vánia* Ástrov tells Sónia how he is being misjudged when people readily label him as a strange, or even as a mentally disturbed person only because he adopts original and idiosyncratic views and practices and does not conform to expected clichés of behaviour. As shown repeatedly in the Book, Chekhov revelled in individuality and abhorred uniformity and sameness in human beings: for him, the former is a *sine qua non* for being human, whereas the latter is intrinsically opposed not only to being human, but also to being alive.

11 The latter two are related, but not identical: thus, a playwright, correctly characterised as inclined to *Realism*, for instance, can author plays that are *non-realistic* (Ibsen is a typical case in point), just as a playwright famous for *tragedies* can author also *comedies* (Shakespeare is a shining example), etc.

12 Attempts to justify some of Chekhov's plays' *genre*-classifications abound in the literature. More often than not, they try to vindicate Chekhov's own subtitling; in other cases a 'heroic' attempt is made to reverse Chekhov's choices (a case in point is Krook 1969, 119–145, where the author goes out of her way to characterise *The Seagull* and *The Cherry Orchard* — originally subtitled *comedy* — as full fledged *tragedies*). I am not aware, however, of a serious attempt to challenge the very need for, and significance of, such 'matchings' in general, and in Chekhov's case in particular; such an attempt is made in this Chapter.

13 For discussions of the phenomenon of *inevitable circularity* in some relationships between groupings and their defining individual cases, and in other contexts of theoretical reasoning, see Harshav 2007, pp. 1, 3, 264; Krook 1967, 2–6; and in a Chekhovian context, also Stelleman 1992, 13.

14 This *circularity* is also analogous to the concept and procedure of *reversible hierarchies* (see Harshav 2007, 178).

15 A conceptually similar model (in a different context, both substantively and terminologically) is proposed in Krook 1967, 3–6.

16 At this stage I am deliberately ignoring the question whether the playwrights themselves assigned their plays to a group (which they often did). This can add complication to the model, but not undermine it. Moreover, the present discussion is limited to *drama*, but much of it is relevant to other *genres/super-genres*, even to other arts, which will be ignored here.

17 The specifics of this example are beside the point: similar procedures can be applied to other terms (e.g., *comedy*, *Realism*, etc.). It is the process which produces such group labels and nomenclatures and their reception, **in principle**, that is the focus of discussion here.

18 The distinction between (a), (b) and (c) in this model is largely analogous to M.C. Beardsley's distinction between the *work of art*, *criticism* and *aesthetics*, respectively (see Beardsley 1958, especially pp. 3–10). By the way, I am unhappy with the (largely Anglo-American) tradition behind Beardsley's use of the term *criticism*; I subscribe to an alternative (largely East European) tradition that prefers *theory*, *scholarship* and *analysis* (differences between these ignored here) to *criticism* in this sense, relegating

the latter term to less systematic and analytical types of looking at works of art (e.g., reviews, unresearched evaluative essays, etc.).

19 The term 'like us' refers here only to the most elementary fact that they are human beings, whose mental and cognitive processes we can emulate being human ourselves. Thus we are in a position to put ourselves "in their shoes" and challenge them to convince us of their findings, and/or to challenge ourselves to get to the bottom of their processes of reasoning.

20 This 'birthright' — it goes without saying — does not mean replacing, or making superfluous, professional training in the study of the humanities and the arts as academic disciplines. It only means that an initial analogy between people who generate the observed works and people observing them is an important theoretical and analytical point of departure in the humanities. The observation itself is a complex process that cannot be performed without proper training, acquiring methodological tools, etc.

21 This is partly analogous to a question discussed at some length in Chapter 8, especially 8.0, i.e., the interrelationship between what is **specific** to literary art, or its *literariness* (see Harshav 2007, especially 161–173), on the one hand, and what is **important** in it on the other hand.

22 In some studies the explicit subject of investigation is the nature and history of a grouping, which is thus placed at the top of the hierarchy. A case in point is Krook 1967, dedicated to *tragedy*. An inevitable result of its chosen hierarchy is that analyses of specific plays are structurally subordinated to the superordinate theoretical scheme (which is, to my mind, a justified hierarchy of preference in this context). It is by no means an inevitable result of this hierarchy, though, that *tragedy* should be considered superior to other *genres* (as implied in that book), and that plays which its author holds in high esteem (e.g., Chekhov's) are presumed *tragedies* because of their sheer high quality, thereby subordinating their own traits to the genre's (as characterised by the author at that). Such practices are an epitome of 'reading into'.

23 The play was finally accepted for the Theatre's repertoire, expressly in spite these 'shortcomings'. All major biographically-oriented studies of Chekhov give fuller accounts of this Committee's report (quoting the *Ibsenism* 'charge'): see, for instance, Rayfield 1997, 389; Henry 1965, 32; Simmons 1962, 365; and other biographical sources.

24 It is almost certain though that Chekhov himself would have found the term *Chekhovism* laughable: in his first published story (written in the first person), "A Letter to a Learned Neighbour" (1880), the fictional 'author' of the 'letter' writes something like "I passionately love astronomers, poets, metaphysicists, adjunct associate professors, chemists, and other high priests of science". It would fit Chekhov's comic spirit to include *Chekhovists* (or *Chekhovians*) in this ridiculous catalogue.

25 The allusion here is to the title of a famous book by a leading Russian Formalist, Yúriĭ Tyniánov: *Archaists and Innovators* (Tyniánov 1929); I am not aware of an English translation of this book.

26 Caution in this formulation is essential: there can be no total absence of common features between various authors' work; it is a question of **degree**, of 'more *vs.* less' rather than 'yes *vs.* no', as applied to the most crucially specific, defining aspects or features of an author's poetics.

27 It is admittedly difficult, and not altogether consensual, to make fine distinctions between various kinds of -*isms*. Donald Rayfield's characterisation of *The Cherry Orchard* as heralding a "new, arguably **'symbolist' or 'absurdist'** literature" (Rayfield 1994, p. 11) is no exception: quite a few first-rate professional scholars are justifiably inclined to describe Chekhov through a mixture of -*isms* deemed interchangeable in

context (though this interchangeability, in turn, is debatable). My cautious suggestion of *Chekhovism* as a term is admittedly a problematic solution to an insoluble problem.

28 This term (in the original Russian «вторичные моделирующие системы») was coined by members of the Tartu School of Semiotics, mainly Lotman (1977), and constitutes a major concept in their theoretical thinking. These *modelling systems* are deemed *secondary* in relation to the status of *natural languages* as *primary modelling systems*, by which the human brain/mind models its basic/initial perception of the world/reality more directly. One's native language is a primary tool in generating models of the world in one's mind; the actions of other mechanisms that generate models — e.g., *arts*, *myths*, *religions*, *ideologies*, *scientific theorems*, etc. — are modelled, as an 'upper floor', on the workings of *languages* in the 'ground floor'. These analogies and contrasts between *primary* and *secondary modelling systems* are clarified in Lotman's studies, and need not be elaborated here.

29 Harshav's *regulating principle* is presented mainly in the context of the inevitable *circularity*, whereby we glean or reconstruct certain properties from a text, and these 'tell us', cumulatively, something general about it (e.g., that it is *ironic*, *tragic*, even *metrical*, etc.), and then — here comes the *circularity* — this *regulating principle*, in turn, 'tells us in what sense' to read the text from which it was gleaned (thus, the same sequence of words can, in principle, be read *ironically*, *figuratively*, *literally*, etc., and we choose which is more suitable in context, activating the aforementioned *circularity*). This conceptual framework complements the one behind the concept of *secondary modelling system*, which is more central to the present argument.

30 The concept of *Mimesis* (by this or "any other name") has been incessantly discussed in the literature from time immemorial to the present; see Auerbach 1953 for a classical 20th-century study of the subject, which is also discussed in 5.1.2 from a different perspective. By contrast, the concept of *Modelling Systems* is much more recent.

31 By the way, this is not necessarily an 'either-or' situation: one can use both methods complementarily, but I have chosen to focus on the latter, for reasons spelled out in this Section.

32 This statement is not intended to be as negative and judgemental as it appears to be (Chekhov's own 'defence' against demands to answer questions rather than ask them 'correctly' is irrelevant here, because he applies his remark to *artists* and works of art, rather than to scholars and academic studies, as argued in 5.1.6). Moreover, the generalisations and formulations quoted here are unobjectionable as far as they go. Again, some *circularity* in wording and formulation in these matters is to a certain extent inevitable, especially if a *mimesis*-oriented approach is adopted; much of this difficulty can be avoided, or at least mitigated, yet not completely eliminated, if a *modelling systems* approach is adopted instead. The least (and often the most) one can achieve, then, is awareness of the intuitive nature of one's formulations: its inevitability vindicates its use, as long as its corollary fuzziness and subjectivity are taken into account, neither denied nor ignored.

33 An association comes to mind: Michelangelo is reported to have defined the process of sculpting as '*taking a block of stone and removing whatever is superfluous*' (I am not sure of the exact words, but this is the idea). This analogy, concretised by the change of material from airy words into tangible stone, seems to reverse the image of selection in the process, but actually it is an imaginative illustration of selection and modelling shared by various arts.

34 Preoccupation with such issues seems to have been 'in the air' around the turn of the 20th century in various parts of the world. Thus, in his seminal *Aspects of the Novel*, E.M. Forster (1975 [1927], 55–65) says that all people must spend about a third of their

lives in sleep, whereas love (however defined) takes much less of a person's time on earth; yet, no novel would qualify as *realistic* if it dedicated respective portions of its text to these two human preoccupations.

35 For instance, 'trivialities' (e.g., cups of tea, and **undrunk** ones at that [*Three Sisters*, especially Act 2]; cucumbers and literally eaten ones at that [*The Cherry Orchard*, Act 2]), 'irrelevancies' (e.g., "philosophising" everywhere, Balzac's wedding in *Three Sisters*, Act 2), *pauses* galore, when nothing happens, *offstage personages* and other unheard and unseen personages and events, etc.

36 The notion of *art* as used by Chekhov according to this memoir is tricky, as it is in any reference to *realistic illusion*: the portrait is physically real but perceptually a work of art and artifice, whereas the mental three-dimensional image that it creates in the viewers' minds is technically illusory but mentally conceived as 'real'.

37 *Realism in drama*, thus characterised, enjoys the status of '*default*' model, at least within the cultural tradition of the West. In this sense it is analogous to *tonality* and *functional harmony* in music and *perspective* and *figurative* styles in painting: they all are perceived **now, and in the foreseeable future**, as the 'normal', *unmarked model*, which serves for us as a kind of timeless yardstick, since all other models of all periods, both before and after it historically, are measured and characterised in relation to it. While newer styles keep emerging, there is always some creative activity in the style of these '*default*' *models*, in all arts: indeed, works of *realistic* literature/drama, tonal music, perspective-governed figurative painting, etc., have been, are incessantly being, and in all probability will always be, created, alongside other trends that appear and sometimes disappear. Thus, *avant-garde* vogues and fashions come and go (e.g., *dadaism*, *cubism*, *futurism*, *dodecaphonic* and other *serial* music), whereas *tonality*, *Realism* and *perspective* never die. The reasons for the durability and resilience of these 'default' systems are manifold, but *cognitive* ones are undoubtedly paramount among them: they cater more than other systems to acquired, though non-arbitrary, *schemata of perception and cognition*. Western minds will always recognise and respond to *tonality* in music (see all Dalia Cohen's studies in *Works Consulted*), and to comparable types of *default* in other arts.

38 Indeed, the change from *verse* (which for centuries reigned supreme in theatre-acting and play-writing in Europe) to *prose* is of crucial significance in the 'realistic revolution' of the late 19th and early 20th centuries. The *model of reality* of most pre-realistic drama — from ancient Greece via Shakespeare to early 19th century — relied on the presentation on stage of people in position of highest authority, who speak *verse* (*rhymed* or *blank*), in blatant contrast to the way people have been speaking since time immemorial, and will be speaking till doomsday, in reality. As Molière's M. Jourdain discovered to his amazement, people normally 'speak prose'; yet, hardly one century has passed since they began to speak prose on stage as well. However, once they started, roughly a century ago, prose on stage has become the *default*, so much so that we tend to forget that it was a revolutionary innovation.

39 This quote underscores the unequivocally positive attitude to the notion of *verisimilitude* adopted in most of the literature about *Realism*: it is consensually a prime aesthetic ideal, 'a good thing' that everybody — whether a practising playwright or a scholar–analyst — aspires to achieve and/or to praise in others. Various individuals, schools and ideologies differ on how to achieve it and vie for recognition as the closest to it. Historically this is not a foregone conclusion: for centuries of *pre-realistic drama* a 'slice-of-life' effect on stage was not an aim; rather, blatant artifice reigned supreme. It is a comparatively new development that a model of *verisimilitude* has become a major ideal of drama or theatre, a criterion to judge a play's merit by. See below.

40 There is an obvious *asymmetry*, whereby *Chekhovism* and *Realism* are not meaning-fully comparable as terms: the former is explicitly related to a single author, whereas the latter is just as explicitly an umbrella-term for an unspecified number of authors. Within such group-terms as *Realism* one can speak of more partial, individual-name-linked -*ism*s like (early) *Ibsenism*, [*Tennessee*] *Williamsism*, [Edward] *Albeeism*, *Pinterism*, etc. etc. (these terms are not suggested for use, just for illustration) in more recent decades. By the way, the *Ibsenism model*, and comparable ones related to other authors, have their idiosyncratic components that are not part of 'general' *Realism*. Thus, specifically, *Ibsenism* includes a 'hidden dark secret' that comes to light in the course of the play: this essential component of Ibsen's personal poetics is not an essen-tial part of the general model of *Realism*. However, as argued here, not all authors are equally *unique*, a term that is not synonymous with *great*: thus, Ibsen may be regarded by some as *greater* than Chekhov (which is an evaluative position), yet less *unique* — i.e., having more common traits with others (which is a descriptive–analytical position).

41 This restricted usage is anyway prevalent in the literature. There are also other usages, as Jakobson shows; the present argument is only that the restricted sense adopted here has methodological advantages in comparison to broader and vaguer alternatives.

42 An analogical discussion of everyday *vs.* professional usage of terminologies is provided in 4.1

43 It is enough to look into Hamlet's instructions to the players in order to understand how non-*realistic* (or, rather, pre-*realistic*) and *non-mimetic* Shakespeare's vision is: when preaching to them (III, ii, 17–24) about their duty "to hold as 'twere the mirror up to nature", he goes on to interpret what he means by that, which refers almost exclusively to the moral dimension of a message on stage: "to show virtue her feature, scorn her own image", etc.; in other words, to be 'realistic' *à la* Shakespeare/Hamlet one need not speak 'naturally' (*blank verse*, rich *imagery* and *figurative language*, so typical of Shakespeare's style, are indeed blatantly 'unnatural'), nor respond 'naturally' to others, etc., as long as one faithfully reflects the "true" moral dimension.

44 In fact, Konstantín has very peculiar ideas about "dreams" or "visions" (there is a chal-lenging translation problem here); there is hardly a resemblance, however remote, between his play-fragment in Act 1 and any account of people's "dreams" in real life, and even "visions" is problematic in this context. One can say to him kind-of '*speak for yourself: maybe your dreams and visions are like that, but not ours*': frankly, is there anyone known to any reader personally whose dreams or fantasies are related in any significant way to what Konstantín's play is about? This of course is a *mimesis*-inspired exercise, but characterising Konstantín's play as a "dream" is so counter-intuitive that I could not resist the temptation to ask these rhetorical questions.

45 Strindberg, by the way, wrote a manifesto of *Naturalism* as Introduction to *Miss Julie* (Strindberg 1962 [1888]); a close reading of this text can show that in most crucial senses Chekhov did not conform to *Naturalism* as presented by Strindberg.

46 By the way, in his earliest published piece, the comic story "A Letter to a Learned Neighbour", Chekhov treats *Darwinism* (viewed through naïve and ignorant anti-*Darwinism*) as a subject for laughs, rather than as a mindless, frightening monster whose sinister presence controls our lives.

47 A notable exception is Nína's remark to Konstantín in *The Seagull*'s Act 2: looking at the seagull that he had just shot and brought to her, she says to him: "And this seagull here is, apparently, a symbol, but forgive me, I don't understand it... I am too simple to understand you". I shall not try to analyse this amazingly complex and multi-functional *réplique* here — neither in its basically 'realistic' sense, within the *inner plane*, nor in its largely *symbolic* sense, within the *outer plane*. Suffice it to say that it

functions in both, and designed to encourage the addressees to investigate the interaction between the seagull's multiple functions on both these planes of communication. Anyway, this is an example of Chekhov's insistence on providing every *symbol* with *fictional–realistic* substantiation.

48 "Philosophising" is hardly an exception, being usually explicitly shallow (unlike the working of *symbols*) and motivated (as shown in Chapter 8) — both on the *inner/fictional plane* and on the *outer/rhetorical plane* — by needs other than solving problems of incomprehensibility by *symbolic* means. Almost on the contrary: "philosophising" comes in where there are no problems of understanding in sight, and adds to the text hardly any *symbolic* explanations with heuristic powers: it tells us very little we don't know without it in terms of content. Its added semantic value is much more indirect and lies elsewhere, mainly in the text's rhetoric, as shown in Chapter 8.

49 There is one possible exception — the famous sound of the 'snapping string' in *The Cherry Orchard* — but Chekhov does take care to provide some 'realistic' explanation in the text itself, however flimsy it may appear; thus, it does exist as a *real* sound within the play's *fictional* world, and the quest for its possibly *unreal* meaning, perhaps *symbolic* one, is instigated by the personages themselves. For another instance see Marsh 2012.

50 Especially in the cultural context of 19th-century Russia, the two terms — *symbolistic* and *decadent* — were closely related, as demonstrated by Chekhov himself through Arkádina's responses to Konstantín's play in Act 1 of *The Seagull*. See Donchin 1958 and Tabachnikova 2010 for elaborations of this subject.

51 A shining example of this is the 'melancholy waltz' scene in *The Seagull*, Act 4, discussed in 4.3.3.

52 Examples are innumerable: for instance, the careful wording of Trigórin's design for a "seagull story", *The Seagull*, Act 2; the very last sentence of *Three Sisters*; the false impression of vagueness is generated, e.g., in some "philosophising" tirades. A misleading façade of vagueness that hides carefully designed precision may indeed be similar to some *Impressionists'* impeccable technique used to achieve analogous results in painting.

53 In the case of the greatest masters in all arts, and their greatest works, such a conception can be encountered in the literature, with or without appending the suffix *-ism* to their names. Thus, for instance, most books on the history of *drama* and *theatre* discuss Shakespeare on equal footing with whole periods, rather than as just one Elizabethan poet and playwright out of many; Bach and Beethoven are also often categorised in analogy to entire periods in music-history books; The entry *"Mass"* in *The Oxford Companion to Music* regards even a single work — Bach's *B Minor Mass* — as tantamount to an entire *period* in the history of this *genre*.

54 As shown in Chapter 2, of all possible *-isms*, Chekhov's plays are a celebration of *Structuralism*, which is not a school in the arts, but in the disciplines studying them. In other words, the statement that Chekhov is a *Structuralist* may be true only figuratively, in a context totally different from the idea of his being a *Realist*, *Symbolist*, *Impressionist*, etc., which has just been disproved.

55 Neither of them is able to realise that, at least to a certain extent, he exposes himself to ridicule; in Shakespeare's case, it is also unclear how seriously, or jokingly, Polonius takes the *genres* he is blabbering about.

56 It is worth noting that Friedrich Dürrenmatt *genre*-subtitled his *The Visit of the Old Lady* (1952) with the label *tragicomedy*. An analysis of this play proves him right: the play is a carefully designed combination of typical elements of both *tragedy* and *comedy*, which constantly interact in its text, shedding light and providing complementary and

contradictory perspectives on each other, while remaining distinct rather than merged. *Tragicomedy*, then, is an exceptionally apt label for a play that is **both** *tragedy* **and** *comedy*; it is analogous to chemical *mixture*. Chekhov, by contrast, created a blend comparatively similar to a chemical *compound*: a new integrative *genre*-language, which is **neither** *comedy* **nor** *tragedy*, though often reminiscent of either, or both. We can definitely apply this view to all four major plays, regardless of what Chekhov chose for *genre* labels/subtitles for each of them.

57 By the way, this is a kind of **selective** *realisation of potentials* — i.e., another way of activating a major creative–generative mechanism of *Chekhovism*: each of these *genres* is a given potential, out of which Chekhov chooses to realise certain features, according to his changing needs and, above all, his changing visions.

58 The same applies to other arts: thus, in music, Handel, Telemann, even Bach, are para-digmatic representatives of *late baroque* music and can be grouped with others under this 'umbrella' more easily than their contemporary Scarlatti; Haydn is more easily grouped with others under *classicism* than Beethoven, who is partly grouped under *romanticism*, but much less typically so than Schubert or Schumann; etc. In all such cases individualistic *mavericks* do not have a stronger, or weaker, claim to *greatness* by their sheer incompatibility with established *groupings*.

59 Senderovich 1994, for instance, makes a powerful case for the *comedic* nature of the play, characterising it as "a comedy in a very special sense". This means that its genre-subtitle, however justified, is still problematic. The case in Senderovich's article is based primarily on convincing and thought-provoking materials relating to Chekhov himself, rather than to millennia of tradition associated with the term *comedy*: the matter of matching this play with this tradition is far from settled or resolved, to say the least, no matter how one looks at it.

60 Indeed, especially in Russia near Chekhov's time, *drama* was considered much closer to *tragedy* and opposed to *comedy*; however, Chekhov's conscious refusal to label any of his plays *tragedy* is telling.

61 My late teacher, Poet–Professor Lea Goldberg (1911–1970), said in a Chekhov class that I attended in the late 1960s that if the death (especially a violent and unnatural one) of the major protagonist is a *sine qua non* of *tragedy*, the death of Túsenbach in *Three Sisters* does not qualify, as he is not **the** protagonist of the play. Rather, in this context, "the Moscow Dream" — alive and held in high esteem at the play's beginning and virtu-ally murdered towards its ending — is the play's relevant *tragic protagonist*. Even if this imaginative, thought-provoking yet highly debatable statement is rejected, there are other typically *tragedical* features (connecting to the *Greek* rather than the *Shakespearean models* of *tragedy*) that only *Three Sisters*, of all Chekhov's plays, possesses; not least, the function of Ól'ga as the character who utters the first and last words of the play, supplying not only *primacy* and *recency effects*, but also a hesitant yet authoritative overviews of a *choric* nature for the entire play. Lea Goldberg's argu-ment is objectionable, then, on various counts, mainly because of the substitution of a *symbol* and an *idea* for a 'real' personage; but to my mind it does reflect the actual rela-tion between the nature of each play and its subtitle; I would like to re-emphasise that in all likelihood Chekhov never thought of such a downgrading/demoting formula consciously, but this does not invalidate the idea that such a formula did actually operate in his mind.

62 The *tragic protagonist* should have a **capacity** for self-awareness, i.e., a ***potential*** that is typically realised too late. The characteristic *tragic flaw* of the *protagonist* prevents him from **timely** awareness that could have pre-empted his downfall. However, the awakening of self-awareness, however belated, indicates its potential within him, whereas Chekhov's personages typically lack the initial potential.

63 This scheme is based on 'serious' drama only — i.e., excluding *comic genres* and including *tragedy* and cognate genres and types of plays, including the vague notion of *drama* in a narrow sense, defined more 'negatively' as *non-comic* than in any specific 'positive' terms. 'Classical' *Comedy* and its *sub-genres (farce, satire,* etc.), in their established pre-Chekhov meanings, have been ignored here, because of their irrelevance to Chekhov's Four Major Plays. They are relevant to his earlier plays, especially one-acters like "The Bear", "Jubilee", "The Proposal", etc.; but these, in turn, are hardly relevant to the Book's concerns. Reid 2007 virtually labels all Chekhov's major plays as *comedies,* but this is an extremely rare and virtually unexplained and unsubstantiated use of the term. I am not aware of any other study which applies this term to Chekhov's entire later plays so indiscriminately

64 This enormous time-range includes, of course, equally enormous variety on all parameters. It is only in the context of highlighting Chekhov's uniqueness that this 'period' has been grouped together.

65 Admittedly, late 20th-century *drama* is a 'mixed bag' of a lot of different types of poetics, so that generalisations in this scheme have very partial validity in the corpus; they are based primarily on a sample of plays by Beckett, Ionesco, and other *absurd* playwrights, and formulated with highlighting differences and similarities with *Chekhovism* in mind. Moreover, some of the most leading and influential playwrights, who have unique artistic systems of their own, are absent from the comparisons and schemes presented in this Book, notably Brecht, Pirandello, and many others. Arguably, contrastive comparisons with these masters may be less relevant to *Chekhovism,* and in any case their *models* — if incorporated into the Book's argument — would add considerable complication to the argument, possibly without comparable addition to its strength. Comparative–contrastive perspectives on these great authors' poetics in relation to Chekhov's do deserve separate consideration and further study, preferably with authors' expertise in their work (which the present author cannot claim).

66 In early plays (from antiquity to the 19th century) one can occasionally encounter *supernatural elements,* whether characters (gods, ghosts, spirits, etc.) or events (miracles, apparitions, etc.).

67 Curiously enough, some *supernatural elements* returned to the stage, 'via the back door', in some 20th-century plays, in a kind of 'post-realistic backlash', together with the return of the soliloquy (the latter, often reminiscent of the *commedia dell'arte* 'flirting with the audience' more than of the Shakespeare type); thus we meet angels in Brecht, fictionalised characters posing as real ones in Pirandello, etc. Such elements in *pre-realistic* and in *post-realistic* drama are quite different in nature and function: in the former, the text conveys real belief in those phenomena's existence, in the latter their presence does not convey *verisimilitude,* and the belief in their existence is faked in its tone.

68 This parameter relates to the main protagonists' overall stature: early authors shaped their protagonists in their own image in terms of intellectual and verbal capabilities: thus, a Hamlet or Lear possesses the full extent of Shakespeare's own abilities to 'capture the world in words', achieving the highest level of expression in poetic, versified language (which is another reason for the audience to look up to people who speak that way). The gradual decline in the stature of personages, complemented by a comparable rise in the stature of *implied spectators,* as summarised here, is presented in 6.0.

69 Late 20th-century drama is characterised by **variety,** in all parameters. Thus, sometimes against the historical one-way process of lowering the stature of personages, there are occasional moments of verse, song etc., that often elevate the verbal style of personages, without altering the basic trend. Some songs, however, deliberately include lower, sub-standard language.

70 This parameter relates to the **centrality** of language *vis-à-vis* non-verbal components of the theatrical medium as well as to the communicative functioning of language. "Self-oriented" means language that draws attention to itself, which is a typical feature of verse (see Jakobson's 1960/1967 "Poetic function"), sometimes at the expense of its message; 'goal-oriented' language focuses on the communicative content conveyed and away from the verbal message itself.

71 This parameter focuses on differences between 'ping-pong' dialogue with short verbal exchanges and those consisting of relatively longer and self-contained *répliques*. The latter are typical of poetic dialogues, where some *répliques* resemble relatively self-contained poems.

72 "Communication" in Parameters 11 and 12 relates also to *semantic integration* of texts spoken on stage and their comprehensibility. Chekhov typically portrays low-level communication on stage but maintains channels of communication with a thinking, attentive audience. Interestingly, typical late 20th-century plays (of the '*absurd* trend') are inclined to reverse this hierarchy: characters on stage seem to communicate freely with each other, while the audience is 'left in the dark'. Presenting this phenomenon from its *communicational* aspect complements its presentation from its *comprehensibility* and *semantic integration* aspect: there is a direct proportion between the two.

73 Again, a text that resists communicability and comprehensibility requires exceptional cognitive powers to decipher its messages; therefore, the stature of the *implied spectator* in Chekhov, and even more so in the less-communicative *absurd*, is higher. This argument clinches the one presented in 6.0.

74 As I argued in Chapter 2, Note 10, I differ with Beardsley only about the totality of the applicability of his claims in this respect, not about their basic validity

75 A more comprehensive *interart perspective* should have included visual arts, dance, cinema etc., but I, personally, cannot provide any of these competently. Cynthia Marsh (2010–2011 and 2012b) and Valentína Silánt'ïeva (2000) have contributed thought-provoking studies of Chekhov's works from perspectives of visual arts. John Reid's (2007) analogies with *opera* provide a different perspective for comparing Chekhov's work with music, which can be seen as complementary to the present Chapter.

76 This ideal is too great a challenge to achieve in every single case, so that in many cases what we hear is 'fake *independence*' (or 'fake *autonomy*'), just an attempt, often a 'heroic' one, to realise the ideal fully. Bach — undoubtedly the creator of the most complex music ever composed — achieved it more often and more completely than any of his contemporaries, but even in his works there are some instances of such 'fake'.

77 There is no room here for the analysis of actual musical examples; such an analysis would contrast, say, a melodic line isolated from one of the choruses in Bach's *B minor Mass* with a comparable line isolated from Palestrina's *Missa Papae Marcelli*, and would yield a richer inner texture of the former compared to the latter.

78 A third model, of **dependence** of one of the voices upon the others, is not polyphonic (e.g., a Mozart piano-sonata with '*Alberti bass*' that is blatantly uninteresting on its own, or many other types of textures in post-*baroque* music). It is tempting to regard such music as less complex, which is usually the case in its *micro texture*, but not necessarily in its overall *macro structure*. A truly *interart* study of these matters requires, of course, much broader space in a discussion devoted to it as its central subject.

CHAPTER
11

Chekhov and Posterity
CLOSING THE BOOK'S OUTER CIRCLE

Those who will live 100–200 years after us, and for whom we are
now paving the way — will they remember us kindly?

(Ástrov, *Uncle Vánia*, Act 1)

11.0 Preliminary: Closing the Outer Circle[1]

To end this journey through Chekhov's plays and their poetics (with excursuses to
some of his stories), it is worthwhile to take a look at the present and future perspectives of his work and world — the 'interface' between that world and our own
present and future. This last, concluding Chapter is devoted to an examination of
this interface from both its ends: on the one hand, the direct and indirect *presence*
of the future (which is, by definition, yet-*absent at present*) in Chekhov's plays,
and particularly *Three Sisters*, in which this theme has its most powerful explicit
and implicit representations, and on the other hand, a look at the relevance and
significance of the Chekhov phenomenon in our world (which closes the circle
opened in the Epigraph by Robert Louis Jackson at the beginning of this book).

Chekhov approaches the themes of near and distant future — which virtually
take us beyond the horizon of one's own life and death into exploring perspectives
of universally human mortality and posterity — largely through the prism of inter-
generational relationships. Indeed, all his major plays (and many of his stories) are
intensely concerned with a cluster of themes revolving around mortality, which
ultimately amounts to the *absence* of a **personal** future, and posterity, which is the
presence of a **collective** future. His covert yet intense attention is particularly
focused on the challenge of facing the inevitability of our mortality and the
frequent psychological need to ignore or evade it (indeed, it is a major instance of
a general need for *self-delusion*, so typical of Chekhov's personages, as argued in
5.1). This thematic cluster involves direct and indirect views of the shaky/transi-
tory *versus* the constant/durable in life and our experience of *time* and the world.

As seen repeatedly in much of the secondary literature (this Book included),
Chekhov often and typically manages a fusion between intense, precise and subtle

treatment of minute details, on the one hand, and broad, all-encompassing generalisations on the other. The former may equally apply to individual personages and
to specific events, scenes, ideas, theatrical moments, etc.; the latter may equally
apply to various kinds of human collectives (generations, nations, classes, societies etc.), culminating in striking insights into the significance and destiny of
humanity as a whole.[2] Granted, the major plays are focused on a limited number
of individuals, each of whom possesses unique character traits, personal and family
history, and of course very specific constraints of *time* and *place* — i.e., Chekhov's
own Russia in the second half of the 19th century; in short, hardly 'generalisable
material'. Yet, there are few texts in world literature and drama which can match
Chekhov's plays, let alone surpass them, in terms of applicability and relevance to
the most durable universals of human philosophy, psychology, history, society, and
destiny — in short, to the most profound experience of the human condition and
the meaning(fulness) of life.

Thus, Chekhov (perhaps without being fully aware of it, and in all likelihood
without intending it) is saying something to **our** generation, over a century after
his, and to posterity beyond us, by showing a complex vision of inter-generation
relationships, with far-reaching ramifications, way beyond the specific situations
shown on stage. "In two-three hundred [...] a thousand years, the precise period
of time is not the issue," — says Vershínin in Act 2 of *Three Sisters* — "a new,
happy life will dawn"; and in a thousand years from now (assuming that humanity
and the theatre will still be around), a thirty-first century Vershínin will stand on
stage anew, and say "In two-three hundred years" etc. Thus, Chekhov encapsulates
future-oriented content within the time of the theatre, which is by definition ever-
present-tense, potentially yet inherently destined to be re-born and re-activated
time and time again, thus creating an intense effect of chasing the horizon in vain,
pursuing a never-attainable glorious future. This is one manifestation of the interaction between the transitory and the immortal in life in general, and in the
juxtaposition life–art in particular.[3]

11.1 Some Truisms[4] on Inter-Generational Transmissions

11.1.1 On *Heredity*

Every human individual is born into an inter-generational relationship with parents
(and/or parent-substitutes). Later on in life most individuals create such relationships with the new generations they produce. As a result, collectively, human
societies and generations are engaged in complex relationships with older generations (dead and alive) and younger ones (usually alive). A major factor in this
never-ending process involves the transfer of genes from one generation to the
next, which is not exclusive to humans. This is called *Heredity*, and it is responsible for the continued existence of the species, and of more closely knit groupings
within it (e.g. nations, communities, families), transcending, as it were, the tem-
porality and mortality of the individual into the potential timeless continuity and
virtual immortality of the species and its sub-groups. *Heredity*, as we know, is an
involuntary process: we cannot choose our parents, children, siblings, and other

blood relatives, nor do we have any impact on the actual processes and procedures by which *heredity* is realised, or on *family resemblance*, which is perhaps its most obvious hallmark.

11.1.2 On *Inheritance*

By and large, humans tend to have **possessions**, or **property**, much more than other species and beings (inasmuch as such terms can be applied to non-humans in the first place).[5] At any rate, only humans have developed sophisticated systems of law and custom, regulating the possession of property — i.e., material worldly goods — belonging to them. One of the main qualities (or *properties*, in a different sense) of many kinds of property is their potentially permanent durability, at least much above and beyond the life expectancy of their individual human owners. This primarily applies, of course, to genuinely indestructible possessions, like land (cosmic catastrophes notwithstanding), and to nearly as durable ones (if not destroyed by extraordinary physical force) like solid houses, but also to much smaller yet precious possessions like jewels; all of these usually outlive their human possessors. It is common human practice, usually regulated by law, that a dead person's property is transferred to his/her surviving family; in other words, usually the unchosen heirs of the *hereditary genes*[6] are also the chosen heirs of the *inherited property*. This aspect of human life is the major feature or component of what is commonly referred to by the term *Inheritance*. Unlike involuntary *heredity*, potentially-voluntary *inheritance* is exclusively human.

11.1.3 On *Heritage*

Humans — and only humans — create, adopt, perceive and experience a whole array of spiritual, intellectual, artistic, ideological, scientific, religious, philosophical, and other **non-material** possessions/properties. These — including values and beliefs — are made to outlive their individual creators and carriers. Such possessions are inherently indestructible, almost like land, and can live forever, potentially,[7] though they do require some kind of physical object and/or mortal human carrier (usually the brains of humans) in order to exist and survive.[8] The material aspects of works of art and *intellectual property* (e.g. physical objects like books and paintings, prices and copyrights of works of art, patents of scientific inventions) are indeed subject to procedures of *inheritance*, often ensuring that finances will stay with the gene carriers; however, the most distinctly human possessions — e.g. thoughts, beliefs, scientific knowledge, artistic creativity, aesthetic experience, in their original abstract forms as potentials to be realised — are not, and cannot be, inherently restricted to territorial or material enclaves. This part of what human generations pass on to their successors is called *Legacy*, or *Heritage*.[9]

11.1.4 Conclusion: On *the 3Hs*

These three aspects of trans-generational transmission — biological–genetic *heredity*, material–financial *inheritance*, and spiritual–intellectual *heritage* — are part of the never-ending quest of humanity[10] for immortality, to beat death and triumph over time. *Heritage*, the most intrinsically exclusively-human among them, is usually born in the mind of an individual human originator,[11] yet often becomes the intellectual and spiritual possession of human collectives — nations, societies, generations, civilisations[12] — rather than individuals, though one can also speak of the *heritage* that a particular individual receives from an individual predecessor, whether a parent, a teacher, mentor, friend, written materials, scientific and artistic experiences, etc.

Heredity takes place within families and biologically–genetically related *individuals*, but is extended to similarly related groups of individuals (e.g., members of a species); *inheritance* takes place usually within *families*, but not necessarily so;[13] and *heritage* can take place within the entire range between the *individual* and *humanity as a whole*. *Heredity* works its ways in stealth, as it were, divorced from controlling human awareness; *inheritance* and *heritage*, however, are usually transmitted with a great deal of such voluntary awareness. All these phenomena define and manage major aspects in humanity's mental handling of **time**, trying to come to terms (or to grips) with it and regulate it. The main coordinates of human existence are *time* and *place*. It is mainly in this context that Chekhov was so intensely preoccupied with *the 3Hs*.

11.2 *Heredity* and *Heritage* in Chekhov's Plays: Past, Present, Future

11.2.1 Preliminaries

It takes a considerable measure of effacement — of oneself and/or of the other(s) — to define humans, whether individuals or collectives, as merely transitional links between their predecessors (parents, mentors, ancestors) and successors (children, disciples, posterity). Such an approach reduces humans to mere insignificant links in an endless chain, in which all the other links, past and future, are more important than the one to which the individual in question belongs.[14] Maybe this is the way biology treats us all as mere carriers of genes, whose sole *raison d'être* is to preserve and perpetuate groups and species; yet, human consciousness has grown to oppose and reject this biological edict (and this Chapter aims to show the magnitude and determination of Chekhov's rejection of it). The temporal–spatial–deictic expression of this attitude is negating the present *now* in favour of the past and/or future *then*:[15] according to this attitude, the *present* is a poor player, a walking shadow signifying nothing, a flimsy connection between the boundless infinities of *past* and *future*. Such an approach was promoted, *inter alia*, by religious and revolutionary movements, in their endeavour to undermine the self-esteem of *individuals*, sacrificing them to *collectives* (e.g., one's nation, social class, religion, political party); these collectives, in turn, are also encouraged, even brainwashed, to sacrifice themselves for the glorious legacy of their ancestors, and/or for the shining visions of posterity, branding any focus on the present, embodied in an *I*, or even a *We*, as selfish and petty. Of course, such ideologies can be (and have been) challenged, and the hierarchies reversed or at least radically changed, placing the individual and generation living at present in legitimate focus, while defining predecessors and/or successors in relation to them, rather than vice versa, in the spirit of a liberal–individualistic "there is no time like the present", or even a nihilistic "eat, drink and be merry, for tomorrow we may die". In this context, the total disregard for time present, as a constant philosophy or ideology of life, is tantamount to the negation of humanity as a whole, and certainly of all its individuals, because in every generation one can point to a past and/or a future for which the present is supposed to sacrifice its life, or at least its well-being; there is hardly any **logical** substantiation to apply such sacrifices to a particular individual, generation, nation etc. — e.g., Chekhov's 19th-century Russia, late 20th-century France, etc. — which just happens to be one's own by some unlucky coincidence.

Very characteristically, Chekhov presents this theme with its complex ramifications without explicitly embracing any ideology. However, as a person, not through his artistic writing,[16] he did express his much-quoted view of the "Holy of Holies", which implies a clear opposition to any sacrifice of the human individual for collectives, ideologies, etc.[17] Chekhov's views of the subject — to the limited extent that they can be learned from his fictional writings — are much more complex and balanced.[18]

11.2.2 *Heredity* in Chekhov and Others: Present Variations on Past Themes

Out of *the 3Hs*, the presence of *heredity* is the most indirect in Chekhov's plays (as we have seen, especially in 10.1.2.2, in his treatment of the subject Chekhov is fundamentally different from *naturalistic* or 'Darwinian' determinism and negation of the autonomy of the individual). Explicit references to *Heredity*, then, are virtually nonexistent in Chekhov's plays, and even implicit ones are few and far between, hardly noticeable. Moreover, even Chekhov's "philosophisers" hardly ever "philosophise" about *Heredity*. Yet, the subject does play a central role in all of Chekhov's plays, at least indirectly, through the focus on *family* — a feature they all share.

Indeed, the centrality of families is the rule, rather than the exception, in most works of fiction, in narrative prose and drama alike; therefore, an effective way of exposing Chekhov's uniqueness is to place his work and world in a comparative–contrastive perspective. Even a very brief (and inevitably superficial) look at the work of two other major masters in the history of Drama can thus contribute to the characterisation of Chekhov in this context.

11.2.2.1 *Heredity* in Shakespeare
Shakespeare's plays abound in both implicit and explicit statements on the subject. Most of his siblings are markedly different from each other in terms of personality, and they often function as polar opposites, *protagonist* and *antagonist* (e.g. Lear's daughters and Gloucester's sons in *King Lear*, Rosalind's and Celia's respective fathers, and Orlando and his brother in *As You Like It*, Hamlet Senior

and Claudius in *Hamlet*, etc.). The same applies to some parents and their children, and other types of blood relations. Counter examples (i.e. similarity in personality and morals between blood relatives) are usually less prominent.[19] It is not uncommon for a Shakespearean personage to wonder about the dissimilarity between siblings or parents/children, thereby belying the expected similarity between them.[20] In Shakespeare's world, then, the combination of external, visual resemblance (as especially expounded in plays featuring twins, for instance) with contrast in personality traits is a common occurrence.

11.2.2.2 *Heredity* in Ibsen

In Ibsen's prose *realistic–social* plays (e.g. *The Wild Duck*, *Ghosts*, etc.) *heredity* is often an inescapable fate or destiny, and when it surfaces in a play, usually as a result of unearthing the typically Ibsenian dark secret, it is in the form of direct genetics (e.g. hereditary disability or disease; this, indeed, is a *Naturalist* trait in Ibsen's poetics). While Shakespeare allowed visual resemblance between blood relatives to propel some of his plots, especially in the comedies, similar focus cannot be found in Ibsen or in Chekhov. This in all likelihood is a result of differences between the types of theatrical poetics and norms and conventions of *staged reality* in the theatres of Shakespeare's time and those of the late 19th century: Shakespeare knew full well that visual dissimilarities between actors would belie family resemblances in the plot, but it probably did not bother him, whereas both Ibsen and Chekhov cared more for such discrepancies, and refrained from presenting heredity through visual resemblance.

11.2.2.3 *Heredity* in Chekhov (Comparatively)

Chekhov approaches *heredity* in a typically indirect way: family resemblances in his plays are non-visual, often shown through subtle detail, addressing and activating our intuitive perception of the family phenomenon. Thus, very often in his plays personality similarities and differences between family members are likely to make us say to ourselves, as we often do in real life, '*Look how different yet how similar these two siblings are; one can see that they come from the same family*'. This kind of 'saying to ourselves' in real life is more often than not evoked by visual, facial resemblance;[21] Chekhov transfers this intuitive audience response from the external–visual to the internal–mental.

In reality, beyond the undeniable facts of visual family resemblances, there is a permanently irresolvable controversy about the relative importance of *heredity vs. environment* (or *nature vs. nurture*) in shaping our personalities (since most children are raised by their parents, it is often hard to tell the two apart). In Chekhov, family members are usually shaped in the same mental (rather than visual) mould. In *The Seagull* differences and similarities between Konstantín and Arkádina, or between Polína and Másha, are subtle as well as striking, occasionally involving such barely noticeable features as speech rhythms.[22] In *Uncle Vánia* the very title underlines family relationships, though the pivotal source of the uncle–niece relationship — Véra Petróvna — is dead, survived by a brother and a daughter (Véra is indeed an instance of a typically Chekhovian *presence-through-absence* — a quality shared by other *offstage personages*, such as *Three Sisters*'

General Prózorov, *The Cherry Orchard*'s Grísha, etc.). In this particular case, a special bond is created between uncle and niece, family resemblance that is subtle yet undeniable; however, major character traits shared by the two are diametrically opposed to those displayed by the other blood relative, Vánia's old mother. Chekhov is often keen on demonstrating how true generalisations are rare and difficult to establish. Here he shows that there is no rule governing family resemblances: they are unpredictable, and largely work in mysterious ways. It is also remarkable, of course, that Sónia's personality is so remote from her father's and, by comparison, much closer to her uncle's.[23]

The term *family resemblance* always suggests *similarity* that falls short of *sameness*; the analogy of *variations on a theme* naturally comes to mind.[24] In *The Cherry Orchard* family relationships (Ranévskaïa, Gáïev and Ánia) can also be investigated in analogous terms. Indeed, in the case of Chekhov's plays, as in other cases of works of art composed by the same person, one can speak metaphorically of a 'family', whose members are these individual works, with significant similarities and marked differences between its members. The investigation of such differences and resemblances is the stuff much of literary scholarship is made on.

11.2.3 *Heredity* in *Three Sisters*:[25] The Prózorovs, Past and Present

In *Three Sisters*, as in *Uncle Vánia*, the centrality of the family theme is manifest in the title: even without any prior knowledge, one expects a play named *Three Sisters* to be a 'domestic' drama (in fact, it is less exclusively so than one would expect from the title). The Prózorov sisters are the nucleus of a family group, which also includes, of course, one onstage personage, brother Andréï, and two offstage ones, present through their absence: the deceased parents, especially the father, the late General Prózorov, whose powerful personality is crucial in shaping the inherently frustrated and variously powerless and infertile personalities of his four children.[26]

Biological *heredity*, then, is a central implicit theme in *Three Sisters*; and, in a typically Chekhovian way, its centrality largely emanates from its implicitness. It is almost inevitable in plays, in the absence of an explicit authorial voice, that direct statements are made by personages; it is less common that, as in *Three Sisters*, several direct statements about family resemblances are blatantly incorrect. Thus, though some resemblances do exist within the Prózorov family, they hardly come even close to providing a credible basis for Kulýgin's statements equating Másha with her two sisters: with Ól'ga in Act 3, and with Irína in Act 4. To be sure, the effect is comic–ironic: Kulýgin is made to appear ridiculous for thinking that way in the first place, and even more so for exposing those thoughts to others, totally ignoring their absurdity and inappropriateness, especially for a husband, who is expected to be the first to protest his wife's individuality and uniqueness, even if others doubt it. In this case we, the audience, know about Másha's individuality more than her own husband. However, these statements of Kulýgin's, shallow as they are, do serve a purpose, which is — *inter alia*, of course — to give us food for thought, and motivate us to explore the deep, complex dimensions of the true similarities and differences between the sisters: while exposing the false and simplistic nature of Kulýgin's version of these resemblances, the text brings the very topic of sisterly similarity to our attention through him. The text seems to be saying to us, as it were: '*Kulýgin offers a wrong version of family resemblance; what is the right one?*' We are thus prompted to check the sisters' characters, their verbal and non-verbal communications, including typically sisterly innuendoes between any two of them, and among all three; their reactions and responses to others, notably to their brother and his wife; and to events, situations and ideas. All such textual–situational phenomena demonstrate Chekhov's feat in creating human variations on a theme, a family of three (sisters) or four (siblings) sharply individuated personalities, nonetheless exhibiting a deep bond emanating from a shared genetic and environmental mould. A Kulýgin — within the restricted perspective of the *inner plane* — is quite out of his depth facing the magnitude and intricacy of the family picture that emerges from Chekhov's intertwined textual networks; yet, within the broader perspective of the *outer plane*, his simplistic view serves a purpose in throwing these subtleties and complexities of the situation into bold relief.

11.2.4 Prózorov Posterity: Future, *Present*, and *Absent*

The exceptional intricacy of Chekhov's presentation of family similarities and dissimilarities in *Three Sisters* notwithstanding, perhaps the most striking manifestation of *heredity* in the play lies elsewhere, and has little to do with *family resemblances*. Once again, here as elsewhere, the indirect and implicit is typically more significant than the direct and explicit. Thus, it is of great importance to understand how Chekhov creates implicit contrastive analogies between personages who have children and those who do not, representing differences between fertile and infertile people in more ways than one: more significantly, juxtapositions between those who do and those who do not transmit genes from generation to generation apply to literal–biological and to figurative–spiritual 'genes' alike.

Within the Prózorov family, then, one group of *totally absent* 'personages' carries the principle of *presence-through-absence* to the extreme. Indeed, some personages are absent only temporarily (i.e. they are offstage, or rather backstage, only in certain scenes, before entering or after exiting the stage); other are *offstage personages*, absent permanently through 'exclusion from the cast list' (e.g. Protopópov, or Kulýgin's headmaster) or death (e.g. the Prózorov parents). However, on top of these, we have an ultimate case of *nonexistent existence*: the unborn (or, rather, never-to-be-born) Prózorovs — i.e., the children that the sisters are doomed never to have. Those children — though Prózorovs through the maternal line and thus deprived of the family name — could perhaps have carried on the continuity of *heredity*, *inheritance* and *heritage* alike, if Chekhov had decided to grant them fictional–dramatic life. This, however, is "the road not taken" by him. Such hypothetical children[27] are juxtaposed with Natásha's more conventionally offstage *present-through-absence* children, Bóbik and Sófochka, born of Natásha, (presumably)[28] by Andréï: the latter two, absent from the play's *TF*, exist in its *NF*, whereas the former do not exist in any.

The history of the Prózorov *heredity*, then, can be summarised as follows:

Generation 1, offstage (absent personages). General Prózorov and his wife were certainly fertile; they had four children, three girls and one boy. **Generation 2, onstage (present personages).** During the play's action all four siblings are in their twenties, a typically marriageable and reproductive phase in life. However, only one of the four, Brother Andréï, gets married and begets children, a boy and a girl; these are **Generation 3, backstage (absent personages**, but their absence is supposed to be temporary and technical). These children are, then, the only heirs of the Prózorov name and genes.

The diluted quality of the family *heritage* in Andréï, and its total non-existence in Natásha, mean (*inter alia*) that the grandchildren will care very little for that *heritage*, which will die with the middle generation. The biological and nominal continuity of the family is synchronised, with almost symmetrical precision, with its spiritual discontinuity. Thus, the family's limited biological vitality and total spiritual demise are two sides of the same chronological sequence.

11.2.5 General Reflections: One Russian Family *vs.* Humanity as a Whole

As stated above several times, *Three Sisters* is not merely the story of three child-less women in one family; in the play, this childlessness applies not only to the moral, intellectual and spiritual standing of that family, but has far-reaching implications for Chekhov's presentation of the destiny of humanity.

The asymmetry in the second generation of Prózorovs between the fertility of Andréï, and even more so of Natásha, and the childlessness of the sisters, amounts to breaking the mental backbone of the family and tearing its entire spiritual fabric apart in the third generation, leading to the unstoppable decomposition of that fabric in posterity. Now Chekhov takes care to create many subtle but viable analogies between the fate of the Prózorovs and crucial trends and tendencies in human history as a whole. In this context, the powerful analogy between the hereditary–biological and the spiritual–intellectual dimensions of the fertility of General Prózorov and the infertility of his daughters has far-reaching consequences in the play's view of humanity.[29] The inescapable conclusion is that within the selective world of the play only the Natáshas transmit genes to their offspring. *Heritage*, as we have seen, though intrinsically indestructible, cannot survive without living human hosts/carriers, who transmit its content through teaching and other oral and written channels of communication and dissemination. It follows then, that the absence of children brought up in 'the Prózorov spirit' leads inevitably to the permanent extinction of the *heritage*, which in this case, once again, transcends the limits of the Prózorov family and represents much broader ramifications of human values (the term *Prózorov spirit* means here broadening horizons, learning languages, science, music, etc. and also basic human decency at the very least, as reflected *inter alia* in the clash between the sisters and Natásha in their attitudes towards Anfísa in Act 3). Without such *heritage* humans are, according to Andréï himself, living corpses, or at least inhuman animals. In short, inasmuch as the Prózorovs are a reflection of (and on) human destiny, *Three Sisters* shows us a humanity in renunciation of its *heritage*, and therefore doomed to spiritual decay.

This, however, is not the 'final verdict' of the play, if there is one (Chekhov and final verdicts are almost contradictions in terms).[30] For starters, the very existence of texts like *Three Sisters* and the other Chekhov plays, or any other great work of art for that matter, is incompatible with the total spiritual extinction of humanness, and Chekhov — by the very act of writing his plays, particularly *Three Sisters* — showed that he knew it, at least subliminally and intuitively, even while writing the play. The fact that the world appears to be inherited mainly by the literal and metaphorical Natáshas and their offspring blurs and complicates the picture, but does not negate the continued presence of radically different individuals, for whom great art is created; different from the Natáshas, and different from each other.

That said, there are always balancing factors, however subtle, and the pendulum of perspectives to view the formidable complexity of Chekhov's vision moves back and forth endlessly. In the family, however, the trend is clear. It starts with an overbearing, self-confident and fertile father; it proceeds through a middle generation that displays various degrees of wavering and insecurity, and culminates with a generation of grandchildren, which consists of two groups: (a) the present grandchildren, the family's future, bearers of the Natásha-genes, educated by her at home and by the Kulýgins in school (including the town-school's headmaster, a prominent *offstage personage*); (b) the never-to-be grandchildren, unborn to the sisters, who will live only in the unreal Moscow of their *unrealisable dreams* and *ever-unrealised-potential* values. The asymmetry between Natásha's children — the 'alive-and-kicking' Bóbik and Sófochka — and the sisters' unborn ones is of course highly significant; it is just as highly significant that only the fruitless siblings of the middle generation are *present characters* in the play, granted theatrical life by their author, whereas both the biologically and spiritually fertile, overbearing father, on the one hand, and the spiritually depleted grandchildren, born and unborn, on the other hand, are *offstage characters*, theatrically absent. The significance of this authorial choice by Chekhov cannot be overestimated: only the middle generation is the arena for a tacit, subliminal conflict between a feeble *heritage* fighting for its dwindling life and the forces bent on destroying it. This, indeed, is precisely the type of *covert conflict* that is compatible with Chekhov's poetics as presented in Chapter 4. It is characteristic of this poetics, then, that both the father, immune from this conflict, and the grandchildren, devoid of it, are relegated to the role of *offstage personages*, powerfully *present through their absence*, in a scene inhabited by the *onstage personages*, who belong only to the middle, fruitless generation.

This is the magnitude of the subversive interrelationships between the lines of *heredity* and *heritage* in these three generations of Prózorovs. The three sisters — not least by virtue of the play's title, but also by what happens through its entire unfolding — are the heart of the family.[31] Even the circumstances around their childlessness carry the hallmark of *family resemblance*: the life-story of each sister is highly individual, yet all stories share common traits. Thus, Andréï's credible characterisation of their father's authoritative and oppressive education sheds light on its metaphorically emasculating effect on four siblings, each in his or her own way. The resulting Prózorov entity, sensed in all four, is manifest *inter alia* in a problematic attitude to the upbringing of children, whether as parents (Másha, though married, is childless, and her sisters are unmarried as well as childless) or as teachers (consider the apparent malfunctioning at school of weary and burnt-out Ól'ga in the play's present, and of frustrated, embittered Irína in its near future). In Andréï it is reflected in the analogous difficulty to be an educator at home: he speaks (especially in Act 4) with emotional intensity about the spiritual and educational catastrophe visited upon the children of the provincial town, but does absolutely nothing about it, not even with his own children. The Chekhovian principle of *unrealised potential* is thus realised in this family as the combination of *questionable biological potency* with *obvious spiritual impotence* in Andréï, and a complementary combination of *questionable spiritual potency* with *obvious biological barrenness* in the sisters. The symmetrical reversal of these traits in Natásha, who is very viable biologically and totally destructive spiritually, complements the gloomy picture.

As generalised above, all humans can be seen as unique individuals in their own right, but also as mere transitional gene-carriers mediating between their parents and children, in analogy to viewing the present as a time dimension viable on its own or as a mere transition between the past and the future. Chekhov, as we have seen, encapsulates the complexity and magnitude of these all-embracing human matters in one family, framing its chronology in such a way that everything is viewed theatrically from the standpoint of a generation set in the middle. Rather than *re-generation* through the birth of new generations, as the conventional view would have it, we observe a family in gradual *de-generation*. We have seen manifestations of this process in the family's *heredity* and *heritage*; the role of its *inheritance*, and combinations among *the 3Hs*, are just as significant.

11.3 Perspective of *Inheritance*: Parallels and Isomorphisms

11.3.1 *De-Generation* of the House/Home

The Prózorov family's *degeneration* from one generation to the next is also manifest in the fate of their house/home. The potent father, firm believer in values of learning and education, was the owner of an imposing house, as clearly indicated in the initial stage directions: though built in the provincial township, it is the house of a Moscow-born-and-bred army general. The four members of the weakened generation which he begets, "oppressed by education" as Andréï puts it in Act 1, are figuratively inflicted with what may be called *the mule syndrome*: they are spiritually begotten — i.e., educated — by parents, or at least a father, with fertile personalities and presumably by competent teachers in languages, arts and sciences, and thus are capable of carrying their own mental lives to term, but cannot reproduce, or transfer anything of value, to the next generation. The "oppressive education" given to this generation by their army-general father fails its objective, which is to instil valued, viable and durable *heritage* into them; moreover, it results in disabling them in the field of *inheritance* as well. They are crippled as fighters for survival, unable to prosecute a defensive war (let alone an offensive one), which is the domestic equivalent of defending the homeland against enemy invasion. Analogically, they fail to protect their territory from the hostile takeover of the Natáshas and Protopópovs;[32] moreover, while sticking to their guns as it were, preserving much of their father's *heritage* in themselves, they are incapable of disseminating it to others. Their posture in matters of *inheritance* and *heritage* alike oscillates between the defensive and the defenceless, never attempting anything assertive, let alone dominative. At the same time, they are also incapable of disengaging from their heritage, abandoning it by compromising with, or blending into, the hostile provincial environment. The house is degraded, not least through drastic shifts in its theatrical representations, from sunlit centre-stage to hidden offstage.

So much for the first two generations of Prózorovs. Then comes the third generation, Natásha's *offstage children*, whose prospective education, both at home and at school, has been outlined above (especially in 1.2.1 and 8.3.4).[33] Andréï describes such children as living corpses, whose resemblance to each other and to their parents deprives them of any individuality and reduces them to mental *sameness*. Such children, whose future biological fertility or infertility is irrelevant in this context, cannot contribute to the family's re-generation by being (figuratively speaking) torchbearers of its *heritage* and/or carriers of its 'spiritual genes', even if they possess diluted vestiges of its genetic *heredity*, and/or own its material *inheritance*.

Natásha — undoubtedly the single most fertile, or rather most reproductive, personage in the play and in the family — can and does fight with her claws for the house, her territory, in order to facilitate the dissemination of her genes through her children. She is the female procreator of the sole third-generation heirs of the Prózorov *heredity*, *inheritance*, and *heritage*. However, as we have seen, they will not care one bit for that *heritage*, and their *heredity* is also in some doubt. What remains, then, is the *inheritance*, for what it's worth; not much even as far as it goes, when a *Cherry-Orchard*-styled auction awaits this mortgaged house, in all probability.

11.3.2 The Prózorov *Inheritance*: The Venue of *Heredity* and *Heritage*

The Prózorov house is indeed a focal point in *Three Sisters*; its fate and 'history' can serve as a prism through which much of the entire play can be viewed. It is the home of the Prózorovs' genes of *heredity*, the major object of their material *inheritance*, and the venue where their spiritual *heritage* took shape (they were too young to really remember the Moscow house of their childhood). It is a spiritual homeland, a little Moscow encapsulated in everything that makes a house into a home.[34] The fate of the house is commensurate with the fate of the family and its values. The play begins in the big 'public' rooms of the family. The sisters are the ladies of the house: they are the hosts, the rulers of this tiny but precious kingdom. It is light and bright, we are told in the *stage directions*. In Act 2 it is dark; Natásha, the new lady of the house, supervises all goings-on with her candle, that main source of meagre flickering light, and plans her hostile takeover, abusing her status as a mother both by being the family's killjoy and by usurping room after room from the original, morally lawful owners. Her expansionist policy is clear: she does not propose swapping rooms between Bóbik and Irína, because what's hers is hers, and what's not hers as yet will be hers soon enough. In the course of Acts 2 and 3 it becomes clear that Andréï is almost addicted to gambling, and that the house is mortgaged while Natásha has got most of the money. It is also clear that she is having an affair with Protopópov (who, with some stretch of imagination, can be the future buyer of the house from Andréï's creditors — the analogy with the sale of the cherry orchard comes to mind). Andréï compromises and jeopardises the family's *heredity* (through neglecting his children and through ignoring his wife's infidelity and its potential consequences), its *inheritance* (through gambling and mortgaging the house), and its *heritage* (through his rebellion against his father's will that he should become a professor in Moscow, and again through neglecting his children's upbringing and education). Act 3, as we have seen, takes place in the room now jointly shared by the two unmarried sisters, the last stronghold (or, rather, 'weakhold') of the family in the house, and Act 4 — which takes place outdoors while the entire house is pushed, as it were, to an offstage position — seals the fate of the house and completes the sisters' eviction.

This wordless story, as told by the stage design and props, consistently links us — as real and implied audience — with the sisters' *point of view* (literally and metaphorically). At the same time, offstage Protopópov is never 'with us': in Act 1 we share the spacious expanse of the living room with the sisters, while he is not even allowed in.[35] We 'keep company' with the sisters in all four Acts, in a process that culminates in Act 4, when we share their exile out of the house: the spaces they vacate are consistently out of bounds for us. The house has become Natásha's cuckoo-nest; her fledglings usurp the home of the 'legitimate' owners by driving them away. In this subtly effective way, by transferring the concept of *point-of-view* from its figurative–literary sense into a literal–theatrical one, Chekhov encourages us to empathise with the sisters' *point of view* in more ways than one (while not fully adopting it, of course). In other words: theatrically, while we share the sisters' *point-of-view* moving gradually out, Natásha changes positions in the opposite direction: from the outside, via the periphery into the centre. Protopópov is always invisible to us: using Natásha as a bridgehead, he is worming his way into the centre throughout Acts 2 and 3. The final triumph of the two, then, is achieved in Act 4: Natásha and Protopópov in, sisters and audience out (this new status of the house is underscored by Másha's emphatic refusal to ever set foot in it again, as emphasised in 7.4). By this manipulation of our *point of view*, as audience, Chekhov makes us experience the process acutely, through our senses.

11.3.3 Integration of the *3Hs*: "Put Out the Divine Spark"

It is Chekhov's implicit contention, then, that something 'unnatural' happens to the 'natural' processes of transmission from the dead to the living and from the old to the young, if they do not involve and integrate **all** *the 3Hs*. Natásha definitely destroys such integration. She ignores and effectively blocks *heritage*; she maybe subverts and usurps *heredity*, and anyway manipulates a semblance of the latter in order to secure *inheritance*, which is what she is really after; if not for herself then for her children, bearers of her genes. Therefore, she does not activate the natural processes; she twists and abuses them, by putting asunder what is ideally joined together — a harmonious, concerted and synchronised operation of all three. Here, once again, Chekhov shows us how the 'positive' option is an *absent, unrealised potential*. Indeed, the disintegration of the *3Hs* triad, making its components confront each other in discord and mutual disregard, is a crucial technique by which Chekhov produces in the audience the desired effect of dismay and indignation at Natásha's usurpation of the house. Her manipulative cashing-in on her questionable motherhood, presumably to promote the natural rule of preferring the young to the old, offends our intelligence as well as our sense of justice, not only because the sisters are far from being old, but also because it ignores the crucial role played by everything subsumed here under *heritage* in shaping the legitimacy of *inheritance*. At least in Chekhov, it is not only morally and spiritually wrong, but also humanly unnatural, to drive so wide a wedge between *inheritance* and *heritage*.

As we have seen, Chekhov's idea of the meaning of being human and being alive is inseparably linked with the concepts of *individuality* of every human being, *realising* his/her *human potentials* through receptiveness to deeply rooted traditions of creativity in science, art, and intellectual achievement. Not least among these, according to Chekhov's legacy, are values of elementary kindness and decency, all naturally subsumed under *heritage*, which is thus inseparable from being **alive as a human being**. The provincial town's children are, according to Chekhov (as we have repeatedly seen), the "living corpses" Andréï says they are, precisely because they are deprived of this vital human quality and individuality. To quote Andréï, this deprivation creates the mentally and spiritually lethal «пошлое влияние» ("vulgar/sordid influence"), which puts out the children's innate "divine spark"[36] so that they become uniform adults, undistinguishable from each other, i.e., neither alive nor human. A far cry from natural *family resemblance*, visual and/or mental, this type of inhuman *sameness* is not produced by *heredity*, but by **the negation of *heritage***. For Chekhov, the common *heritage* shared by all humans involves the imperative to cherish individuation. Thus, not only the Prózorovs are ejected from their home; humanity worthy of the name (according to Chekhov's values) is evicted and exiled with them.[37] The house, the family's *inheritance*, is no longer a human dwelling if no human *heritage* resides in it. "Put out the Divine Spark, and then put out the Divine Spark" (see Shakespeare, *Othello* V, ii, 7) is the inescapable result of *Heritage-free* education.

Selfish Natásha, who cares little even for her children[38] (beside using them for her territorial expansion), succeeds in dehumanising the house and replacing the sisters' values with her own, such as they are. This is underscored by at least three juxtapositions in the play: (a) the foreign languages that the Prózorov siblings have studied seriously and thoroughly *vs.* Natásha's stilted French and Kulýgin's fossilised Latin; (b) the serious music that Másha used to excel in playing before her father's death *vs.* Natásha's ludicrous playing of *The Virgin's Prayer* to Protopópov inside the house (see Golomb 1984); (c) the milk of human kindness shown, for instance, by the sisters (especially Ól'ga) to Anfísa and to the victims of the fire, *vs.* Natásha's callous brutality towards Anfísa, accompanied by hypocritical clichés about the social duties of the rich and their responsibilities for the poor. Through all of this wealth of interactions between personages, ideas, events, and thematic materials associated with them, Chekhov is saying to us that biology — arguably the stuff *heredity* is made of, as manifest, *inter alia*, in being a parent, being young etc. — is not enough for determining human value (so closely linked to *heritage*), or indeed for earning the right to a family's *inheritance*. Property is wasted if placed in the hands of "living corpses", or "inhuman animals" (again, as Andréï characterises Natásha in Act 4). Investment in such people is ill-conceived and bears no fruit, and no Natásha-held candle-light, nor even real sunlight, can help when the "divine spark" is put out in the children's souls. Frustrated Irína in her early twenties, and even hopeless Másha in her mid-twenties and burnt-out Ól'ga in her late-twenties, have more *human potential* than *spark-deprived* Bóbik in the nursery. Therefore, evicting any of them for him is a wrong choice, a bad investment in the future.

It should be re-emphasised that this implicit view of Chekhov's — a view, whose explicit verbalisation above is inferable only from textual analogies and interactions — is inseparably linked with his *potential–(non)realisation* modelling of reality, with his belief in innate "*divine spark*", and his observation that this spark is almost always doomed to be put out at an early stage in life. It is not an expression of Chekhov's aristocratic, or even meritocratic, condescension towards those who do not care for *heritage*; rather, it is an expression of his exasperation at any act of depriving people, young or adult, of the potential ability to become not only *originators of heritage* (i.e., artists, scientists etc.), but even its *transmitters* or *carriers* (i.e., those who emulate or appreciate such originators and their work and make up an educated audience of perceivers of literature, music or theatre, science enthusiasts, etc.). It is those whose *spark* was put out in childhood who grow up into becoming the likes of Kulýgin and his Headmaster. They are not only beyond redemption by sunshine and clear air; they are the ones who put out the *spark* in others. Thus, for instance, consider the Headmaster's expected objection, transmitted by Kulýgin, to Másha's giving a concert; Nína's parents' rejection of the theatre in *The Seagull*; or Professor Serebriakóv's refusal to let Yeléna play the piano in *Uncle Vánia* (though the latter case is more complex). It is the potential to stifle potentials that must not be allowed to be realised, if Chekhov's values (which he held as a writer and as a man alike) can prevail.

11.4 Conclusion: Mortal Chekhov's Immortal *Heritage*

By integrating *Heredity*, *Inheritance* and *Heritage* as he did, Chekhov did not only make a crucial impact on his own poetics in general and that of *Three Sisters* in particular;[39] he also contributed, quite inadvertently, to a complex and comprehensive view of an important aspect of his own lasting *heritage*.

As argued above, *the 3Hs'* major function in human life is to come to terms with the challenges of the perceptions of *time* as the representative of our *mortality*, and to control them as much as possible. In *Three Sisters* Chekhov brings together the two complementary ways in which humans look at *time*: linear–directional and cyclic–periodical (see a different and largely complementary way of looking at *time* in this play in Marsh 2005). *Heredity* is linear–directional: genes can only be transmitted one-way, from parent–begetter to child–begotten. However, we tend to perceive the very phenomenon of birth and death in nature, as opposed to birth and death of an individual, as *cyclic*: we tend to speak (usually very positively) of *re-birth* and *re-generation*. This is the very cycle which in the life of humans, unlike the life of any other species, is viewed by Chekhov as worthless in the *absence* of the elements of *heritage*: "[in this town] there is no scholar, no artist, no man of distinction [...] people only eat, drink, sleep, then die... others are born, and they too eat, drink, and sleep", says Andréï in Act 4. Humans and animals alike are subject to this cycle of eat–drink–sleep–beget–die (which has linear as well as cyclic elements in it); only humans, however, look for the outstanding and the unique, and for their own individuality; and only humans, like Andréï, question and ponder such subjects. Chekhov shows us that the cyclic–periodical and the linear–directional are mutually complementary in a variety of ways.

Each of these two ways of experiencing *time* has a 'positive' and a 'negative' aspect, in terms of conventional human values. On the one hand, *linear–directional time* moves forward, does not look back, and is perceived as synonymous with the conventionally positive concept of *progress*; by the same token, *periodicity* is regarded as negative: going 'back to square one', 'running in circles', etc. — all associated with circular movements — have a self-evident bad reputation. On the other hand, *linear–directional progression* is the course of all living beings from birth to death; it is an irresistible brute force that — in the final analysis — imposes on us old age and ultimate extinction. In this context, then, *directional linearity* is a 'negative' force, especially if it is constantly on our minds; it can cause stagnation, depression and despair. By the same token, *periodicity* can be seen as a 'positive' element in human life: we cannot really function without the convenient cyclic–periodical time units that humans have partly discovered in nature and partly devised for themselves (e.g. the twenty-four hour clock; the seven days of the week; the twelve months; the four seasons; the year as a basis for holidays, birthdays, anniversaries, centenaries, etc.; see Marsh 2005). The *cyclic movement* of time, albeit often delusional or illusory, complements its *linear, one-way movement* in our minds. One birthday or anniversary may be over, but there will be another one (though the year-figure marked by it will always move one-way, only forward); there will always be a next sunrise, a next evening/month/year. A class assignment, for instance, not performed as scheduled on a particular Wednesday (in a course that takes place on Wednesdays), can still be accomplished on the following Wednesday. *Cyclic time*, then, can be kinder to us than *linear time*; it allows some temporary respite, however illusory it may be, from the depressing constant awareness of stampeding directionality.

Chekhov's concept of time is primarily *linear–directional*, but it is also significantly *cyclic–periodical*, though the former is much more powerful. In the context of *Three Sisters*, a case in point is the *unrealisable potential* inherent in the sisters' desperate need **to restore in the Moscow of their future what now, in their provincial present, they delude themselves that they used to have in the Moscow of their past**. This delusion is the core of their Moscow dream, which is so vital for their spiritual life, yet produces such a deadly effect on their reality. The brutality of linearity's assault on the dreams of perpetual periodicity is further underscored by Natásha's felling of the tree that adorns Túsenbach's last daydream. That said, it is undeniable that the hopeful dreams of *periodicity* are there in the air, mentally indestructible in the text's discourse with its addressees (i.e., in the *outer/rhetorical plane*). Moreover, Chekhov's text itself (i.e., *Three Sisters*), through this text-to-audience discourse, realises potentials of *theatrical periodicity* and *human heritage* alike. In that context, the gloomy aspects of the fictional world, however dominant, are complemented by the inevitably brighter aspects of the actual act of creating, conceiving and perceiving great art. Granted, this aspect of human rejuvenation was probably far from Chekhov's conscious mind while writing *Three Sisters*; however, this does not diminish the validity of the contention that he contributed quite decisively to the demonstration of its enormous force.[40]

The *complexity* of the fusion between the two aforementioned perceptions of time — the *linear–directional* and the *cyclic–periodical* — is complemented by the seeming *simplicity* of the human vision, which accommodates the existential need for some degree of self-delusion. It is all a matter of degree: to wallow forever in paralysing self-delusion is of course destructive; to allow oneself moments of repose resulting from short-term denials of death-bound linearity is vital for mental survival. This is the difference, for instance, between the sisters' paralysing fixation on the Moscow dream, on the one hand, and Másha's moment of looking up to the sky, contemplating the periodicity of the birds' migration cycle in Act 4, on the other hand. Even the futile *philosophising* of some of the male personages (notably Vershínin and Túsenbach in *Three Sisters*, but occasionally also Trigórin in *The Seagull*, Ástrov in *Uncle Vánia*, Trofímov in *The Cherry Orchard*, and quite a few others) has different dimensions to it, when it **replaces** any other activity on the one hand, or when it **complements** such activities, on the other.

As we have seen, the *time of heredity* is practically linear; in *Three Sisters* the *time of inheritance* is a mock-application of the *time of heredity*, for the wrong reasons and in the wrong context.[41] The *time of heritage* is genuinely human: it is the *linear time* of scientific progress, but also the time of learning languages, arts, or sciences, of experimentation and contemplation, which is complex, *multidimensional, cyclic and directional alike*; it is also the time of artistic creativity, in which there is no progression or regression, just an endless quest for truths and a boundless search for experience and knowledge. It is thus directional and innovative, and also repetitive–exploratory, as well as (occasionally) retrospective–evocative in drawing on past traditions, both for the individual and for humanity as a whole. It is also the *linear time* of history and the *multi-dimensional time* of contemplating it. It is the most complex time-experience imaginable.

Chekhov's art is part of our *heritage*; Vladímir Katáïev (2002, p. ix) is right to speak of it, in this context, in terms of "immortality" and timelessness. As such it is subject to the *multi-dimensional* time just introduced, *linear as well as periodical*. We try to reach a deep core in it, attempting — or maybe pretending, possibly through self-delusion — to pursue relentlessly a one-way quest for *a truth*.[42] Yet, this also involves returning to it again and again, retracing our tracks, often finding ourselves in a "back to square one" position, as a precondition for a fresh start in our search for Chekhovian truths. Indeed, this can of course be said of every great art. However, in Chekhov's art it happens time and again (a cyclic term!), that much in it is mirrored, directly or inversely, in the process of its own afterlife, the ways in which it functions within our cultural and psychological consciousness and our own world (see, for instance, Robert Louis Jackson's Epigraph to this Book).

It is not superfluous in these closing remarks of the Book to reiterate an idea presented in its opening, that Chekhov's is an art which speaks in a complex way about *potentials that are inescapably unrealisable*, while it belies its very premise and message by *realising its own potentialities to near-perfection*. It is an art which shows us a world of values in decline, focusing mainly on the diminishment of art in *The Seagull*, the diminishment of hope for change in *Uncle Vánia*, the diminishment of the values connected with *the 3Hs* in *Three Sisters*, and the diminishment of hope for understanding and communication between individuals, social classes, genders and generations, etc., in *The Cherry Orchard*. Yet, the very existence of this art and the nature of its communication with its audiences can have an uplifting quality, which embodies an *ascent of man*. Indeed, Chekhov's art shows processes characterisable, or at least perceived, as deterioration and degeneration in families. This is true, actually, in all four major plays (as well as in earlier plays and many stories). This process of diminishment in reality is usually juxtaposed with tirades delivered by some of the personages: shallow optimistic *philosophising* about progress and bright future for posterity. This contrast seems to expose the hollowness of the talk of progress in the face of deterioration and degeneration. Yet, it is not quite so simple. First, as argued here, the sheer greatness of Chekhov's art undermines the totality of desperation. Moreover, the seeds of the optimistic ideas also take root in our minds, and we are prompted to critically explore them: of course, not to take them at face value, but also not to dismiss them offhand, without giving them a thought. Such exploration yields exceptionally complex and inherently undecided views. Moreover, in Chekhov's world wishes and aspirations count for much, often for more than deeds and facts. "Tell me what you want, and I will tell you who you are", says his Prof. Nikoláï Stepánovich in "A Dreary Tale" («Скучная история»), as discussed in greater detail in 1.3 and quite extensively throughout the Book. And indeed, people who want, who aspire, who aim high, even people who feel the need, albeit a futile one, to talk and think **about** aiming high — such people are the infrastructure of any progress.

Chekhov's art accommodates the high-spirited talk of dreams, wishes and aspirations, alongside the bleak reality, both constituting an integral part of the human world and condition. A world where people think and speak of hope, even from the depth of suffering, misery and despair, is (almost technically and by definition) not totally devoid of hope. Imagine Chekhov's texts and plots without those expressions of hope: how much duller, greyer and shallower his world would have become without them! Indeed, these expressions of hope often make Chekhov's world excruciatingly painful, because reality crushes those hopes so cruelly,[43] and lends them a definite air of bitter, poignant irony, even of despair, in the minds of the audience. Yet the very existence of these hopes is indestructible, and it resonates with the dignity of being human in ways incompatible with totally bleak hopelessness. This uniquely Chekhovian combination breaks one's heart and lifts one's spirit at the same time; another one of the inherent paradoxes and oxymorons of Chekhov's art, which create his unparalleled uniqueness.

Thus, the afterlife role of Chekhov's art, the way it functions in our consciousness, and in 20th-century dramatic and narrative literature, is characterised by growth and fertilisation, rather than diminishment and futility. Just as *family resemblance* never means *sameness*, and just as *heredity* does not reproduce the procreator *in toto*, Chekhov-inspired works composed in later generations are never really Chekhovian. There is something genuinely irreproducible in his evasive complexities, notably his unique blend of *unrealised potentials* and *present absences*. Major trends in 20th-century theatre and drama would not have been the same without the powerful presence of Chekhov's plays, but this does not mean that these trends are a real continuation of Chekhov's poetics in equally emphasising the strength of potentials and the forces that stifle and undermine them, as well as in other ostensible paradoxes and contradictions of his art

As Túsenbach says about the dead tree that sways in the wind with the living ones, dead Chekhov continues his presence among the living. And though Natásha orders this tree to be chopped down, Irína, who hears Túsenbach's words, remembers them, so that even within the fictional world of the play Túsenbach goes on living in and through her. And, what's more important for our purpose, we — as readers or spectators — read and hear those words, and they live through us. Indeed, great art always outlives its creator, but Chekhov's art has a special way of interaction between its inner content and its outer existence. It includes Ól'ga's quest for knowledge ("If it were only possible to know")[44] with Chebutýkin's nihilistic «всё равно» ("it's all the same"). As explained in 9.2.4. in greater detail, "If it were only possible to know" means: we know that we will never know, but, knowing that, we still **want** to know everything that we will never know. The unquenchable thirst for knowledge and understanding, even for unattainable knowledge, the perpetual dissatisfaction with any present state of knowledge and the urge to expand it, is a crucial part of being human, according to Chekhov's world and poetics. What we do know for sure is that «не всё равно»: it's **not** all the same, just as living human beings are never, and must not ever be, "all the same".

It has to be reiterated that in Act 4 Andréï claims that (a) in the provincial town all people are "the same"; (b) as a result, all of them are "living corpses"; (c) his wife, Natásha (who was born and bred in this town), is reduced to a blind, senseless animal, and at any rate she is "not a human being". Thus, *sameness* is both deadly and inhuman. Against this carefully prepared background, Chekhov gives us a double message: Chebutýkin's senseless refrain ("ta-ra-ra-bumbia"),[45] combined with the *sense-negating* "it's all the same", are confronted with Ól'ga's *sense-pursuing* "If it were only possible to know" (or "If only we could know"). This ending is polyphonically orchestrated, with the two *quasi melodic lines* — Chebutýkin's and Ól'ga's — unaware of each other, weaving their intrinsically contrastable threads concurrently (in terms of compositional technique, the ending here closes the circle begun in the play's first scene, where different lines are also performed concurrently, as if not taking each other into account). Still it is significant that the final word is given to Ól'ga, whose pursuit of knowledge and understanding, as it were, overrules Chebutýkin's nihilism of "it's all the same"; yet, it is of crucial significance that the audience should integrate both conflicting messages and let them perpetually resonate concurrently, negating and complementing each other. Thus, the two opposing messages collaborate in producing the play's final verbal and visual tableau; and though Ól'ga, being the last speaker (and also the first one, as a *Greek chorus* that is charged with opening the play and concluding it as well), has the final word, which gives her an edge over Chebutýkin, her message does not cancel out his.

Be that as it may, our *heredity* comes from our parents and ancestors, and they are usually the source of our *inheritance* as well; but our *heritage* comes mainly from great artists, scholars, scientists, thinkers, those who make a difference, those who **are** different, those who make eating, drinking and sleeping not the be-all and end-all, but only an absolutely necessary and totally insufficient condition for a life that is **humanly** worth living. Chekhov is one of those great artists, who know how *the 3Hs* can be intertwined to give life a meaning.

This is part, just part, of what makes his art so specific, individual, unlike any other great art, and immortal in its absolutely unique, unprecedented, inimitable and irreproducible way. Typically-paradoxically, though, this is part, just part, of what makes his art so universal, potentially transcending every boundary of whatever type, so genuinely shareable by/with all human beings, wherever they may live on earth, and whenever they may live in time.

For the twentieth century, for the twenty-first, and beyond.

Notes

1 This concluding Chapter is designed to close the entire 'Outer Circle' of the Book's argument; it inevitably includes short reminders and repeats, referring back to statements made previously, especially in Chapter 1, which opened the same Circle.
2 This distinction is different from the one between individual/collective/universal characterisation offered in 5.0.2; in the present context *single* (individual) is simply opposed to *many*, within an elementary scale of *more* vs. *less*.
3 Art–life interrelationships in Chekhov are discussed in greater detail in the Appendix.
4 Most statements in this Section are admittedly well-known truisms, perhaps too trivial to merit re-stating; yet grouping them together, with the aim of integrating isolated trivialities into a meaningful sequence, provides an essential point of departure for investigating Chekhov's treatment of a crucial thematic cluster in his work.
5 Perhaps the ways in which territory and some foods are acquired, identified and protected in some species can be equated to the ways in which possessions and property function in humans.
6 Marital and other *spouse/life-partner* relationships are only marginally an exception: the individual partner is indeed humanly chosen, unlike blood relatives, and does not share his/her partner's genes; but given the inevitably sexual nature of gene-transmission, the actual need for **a** partner is not a matter of choice. Other types of dual partnership are extensions of the male–female dyad, which is an involuntary precondition for transmitting genes.
7 It is another matter altogether whether they really attain such everlasting life; this

largely depends on whether, and for how long, people feel that these non-material possessions deserve such immortality and engage in their dissemination and perpetuation. The point here is that they are indestructible and immortal **in principle**, technically and potentially.

8 I am not going to engage in philosophical discussions about the abstract nature and ontology of such possessions; I am just observing what is experienced by humans, empirically and intuitively.

9 For the purpose of this discussion I prefer the latter term, *Heritage*, mainly because of its phonetic and etymological closeness to the other two key terms — *Heredity* and *Inheritance*. The latter term's spelling notwithstanding, I shall use the term *The 3Hs* to refer to the entire cluster of the three terms/concepts.

10 This human reference applies to *heredity* as well: though the phenomenon itself is, once again, not exclusively human, only humans conceive of **all** *3Hs* as "an opening to immortality" (to paraphrase the subtitle of Gilman 1995).

11 Even ancient works traditionally accepted as collective creations — verbal texts (e.g., epics), paintings, songs, etc., whose authors are forever unidentifiable — were created, perhaps in parts and piecemeal, by some collaborating individuals. The eternal question about the creation of language itself is outside the scope of this discussion.

12 Potentially and technically, once again, *heritage* can be universal and timeless; yet in practice large parts of it are perceived as belonging to particular groups of people, and even as dividing between those who embrace and those who reject specific bodies of *heritage* (the rejection of holy scriptures of one religion by believers of another is a case in point; in a simpler context, verbal texts written in a language 'belong' to its native users more than to any other group, and are simply out of the reach of the 'linguistically uninitiated', unless and until a translation is provided).

13 The problem of relating *heredity* to race and other collective groups, and relating *inheritance* (e.g., of *territories*, precious relics etc.) to nations, states etc., is tricky and complicated, and cannot be discussed here, especially as it is almost totally unrelated to Chekhov's poetics of focusing on the *individual* and the *universal* in preference to the *group/collective*.

14 By the way, this is the rationale behind the unfortunate term *the Middle Ages*, which has become so prevalent that we are permanently stuck with it. It is blatantly untenable to regard a thousand years of history, with everyone who lived in those thousand years, as being "in the middle" between 'real' historical periods.

15 The complementary coordinates of place/space — *here* as opposed to *there* — also operate powerfully in Chekhov's plays; thus, in *Three Sisters*, virtually all the Prózorovs (in differing ways and degrees) negate both the *time* and the *place* of their present, idealising the Moscow of their past childhood and of their envisioned future.

16 This is a deliberate choice on Chekhov's part. In a letter to A.S. Suvórin dated October 1888, mentioned and extensively discussed above, he insists that artists should commit themselves to the "correct presentation" of questions **rather than** to answering them.

17 In a letter to A.N. Pleshchéïev (1889), after emphatically refusing to identify himself with any group or ideology, Chekhov writes: "My holy of holies is the human body, health, intelligence, talent, inspiration, love, and the most absolute freedom [...] from violence and lying" (Friedland 1965, 63). It could not cross the mind of any other 19th-century Russian classic — least of all, arguably, the greatest ones, Dostoïévskiï and Tolstóï — to associate the concept of 'holiness' with such a secular–humanistic list, significantly beginning with the human **body**.

18 Thus, Yeléna praises Dr. Ástrov for his total dedication to posterity, with Chekhov's seeming authorial consent (*Uncle Vánia*, Act 2); yet other, present-time-focused aspects

in Ástrov's character, seem to call into subtle doubt Yeléna's judgement of character, or at least to slightly contrast her 'ideological' praise for dedication to posterity with the partiality of her view of Ástrov, let alone her own entangled conflict between living the present moment and sacrificing it to ideals of honour and fidelity, which gives a highly complex perspective to her views of Ástrov. More significant is Ástrov's own character, with its subtle and complex combinations of present- and future-oriented elements, e.g., his treatment of patients of different ages and views of those treatments, and of course the crucial temporal dimension of his views and actions concerning the forestation of Russia.

19 An interesting case is Malcolm, son and heir to the murdered King Duncan in *Macbeth*, who at first wrongly maligns his own character as being diametrically opposed to his father's, and then discloses the true mental and spiritual affinity between father and son.

20 In Hamlet's words: "My father's brother, but no more like my father/ Than I to Hercules" (*Hamlet*, I, ii, 152–153). In few productions of *Hamlet*, though, the same actor is cast in the dual role of the two brothers, thus accentuating their visual resemblance. Shakespeare facilitates this practice — which, by the way, is also more economical for the theatre — because the two never meet on stage.

21 The notion of *family resemblance* is applied metaphorically in quite a few disciplines of philosophical and scientific investigation, which are irrelevant to the present discussion.

22 Consider, for instance, the rhythmical characterisation of Arkádina and her son Konstantín. Such features betray similarity as well as dissimilarity between mother and son. Tensions between the two reflect other elements of similarity, like being obstinate and opinionated (this particular character trait invokes discord rather than accord between persons who share it). Gáïev and Ranévskaïa, the four Prózorovs, and others, naturally come to mind.

23 A similar case is the lack of resemblance between Sórin on the one hand and the common traits of Arkádina and Konstantín on the other hand in *The Seagull*; in both cases old age seems to prevail over genetics in shaping certain character traits, but in matters of age, too, no schematic rule is ever applied by Chekhov consistently (consider, for instance, the dearth of shared character traits between such old people as the Professor, Vánia's mother and Marína from *Uncle Vánia*, or between youngsters like Yásha and Trofímov from *The Cherry Orchard*). Indeed, Chekhov's aversions to consistent dogmatism/schematicism and to characterisation by *groups* or *collectives* go hand in hand.

24 In this particular context one can speak of *enigma variations*: the whole phenomenon is **enigmatic**, and — as in Elgar's work — the '*variations*' are *present*, whereas the '*theme*' is *absent*, and should be extracted from them.

25 *Three Sisters* is demonstrably the most paradigmatic Chekhov play in this context; it is also the most powerful example of the way Chekhov binds together the themes of *heredity*, *inheritance* and *heritage*, though *the 3Hs* are closely interconnected in all of his major plays. The present Subsection singles out this play for closer analysis.

26 Other offstage Prózorovs — notably the third generation, Bóbik and Sófochka — will be discussed later on.

27 By the way, these children's nonexistence is substantially different from that of Ól'ga's would-have-been husband (Acts 1 and 3) or Irína's dreamed-of Moscow beloved (Act 3): the major difference is that these unborn children are never mentioned by any personage, not even as admittedly unrealisable dreams.

28 It is not necessary for the present discussion to make a stand on the speculation that Sófochka is biologically Protopópov's child. The idea that the same applies even to

Bóbik is less likely, for chronological considerations; but for the present argument both are irrelevant, since the family's heritage is doomed to extinction even if both of Natásha's children carry Andréï's genes.

29 Analogies between begetting children and generating products of the mind abound in human consciousness, language and literature everywhere. Consider, for instance, the term *brainchild* in English, and the powerfully explicit analogies between child and book in Ibsen's *Hedda Gabler*.

30 Let us remember, once again, Chudakóv's (1983 [1971]) dictum: "The single dogmatic feature in Chekhov is his condemnation of dogmatism" (p. 204).

31 This crucial status of the sisters is just too obvious to dwell on; however, one can point out further corroboration for it: thus, the phrase *three sisters* is uttered several times throughout the play, by members of the family (Andréï, Irína) and other personages (e.g., Vershínin) alike; in all these cases the very existence of Andréï is ignored.

32 Laurence Senelick, in his 2009 "Money in Chekhov's Plays", says: "Natásha is the prime mover of the loss of the house, her sense of proprietorship far more lethal than the mortgage to the bank". Naum Berkóvskiï is quoted in the same paper as saying: "the sisters lose because they will not get engaged in property litigation with her — this would put the sisters on her level, and that would be disgraceful for them". I fully concur with these statements. In the Prózorov family, *Heritage* blocks *Inheritance*.

33 The role of *education and learning*, as personified in teachers, in transmitting *heritage* (in parallel to the role of parents in transmitting *heredity*) is a subject that merits separate treatment. Chekhov portrays teachers very often, in his plays and stories alike, and discussions of these personages abound in the literature. See for instance Popkin 1993, 17–52, for a particularly illuminating discussion of one of Chekhov's fictional teachers.

34 In the *Three Sisters* film of the National Theatre of Great Britain, based on the legendary stage production directed by Laurence Olivier, this idea is rendered visually: the family's clock (which represents time) is shaped like the famous St. Vasíliï Basilica in the Red Square — an image, which signals *Moscow* to many westerners as well — so that the sisters' house is stage-designed to bring the proverbial Kremlin to the spectator's mind, and to emphasise that the family takes its cues from Moscow, in time and space alike. The grandeur of the house in that film, much in tune with the spirit of Chekhov's stage directions, smacks of aristocracy and traditional good taste, that blend with the characterisation of the late General and his system of values, education etc.

35 Másha shows her contempt for him by explicitly and emphatically endorsing Irína's decision not to invite him to her birthday party, and contemptuously forgetting–distorting his name and patronymic.

36 There is a relevant contrastive analogy connecting Andréï's "divine spark" with the almost ever-present candle in Natásha's hands: the figurative light of the former is much brighter and more real than the literal light of the latter, spreading as it does *figurative darkness*. A Shakespearean analogy was created extra-textually by Chekhov himself, when he instructed the first Natásha-actress to walk with her candle "*à la* Lady Macbeth" (see Senelick 2006, 936).

37 As the Schoolmaster, teacher of classics and humanities, in Dürrenmatt's *The Visit of the Old Lady* says cynically, when his protest is silenced with 'Sit down!': 'Humanitarianism has to sit down'. See Friedrich Dürrenmatt, *The Visit: A Tragicomedy*, translated from the German by Patrick Bowles (London: Jonathan Cape, 1962), p. 74.

38 In order to drive this point home Chekhov introduces the song of Bóbik's Nanny in Act 2: while Natásha, after being the family's killjoy presumably for the sake of Bóbik's health, goes out to pursue her affair with Protopópov, the Nanny is the one who really

takes care of the child. This is arguably the sole reason for bringing the Nanny's song to the attention of the audience. See Golomb 1984, 187–188.

39 *Three Sisters* is indeed often chosen for detailed case studies in this Book, because in many respects Chekhov's poetics is epitomised in it more than in other plays; however *the 3Hs* are intertwined in all of the four major plays: in *The Seagull* we have intricate interrelationships between the *heredity* of character traits and talents, the *inheritance* of estates, and literary and theatrical *heritage*; similar interrelationships pervade the spiritual and theatrical spaces of *Uncle Vánia* (e.g., once again, *hereditary* character traits, Véra Petróvna's *inheritance*, the *heritage* of such personages as the Professor and Ástrov, and its lamented absence in Vánia) and *The Cherry Orchard* (along analogous lines). The *Three Sisters*-based analyses in this Chapter can readily be extended into analogous analyses of other plays, of course subject to whatever adjustment is needed for each separate case.

40 See Appendix for a demonstration of another form of *presence* of this power-of-art focus within Chekhov's "*Realm of Ideas*" — the English title of the last chapter in Chudakóv 1983 [1973].

41 There is an analogy between the sale of the cherry orchard (*The Cherry Orchard*, Act 3), the inevitable mortgaging of the Prózorov house (see *Three Sisters*, Acts 3 and 4) and the stuffing of the seagull (*The Seagull*, Act 4): all of them reduce the vital linear and periodical aspects of the time of the living to the "dusty death" of still life, capturing the shell of external beauty while "killing in the shell" the vibrant life that used to inhabit it.

42 Rather than *the truth*; the point is elaborated in Chapter 5, Note 43.

43 At a remarkably early stage of *Three Sisters*, in Act 1, it is seemingly naïvely happy Irína, on her twentieth birthday, who says: "for us three sisters life has not been beautiful; it has stifled us like weeds" and almost bursts into tears after making this statement.

44 This is a more accurate rendition of the original Russian phrase, though it is admittedly inferior as an English one; see 9.2.4.

45 Several interpretations and etymologies for these nonsense rhymes have been suggested, but I intentionally ignore them here, since Chekhov clearly juxtaposes Chebutýkin's obviously nonsensical text with Ól'ga's obviously meaningful and meaning-seeking one. This juxtaposition is much more significant than any signification that may be attributed to the former, or even to the latter, in isolation. Chebutýkin's phrase clearly negates any meaning, or search for meaning (I am echoing here Másha's dictum in Act 2, when she says that every person has to believe in something, or at least search for such belief).

APPENDIX

Reflecting (on) Chekhovian "(Auto)Biographophobia"
Nína Zaréchnaïa's Medallion under a Magnifying Glass[1]

Art is not a copy of the real world:
one of the damn things is enough.
(Quoted by Nelson Goodman [1968, p. 3])

1 Delimiting the Unit of the *'Medallion Scene'*

As I have argued in Chapter 2, Chekhov's poetics is characterised, *inter alia*, by the creation of intense, powerful and meaningful networks of interrelationships among elements, that can be described in turn as relatively 'weak' or 'depleted' if viewed in isolation.[2] In Chekhov the whole is usually not merely 'more than' the sum-total of its parts; its very strength is largely derived from the weakness of the parts, and it grows **at their expense**. The scene discussed in this study is a case in point. Its main force, complexity and significance emanate from dense networks of relationships that build up around it, rather than from its own content, or from any single element making up those networks. These generalisations will be demonstrated below.

My basic text is 'The Medallion Scene' in Act 3. It is a discrete, unified and coherent unit, and it is definitely a *scene*, in terms of Chekhov's typical simulta-neous, 'polyphonic' patterning of dramatic texture; yet, it characteristically defies most conventional classifications of scene division. It is a *discontinuous scene*, an *ad hoc* term based on the more general notion of the 'discontinuous pattern' as proposed and developed in several studies by Benjamin Harshav (see, for example, Harshav 1988, p. 640; 2007, p. 179). In this particular instance, the scene is held together by several (not necessarily Aristotelian) 'unities': the continuous actions of a single personage, preoccupied (in thought) with one topic, or subject, which in turn is associated with one physical object. It is this object, a medallion, that actually delimits the scene: it is introduced by the object's first appearance and ends when the last suggestion for direct action embedded in the object[3] has been realised, and its direct role has thereby terminated. Viewed in this way, it is a well-established scene. However, it lacks unity (or, rather, continuity and contiguity): it consists of two segments separated by wedges featuring other personages and themes. Some of them occupy the stage's "mimetic space", while the personages, themes, and physical object of the medallion scene temporarily retreat into suspension in the "diegetic space" offstage,[4] and then the new occupants of the stage clear off to make way for the completion of the scene. This kind of oscillation between alternating scene-generating elements creates a typically Chekhovian effect of quasi-simultaneous 'polyphony', without "sinning against" the constraints imposed by the linear, successive nature of the verbal component of the theatrical medium.[5]

2 An Exposition of the *'Medallion Scene'*

The discontinuous scene under discussion is delimited, then, by the (physical and mental) entrance and exit of a stage prop: an engraved medallion, whose scene-unifying force is derived from the meaning embedded in it, or its "semantisation" (see Avigal & Rimmon-Kenan 1981), rather than from its sheer physical presence. As long as things on stage are directly connected with the medallion and its inscription, this force is still in operation.

The scene starts soon after the beginning of Act 3. Young Nína Zaréchnaïa is about to make two crucial decisions about her life, which become increasingly interconnected: (a) whether to steal away from her father's and stepmother's rural estate and go to Moscow in order to become an actress and (b) whether to follow her heart and deepen her emotional involvement with the successful writer Trigórin. Soon enough, she decides in the affirmative on both. However, at the beginning of the scene, she meets Trigórin and asks for his advice on "whether to go on the stage or not" (p. 259).[6] After he refuses to commit himself to any advice, she hands him a medallion as a gift, saying: "I had your initials engraved on it, and there's the title of your book *Days and Nights* on the other side" (*ibid.*). Trigórin takes the medallion and kisses it; and when Nína has left the stage he discovers that there is more to the inscription than she cared to specify orally: the inscribed text is "*Days and Nights*, page 121, lines 11 and 12" (*ibid.*). Somewhat later, 'The Medallion Scene' continues:

> TRIGÓRIN [*To himself*]: "Page 121, lines 11 and 12". I wonder what those lines
> are. [*To Arkádina*] Are there any of my books in the house?
> ARKÁDINA: Yes, in the corner bookcase in my brother's study.
> TRIGÓRIN: "Page 121..." [*Goes out*]. (p. 260)

Here Trigórin exits, moving with his medallion to the *diegetic space* offstage; the scene, then, is temporarily suspended. The *mimetic space* (see Issacharoff 1981) onstage is cleared, to accommodate other personages, themes, and even a new scene-unifying stage prop — a bandage. Following 'The Bandage Scene' (which, unlike the *medallion scene*, is a continuous one) Trigórin comes back onstage for the remainder of 'The Medallion Scene' (p. 264):

> TRIGÓRIN [*Looking in a book*]:[7] Page 121, lines 11 and 12. Ah. [*Reads*]. "If you should ever need my life, then come and take it."

Subsequently Trigórin repeats this sentence twice more, reading it from his own book; always to himself, yet always "within Arkádina 's hearing" (Styan 1971, p. 67), always in contrapuntal oscillation between those echoing, self-directed 'asides' and Arkádina's demands for dialogic communication that become increasingly annoying and meaningless to him:[8]

> ARKÁDINA [*Glancing at her watch*]: The carriage will be here soon.
> TRIGÓRIN [To himself]: "If you should ever need my life, then come and take it."
> ARKÁDINA: I hope all your things are packed.
> TRIGÓRIN [*Impatiently*]. Yes, yes. [*Thoughtfully*] This appeal from a pure soul — why does it sound so sad? Why does it wring my heart so painfully? "If you should ever need my life, then come and take it." [*To Arkádina*] Let's stay another day! (p. 264)

Here ends 'the medallion *discontinuous scene*' as a textual unit, never to be explicitly mentioned again in the play.[9] I am not going to discuss the compositional merits of this scene,[10] nor shall I expand this study to offer a comprehensive analysis of it, viewed in isolation as a discrete unit. Rather, I shall confine myself to the diverse discontinuous patterns that intersect at this scene, thus viewing it as 'junction'.[11] The analysis will be divided into two main parts: intra-textual (enclosed within the confines of the fictional world of the play) and inter- or extra-textual (drawing on relevant material from Chekhov's life, integrating and juxtaposing it with the former part).

3 The Medallion in the Fictional World of *The Seagull*

3.1 The '*Literariness*' of *The Seagull*

The Seagull has rightly earned the reputation of being Chekhov's most literary play. Chekhov himself, in the letter to Suvorin mentioned above, illustrates his alleged "sinning terribly against the tenets/conventions of the theatre" by saying that there is "lots of talk about literature" in the play (often quoted in the literature; e.g., Henry 1965, p. 17). S. D. Balukhátyï [Balukhaty], whose book on Chekhov's drama (1927) is "the only full-length study in this field [dramatic theory] made along Formalist or near-Formalist lines",[12] published in 1938 a critical edition of *The Seagull* with Stanislavsky's full production score. In the Introduction to that book he writes:

[...] Chekhov included long theoretical statements about the theatre in the play [... He] discusses the problems of the new drama by, as it were, deliberately making his characters talk about the questions in which he was himself so deeply interested. (Balukhaty 1952 [1938], p. 18)

Balukhátyï somewhat naïvely takes some speeches by the two writers in the play — Konstantín and Trigórin — for "an exposition of his [Chekhov's] own ideas on the subject".[13] Yet, one need not adopt this view at face value in order to notice the play's constant preoccupation with literary problems. 'Literariness',[14] then, is indeed a dominant feature of the play, in more ways than one (as will be shown in the following pages); much more so than would be suggested by any list enumerating all explicit references to literary works or topics that can be found in the text. I doubt whether even the task of such mere listing has been carried out exhaustively.[15] A few studies devoted to isolated cases (for example, Jackson 1967; Chances 1977; Winner 1956; Golomb 1986) naturally tend to be more thorough. However, a structurally or semiotically oriented analysis of literary topics in the play, as an underlying thematic network, has hardly been attempted, to the best of my knowledge.

3.2 The Complexity of the Medallion

Even without taking the entire scene into account, the medallion itself — i.e., the physical object — contains quite a complex referential mechanism. As an object fulfilling the relevant requirements (see Avigal & Rimmon-Kenan 1981, esp. p. 13), it is obviously a *referent* of the stage-directions. However, it is also a referent of Nína's and Trigórin's "auditory discourse" (Issacharoff 1981, 215). By giving it as a present the way she does, Nína endows it with explicitly-literary meanings. By accepting it as he does, with the explicit reference to 'The Seagull-story scene' (i.e., the beginning of Act 3, p. 259, referring back to the final scene of Act 2, p. 257, activating a multi-dimensional analogy), Trigórin adds much to its referential load.[16]

Now the referential status of the medallion is far more complex than suggested so far, since it is an object in which Nína, through a verbal inscription, directly refers to a specific scene and sentence in a book. But her act of referring, viewed pragmatically, is even more complex, since the book to which she is referring was authored by her addressee. The roles of *addresser* and *addressee*, then, are here in perpetual oscillation or reversal: he, when writing the sentence, had addressed it to her (though impersonally), as a reader; she, as the giver of the gift and designer of the medallion, boomerang-like, addressed it back to him. In this context, she is directly expressing her emotions as a woman, but also, indirectly, as a reader and would-be actress emotionally moved by a writer whom she had admired before she ever dreamed of meeting (this aspect of their relationship is amply substantiated in the play). It is **as if** she is saying to him something like: '*it is not I saying these words, but you; even if I tried hard, I could not find better ones to express my emotions*'. Moreover, she implies that he must assume responsibility for the pragmatic power of his own words. And, to conclude, one can reconstruct

Trigórin's side at the receiving end of this communication-through-reference, recognising the new *referents* that his words acquired in the new pragmatic context, which he in all likelihood had never thought about when writing these words or afterwards; however, this kind of effect on a reader can potentially be foreseen in any act of writing for public consumption.

3.3 Pragmatic and Fictional Dimensions of the Medallion Scene

The most fascinating thing about the referential functioning of the medallion lies, perhaps, in the way it is integrated into the play's network of interrelationships between *art* (and/or *drama, literature, fiction*, the *theatre*, etc.) on the one hand, and *life* (and/or *fact, reality*, the *real world*, etc.),[17] on the other hand.

Fictionality (whether by this or "any other name"), especially in its relation to *reality*, is an exceptionally complex concept; problems related to it are eternal, and have been discussed in the professional literature of several cognate disciplines from time immemorial. In this specifically literary context, though, a theoretical framework conceived with literature in mind seems more adequate than a linguistically or philosophically oriented framework (e.g., Doležel 1980, especially p. 8). I prefer, then, to use two complementary terms proposed by Benjamin Harshav: '(*Internal* or *External*) *Fields of Reference*' (*IFR* and *ExFR*, respectively). This set of terms, whether or not explicitly mentioned, constitutes a conceptual framework underlying my discussion.[18]

By way of a simplified introduction to Harshav's terminology and conceptual framework, *IFR* (*Internal Field of Reference*) is the distinctive feature of the unique kind of referring and denotation typical of the fictional world in a work of verbal art: within it, most of the *referents* (i.e., whatever is *referred to* in the text) do not exist in the 'real world', but create the work's own *Field of Reference*.[19] The term *ExFR* (*External Field of Reference*) is used when a (fictional) text refers to fact, reality, 'real-life' etc. (e.g., when the fictional text of Tolstói's *War and Peace* refers to Napoleon, Kutuzov, or the battle of Borodino). Thus, for Chekhov, as the author of *The Seagull*, all the play's personages belong to an *IFR* that he created, while for Trigórin the personages in his fictional works belong to an *IFR* that **he** created. Trigórin creates a subtle blend of *IFR* and *ExFR* when he plans to include a Nína-like character in a new story. Chekhov creates an analogous blend when *The Seagull* partly refers to his **real** relationship with Lídiïa Avílova (see below).

The medallion inscription is a link in a causal chain of events and phenomena, relating to each other in terms of *fiction/reality* relationships. It is a causal chain, because this inscription has an 'ancestry' (or a genesis) responsible for 'begetting' it, as well as its own 'offspring'. What can a *Seagull* spectator know about the ancestry of the medallion-inscription? Where does the sentence inscribed there come from,[20] and how was it composed? It is typical of Chekhov's treatment of the subject that the best answer to this question is somewhat paradoxical: we know for a **fact** that this 'ancestry' is a piece of **fiction** (of a 'secondary' order, i.e., fiction embedded within a 'primary' fictional world); yet, we can construct a **fictive** hypothesis according to which this sentence is based in **fact** (within that primary fictional world).

In less cryptic terms: let us forget for a moment that the actual text of *The Seagull* is fictional in the first place (i.e., let us ignore the 'primary' fictional world). Within the 'reality' of the world of the play, the quotation cites a fictional text, namely, Trigórin's imagined book, *Days and Nights*. The actual words were originally spoken, presumably, by a fictional character in a fictional context or situation. However, we can quite safely speculate, using techniques of **analogy** and **gap-filling** (see Perry 1968; Perry & Sternberg 1986), that these words had been originally spoken in 'real life', echoing something that Trigórin had heard before (or while) writing his alleged *Days and Nights*. Now this is undeniably a speculation; but as speculations go, it is a solid one: Chekhov spares no effort to put us on the track leading to it. Trigórin's *modus operandi* as a writer is to go always and everywhere with a notebook, in which he records obsessively whatever he hears and sees — words, sights, scenes, events, ideas, etc. — that might come in handy some day as raw-material for his writing. Chekhov lets us watch Trigórin work like that on several totally different and even contrastable occasions: during stormy arguments, romantic scenes, quiet conversations, etc. Especially striking are the two following examples. (1) On p. 266: right after the scene toward the end of Act 3, where Arkádina melodramatically persuades him to stay with her — a crucial and emotionally loaded scene, by 'normal' human standards — Trigórin, as if nothing has happened, writes down a verbal association for potential employment in a future book.[21] (2) On p. 274: in Act 4, Trigórin plans to see the stage-upon-a-stage, originally constructed for the performance of Konstantín's play. This makeshift stage is loaded with memories of his own love affair with Nína, which terminated after the death of their baby, and Nína is indeed moved to sobbing by the sheer sight of it. However, Trigórin plans to visit the place only in order to collect material for a story. These are cases of extreme insensitivity; they can be accounted for mainly in terms of a self-centred, uncontrollable writing obsession.[22] Moreover, Trigórin himself, in moments of candid, confession-like self-characterisation, indeed describes his writing passion as real addiction (without using the word; see pp. 255, 274). Another two 'Trigórin-items' in the play are relevant here: (1) his complaint that, not knowing how young women feel and think, his young female characters strike a false note, or at least are not convincing (p. 254 — see 3.6.1 below); (2) his planned 'seagull story' (p. 274), which seems to be freely modelled on the Nína–Konstantín–Trigórin interrelationships themselves. All this material lays a solid foundation for reasonably speculating that Trigórin must have heard the phrase inscribed on the medallion somewhere in real life before committing it to paper in his fictional book, *Days and Nights*.

3.4 Chains of Factual, Fictional and Referential Events

Here, then, is the chain of factual and literary events that explicitly or implicitly happen in and around 'The Medallion Scene', link by link:

1. Trigórin hears (about) someone (probably, a young woman) saying, in real life, something like "If you should ever need my life, then come and take it".

2. He finds a point in the narrative of his story where this sentence seems appropriate, and writes it (probably, spoken or written by a fictional female character).

3. Nína reads the story and is so deeply moved by it that she memorises and internalises certain phrases (see her enthusiasm as a Trigórin reader in Act 2, pp. 238, 254–256).

4. Her infatuation with Trigórin, soon developing into powerful romantic involvement, brings the sentence to her mind as expressing her feelings about him (using his own words suggests genuine kinship of minds).

5. She orders a medallion with the referring inscription on it, in order to convey her feelings to him, and presents it to him.

6. Having read his own words as embedded in the medallion presented by her, he responds to the pragmatics of the reference and starts an affair with her.

7. Less than two years later, he abandons her at his convenience, after the birth and death of their child. Thus Trigórin subconsciously takes full advantage of the licence implied in the inscription ("take my life IF you ever need it" implies also "you may leave me if, and when, you no longer need it"). Nína is apparently less literal, more literary than Trigórin: to her, the conditional sentence from *Days and Nights* was not so conditional...

8. Trigórin's behaviour at later stages implies that he regards (parts of) this chain of events as a proper subject for a new story that he plans to write, using the original locations of the 'real' events (i.e., belonging to the 'primary' order of fictionality) as setting for the designed plot on the 'secondary' order of fictionality (p. 274). In other words, the true story of their lives is once more planned to be embedded in a work of fiction, which, in turn, is eventually 'embeddable' in future life-stories of prospective readers of Trigórin's newly written fictional story. Such readers, of course, can respond in various ways, in their own lives, to the story they have read, not least by writing fictional stories, and so on *ad infinitum* (this last point will be developed in the next Subsection).

Now everything described so far, except the last phrase, is based on the false premise that all *The Seagull*'s events take place in reality. In reality, however, all is embedded in one fictional discourse (the text of *The Seagull*, which is Chekhov's *IFR*) embedding, in turn, another (Trigórin's *Days and Nights*, i.e., **his** *IFR* within Chekhov's) and occasionally referring to others — i.e., the stories that Trigórin plans to write (his *IFR*), using the materials (fictional for Chekhov, real for Trigórin) that he keeps collecting.

Taking the various planes of reality and fiction with their implications into account, the preceding 'chain of events' can be re-stated in more formal referential terms as follows (retaining the original numbering):

1. Trigórin's real life, Chekhov's speculative/virtual *IFR*.
2. Trigórin's *IFR* (i.e., the same words now refer to an *Internal Field of Reference*).
3. Trigórin's *IFR* internalised in Nína's real-life.[23]

4. Nína's mind creates a virtual *ExFR*, making Trigórin's *IFR* refer to it.
5. Nína uses a real-life object[24] as a speech-act designed to turn Trigórin's *IFR* into *ExFR*, as if he referred in his book to their real-life situation.
6. The de-fictionalised sentence refers to *ExFR* for both of them.
7. Now the sentence functions in real life for Trigórin; for Nína, the same sentence is a borderline case between *IFR* and *ExFR*, referring to both.
8. Events have virtually come full circle: the entire 'happening', once taking place in reality (of course — it must be kept in mind — within the fiction of *The Seagull*), can 're-refer' to fresh contexts, both *IFRs* and *ExFRs*, in future perceivers' minds and lives.

Thus 'the referential pendulum' — moving to and fro between fact and fiction, separating them, merging them, subordinating them to each other, emancipating them from such subordination, etc. — delineates wider and narrower circles around the medallion. The chain just outlined, then, demonstrates the complexity, subtlety and evasiveness of fiction–reality interactions and reciprocal reflections in the play.

3.5 Chekhov's Poetics of the Implicit: Functions of "philosophising"

This Section focuses on one of the main techniques that Chekhov uses to maintain permanent superiority — which, in the final analysis, he shares with his audience — over his characters.[25] As shown throughout the Book, the later Chekhov always makes his own points through structural, thematic and/or psychological relationships — which the audience has to spot, construct, integrate and interpret — rather than through isolated elements that are fully formulated and ready for instant use. Such direct formulations are particularly characteristic of the "philosophising" tirades of individual personages/speakers, who generalise about life, art, society, the future and destiny of mankind, etc., as analysed mainly in Chapter 8. Thus it is a composite textual entity (e.g., the *medallion scene*), rather than any individual personage (e.g., Konstantín or Trigórin and their plain "philosophising" platitudes), that represents Chekhov's authorial attitude towards the theme at hand. Chekhov's attitudes reside in the level of the final, fullest textual integration; it is the level of the overview, under which all statements and relationships, explicit and implicit, have gone through processes of reciprocal reflection, interaction and modification in the perceiver's mind. It cannot be spotted at any point in the text.

What we have seen so far is a case in point. The chain of metamorphoses that unfolds in the play through the medallion and its indirect consequences shows us how art can function in life and vice versa; how a phrase uttered somewhere, perhaps inadvertently, can become meaningful once embedded in a work of art, realising additional referring potentials; and how, after this embedding has taken place, it can affect a reader so powerfully that it can change the course of his/her life. The play is full of explicit statements by various personages about the nature and importance of art (see Note 23). However, most of them sound hollow and shallow in comparison to the indirect, yet powerful and inexhaustively complex and multi-dimensional messages emanating from the *medallion scene*, such as the seagull imagery, the multi-functioning of the stage-upon-a-stage and the play-within-a-play, the lake, or the allusions to *Hamlet* and other literary sources. It is through this type of densely semanticised relationships that the powers of reference and representation in art are not only demonstrated, but also brought home to the addressee by activating a direct emotional experience in him/her. As I have pointed out, no addressee is necessarily the last link at the potentially endless chain of ... →*life*→*art*→*life*→*art*→ ... embeddings, as one would tend to think. This is so simply because a *potentially endless chain*, as such, may have no last link at all. Addressees presumed 'last link in the chain', once again, can react to the impact of the work of art that they have experienced (e.g., *The Seagull*) by modifying their actions, thoughts, emotions and attitudes; potentially, such reactions can include creating their own fictional worlds, and non-fiction ones, in writing, to be read by further addressees. By the way, the present study itself is a case in point: it can have its impact on you, its readers, from this very moment of your reading it and on; each and every one of you can of course say, do, write, or otherwise generate a response to this study, which can potentially affect other people at your future 'receiving end' — as listeners, readers, spectators etc. — and they, too, can say, write, do, etc., addressing their own addressees, till doomsday.

Yet, for all their shallowness, the explicit "philosophising" remarks made by personages (e.g., preaching for or against "new forms"), do serve a purpose, as argued in Chapter 8. These superficial tirades define and delineate a thematic target, like an arrow pointing to a direction, whereas the real treatment of the thematic complex is carried out by each of the respective plays' semantic and structural networks. It is through these networks and relationships that the actual job of saying something meaningful and uncompromisingly truthful about crucial phenomena in life is carried out. Each of the plays concentrates on its own complex of themes, and in each we have this mutually complementary employment of the explicit and the implicit, the superficial and the profound, each fulfilling its own indispensable function.

3.6 Additional Functions of the Medallion Scene

3.6.1 Characterising Trigórin as a Writer

Konstantín and Trigórin are writers, and their art is crucial to them and to the play. There are quite a few instances when various personages explicitly evaluate the literary quality of these writers' work; on some occasions the writers themselves also engage in self-evaluation (by the way, the two actresses in the play, too, evaluate themselves, each other, and the two writers). Yet, we are hardly given an opportunity to judge the artistic merit of their work for ourselves, based on first-hand impression, since very little of the alleged texts is quoted.[26] In the absence of other evidence, one of the functions of the sentence "If you should ever need my life, then come and take it" is to serve as a synecdochical representation of Trigórin's entire literary output, being the only Trigórin text actually supplied.[27] Bearing in mind the lack of other evidence and the powerful emotional impact and sentimentality of the gesture implied by the phrase, one is encouraged to speculate about the type of fictional heroine who presumably uttered it in Trigórin's alleged book: he himself, by the way, confesses to Nína in Act 2, that his young heroines strike a false note (Act 2; see 3.3 above).[28] One is also likely to wonder about the situation in which the sentence was uttered in *Days and Nights*, etc., asking oneself which of the contradictory evaluations of Trigórin's writing (by Konstantín, Nína, Arkádina, Trigórin himself, and indirectly by others as well) is most compatible with this sentence.

Here is an interesting case of specifically literary referring: a sentence in a work of fiction (of primary order) refers to a nonexistent work of fiction (of secondary order), of which it is the only 'realistically' existing sentence... To be more precise: if the events of *The Seagull* were real, *Days and Nights* would be a **real** work of **fiction**, and the quote would be just one sentence out of that work, the rest of the text being accessible to everyone in the world in bookshops, libraries etc. It is the initial fictionality of *The Seagull* that makes *Days and Nights* nonexistent; thus all of 'it' but the quoted sentence is inaccessible to anyone in the world. The quotation does exist as a sentence in *The Seagull* proper, thus representing the existence of *Days and Nights* in the same status as all other objects and persons in the play. On stage, Trigórin holds a tangible book in his hands, a prop purported to be his *Days and Nights*; yet, as a work of fictional verbal art — or, in other words, **as a novel** — the book is nonexistent; it becomes partially existent, though, through this single quotation, which serves as evidence that it consists of real, quotable verbal material. In this sense the verbality of the quote contributes to the novel's existence much more than the physicality of the prop-volume on the stage.

Moreover, one can contrast this quote with Konstantín's play, and with *The Seagull* itself, thus comparing three writers: Chekhov,[29] Konstantín and Trigórin. Konstantín's 'oeuvre' is represented by his fragment-play, and Trigórin's — by that single sentence, to which the inscription on the medallion refers. Yet it is through his authorial decision, as the creator of the world of *The Seagull* in its entirety, that Chekhov chose to give us those samples — nothing more, yet nothing less — to represent the writing of his two writers–characters, Konstantín and Trigórin. Focusing on the latter as the subject of the present study, one can say that this authorial decision validates our attempts to learn whatever we can from this single sentence, in the absence of any other direct evidence, about Trigórin's 'poetics', about his aesthetic–artistic, moral, psychological, emotional and other qualities as a writer.

What strikes a reader of the sentence, especially when considered in isolation, is the total dedication that it expresses, to the point of utter submission and readiness for self-effacing sacrifice. A reasonable speculation, then, is that the 'world' of a Trigórin story is at least partly inhabited by people, perhaps mainly women, who make speeches, gestures and actions of total love and ultimate devotion and sacrifice. As a verbal proclamation this sentence is a grand theatrical gesture, but as a speech act with pragmatic implications it is the epitome of *passivity*: a speaker of such a sentence makes an active decision to impose his/her total passivity and apparent lack of will upon his/her addressee.[30] At any rate, the least one can gather from this sentence is that Trigórin's works include sentimental presentations of such qualities as gestural theatricality, total devotion, false or genuine self-effacement, and passivity; in considerable likelihood, these qualities apply mainly to his women-personages.

3.6.2 Characterising Trigórin as a Man: the Fisherman, the Lover, and the Writer

I shall confine myself to one trait in Trigórin's character — namely, passivity — that Chekhov convincingly connects with the former's writing and with the single specimen of it that he provides us with. This is a very central character-trait of Trigórin's throughout the play (see especially his submissiveness to Arkádina in Act 3, explicitly saying: "I've no will of my own [...] I'm a flabby, spineless creature" etc. [p. 265]). Yet, the 'Medallion Scene' decisively contributes to the analogical link between his passivity as a man and as a writer. At first, he appears as a dynamic, restless, obsessively hardworking writer; almost the epitome of activity. But when one looks more closely into his working habits one can see subtly camouflaged passivity there too. Trigórin does not go looking for his materials, but waits patiently in his writer's ambush, pen and notebook ready; and when 'something writable' comes his way — he 'strikes', by capturing this 'something' and depositing it in his notebook. It is no wonder that he loves fishing so passionately, deluding himself that this hobby is diametrically opposed to his profession (see his own description, p. 255, and Rozik 1988). In fact, he practises the very same passive-ambush technique when he functions as a fisherman, a lover, and a writer: his love-affairs with both Arkádina and Nína are dominated by these active women, while Trigórin waits until they come to pick him up.[31]

It is in this latter context that the medallion comes in. The sentence to which its engraved inscription refers is subtly representative of Trigórin's nature: a fisherman's frame of mind is compatible with such a passive and submissive offer of love. As I have pointed out, it is a highly convincing paradox that Nína — by far, the most active major character in the play, and one of Chekhov's rare genuinely changing and developing characters — decides to offer herself as a passive fish waiting motionless for the fishing rod of love to catch her, or, in fact, to destroy her life (the reference here is, of course, to Trigórin's "idea for 'the seagull' story"). In partial analogy, in the beginning of Act 3, Másha explicitly offers herself to Trigórin as literary material, after he has written about her in his notebook. Here, too, Trigórin waits passively for the fish to come to his net; yet the nature of the offer is radically different.

The analogy between the medallion inscription and Trigórin's planned 'Seagull story', however, is striking and illuminating: the life of a fictitious happy girl, the heroine of Trigórin's potential book, is destroyed by a fictitious man out of idleness, **having nothing better to do** ("от нечего делать"); a fisherman-character. In order to communicate with Trigórin on his own psychological terms, Nína adopts his stance through that sentence of his. Thus passivity and fishing become covert *Fields of Reference*, to which the medallion inscription refers.

3.6.3 The Medallion and the 'Seagull Story'

This coupling may be the most interesting function of the medallion. 'The seagull story' (p. 257) seems to me a case of *mise-en-abîme*, connected by innumerable links to many aspects of the play. I shall confine myself to three: (1) the semanticised physical object; (2) the fictional double-embedding; and (3) the potentially destructive passivity.

(1) Trigórin sees the seagull that Konstantín has killed. This inspires him to think of a girl who is free and happy like Nína, and loves the lake like a seagull. "But a man comes along, sees her, and having nothing to do, destroys her, as happened to this seagull". In both cases a physical object — a stage-prop medallion, a stage-prop seagull[32] — is endowed with meaning. (2) In both cases we have a network of literary references to fiction-within-fiction (here Act 1's play-within-a-play is powerfully invoked). (3) In both cases passivity is linked with destruction.[33] Trigórin — considering himself a hardworking writer, unlike the 'idle' Konstantín — fails to realise that in the '**real** story' (i.e., in Nína's life), in both its 'seagull' and 'medallion' versions, his own actions/inactions and his own character (rather than Konstantín's) determine the 'plot' (the actual chain of events). And, indeed, he eventually takes Nína's life offered to him and destroys it; not because he wants to, but because, in spite of his obsessive incessant work, he is a type of person who, out of passivity, destroys beautiful things that come his way. In other words, while the fictitious man in the "Seagull-story" was clearly modelled on Konstantín **in Trigórin's mind**, in fact he was characterising himself more than any other person by inventing this personage. Trigórin may have been only half-consciously aware of the implied message he was conveying to Nína, that sometimes passivity can be more destructive than active violence (like the killing of the real seagull by Konstantín); Chekhov, obviously, was fully aware of this message when he conveyed it to us.[34]

The play abounds in other materials that work for the thematic centrality and referential polyvalence of the engraved medallion. But once the point has been demonstrated in principle, I come to the last part of my discussion.

4 The Biographical Genesis of 'The Medallion Scene'

Critics, text-analysts and biographers have accumulated impressive evidence concerning the abundance of autobiographical material in *The Seagull*. I share the view that extreme caution should be exercised in bringing events and statements from writers' lives to bear upon the analysis of their fictional writings. Chekhov is a strong case in point; he had a conscious dislike of biographical 'meddling' with his artistic work, which is consistent with his personality and 'privacy policy'.[35] However, as we shall see, 'the Medallion Scene' is an exception, and a fascinating one. Here textual analysis and interpretation can benefit from the integration of fictional and biographical materials.

4.1 The Biographical Source of the Medallion Scene

From various biographical sources[36] I have synthesised a factual narrative, which runs as follows:

Several years before writing *The Seagull* Chekhov met a young lady-writer, (Mrs.) Lídiïa Avílova. She fell in love with him, and after intensive heart-searching felt she was ready to link her life with his. To inform Chekhov of her feelings, she ordered a medallion in the form of a book, on which she commissioned the engraved inscription: "**A. P. Chekhov:** *Collected Stories*, **p. 267, lines 6 and 7**". Those lines refer precisely to **Chekhov's** sentence "If you should ever need my life, then come and take it", as it appears in the story "Neighbours" (1892). Chekhov did not respond. However, a few months before the premiere of *The Seagull*, he met Avílova in costume at a masquerade party. He recognised her, and encouraged her to go to the theatre for the premiere of *The Seagull*, saying that he would answer her from the stage. She did. When the Medallion Scene came, her heart skipped a beat: she identified this scene as a re-enactment of her presentation of the medallion to Chekhov; yet she noticed that the page and line references had been altered.[37] Having returned home, she looked the new reference up in Chekhov's book, and the result — "What are you looking at me with such admiration? Do you like me?"[38] — did not strike her as significant enough. However, in her own book of stories that she had sent to Chekhov, the same page and line numbers refer to the sentence: "It is improper for young girls to attend a masquerade party". These two possibilities are quite contradictory, each 'turned against' its respective author; however, they are both potentially relevant.

The study of such strange, almost supernatural coincidence is outside the competence of any academic discipline known to me. At any rate, whether Chekhov intended to refer "from the stage" to his own text or to Avílova's (my guess, which is as good as anyone's, is that the former is more probable), one thing is clear: his text, within its fictional *IFR*, evoked an *ExFR* (which, in itself, happens to be part of an *IFR*...) known only to him and her, as a private communication between them above the heads of an unsuspecting audience. At the same time, the official text communicated to the audience has its own complex networks of *IFR* mechanisms (as shown above). Probably nobody but Chekhov and Avílova themselves knew at the time about this *ExFR*. In all likelihood, Chekhov died thinking that nobody would ever know: he could not foresee that Avílova would write her memoirs long after his death, and that these would be published (1947) after hers (1943), and translated to other languages. Granted, most Chekhov biographers question the reliability of Avílova's memoirs as a source of information on his life, but the part concerning 'the Medallion Scene' is accepted as fundamentally true by general consent, being corroborated by other evidence.[39] Be that as it may, the entire Avílova story has nothing to do with the discourse between the text of *The Seagull* and its audience, wherever and whenever this audience lives. In this context, we are cast in the questionable role of posthumous eavesdroppers. Evidence thus obtained, albeit 'admissible' in a 'court of biography', is inadmissible in a 'court of textual analysis' — once again, on grounds of genuine irrelevance. Or is it 'admissible' after all in the latter 'court' too?

4.2 Interdependence between Biographical and Textual Perspectives

In fact, there are two separate questions here: (1) Does this background-story necessarily **alter** an analysis and interpretation of *The Seagull* and the Medallion Scene within it? (2) Does it **add** to the textual analysis of the Scene?

The answer to question (1) is "No", for 'negative' as well as 'positive' reasons.

'Negatively', there is no reason why the meaning of the play — which is a self-sufficient, autonomous text and work of art — should in any way be affected by the additional biographical knowledge, which is genuinely and fundamentally extraneous to it. 'Positively', the Medallion Scene is firmly rooted in the play: I hope to have shown throughout Section 3 above that this is one of the best-integrated and convincingly motivated short scenes in world drama. Strictly speaking, from the standpoint of the explication of the text, the biographical story adds nothing relevant. Moreover, it is potentially distracting, tempting the analyst to substitute the pursuit of intriguing and easily accessible gossip for the difficult task of analysing complex artistic texts. Therefore it is wrong to assign to it a role within semiotic–communicational processes that are 'legitimately' embedded in the text or activated by it.

The answer to question (2), however, is "Yes".

Adding the biographical dimension to the textual one confronts us with a uniquely complex and challenging object of study. Our concern need not be confined only to the analysis and explication of the text. It may spread also to communicational–semiotic processes: e.g., referring in literature; the dynamics of sign systems; the chain of addressers and addressees in human communication in general and in artistic, literary and theatrical communication in particular. Within these perspectives of interest, the biographical story can integrate in our minds with the richness and complexity of the multiply meaningful fictional text. They will then constitute together a semiotic network characterised by complexity of the highest order. And, besides, once a piece of information comes to our knowledge, through whatever channel, barring it from playing an enriching role in our cognitive and mental processes is in itself 'illegitimate', smacking as it does of censorship. One has to find the most convincing framework for integrating such information, but one cannot wait for it to go away.

4.3 Chekhovian Self-Reference

In what follows I shall try to suggest where and how the biographical and the textual can integrate fruitfully. First, consider the fact that the engraved sentence came from a previously published story by Chekhov himself. This way, one element of Chekhov's fiction (a story) is transplanted into another (a play) through an element of his life (this works for those familiar with the Avílova affair) or without real-life interference (for those familiar with both texts but ignorant of the real-life element).

Knowing this information could complicate matters considerably. The story's publication date preceded the play's, thus enjoying public-domain availability by the day of the latter's premiere; therefore, this aspect of self-allusion — unlike the aspect of private communication between Chekhov and Avílova — cannot be totally ignored when considering possible responses of the original audience. When writing the *medallion scene*, then, Chekhov could envisage a spectator who would recognise the quotation, interpreting it as an invitation to draw analogies between Chekhov and Trigórin, at least as writers, and maybe also as men, lovers, ideologists of art, etc. Chekhov also ran the risk that the text would mean quite different things to spectators familiar with his story "Neighbours" and those who are unfamiliar with it (or at least not familiar enough to recognise the quotation). In fact, my own rhetorical strategy, as adopted in most of the present study, is a case in point: I have suspended the identification of the Chekhovian source of the quotation until this late stage in my discussion. This strategy is based on my decision to make my readers really sense that *The Seagull* is an autonomous, self-sufficient work, a play for theatre audiences that need not consist of scholars specialising in Chekhov studies. At any rate, Chekhov could hardly expect most of his prospective spectators to be familiar enough with the story "Neighbours" to make a positive identification of a single sentence from that story upon hearing it uttered in a fleeting moment on the stage.

Arguably, for Chekhov such identification was a price he was reluctantly ready to pay, rather than an added benefit he expected to enjoy, i.e., a liability rather than an asset: Chekhov clearly dissociates himself from Trigórin, as a writer and as a human being.[40] On the other hand, it has also been noticed that Chekhov supplies another tangible basis for identifying him with Trigórin: on p. 277 Konstantín summarises a description of a moonlit night in a story by Trigórin, without actually quoting from it. The verbal–visual summary itself, however, refers to a specific description in a previous Chekhov story, "Wolf" (1886).[41] Whatever Chekhov's conscious or subconscious considerations, the effect resulting from such self-allusions is mixed: despite striking differences between him and Trigórin, a Chekhov-informed reader is made to find in Trigórin certain Chekhovian qualities, at least as a **literary craftsman**. I have an unsubstantiated suspicion that Chekhov might have secretly but consciously enjoyed challenging, teasing, and even misleading, certain types of prospective readers–spectators, as well as critics[42] — particularly those inclined to waste energy on looking for real-life gossip behind personages and events in literature generally, and in a play like *The Seagull*, full of writers and actresses, in particular.

A more striking example of the futility of the indiscriminate insistence on looking for biographical bases for fictional events concerns the love affair between Chekhov's close lady-friend, Líka Mizínova, and the married writer Ignáti Potápenko. The two had an illegitimate baby-girl, born in autumn 1894. He stayed married to his wife and abandoned Líka. Their daughter died at the age of two, in November 1896, about a month after the premiere of *The Seagull*; thus, with hindsight, the fictional death of Nína's and Trigórin's child can be seen as an ominous premonition.[43] Yet a similar sequence of events is told in Chekhov's famous story "A Dreary Tale" (1889),[44] which had been published five years before the Potápenko–Mizínova affair occurred in real life. There is greater similarity in terms of significant factual details between the two Chekhov works of fiction than between any of them and the real-life events. To the best of my knowledge, this astounding triad (in chronological order: story, reality and play) has hardly been noticed in its entirety in the literature. Most biographers dwell on *The Seagull*'s ostensible origins in the Potápenko–Mizínova affair, whereas other critics (e.g.,

Gilman 1995, 92–94) point out the link between Chekhov's earlier story and later play (Rayfield 1997, 356 mentions the two works almost in the same breath, but does not dwell on the similarity between the story's Katia and the play's Nína in their unhappy love affairs ending with dead infants). Moreover, no writer known to me has placed this triad in the theoretical contexts of biography *vis-à-vis* fiction and art–life interactions. The undoubted chronological sequence (worth reiterating: *fictional story→real life love-affair→fictional play→death of real baby*), then, is another proof of the polyvalence of art–life interactions: they breed, inspire and reflect each other with infinite variety of unpredictable ways.

At any rate, the reason for the inclusion of these self-oriented allusions in the text is probably that they seemed to Chekhov useful and functional for the textual passages in which he placed them. Thus, he seems to have attached more importance to this immediate, local functionality (which includes an intra-*Seagull*, intra-Konstantín link between the moonlight description in "Wolf" and the role of moonlight in Konstantín's play) than to preventing possible false identification between Chekhov and Trigórin, which his text anyway takes care to undermine. If, however, anyone sees the inclusion of the ready-made moonlight description in *The Seagull* as a minor flaw in this masterpiece of world drama, I would not contest such a view. The case of the actual text of the medallion inscription is different: this previously-published text is absolutely irreplaceable, as we have seen.

4.4 The Origin of the Inscribed Sentence: *Crime and Punishment*

I am gratefully indebted to my colleague Michael Finke, Professor of Russian (now at the University of Illinois, Urbana-Champaign), for pointing out an astounding reference to me. As he wrote to me in a private e-mail communication, "So far as I know, nobody has ever noticed this, as unlikely as that seems". And indeed it is strange that this reference escaped the watchful eyes of experts who have otherwise successfully unearthed lots of literary allusions and references in *The Seagull*.

In Part V, Chapter 5, of Dostoïévskiï's *Crime and Punishment* (Dostoevsky 1975, p. 359) Dúnia, Raskól'nikov's sister, visits her brother, and what she says to him is strikingly similar to the sentence that Chekhov wrote in "Neighbours" and self-quoted in *The Seagull*. The relevant quote from *Crime and Punishment* runs as follows: "if you should happen to need me, or need... all my life, or anything... you must call me and I will come" [«если, на случай, я тебе в чем понадоблюсь или понадобится тебе... вся моя жизнь, или что... то кликни меня, я приду.»][45]

The similarity between the two texts, Dostoïévskiï's and Chekhov's, is so striking that a coincidence is extremely unlikely and must be ruled out. *Crime and Punishment* is a product of the late 1860s; its first publication as a separate book dates to 1867 (when Chekhov was seven). Chekhov, of course, knew this novel very well, as did (and still does) any person with literary education, at least in Russia.[46] At any rate, Chekhov was most probably affected by Dúnia's words when he read the novel.

Actually, there are two possibilities: Chekhov could have alluded to Dúnia's words either consciously or subconsciously (his word-by-word self-quote from "Neighbours" in *The Seagull* must have been conscious). Now for our purpose it makes little difference which of the two is factually correct. In a way, the subconscious possibility, though unlikely, makes the art–life interaction even more impressive: in that hypothetical case, Chekhov would have demonstrated in his own life how words of fiction can affect a reader in reality, and influence such a reader's writing (if s/he is a writer). At any rate, Chekhov could envisage spectators who would recognise his own "Neighbours" and not recognise *Crime and Punishment*, or vice versa, or both, or neither, when hearing the sentence 'written by Trigórin' spoken on the stage. This adds considerably to the enormous complexity of this case, above and beyond the perspectives already outlined and analysed above.

4.5 Art–Reality Interactions as a Matter of Life and Death: Futility *vs.* Fertility

Let me come back to the actual content of the engraved sentence "If you should ever" etc. In addition to the interpretations of this inscription offered in Section 3 above, one may see the expanded chain of actions, addressers and addressees in the thematic perspective of **futility *vs.* fertility**. Trigórin's text here is indeed an epitome of stereotyped feminine passivity; yet, paradoxically, its powerful effect is one of **hyper-activity,** due to the totality of the submission it expresses. Moreover, metaphorically, as a text, *Days and Nights* (and this quote in particular) penetrates Nína's mind, thereby 'fertilising' her mental processes; as a result, she bears **it** a figurative 'child' of thought and feelings of love.[47] Analogically, the same happens later, literally and biologically, when she bears the (fictitiously) real man Trigórin a (fictitiously) real child. The death of that child and Trigórin's subsequent abandonment of Nína are powerful events by real-life standards, and their impact in human terms may make the figuratively fertilising powers of art look futile as well.[48] Yet, such an expected response by members of the audience involves (at least temporarily) the (un)willing suspension of their potential sophistication and ignores the very essence of this specific play's uniqueness.

And indeed, this human impact does not amount to a conclusive negation of art's potential fertility. Rather, it complements the naïve view of the fertilising powers of art, implied by the young Nína of the beginning of the play, and modified by the more mature, disillusioned, but still believing Nína of its ending. Thus the medallion is a pivotal core in a comprehensive view of the endless reciprocal interaction of art and life: the two are capable of fertilising and sterilising, begetting and emasculating, invigorating and smothering each other, with potentially comparable intensity. In each specific case, an infinite variety of circumstances can weaken or strengthen any of these 'positive' and 'negative' forces. Our knowledge that events of similar nature happened in the lives of Chekhov and members of his close circle of friends makes us keenly aware of both figurative and literal cases of life and death, and of life begetting art and vice versa. This knowledge is the most important contribution of the biographical information to the understanding of the text of *The Seagull* and its human as well as theoretical ramifications. It negates the naïvely human immediate response described in the previous paragraph, and gives the entire referential chain, which includes the birth and death of a real infant, an aura of almost tangible awe.

By viewing the engraved sentence in its dual perspective, biographical and textual, then, we gain a new insight into a host of ever-balanced contradictions. An insight of this nature even Chekhov could not give us through any of his works. This is so because the overall perspective discussed here encompasses (most probably against Chekhov's own will) both his inexhaustively complex text and parts of his private life-story. The latter include the actions of other real people, like Lídiïa Avílova, that he could not possibly control (not while alive, and certainly not after his death), and, by analogy, the stories of **our** lives as well, at least as long as we function as readers/spectators of *The Seagull* and its derivatives (present study included). For this to happen he had no choice but to actively 're-cycle' the idea of total passivity from his previously-published story (probably originating in his own early response, as a reader, to Dostoïévskiï's *Crime and Punishment*). Indeed, the sentence from the story functions in its new environment in *The Seagull* much more powerfully than it ever did in its 'native terrain', in "Neighbours" (and more powerfully than its Dostoïévskiïan source functioned within *Crime and Punishment*, for that matter, though evaluating that is quite beyond my charter in this study). No wonder, then, that to achieve his part in an insight of such magnitude Chekhov was prepared (whether consciously or not) to risk a false identification between Trigórin and himself by occasional well-informed Chekhov enthusiasts in the audience. Spectators who would recognise the *Crime and Punishment* quote, however few as they may be — with or without recognising Chekhov's story — would have a sharper sense of the experience that he is likely to have had in mind. He may have taken pleasure, though, in the knowledge that even the best informed and most inquisitive members of the audience could never guess the **entire** makeup of the genesis of the scene and the inscription (ironically, this includes Avílova herself, who in all likelihood missed the Dostoïévskiï reference). Be that as it may, luckily for Chekhov, his cherished, closely guarded privacy was in this case violated only many years after his death. Luckily for us, though, we were allowed to learn about Avílova's medallion. This acquired knowledge, as we have seen, gives us some safeguards against hasty art–life analogies, which the original audience did not have. Moreover, it sharpens our awareness of crucial matters of human, textual and referential significance, and gives us more adequate tools to reflect on them theoretically.

4.6 Potentialities and Limitations of *Referential Reflection*

Alongside the awesome existential dimensions of the case, a down-to-earth juxtaposition of the two Chekhov texts involved would cut at least one aspect of the entire picture to size. The 'intra-Chekhov' reference that Chekhov created between two of his own texts does not amount to a full-fledged literary allusion.[49] It seems to me, that the story "Neighbours" has no function in *The Seagull*; readers' acquaintance with it is not necessary for understanding the play, and the original context of the famous sentence has no bearing on the new one. Even the effect of characterising Trigórin through this single sentence is not seriously affected by the fact (or the knowledge of the fact) that Chekhov the short-story writer was its original author. In *The Seagull* Chekhov the playwright embeds it in Trigórin's writing, thereby dissociating himself from it. Such dissociation functions in "Neighbours" itself as well: there it was uttered by a sentimental and not-too-bright character, a particularly unlikely choice to play the role of Chekhov's mouthpiece (as I stressed above, this is a role that he anyway used to deny even the most authoritative among his personages).[50] In the context of art–life embeddings within *The Seagull*, *Crime and Punishment* demonstrates the potentially 'fertilising' powers of art much more significantly than "Neighbours".

Be that as it may, it has to be re-emphasised that the offer of ultimate self-submission is made in three radically different meanings in the three texts in which it appears. In *Crime and Punishment* the offer is made by a sister to her brother about to be accused of murder; the message is one of unconditional selfless sisterly love and trust, of being "there for him" whatever the consequence. In "Neighbours" it is made by a lover-seducer to his mistress's brother; the message is one of shame and guilt. In Trigórin's *Days and Nights*, of course, we do not and cannot know by whom, to whom and in what context these words are uttered; even Chekhov, probably, didn't know for sure... Only in *The Seagull* the sentence is used romantically. Addressed by Nína (though through a complex disguise, as we have seen) to Trigórin, it expresses a woman's passive devotion and submission to the man she loves. Yet, it is a resolute and assertive act of involvement, of assuming one's own responsibility while actively placing the other's share of responsibility on his shoulders. The words are indeed identical (in Chekhov), or almost-identical (with Dostoïévskiï); yet, when reflected within different contexts and perspectives, they are worlds apart, despite the common trait of selfless offering. Matching artistic mirroring and textual borrowing with closeness of content and emotion is very partial here.

One could construct, then, a longer and more complex chain of embeddings for the combination of the Avílova affair with the Nína–Trigórin affair along the lines proposed in 3.4 above. It might run along the following lines: **Stage 1** (doubtful and speculative): Dostoïévskiï hears or reads somewhere: "If ever", etc. **Stage 2:** he writes the sentence in *Crime and Punishment*. **Stage 3:** Chekhov reads *Crime and Punishment* and is affected by this sentence. **Stage 4:** Chekhov makes a character in the story "Neighbours" use a similar phrase. **Stage 5:** he is surprised by Lídiïa Avílova's gift and inscription. **Stage 6:** he creates the Medallion Scene in *The Seagull*. From this point on one can add stages from Section 3.4 above, with some adjustments. A precise chain of potential art–life links would be even fuller and more complex, but there is no need to spell it out in detail: the basic principle is quite clear.

One could go on to analyse the precise factual or fictional status of each component in the complex. Thus, for instance, the original medallion given to Chekhov by Avílova, and actually used on stage as Nína's present to Trigórin in the first St. Petersburg production, bears the original inscription. However, it serves as cue for the new page and line reference; thus, it belongs simultaneously to several referential sets, serving in a different capacity in each. In that 1896 St. Petersburg premiere evening, then, the combination of page and line reference carried a private communication — an autonomous referential set — superimposed on the complex as already described in the play proper. Thus we have a succession of *Frames* and *Fields of Reference*, some of which are *Internal* and *External* at the same time, on different planes.

5 Concluding Remarks on Fictionality and (Im)Perfection

I hope to have shown through this rare example some general principles of art–reality embedding, demonstrating how art can function in life and vice versa.

The features of this case are rare, probably unique; yet, at the same time, the case is also typical, as it demonstrates a basic mechanism of the function of fiction in literature and drama, and, when assigned a thematic role, also in real life, and vice versa. This mechanism, if activated fully, reproducing itself potentially endlessly, is so complex that it makes heavy demands on the integrating cognitive functioning of the brain of the perceiver; and, as we have seen, it did require the brain of a genius to produce. This may be one of the reasons why examples of this mechanism activated to full capacity are so rare.

Moreover, the medallion scene derives much of its strength from the fact that *The Seagull* as a whole is a self-referential work of *ars poetica.* It is a play about plays, and a piece of theatre about the theatre; a work of art about art, and a work of fiction about fictionality. It is one of the pioneering works in a trend developed in the first half of the 20th century, of theatre looking at itself (continued in radically different ways, but with comparable complexity, by Pirandello, and perhaps with lesser self-referential complexity by Brecht and other masters). Only in this kind of self-oriented literature can this type and degree of complexity be achieved.

The specificity of Chekhov's contribution to this 20th-century tradition is perhaps found in his unique blend of complexities on many planes, thematic and compositional; in the inimitable combination of meaningful human and psychological networks of relationships and events with just as meaningful structural quasi-technical networks by which he builds a text; and, last but not least, in the overall patterns that he creates in order to connect between these heterogeneous networks (e.g., the analogies of *fertility–futility*, or *passivity–activity*, on human and artistic planes).

Yet, above all, Chekhov seems to have known that, in the true hierarchy of values that governs literary and dramatic art, the validity and efficiency of complex artistic mechanisms are judged and tested, above all, by the extent of their contribution to penetrating insights into the human condition, i.e., by generating moving emotional experiences of the addressees. The uniqueness of great works of literary (including dramatic) art lies not only in their compositional complexity and multi-layered organisation, but also in the depth, intensity and subtlety of human experiences that they convey and generate. The former's major role is to serve the latter. Such human experience, however, cannot be achieved or reproduced without such intensity and complexity of artistic organisation, as argued in 8.0.

Chekhov is one of the greatest creators of compositional perfection in the service of human imperfection. Not least for this reason, his poetics is a major land-mark in the endless quest for the reciprocal reflection of art and humanity.

6 Reflecting on Reflection: Biblical and Mythological Ramifications (an Epilogue)[51]

The 'Medallion Scene', as analysed above, activates intense mechanisms of *mirroring* and *reflection*; such mechanisms provide additional ways of looking at this scene, through perspectives of ancient mythologies central to Western culture.

Narcissus fatally fell in love with himself by looking at his *reflection* in the water, and unwittingly committed suicide by trying to embrace his own captivat-ingly beautiful image. Without going into the strictly psychoanalytical and psychological ramifications of this myth, I would like to point out its obvious char-acteristic of bringing together the concepts of beauty, mirroring, (self-) love, and death (including suicide and unconscious death-wish). All of these concepts have also been connected throughout the ages, in different forms and degrees, with the phenomenon of *art* and its crucial presence in the world of humans from time immemorial, and in all probability till doomsday. Throughout the ages all arts have often been discussed and characterised in terms of *mimesis* (i.e., imitation of *life* or the *real world*) — whether, how, and to what extent a given art in general, or any specific work of art in particular, is engaged in *imitating*, or *reproducing*, or *modelling*, life/reality/the 'real world', etc. Arts have also been classified *inter alia* according to the mimetic criterion (e.g., labelling visual arts as *mimetic*, and music as *non-mimetic*, in principle). Analogies between art and **materials** capable of reflecting, mainly glass (of which mirrors are made) and water (of which pools, ponds, lakes, seas and oceans are made), have been common in texts of art and about it. It is no wonder that Chekhov, too, challenged his genius to cope with this eternal complex of topics. As one would expect, he did so in ways that mainly shed his own light on this theme, while partly reflecting what his predecessors had done before him since time immemorial. Nowhere in his oeuvre is this attempt more apparent than in *The Seagull*, and nowhere in this play is it more obvious and focused than in the 'Medallion Scene'.

Four major personages in *The Seagull* are artists: Konstantín and Trigórin are writers, and Nína and Arkádina are actresses, and all of them share marked narcis-sistic traits, despite striking differences between their personalities, and indeed between the specific types of their respective narcissistic traits (which outweigh their similarities). Arguably the most narcissistic of them, Konstantín, is the author of the play-within-the-play (a typically imperfect mirroring device), and he is inescapably and obsessively preoccupied — as an ever-frustrated son, man, writer and man of the theatre — with subjects of art in its relation to reality. His suicide at the end of the play shows how fatal such an obsession can be, not only for every human being in general, but for an artist in particular, in the context of his art; how the absence and/or (manner of) presence of life within art can render this art vibrant or lifeless, and, by the same token, how the absence and/or (manner of) presence of art within (a) life can render (such a) life vibrant or lifeless. This incomparably powerful presence of most arts in human reality, its life-affirming and life-negating force, is largely derived from its reflective, mirroring capacity, and from its inseparable link with the concept of beauty and the quest for it; from the constant need to compare, contrast, and juxtapose between the two worlds, the 'god-made' world of reality and the man-made world of art. "Mirror mirror on the wall, who's the fairest of them all?" is a question asked not only by Snow-White's envious stepmother, but much more significantly by mankind as a whole when looking at itself in the inescapably subjective and inaccurate mirror of art. The urge to ponder the mystery of art and beauty and to find out to what extent the former reflects or distorts reality is one of the ways to come to grips with the innermost truth and essence of life and the world. The deepest manifestations of the universally human urge to experience art, then, can be also described as analogous to narcissistic mirroring and fatally uncontainable self-love and to the seductive powers of the suggestion of redemptive depth-under-water, that may prove treacherous and deadly if one dares to plunge into it and check for oneself. This, in a nutshell, is the relevance of that Greek myth to a central complex of problems one encounters in the analysis of the 'Medallion Scene'.

Indeed, such an attempt to confront this type of mystery may be a dangerous enterprise, perhaps 'punishable by (self-inflicted) death'; and here comes also a myth derived from the Biblical Judaeo-Christian sources. Thus, the ancient divine taboo — "there shall no man see Me [=see God] and live" (*Exodus* 33:20) — can be re-interpreted and charged with additional, multi-dimensional meanings in the light of some of the awesome combinations unravelled here. Consider such concepts as reflection–mirroring; self-love; the urge to become one with the object of love; the life-imitating and life-generating qualities attributed to art; the four-way fatal connection of art, love, beauty and death; and other related qualities. Now consider how closely all of them are related to the concept of the identity of God and man ("So God created man in His own image, in the image of God created He him" — *Genesis* 1:27), and to the death penalty that hangs over man when he tries to look into the image of God, which (paradoxically?) is his own image. Ancient Biblical– monotheistic and Greek–pagan mythological taboos, then, reflect each other in instilling the dread of looking at the mirror in their believers. Of course, one can make distinctions between similarity and identity, between various kinds of love, beauty, and reflection, as well as between the human and the divine, selfish and selfless love, etc. etc.; regardless of these crucial subtleties, the 'bottom line' is that the fateful Gordian connection between all these concepts is deeply rooted in our collective consciousness and cannot ever be completely disentangled.

Keeping these vast perspectives in mind, let us return to Chekhov's *The Seagull*. In this play, the endless reflecting powers residing in art–life interactions are the core of the 'Medallion Scene', whereas its fatal potentials are finally realised in Konstantín's suicide (whose more explicit and conventional causes, like frustrations in the realms of romantic love and personal artistic calling, are more apparent on the surface of the play). The purpose of these remarks, then, is to reflect upon a deeper and more comprehensive background to the connection between *The Seagull* and narcissistic/fatal reflection.

As an epilogue, let me close the circle and re-connect to the beginning of this

Appendix and to its Epigraph (quoted from Nelson Goodman). I am proposing an *ad hoc* working distinction between the concepts of *mirroring* and *reflection*, although in the body of the study they have been used interchangeably, i.e., "mirroring/reflecting" each other... I suggest to assign to the former — i.e., *mirroring* — the sense of an *object*, that is the precise copy or duplication of another one (colloquially, its "spitting image"); such a duplication means that the two totally identical objects are actually one and the same. *Reflection*, however, according to this distinction, is in fact *reflecting*; it is a *process*, through which an object is reproduced by, through, or within a reflecting substance, such as glass or water (or something that functions analogously, e.g., the mechanisms of *mimetic art*). Such a *reflecting substance* is dynamic, and has its own qualities, which in turn has an impact on the resulting (reflected) object. The latter is, of course, similar to the 'original', sometimes hardly distinguishable from it, but not totally identical with it in the final analysis. Of course, to the doubtful extent that mimetic art 'imitates' real life, it does not copy it, and the two are easily differentiated.

Thus, aspects of the art–life embeddings in and around 'The Medallion Scene' in particular, and *The Seagull* in general, have been likened above both to the static state of endless reflections by two mirrors facing each other and to a dynamic, temporal chain of causes and effects. The gap between the two visions is somewhat bridged by the image of the *pendulum*, moving back and forth, as it were, between two fixed poles. These descriptions are mutually complementary, rather than contradictory. Thus, *mirroring* betrays a binary vision, *art* vs. *life* — extracting from each specific instance its 'art-like' or 'life-like' quality, and viewing this quality as dominant, while ignoring other, specific and distinctive components of the instance under discussion; *reflection*, conversely, is attentive precisely to these components (e.g., to differences **within** each group of 'Stages' as presented in 3.4 above, beyond their common traits as 'factual' or 'fictional').

A more comprehensive analysis of these complexities requires much more time and space than can be given to it at this point. Let me end this discussion, with reference to its witty Epigraph, by saying that art does not and cannot 'copy', 'mirror', or 'reproduce' the real world, not only because the latter is a 'damn thing', but also and mainly because art is produced by an active human mind, which cannot merely emit precisely what it takes in; it cannot help being creative and add its own input. The analogies of juxtaposed mirrors and of the pendulum movement, then, are designed to clarify the vision of the inexhaustible complexity of the phenomena involved, to make it just a tiny bit less mind-boggling; however, they cannot do justice to the endless, perpetual process of art and life begetting and recreating, rather than merely mirroring, or even reflecting, each other. The a-temporal vision of two mirrors facing each other, then, cannot stand alone unless it is complemented by the temporal chain, where no two 'stages'— whether dominated by 'fact' or by 'fiction' — can be entirely identical.

Chekhov's *The Seagull* is undoubtedly one of the most striking achievements in the quest of mankind to look at itself, at the facts of its life and the fictions of its creative mind, at its own humanly-divine and divinely-human image, without breaking the mirror or drowning in the water, being sucked-in to its fatally unknown depths by its seductive and treacherous smooth, reflecting surface.

In and through art, human beings **can** see themselves, even look at themselves, **and go on living.**

Notes

1 This single-scene-analysis is a unified and newly re-edited version of Golomb 2000 and Golomb 2012, inclusive of additions from a guest-lecture I was invited to deliver in the Summer School of the East European Psychoanalytical Institute, Odessa 2010. This Appendix is printed here as a separate study, organised as a series of concentric circles focused on a short single scene in Chekhov's *The Seagull*; it is an Appendix because (a) it is focused on a textual unit (a scene) rather than on a general theme in Chekhov's poetics; (b) it is not integrated into the Book's line of argument and principles of construction, though based on its premises. To maintain the relative autonomy of this study as object for self-contained reading, some materials repeating other parts of the Book have been retained.

2 An 'element' in this context is any isolated component of a composite whole (or aggregate) of a higher order, in relation to that whole: a single character in relation to a group of characters, to all characters, or even to the conception of mankind as a whole in a given work; a single theme within the thematic 'world' of a play; a single scene in relation to any group of scenes; etc.

3 For a demonstration of how speech acts can be embedded in objects, see Harshav 1979, 365–368.

4 For these terms see Issacharoff 1981 (especially pp. 215–218), and Golomb & Heskia 1990.

5 See Harshav 1979, p. 375. Chekhovian simultaneity is discussed in greater detail in Golomb 1984 and 1987, and in this Book, especially Chapters 5, 6, 8, and 9 and Subsection 10.4.2.

6 Quotations from *The Seagull* are largely based on Ronald Hingley's *OXFORD CHEKHOV* translation (Hingley 1964 etc.) as a major source; page-references are made to this edition.

7 Here the medallion itself is no longer present: once it has discharged its direct referential powers, the book referred to **via** the medallion takes its place. This will be discussed below in greater detail. In addition, note that the book, with Trigórin holding it upon his re-entrance, functions explicitly as a link connecting the *medallion scene* with the allusions to *Hamlet,* and especially to the character of Hamlet, in *The Seagull* (see Scolnicov 1991 and Golomb 1986).

8 The complexity of human communication as depicted by Chekhov is evident in the apparent paradox that Trigórin's 'twofold monologue' — reading his own lines to himself — is more communicative in its effect than his technical dialogue with Arkádina . This is of course the result of the centrality of his relationship with Nína at this point, to which Arkádina is totally extraneous. See my more detailed discussion of Chekhovian communication-paradoxes in Golomb 1987.

9 In a wider and much less formal sense, the scene extends far beyond its technical boundaries, for as long as Trigórin "needs Nína's life", and even beyond that, to the end of the play (re-activated by Nína's last monologue). While a case for such an extension can be made on thematic and psychological grounds, it is counter-productive for meaningful text-analysis: once the scene is so vaguely defined, it becomes virtually co-extensive with the entire play, thus rendering any reference to it meaningless.

10 'The Medallion Scene' is particularly interwoven with 'The Bandage Scene', with the

Hamlet inter-textual allusion (Golomb 1986; Scolnicov 1991, Winner 1956), and with Trigórin's planned 'Seagull-story' (see Sections 3 and especially 4, below).

11 For a fuller presentation of this term see Harshav 1976, pp. 9–11; for an updated discussion of these matters see Harshav 2007, pp. 174–209.

12 Erlich 1969, p. 241, n. 52. Erlich refers to the early formalism of the 1920s, whereas in more recent phases of East European Formalist–Structuralist scholarship, and in Western scholarship inspired by it, interest in the theory of theatre and drama has been growing, with Chekhov's plays receiving their share in this activity. Yúriï Shcheglóv in Russian, Tadeusz Kowzan in Polish and French, Jiří Veltruský in Czech and English, and Herta Schmid in German and English — to cite a random selection of names of scholars whose work is partially available in English, at least in translation — are part of this trend in recent decades.

13 As shown throughout the Book, Chekhov virtually never trusts any of his characters to express his own ideas on any subject. There are few genuine exceptions to the aphoristic 'rule' formulated by Nilly Mirsky (1991), saying that "The very fact that a Chekhov character expresses an idea is reason enough to dissociate Chekhov from it" [see the Book's Chapter 5, where this saying is given as Epigraph]. See below, Section 4.3.

14 For a general discussion of this concept see Harshav 2007, 161–174.

15 For impressively detailed accounts of the play's allusions to literary texts (by Chekhov himself and other writers) see Rayfield 1975, 204–205; Magarshack 1952a, 175–178; Balukhaty 1927, 104–105; to cite just a few studies available in English from the rich literature on the subject.

16 This is a striking example of the pragmatic aspects of reference as presented in Tanya Reinhart's (1981, manuscript) discussion of D. Kaplan's (1971) three-place relation of representation, whereby an expression represents a reference specifically for a given person, and of Strawson's (1950) view of reference as something done by the user of the expression rather than by the expression itself (see also Lyons 1977, Vol. I, p. 177).

17 I shall deliberately ignore the differences between members of each group of terms, since for my present purpose they can, and will, be used interchangeably.

18 B. Harshav has explained and demonstrated these terms extensively in several studies; the most recent is Harshav 2007, especially pp. 1–31, 113–139, and 174–210. Although he often speaks of (parts of) the text itself, rather than the persons perceiving it, as performing the act of referring, this is not always the case in his analyses (see, for instance, Harshav 1976, p. 19); moreover, this difference can be dismissed on grounds of technical convenience and in terms of "the Interdependence of the First Two Dimensions" (Harshav 1979, 374). See also Lyons 1977, Vol. I, p. 180.

19 There is of course a kinship between *IFR* and the concept of *possible worlds*, preferred mostly in philosophical discourse. This is not the place to contrast these concepts and terminologies and weigh their respective pros and cons. Suffice it to draw attention the differences between the terms themselves: whereas *possible worlds* focuses on the potential (im)possibility of a 'world', *IFR* and *ExFR* are concerned with mechanisms of *referring*, activated by texts and their authors. Basically, the main difference resides in the type of (implicit or explicit) questions, which different strategies of textual analysis aim to answer. This can also yield differences in the applicability of certain categories of referring, or of 'possible worlds', to certain types of textual phenomena. Regrettably, these theoretical points cannot be clarified here by specific textual illustrations, as they are hardly applicable to the case discussed in this article.

20 I am referring now to the uninformed spectator, for whom the text of the play is the only source of knowledge, deliberately ignoring the fact that the sentence comes from a

previous Chekhov story, with probable roots in a Dostoïévskiï novel. This will be discussed later on, in Section 4.

21 This obsessions of Trigórin's has been discussed, *inter alia*, in Rozik 1988.

22 In Chekhov's next major play, *Uncle Vania*, Professor Serebriakóv is characterised by Vánia as a 'writing machine'. Despite numerous cardinal differences between Trigórin and Serebriakóv as persons and writers, the term 'writing machine' itself could be applied to Trigórin in both its obsessive and inhuman connotations.

23 It should be noted that for Nína, at this early and naïve stage in her life, plays and novels are the true world in which she 'really' lives, whereas reality is, by comparison, insignificant, unreal 'fiction': this 'upside-down' hierarchy is apparent in her notions about fame and glory (254–257), about Trigórin's writing (p. 238) and about what we would term *literary thematics* in general (*ibid.*). In *The Seagull* almost all characters, including 'non-artists', generalise about the importance of art and artists as one of the most 'real' aspects of reality. It is quite typical of Chekhov to create reversals of roles and hierarchies between art and life, delusion and reality (see, for instance, the ending of his story "A Little Joke", as discussed in the Book's 5.1).

24 As a **dramatic** object in the text, the medallion belongs to *IFR*; as a **theatrical** object it becomes a referent not only in Chekhov's, but also in the audience's real-life, blurring fact/fiction boundaries. Some of these theoretical complexities, however, are part and parcel of any discussion of the status of tangible objects in the theatre (e.g., Issacharoff 1981).

25 A further ramification of this technique is that in the very final analysis, at the end of an extremely subtle and complex mental process that Chekhov's texts are made to produce in their addressees, Chekhov makes us realise the common limitations of all human beings, shared of course by all parties to the artistic communication — author, text and its fictional inhabitants, and the audience of addressees. This point is elaborated in Chapters 5 (especially 5.1.2) and 6.

26 The evaluative function of Konstantín's play is discussed, *inter alia*, in the Book's Chapter 6, Note 9, and in Jackson 1967.

27 Towards the end of the play Konstantín mentions a description in another Trigórin story, but this instance of indirect speech does not amount to a real quote; I am deliberately ignoring here the added ramification of this textual description's reference to an earlier Chekhov story. See Section 4 below.

28 Styan 1971, p. 67, comments on "the falseness of his [Trigórin's] art and perhaps his own insincerity" in connection with this sentence and his reading it from his own book. I suspect that Styan would have exercised some caution about this "insincerity" had he been aware of the undoubtedly Chekhovian and possible Dostoïévskiïan authorship of this sentence... See below, Section 4.

29 Chekhov himself does make a stand, implicitly but powerfully, on the controversial issues of artistic ideology mentioned in the play: he does that simply by writing the play *The Seagull*. Thus, for instance, if Nína says that there must be love in a play, and Konstantín says that plays should describe our dreams rather than our realities and wishes, one can infer Chekhov's stand on these issues by examining which of the views is more compatible with what he actually did, as an author, in writing *The Seagull* itself. According to this simple criterion it is unequivocally clear that when writing *The Seagull* Chekhov was much closer in his aesthetics to views expressed by Nína and Trigórin than to those expressed by Konstantín; moreover, in terms of actual poetics, there is an unbridgeable gap between Konstantín's play and *The Seagull*.

30 From this standpoint, there is an analogous case in Act 3 of *The Cherry Orchard*: when Liubóv' Andréïevna Ranévskaïa asks the old servant Firs where he would go if the estate

is sold, he answers — in amazement at the very question — that he would go wherever she would tell him. For him this is the obvious, and the only, answer that a loyal servant can give to his masters. Ranévskaïa, however, cannot face the responsibility that his unsolicited submission places upon her shoulders. Trigórin, likewise, did not ask for Nína's passive submission, which she actively imposed on him; yet, he was passive enough not to reject it, leaving the entire responsibility for the consequences to her. It does not even occur to him that once he enjoyed some pleasures that came with the offer, he can be held accountable for some of the same offer's less palatable implications (from his perspective). A subtle, evasive, and largely subconscious game of assuming, shirking, and placing responsibilities on one's own as well as on the other's shoulders, is played here between these two personages.

31 The contrastive analogy between Trigórin's passive ambushing and fishing and Konstantín's active pursuing and hunting characterises their respective attitudes to several aspects of life, notably in their behaviour as writers and lovers. Just as illuminating is Trigórin's wish to stuff the seagull that Konstantín had hunted and killed. Some of these matters have been pointed out time and again in the literature (e.g., in Gilman 1995; Golomb 1996; Jackson 1967; Magarshack 1952a; Rozik 1988; and many others), each with his emphases and hierarchies.

32 Another meaningful yet somewhat enigmatic Chekhovian stage-prop — Vánia's map of Africa in Act 4 of *Uncle Vánia* — is discussed in Marsh 2012.

33 Another analogy is supplied in the beginning of Act 3, when Arkádina contrasts herself with Másha, as epitomes of *activity* vs. *passivity*, respectively.

34 Another eternally unanswerable question is strongly posed here; it concerns the relation between the personalities of authors and characters: what does it take, in terms of personality, for an author to invent a Konstantín, a Hamlet, a Madam Bovary, etc.? Here Chekhov characterises Trigórin, partially, by making him create that fictitious idle man who destroys the fictitious young woman in his unwritten story. Inadvertently, though, Chekhov himself cannot escape some degree of self-characterisation by creating all his characters, including the 'secondary order' fictitious personages created, in turn, by his own 'primary-order' fictional ones. This question is, of course, outside the scope of this Book.

35 In a letter (1899, to Rossolimo) Chekhov writes: "I have a disease: 'Autobiographophobia'" («У меня болезнь: 'автобиографофобия'»). However, the quoted sentence, in context, expresses Chekhov's reluctance, even aversion, to personally engage in **writing his own biography**; it has nothing to do with his views on the potential relevance of his biography to the analysis of his work — a subject that he hardly ever spoke explicitly about. Rather than this remark, especially if used out of context, then, it is the truly autonomous nature of his fiction, in narrative and drama alike, that require us to be cautious, even suspicious, especially in his case, in assessing the relevance of biographical material to textual analysis. In this context one can recall his adamant insistence on guarding his precious privacy, and his sharp distinction between the roles of the creative literary artist and that of the philosopher, ideologist, or preacher. That said, caution and suspicion are safeguards against making hasty and thoughtless connections, rather than an absolute prohibition of making any kind of such connection, ever.

36 My main sources are: Avílova 1950, pp. 75–95; Hingley 1976, pp. 196–199; Khanílo 1994–1995; Llewellyn-Smith 1973, pp. 97–108; Magarshack 1952b, pp. 283, 290; Rayfield 1975, p. 204; Rayfield 1997, pp. 340, 369, 398, 616 (n. 5), and 620 (n. 54); Simmons 1962, pp. 207–209, 335–341, 357, 374–375; Troyat 1986, pp. 178, 183, 191–192. All studies devoted to the analysis of the play (as distinct from Chekhov's

biography) tell, basically, the same story. Biographies vary in some points of fact and interpretation, but these differences are of little importance for the present discussion.

37 She probably sat too far back and/or was too agitated to notice that the actual pendant she had sent to Chekhov was being used on the stage as a prop-medallion: Chekhov had lent it to Vera Komissarzhévskaïa, the Nína-actress of the St. Petersburg premiere (1896), who returned it to him long after the play closed on the Petersburg stage. He had repeatedly forgotten to answer her when she kept asking him where to send it, in apparent lack of interest to get it back. Alla Khanílo (1994–1995) gives a full account of the 'biography' of the medallion itself, as a physical object. After Chekhov's death, it was deposited in a bank safe, together with other Chekhov valuables, and 'nationalised' (i.e., 'snitched') in the wake of the Revolution (this was the fate of the content of many a private bank-safe). There has been no trace of it ever since. There is no public or academic knowledge whether or where it still exists anywhere in someone's possession.

38 The quote is from Chekhov's famous story "The Black Monk", which is focused on a case of pathological fantasising, explicitly characterised in the story itself as *hallucination*. Chapter 5, Note 30, refers to potential connections between this unique story on the one hand and themes and matters discussed elsewhere in the Book on the other hand.

39 Various biographies imply that some members of Chekhov's closest circle learned at a later stage about the Avílova–Chekhov affair (or actually, in another sense, the Avílova–Chekhov **non-affair**), and perhaps even about the medallion and its role in the text of *The Seagull*. At the time of the original Petersburg premiere, however, Chekhov and Avílova were probably the only people who knew the matter with all its up-to-that-date ramifications. Rayfield (1997, 620, n. 54) observes: "Lidia Avilova was convinced that [the 1898 story] 'About Love' told of Chekhov's renunciation of love for her. She angered Anton, by accusing him of exploiting intimate secrets for literary gain". It is remarkable that (a) she apparently made no such claim in connection with *The Seagull*; (b) Chekhov was angered for being branded with the very kind of behaviour, which he liberally 'gave to' Trigórin.

40 Dissociating himself from virtually all his personages is one of Chekhov's most typical traits. See above, Note 13. In Golomb 1987, p. 10, I discussed this subject more fully, as I do in the Book's Chapter 5.

41 This self-allusion is identified by almost all writers on *The Seagull* (e.g., Henry 1965, pp. 116–117; Rayfield 1975, p. 203).

42 Admittedly highly speculative, this idea is based on the type of sense of humour that Chekhov often displayed. Particularly intriguing, and relevant to this study, is his joking yet callous offer to one of his dear lady-friends, Líka Mizínova, to give her a medallion with a page-and-line-number inscription, alluding in a sarcastic manner to the writer Potápenko and the disastrous love-affair that she had had with him. This use of the medallion idea is mentioned in several biographies (see, for instance Troyat 1986, 192; Rayfield 1997, 403).

43 The sad sequence of events is told in great detail, blow by blow (alongside concurrent events in Chekhov's life), in Rayfield 1997, throughout pages 305–404. Rayfield also elaborates on the connection between this real-life story and *The Seagull*.

44 This story's title and problems of translating it into English are discussed in the Book's Chapter 1, Note 4.

45 The originally supplied '...' in all likelihood indicate Dúnia's hesitation pauses.

46 In 1894, in Milan, Chekhov watched a dramatisation of *Crime and Punishment* (see Simmons 1962, p. 325; Rayfield 1997, p. 329) — an event which refreshed his memory

of the novel and interest in it. At that stage he had initial thoughts about *The Seagull*; "Neighbours", however, had already been published, and this fact minimises the potential importance of Chekhov's attendance of the Milan production for our purpose. Moreover, it is doubtful whether this particular sentence was spoken on stage (and in Italian at that!).

47 Chekhov presents a similar idea, though in a deliberately comic and clumsy manner, in the way Medvedénko talks to Másha in *The Seagull*'s opening dialogue, when he views the artistic co-operation between Nína and Konstantín as born out of their love. The ironies and analogies generated by this saying — of all people, by Medvedénko and to Másha — and its interaction with later events in the play, are yet another ramification that cannot be developed here. By the way, in Ibsen's *Hedda Gabler* — a play known to Chekhov (see Rayfield 1997, p. 582) — a destroyed manuscript is likened to a dead child, and it was in connection with *The Seagull* (though probably not with *Hedda Gabler*) that Chekhov was accused of "Ibsenism" (this was elaborated in 10.1.1.2; see also Henry 1965, p. 32).

48 Similarly, soon after Nína says in Act 1 that she is drawn to the lake (which Konstantín rightly interprets as analogous to the artistic world which they share) like a seagull, Konstantín realises that she has fallen out of love with him, and subsequently goes hunting and kills a seagull. This killing is for him analogous to the figurative murder of their love by Nína. The dead seagull and the dead child are analogous-yet-different, as are the romantic and artistic affairs between Nína and each of the men. This, again, requires elaboration elsewhere.

49 Ben-Porat 1976, especially pp. 107–110, offers a clear statement of what a literary allusion is.

50 In "Neighbours" the sentence is addressed by a man 'living in sin' to the distressed and indignant brother of his mistress, in a sentimental confession of guilt. The message (in my words) is: '*you have the right to kill me whenever you like*'. In *The Seagull* the same sentence means something totally different; forcing the meaning of the sentence as contextualised in "Neighbours" down the throat of *The Seagull* is a gross misinterpretation of the play. "Neighbours" is relevant to *The Seagull* only inasmuch as any work is potentially relevant to all other works by the same author.

51 This Section is based on my guest-lecture (Odessa 2010; see Note 1).

A *Guide* to the Structure of Names, Their Transliteration and Pronunciation*

Introduction

The current scene of 'Chekhoviana' in English is very rich and varied: it includes numerous translations of his own *oeuvre*, as well as thousands of works about him written originally in English or translated into it; countless live and recorded (filmed/televised) performances of his plays and dramatised originally-narrative works in English; etc. One result of this enormous body of texts is a maze of a large number of different transliterations of the same Russian words and names, creating confusion among performers, audiences, and even scholars and critics uninitiated in Russian language, literature and culture.[1] This multiplicity of solutions indicates the existence of a real and, in fact, insoluble problem: there is no single once-and-for-all fool-proof way to transliterate Russian into the Latin alphabet (for English or any other language using it).[2] No claim is made that the systems adopted in this Book in general, and in this *Guide* in particular, are superior to all existing alternatives: like all other systems, they have their faults and merits and can produce, at best, a reasonable approximation; they lack unified consistency, and reflect a compromise, resulting from the attempt to reconcile conflicting needs and preferences and to create a hierarchy between them. It is the aim of the present *Guide* to offer a helping hand to interested readers[3] who wish to find their way around in this maze without referring them to the literature that specialises in teaching and researching the sounds of Russian. Some sources taken from such literature — mainly English-language teach-yourself-Russian books — were consulted, but not copied, in the process of preparing this *Guide*. The main source, however, is my personal experience: having been exposed from early childhood to Russian as a foreign language, I have listened attentively to the speech of its educated native speakers and consulted them for many years, also while writing this *Guide*.

Indeed, it is quite impossible to reproduce phonetic and phonological systems of a source language (in this case, Russian), and their interactions with the traditions of its orthography, within comparable systems and interactions in a target language (in this case, English). Many attempts have been made to guide users

---

* The word *Guide*, capitalised and italicised, is used throughout the Book to refer to this *Guide*.

of English through the sounds of Russian, inevitably manipulating the Latin alphabet for this purpose.[4] No technique of transliteration (in this case, of Russian into the Roman alphabet with an English slant) can match the effectiveness of recurring oral demonstrations (preferably repeated several times) by linguistically conscious and competent native speakers (of Russian). Granted, such demonstrations rarely achieve successful reproductions by uninitiated listeners–imitators, but they can at least make the latter more attentive to, and then aware of, specific sounds and phonetic or phonological distinctions when they hear them, and enable them to some extent to develop a working sound image of those phonetic distinctions, at least passively, in their minds' ears, even if they are unable to reproduce them actively, in their own speech. Moreover, a major reason for the impossibility of finding a single consistent and fool-proof system of transliteration (here, of Russian into English-conditioned Roman alphabet) is that the various goals of such a system are irreconcilable, largely undermining each other. These goals include phonetic accuracy, phonological functionality, orthographic clarity resulting in easy auditory recognition, and respect for time-honoured traditions of transliteration (with which educated native users of English are likely to be familiar); such traditions take into account Russian's own orthographic traditions, as well as its sound system. Thus it is hoped that whatever texts by and about Chekhov the reader may consult in English, the Latinised Russian transliteration practice adopted in each of them would become more reader-friendly after reading this *Guide*.

The Book's transliteration policies are applied to most Russian names mentioned in it. Preferences of real Russian people (e.g., Chekhov scholars) in transliterating their names in Latin characters are respected, though these are usually followed by the Book's transliteration in square brackets, at least when first introduced (e.g., Kataev [Katáïev]); thereafter the Book's preferences are inconsistently applied (in some cases consistency results in awkward spellings, which are not always applied). Similar practices are adopted in the bibliographical list at the end of the Book (*Works Consulted*), where the reader can find both transliterations — the author's own and the Book's — side by side. When there is no evidence of a Russian author's transliteration preference, the Book's transliteration is the only one supplied, beside the original Russian–Cyrillic.

By and large, the approach adopted here can be characterised as deliberately diametrically-opposed to the one adopted in the nine volumes of *THE OXFORD CHEKHOV*, Ronald Hingley's monumental project (Hingley 1964 etc.). Thus, whereas Hingley does his utmost (though not totally consistently) to Anglicise Russian names (*Andrew* for *Andréï*, *Helen* for *Yeléna*, *Theodore* for *Feódor*, etc.), and to ignore linguistic–cultural Russian traditions like *Patronymics* (see Subsection 3.2 below), my goal is to retain the names' Russianness to the best of my ability, even at the cost of making them flagrantly strange to the English reading eye. This is done, however, while the phonology and sound associations of native speakers of English serve as point of departure for transliteration preferences. It is my express purpose, then, to constantly remind the reader that the texts discussed here were written by a Russian writer, in Russian, about Russia(ns). Granted, the Book is basically addressed to monolingual users of

English, yet it tries to cater to the needs of those interested in exposing themselves, via English, to the peculiarities of Chekhov's original language — and, to some extent, to his original culture.

To achieve this goal two distinct systems of transliteration are used: (1) *Phonetic Transliteration* and (2) *Text Transliteration.* (1) is employed **only in this *Guide*** and for its specific purpose, namely, to suggest a hopefully achievable approximation of Russian sound systems to English readers' minds' ears, i.e., to their phonetic and phonological imaginative awareness. In this *Phonetic Transliteration* the interests of reading fluency and the orthographic traditions of both languages are largely sidestepped. Instances of this *transliteration*, whenever used within the *Guide* and very rarely elsewhere in the Book, are inserted between two slashes.[5] (2) Conversely, *Text Transliteration* is adopted in the main body of the Book; it is simpler and more English-user-friendly than (1), taking into account some of the orthographic traditions of both languages as well as transliterations commonly used in previous texts by and about Chekhov[6] in English, to which Chekhov-initiated readers may be accustomed. Neither of these transliterations claims integrative and iron-clad consistency and, naturally, both are imperfect. Moreover, some fine subtleties of Russian speech — especially if they are part of linguistic systems too intricate to be explained here, and if their value for the phonetic reproduction of names in Chekhov's texts is negligible — are ignored in this *Guide*, or just mentioned briefly and admittedly inconsistently.[7]

The *Guide* is divided into four parts, addressing the following issues: (1) phenomena in Russian phonetics and phonology that are highly relevant to the native pronunciation of Chekhov's names, with special reference to the *palatalisation* ("*softening*") of consonants. (2) A 'conversion table' of Cyrillic characters and the sounds they represent into the two *transliteration systems* used in this Book. (3) The structure of Russian names and basic forms of addressing another person. (4) A list of the names of personages in Chekhov's Four Major Plays, transliterated through both systems. The sign § in this *Guide* refers to numbered items in the 'conversion table'.

1 On 'Chekhov-relevant' Elements in Russian Pronunciation

1.1 Stress and Stress-Related Features

The stress system of Russian is very intricate indeed. As in English, stress in Russian is variable and phonological (i.e., there are pairs of words that can be told apart only by the location of the stress in them, as in the pronunciation of *désert* [noun] vs. *desért* [verb] or *cóntent* vs. *contént* in English); and, once again as in English, almost any syllable in a multi-syllabic word, from the fifth before a word's end to its last syllable, can **potentially** be phonologically stressed (consider, for instance, the placement of stress in English words like *cértifiably*, *pérmanently*, *térribly*, *máinly* and *appellée*). The interested reader can simply note, memorise and internalise the correct stress of all names of Chekhov's personages listed below; this is a comparatively easy task for any competent and linguistically aware user of English: stress-related features are quite similar in the two languages, unlike many other features of phonetics. It is therefore strange, to say the least, that in many English-language productions of Chekhov's plays, even by most prestigious casts on both sides of the Atlantic, actors and directors seem to be oblivious of Russian stress, and err consistently, as if on purpose.[8] In popular pronunciation of Russian words and names by lay speakers of English the situation is even worse, but that is hardly surprising; it is even somehow legitimate in non-professional usage. Because of the crucial importance of stress in Russian, all names of Chekhov's personages and other Russian names are printed in this Book always with the stressed vowel marked by an accent (e.g., *Yeléna*), the single notable exception being the name *Chekhov* itself (rather than *Chékhov*).

Another stress-related feature of Russian that is phonologically similar to English (although its actual phonetic execution sounds quite different) is a tendency to distinguish sharply between stressed and unstressed vowels in terms of phonetic clarity/distinctiveness/discreteness: consider the obscure nature of the second and third vowels in a word like *different* in English, compared to the clear distinctiveness of its first, stressed vowel, or to the clarity acquired by its third syllable when it becomes stressed in *differéntiate*. In Russian, too, many vowels are obscured when unstressed; thus, for instance, unstressed *e* and *i* are often barely distinguishable.[9]

A special case in Russian is the vowel *O*, which is fully and distinctively pronounced as such only when stressed; it is consistently pronounced as *a* [as in the English words *father* or *calm*] in the position preceding the stress, whereas in syllables more remote from the stress (whether before or after it) sometimes an obscured version of the original *o* is heard, somewhat resembling the sound of *o* in the suffix *-ion* in English (as in the last syllable of *enunciation*, for instance). This point is discussed here at some length only because of its relevance to the original pronunciation of quite a few names in Chekhov's texts. Thus, in spelling the name of Lopákhin in *The Cherry Orchard*, with *o* as the second character, **all** English translations follow the Russian original only in orthography, but not in pronunciation, since the name really sounds /lapáxin/. The case of unstressed *O* is so crucial, that **all** its occurrences are italicised in the text of this Book, to make the reader aware of the problematic nature of this vowel (the matter is further discussed under §16 in Section 2.1 below). This is one of the instances of inconsistent compromise adopted in this Book: using the vowel *a* for such names (e.g., *Lapákhin*) would have been more correct phonetically, but at odds with many decades of transliterations in all English versions of the play.

1.2 Consonants, *"Soft"* and *"Hard"*:[10] *Palatalisation*

A crucial feature of Russian phonetics and phonology is *palatalisation*, also known as *"softening"* of consonants. This is the virtually **simultaneous** articulation of any given consonant with the sound marked in this Book by the character *ĭ* (but usually recorded in English writing by the character *y* as in *yes*, or *i* as in *Iago*).[11] The most crucial element here is indeed the *simultaneity*: the *softening sound* /ĭ/ is not heard separately after the consonant (as it is heard in English after /k/ in *cute* or after /p/ in *pure*), but the basic sound of the given consonant itself appears to be "softened", by being co-articulated with a 'hidden' but definitely audible /ï/, which lacks an autonomous 'life of its own'.

One of the confusing aspects of this phenomenon is the relation between phonetics–phonology on the one hand and orthography on the other: phonologically, and usually phonetically,[12] **all** Russian consonants have to be either *hard* or *soft*, yet there are no separate graphic signs for soft and hard variants of each consonant; instead, the Russian–Cyrillic alphabet supplies parallel sets of **vowels**. Thus, in Russian orthography there are pairs of graphic signs *a* vs. я, *y* vs. ю (/a/ vs. /ïa/ or /ia/, /u/ vs. /ïu/ or /iu/, respectively, in the *Phonetic Transliteration*). Phonetically, then, it is incorrect to regard them as hard *vs.* soft **vowels**, because the sheer vowel-sounds are identical within each pair. Indeed, the second in each pair of vowels above is in fact *softening*, or *palatalising*, rather than *soft(ened)* or *palatalised*, since its *raison d'être* is **to soften the consonant preceding it**. However, when such a *softening vowel* is not preceded by a consonant — i.e., when it begins a word, or follows a *vowel* (as in *Dostoïévskiï* spelled in Russian *Dostoévskiï* if transliterated letter by letter), or a *wedge* (*hard* or *soft sign*; see §28 and §30 in Section 2.1) — its execution starts with a distinct, autonomously audible /ï/ sound, as in Yeléna (/ïeléna/),[13] the Professor's wife in *Uncle Vánia*, or Il'ïá (/ilïá/, the forename of Shamráïev in *The Seagull* and Telégin in *Uncle Vánia*). In this Book, the *i*-transliterations of the *softening vowels* apply to the former case (when they really *soften* a preceding vowel), whereas the *ï*-transliterations apply to the latter (when they have nothing to soften and their initial *ï*-sound is distinctly audible).

Russian orthography, then, rarely concedes that *palatalisation* is a feature of consonants (rather than vowels). This is of significance for the *Guide* because, as a rule, well-established transliterations of Chekhovian names (and Russian words in general) prefer this orthographic inaccuracy to the realities of Russian pronunciation. An exception to this rule is *the soft sign* (ь), reflected in the *Phonetic Transliteration* by the italicisation of the relevant consonant, and in the *Text Transliteration* by the **vertical** prime-sign (')[14] after the relevant consonant. This sign is used in three cases that preclude the 'default' use of the *softening vowel*: (a) at the end of words, as in Liubóv' /lubóv/, the forename of Ranévskaïa from *The Cherry Orchard*: here there is simply no vowel after the soft consonant; (b) when the soft consonant is followed by another consonant (rather than a vowel), as in Ól'ga /ólga/, the eldest of the three sisters; (c) when the soft consonant is followed by a genuine /ï/ sound, as in Il'ïá /ilïá/, the forename of Telégin in *Uncle Vánia* and Shamráïev in *The Seagull*: in such cases the *soft sign* is needed as a *wedge* separating between the hidden /ï/ sound incorporated in the soft consonant and the full-fledged /ï/ sound following it. Such a *wedge* is also needed rarely but significantly before the vowel и (/i/), as in Il'ích /ilích/, the patronymic of the former personage.

Apart from the cardinal issue of *palatalisation*, the inventory of consonant signs in the Roman alphabet, as it functions in most Western languages, is adequate for transliterating Russian consonants.

1.3 Vowels

The vowel system of Russian consists of six vowel sounds, five of which are virtually identical with sounds represented by the original Latin system of five graphic vowel-characters: *A, E, I, O,* and *U*.[15] As explained above, the existence in Russian of twice as many graphic signs for vowels is an orthographic substitute for creating separate signs for hard and soft variants of each consonant (which would have added some 20 characters to the alphabet).[16] As explained below (§6 and §31), *e* is treated differently from other pairs of vowels within the Book's inescapable inconsistencies: instead of *e:ïe* and *e:ie* we have *è:e* for *non-palatalising:palatalising* e-sound, respectively.

The case of /i/ is unique in a different sense, since its hard counterpart is a phonetically distinct sound, which is why Russian has six (not five) vowel sounds: *u* is similar to the vowel in *beet*, but it is a *softening/palatalising* vowel,[17] while its hard counterpart, marked in the Russian–Cyrillic alphabet by the character ы, is different in its phonetic quality, not only in its phonological function (see §10 and §29 below).

2 Guide to Russian Sounds and Their Transliterations

2.1 Notes and Explanations (referring to the §-numbers[18] in the Table)[19]

§1. [A][20] This sound in Russian **invariably** resembles *a* as in *father, calm* etc. Caution to native users of English: **never** read a Russian *a* in the way that this graphic character is executed in English words like *rat, rate, rare, raw, many, all,* or any other phonetic execution that is different from its sound in *father*.

§6. [E] This sound is invariably (taking Note 11 into account) a *palatalising vowel* in Russian words: any consonant preceding it is softened, and whenever it is not preceded by a consonant a full-fledged /ï/ sound is heard. A truly systematic and consistent *Text Transliteration* should have decreed that this vowel be always written as *ie*, but here the adoption of an admittedly inconsistent compromise was quite inevitable, for the sake of preservation of time-honoured cultural traditions and conventions, as well as for the interests of reading fluency alike. Thus, such cumbersome spellings as *Miedviediénko* (from *The Seagull*), *Tieliégin, Sieriebriakóv* (both from *Uncle Vánia*), and, indeed, *Chiekhov*'s own name (see Note 6), were scrapped in favour of *Medvedénko, Telégin, Serebriakóv*,[21] and, of course, *Chekhov*. The reader is advised, however, that any *e* in Russian names in the Book — with the only exceptions of §§ 8, 24 and 26 — in fact stands for *ie* and is pronounced accordingly in native Russian speech (listen, for instance, to the first consonant in *Chekhov* as pronounced by native speakers). In Cyrillic transliteration of foreign words and names in Russian, however, this character often does not palatalise the preceding consonant, as if it were §30 (see Note 29). This is one of the matters in which Russian practice is simply inconsistent.

2.2 A 'Conversion Table'[22]

Cyrillic	Phonetic Transliteration	Text Transliteration
§1. А/а	a	a
§2. Б/б	b	b
§3. В/в	v	v
§4. Г/г	g	g
§5. Д/д	d	d
§6. Е/е	*e* prec. by ital. cons. or ï	e; *ye* at word-start
§7. Ё/ё	*o* prec. by ital. cons. or ï	*io, ïo*; *yo* at word-start
§8. Ж/ж	zh	zh
§9. З/з	z	z
§10. И/и	i prec. by ital. cons.	i
§11. Й/й	ï	*ï*; *y* at word-start
§12. К/к	k	k
§13. Л/л	l	l
§14. М/м	m	m
§15. Н/н	n	n
§16. О, о	o, a, *o*	o, *o*
§17. П/п	p	p
§18. Р/р	r	r
§19. С/с	s	s
§20. Т/т	t	t
§21. У/у	u	u
§22. Ф/ф	f	f
§23. Х/х	x	kh
§24. Ц/ц	ts	ts
§25. Ч/ч	ch	ch
§26. Ш/ш	sh	sh
§27. Щ/щ	sh*sh*, sh*ch*	shch
§28. ъ [23]	rt cons.	_ [24]
§29. ы	y	y [25]
§30. ь	ital. cons.	'
§31. Э/э	e prec. by rt cons.	è
§32. Ю/ю	u prec. by ital. cons. or ï	*iu* or *ïu* ; *yu* at word-start
§33. Я/я	a prec. by ital. cons. or ï	*ia* or *ïa*; *ya* at word-start

§7. [Ё] This vowel is always stressed, and is closely linked with the former one (§6) in Russian grammar and phonology, in complex and often inconsistent ways that do not concern this discussion; phonetically, however, it is simply a '*palatalising O*', relating to *O* itself precisely as *ia* relates to *a*, or *iu* to *u*. Its *i*-element is more or less audible according to the phonetic nature of the preceding sound.

§8. [Ж] This consonant sounds like the *s* in English words like *pleasure, vision* etc. A peculiarity of this sound is that it retains its "*hardness*" even when followed by a *palatalising vowel*; specifically, the vowel /i/ after it sounds like the vowel /y/ (§29), regardless of how it is spelled. See §24 and §26.

§10. [И] This vowel is very similar to *ee* as in *see* or *beet*, though not totally identical with it; as stated above, in Russian it is a *palatalising vowel* (of course, if preceded by a consonant; see §6, §28 and §30), *softening* the preceding consonant, unless the latter is §8, §24 or §26 (see also Note 11).

§11. [Й] This graphic character stands for the consonant sound that begins the word *yes* and ends the word *boy* in English. In Russian orthography it is almost always *post-vocalic*, i.e., it ends a syllable/word, and hardly ever begins it (exceptions are almost invariably Cyrillic transliterations of foreign words). However, the sound represented by it often starts words or syllables (after another vowel, or after a *wedge* consisting of the *soft sign* or the *hard sign*, see §28 and §30), but then its graphic representation is incorporated into one of the *palatalising vowels*; hence the various contradictory transliteration-practices adopted in the literature in the names of the following *Cherry Orchard* personages: *Epikhodov* and *Gaev* (affected by spelling, but distorting the pronunciation), or *Yepikhodov* and *Gaiev* or *Gayev* (doing the reverse; there are analogous cases in other plays). Once again, in this *Guide* the sign *ï* is used in all these cases, regardless of Russian spellings, and in the text of the Book the character *Y* is used in the beginning of names (e.g., *Yeléna, Yepikhódov*), and the character *ï* is used in other positions (e.g., *Gáïev*).

§13. [Л] The Russian hard *L* is pronounced with the tongue 'deeper' or 'lower' than *L* in most English accents, whereas in the soft *L* the tongue is raised towards the palate, closer to the /ï/ sound (which, as in all soft sounds, is 'hidden' and co-articulated with it).[26] Phonetically, most executions of *L* in all native English accents are located between these two extremes.[27]

§16. [О] This is the trickiest among Russian vowels, and the one most affected by stress (see 1.1 above for a fuller discussion of this vowel). Native English speakers should be cautioned that Russian *O* **never** sounds like the English diphthongal *O* (as the vowel in *go*, or *blow*, etc., is pronounced in **any** variant of native spoken English); moreover, **stressed** Russian *O* never resembles /a/-like pronunciations adopted by some native speakers of English, especially Americans, in words like *hot, got, shop* etc. (note that Americans tend to make this /a/-like sound only when the *o* is stressed, which is the **exact opposite** of the Russian practice). Stressed Russian *O* is much closer to the British pronunciation of the latter words, or to the *o*-vowel in most English accents in words like *long* or *soft* (occasionally and 'unofficially', stressed Russian *O* is pronounced with very slight diphthongal effect that is **the reverse** of the diphthongal order of *O* in English, i.e., a slight /u/-component stealthily **precedes** the /o/-component, but much less perceptibly than in the first syllable of the Italian *uomo*, for instance).

The problematic nature of the unstressed *O* in Russian is reflected in this Book in that most of its occurrences are transliterated with an italicised character (L*o*pákhin, Yepikhód*o*v, etc.), in order to indicate a phonetic caution to the reader.

Unstressed *o* is italicised in all Russian names mentioned in the Book, whether dead, alive or fictional, except Chekhov, being the Book's most frequently mentioned name and its unchallenged protagonist, so to speak. All *O*'s in Russian names in the Book, then, are either accented (=ó), when stressed, or italicised (*o*), when unstressed.

§18. [P] Russian *R* is *trilled*: it does not sound like the execution of its equivalent in most English pronunciations; rather, it resembles the *R*'s in some Scottish accents, and in languages like Italian or Spanish. Native speakers of British and British-influenced English should be particularly cautioned that Russian *R* is **always an audible, fully articulated consonant**; it is **never** silent. The phonetic distinction between its *hard* and *soft* variants is quite audible (for the latter, consider both *R*'s in the surname of Professor Serebriakóv /se*r*ebrakóv/, the *Uncle Vánia* personage), but this is one of the most difficult phonetic distinctions for non-native speakers to execute, especially when the *soft r* is not followed by a vowel (e.g., Vár'ka /vá*r*ka/, the child-protagonist of the story "Sleepy", or Khár'kov /xá*r*kov/, the now-Ukrainian town mentioned, e.g., in *The Seagull*). Here, again, a demonstration by a native speaker is the only way to perceive this distinction. Passive perception and recognition, rather than active execution, is the modest goal of this *Guide*.

§21. [У] This vowel is almost identical with the *u* in English words like *prune*. It tends to remain virtually unchanged and quite distinct, whether stressed or unstressed.

§23. [X] This sound does not exist in English proper, but it is heard in the original pronunciations of Scottish words like *loch*. It is very similar to the last consonant in the German *doch*, though it usually sounds in Russian milder than in German; speakers of English often mispronounce it either as *h* or as *k* (the latter is typically chosen by speakers of French or Italian, who do not have the *h* option). It is of course the middle consonant in *Chekhov*, and appears in names of quite a few Chekhovian personages. Its transliteration here is *kh* in *text transliteration* and /*x*/ in *phonetic transliteration*.

§24. [Ц] An airtight combination of *t* and *s*, this is the second consonant in the name of Mozart, for instance; in English it is not a phoneme, but can easily be heard in the plural of nouns, and in the third person singular (present tense) of verbs, ending with *t* (e.g., the last consonant in *dots* or *gets*). A peculiarity of this sound is that it retains its "*hardness*" even when followed by a *palatalising vowel*; specifically, the vowel /i/ after it sounds like the vowel /y/ (§29), regardless of how it is spelled. See §8 and §26.

§25. [Ч] An airtight combination of *t* and *sh*, it is like the English *ch* in *Church*; the first consonant in Chekhov's name, it is transliterated invariably *ch* in this Book.

§26. [Ш] This sound is identical with the English *sh* in *show*. A peculiarity of this sound is that it retains its "*hardness*" even when followed by a *palatalising vowel*; specifically, the vowel /i/ after it sounds like the vowel /y/ (§29), regardless of how it is spelled. See §8 and §24. A case in point is the surname of the *Three Sisters* personage Vershínin, pronounced /vershýnin/.

§27. [Щ] Formally, or at least traditionally, it is supposed to be a compound, or even a sequence, of the two previous sounds, in reverse order: first *sh* [=§26] and then *ch* [=§25]; since the latter is a combination of *t+sh*, we are actually talking about an ostensible sequence of *shtsh*. An approximation of this sequence for an English mind's ear would be the transition between the two words that make up the noun-phrase *fish chowder*; this is the way this character and the sound(s) that it reprcscnts are traditionally rendered in the Latin alphabet by universal consent: not only in English, but in most other non-Russian languages. This practice — sanctioned in most transliterations adopted by Russians when transliterating their language for foreign consumption — is also adopted in this Book's *Text Transliteration*. However, in actual Russian speech the *ch* component is hardly ever heard as such (actually, to be precise, we are talking about the *t*-element within the ostensible sequence *shtsh*). Instead of this absent *t/ch* sound, what one really hears is a prolongation, and usually also a softening, of the *sh* component. In other words, this sound is frequently pronounced like a protracted /sh/, at first "hard", and later (in a split second) sliding into "soft" (*palatalised*) execution of the same /sh/, especially if followed by *softening* vowels like /i/ or /e/ (it should be re-emphasised that the regular /sh/ remains *hard* even when followed by these vowels, as just explained in §26). The bottom line is that the difference between a regular /sh/ and this ostensible *shch* sound is hardly audible in most circumstances. Whether (and to what extent) there is any difference between the two, then, is largely determined by the adjacent/surrounding phonetic environment. This, too, is one of the sounds that can only be learned passively, let alone actively, by attentive listening to demonstrations by native speakers. The full intricacy of the interrelations between §§ 25-27 cannot be described here, and it is not needed for the limited purpose of this *Guide*. In fact, this description is necessary 'for the record', only because this sound features in the name of the *Cherry Orchard* personage Semeónov-Píshchik (roughly, /semeónov-píshshik/), but in fact one should not bother 'on his account', so to speak, because he is never addressed by surname in the play.

§28. [ъ] This graphic character is *the hard sign*; it has no direct sound value of its own, but it is phonetically significant as a *wedge* between a hard consonant and a *palatalising* vowel. Its insertion indicates an autonomous /ï/ component of the vowel, distinct from the preceding hard consonant; the latter stays hard and unpalatalised, unaffected by the discrete /ï/ sound that follows (as it happens, for instance, in English words like *few* or *view*, which could be transliterated in Russian as *фъю* or *въю*, and then be back-transliterated as /fïu/ or /vïu/ under the system of *phonetic transliteration* as adopted in this Book).[28]

§29. [ы] This vowel-sound is unique to Russian (to the best of my knowledge). Phonologically, it is the "hard", *non-palatalising* equivalent of /i/, but phonetically the two sounds are quite distinct. The best way users of English can create a mental image of this sound is to listen to native speakers of Russian demonstrate it. A rough approximation would be that the sound of *i* in *bit* (which does not exist in Russian) is somewhat halfway between the sound of *ee* in *beet* (the Russian и, transliterated /i/, §10 in this Guide) and the sound of ы, transliterated /y/, as in /chebutýkin/, the doctor from *Three Sisters*. Thus, the distinction between these two vowels in Russian is phonetically sharper than the one between the vowels of *beet* and *bit* in English.

§30. [ь] This is *the soft sign*; it indicates that the consonant preceding it is soft (*palatalised*) without being directly followed by a vowel. This applies, of course, in word endings (e.g., /lubóv/, the forename of Ranévskaïa in *The Cherry Orchard*), but also when a *wedge* is needed between a *palatalised* consonant and an autonomous /i/ sound following it, as in Il'ïá /Iljá/ the forename of Telégin in *Uncle Vania* and of Shamráïev in *The Seagull*.

§31. [Э] This is the "*hard*", *non-palatalising*, /i/-less and /i/-less counterpart of the vowel /e/; it sounds like the vowel *e* in English words like *ebb* or *elf*.[29]

§32. [Ю] This is the *palatalising* counterpart of §21.

§33. [Я] This is the *palatalising* counterpart of §1.

3 The Structure of Russian Names and Forms of Address

The name of every Russian person, without exception, consists of three parts: (1) *forename* (i.e., given/Christian name);[30] (2) *patronymic* (i.e., the person's father's forename, followed by a suffix indicating its patronymic function in the context of being preceded by the person's own *forename*); (3) *surname* (family name). For users of English it may be remarkable that the universal existence of *patronymics* makes middle names virtually nonexistent in Russian language and culture: the three parts of Russian names gives them the same tripartite rhythm that the conventional structure of *forename+middle name+surname* gives to names in the English-speaking culture.

3.1 Forenames

In the use of *forenames* one has to be aware of an elaborate system of suffixes of diminution, usually indicating affection, endearment, familiarity, intimacy, and other subtleties of emotional attitude of the speaker to the person addressed (in the second person), or referred to (in the third), by his/her *forename* (Chekhov's texts contain quite a few examples of this kind). Nicknames are not foreign to users of English, whether they are derived from the formal full forename organically (e.g.,

Pam for *Pamela*, *Dave* for *David*, *Sue* for *Susan*, *Mike* for *Michael*, etc.) or less obviously, though universally, related to it (e.g., *Dick* for *Richard*, *Bob* for *Robert*); however, the Russian system is much more refined, elaborate, and potentially multi-layered. Thus, for instance, the Russian versions of *Alexander* and *Alexandra* (/Aleksándr/, /Aleksándra/) are regularly–automatically 'endeared' as *Sásha*, but this regular diminutive, in turn, can be 'padded' with additional layers of suffixes of diminution and affection (e.g., /Sáshechka/, /Sáshenka/), exhibiting common endearment suffixes like *sha, chka, n'ka, shka*, potentially preceded by more than one optional vowel. The suffix *ka*, if added on its own (in the case of *Sásha* it would be *Sáshka*), often *palatalising* (softening) a preceding consonant, usually means familiarity of a less charitable kind, possibly implying a patron-ising–condescending attitude, especially (but not exclusively) if spoken by a senior to or about a junior.[31] Moreover, some suffixes of diminution/endearment are appli-cable to both genders (e.g., *-sha*), others are gender-specific (e.g., *-chka* for females, *-chik* for males); there is also room for momentary individual creativity .in rearranging and compounding such suffixes. For instance, in the beginning of Act 2 of *Three Sisters* Natásha addresses her husband Andréï as "Andriushánchik" /andrushánchik/. This is a combination of one of the commonest nicknames for an Andréï — *Andriúsha* /andrúsha/ — with another suffix of diminutions for males, *-chik*: each of the two is familiar to any Russian, but their combination is not, and sounds like a momentary intuitive invention; in the context, this implies an affected intimacy, coquettish attempt to flatter, and an overtone of addressing an adult as if he were a child.

This is by no means an exhaustive list of the relevant repertory in Russian in general, or in Chekhov in particular; the only purpose here is to make the reader aware of, rather than really acquainted with, the richness of Russian in this respect, which is also reflected in the ways Chekhov's personages address each other.[32]

3.2 Patronymics

Patronymics are produced by the addition of a suffix to the forename of the person's father: it is usually *-vich* (*-ich* or *-ych* is obligatory) for a male, and *-vna* (*-na* is idnispesnable) for a female, both often preceded by a vowel, usually *o*. Thus, Iván Ivánovich is Iván whose father's name is also Iván; Galína Aleksándrovna is Galína whose father's name is Aleksándr. There are quite a few variants to patronymics, produced by a combination of phonetic, phonological and morpho-phonemic reasons;[33] it is enough for the reader of this Book who wants to understand some basics about Russian names encountered in English translations to be aware of their tripartite structure and *-ch* and *-na* endings.

Another important aspect of this structure is its socio-linguistic function: by addressing (or referring to) a person with *forename* plus *patronymic* all the formal requirements of etiquette and decorum are met. This is slightly analogous to addressing a holder of the title *Sir* or *Dame* (in the United Kingdom and its domin-ions) with the combination of this title and the person's forename, omitting his/her surname; this omission is consistent with decorum, not at all a sign of familiarity (this partial analogy applies only in the latter sense — the omission of the surname without an effect of closeness or familiarity; otherwise there is no analogy at all, patronymic is part of every name, and has nothing to do with knighthood). The form of address *Mr./Mrs./Miss/Ms.* + *surname* is well known and occasionally used in Russia(n), but it is perceived as an 'imported' foreign/western format, whereas the genuine Russian formal address is forename + patronymic. In this context, surnames are optional extras; they are more often used in the third person, i.e., when referring to a person, rather than when addressing him/her in the second person (e.g., when Kóstia in Act 1 of *The Seagull* inquires about Nína with the question "Where is Zaréchnaïa?", or when he summarises Nína's life story to Dorn and refers to Trigórin by surname).

3.3 Surnames

Some surname endings (e.g., -ov, -skiï,[34] -in, etc.) are considered masculine, and if the bearer of such a surname is a woman the ending should change to the appropriate feminine form (e.g., a woman whose surname is Chékhov is called Chékhova, Púshkin becomes Púshkina, Dostoïévskiï becomes Dostoïévskaïa). The process is reversible: if the surname of a female personage has a feminine ending, the surname of male members of her immediate family (husband, father, brother, as applicable) can be automatically inferred. Thus, the surname of *The Seagull*'s Nína Zaréchnaïa's father (an absent, offstage personage), and any other male members of the family, is Zaréchnyï, and the surname of the late husband of *The Cherry Orchard*'s Ranévskaïa is Ranévskiï.[35]

4 Pronouncing Personages' Names
in Chekhov's Major Plays[36]

[The left column is written in *Text Transliteration*; the right column in *Phonetic Transliteration*]

4.1 *The Seagull*

1	Irína Nikoláïevna Arkádina [Trépleva]	irína nikaláïevna arkádina [trépleva]
2	Konstantín Gavrílovich Tréplev[37]	konstantín gavrílovich tréplev [kósta] [Kóstia]
3	Piotr Nikoláïevich Sórin	potr nikaláïevich sórin
4	Nína Mikháïlovna Zaréchnaïa	nina mixáïlovna zaréchnaïa
5	Il'iá Afanás'ievich Shamráïev	il'iá afanásievich shamráïev
6	Polína Andréïevna	palína andréïevna
7	Másha [Máriïa Il'ínichna]	másha [máriïa ilínichna]
8	Borís Alekséïevich Trigórin	barís alekséïevich trigórin
9	Yevgéniï Sergéïevich Dorn	ïevgéniï sergéïevich dorn
10	Semión Semiónovich Medvedénko	semón semónovich medvedénko
11	Yákov	ïákov

4.2 Uncle Vánia

1 Aleksándr Vladímirovich Serebriakóv   a*l*eksándr vla*d*ímirovich *s*erebrakóv
2 Yeléna Andréïevna   ïe*l*éna and*r*éïevna
3 Sóf'ïa Aleksándrovna [Sónia]   só*f*ïa a*l*eksándrovna [Só*n*a]
4 Máriïa Vasíl'ïevna Voïnítskaïa   má*r*iïa va*síl*'ïevna *v*aï*n*ítskaïa
5 Iván Petróvich Voïnítskiï [Vánia]   iván *p*etróvich vaï*n*íts*k*iï [vá*n*a]
6 Mikhaíl L'vóvich Ástrov   *m*ixaíl *l*vóvich ástrov
7 Il'ïá Il'ích Telégin   i*l*'ïá i*l*ích *t*elégin
8 Marína   ma*r*ína

4.3 Three Sisters

1 Andréï Sergéïevich Prózorov   and*r*éï *s*ergéïevich prózo*r*ov
2 Natál'ïa Ivánovna [Natásha]   natá*l*'ïa ivánovna [natásha]
3 Ól'ga [Ól'ga Sergéïevna]   ó*l*ga [ó*l*ga *s*ergéïevna]
4 Másha [Máriïa Sergéïevna]   másha [má*r*iïa *s*ergéïevna]
5 Irína [Irína Sergéïevna]   i*r*ína [i*r*ína *s*ergéïevna]
6 Fiódor Il'ích Kulýgin   *f*ódor i*l*'ích kulýgin
7 Aleksándr Ignát'ïevich Vershínin   a*l*eksándr ignát*ï*ievich *v*ershý*n*in
8 Nikoláï L'vóvich Túsenbach   *n*ikaláï *l*vóvich túzenbax
9 Vasíliï Vasíl'ïevich Soliónyï   va*s*íliï va*síl*'ïevich sa*l*ónyï
10 Iván Románovich Chebutýkin   iván ramánovich *ch*ebutý*k*in
11 Alekséï Petróvich Fedótik   a*l*ekséï petróvich *f*edó*t*ik
12 Vladímir Kárlovich Rodè   vla*d*ímir kár*l*ovich radè
13 Ferapónt [Ferapónt Spiridónych]   *f*erapónt [*f*erapónt s*p*iridónych]
14 Anfísa   an*f*ísa

4.4 The Cherry Orchard

1 Liubóv' Andréïevna Ranévskaïa   *l*ubóv and*r*éïevna ra*n*évskaïa
2 Ánia   á*n*a
3 Vária [Varvára Mikháïlovna]   vá*r*a [varvára *m*ixáïlovna]
4 Leoníd Andréïevich Gáïev   *l*ea*n*íd and*r*éïevich gáïev
5 Yermoláï Alekséïevich Lopákhin   ïermaláï a*l*ekséïe*v*ich lapáxin
6 Piotr [Pétia] Trofímov   potr [*p*éta] tra*f*ímov
7 Borís Borísovich Semeónov-Píshchik   ba*r*ís ba*r*ísovich *s*emeónov-*p*ish*sh*ik
8 Charlótta Ivánovna   sharlótta ivá*n*ovna
9 Semión Panteléïevich Yepikhódov   *s*emón pan*t*e*l*éïe*v*ich ïe*p*ixódov
10 Duniásha   du*n*ásha
11 Firs [Firs Nikoláïevich]   *f*irs [*f*irs *n*ikaláïevich]
12 Yásha   ïásha

4.5 Additional Notes to the Names

Names originating in western languages that appear in Chekhov's texts in Russian transliteration are restored in this Book to their source spelling, but retain their Russianised form phonetically; e.g., *Charlótta* (rather than *Sharlotta* or *Charlotte*), *Túsenbach* (rather than Tuzenbakh), etc.

Certain suffixes of patronymics are occasionally given in Chekhov's plays in a colloquial–rural variant, to reflect the dialect of his personages in dialogue. These sub-standard variants alternate freely with the formally correct ones. The following are the colloquial variants actually used in Chekhov's four major plays (first the full formal form, in bold type, then, after a colon, the colloquial variant, the latter in both transliterations):

Gavrílovich: Gavrílych, /gavrílych/; **Nikoláïevich**: Nikoláich /nikaláich/;
Afanás'ïevich: Afanás'ich, /afanás'ich/; **Alekséïevich**: Alekséich, /alekséich/;
Sergéïevich: Sergéich /sergéich/; **Semiónovich**: Semiónych /semónych/;
Ignát'ïevich: Ignát'ich /ignát'ich/; **Vasíl'ïevich**: Vasíl'ich /vasíl'ich/;
Románovich: Románych /ramánych/; **Andréïevich**: Andréich /andréich/;
Spiridónovich: Spiridónych /spiridónych/.

Notes

1 Out of the great 19th-century Russian classics, Chekhov is undoubtedly the most intensely studied by scholars and critics who have no access to his work in its original Russian.

2 In Act 1 of *The Cherry Orchard* Gáïev says, that a large number of suggested cures for an illness is an indication that the illness is incurable. "Same here".

3 The *Guide* is merely a practical tool, albeit a reasoned one. A potential aid to some readers, it is not a study in Russian phonetics, phonology, grammar, or social etiquette. It is addressed to readers whose linguistic frame of reference is English and who, though having no knowledge of Russian, are still interested in learning how names mentioned in Chekhov's texts should sound, and in understanding the rationale behind different solutions to problems of transliteration, as attempted here and elsewhere. Readers who are not intrigued by such subjects can simply ignore this *Guide*, partly or completely. Their comprehension of the main body of this Book will not be impaired in any way as a result of skipping the *Guide*. That said, however, such readers may still lose something: they may find certain transliterations adopted in this Book bewildering without the *Guide*'s explanations.

4 Granted, the alphabet and orthography adopted in any language is, for starters, a compromise product of its own traditions and conventions; it emanates from facing a formidable challenge of recording the flexible dynamics of ever-changing verbal sound within a rigid system of static sign system of graphic characters. The latter allows the history of a language leave its mark on the end product, while actual pronunciation has moved on, ignoring the old history that it has left behind. English and French, for instance, are notorious for the lack of correspondence between their conservative, antiquated orthographies on the one hand and their contemporary pronunciations on the other hand. Other languages, with 'better reputation' in this area — e.g., German, Italian, and indeed Russian — are also far from creating a consistent match between the written–graphic and the oral–phonetic traditions. Educated native users of any language possess the right 'keys' that enable them to make smooth transitions between their oral and written practices and traditions; thus, native users of English would have an immediate phonetic image in their minds' ears, and translate it readily to a sequence of spoken sounds, upon seeing the sequence of written characters t-h-r-o-u-g-h or t-h-o-u-g-h on the page. For such native users these keys are activated casually and automatically, whereas for non-native users the correspondence (or lack thereof)

between speech and writing is a serious and conscious stumbling block in the process of language acquisition. Foreign users, as a rule, find it more difficult than native ones to ignore orthography in their speech (not least, because they are often exposed to the foreign language through reading its written text before hearing it pronounced); and, paradoxically, they often delude themselves that they speak the foreign language more 'correctly' than the natives, inasmuch as their speech is more affected by its orthography.

5 The *International Phonetic Alphabet* (*IPA*) has been consulted, but rarely adopted, since the frame of reference here is practical and English-specific, rather than scientific and universal. However, in certain cases, in the *Phonetic Transliteration* only, an *IPA* transliteration is retained (thus, /x/ stands for what the *Text Transliteration* renders as *kh*, e.g., /mixaíl/ *vs. Mikha*íl, /xárkov/ *vs.* Khár'kov, etc.).

6 The transliteration of Chekhov's own surname is a case in point. Only the two vowels, *e* and *o*, are accepted by universal consent in all versions of this name in Roman alphabet known to me (although both of them, and particularly *o*, are problematic in Russian speech; see below in this Subsection, and items §6 and §16 in Section 2.1 and 2.2). However, as for the name's three consonants, in major Western languages (e.g., English, French, German, Spanish, Italian) one can encounter quite a few versions of each, the major ones (listed here in arbitrary order) being: *Ch, C, Tch, Tsh, Tsch, Č, Tš, Tsc* for the first consonant; *kh, k, h, x, ch, j, c,* for the second; and *v, w, f* and *ff* for the third. Many of the mathematically possible combinations of these options can be actually encountered in the literature, though probably not all of them. Note that although the first consonant is palatalised in Russian (see below), I have encountered no transliteration reflecting this fact (e.g., *Chiekhov, Čiexov,* etc.), nor have I adopted one in this Book, for reasons spelled out below.

7 Thus, the consistent practice in Russian of voiceless execution of voiced consonants at the end of words (e.g., /f/ for /v/, /t/ for /d/, /s/ for /z/ etc., which would result, for instance, in ending Chekhov's name with *f* or *ff* rather than *v*), is one of the subtle features ignored completely in the transliterations adopted in this Book, even in this *Guide* (a major reason for this is that final consonants tend very often to regain their voicing in context, when followed by a vowel). Other features ignored here include the interchangeability of some sounds in unstressed syllables (see Note 9 below). Other, more significant cases of discrepancy between written and spoken practices — e.g., the grammatical suffixes written *ogo/ago* and pronounced *ovo* or *avo*, the reading of the Cyrillic character *Γ* (normally /g/) at the end of words or in some post-vocalic positions as if it were a Russian *X* (i.e., /x/), and a number of other cases — are ignored in this *Guide* because of their irrelevance to the sound of Chekhovian names.

8 In a largely thoughtful and sensitive production of *The Seagull* directed by Trevor Nunn (the Royal Shakespeare Company [RSC], London, 2007), for instance, the Trigórin-actor stressed the name of the great Russian writer Turgénev correctly, whereas the Nína-actress stressed it (twice) flagrantly incorrectly (she said *Túrgenev*, i.e., stressing the first syllable, and with a British silent r at that, as if she would pronounce the first syllable in an English word like *turbulent* in the British way). The director, otherwise attentive to many subtleties in this production, seems to have been deaf to the annoying, not to say infuriating, negligence that this error betrays and to the discrepancy between the pronunciations of the same name by two actors within the same production. This instance of gratuitous inconsistency and unprofessionalism is indicative of the prevalent lack of effort to ascertain even the most easily executable features of Russian in English-speaking theatres. It is quite obvious that no one took the trouble to invite a native speaker to coach the actors, as if even striving towards correct pronunciation is

not a crucially important part of their trade. It is unimaginable, for instance, that a professional opera singer would get away with such blatant ignorance-generated errors when singing a text in a foreign language, though such errors are much less audible in listening to operatic singing than to speech enunciation on stage.

9   By analogy, in some pronunciations of English the past-tense suffix in regular verbs, spelled *-ed*, is often pronounced by native speakers like *id*, yet like *ed* by others, or in different circumstances. Usually there is no conscious distinction between these two pronunciations: thus, in words like *printed* or *added* the final, unstressed syllables are variously pronounced in both ways, while the ear of the native speaker is trained to accept both as two correct and hardly distinguishable variants (*allophones*) of the same vowel (*phoneme*), though under other circumstances /i/ and /e/ are two different phonemes in English, especially when stressed (e.g., consider the crystal-clear distinction between *bet* and *bit*).

10   Double quotation marks should be applied here to the terms "*soft*" and "*hard*", because in this context they are intuitive, synaesthetic metaphors, rather than scientific facts (though used consistently in Russian phonetic terminology, hence the *double* quotation marks); however, for reading fluency these quotation marks will often be dropped henceforward from these adjectives and their derivatives, but should be assumed by the reader.

11   The graphic sign *y* is indeed a natural choice for transliterating this sound in English; however, since this sign is traditionally (and in this Book) assigned to the radically-different vowel-sound ы (see §29 in Sectiom 2.1), it is not used for this sound in the Book's text, except in initial positions, where it cannot be confused with the ы-sound (the latter never begins a word in Russian); therefore, the graphic symbol *ï* has been chosen for this sound instead.

12   Phonetically, not all consonants are equally susceptible to audible softening. Thus, one hears very clearly the difference between hard and soft consonants like /t/, /l/ or /n/, whereas the difference is not so clear in cases like /b/ or /p/, even less so in /k/, /g/, /sh/, /ts/, or /zh/, especially when not followed by a vowel (i.e., mostly at the end of a word). The latter three consonants, by the way, are often not even supposed to be palatalised (see §§ 8, 24 and 26 and the appropriate Notes and explanations therein). One can say that, as a rule, the *phonological command* to "soften" applies equally to almost all consonants, but the *phonetic execution* and the *auditory recognition* of this command depend on the oral–physical articulation qualities of each consonant, which in some cases 'neutralise' it.

13   This forename can illustrate the point, since there are two graphic *e*'s in it, the first indicates an autonomous /ï/ sound, since it is not preceded by a consonant so there is nothing to soften, whereas the second causes a hidden /ï/ sound to soften the preceding /l/.

14   In contradistinction to the rounded ', used to indicate the possessive case, single quotation marks etc.

15   In English they would be represented, roughly, by the vowels in the following monosyllables (respectively, of course): *alms, elm, chief, soft, rule*. None of these correspondences is perfect, as there are subtle differences: thus, speakers of Russian often precede their stressed /o/ with a faint, hardly noticeable sound of /u/, which does not amount to making it a diphthong; other individual, regional and dialectal differences between speakers exist in both languages, but the approximations described here are basically valid.

16   Yet, hypothetically, there could have been another solution to the problem — the use of a single character, *the soft sign*, in conjunction with every consonant (to denote its softening), followed by one of the regular vowels i.e., a combination of ьа and ьу —

'*a* and '*u* — instead of the characters я and ю (*ia* and *iu*, respectively). This could have made some sense, but historically it is "the road not taken" in the formative stages of Russian orthography, and for a reason: adopting this system would have made Russian words with palatalised sounds much longer and awkward in writing (e.g., Сьэрьэбрьаќов [S'èr'èbr'akóv] instead of the relatively much shorter and simpler Серебряќов [Serebriakóv]. See §§ 6, 10 and 30, and their Notes.

17   Anyone with attentive ears can notice the tendency of native Russian speakers to soften consonants followed by this vowel-sound when they speak other languages, e.g., English (imagine, for instance, how the d in *deep*, the l in *leap*, etc., would be pronounced in the English speech of many native Russian speakers).

18   Any sound that is not commented upon is a straightforward one, as in English and most other European languages. This applies to most consonants and to some vowels.

19   Since unstressed vowels are often obscured or indeterminate, all comments on vowels apply mainly to their stressed execution, unless otherwise stated.

20   In this Subsection graphic characters inside square brackets are Cyrillic uppercase letters, unless otherwise stated.

21   The latter name illustrates the inconsistency most vividly: consistency would have produced either *Serebrakóv* or *Sieriebriakóv*, but there is a consistent tradition of ignoring the /i/ element in transliterating *e* while retaining it in transliterating я [*ia*] or ю [*iu*]. This tradition, by the way, is not arbitrary, since the palatalising *e* is the Russian default for this vowel sound, as used in transliterating most non-Russian words and names into Cyrillic alphabet, whereas the non-palatalising version is the default for the vowel-sounds of *a* and *u*. See above, Note 16.

22   Abbreviations in Table: *prec.* = preceded; *rt* = Roman Type; *ital.* = italicised; *cons.* = consonant. *Italics* in this Table are used to draw attention to peculiar cases, discussed in the text of the *Guide*.

23   The three graphic characters §§ 28–30 never begin a word; therefore they are presented here in lowercase forms.

24   Since this sign does not appear in personages' names in Chekhov's plays, there was no need to provide a transliteration for it. A cursory explanation of its function is supplied in §28.

25   Since this sound never begins a word, the graphic character *Y* is used for the ï-sound in beginnings of words only, where it cannot be misinterpreted as signalling the ы sound, represented in this Book consistently and exclusively by the graphic character *y*. Thus traditional transliterations of names like *Yeléna* or *Yepikhódov* is preserved (rather than *Ïeléna* or *Ïepikhódov*: it seems that the character *Ï* in the beginning of a word looks stranger than in the middle or end of a word within an English context).

26   The closeness between these two sounds, /l/ and /i/, is a phonetic universal, affecting pronunciation peculiarities in several languages; thus, in Italian a process of assimilation produced forms like *piazza* or the name *Chiara* (in Spanish, in which this particular process did not take place, the analogous forms are *plaza* and *Clara*).

27   Usually in Russian the hard forms are the unmarked/default ones used to transliterate consonants in non-Russian words, but *L* is an exception: its soft variant, with the *soft sign* or a *palatalising vowel*, is used to transliterate most of its occurrences in non-Russian words and names. Apparently, Russians perceive the sound of *L* in western languages as closer to their own soft variant than to the hard one. In this Book (including the *Guide*), *L*'s *hard* version is the unmarked default, i.e., it is treated as all other consonants in this respect.

28   In pre-revolutionary Russian orthography (adopted, of course, by Chekhov who died before the revolution), every word-ending consonant had to be followed either by this

hard sign or — if that last consonant was palatalised — by the *soft sign* (ь). In other words, no word could be spelled with a graphic character representing a consonant at its end without either one of the signs, *soft* or *hard* (Chekhov's own tripartite name is, of course, no exception: all three components — *Anton, Pavlovich,* and *Chekhov* — were spelled by Chekhov and his generation with a *hard sign* at the end of each). An essential orthographic reform introduced after the October 1917 Revolution abolished the use of the *hard sign* at the end of words, alongside other changes intended to rationalise the spelling and eliminate redundancies; so that now the *"hardness"* of a last consonant is the unmarked default, indicated by the sheer absence of a *soft sign.* All pre-revolutionary Russian literature has been retyped during and after the 1920s, and is now printed under the new rules of spelling.

29   Unlike other comparable pairs, here the *palatalising/softening* variant is the default, whereas the hard one is much rarer, and exists mainly in transliterating the *e*-sound in some non-Russian words, especially when the foreign word begins with this vowel. Yet, in most non-Russian words this sound is transliterated with the default *e* /ie/, rather than with the phonetically more correct *è* /e/, and it is often (but not always) pronounced accordingly. Thus, the Russian word for *Europe* is Yevrópa /ïevrópa/, the word for *telephone* is pronounced /telefón/, i.e., with softened /t/ and /l/. This sound and written character end the surname of the officer Rodè (personage № 12 in *Three Sisters,* 4.3); however, he is one of Chekhov's personages whose names are never pronounced on stage.

30   It was, and to a large extent still is, a widely accepted but non-binding cultural norm to associate a person's name with the name of a saint in the Pravoslav (Orthodox) calendar, celebrated on or close to his/her birthday. Birthdays are often referred to as *name-days,* i.e., on the day of the christening, when the sainted name is celebrated. Irína's *name-day,* celebrated in Act 1 of *Three Sisters,* is a case in point.

31   For instance, Ván'ka, Vár'ka (the children-protagonists of stories discussed in Chapter 9 — see Note 9 to that Chapter). A subtle case is Irína's sisterly reproach to Másha in Act 2 of *Three Sisters.* Irína is the youngest, but this is immaterial here: when rebuking her sister, saying to her "You, Máshka, are bad" (or: "You are a bad one, Máshka") she assumes the attitude of scolding a child with awareness that the addressee is an adult; at least, the speaker is looking down on the addressee of the rebuke (although *bad* is uttered point blank, as a single word, most translations into English render it here as "in bad temper" and similar phrases). The word *bad* is spoken here half-jokingly, like saying to an adult "you are a bad boy/girl". Specifically within the intimate interaction between sisters, this particular form of nicknaming together with name-calling is appropriate and nuanced. It is later echoed in the exchange between Ól'ga and Másha in Act 3, when the two chide each other with *"silly"*, again with nickname subtleties, as analysed in 6.2.1. Both adjectives — *bad* and *silly* — hurled by two sisters at each other, are neither meant nor taken literally; but the former is just a bit more seriously intended than the latter. All these nuances function as a present tip of the absent iceberg of decades of intimacy between sisters.

32   Some translators of Chekhov's plays ignore such Russian subtleties; others simply keep them as they are, unchanged and unexplained, by merely transliterating their Russian forms, whereas some others take care to add the odd footnote (a luxury that translators for stage productions do not enjoy). In such cases over-accuracy fails in its communicative function, since a non-Russian user of the translated text is likely to be bewildered rather than enlightened by an unexplained 'endearing suffix'. Again, it is not the purpose of this *Guide* to discuss translation problems, but rather to make readers aware of them.

33 Depending on the structure of the father's full forename, especially its ending, the form of the suffix may vary radically; e.g., the son and daughter of *Iván* are *Ivánovich* and *Ivánovna*, respectively (this added *o* between the father's forename and the patronymic suffix often applies to names ending with a consonant), whereas the son and daughter of *Nikoláï* are *Nikoláïevich* and *Nikoláïevna*, and the son and daughter of *Sergéï* are *Sergéïevich* and *Sergéïevna* (respectively, of course). Certain names, especially mono-syllabic ones and those ending with a stressed vowel (but other names too), produce particular patronymic endings; thus, the son and daughter of *Il'iá* are *Il'ích* and *Il'ínichna* (all these patronymics exist in Chekhov's plays!). Another peculiarity is that certain forenames change internally when the patronymic suffix is added to them, as in Chekhov's own case: his father's name was *Pável*, but in the patronymic setting it becomes *Pávlovich*, omitting the *e* between the *v* and the *l* (the same applies to *L'vóvich* and *L'vóvna*, patronymics derived from *Lev*). In certain cases a shorter form -ych is adopted, rather than -vich (e.g., *Iónych*, which happens to be the title of a famous story by Chekhov; see a full list of these variants as they appear in Chekhov's four major plays at the end of this *Guide*). All these peculiarities need not be studied thoroughly in order to understand and identify the basic structures passively, when encountered in a written text. Again, the sole reason for this explanation here is the existence of many patronymics in Chekhov's plays, and the insistence of some translators to retain them without explaining this practice to their readers.

34 The latter suffix, a grammatical ending frequent in Russian surnames, is usually translit-erated -*sky* or -*ski* in the Roman alphabet (this is also the practice in some non-Russian and non-Cyrillic Slavic languages like Polish and Czech). Although the final ï-element is hardly audible even in Russian, the more accurate form, *skiï*, is adopted in this Book, following the practice of most western linguists, who transliterate this ending as -*skij*; since the graphic character *j* is likely to be misread by users of English as in the name *Jack* or the noun *jury*, it has been consistently replaced by *ï* in this Book (see § 11).

35 In fact, these are the only male-ending surnames in Chekhov's major plays inferable solely from female-ending ones; however, some female surnames can be learned from male ones, e.g., *The Cherry Orchard*'s Ranévskaïa's maiden name was Gáïeva (infer-able from her brother's surname). A special case is *The Seagull*'s Arkádina: this is neither a married name (which was Trépleva, according to the list of personages), nor a maiden name (Sórina), but an invented stage-name. Yet, its feminine ending presup-poses a Mr. Arkádin (father or husband), a pure figment of her imagination. Incidentally, quite a few of Chekhov's surnames are never uttered on stage (people address each other without them, see 3.1 and 3.2 in this *Guide*). In Chekhov scholarship and criticism, though, it is customary to mention some personages by their surnames, and we tend to identify them to ourselves that way, ignoring the fact that a number of these surnames (e.g., *Tréplev* in *The Seagull*, *Voïnítskiï* in *Uncle Vánia*, and many others) are never uttered on stage or heard by audiences.

36 Personages are presented here in the order determined by Chekhov in the lists of char-acters preceding each play.

37 As just stated (Note 35), this surname is never pronounced on stage, but is referred to in the secondary literature, following Chekhov's list of personages. There are two versions of pronouncing it: tréplev /tréplev/, as adopted here, and Treplióv /treplóv/ (the latter interprets §6 as if it were §7 — it is common practice to omit the two *Umlaut*-like dots that tell these two characters apart). I have consulted several (written and oral) sources and authorities, Russian specialists and western Slavists; the Russians are unan-imous in preferring the former version, whereas the latter was advocated only by some westerners — e.g., Laurence Senelick in his 2005 and 2006 English versions of

Chekhov's plays. Peter Henry indeed prefers the latter in his earlier edition of the play (Henry 1965, p. 56 & passim), but resorts to the former in his 1993 updated version of the same work (London and Bristol: Bristol Classical Press), p. 52 & passim: this revision must be the result of consultations with native specialists. Far from being a native user of Russian, I am unqualified to make a choice in this case, and, frankly, I don't care one way or the other; however, reliable than foreign ones in determining such strictly linguistic matters, hence my preference for the former pronunciation.

Works Consulted

[Afanás'ïev 1997] Афанасьев, Э. С., 1997. *Творчество А.П. Чехова: Иронический модус*. Ярославль: Ярославский государственный педагогический университет.

Allen, David, 2000. *Performing Chekhov*. London and New York: Routledge.

Apollonio, Carol, and Angela Brintlinger (eds.), 2012. *Chekhov for the 21ˢᵗ Century*. Bloomington, Indiana: Slavica.

Auerbach, Erich, 1953. *Mimesis: The Representation of Reality in Western Literature* (translated from the German by Willard R. Trask). Princeton: Princeton University Press.

Avigal, Shoshana, and Shlomith Rimmon-Kenan, 1981. "What Do Brook's Bricks Mean? — Towards a Theory of 'Mobility' of Objects in Theatrical Discourse". *Poetics Today*, Vol. 2, № 3, 11–34.

Avílova, Lydia [Lídiïa], 1989. *Chekhov in My Life: A Love Story* (translated with an Introduction by David Magarshack). London: Methuen. [First published in 1950 by John Lehmann, London; Russian original published 1947 in Moscow]. See also Senelick 2005a.

Baluchatyj [=Balukhátyï; Balukhaty], Sergéï, 1969 [1927]. *Čechov* (Slavische Propiläen 68). München [Munich]: Wilhelm Fink Verlag. [originally: Балухатый, Сергей Дмитриевич, 1927. *Проблемы Драматургического Анализа: Чехов*. Ленинград: Academia].

——, 1926. «Этюды по истории текста и композиции чеховских пьес». *Поэтика: Временник отдела словесных искусств*. Ленинград: Academia.

——, ed., 1952 [1938]. *'The Seagull' Produced by Stanislavsky* (translated by David Magarshack). London: D. Dobson.

Barricelli, Jean-Pierre (ed.), 1981. *Chekhov's Great Plays: A Critical Anthology* (Edited with an Introduction by Jean-Pierre Barricelli). New York and London: New York University Press.

Bartlett, Rosamund, 2004. *Chekhov: Scenes from a Life*. London: Free Press.

——, 2004a. *Chekhov: A Life in Letters* (translated by Rosamund Bartlett and Anthony Phillips). London: Penguin.

—— (Translator and Editor), 2008. *Anton Chekhov: The Exclamation Mark and Other Stories*. London: Hesperus.

Bauer, Roger, and Douwe Fokkema (eds.), 1990. *Space and Boundaries: Proceedings of the 12th Congress of ICLA, Munich 1988*. Munich: Iudicium.

Beardsley, Monroe C., 1958. *Aesthetics: Problems in the Philosophy of Criticism*. New York and Burlingame: Harcourt, Brace & World

——, 1966. *Aesthetics: From Classical Greece to the Present — A Short History*. New York and London: Macmillan.

Ben-Porat, Ziva, 1976. "The Poetics of Literary Allusion". *PTL* 1, pp. 105–128.

[Bérdnikov 1981] Бердников, Г. Б., 1981. *Чехов-Драматург: Традиции и новаторство в драматургии А. П. Чехова*. Москва: Исскуство.

Berghaus, Günther (ed.), 2001. *New Approaches to Theatre Studies and Performance Analysis*. Tübingen: Max Niemeyer Verlag.

Bitsilli, Peter M., 1983. *Chekhov's Art: A Stylistic Analysis* (translated by Toby W. Clyman & Edwina J. Cruise). Ann Arbor: Ardis.

Björklund, Martina, 1993. *Narrative Strategies in Čechov's "The Steppe": Conclusion, Grounding and Point of View*. Åbo: Åbo Akademis Förlag — Åbo Akademi University Press.

Booth, Wayne C., 1961. *The Rhetoric of Fiction*. Chicago and London: University of Chicago Press.

Borny, Goeffrey, 2006. *Interpreting Chekhov*. Canberra: ANU E-Press.
    [downloadable from http://epress.anu.edu.au/chekhov/pdf/chekhov-whole.pdf]

Brahms, Caryl, 1976. *Reflections in a Lake: A Study of Chekhov's Four Greatest Plays*. London: Weidenfeld and Nicolson.

Bristow, Eugene K., 1977. *Anton Chekhov's Plays: The Seagull * Uncle Vánia * Three Sisters * The Cherry Orchard; with Background and Criticism*. New York and London: W. W. Norton.

Brooke-Rose, Christine, 1981. *A Rhetoric of the Unreal: Studies in Narrative & Structure, Especially of the Fantastic*. Cambridge: Cambridge University Press.

Callow, Philip, 1998. *Chekhov — The Hidden Ground: A Biography*. London: Constable & Co.

Chances, Ellen, 1977. "Chekhov's Seagull: Ethereal Creature or Stuffed Bird?" in Debreczeny & Eekman 1977, 27–35.

Chatman, Seymour, and Samuel R. Levin (eds.). *Essays on the Language of Literature*. Boston: Houghton Mifflin.

Chudakóv, A. P., 1983 [1973]. *Chekhov's Poetics* (translated by Edwina Jannie Cruise and Donald Dragt). Ann Arbor: Ardis.

——, 2012. "Вторая реплика". In Nohejl and Setzer 2012, pp. 152–160.

Chvany, Catherine V., 1985. "Background Perfectives and Plot Line Imperfectives: Toward a Theory of Grounding in Text", in M. S. Flier and A. Timberlake (eds.), *The Scope of Slavic Aspect* (ULA Slavic Studies, 12) (Columbus: Slavica), 247–273.

Clarke, Charanne Carroll, 1977. "Aspects of Impressionism in Chekhov's Prose". In Debreczeny & Eekman 1977, 123–133.

Clayton, J. Douglas (ed.), 1997. *Chekhov Then and Now: The Reception of Chekhov in World Culture* (Middlebury Studies in Russian Language and Literature, 7). New York: Peter Lang.

——, (ed.), 2006. *Chekhov: Poetics • Hermeneutics • Thematics*. Ottawa: The Slavic Research Group of the University of Ottawa. `

——, 2006. "'Words, Words, Words': On the Emptiness of Speech and the Fullness of Songs". In Clayton (ed.) 2006, 35–46.

Clyman, Toby W. (ed.), 1985. *A Chekhov Companion*. Westport (Connecticut) and London: Greenwood Press.

Cohen, Dalia, 1971. "Palestrina Counterpoint — A Musical Expression of Unexcited Speech". *Journal of Music Theory*, Vol. 15, pp. 84–111.

——, 1983. "Birdcalls and the Rules of Palestrina Counterpoint: Towards the Discovery of Universal Qualities in Vocal Expression". *Israel Studies in Musicology*, Vol. 3, pp. 96–123.

——, 1998. "Order/Disorder as a Factor in Shaping a Style: Schemata of Repetition and Form". *Symmetry, Culture and Science*, Vol. 9, № 2–4, pp. 143–164.

——, and Naftali Wagner, 2000. "Concurrence and Nonconcurrence between Learned and

Natural Schemata: The Case of Johann Sebastian Bach's *Saraband in C Minor for Cello Solo*". *New Music Research*, Vol. 29, № 1, pp. 23–36.

Culler, Jonathan, 1975. *Structuralist Poetics: Structuralism, Linguistics and the Study of Literature*. London: Routledge & Kegan Paul.

Davidson, J. M. C. (ed.), 1962. *A. P. Chekhov:* 'Три Сестры — Three Sisters' [original text in Russian], *Edited with Introduction, Notes and Vocabulary* [in English] (The Library of Russian Classics). Letchworth, Hertfordshire: Bradda Books.

——, (ed.), 1962a. *A. P. Chekhov:* 'Вишнёвый Сад — The Cherry Orchard' [original text in Russian], *Edited with Introduction, Notes and Vocabulary* [in English] (The Library of Russian Classics). Letchworth, Hertfordshire: Bradda Books.

——, (ed.), 1963. *A. P. Chekhov:* 'Дядя Ваня — Uncle Vánia' [original text in Russian], *Edited with Introduction, Notes and Vocabulary* [in English]. (The Library of Russian Classics). London: Bradda Books.

Debreczeny, Paul, and Thomas Eekman (eds.), 1977. *Chekhov's Art of Writing: A Collection of Critical Essays*. Columbus, Ohio: Slavica.

Dixon, Ros, and Irina Ruppo Malone (eds.), 2012. *Ibsen and Chekhov in Ireland*. Dublin: Carysfoot Press.

[Dóbin 1981] Добин, Ефим С., 1981. *Сюжет и действительность: Искусство детали*. Ленинград: Советский писатель.

Doležel, Lubomír, 1980. "Truth and Authenticity in Narrative". *Poetics Today*, Vol. 1, № 3, pp. 7–25.

[Dománskiï 2005]. Доманский, Юрий В., 2005. *Вариативность драматургии А. П. Чехова: монография*. Тверь: «Лилия Принт».

——, 2012. "Финал *Вишнёвого сада*: драма и театр". In Nohejl and Setzer 2012, pp. 249–255.

Donchin, Georgette, 1958. *The Influence of French Symbolism on Russian Poetry* (Slavistic Printings and Reprintings XIX). 's-Gravenhage [The Hague]: Mouton.

Dostoevsky [Dostoïévskiï], Feodor, 1975 [1867]. *Crime and Punishment (Revised): The Coulson Translation, Backgrounds and Sources, Essays in Criticism*. [A Norton Critical Edition, translated by Jessie Coulson] New York: W.W. Norton & Company.

Edgar, David, 2009. *How Plays Work*. London: Nick Hern Books.

Eekman, Thomas A. (ed.), 1989. *Critical Essays on Anton Chekhov*. Boston, Mass.: G. K. Hall & Co.

Eichenbaum, Boris [Eïkhenbaum, Borís], 1963 [1918]. "The Structure of Gogol's Overcoat" (translated by Beth Paul and Muriel Nesbitt). *Russian Review*, Vol. 22, № 4, 377–399.

——, 1974 [1924]. "How Gogol's 'Overcoat' is Made" [a more recent English translation, with a new title, of a later version of the Russian original of the previous item]. In Maguire 1974, 269–291.

Erlich, Victor, 1965. *Russian Formalism: History — Doctrine*. The Hague: Mouton.

Esslin, Martin, 1985. "Chekhov and the Modern Drama". In Clyman 1985, 135–145.

——, 1987. *The Field of Drama: How the Signs of Drama Create Meaning on Stage & Screen*. Reading: Methuen Drama.

Finke, Michael C., 2005. *Seeing Chekhov: Life and Art*. Ithaca and London: Cornell University Press.

Forster, E. M., 1975 [1927]. *Aspects of the Novel*. London: Penguin Books [A Pelican Book]

Friedland, Louis S. (ed.), 1965. *Letters on the Short Story, the Drama and Other Literary Topics by Anton Chekhov* (Selected and Edited by Louis S. Friedland, with a Preface by Ernest J. Simmons). London: Vision.

Garnett, Constance (Translator and Editor), 1926. *The Letters of Anton Pavlovich Chekhov to Olga Leonardovna Knipper*. London: Chatto & Windus.

Garvin, Paul (ed.), 1964. *A Prague School Reader on Esthetics, Literary Structure, and Style*. Washington: Georgetown University Press.

Gilman, Richard, 1995. *Chekhov's Plays: An Opening into Eternity.* New Haven and London: Yale University Press.

Golomb, Harai, 1979. *Enjambment in Poetry: Language and Verse in Interaction* (Meaning and Art, 3). Tel Aviv: The Porter Institute for Poetics and Semiotics, Tel Aviv University.

——, 1984. "Music as Theme and as Structural Model in Chekhov's *Three Sisters*". In Schmid & van Kesteren 1984, 174–196.

——, 1986. "*Hamlet* in Chekhov's Major Plays: Some Perspectives of Literary Allusion and Literary Translation". *New Comparison*, № 2 (Autumn), 69–88.

——, 1987. "Communicating Relationships in Chekhov's *Three Sisters*". In Senderovich and Sendich 1987, pp. 9–33.

——, 2000. "Referential Reflections around a Medallion: Reciprocal Art/Life Embeddings in Chekhov's *The Seagull*". *Poetics Today*, Vol. 21, № 4, 681–709.

——, 2001. "Chekhovian Plays Viewed through Implied Actors: Part-Readings in *Three Sisters* and *The Cherry Orchard*". *ТЕАТРЪ: Russian Theatre Past and Present*, № 2, 13–29.

——, 2005. "Heredity, Inheritance, Heritage: Human De- and Re-Generation in Chekhov's Major Plays (with Special Reference to *Three Sisters*)". *Essays in Poetics* 30 (*EIP* Publications 10 — Chekhov Special Issue, 1), 75–103.

——, 2006. "The Whole at the Expense of its Parts: Chekhov's Plays as Structuralists' Paradise". *Essays in Poetics* 31 (*EIP* Publications 11, Chekhov Special Issue, 2), 151–179.

——, 2012. "Reflecting on Chekhovian '(Auto)biographophobia': Nina's Medallion and Reciprocal Art/Live Embeddings in *The Seagull*" [Based on a revised, enlarged and updated version of Golomb 2000]. In Schönle *et al.*, pp. 31–70. [Reprinted with minor revisions as Appendix in this Book]

——, 2012a. "'No Joking Matter': (Day-)Dreaming, Reality and Fictionality in Chekhov's 'A Little Joke' [«Шуточка»] (1886/1899)". *Bulletin of the North American Chekhov Society*, Vol. XVIII, № 2 (Winter 2012), 2–30 [An autonomous article, based on Section 5.1 in this Book] (available also online at:
  http://chekhbul.com/issues/4d6c88166134a274e4d0303d5c1de082.pdf)

——, 2012b. "Dramaticality, Theatricality and Dual Fictionality in Chekhov's Major Plays". In Nohejl and Setzer 2012, pp. 121–143.

——, 2015. "Bach's Complexity Viewed from a Literary Perspective". *Understanding Bach* № 10 (forthcoming).

——, and Karin Heskia, 1990. "Onstage and Offstage in Chekhov's Plays". In Bauer & Fokkema 1990, pp. 124–130.

Goodman, Nelson, 1968. *Languages of Art: An Approach to a Theory of Symbols*. Indianapolis and New York: The Bobbs-Merrill Co.

[Gornfel'd 1939] Горнфельд, Аркадий Георгиевич, 1939. «Чеховские финалы». *Красная новь* № 8–9, 286–300.

Grossman, Leonid, 1967 [1914]. "The Naturalism of Chekhov". In Jackson 1967, pp. 32–48.

[Gvozdeï 1999] Гвоздей, В. Н., 1999. *Секреты чеховского художественного текста: Монография*. Астрахан: Издательство Астраханского педагогического университета.

Hahn, Beverley, 1977. *Chekhov: A Study of the Major Stories and Plays*. Cambridge, London, New York and Melbourne: Cambridge University Press.

Harshav [Hrushovski], Benjamin, 1976. *Segmentation and Motivation in the Text Continuum of Literary Prose: The First Episode of* War and Peace. (PPS 5). Tel Aviv: The Porter Institute for Semiotics and Poetics, Tel Aviv University.

——, 1979. "The Structure of Semiotic Objects: A Three-Dimensional Model". *Poetics Today*, Vol. 1, № 1–2, pp. 363–76.

——, 1980. "The Meaning of Sound Patterns in Poetry: An Interaction Theory". *Poetics Today* vol. 2, № 1a, pp. 39–56.

——, 1982. "An Outline of Integrational Semantics: An Understander's Theory of Meaning in Context". *Poetics Today*, Vol. 3, № 4, pp. 59–88.

——, 1984. "Fictionality and Fields of Reference: Remarks on a Theoretical Framework". *Poetics Today* vol. 5, № 2, pp. 227–251.

——, 1988. "Theory of the Literary Text and the Structure of Non-Narrative Fiction: The First Episode of *War and Peace*". *Poetics Today*, Vol. 9, № 3, pp. 635–666.

——, 2007. *Explorations in Poetics*. Stanford, California: Stanford University Press.

Henry, Peter (ed.), 1965. *A. P. Chekhov*: 'Чайка — The Seagull' [original text in Russian], *Edited with an Introduction, Notes, and Vocabulary* [in English] (The Library of Russian Classics). Letchworth, Hertfordshire: Bradda Books. [Revised and updated, London and Bristol: Bristol Classical Press, 1993].

Hercher, Jutta, and Peter Urban (eds.), 2012 [2004]. *Chekhov on Theatre* (translated with introduction and commentary by Stephen Mulrine) [originally published in D-Frankfurt am Main: Verlag der Autoren]. London: Nick Hern Books.

Herrnstein Smith, Barbara, 1968. *Poetic Closure: A Study of How Poems End*. Chicago and London: University of Chicago Press.

——, 1979. "Fixed Marks and Variable Constancies: A Parable of Literary Value". *Poetics Today*, Vol. 1, № 1–2, pp. 7–22.

Hingley, Ronald, 1950. *Chekhov: A Biographical and Critical Study*. London: Allen and Unwin.

——, 1976. *A New Life of Anton Chekhov*. London: Oxford University Press.

——, (Translator and Editor), 1964 etc. *THE OXFORD CHEKHOV: A Selection of Stories and Plays, in Nine Volumes (translated and edited by Ronald Hingley)*. London, New York and Toronto: Oxford University Press.

Holland, Peter, 1991. "Reading to the Company". In Scolnicov & Holland 1991, 8–29.

Hrushovski, Benjamin. *See* Harshav

Innes, Christopher (ed.), 2000. *A Sourcebook on Naturalist Theatre*. London and New York: Routledge.

Iser, Wolfgang, 1974. *The Implied Reader: Patterns of Communication in Prose Fiction from Bunyan to Beckett*. Baltimore: Johns Hopkins University Press.

Issacharoff, Michael, 1981. "Space and Reference in Drama". *Poetics Today*, Vol. 2, № 3, pp. 211–224.

Jackson, Robert Louis (ed.), 1967. *Chekhov: A Collection of Critical Essays*. Englewood Cliffs, New Jersey: Prentice-Hall.

——, 1967a. "Chekhov's *Seagull*: The Empty Well, the Dry Lake, and the Cold Cave". In Jackson 1967, pp. 99–111.

— (ed.), 1993. *Reading Chekhov's Text* (Studies in Russian Literature and Theory). Evanston, Illinois: Northwestern University Press.

——, 1999. "Russian Man at the Rendezvous: The Narrator of Chekhov's 'A Little Joke'". In Manger 1999, pp. 151–158.

———, 2012. "What Time Is It? Where Are We Going? — Chekhov's *Cherry Orchard*: The Story of a Verb". In Nohejl & Setzer 2012, pp. 33–327.

Jakobson, Roman, 1960. "Closing Statement: Linguistics and Poetics". In Sebeok 1960, pp. 350–377. [Reprinted under the title "Linguistics and Poetics" in Chatman and Levin 1967, pp. 296–322.]

———, 1971. "On Realism in Art". In Matejka & Titunik 1971, 38–46.

Johnson, Ronald L., 1993. *Anton Chekhov: A Study of the Short Fiction*. New York, Toronto, Singapore and Sydney: Twayne Publishers, Maxwell Macmillan International.

Kaplan, David, 1971. "Quantifying In". In Linsky 1971, pp. 112–144.

Karlinsky, Simon, 1981. "Huntsmen, Birds, Forests, and Three Sisters". In Barricelli 1981, 144–160.

———, 1984. "Russian Anti-Chekhovians". *Russian Literature*, Vol. XV, pp. 183–202.

[Kataev (=Katáïev) 1998]. Катаев, Владимир Борисович, 1998. *Сложность простоты: рассказы и пьесы Чехова*. Москва: Издательство Московского университета.

———, 2002. *If Only We Could Know! — An Interpretation of Chekhov* (Translated from the Russian and Edited by Harvey Pitcher). Chicago: Ivan R. Dee.

———, 2006. "'A Cruel Audacity': The Poetics of Deceived Expectation". In Clayton 2006, 193–205.

Kaynar, Gad, 1997. "The Actor as Performer of the Implied Spectator's Role". *TRI* [*Theatre Research International*], Vol. 22, № 1 (Spring), pp. 49–62.

———, 2001. "Audiences and Response-Programming Research and the Methodology of the Implied Spectator". In Berghaus 2001, pp. 159–173.

Kelly, Michael (ed.), 1998. *Encyclopedia of Aesthetics*. Oxford and New York: Oxford University Press.

Khanilo, Alla, 1994–1995. "Anton Chekhov — Some Personal Effects" (translated by Peter Henry). *Slavonica*, Vol. 1, № 2, pp. 94–97.

[Kiríllova 1985] Кириллова, И.: "Пьеса Константина Треплева в поэтической структуре *Чайки*". In Nínov 1985, pp. 97–117.

Kirk, Irina, 1981. *Anton Chekhov*. Boston: Twayne Publishers.

Knipper-Chekhova, Olga. "A Few Words about Chekhov". In: Garnett 1926.

Kreitler, Hans and Shulamith, 1972. *Psychology of the Arts*. Durham, N.C.: Duke University Press.

Krinicyn, Aleksandr, 2012. "Поэтика и семантика пауз в драматургии Чехова". In Nohejl and Setzer 2012, pp. 176–185.

Krook, Dorothea, 1969. *Elements of Tragedy*. New Haven: Yale University Press.

Lahr, John, 1968. "Pinter and Chekhov: The Bond of Naturalism". *The Drama Review – TDR*, Vol. 13, № 2 (Winter), 137–145.

Lantz, Kenneth A., 1985. "Chekhov's Cast of Characters". In Clyman 1985, 71–85

Levitan, Olga, and Harai Golomb, 2007. A Review of Stepánov 2005. *Bulletin of the North American Chekhov Society*, Vol. XV, № 1, 26–29 (available also online: http://chekhbul.com/issues/1ff0408da3dc61df35e2fa44eda47faa.pdf).

Linsky, Leonard (ed.), 1971. *Reference and Modality*. Oxford: Oxford University Press.

Llewellyn Smith, Virginia, 1973. *Anton Chekhov and the Lady with the Dog*. Oxford: Oxford University Press.

Loehlin, James N., 2006. *Chekhov: The Cherry Orchard*. In: PLAYS IN PRODUCTION Series, ed. Michael Robinson. Cambridge and New York: Cambridge University Press.

———, 2010. *The Cambridge Introduction to Chekhov*. Cambridge: Cambridge University Press.

Lotman, Jurij [=Lótman, Yúrii], 1976 [1966]. "The Modelling Significance of the Concepts of 'End' and 'Beginning' in Artistic Texts" (translated by Wendy Rosslyn). In *Russian*

Poetics in Translation, Volume 3: *General Semiotics* (Oxford: Holdan Books), pp. 7–11 [See Tomashevsky 1978].

——, [=Lótman, Yury], 1976 [1972]. *Analysis of the Poetic Text* (Edited and Translated by D. Barton Johnson). Ann Arbor: Ardis.

——, [=Lótman, Yúriï], 1977 [1971]. *The Structure of the Artistic Text* (translated from the Russian by Gail Lenhoff and Ronald Vroon) [Original Russian text published in 1971]. (Michigan Slavic Contributions 7). Ann Arbor: University of Michigan, Department of Slavic Languages and Literatures.

Lyons, John, 1977. *Semantics*. Cambridge: Cambridge University Press.

Magarshack, David, 1952. *Chekhov the Dramatist*. London: John Lehmann. [Re-published 1980, London: Eyre Methuen.]

——, 1952a. *Chekhov: A Life*. London: Faber and Faber.

——, 1972. *The Real Chekhov: An Introduction to Chekhov's Last Plays*. London: George Allen & Unwin.

See also Avílova 1989; Baluchatyj 1952.

Maguire, Robert A., 1995. *Gogol from the Twentieth Century: Eleven Essays — Selected, Edited, Translated and Introduced by Robert A. Maguire*. Princeton: Princeton University Press.

Manger, Klaus (ed.), 1999. *Die Wirklichkeit der Kunst und das Abenteuer der Interpretation: Festschrift für Horst-Jürgen Gerick*. Heidelberg: Universitätsverlag C. Winter.

Marsh, Cynthia, 2005. "Two-Timings Time in *Three Sisters*". In *Chekhov 2004: Special Issue, Volume 1. Essays in Poetics*, Volume 30. Keele: EIP Publications (10), 104–115.

——, 2010–2011. "Chekhov after Magritte". Lecture Presented at the Chekhov Working Group, Annual (2010) Conference of *IFTR* [International Federation for Theatre Research], Munich. Re-Presented at the Conference *Complexities in Verbal, Musical and Performative Arts*, Faculty of Arts, Tel Aviv University, 2011.

——, 2012. "Vania's Map". In Schönle *et al.*, 72–86.

——, 2012a. "Making Foreign Theatre or Making Theatre Foreign: Russian Theatre in English". In Dixon & Ruppo Malone 2012, pp. 113–126.

——, 2012b. "*Three Sisters* as a Case Study for 'Making Foreign Theater or Making Theater Foreign'". In Apollonio & Brintlinger 2012, pp. 269–281; illustrations, pp. 210–211.

Matejka, Ladislav, and Krystyna Pomorska (eds.), 1971. *Readings in Russian Poetics: Formalist and Structuralist Views*. Cambridge, Mass.: MIT Press.

——, and Irwin R. Titunik (eds.), 1976. *Semiotics of Art: Prague School Contributions*. Cambridge, Mass.: MIT Press.

Meerzon, Yana, 2006. "Three Degrees of Defamiliarization: Rhythm and Action in Anton Chekhov's Drama". In Clayton 2006, 207–225.

Meijer, Jan, 1978 [co-author]. See Van der Eng.

Meisel, Martin, 2007. *How Plays Work: Reading and Performance*. Oxford: Oxford University Press.

Meyerhold, Vsévolod, 1967 [1908]. "Naturalistic Theater and Theater of Mood". In Jackson 1967, 62–68.

——, 1978 [1913]. *On Theatre* (translated by Edward Brown). London: Methuen.

Miles, Patrick, 2003. *Mikhail Gromov, Chekhov Scholar and Critic: An Essay in Cultural Difference*. Nottingham: Astra Press, 2003.

——, 2008. *Brief Lives: Anton Chekhov*. London: Hesperus Press.

Nabokov, Vladimir, 1944. *Nikolai Gogol*. New York: New Directions Publishing Corporation.

[Nínov 1985] Нинов, А. А. (ответственный редактор). *Чехов и театральное искус-*

ство: сборник научных трудов. Ленинград: Ленинградский государственный институт театра, музыки и кинематографии им. Н. К. Черкасова.

Nohejl, Regine, and Heinz Setzer (eds.), 2012. *Anton P. Čechov — der Dramatiker : Drittes internationales Čechov-Symposium, Badenweiler im Oktober 2004*. (DIE WELT DER SLAVEN SAMMELBÄNDE • СБОРНИКИ, Band 44). München–Berlin–Washington, D.C.: Verlag Otto Sanger.

Nowottny, Winifred, 1965. *The Language Poets Use*. London: The Athlone Press, University of London.

[Papérnyĭ 1982]. Паперный, Зиновий. «*Вопреки всем Правилам...* »: *Пьесы и водевили Чехова*. Москва: «Искусство».

——, 1989 [1982]. "Microsubjects in *The Seagull*" (translated by David Woordruff). In Eekman 1989, 160–169 [a translation from Papérnyĭ 1982].

Pavis, Patrice, 1982. *Languages of the Stage: Essays in the Semiology of the Theatre*. New York: Performing Arts Journal Publications.

——, 1998. *Dictionary of the Theatre: Terms, Concepts, and Analysis* (translated by Christine Shantz). Toronto and Buffalo: University of Toronto Press.

——, 2003. *Analyzing Performance: Theater, Dance, and Film* (translated by David Williams). Ann Arbor: The University of Michigan Press.

Peace, Richard, 1983. *Chekhov: A Study of the Four Major Plays*. New Haven and London: Yale University Press.

Pennington, Michael, 2007. *Chekhov's* Three Sisters: *A Study Guide* (Page to Stage Series). London: Nick Hern Books.

Perlstein, Moshe, 2009. "It's About Time: The Temporal Evolution of Order". *Theatre Research International*, Vol. 34, № 2, pp. 131–137.

Perry, Menakhem, 1968. "Analogy and its Role as a Structural Principle in the Novels of Mendele Moykher Sforim". *Hasifrut*, Vol. 1, № 1, pp. 65–100 [in Hebrew; English abstract, pp. VIII–X].

——, 1979. "Literary Dynamics: How the Order of a Text Creates its Meanings [With an Analysis of Faulkner's 'A Rose for Emily']". *Poetics Today*, Vol. 1, № 1–2, pp. 35–64, 311–361.

——, 1979a. "Alternative Patterning: Mutually Exclusive Sign-sets in Literary Texts". *Versus* 24, pp. 83–106.

——, and Meir Sternberg, 1986. "The King through Ironic Eyes: Biblical Narrative and Literary Reading Process". *Poetics Today*, Vol. 7, № 2, pp. 275–322.

[Petróvskiĭ 1927] Петровский, М. А. (ed.), 1927. *Ars Poetica: Сборник статей, под редакцией М. А. Петровского*. Москва: Государственная академия художественных наук.

——, 1927a. «Морфология новеллы». In Petróvskiĭ 1927, pp. 28–35

Pfister, Manfred, 1988 [1977]. *The Theory and Analysis of Drama* (translated by John Halliday from the 1977 German original). Cambridge: Cambridge University Press.

Phelan, James, and Peter Rabinowitz (eds.), 2005. *A Companion to Narrative Theory* (Oxford: Blackwell).

Pitcher, Harvey, 1973. *The Chekhov Play: A New Interpretation*. Berkeley, Los Angeles and London: University of California Press.

——, 2010. *Responding to Chekhov: The Journey of a Lifetime*. Cromer: Swallow House Books.

[Pólotskaïa 2000] Полоцкая, Эмма Артемьевна, 2000. *О Поэтике Чехова*. Москва: Наследие.

——, 2003. *Вишнёвый Сад: Жизнь во Времени*. Москва: Наука.

——, 2006. *О Чехове и не только о нём: Статьи разных лет*. Москва: Типография Россельхозакадемии.

• , "Принцип неопределённости в пьесах Чехова", pp. 11–25. [this study is printed also in Nohejl and Setzer 2012, pp. 144–151]

• , "Вокруг Ялтинской редакции 'Шуточки'", pp. 39–61.

Popkin, Cathy, 1993. *The Pragmatics of Insignificance: Chekhov, Zoshchenko, Gogol*. Stanford, California: Stanford University Press.

——, "Restor(y)ing Health: Case History of 'A Nervous Breakdown'". In Clayton 2006, 107–124.

Preminger, Alex, and T.V.F. Brogan (eds.), 1993. *The New Princeton Encyclopedia of Poetry and Poetics*. Princeton: Princeton University Press.

Pritchett, V. S., 1988. *Chekhov: A Spirit Set Free*. London, Sydney, Auckland & Toronto: Hodder & Stoughton.

[Rabeneck 1958] Рабенек, Лев Людвигович [Львович], 1958. "Последние минуты Чехова". *Возрождение*, № 84, 28–35.

——, 2005. "Chekhov's Last Moments" (translated by Harvey Pitcher) [a new translation into English of Rabeneck 1958]. *The Bulletin of the North American Chekhov Society*, Vol. XIII, № 1 (Summer–Autumn), pp. 1–5. [This English version is also available online: http://chekhbul.com/issues/aa1651adb8d678cec7f14827ca2bae60.pdf]

Rayfield, Donald, 1975. *Chekhov: The Evolution of his Art*. London: Paul Elek.

——, 1994. *The Cherry Orchard: Catastrophe and Comedy* (Twayne's Masterwork Studies). New York: Twayne Publishers.

——, 1995. *Chekhov's* Uncle Vanya *and* The Wood Demon: *A Critical Study*. Bristol: Bristol Classical Press.

——, 1997. *Chekhov: A Life*. London: HarperCollins.

——, 1999. *Understanding Chekhov: A Critical Study of Chekhov's Prose and Drama*. London: Gerald Duckworth, and Madison: University of Wisconsin Press.

See also Schönle *et al.* 2012.

[Razúmova 2001]. Разумова, Нина Евгеньевна. *Творчество А.П. Чехова в аспекте пространства*. Томск: Томский государственный университет.

Reid, John McKellor, 2007. *The Polemical Force of Chekhov's Comedies: A Rhetorical Analysis*. Lewiston (New York, USA), Queenston (Ontario, Canada) and Lampeter (Wales, UK): The Edwin Mellen Press.

Reinhart, Tanya, 1981. "Some Pragmatic Aspects of Referential Expressions" (Unpublished Manuscript, Tel Aviv University).

Rimmon-Kenan, Shlomith, 1977. *The Concept of Ambiguity — The Example of James*. Chicago: University of Chicago Press.

Rozik, Eli, 1988. "The Interpretative Function of the 'Seagull' Motif in *The Seagull*". *Assaph: Studies in the Theatre*, Vol. 4, pp. 55–81.

——, 1992. *The Language of the Theatre*. Glasgow: Theatre Studies Publications.

——, 2008. *Generating Theatre Meaning*. Brighton and Portland: Sussex Academic Press.

Schmid, Herta, 1976. "Ist die Handlung die Konstruktionsdominante im Drama? Čechovs *Drei Schwestern* als Beginn einer Paradigmaenerweiterung des Dramas". *Poetica* 82, pp. 177–207.

——, and Aloysius van Kesteren (eds.), 1984. *Semiotics of Drama and Theatre* (LLSEE 10). Amsterdam: John Benjamins.

——, 1978 [co-author]. *See* van der Eng.

——, 2006. "Variations on the Man in a Case in Chekhov's 'Man in a Case' and 'On the Harmfulness of Tobacco'". In Clayton 2006, 151–178.

Schönle, Andreas, Olga Makarova, and Jeremy Hicks (eds.), 2012. *When the Elephant*

Broke Out of the Zoo: A Festschrift for Donald Rayfield (Stanford Slavic Studies, 39). Stanford: The Department of Slavic Languages and Literatures, Stanford University.

Scolnicov, Hanna, 1991. "Chekhov's Reading of *Hamlet*". In Scolnicov & Holland 1991, 192–205.

——, and Peter Holland (eds.), 1989. *The Play Out of Context: Transferring Plays from Culture to Culture*. Cambridge: Cambridge University Press.

——, (eds.), 1991. *Reading Plays: Interpretation and Reception*. Cambridge and New York: Cambridge University Press.

Sebeok, Thomas A. (ed.), 1960. *Style in Language*. New York & London: The Technology Press of MIT and John Wiley & Sons.

Senderovich, Savely, 1977. "Chekhov and Impressionism: An Attempt at a Systematic Approach". In Debreczeny and Eekman 1977, pp. 134–152.

——, 1994. "*The Cherry Orchard*: Chekhov's Last Testament." *Russian Literature* (North-Holland), Vol. XXXV, pp. 223–242.

—— and Munir Sendich (eds.), 1987. *Anton Chekhov Rediscovered: A Collection of New Studies with a Comprehensive Bibliography* (East Lansing, Michigan: *Russian Language Journal*).

Senelick, Laurence, 1985. *Anton Chekhov.* London: Macmillan [Macmillan Modern Dramatists].

——, 1997. *The Chekhov Theatre: A Century of the Plays in Performance*. Cambridge: Cambridge University Press.

—— (Translator and Editor), 2005. *Anton Chekhov's Selected Plays* (A Norton Critical Edition). New York and London: W.W. Norton & Company.

——, 2005a. "Bleeding Hearts and Mocking Darts: A Suppositious Parody of Lidiya Avilova" [see Avilova 1989]. *The Bulletin of the North American Chekhov Society*, Vol. XIII, № 1 (Summer/Autumn), 1–5.

——, (Translator and Editor), 2006. *The Complete Plays of Anton Chekhov.* New York and London: W.W. Norton & Company.

—— 2009. "Money in Chekhov's Plays". *Studies in Theatre and Performance*, Vol. 29, № 3, pp. 327–337.

[Shátin 1993]. Шатин, Ю. «Речевая деятельность персонажей как средство комического в пьесе *Вишневый сад*». In Sobénnikov 1993, pp. 251–261.

[Silánt'ieva 2000] Силантьева, В. И. *Художественное мышление переходного времени (литература и живопись): А. П. Чехов, И. Левитан, В. Серов, К. Коровин*. Одесса: Астропринт.

Simmons, Ernest J., 1962. *Chekhov: A Biography*. London: Jonathan Cape.

Smith, Barbara Herrnstein. *See* Herrnstein Smith, Barbara.

Smith, Omry, 2009. *Reason Not: Emotional Appeal in Shakespeare's Drama*. Oxford: Peter Lang.

[Sobénnikov 1993] Собенников, Анатолий Самуилович (ред.), 1993. *О поэтике Чехова*. Иркутск: Издательство Иркутского Университета.

Stanislavski, Constantin [=Stanislavsky, Konstantin; Stanislávskiï, Konstantín], 1949. *Building a Character* (translated by Elizabeth Reynolds Hapgood). London: Methuen (University Paperbacks).

——, 2008 [1926]. *My Life in Art* (translated and edited by Jean Bendedetti). London & New York: Routledge.

Stelleman, Jenny, 1992. *Aspects of Dramatic Communication: Action, Non-action, Interaction (A. P. Čechov, A Blok, D. Charms)* (Studies in Slavic Literature and Poetics, 16). Amsterdam & Atlanta, Georgia: Rodopi.

[Stepánov 2005] Степанов, Андрей Д., 2005. *Проблемы коммуникации у Чехова*.

Москва: Языки славянской Культуры. [English summary, pp. 391–396] See also Levitan & Golomb 2007.

Sternberg, Meir, 1978. *Expositional Modes and Temporal Ordering in Fiction*. Baltimore and London: Johns Hopkins.

——, 1985. *The Poetics of Biblical Narrative: Ideological Literature and the Drama of Reading*. Bloomington: University of Indiana Press.

[co-author] See Perry, Menakhem.

Stowell, H. Peter, 1980. *Literary Impressionism, James and Chekhov*. Athens: University of Georgia Press.

Strawson, Peter Frederick, 1950. "On Referring". *Mind* 59 (New Series), pp. 320–344.

Strindberg, August, 1962 [1888]. "Author's Foreword [to *Miss Julie*]". In *Plays: Translated from the Swedish by Elizabeth Sprigge* (Chicago: ALDINE Publishing Company), pp. 59–73.

Struve, Gleb, 1961. "On Chekhov's Craftsmanship: The Anatomy of a Story". *Slavic Review*, Vol. 20, № 3 (October), pp. 465–476.

Styan, J.L., 1969. *The Elements of Drama*. Cambridge: Cambridge University Press.

——, 1971. *Chekhov in Performance*. Cambridge: Cambridge University Press.

[Sukhikh 2010] Сухих, Игорь, 2010. *Чехов в жизни: сюжет для небольшого романа*. Москва: Время.

Tabachnikova, Olga (ed.), 2010. *Anton Chekhov through the Eyes of Russian Thinkers: Vasilii Rozanov, Dmitrii Merezhkovskii and Lev Shestov*. London, New York and Delhi: Anthem Press.

Tait, Peta, 2002. *Performing Emotions: Gender, Bodies, Spaces, in Chekhov's Drama and Stanislavski's Theatre*. Aldershot: Ashgate.

Tiupa, Valery, 2006. "The Communicative Strategy of Chekhov's Poetics". In Clayton 2006, pp. 1–19.

Tomashevsky, Boris [=Tomashévskiï, Borís], 1978 [1928]. "Literary Genres" (translated by L.M. O'Toole). In *Russian Poetics in Translation*, Volume 5: *Formalism: History , Comparison, Genre* (Oxford: Holdan Books), pp. 52–93. "1. Dramatic Genres", pp. 55–74.

Troyat, Henri, 1986 [1984]. *Chekhov* (translated from the French by Michael Henry Heim). London: Hamish Hamilton Paperbacks.

Tsur, Reuven, 1987. *How Do the Sound Patterns Know They Are Expressive: The Poetic Mode of Speech-Perception*. Jerusalem: Israel Science Publishers.

——, 1998. "'To Be or Not to Be' — That is the Rhythm: A Cognitive–Empirical Study of Poetry in the Theatre". *Assaph — Studies in the Theatre*, № 13, 95–122.

Tulloch, John, 1980. *Chekhov: A Structuralist Study*. London: Macmillan.

——, 2005. *Shakespeare and Chekhov in Production and Reception: Theatrical Events and Their Audiences*. Iowa City: University of Iowa Press.

Turner, C. J. G., 1994. *Time and Temporal Structure in Chekhov* (Birmingham Slavonic Monographs 22). Birmingham: Birmingham University Press.

[Tyniánov 1929] Тынянов, Юрий Николаевич, 1929. *Архаисты и новаторы*. Ленинград: Прибой.

Urban, Peter, *see* Hercher

Urbanski, Henry, 1979. *Chekhov as Viewed by his Russian Literary Contemporaries*. Wrocław: Wrocław University Press.

Valency, Maurice, 1966. *The Breaking String: The Plays of Anton Chekhov*. New York: Oxford University Press.

Van der Eng, Jan, Jan Meijer, and Herta Schmid, 1978. *On the Theory of Descriptive Poetics: Anton P. Chekhov as Story-Teller and Playwright*. Lisse: Peter de Ridder Press.

Veltruský, Jiří, 1977. *Drama as Literature*. Lisse: Peter de Ridder Press.

Volchkevich, Maya, 2007 [2005]. *'The Seagull': A Comedy of Delusions* (translated from the Russian by Svetlana le Fleming). Moscow: "Probel-2000".

Wellek, René, and Austin Warren, 1963. *Theory of Literature*. London: Penguin Books/Peregrine Books.

Wellek, René and Nonna D. (eds.), 1984. *Chekhov: New Perspectives*. Englewood Cliffs, N.J.: Prentice Hall.

Wellek, René, 1984. "Introduction: Chekhov in English and American Criticism". In Wellek R. & N. 1984, 1–30.

Whyman, Rose, 2011. *Anton Chekhov*. [Routledge Modern and Contemporary Dramatists Series]. London and New York: Routledge.

Williames, Lee J., 1989. *Anton Chekhov the Iconoclast*. Scranton, Pa.: University of Scranton Press.

Winner, Thomas G., 1956. "Chekhov's *The Seagull* and Shakespeare's *Hamlet*: A Study of a Dramatic Device". *American Slavic and East European Review*, Vol. xv, pp. 103–111. Reprinted in Bristow 1977, pp. 341–349, and in Wellek 1984, pp. 107–117.

——, 1966. *Chekhov and his Prose*. New York, Chicago and San Francisco: Holt, Rinehart and Winston.

——, 1977. "Syncretism in Chekhov's Art: A Study of Polystructured Texts". In Debreczeny and Eekman 1977, pp. 153–166.

Yacobi, Tamar, 2001. "Package-Deals in Fictional Narrative: The Case of the Narrator's (Un)Reliability". *Narrative* 9, pp. 223–229.

——, 2005. "Authorial Rhetoric, Narratorial (Un)Reliability, Divergent Readings: Tolstoy's *Kreutzer Sonata*". In Phelan and Rabinowitz 2005, pp. 108–121.

[Záïtsev 1954] Зайцев, Борис К., 1954. *Чехов: Литературная биография*. Нью Йорк: Издательство имени Чехова.

[Zingerman 1988] Зингерман, Б. В., 1988. *Театр Чехова и его мировое значение*. Москва: Наука.

Žirmunskij [=Zhirmúnskiĭ; Zhirmunsky], Viktor M., 1966 [1925]. *Introduction to Metrics: The Theory of Verse* (translated from the Russian by C. V. Brown, edited with an Introduction by E. Stankiewicz and W. N. Vickery) (Slavistic Printings and Reprintings, LVIII). The Hague, London and Paris: Mouton.

[Zótov 2010] Зотов, С. Н. (Ответственный редактор), 2010. *Творчство А. П. Чехова*. Таганрог: Издательство ГОУВПО («Таганрогский государственный педагогический институт»).

Zubareva, Vera, 1997. *A Systems Approach to Literature: Mythopoetics of Chekhov's Four Major Plays*. (Contributions to the Study of World Literature, № 75). Westford, Connecticut, and London: Greenwood Press.

Zviniatskovsky, Vladimir, 2006. "If You Listened to Me, I Would Not Talk to You: On a Structural Device in Chekhov's Drama". In Clayton 2006, 21–33.

Index

Page references under the entry "Chekhov, Anton" are restricted to personal/biographical/historical information only.

All short stories and plays by Chekhov are listed under the name of the short story or play, e.g. *Three Sisters* or "A Little Joke". Works by other authors are indexed under the author's name, e.g. Ibsen's play *Hedda Gabler* will be found under Ibsen.

Noun phrases comprising an adjective and a noun are indexed under the former, e.g. "implied author" rather than "author, implied".

Page references to major discussions of a topic are given in **bold**. In certain cases such references are given under a topic, even if the entry-word does not appear on the page. References to a note-text are followed by an italicised *n* after the page-number; thus, "185*n*" refers to a note-text printed on page number 185.

The names of fictional personages are enclosed in single quotation marks, followed by the name of the play/short story; e.g., 'Arkádina' (*The Seagull*). Possessive-case instances of such names are given as: 'Arkádina's'. Fictional personages are indexed under the name most often used in the text, usually the forename. Thus, Andréï Prózorov will be found under "'Andréï' (*Three Sisters*)", rather than "Prózorov, Andréï (*Three Sisters*)". According to the same principle, however, some personages are indexed under their surname, e.g., Trigórin.

The index has been compiled by Sussex Academic Press editors.

About the Author

Harai Golomb has retired as Professor at Tel Aviv University's Faculty of Arts, where he taught at the Departments of Theatre, Literature and Musicology, and at the Programme for Multidisciplinary ('Interart') Studies. Though he has lectured and published extensively on a large variety of subjects — including Hebrew Poetry and Prosody, Interactions between Drama and Music in Opera, and Translation Analysis — the study of Chekhov's plays has been his major field of research and teaching in recent decades. This is his first book-length study on the subject.